W9-AVY-461

Human Nutrition and Metabolism

Custom Edition for Kin 3Y03

NELSON EDUCATION

NELSON EDUCATION

COPYRIGHT © 2009 by Nelson Education Limited.

Printed and bound in Canada
2 3 4   11 10 09

For more information contact Nelson Education Limited 1120 Birchmount Road, Toronto, Ontario, M1K 5G4. Or you can visit our internet site at http://www.nelson.com

ALL RIGHTS RESERVED.
No part of this work covered by the copyright hereon may be reproduced, transcribed, or used in any form or by any means – graphic, electronic, or mechanical, including photocopying, recording, taping, web distribution or information storage and retrieval systems – without the written permission of the publisher.

For permission to use material from this text or product, submit all requests online at www.cengage.com/permissions.

Further questions about permissions can be emailed to permissionrequest@cengage.com.

Every effort has been made to trace ownership of all copyrighted material and to secure permission from copyright holders. In the event of any question arising as to the use of any material, we will be pleased to make the necessary corrections in future printings.

This textbook is a Nelson custom publication. Because your instructor has chosen to produce a custom publication, you pay only for material that you will use in your course.

ISBN-13: 978-0-17-647801-8
ISBN-10: 0-17-647801-9

Consists of Selections from:

Understanding Nutrition
Eleventh Edition
Whitney/Rolfes
ISBN 10: 0-495-11686-6
© 2008/2005

Practical Sports Nutrition
Burke
ISBN 10: 0-7360-4695-X
© 2007 Human Kinetics, Inc.

Sport Nutrition : An Introduction to Energy Production and Performance
Jeukendrup/Gleeson
ISBN 10: 0-7360-3404-8
© 2004 Human Kinetics, Inc.

Contents

Chapter 1   **Understanding Nutrition,** *Eleventh Edition*
An Overview of Nutrition .... page   2
Food Choices .... page   3
The Nutrients .... page   5
The Science of Nutrition .... page   11
Dietary Reference Intakes .... page   16
Nutrition Assessment .... page   20
Diet and Health .... page   24
Highlight: Nutrition Information and Misinformation .... page   30

Chapter 2   **Understanding Nutrition,** *Eleventh Edition*
Planning a Healthy Diet .... page   36
Principles and Guidelines .... page   37
Diet-Planning Guides .... page   41
Food Labels .... page   54
Highlight: Vegetarian Diets .... page   64

Chapter 1   **Practical Sports Nutrition**
Training and Competition Nutrition .... page   1
Goals of Training Nutrition .... page   1

Chapter 3   **Understanding Nutrition,** *Eleventh Edition*
Digestion, Absorption, and Transport .... page   70
Digestion .... page   71
Absorption .... page   80
The Circulatory Systems .... page   83
The Health and Regulation of the GI Tract .... page   86
Highlight: Common Digestive Problems .... page   92

Chapter 7   **Understanding Nutrition,** *Eleventh Edition*
Metabolism: Transformations and Interactions .... page   212

Chemical Reactions in the Body .... page   214

Breaking Down Nutrients for Energy .... page   217

Energy Balance .... page   230

Highlight: Alcohol and Nutrition .... page   238

Chapter 5   **Sport Nutrition**
Carbohydrate .... page   101

History • Role of Carbohydrate • Carbohydrate Before Exercise •
Carbohydrate During Exercise • Carbohydrate After Exercise • What
Athletes Really Do • Key Points • Key Terms • Recommended Readings

Chapter 6   **Sport Nutrition**
Fat .... page   127

Fat Metabolism During Exercise • What Limits Fat Oxidation •
Fat As A Fuel During Exercise • Regulation of Carbohydrate and
Fat Metabolism • Fat Supplementation and Exercise • Effect of Diet on Fat
Metabolism and Performance • Supplements That Increase Fat Oxidation •
Key Points • Key Terms • Recommended Readings

Chapter 7   **Sport Nutrition**
Protein and Amino Acids .... page   147

Amino Acids • Techniques to Study Protein and Amino Acid Metabolism •
Protein Requirements for Exercise • Training and Protein Metabolism •
Effect of Protein Intake on Protein Synthesis • Amino Acids As Ergogenic
Aids • Protein Intake and Health Risks • Key Points • Key Terms •
Recommended Readings

Chapter 8   **Sport Nutrition**
Water Requirements and Fluid Balance .... page   169

Thermoregulation and Exercise in the Heat • Effects of Dehydration on
Exercise Performance • Mechanisms of Heat Illness • Effects of Fluid Intake
on Exercise Performance • Daily Water Balance • Fluid Requirements for
Athletes • Key Points • Key Terms • Recommended Readings

Chapter 11   Sport Nutrition
Weight Management .... page   267
*Ideal Body Weight and Composition ▪ Weight Loss ▪ Making Weight
and Rapid Weight-Loss Strategies ▪ Key Points ▪ Key Terms ▪
Recommended Readings*

Dietary Reference Intakes (DRI) .... page   A

**Recommended Dietary Allowances (RDA) and Adequate Intakes (A1)
for Vitamins and Minerals** .... page   B

Tolerable Upper Intake Levels (UL) for Vitamins and Minerals .... page   C

Appendix A   Cells, Hormones, and Nerves .... page   A-2

Appendix C   Biochemical Structures and Pathways .... page   C-1

Appendix D   Measures of Protein Quality .... page   D-1

Appendix F   Physical Activity and Energy Requirements .... page   F-1

**Appendix I   WHO: Nutrition Recommendations
Canada: Guidelines and Meal Planning** .... page   I-1

Key Sanders/Getty Images

Nutrition in Your Life

Believe it or not, you have probably eaten at least 20,000 meals in your life.

Without any conscious effort on your part, your body uses the nutrients from

those foods to make all its components, fuel all its activities, and defend itself

against diseases. How successfully your body handles these tasks depends, in

part, on your food choices. Nutritious food choices support healthy bodies.

Thomson NOW! Throughout this chapter, the ThomsonNOW logo indicates an opportunity for online self-study, linking you to interactive tutorials and videos based on your level of understanding.

www.thomsonedu.com/thomsonnow

How To: Practice Problems

Nutrition Portfolio Journal

Nutrition Calculations: Practice Problems

An Overview of Nutrition

CHAPTER OUTLINE

Food Choices

The Nutrients • Nutrients in Foods and in the Body • The Energy-Yielding Nutrients: Carbohydrate, Fat, and Protein • The Vitamins • The Minerals • Water

The Science of Nutrition • Conducting Research • Analyzing Research Findings • Publishing Research

Dietary Reference Intakes • Establishing Nutrient Recommendations • Establishing Energy Recommendations • Using Nutrient Recommendations • Comparing Nutrient Recommendations

Nutrition Assessment • Nutrition Assessment of Individuals • Nutrition Assessment of Populations

Diet and Health • Chronic Diseases • Risk Factors for Chronic Diseases

HIGHLIGHT 1 Nutrition Information and Misinformation—On the Net and in the News

Welcome to the world of **nutrition**. Although you may not always have been aware of it, nutrition has played a significant role in your life. And it will continue to affect you in major ways, depending on the **foods** you select.

Every day, several times a day, you make food choices that influence your body's health for better or worse. Each day's choices may benefit or harm your health only a little, but when these choices are repeated over years and decades, the rewards or consequences become major. That being the case, paying close attention to good eating habits now can bring you health benefits later. Conversely, carelessness about food choices can contribute to many chronic diseases ◆ prevalent in later life, including heart disease and cancer. Of course, some people will become ill or die young no matter what choices they make, and others will live long lives despite making poor choices. For the majority of us, however, the food choices we make each and every day will benefit or impair our health in proportion to the wisdom of those choices.

Although most people realize that their food habits affect their health, they often choose foods for other reasons. After all, foods bring to the table a variety of pleasures, traditions, and associations as well as nourishment. The challenge, then, is to combine favorite foods and fun times with a nutritionally balanced **diet**.

◆ In general, a **chronic** disease progresses slowly or with little change and lasts a long time. By comparison, an **acute** disease develops quickly, produces sharp symptoms, and runs a short course.
- **chronos** = time
- **acute** = sharp

nutrition: the science of foods and the nutrients and other substances they contain, and of their actions within the body (including ingestion, digestion, absorption, transport, metabolism, and excretion). A broader definition includes the social, economic, cultural, and psychological implications of food and eating.

foods: products derived from plants or animals that can be taken into the body to yield energy and nutrients for the maintenance of life and the growth and repair of tissues.

diet: the foods and beverages a person eats and drinks.

Food Choices

People decide what to eat, when to eat, and even whether to eat in highly personal ways, often based on behavioral or social motives rather than on an awareness of nutrition's importance to health. Many different food choices can support good health, and an understanding of nutrition helps you make sensible selections more often.

Personal Preference As you might expect, the number one reason people choose foods is taste—they like certain flavors. Two widely shared preferences are for the sweetness of sugar and the savoriness of salt. Liking high-fat foods also appears to be a universally common preference. Other preferences might be for the hot peppers

An enjoyable way to learn about other cultures is to taste their ethnic foods.

common in Mexican cooking or the curry spices of Indian cuisine. Some research suggests that genetics may influence people's food preferences.[1]

Habit People sometimes select foods out of habit. They eat cereal every morning, for example, simply because they have always eaten cereal for breakfast. Eating a familiar food and not having to make any decisions can be comforting.

Ethnic Heritage or Tradition

Among the strongest influences on food choices are ethnic heritage and tradition. People eat the foods they grew up eating. Every country, and in fact every region of a country, has its own typical foods and ways of combining them into meals. The "American diet" includes many ethnic foods from various countries, all adding variety to the diet. This is most evident when eating out: 60 percent of U.S. restaurants (excluding fast-food places) have an ethnic emphasis, most commonly Chinese, Italian, or Mexican.

Social Interactions Most people enjoy companionship while eating. It's fun to go out with friends for pizza or ice cream. Meals are social events, and sharing food is part of hospitality. Social customs invite people to accept food or drink offered by a host or shared by a group.

Availability, Convenience, and Economy People eat foods that are accessible, quick and easy to prepare, and within their financial means. Today's consumers value convenience and are willing to spend more than half of their food budget on meals that require little, if any, further preparation.[2] They frequently eat out, bring home ready-to-eat meals, or have food delivered. Even when they venture into the kitchen, they want to prepare a meal in 15 to 20 minutes, using less than a half dozen ingredients—and those "ingredients" are often semiprepared foods, such as canned soups. This emphasis on convenience limits food choices to the selections offered on menus and products designed for quick preparation. Whether decisions based on convenience meet a person's nutrition needs depends on the choices made. Eating a banana or a candy bar may be equally convenient, but the fruit offers more vitamins and minerals and less sugar and fat.

Positive and Negative Associations People tend to like particular foods associated with happy occasions—such as hot dogs at ball games or cake and ice cream at birthday parties. By the same token, people can develop aversions and dislike foods that they ate when they felt sick or that were forced on them.[3] By using foods as rewards or punishments, parents may inadvertently teach their children to like and dislike certain foods.

Emotional Comfort Some people cannot eat when they are emotionally upset. Others may eat in response to a variety of emotional stimuli—for example, to relieve boredom or depression or to calm anxiety.[4] A depressed person may choose to eat rather than to call a friend. A person who has returned home from an exciting evening out may unwind with a late-night snack. These people may find emotional comfort, in part, because foods can influence the brain's chemistry and the mind's response. Carbohydrates and alcohol, for example, tend to calm, whereas proteins and caffeine are more likely to activate. Eating in response to emotions can easily lead to overeating and obesity, but it may be appropriate at times. For example, sharing food at times of bereavement serves both the giver's need to provide comfort and the receiver's need to be cared for and to interact with others, as well as to take nourishment.

Values Food choices may reflect people's religious beliefs, political views, or environmental concerns. For example, many Christians forgo meat during Lent (the period prior to Easter), Jewish law includes an extensive set of dietary rules that govern the use of foods derived from animals, and Muslims fast between sunrise and sunset during Ramadan (the ninth month of the Islamic calendar). A concerned consumer may boycott fruit picked by migrant workers who have been exploited. People may buy vegetables from local farmers to save the fuel and environmental costs of foods shipped in from far away. They may also select foods packaged in containers that can be reused or recycled. Some consumers accept or reject foods that have been irradiated or genetically modified, depending on their approval of these processes (see Chapter and Highlight 19 for a complete discussion).

Body Weight and Image Sometimes people select certain foods and supplements that they believe will improve their physical appearance and avoid those they believe might be detrimental. Such decisions can be beneficial when based on sound nutrition and fitness knowledge, but decisions based on fads or carried to extremes undermine good health, as pointed out in later discussions of eating disorders (Highlight 8) and dietary supplements commonly used by athletes (Highlight 14).

Nutrition and Health Benefits Finally, of course, many consumers make food choices that will benefit health. Food manufacturers and restaurant chefs have responded to scientific findings linking health with nutrition by offering an abundant selection of health-promoting foods and beverages. Foods that provide health benefits beyond their nutrient contributions are called **functional foods**.[5] Whole foods—as natural and familiar as oatmeal or tomatoes—are the simplest functional foods. In other cases, foods have been modified to provide health benefits, perhaps by lowering the fat contents. In still other cases, manufacturers have fortified foods by adding nutrients or **phytochemicals** that provide health benefits (see Highlight 13). ◆ Examples of these functional foods include orange juice fortified with calcium to help build strong bones and margarine made with a plant sterol that lowers blood cholesterol.

Consumers typically welcome new foods into their diets, provided that these foods are reasonably priced, clearly labeled, easy to find in the grocery store, and convenient to prepare. These foods must also taste good—as good as the traditional choices. Of course, a person need not eat any of these "special" foods to enjoy a healthy diet; many "regular" foods provide numerous health benefits as well. In fact, "regular" foods such as whole grains; vegetables and legumes; fruits; meats, fish, and poultry; and milk products are among the healthiest choices a person can make.

© Ariel Skelley/CORBIS

To enhance your health, keep nutrition in mind when selecting foods.

◆ Functional foods may include whole foods, modified foods, or fortified foods.

IN SUMMARY

A person selects foods for a variety of reasons. Whatever those reasons may be, food choices influence health. Individual food selections neither make nor break a diet's healthfulness, but the balance of foods selected over time can make an important difference to health.[6] For this reason, people are wise to think "nutrition" when making their food choices.

The Nutrients

Biologically speaking, people eat to receive nourishment. Do you ever think of yourself as a biological being made of carefully arranged atoms, molecules, cells, tissues, and organs? Are you aware of the activity going on within your body even as you sit still? The atoms, molecules, and cells of your body continually move and change, even though the structures of your tissues and organs and your external appearance remain relatively constant. Your skin, which has covered you since your birth, is replaced entirely by new cells every seven years. The fat beneath your skin is not the

functional foods: foods that contain physiologically active compounds that provide health benefits beyond their nutrient contributions; sometimes called *designer foods* or *nutraceuticals*.

phytochemicals (FIE-toe-KEM-ih-cals): nonnutrient compounds found in plant-derived foods that have biological activity in the body.

• **phyto** = plant

Foods bring pleasure—and nutrients.

◆ As Chapter 5 explains, most lipids are fats.

same fat that was there a year ago. Your oldest red blood cell is only 120 days old, and the entire lining of your digestive tract is renewed every 3 to 5 days. To maintain your "self," you must continually replenish, from foods, the **energy** and the **nutrients** you deplete as your body maintains itself.

Nutrients in Foods and in the Body

Amazingly, our bodies can derive all the energy, structural materials, and regulating agents we need from the foods we eat. This section introduces the nutrients that foods deliver and shows how they participate in the dynamic processes that keep people alive and well.

Composition of Foods Chemical analysis of a food such as a tomato shows that it is composed primarily of water (95 percent). Most of the solid materials are carbohydrates, lipids, ◆ and proteins. If you could remove these materials, you would find a tiny residue of vitamins, minerals, and other compounds. Water, carbohydrates, lipids, proteins, vitamins, and some of the minerals found in foods are nutrients—substances the body uses for the growth, maintenance, and repair of its tissues.

This book focuses mostly on the nutrients, but foods contain other compounds as well—fibers, phytochemicals, pigments, additives, alcohols, and others. Some are beneficial, some are neutral, and a few are harmful. Later sections of the book touch on these compounds and their significance.

Composition of the Body A complete chemical analysis of your body would show that it is made of materials similar to those found in foods (see Figure 1-1). A healthy 150-pound body contains about 90 pounds of water and about 20 to 45 pounds of fat. The remaining pounds are mostly protein, carbohydrate, and the major minerals of the bones. Vitamins, other minerals, and incidental extras constitute a fraction of a pound.

FIGURE 1-1 Body Composition of Healthy-Weight Men and Women

The human body is made of compounds similar to those found in foods—mostly water (60 percent) and some fat (13 to 21 percent for young men, 23 to 31 percent for young women), with carbohydrate, protein, vitamins, minerals, and other minor constituents making up the remainder. (Chapter 8 describes the health hazards of too little or too much body fat.)

Key:
◼ % Carbohydrates, proteins, vitamins, minerals in the body

◼ % Fat in the body

◼ % Water in the body

© Photodisc/Getty Images

energy: the capacity to do work. The energy in food is chemical energy. The body can convert this chemical energy to mechanical, electrical, or heat energy.

nutrients: chemical substances obtained from food and used in the body to provide energy, structural materials, and regulating agents to support growth, maintenance, and repair of the body's tissues. Nutrients may also reduce the risks of some diseases.

Chemical Composition of Nutrients The simplest of the nutrients are the minerals. Each mineral is a chemical element; its atoms are all alike. As a result, its identity never changes. For example, iron may have different electrical charges, but the individual iron atoms remain the same when they are in a food, when a person eats the food, when the iron becomes part of a red blood cell, when the cell is broken down, and when the iron is lost from the body by excretion. The next simplest nutrient is water, a compound made of two elements—hydrogen and oxygen. Minerals and water are **inorganic** nutrients—which means they do not contain carbon.

The other four classes of nutrients (carbohydrates, lipids, proteins, and vitamins) are more complex. In addition to hydrogen and oxygen, they all contain carbon, an element found in all living things. They are therefore called **organic** ◆ compounds (meaning, literally, "alive"). Protein and some vitamins also contain nitrogen and may contain other elements as well (see Table 1-1).

Essential Nutrients The body can make some nutrients, but it cannot make all of them. Also, it makes some in insufficient quantities to meet its needs and, therefore, must obtain these nutrients from foods. The nutrients that foods must supply are **essential nutrients.** When used to refer to nutrients, the word *essential* means more than just "necessary"; it means "needed from outside the body"—normally, from foods.

The Energy-Yielding Nutrients: Carbohydrate, Fat, and Protein

In the body, three organic nutrients can be used to provide energy: carbohydrate, fat, and protein. ◆ In contrast to these **energy-yielding nutrients,** vitamins, minerals, and water do not yield energy in the human body.

Energy Measured in kCalories The energy released from carbohydrates, fats, and proteins can be measured in **calories**—tiny units of energy so small that a single apple provides tens of thousands of them. To ease calculations, energy is expressed in 1000-calorie metric units known as kilocalories (shortened to kcalories, but commonly called "calories"). When you read in popular books or magazines that an apple provides "100 calories," it actually means 100 kcalories. This book uses the term kcalorie and its abbreviation kcal throughout, as do other scientific books and journals. ◆ The "How to" on p. 8 provides a few tips on "thinking metric."

◆ In agriculture, *organic* farming refers to growing crops and raising livestock according to standards set by the U.S. Department of Agriculture (USDA). Chapter 19 presents details.

◆ Carbohydrate, fat, and protein are sometimes called **macronutrients** because the body requires them in relatively large amounts (many grams daily). In contrast, vitamins and minerals are **micronutrients,** required only in small amounts (milligrams or micrograms daily).

◆ The international unit for measuring food energy is the **joule,** a measure of *work* energy. To convert kcalories to kilojoules, multiply by 4.2; to convert kilojoules to kcalories, multiply by 0.24.

inorganic: not containing carbon or pertaining to living things.
• **in** = not

organic: in chemistry, a substance or molecule containing carbon-carbon bonds or carbon-hydrogen bonds. This definition excludes coal, diamonds, and a few carbon-containing compounds that contain only a single carbon and no hydrogen, such as carbon dioxide (CO_2), calcium carbonate ($CaCO_3$), magnesium carbonate ($MgCO_3$), and sodium cyanide (NaCN).

essential nutrients: nutrients a person must obtain from food because the body cannot make them for itself in sufficient quantity to meet physiological needs; also called **indispensable nutrients.** About 40 nutrients are currently known to be essential for human beings.

energy-yielding nutrients: the nutrients that break down to yield energy the body can use:
• Carbohydrate
• Fat
• Protein

calories: units by which energy is measured. Food energy is measured in **kilocalories** (1000 calories equal 1 kilocalorie), abbreviated **kcalories** or **kcal.** One kcalorie is the amount of heat necessary to raise the temperature of 1 kilogram (kg) of water 1°C. The scientific use of the term *kcalorie* is the same as the popular use of the term *calorie.*

TABLE 1-1	Elements in the Six Classes of Nutrients				

Notice that organic nutrients contain carbon.

	Carbon	Hydrogen	Oxygen	Nitrogen	Minerals
Inorganic nutrients					
Minerals					✓
Water		✓	✓		
Organic nutrients					
Carbohydrates	✓	✓	✓		
Lipids (fats)	✓	✓	✓		
Proteins[a]	✓	✓	✓	✓	
Vitamins[b]	✓	✓	✓		

[a] Some proteins also contain the mineral sulfur.
[b] Some vitamins contain nitrogen; some contain minerals.

HOW TO Think Metric

Like other scientists, nutrition scientists use metric units of measure. They measure food energy in kilocalories, people's height in centimeters, people's weight in kilograms, and the weights of foods and nutrients in grams, milligrams, or micrograms. For ease in using these measures, it helps to remember that the prefixes on the grams imply 1000. For example, a *kilo*gram is 1000 grams, a *milli*gram is 1/1000 of a gram, and a *micro*gram is 1/1000 of a milligram.

Most food labels and many recipe books provide "dual measures," listing both household measures, such as cups, quarts, and teaspoons, and metric measures, such as milliliters, liters, and grams. This practice gives

people an opportunity to gradually learn to "think metric."

A person might begin to "think metric" by simply observing the measure—by noticing the amount of soda in a 2-liter bottle, for example. Through such experiences, a person can become familiar with a measure without having to do any conversions.

To facilitate communication, many members of the international scientific community have adopted a common system of measurement—the International System of Units (SI). In addition to using metric measures, the SI establishes common units of measurement. For example, the SI unit for measuring food energy is the joule (not the kcalorie). A joule

is the amount of energy expended when 1 kilogram is moved 1 meter by a force of 1 newton. The joule is thus a measure of *work* energy, whereas the kcalorie is a measure of *heat* energy. While many scientists and journals report their findings in kilojoules (kJ), many others, particularly those in the United States, use kcalories (kcal). To convert energy measures from kcalories to kilojoules, multiply by 4.2. For example, a 50-kcalorie cookie provides 210 kilojoules:

$$50 \text{ kcal} \times 4.2 = 210 \text{ kJ}$$

Exact conversion factors for these and other units of measure are in the Aids to Calculation section on the last two pages of the book.

Volume: Liters (L)

1 L = 1000 milliliters (mL)
0.95 L = 1 quart
1 mL = 0.03 fluid ounces
240 mL = 1 cup

A liter of liquid is approximately one U.S. quart. (Four liters are only about 5 percent more than a gallon.)

One cup is about 240 milliliters; a half-cup of liquid is about 120 milliliters.

Weight: Grams (g)

1 g = 1000 milligrams (mg)
1 g = 0.04 ounce (oz)
1 oz = 28.35 g (or 30 g)
100 g = 3½ oz
1 kilogram (kg) = 1000 g
1 kg = 2.2 pounds (lb)
454 g = 1 lb

A kilogram is slightly more than 2 lb; conversely, a pound is about ½ kg.

A half-cup of vegetables weighs about 100 grams; one pea weighs about ½ gram.

A 5-pound bag of potatoes weighs about 2 kilograms, and a 176-pound person weighs 80 kilograms.

ThomsonNOW
To practice thinking metrically, log on to **www.thomsonedu.com/thomsonnow**, go to Chapter 1, then go to How To.

◆ Foods with a high energy density help with weight gain, whereas those with a low energy density help with weight loss.

energy density: a measure of the energy a food provides relative to the amount of food (kcalories per gram).

Energy from Foods The amount of energy a food provides depends on how much carbohydrate, fat, and protein it contains. When completely broken down in the body, a gram of carbohydrate yields about 4 kcalories of energy; a gram of protein also yields 4 kcalories; and a gram of fat yields 9 kcalories (see Table 1-2). Fat, therefore, has a greater **energy density** than either carbohydrate or protein. Figure 1-2 compares the energy density of two breakfast options, and later chapters describe how considering a food's energy density can help with weight management. ◆ The "How to" on p. 9 explains how to calculate the energy available from foods.

One other substance contributes energy—alcohol. Alcohol is not considered a nutrient because it interferes with the growth, maintenance, and repair of the body, but it does yield energy (7 kcalories per gram) when metabolized in the body. (Highlight 7 and Chapter 18 present the potential harms and possible benefits of alcohol consumption.)

FIGURE 1-2 Energy Density of Two Breakfast Options Compared

Gram for gram, ounce for ounce, and bite for bite, foods with a high energy density deliver more kcalories than foods with a low energy density. Both of these breakfast options provide 500 kcalories, but the cereal with milk, fruit salad, scrambled egg, turkey sausage, and toast with jam offers three times as much food as the doughnuts (based on weight); it has a lower energy density than the doughnuts. Selecting a variety of foods also helps to ensure nutrient adequacy.

LOWER ENERGY DENSITY
This 450-gram breakfast delivers 500 kcalories, for an energy density of 1.1
(500 kcal ÷ 450 g = 1.1 kcal/g).

HIGHER ENERGY DENSITY
This 144-gram breakfast delivers 500 kcalories, for an energy density of 3.5
(500 kcal ÷ 144 g = 3.5 kcal/g).

Most foods contain all three energy-yielding nutrients, as well as water, vitamins, minerals, and other substances. For example, meat contains water, fat, vitamins, and minerals as well as protein. Bread contains water, a trace of fat, a little protein, and some vitamins and minerals in addition to its carbohydrate. Only a few foods are exceptions to this rule, the common ones being sugar (pure carbohydrate) and oil (essentially pure fat).

Energy in the Body The body uses the energy-yielding nutrients to fuel all its activities. When the body uses carbohydrate, fat, or protein for energy, the bonds between

HOW TO Calculate the Energy Available from Foods

To calculate the energy available from a food, multiply the number of grams of carbohydrate, protein, and fat by 4, 4, and 9, respectively. Then add the results together. For example, 1 slice of bread with 1 tablespoon of peanut butter on it contains 16 grams carbohydrate, 7 grams protein, and 9 grams fat:

16 g carbohydrate × 4 kcal/g = 64 kcal
7 g protein × 4 kcal/g = 28 kcal
9 g fat × 9 kcal/g = 81 kcal
Total = 173 kcal

From this information, you can calculate the percentage of kcalories each of the energy nutrients contributes to the total. To determine the percentage of kcalories from fat, for example, divide the 81 fat kcalories by the total 173 kcalories:

81 fat kcal ÷ 173 total kcal = 0.468
(rounded to 0.47)

Then multiply by 100 to get the percentage:

0.47 × 100 = 47%

Dietary recommendations that urge people to limit fat intake to 20 to 35 percent of kcalories refer to the day's total energy intake, not to individual foods. Still, if the proportion of fat in each food choice throughout a day exceeds 35 percent of kcalories, then the day's total surely will, too. Knowing that this snack provides 47 percent of its kcalories from fat alerts a person to the need to make lower-fat selections at other times that day.

ThomsonNOW™
To practice calculating the energy available from foods, log on to **www.thomsonedu.com/ thomsonnow**, go to Chapter 1, then go to How To.

TABLE 1-2 kCalorie Values of Energy Nutrients[a]

Nutrients	Energy (kcal/g)
Carbohydrate	4
Fat	9
Protein	4

NOTE: Alcohol contributes 7 kcalories per gram that can be used for energy, but it is not considered a nutrient because it interferes with the body's growth, maintenance, and repair.
[a]For those using kilojoules: 1 g carbohydrate = 17 kJ; 1 g protein = 17 kJ; 1 g fat = 37 kJ; and 1 g alcohol = 29 kJ.

◆ The processes by which nutrients are broken down to yield energy or used to make body structures are known as **metabolism** (defined and described further in Chapter 7).

the nutrient's atoms break. As the bonds break, they release energy. ◆ Some of this energy is released as heat, but some is used to send electrical impulses through the brain and nerves, to synthesize body compounds, and to move muscles. Thus the energy from food supports every activity from quiet thought to vigorous sports.

If the body does not use these nutrients to fuel its current activities, it rearranges them into storage compounds (such as body fat), to be used between meals and overnight when fresh energy supplies run low. If more energy is consumed than expended, the result is an increase in energy stores and weight gain. Similarly, if less energy is consumed than expended, the result is a decrease in energy stores and weight loss.

When consumed in excess of energy needs, alcohol, too, can be converted to body fat and stored. When alcohol contributes a substantial portion of the energy in a person's diet, the harm it does far exceeds the problems of excess body fat. (Highlight 7 describes the effects of alcohol on health and nutrition.)

Other Roles of Energy-Yielding Nutrients In addition to providing energy, carbohydrates, fats, and proteins provide the raw materials for building the body's tissues and regulating its many activities. In fact, protein's role as a fuel source is relatively minor compared with both the other two nutrients and its other roles. Proteins are found in structures such as the muscles and skin and help to regulate activities such as digestion and energy metabolism.

The Vitamins

The **vitamins** are also organic, but they do not provide energy. Instead, they facilitate the release of energy from carbohydrate, fat, and protein and participate in numerous other activities throughout the body.

Each of the 13 different vitamins has its own special roles to play.* One vitamin enables the eyes to see in dim light, another helps protect the lungs from air pollution, and still another helps make the sex hormones—among other things. When you cut yourself, one vitamin helps stop the bleeding and another helps repair the skin. Vitamins busily help replace old red blood cells and the lining of the digestive tract. Almost every action in the body requires the assistance of vitamins.

Vitamins can function only if they are intact, but because they are complex organic molecules, they are vulnerable to destruction by heat, light, and chemical agents. This is why the body handles them carefully, and why nutrition-wise cooks do, too. The strategies of cooking vegetables at moderate temperatures for short times and using small amounts of water help to preserve the vitamins.

The Minerals

In the body, some **minerals** are put together in orderly arrays in such structures as bones and teeth. Minerals are also found in the fluids of the body, which influences fluid properties. Whatever their roles, minerals do not yield energy.

Only 16 minerals are known to be essential in human nutrition.** Others are being studied to determine whether they play significant roles in the human body. Still other minerals are environmental contaminants that displace the nutrient minerals from their workplaces in the body, disrupting body functions. The problems caused by contaminant minerals are described in Chapter 13.

Because minerals are inorganic, they are indestructible and need not be handled with the special care that vitamins require. Minerals can, however, be bound by substances that interfere with the body's ability to absorb them. They can also be lost during food-refining processes or during cooking when they leach into water that is discarded.

vitamins: organic, essential nutrients required in small amounts by the body for health.

minerals: inorganic elements. Some minerals are essential nutrients required in small amounts by the body for health.

---

* The water-soluble vitamins are vitamin C and the eight B vitamins: thiamin, riboflavin, niacin, vitamins B_6 and B_{12}, folate, biotin, and pantothenic acid. The fat-soluble vitamins are vitamins A, D, E, and K. The water-soluble vitamins are the subject of Chapter 10 and the fat-soluble vitamins, of Chapter 11.
** The major minerals are calcium, phosphorus, potassium, sodium, chloride, magnesium, and sulfate. The trace minerals are iron, iodine, zinc, chromium, selenium, fluoride, molybdenum, copper, and manganese. Chapters 12 and 13 are devoted to the major and trace minerals, respectively.

Water

Water, indispensable and abundant, provides the environment in which nearly all the body's activities are conducted. It participates in many metabolic reactions and supplies the medium for transporting vital materials to cells and carrying waste products away from them. Water is discussed fully in Chapter 12, but it is mentioned in every chapter. If you watch for it, you cannot help but be impressed by water's participation in all life processes.

Water itself is an essential nutrient and naturally carries many minerals.

© Corbis

> **IN SUMMARY**
>
> Foods provide nutrients—substances that support the growth, maintenance, and repair of the body's tissues. The six classes of nutrients include:
>
> · Carbohydrates
> · Lipids (fats)
> · Proteins
> · Vitamins
> · Minerals
> · Water
>
> Foods rich in the energy-yielding nutrients (carbohydrates, fats, and proteins) provide the major materials for building the body's tissues and yield energy for the body's use or storage. Energy is measured in kcalories. Vitamins, minerals, and water facilitate a variety of activities in the body.

Without exaggeration, nutrients provide the physical and metabolic basis for nearly all that we are and all that we do. The next section introduces the science of nutrition with emphasis on the research methods scientists have used in uncovering the wonders of nutrition.

The Science of Nutrition

The science of nutrition is the study of the nutrients and other substances in foods and the body's handling of them. Its foundation depends on several other sciences, including biology, biochemistry, and physiology. As sciences go, nutrition is young, but as you can see from the size of this book, much has happened in nutrition's short life. And it is currently entering a tremendous growth spurt as scientists apply knowledge gained from sequencing the human **genome.** The integration of nutrition, genomics, and molecular biology has opened a whole new world of study called **nutritional genomics**—the science of how nutrients affect the activities of genes and how genes affect the interactions between diet and disease.[7] Highlight 6 describes how nutritional genomics is shaping the science of nutrition, and examples of nutrient–gene interactions appear throughout later sections of the book.

Conducting Research

Consumers may depend on personal experience or reports from friends ◆ to gather information on nutrition, but researchers use the scientific method to guide their work (see Figure 1-3 on p. 12). As the figure shows, research always begins with a problem or a question. For example, "What foods or nutrients might protect against the common cold?" In search of an answer, scientists make an educated guess (**hypothesis**), such as "foods rich in vitamin C reduce the number of common colds." Then they systematically conduct research studies to collect data that will test the hypothesis (see the glossary on p. 14 for definitions of research terms). Some examples of various types of research designs are presented in Figure 1-4 (p. 13). Each type of study has strengths and weaknesses (see Table 1-3 on p. 14). Consequently, some provide stronger evidence than others.

◆ A personal account of an experience or event is an **anecdote** and is not accepted as reliable scientific information.
  • **anekdotos** = unpublished

> **genome** (GEE-nome): the full complement of genetic material (DNA) in the chromosomes of a cell. In human beings, the genome consists of 46 chromosomes. The study of genomes is called **genomics.**
>
> **nutritional genomics**: the science of how nutrients affect the activities of genes (**nutrigenomics**) and how genes affect the interactions between diet and disease (**nutrigenetics**).

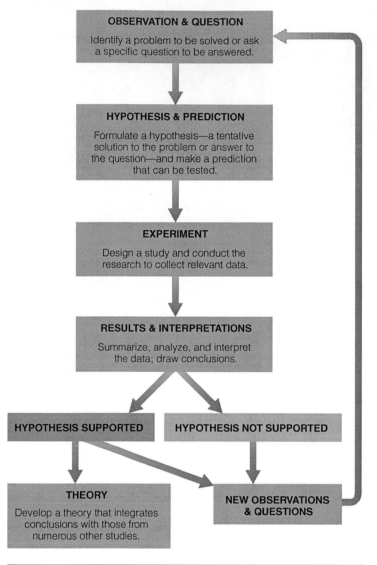

FIGURE 1-3 The Scientific Method

Research scientists follow the scientific method. Note that most research generates new questions, not final answers. Thus the sequence begins anew, and research continues in a somewhat cyclical way.

OBSERVATION & QUESTION

Identify a problem to be solved or ask a specific question to be answered.

HYPOTHESIS & PREDICTION

Formulate a hypothesis—a tentative solution to the problem or answer to the question—and make a prediction that can be tested.

EXPERIMENT

Design a study and conduct the research to collect relevant data.

RESULTS & INTERPRETATIONS

Summarize, analyze, and interpret the data; draw conclusions.

HYPOTHESIS SUPPORTED

HYPOTHESIS NOT SUPPORTED

THEORY

Develop a theory that integrates conclusions with those from numerous other studies.

NEW OBSERVATIONS & QUESTIONS

In attempting to discover whether a nutrient relieves symptoms or cures a disease, researchers deliberately manipulate one variable (for example, the amount of vitamin C in the diet) and measure any observed changes (perhaps the number of colds). As much as possible, all other conditions are held constant. The following paragraphs illustrate how this is accomplished.

Controls In studies examining the effectiveness of vitamin C, researchers typically divide the **subjects** into two groups. One group (the **experimental group**) receives a vitamin C supplement, and the other (the **control group**) does not. Researchers observe both groups to determine whether one group has fewer or shorter colds than the other. The following discussion describes some of the pitfalls inherent in an experiment of this kind and ways to avoid them.

In sorting subjects into two groups, researchers must ensure that each person has an equal chance of being assigned to either the experimental group or the control group. This is accomplished by **randomization;** that is, the subjects are chosen randomly from the same population by flipping a coin or some other method involving chance. Randomization helps to ensure that results reflect the treatment and not factors that might influence the grouping of subjects.

Importantly, the two groups of people must be similar and must have the same track record with respect to colds to rule out the possibility that observed differences in the rate, severity, or duration of colds might have occurred anyway. If, for example, the control group would normally catch twice as many colds as the experimental group, then the findings prove nothing.

In experiments involving a nutrient, the diets of both groups must also be similar, especially with respect to the nutrient being studied. If those in the experimental group were receiving less vitamin C from their usual diet, then any effects of the supplement may not be apparent.

Sample Size To ensure that chance variation between the two groups does not influence the results, the groups must be large. For example, if one member of a group of five people catches a bad cold by chance, he will pull the whole group's average toward bad colds; but if one member of a group of 500 catches a bad cold, she will not unduly affect the group average. Statistical methods are used to determine whether differences between groups of various sizes support a hypothesis.

Placebos If people who take vitamin C for colds *believe* it will cure them, their chances of recovery may improve. Taking anything believed to be beneficial may hasten recovery. This phenomenon, the result of expectations, is known as the **placebo effect.** In experiments designed to determine vitamin C's effect on colds, this mind-body effect must be rigorously controlled. Severity of symptoms is often a subjective measure, and people who believe they are receiving treatment may report less severe symptoms.

One way experimenters control for the placebo effect is to give pills to all participants. Those in the experimental group, for example, receive pills containing vitamin C, and those in the control group receive a **placebo**—pills of similar appearance and taste containing an inactive ingredient. This way, the expectations of both groups will be equal. It is not necessary to convince all subjects that they are receiving vitamin C, but the extent of belief or unbelief must be the same in both groups. A study conducted under these conditions is called a **blind exper-**

FIGURE 1-4 Examples of Research Designs

EPIDEMIOLOGICAL STUDIES

CROSS-SECTIONAL	CASE-CONTROL	COHORT

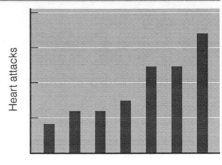

Heart attacks

Blood cholesterol

Researchers observe how much and what kinds of foods a group of people eat and how healthy those people are. Their findings identify factors that might influence the incidence of a disease in various populations.

Example. The people of the Mediterranean region drink lots of wine, eat plenty of fat from olive oil, and have a lower incidence of heart disease than northern Europeans and North Americans.

Researchers compare people who do and do not have a given condition such as a disease, closely matching them in age, gender, and other key variables so that differences in other factors will stand out. These differences may account for the condition in the group that has it.

Example. People with goiter lack iodine in their diets.

Researchers analyze data collected from a selected group of people (a cohort) at intervals over a certain period of time.

Example. Data collected periodically over the past several decades from over 5000 people randomly selected from the town of Framingham, Massachusetts, in 1948 have revealed that the risk of heart attack increases as blood cholesterol increases.

EXPERIMENTAL STUDIES

LABORATORY-BASED ANIMAL STUDIES	LABORATORY-BASED IN VITRO STUDIES	HUMAN INTERVENTION (OR CLINICAL) TRIALS

Researchers feed animals special diets that provide or omit specific nutrients and then observe any changes in health. Such studies test possible disease causes and treatments in a laboratory where all conditions can be controlled.

Example. Mice fed a high-fat diet eat less food than mice given a lower-fat diet, so they receive the same number of kcalories—but the mice eating the fat-rich diet become severely obese.

Researchers examine the effects of a specific variable on a tissue, cell, or molecule isolated from a living organism.

Example. Laboratory studies find that fish oils inhibit the growth and activity of the bacteria implicated in ulcer formation.

Researchers ask people to adopt a new behavior (for example, eat a citrus fruit, take a vitamin C supplement, or exercise daily). These trials help determine the effectiveness of such interventions on the development or prevention of disease.

Example. Heart disease risk factors improve when men receive fresh-squeezed orange juice daily for two months compared with those on a diet low in vitamin C—even when both groups follow a diet high in saturated fat.

iment—that is, the subjects do not know (are blind to) whether they are members of the experimental group (receiving treatment) or the control group (receiving the placebo).

Double Blind When both the subjects and the researchers do not know which subjects are in which group, the study is called a **double-blind experiment.** Being fallible human beings and having an emotional and sometimes financial investment

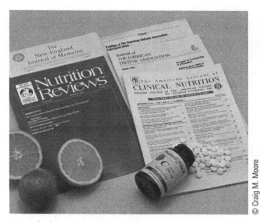

Knowledge about the nutrients and their effects on health comes from scientific study.

© Craig M. Moore

TABLE 1-3	Strengths and Weaknesses of Research Designs	
Type of Research	**Strengths**	**Weaknesses**
Epidemiological studies determine the incidence and distribution of diseases in a population. Epidemiological studies include cross-sectional, case-control, and cohort (see Figure 1-4).	• Can narrow down the list of possible causes • Can raise questions to pursue through other types of studies	• Cannot control variables that may influence the development or the prevention of a disease • Cannot prove cause and effect
Laboratory-based studies explore the effects of a specific variable on a tissue, cell, or molecule. Laboratory-based studies are often conducted in test tubes (in vitro) or on animals.	• Can control conditions • Can determine effects of a variable	• Cannot apply results from test tubes or animals to human beings
Human intervention or **clinical trials** involve human beings who follow a specified regimen.	• Can control conditions (for the most part) • Can apply findings to some groups of human beings	• Cannot generalize findings to all human beings • Cannot use certain treatments for clinical or ethical reasons

in a successful outcome, researchers might record and interpret results with a bias in the expected direction. To prevent such bias, the pills would be coded by a third party, who does not reveal to the experimenters which subjects were in which group until all results have been recorded.

Analyzing Research Findings

Research findings must be analyzed and interpreted with an awareness of each study's limitations. Scientists must be cautious about drawing any conclusions until they have accumulated a body of evidence from multiple studies that have used various types of research designs. As evidence accumulates, scientists begin to develop a **theory** that integrates the various findings and explains the complex relationships.

GLOSSARY OF RESEARCH TERMS

blind experiment: an experiment in which the subjects do not know whether they are members of the experimental group or the control group.

control group: a group of individuals similar in all possible respects to the experimental group except for the treatment. Ideally, the control group receives a placebo while the experimental group receives a real treatment.

correlation (CORE-ee-LAY-shun): the simultaneous increase, decrease, or change in two variables. If A increases as B increases, or if A decreases as B decreases, the correlation is **positive.** (This does not mean that A causes B or vice versa.) If A increases as B decreases, or if A decreases as B increases, the correlation is **negative.** (This does not mean that A prevents B or vice versa.) Some third factor may account for both A and B.

double-blind experiment: an experiment in which neither the subjects nor the researchers know which subjects are members of the experimental group and which are serving as control subjects, until after the experiment is over.

experimental group: a group of individuals similar in all possible respects to the control group except for the treatment. The experimental group receives the real treatment.

hypothesis (hi-POTH-eh-sis): an unproven statement that tentatively explains the relationships between two or more variables.

peer review: a process in which a panel of scientists rigorously evaluates a research study to assure that the scientific method was followed.

placebo (pla-SEE-bo): an inert, harmless medication given to provide comfort and hope; a sham treatment used in controlled research studies.

placebo effect: a change that occurs in reponse to expectations in the effectiveness of a treatment that actually has no pharmaceutical effects.

randomization (RAN-dom-ih-ZAY-shun): a process of choosing the members of the experimental and control groups without bias.

replication (REP-lih-KAY-shun): repeating an experiment and getting the same results. The skeptical scientist, on hearing of a new, exciting finding, will ask, "Has it been replicated yet?" If it hasn't, the scientist will withhold judgment regarding the finding's validity.

subjects: the people or animals participating in a research project.

theory: a tentative explanation that integrates many and diverse findings to further the understanding of a defined topic.

validity (va-LID-ih-tee): having the quality of being founded on fact or evidence.

variables: factors that change. A variable may depend on another variable (for example, a child's height depends on his age), or it may be independent (for example, a child's height does not depend on the color of her eyes). Sometimes both variables correlate with a third variable (a child's height and eye color both depend on genetics).

Correlations and Causes Researchers often examine the relationships between two or more **variables**—for example, daily vitamin C intake and the number of colds or the duration and severity of cold symptoms. Importantly, researchers must be able to observe, measure, or verify the variables selected. Findings sometimes suggest no **correlation** between variables (regardless of the amount of vitamin C consumed, the number of colds remains the same). Other times, studies find either a **positive correlation** (the more vitamin C, the more colds) or a **negative correlation** (the more vitamin C, the fewer colds). Correlational evidence proves only that variables are associated, not that one is the cause of the other. People often jump to conclusions when they notice correlations, but their conclusions are often wrong. To actually prove that A causes B, scientists have to find evidence of the *mechanism*—that is, an explanation of how A might cause B.

Cautious Conclusions When researchers record and analyze the results of their experiments, they must exercise caution in their interpretation of the findings. For example, in an epidemiological study, scientists may use a specific segment of the population—say, men 18 to 30 years old. When the scientists draw conclusions, they are careful not to generalize the findings to all people. Similarly, scientists performing research studies using animals are cautious in applying their findings to human beings. Conclusions from any one research study are always tentative and take into account findings from studies conducted by other scientists as well. As evidence accumulates, scientists gain confidence about making recommendations that affect people's health and lives. Still, their statements are worded cautiously, such as "A diet high in fruits and vegetables *may* protect against *some* cancers."

Quite often, as scientists approach an answer to one research question, they raise several more questions, so future research projects are never lacking. Further scientific investigation then seeks to answer questions such as "What substance or substances within fruits and vegetables provide protection?" If those substances turn out to be the vitamins found so abundantly in fresh produce, then, "How much is needed to offer protection?" "How do these vitamins protect against cancer?" "Is it their action as antioxidant nutrients?" "If not, might it be another action or even another substance that accounts for the protection fruits and vegetables provide against cancer?" (Highlight 11 explores the answers to these questions and reviews recent research on antioxidant nutrients and disease.)

Publishing Research

The findings from a research study are submitted to a board of reviewers composed of other scientists who rigorously evaluate the study to assure that the scientific method was followed—a process known as **peer review.** The reviewers critique the study's hypothesis, methodology, statistical significance, and conclusions. If the reviewers consider the conclusions to be well supported by the evidence—that is, if the research has **validity**—they endorse the work for publication in a scientific journal where others can read it. This raises an important point regarding information found on the Internet: much gets published without the rigorous scrutiny of peer review. Consequently, readers must assume greater responsibility for examining the data and conclusions presented—often without the benefit of journal citations.

Even when a new finding is published or released to the media, it is still only preliminary and not very meaningful by itself. Other scientists will need to confirm or disprove the findings through **replication.** To be accepted into the body of nutrition knowledge, a finding must stand up to rigorous, repeated testing in experiments performed by several different researchers. What we "know" in nutrition results from years of replicating study findings. Communicating the latest finding in its proper context without distorting or oversimplifying the message is a challenge for scientists and journalists alike.

With each report from scientists, the field of nutrition changes a little—each finding contributes another piece to the whole body of knowledge. People who know how science works understand that single findings, like single frames in a movie, are just small parts of a larger story. Over years, the picture of what is "true" in nutrition gradually changes, and dietary recommendations change to reflect the current understanding of scientific research. Highlight 5 provides a detailed look at how dietary fat recommendations have evolved over the past several decades as researchers have uncovered the relationships between the various kinds of fat and their roles in supporting or harming health.

> **IN SUMMARY**
>
> Scientists learn about nutrition by conducting experiments that follow the protocol of scientific research. Researchers take care to establish similar control and experimental groups, large sample sizes, placebos, and blind treatments. Their findings must be reviewed and replicated by other scientists before being accepted as valid.

The characteristics of well-designed research have enabled scientists to study the actions of nutrients in the body. Such research has laid the foundation for quantifying how much of each nutrient the body needs.

Dietary Reference Intakes

Using the results of thousands of research studies, nutrition experts have produced a set of standards that define the amounts of energy, nutrients, other dietary components, and physical activity that best support health. These recommendations are called **Dietary Reference Intakes (DRI),** and they reflect the collaborative efforts of researchers in both the United States and Canada.*[8] The inside front covers of this book provide a handy reference for DRI values.

Establishing Nutrient Recommendations

The DRI Committee consists of highly qualified scientists who base their estimates of nutrient needs on careful examination and interpretation of scientific evidence. These recommendations apply to healthy people and may not be appropriate for people with diseases that increase or decrease nutrient needs. The next several paragraphs discuss specific aspects of how the committee goes about establishing the values that make up the DRI:

- Estimated Average Requirements (EAR)
- Recommended Dietary Allowances (RDA)
- Adequate Intakes (AI)
- Tolerable Upper Intake Levels (UL)

Estimated Average Requirements (EAR) The committee reviews hundreds of research studies to determine the **requirement** for a nutrient—how much is needed in the diet. The committee selects a different criterion for each nutrient based on its various roles in performing activities in the body and in reducing disease risks.

An examination of all the available data reveals that each person's body is unique and has its own set of requirements. Men differ from women, and needs change as people grow from infancy through old age. For this reason, the committee clusters its recommendations for people into groups based on age and gender. Even so, the exact requirements for people of the same age and gender are likely to be different. For example, person A might need 40 units of a particular nutrient each day; person B might need 35; and person C, 57. Looking at enough people might reveal that their individual requirements fall into a symmetrical distribution,

Don't let the DRI "alphabet soup" of nutrient intake standards confuse you. Their names make sense when you learn their purposes.

© PhotoDisc/Getty Images

Dietary Reference Intakes (DRI): a set of nutrient intake values for healthy people in the United States and Canada. These values are used for planning and assessing diets and include:
- Estimated Average Requirements (EAR)
- Recommended Dietary Allowances (RDA)
- Adequate Intakes (AI)
- Tolerable Upper Intake Levels (UL)

requirement: the lowest continuing intake of a nutrient that will maintain a specified criterion of adequacy.

---

* The DRI reports are produced by the Food and Nutrition Board, Institute of Medicine of the National Academies, with active involvement of scientists from Canada.

with most near the midpoint and only a few at the extremes (see the left side of Figure 1-5). Using this information, the committee determines an **Estimated Average Requirement (EAR)** for each nutrient—the average amount that appears sufficient for half of the population. In Figure 1-5, the Estimated Average Requirement is shown as 45 units.

Recommended Dietary Allowances (RDA) Once a nutrient *requirement* is established, the committee must decide what intake to *recommend* for everybody—the **Recommended Dietary Allowance (RDA).** As you can see by the distribution in Figure 1-5, the Estimated Average Requirement (shown in the figure as 45 units) is probably closest to everyone's need. However, if people consumed exactly the average requirement of a given nutrient each day, half of the population would develop deficiencies of that nutrient—in Figure 1-5, for example, person C would be among them. Recommendations are therefore set high enough above the Estimated Average Requirement to meet the needs of most healthy people.

Small amounts above the daily requirement do no harm, whereas amounts below the requirement may lead to health problems. When people's nutrient intakes are consistently **deficient** (less than the requirement), their nutrient stores decline, and over time this decline leads to poor health and deficiency symptoms. Therefore, to ensure that the nutrient RDA meet the needs of as many people as possible, the RDA are set near the top end of the range of the population's estimated requirements.

In this example, a reasonable RDA might be 63 units a day (see the right side of Figure 1-5). Such a point can be calculated mathematically so that it covers about 98 percent of a population. Almost everybody—including person C whose needs were higher than the average—would be covered if they met this dietary goal. Relatively few people's requirements would exceed this recommendation, and even then, they wouldn't exceed by much.

Adequate Intakes (AI) For some nutrients, there is insufficient scientific evidence to determine an Estimated Average Requirement (which is needed to set an RDA). In these cases, the committee establishes an **Adequate Intake (AI)** instead of an RDA. An AI reflects the average amount of a nutrient that a group of healthy people consumes. Like the RDA, the AI may be used as nutrient goals for individuals.

FIGURE 1-5 Estimated Average Requirements (EAR) and Recommended Dietary Allowances (RDA) Compared

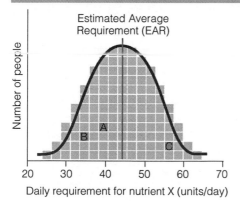

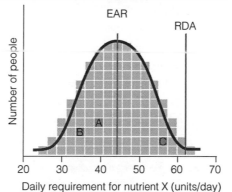

Each square in the graph above represents a person with unique nutritional requirements. (The text discusses three of these people—A, B, and C.) Some people require only a small amount of nutrient X and some require a lot. Most people, however, fall somewhere in the middle. This amount that covers half of the population is called the Estimated Average Requirement (EAR) and is represented here by the red line.

The Recommended Dietary Allowance (RDA) for a nutrient (shown here in purple) is set well above the EAR, covering about 98% of the population.

Estimated Average Requirement (EAR): the average daily amount of a nutrient that will maintain a specific biochemical or physiological function in half the healthy people of a given age and gender group.

Recommended Dietary Allowance (RDA): the average daily amount of a nutrient considered adequate to meet the known nutrient needs of practically all healthy people; a goal for dietary intake by individuals.

deficient: the amount of a nutrient below which almost all healthy people can be expected, over time, to experience deficiency symptoms.

Adequate Intake (AI): the average daily amount of a nutrient that appears sufficient to maintain a specified criterion; a value used as a guide for nutrient intake when an RDA cannot be determined.

FIGURE 1-6 Inaccurate versus Accurate View of Nutrient Intakes

The RDA or AI for a given nutrient represents a point that lies within a range of appropriate and reasonable intakes between toxicity and deficiency. Both of these recommendations are high enough to provide reserves in times of short-term dietary inadequacies, but not so high as to approach toxicity. Nutrient intakes above or below this range may be equally harmful.

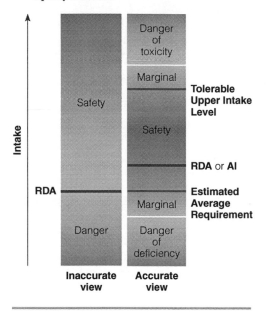

◆ Reference adults:
  • Men: 19–30 yr, 5 ft 10 in., and 154 lb
  • Women: 19–30 yr, 5 ft 4 in., and 126 lb

Tolerable Upper Intake Level (UL): the maximum daily amount of a nutrient that appears safe for most healthy people and beyond which there is an increased risk of adverse health effects.

Estimated Energy Requirement (EER): the average dietary energy intake that maintains energy balance and good health in a person of a given age, gender, weight, height, and level of physical activity.

Acceptable Macronutrient Distribution Ranges (AMDR): ranges of intakes for the energy nutrients that provide adequate energy and nutrients and reduce the risk of chronic diseases.

Although both the RDA and the AI serve as nutrient intake goals for individuals, their differences are noteworthy. An RDA for a given nutrient is based on enough scientific evidence to expect that the needs of almost all healthy people will be met. An AI, on the other hand, must rely more heavily on scientific judgments because sufficient evidence is lacking. The percentage of people covered by an AI is unknown; an AI is expected to exceed average requirements, but it may cover more or fewer people than an RDA would cover (if an RDA could be determined). For these reasons, AI values are more tentative than RDA. The table on the inside front cover identifies which nutrients have an RDA and which have an AI. Later chapters present the RDA and AI values for the vitamins and minerals.

Tolerable Upper Intake Levels (UL)   As mentioned earlier, the recommended intakes for nutrients are generous, and they do not necessarily cover every individual for every nutrient. Nevertheless, it is probably best not to exceed these recommendations by very much or very often. Individual tolerances for high doses of nutrients vary, and somewhere above the recommended intake is a point beyond which a nutrient is likely to become toxic. This point is known as the **Tolerable Upper Intake Level (UL)**. It is naive—and inaccurate—to think of recommendations as minimum amounts. A more accurate view is to see a person's nutrient needs as falling within a range, with marginal and danger zones both below and above it (see Figure 1-6).

Paying attention to upper levels is particularly useful in guarding against the overconsumption of nutrients, which may occur when people use large-dose supplements and fortified foods regularly. Later chapters discuss the dangers associated with excessively high intakes of vitamins and minerals, and the inside front cover (page C) presents tables that include the upper-level values for selected nutrients.

Establishing Energy Recommendations

In contrast to the RDA and AI values for nutrients, the recommendation for energy is not generous. Excess energy cannot be readily excreted and is eventually stored as body fat. These reserves may be beneficial when food is scarce, but they can also lead to obesity and its associated health consequences.

Estimated Energy Requirement (EER)   The energy recommendation—called the **Estimated Energy Requirement (EER)**—represents the average dietary energy intake (kcalories per day) that will maintain energy balance in a person who has a healthy body weight and level of physical activity. ◆ Balance is key to the energy recommendation. Enough energy is needed to sustain a healthy and active life, but too much energy can lead to weight gain and obesity. Because *any* amount in excess of energy needs will result in weight gain, no upper level for energy has been determined.

Acceptable Macronutrient Distribution Ranges (AMDR)   People don't eat energy directly; they derive energy from foods containing carbohydrate, fat, and protein. Each of these three energy-yielding nutrients contributes to the total energy intake, and those contributions vary in relation to each other. The DRI committee has determined that the composition of a diet that provides adequate energy and nutrients and reduces the risk of chronic diseases is:

• 45–65 percent kcalories from carbohydrate
• 20–35 percent kcalories from fat
• 10–35 percent kcalories from protein

These values are known as **Acceptable Macronutrient Distribution Ranges (AMDR).**

Using Nutrient Recommendations

Although the intent of nutrient recommendations seems simple, they are the subject of much misunderstanding and controversy. Perhaps the following facts will help put them in perspective:

1. Estimates of adequate energy and nutrient intakes apply to *healthy* people. They need to be adjusted for malnourished people or those with medical problems who may require supplemented or restricted intakes.

2. *Recommendations* are not minimum requirements, nor are they necessarily optimal intakes for all individuals. Recommendations can only target "most" of the people and cannot account for individual variations in nutrient needs—yet. Given the recent explosion of knowledge about genetics, the day may be fast approaching when nutrition scientists will be able to determine an individual's optimal nutrient needs.[9] Until then, registered dietitians ◆ and other qualified health professionals can help determine if recommendations should be adjusted to meet individual needs.

3. Most nutrient goals are intended to be met through diets composed of a variety of *foods* whenever possible. Because foods contain mixtures of nutrients and nonnutrients, they deliver more than just those nutrients covered by the recommendations. Excess intakes of vitamins and minerals are unlikely when they come from foods rather than supplements.

4. Recommendations apply to *average* daily intakes. Trying to meet the recommendations for every nutrient every day is difficult and unnecessary. The length of time over which a person's intake can deviate from the average without risk of deficiency or overdose varies for each nutrient, depending on how the body uses and stores the nutrient. For most nutrients (such as thiamin and vitamin C), deprivation would lead to rapid development of deficiency symptoms (within days or weeks); for others (such as vitamin A and vitamin B_{12}), deficiencies would develop more slowly (over months or years).

5. Each of the DRI categories serves a unique purpose. For example, the Estimated Average Requirements are most appropriately used to develop and evaluate nutrition programs for *groups* such as schoolchildren or military personnel. The RDA (or AI if an RDA is not available) can be used to set goals for *individuals*. Tolerable Upper Intake Levels serve as a reminder to keep nutrient intakes below amounts that increase the risk of toxicity—not a common problem when nutrients derive from foods, but a real possibility for some nutrients if supplements are used regularly.

With these understandings, professionals can use the DRI for a variety of purposes.

◆ A **registered dietitian** is a college-educated food and nutrition specialist who is qualified to evaluate people's nutritional health and needs. See Highlight 1 for more on what constitutes a nutrition expert.

Comparing Nutrient Recommendations

At least 40 different nations and international organizations have published nutrient standards similar to those used in the United States and Canada. Slight differences may be apparent, reflecting differences both in the interpretation of the data from which the standards were derived and in the food habits and physical activities of the populations they serve.

Many countries use the recommendations developed by two international groups: FAO (Food and Agriculture Organization) and WHO (World Health Organization). ◆ The FAO/WHO recommendations are considered sufficient to maintain health in nearly all healthy people worldwide.

◆ Nutrient recommendations from FAO/WHO are provided in Appendix I.

IN SUMMARY

The Dietary Reference Intakes (DRI) are a set of nutrient intake values that can be used to plan and evaluate diets for healthy people. The Estimated Average Requirement (EAR) defines the amount of a nutrient that supports a specific function in the body for half of the population. The Recommended Dietary Allowance (RDA) is based on the Estimated Average Requirement and establishes a goal for dietary intake that will meet the needs of almost all healthy people. An Adequate Intake (AI) serves a similar purpose when an RDA cannot be determined. The Estimated Energy Requirement (EER) defines the average amount of energy intake needed to maintain energy balance, and the Acceptable Macronutrient Distribution Ranges (AMDR) define the proportions contributed by carbohydrate, fat, and protein to a healthy diet. The Tolerable Upper Intake Level (UL) establishes the highest amount that appears safe for regular consumption.

Nutrition Assessment

What happens when a person doesn't get enough or gets too much of a nutrient or energy? If the deficiency or excess is significant over time, the person exhibits signs of **malnutrition**. With a deficiency of energy, the person may display the symptoms of **undernutrition** by becoming extremely thin, losing muscle tissue, and becoming prone to infection and disease. With a deficiency of a nutrient, the person may experience skin rashes, depression, hair loss, bleeding gums, muscle spasms, night blindness, or other symptoms. With an excess of energy, the person may become obese and vulnerable to diseases associated with **overnutrition** such as heart disease and diabetes. With a sudden nutrient overdose, the person may experience hot flashes, yellowing skin, a rapid heart rate, low blood pressure, or other symptoms. Similarly, over time, regular intakes in excess of needs may also have adverse effects.

Malnutrition symptoms—such as diarrhea, skin rashes, and fatigue—are easy to miss because they resemble the symptoms of other diseases. But a person who has learned how to use assessment techniques to detect malnutrition can identify when these conditions are caused by poor nutrition and can recommend steps to correct it. This discussion presents the basics of nutrition assessment; many more details are offered in later chapters and in Appendix E.

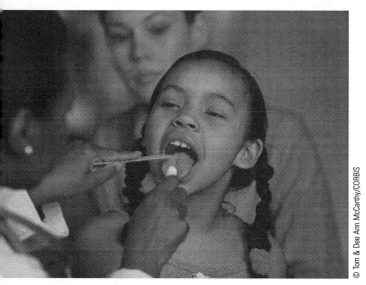

© Tom & Dee Ann McCarthy/CORBIS

A peek inside the mouth provides clues to a person's nutrition status. An inflamed tongue may indicate a B vitamin deficiency, and mottled teeth may reveal fluoride toxicity, for example.

malnutrition: any condition caused by excess or deficient food energy or nutrient intake or by an imbalance of nutrients.

• **mal** = bad

undernutrition: deficient energy or nutrients.

overnutrition: excess energy or nutrients.

nutrition assessment: a comprehensive analysis of a person's nutrition status that uses health, socioeconomic, drug, and diet histories; anthropometric measurements; physical examinations; and laboratory tests.

Nutrition Assessment of Individuals

To prepare a **nutrition assessment,** a registered dietitian or other trained health care professional uses:

- Historical information
- Anthropometric data
- Physical examinations
- Laboratory tests

Each of these methods involves collecting data in various ways and interpreting each finding in relation to the others to create a total picture.

Historical Information One step in evaluating nutrition status is to obtain information about a person's history with respect to health status, socioeconomic status, drug use, and diet. The health history reflects a person's medical record and may reveal a disease that interferes with the person's ability to eat or the body's use of nutrients. The person's family history of major diseases is also noteworthy, especially for conditions such as heart disease that have a genetic tendency to run in families. Economic circumstances may show a financial inability to buy foods or inadequate kitchen facilities in which to prepare them. Social factors such as marital status, ethnic background, and educational level also influence food choices and nutrition status. A drug history, including all prescribed and over-the-counter medications as well as illegal substances, may highlight possible interactions that lead to nutrient deficiencies (as described in Highlight 17). A diet history that examines a person's intake of foods, beverages, and supplements may reveal either a surplus or inadequacy of nutrients or energy.

To take a diet history, the assessor collects data about the foods a person eats. The data may be collected by recording the foods the person has eaten over a period of 24 hours, three days, or a week or more or by asking what foods the person typically eats and how much of each. The days in the record must be fairly typical of the person's diet, and portion sizes must be recorded accurately. To determine the amounts of nutrients consumed, the assessor usually enters the foods and their portion sizes into a computer using a diet analysis program. This step can also be done manually by looking up each food in a table of food composition such

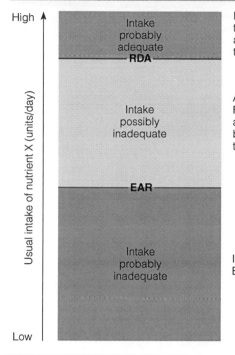

FIGURE 1-7 Using the DRI to Assess the Dietary Intake of a Healthy Individual

High

Usual intake of nutrient X (units/day)

Intake probably adequate

RDA

Intake possibly inadequate

EAR

Intake probably inadequate

Low

If a person's usual intake falls above the RDA, the intake is probably adequate because the RDA covers the needs of almost all people.

A usual intake that falls between the RDA and the EAR is more difficult to assess; the intake may be adequate, but the chances are greater or equal that it is inadequate.

If the usual intake falls below the EAR, it is probably inadequate.

as Appendix H in this book. The assessor then compares the calculated nutrient intakes with the DRI to determine the probability of adequacy (see Figure 1-7).[10] Alternatively, the diet history might be compared against standards such as the USDA Food Guide or *Dietary Guidelines* (described in Chapter 2).

An estimate of energy and nutrient intakes from a diet history, when combined with other sources of information, can help confirm or rule out the *possibility* of suspected nutrition problems. A sufficient intake of a nutrient does not guarantee adequacy, and an insufficient intake does not always indicate a deficiency. Such findings, however, warn of possible problems.

Anthropometric Data A second technique that may help to reveal nutrition problems is taking **anthropometric** measures such as height and weight. The assessor compares a person's measurements with standards specific for gender and age or with previous measures on the same individual. (Chapter 8 presents information on body weight and its standards.)

Measurements taken periodically and compared with previous measurements reveal patterns and indicate trends in a person's overall nutrition status, but they provide little information about specific nutrients. Instead, measurements out of line with expectations may reveal such problems as growth failure in children, wasting or swelling of body tissues in adults, and obesity—conditions that may reflect energy or nutrient deficiencies or excesses.

Physical Examinations A third nutrition assessment technique is a physical examination looking for clues to poor nutrition status. Every part of the body that can be inspected may offer such clues: the hair, eyes, skin, posture, tongue, fingernails, and others. The examination requires skill because many physical signs reflect more than one nutrient deficiency or toxicity—or even nonnutrition conditions. Like the other assessment techniques, a physical examination alone does not yield firm conclusions. Instead, physical examinations reveal possible imbalances that must be confirmed by other assessment techniques, or they confirm results from other assessment measures.

Laboratory Tests A fourth way to detect a developing deficiency, imbalance, or toxicity is to take samples of blood or urine, analyze them in the laboratory, and compare the results with normal values for a similar population. ◆ A goal of nutrition

◆ Assessment may one day depend on measures of how a nutrient influences genetic activity within the cells, instead of quantities in the blood or other tissues.

anthropometric (AN-throw-poe-MET-rick): relating to measurement of the physical characteristics of the body, such as height and weight.
- **anthropos** = human
- **metric** = measuring

FIGURE 1-8 Stages in the Development of a Nutrient Deficiency

Internal changes precede outward signs of deficiencies. However, outward signs of sickness need not appear before a person takes corrective measures. Laboratory tests can help determine nutrient status in the early stages.

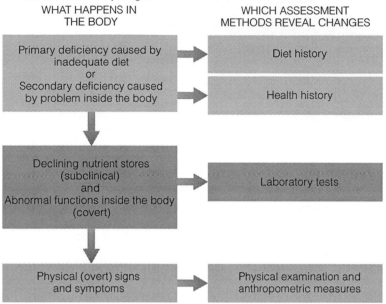

assessment is to uncover early signs of malnutrition before symptoms appear, and laboratory tests are most useful for this purpose. In addition, they can confirm suspicions raised by other assessment methods.

Iron, for Example The mineral iron can be used to illustrate the stages in the development of a nutrient deficiency and the assessment techniques useful in detecting them. The **overt,** or outward, signs of an iron deficiency appear at the end of a long sequence of events. Figure 1-8 describes what happens in the body as a nutrient deficiency progresses and shows which assessment methods can reveal those changes.

First, the body has too little iron—either because iron is lacking in the person's diet (a **primary deficiency**) or because the person's body doesn't absorb enough, excretes too much, or uses iron inefficiently (a **secondary deficiency**). A diet history provides clues to primary deficiencies; a health history provides clues to secondary deficiencies.

Next, the body begins to use up its stores of iron. At this stage, the deficiency might be described as **subclinical.** It exists as a **covert** condition, and although it might be detected by laboratory tests, no outward signs are apparent.

Finally, the body's iron stores are exhausted. Now, it cannot make enough iron-containing red blood cells to replace those that are aging and dying. Iron is needed in red blood cells to carry oxygen to all the body's tissues. When iron is lacking, fewer red blood cells are made, the new ones are pale and small, and every part of the body feels the effects of oxygen shortage. Now the overt symptoms of deficiency appear—weakness, fatigue, pallor, and headaches, reflecting the iron-deficient state of the blood. A physical examination will reveal these symptoms.

Nutrition Assessment of Populations

To assess a population's nutrition status, researchers conduct surveys using techniques similar to those used on individuals. The data collected are then used by various agencies for numerous purposes, including the development of national health goals.

National Nutrition Surveys The National Nutrition Monitoring program coordinates the many nutrition-related surveys and research activities of various federal agencies. The integration of two major national surveys ◆ provides comprehensive data efficiently.[11] One survey collects data on the kinds and amounts of foods people eat.* Then researchers calculate the energy and nutrients in the foods and compare the amounts consumed with a standard. The other survey examines the people themselves, using anthropometric measurements, physical examinations, and laboratory tests.**[12] The data provide valuable information on several nutrition-related conditions, such as growth retardation, heart disease, and nutrient deficiencies. National nutrition surveys often oversample high-risk groups (low-income families, pregnant women, adolescents, the elderly, African Americans, and Mexican Americans) to glean an accurate estimate of their health and nutrition status.

The resulting wealth of information from the national nutrition surveys is used for a variety of purposes. For example, Congress uses this information to establish

◆ The new integrated survey is called *What We Eat in America.*

overt (oh-VERT): out in the open and easy to observe.
  • **ouvrir** = to open
primary deficiency: a nutrient deficiency caused by inadequate dietary intake of a nutrient.
secondary deficiency: a nutrient deficiency caused by something other than an inadequate intake such as a disease condition or drug interaction that reduces absorption, accelerates use, hastens excretion, or destroys the nutrient.
subclinical deficiency: a deficiency in the early stages, before the outward signs have appeared.
covert (KOH-vert): hidden, as if under covers.
  • **couvrir** = to cover

---

* This survey was formerly called the Continuing Survey of Food Intakes by Individuals (CSFII), conducted by the U.S. Department of Agriculture (USDA).
** This survey is known as the National Health and Nutrition Examination Survey (NHANES), conducted by the U.S. Department of Health and Human Services (DHHS).

public policy on nutrition education, food assistance programs, and the regulation of the food supply. Scientists use the information to establish research priorities. The food industry uses these data to guide decisions in public relations and product development.[13] The Dietary Reference Intakes and other major reports that examine the relationships between diet and health depend on information collected from these nutrition surveys. These data also provide the basis for developing and monitoring national health goals.

National Health Goals Healthy People is a program that identifies the nation's health priorities and guides policies that promote health and prevent disease. At the start of each decade, the program sets goals for improving the nation's health during the following ten years. The goals of Healthy People 2010 focus on "improving the quality of life and eliminating disparity in health among racial and ethnic groups."[14] Nutrition is one of many focus areas, each with numerous objectives. Table 1-4 lists the nutrition and overweight objectives for 2010, and Appendix J includes a table of nutrition-related objectives from other focus areas.

At mid-decade, the nation's progress toward meeting its nutrition and overweight Healthy People 2010 goals was somewhat bleak. Trends in overweight and obesity worsened. Objectives to eat more fruits, vegetables, and whole grains and to increase physical activity showed little or no improvement. Clearly, "what we eat in America" must change if we hope to meet the Healthy People 2010 goals.

National Trends What do we eat in America and how has it changed over the past 30 years?[15] The short answer to both questions is "a lot." We eat more meals away from home, particularly at fast-food restaurants. We eat larger portions. We drink more sweetened beverages and eat more energy-dense, nutrient-poor foods such as candy and chips. We snack frequently. As a result of these dietary habits, our energy intake has risen and, consequently, so has the incidence of overweight and obesity. Overweight and obesity, in turn, profoundly influence our health—as the next section explains.

Surveys provide valuable information about the kinds of foods people eat.

TABLE 1-4	Healthy People 2010 Nutrition and Overweight Objectives

- Increase the proportion of adults who are at a *healthy weight.*
- Reduce the proportion of adults who are *obese.*
- Reduce the proportion of children and adolescents who are *overweight* or *obese.*
- Reduce *growth retardation* among low-income children under age 5 years.
- Increase the proportion of persons aged 2 years and older who consume at least two daily servings of *fruit.*
- Increase the proportion of persons aged 2 years and older who consume at least three daily servings of *vegetables,* with at least one-third being dark green or orange vegetables.
- Increase the proportion of persons aged 2 years and older who consume at least six daily servings of *grain products,* with at least three being whole grains.
- Increase the proportion of persons aged 2 years and older who consume less than 10 percent of kcalories from *saturated fat.*
- Increase the proportion of persons aged 2 years and older who consume no more than 30 percent of kcalories from *total fat.*

- Increase the proportion of persons aged 2 years and older who consume 2400 mg or less of *sodium.*
- Increase the proportion of persons aged 2 years and older who meet dietary recommendations for *calcium.*
- Reduce *iron deficiency* among young children, females of childbearing age, and pregnant females.
- Reduce *anemia* among low-income pregnant females in their third trimester.
- Increase the proportion of children and adolescents aged 6 to 19 years whose intake of *meals and snacks at school* contributes to good overall dietary quality.
- Increase the proportion of worksites that offer *nutrition or weight management classes or counseling.*
- Increase the proportion of physician office visits made by patients with a diagnosis of cardiovascular disease, diabetes, or hyperlipidemia that include *counseling or education related to diet and nutrition.*
- Increase *food security* among U.S. households and in so doing reduce hunger.

Note: "Nutrition and Overweight" is one of 28 focus areas, each with numerous objectives. Several of the other focus areas have nutrition-related objectives, and these are presented in Appendix J.
SOURCE: Healthy People 2010, **www.healthypeople.gov**

Healthy People: a national public health initiative under the jurisdiction of the U.S. Department of Health and Human Services (DHHS) that identifies the most significant preventable threats to health and focuses efforts toward eliminating them.

IN SUMMARY

People become malnourished when they get too little or too much energy or nutrients. Deficiencies, excesses, and imbalances of nutrients lead to malnutrition diseases. To detect malnutrition in individuals, health care professionals use four nutrition assessment methods. Reviewing dietary data and health information may suggest a nutrition problem in its earliest stages. Laboratory tests may detect it before it becomes overt, whereas anthropometrics and physical examinations pick up on the problem only after it causes symptoms. National surveys use similar assessment methods to measure people's food consumption and to evaluate the nutrition status of populations.

Diet and Health

Diet has always played a vital role in supporting health. Early nutrition research focused on identifying the nutrients in foods that would prevent such common diseases as rickets and scurvy, the vitamin D– and vitamin C–deficiency diseases. With this knowledge, developed countries have successfully defended against nutrient deficiency diseases. World hunger and nutrient deficiency diseases still pose a major health threat in developing countries, however, but not because of a lack of nutrition knowledge (as Chapter 20 explains). More recently, nutrition research has focused on **chronic diseases** associated with energy and nutrient excesses. Once thought to be "rich countries' problems," chronic diseases have now become epidemic in developing countries as well—contributing to three out of five deaths worldwide.[16]

Chronic Diseases

Table 1-5 lists the ten leading causes of death in the United States. These "causes" are stated as if a single condition such as heart disease caused death, but most chronic diseases arise from multiple factors over many years. A person who died of heart disease may have been overweight, had high blood pressure, been a cigarette smoker, and spent years eating a diet high in saturated fat and getting too little exercise.

Of course, not all people who die of heart disease fit this description, nor do all people with these characteristics die of heart disease. People who are overweight might die from the complications of diabetes instead, or those who smoke might die of cancer. They might even die from something totally unrelated to any of these factors, such as an automobile accident. Still, statistical studies have shown that certain conditions and behaviors are linked to certain diseases.

Notice that Table 1-5 highlights five of the top six causes of death as having a link with diet or alcohol. During the past 30 years, as knowledge about these diet and disease relationships grew, the death rates for four of these—heart disease, cancers, strokes, and accidents—decreased.[17] Death rates for diabetes—a chronic disease closely associated with obesity—increased.

Risk Factors for Chronic Diseases

Factors that increase or reduce the *risk* of developing chronic diseases can be identified by analyzing statistical data. A strong association between a **risk factor** and a disease means that when the factor is present, the *likelihood* of developing the disease increases. It does not mean that all people with the risk factor will develop the disease. Similarly, a lack of risk factors does not guarantee freedom from a given disease. On the average, though, the more risk factors in a person's life, the greater that person's chances of developing the disease. Conversely, the fewer risk factors in a person's life, the better the chances for good health.

TABLE 1-5 Leading Causes of Death in the United States

	Percentage of Total Deaths
1. Heart disease	28.0
2. Cancers	22.7
3. Strokes	6.4
4. Chronic lung diseases	5.2
5. Accidents	4.5
6. Diabetes mellitus	3.0
7. Pneumonia and influenza	2.7
8. Alzheimer's disease	2.6
9. Kidney diseases	1.7
10. Blood infections	1.4

NOTE: The diseases highlighted in green have relationships with diet; yellow indicates a relationship with alcohol.
SOURCE: National Center for Health Statistics: www.cdc.gov/nchs

chronic diseases: diseases characterized by a slow progression and long duration. Examples include heart disease, cancer, and diabetes.

risk factor: a condition or behavior associated with an elevated frequency of a disease but not proved to be causal. Leading risk factors for chronic diseases include obesity, cigarette smoking, high blood pressure, high blood cholesterol, physical inactivity, and a diet high in saturated fats and low in vegetables, fruits, and whole grains.

Physical activity can be both fun and beneficial.

Factors	Percentage of Deaths
Tobacco	18
Poor diet/inactivity	15
Alcohol	4
Microbial agents	3
Toxic agents	2
Motor vehicles	2
Firearms	1
Sexual behavior	1
Illicit drugs	1

TABLE 1-6 Factors Contributing to Deaths in the United States

SOURCE: A. H. Mokdad and coauthors, Actual causes of death in the United States, 2000, *Journal of the American Medical Association* 291 (2004): 1238–1245, with corrections from *Journal of the American Medical Association* 293 (2005): 298.

Risk Factors Persist Risk factors tend to persist over time. Without intervention, a young adult with high blood pressure will most likely continue to have high blood pressure as an older adult, for example. Thus, to minimize the damage, early intervention is most effective.

Risk Factors Cluster Risk factors tend to cluster. For example, a person who is obese may be physically inactive, have high blood pressure, and have high blood cholesterol—all risk factors associated with heart disease. Intervention that focuses on one risk factor often benefits the others as well. For example, physical activity can help reduce weight. The physical activity and weight loss will, in turn, help to lower blood pressure and blood cholesterol.

Risk Factors in Perspective The most prominent factor contributing to death in the United States is tobacco use, ◆ followed closely by diet and activity patterns, and then alcohol use (see Table 1-6).[18] Risk factors such as smoking, poor dietary habits, physical inactivity, and alcohol consumption are personal behaviors that can be changed. Decisions to not smoke, to eat a well-balanced diet, to engage in regular physical activity, and to drink alcohol in moderation (if at all) improve the likelihood that a person will enjoy good health. Other risk factors, such as genetics, gender, and age, also play important roles in the development of chronic diseases, but they cannot be changed. Health recommendations acknowledge the influence of such factors on the development of disease, but they must focus on the factors that are changeable. For the two out of three Americans who do not smoke or drink alcohol excessively, the one choice that can influence long-term health prospects more than any other is diet.

◆ Cigarette smoking is responsible for almost one of every five deaths each year.

IN SUMMARY

Within the range set by genetics, a person's choice of diet influences long-term health. Diet has no influence on some diseases but is linked closely to others. Personal life choices, such as engaging in physical activity and using tobacco or alcohol, also affect health for the better or worse.

The next several chapters provide many more details about nutrients and how they support health. Whenever appropriate, the discussion shows how diet influences each of today's major diseases. Dietary recommendations appear again and again, as each nutrient's relationships with health is explored. Most people who follow the recommendations will benefit and can enjoy good health into their later years.

ThomsonNOW™
www.thomsonedu.com/thomsonnow

 Nutrition Portfolio

Each chapter in this book ends with simple Nutrition Portfolio activities that invite you to review key messages and consider whether your personal choices are meeting the dietary goals introduced in the text. By keeping a journal of these Nutrition Portfolio assignments, you can examine how your knowledge and behaviors change as you progress in your study of nutrition.

Your food choices play a key role in keeping you healthy and reducing your risk of chronic diseases.

■ Identify the factors that most influence your food choices for meals and snacks.

■ List the chronic disease risk factors and conditions (listed in the definition of risk factors on p. 24) that you or members of your family have.

■ Describe lifestyle changes you can make to improve your chances of enjoying good health.

NUTRITION ON THE NET

ThomsonNOW™
For further study of topics covered in this chapter, log on to **www.thomsonedu .com/thomsonnow.** Go to Chapter 1, then to Nutrition on the Net.

- Search for "nutrition" at the U.S. Government health and nutrition information sites: **www.healthfinder.gov** or **www.nutrition.gov**

- Learn more about basic science research from the National Science Foundation and Research!America: **www.nsf.gov** and **researchamerica.org**

- Review the Dietary Reference Intakes: **www.nap.edu**

- Review nutrition recommendations from the Food and Agriculture Organization and the World Health Organization: **www.fao.org** and **www.who.org**

- View Healthy People 2010: **www.healthypeople.gov**

- Visit the Food and Nutrition section of the Healthy Living area in Health Canada: **www.hc-sc.gc.ca**

- Learn about the national nutrition survey: **www.cdc.gov/nchs/nhanes.htm**

- Get information from the Food Surveys Research Group: **www.barc.usda.gov/bhnrc/foodsurvey**

- Visit the food and nutrition center of the Mayo Clinic: **www.mayohealth.org**

- Create a chart of your family health history at the U.S. Surgeon General's site: **familyhistory.hhs.gov**

NUTRITION CALCULATIONS

ThomsonNOW For additional practice, log on to www.thomsonedu.com/thomsonnow. Go to Chapter 1, then to Nutrition Calculations.

Several chapters end with problems to give you practice in doing simple nutrition-related calculations. Although the situations are hypothetical, the numbers are real, and calculating the answers (check them on p. 29) provides a valuable nutrition lesson. Once you have mastered these examples, you will be prepared to examine your own food choices. Be sure to show your calculations for each problem.

1. Calculate the energy provided by a food's energy-nutrient contents. A cup of fried rice contains 5 grams protein, 30 grams carbohydrate, and 11 grams fat.
   a. How many kcalories does the rice provide from these energy nutrients?

   —————————— = —— kcal protein
   —————————— = —— kcal carbohydrate
   —————————— = —— kcal fat

   Total = —— kcal

   b. What percentage of the energy in the fried rice comes from each of the energy-yielding nutrients?

   —————————— = —— % kcal from protein
   —————————— = —— % kcal from carbohydrate
   —————————— = —— % kcal from fat

   Total = —— %

   Note: The total should add up to 100%; 99% or 101% due to rounding is also acceptable.
   c. Calculate how many of the 146 kcalories provided by a 12-ounce can of beer come from alcohol, if the beer contains 1 gram protein and 13 grams carbohydrate. (Note: The remaining kcalories derive from alcohol.)

   1 g protein = —— kcal protein
   13 g carbohydrate = —— kcal carbohydrate
   = —— kcal alcohol

   How many grams of alcohol does this represent?
   —— g alcohol

2. Even a little nutrition knowledge can help you identify some bogus claims. Consider an advertisement for a new "super supplement" that claims the product provides 15 grams protein and 10 kcalories per dose. Is this possible? —— Why or why not? ——————— = —— kcal

STUDY QUESTIONS

ThomsonNOW
To assess your understanding of chapter topics, take the Student Practice Test and explore the modules recommended in your Personalized Study Plan. Log onto www.thomsonedu.com/thomsonnow.

These questions will help you review this chapter. You will find the answers in the discussions on the pages provided.

1. Give several reasons (and examples) why people make the food choices that they do. (p. 3–5)

2. What is a nutrient? Name the six classes of nutrients found in foods. What is an essential nutrient? (pp. 6–7)

3. Which nutrients are inorganic, and which are organic? Discuss the significance of that distinction. (pp. 7, 10)

4. Which nutrients yield energy, and how much energy do they yield per gram? How is energy measured? (pp. 7–10)

5. Describe how alcohol resembles nutrients. Why is alcohol not considered a nutrient? (pp. 8, 10)

6. What is the science of nutrition? Describe the types of research studies and methods used in acquiring nutrition information. (pp. 11–16)

7. Explain how variables might be correlational but not causal. (p. 15)

8. What are the DRI? Who develops the DRI? To whom do they apply? How are they used? In your description, identify the categories of DRI and indicate how they are related. (pp. 16–19)

9. What judgment factors are involved in setting the energy and nutrient recommendations? (pp. 17–18)

10. What happens when people get either too little or too much energy or nutrients? Define malnutrition, undernutrition, and overnutrition. Describe the four methods used to detect energy and nutrient deficiencies and excesses. (pp. 20–22)

11. What methods are used in nutrition surveys? What kinds of information can these surveys provide? (pp. 22–23)

12. Describe risk factors and their relationships to disease. (pp. 24–25)

These multiple choice questions will help you prepare for an exam. Answers can be found on p. 29.

1. When people eat the foods typical of their families or geographic region, their choices are influenced by:
   a. habit.
   b. nutrition.
   c. personal preference.
   d. ethnic heritage or tradition.

2. Both the human body and many foods are composed mostly of:
   a. fat.
   b. water.
   c. minerals.
   d. proteins.

3. The inorganic nutrients are:
   a. proteins and fats.
   b. vitamins and minerals.
   c. minerals and water.
   d. vitamins and proteins.

4. The energy-yielding nutrients are:
   a. fats, minerals, and water.
   b. minerals, proteins, and vitamins.
   c. carbohydrates, fats, and vitamins.
   d. carbohydrates, fats, and proteins.

5. Studies of populations that reveal correlations between dietary habits and disease incidence are:
   a. clinical trials.
   b. laboratory studies.
   c. case-control studies.
   d. epidemiological studies.

6. An experiment in which neither the researchers nor the subjects know who is receiving the treatment is known as:
   a. double blind.
   b. double control.
   c. blind variable.
   d. placebo control.

7. An RDA represents the:
   a. highest amount of a nutrient that appears safe for most healthy people.
   b. lowest amount of a nutrient that will maintain a specified criterion of adequacy.
   c. average amount of a nutrient considered adequate to meet the known nutrient needs of practically all healthy people.
   d. average amount of a nutrient that will maintain a specific biochemical or physiological function in half the people.

8. Historical information, physical examinations, laboratory tests, and anthropometric measures are:
   a. techniques used in diet planning.
   b. steps used in the scientific method.
   c. approaches used in disease prevention.
   d. methods used in a nutrition assessment.

9. A deficiency caused by an inadequate dietary intake is a(n):
   a. overt deficiency.
   b. covert deficiency.
   c. primary deficiency.
   d. secondary deficiency.

10. Behaviors such as smoking, dietary habits, physical activity, and alcohol consumption that influence the development of disease are known as:
   a. risk factors.
   b. chronic causes.
   c. preventive agents.
   d. disease descriptors.

REFERENCES

1. J. A. Mennella, M. Y. Pepino, and D. R. Reed, Genetic and environmental determinants of bitter perception and sweet preferences, *Pediatrics* 115 (2005): e216.
2. J. E. Tillotson, Our ready-prepared, ready-to-eat nation, *Nutrition Today* 37 (2002): 36-38.
3. D. Benton, Role of parents in the determination of the food preferences of children and the development of obesity, *International Journal of Obesity Related Metabolic Disorders* 28 (2004): 858-869.
4. L. Canetti, E. Bachar, and E. M. Berry, Food and emotion, *Behavioural Processes* 60 (2002): 157-164.
5. Position of the American Dietetic Association: Functional foods, *Journal of the American Dietetic Association* 104 (2004): 814-826.
6. Position of the American Dietetic Association: Total diet approach to communicating food and nutrition information, *Journal of the American Dietetic Association* 102 (2002): 100-108.
7. L. Afman and M. Müller, Nutrigenomics: From molecular nutrition to prevention of disease, *Journal of the American Dietetic Association* 106 (2006): 569-576; J. Ordovas and V. Mooser, Nutrigenomics and nutrigenetics, *Current Opinion in Lipidology* 15 (2005): 101-108; D. Shattuck, Nutritional genomics, *Journal of the American Dietetic Association* 103 (2003): 16, 18; P. Trayhurn, Nutritional genomics-"Nutrigenomics," *British Journal of Nutrition* 89 (2003): 1-2.
8. Committee on Dietary Reference Intakes, *Dietary Reference Intakes for Water, Potassium, Sodium, Chloride, and Sulfate* (Washington, D.C.: National Academies Press, 2005); Committee on Dietary Reference Intakes, *Dietary Reference Intakes for Energy, Carbohydrate, Fiber, Fat, Fatty Acids, Cholesterol, Protein, and Amino Acids* (Washington, D.C.: National Academies Press, 2005); Committee on Dietary Reference Intakes, *Dietary Reference Intakes for Vitamin A, Vitamin K, Arsenic, Boron, Chromium, Copper, Iodine, Iron, Manganese, Molybdenum, Nickel, Silicon, Vanadium, and Zinc* (Washington, D.C.: National Academy Press, 2001); Committee on Dietary Reference Intakes, *Dietary Reference Intakes for Vitamin C, Vitamin E, Selenium, and Carotenoids* (Washington, D.C.: National Academy Press, 2000); Committee on Dietary Reference Intakes, *Dietary Reference Intakes for Thiamin, Riboflavin, Niacin, Vitamin B6, Folate, Vitamin B12, Pantothenic Acid, Biotin, and Choline* (Washington, D.C.: National Academy Press, 1998); Committee on Dietary Reference Intakes, *Dietary Reference Intakes for Calcium, Phosphorus, Magnesium, Vitamin D, and Fluoride* (Washington, D.C.: National Academy Press, 1997).
10. S. P. Murphy, S. I. Barr, and M. I. Poos, Using the new Dietary Reference Intakes to assess diets: A map to the maze, *Nutrition Reviews* 60 (2002): 267-275.
12. J. Dwyer and coauthors, Collection of food and dietary supplement intake data: What we eat in America-NHANES, *Journal of Nutrition* 133 (2003): 590S-600S.
13. S. J. Crockett and coauthors, Nutrition monitoring application in the food industry, *Nutrition Today* 37 (2002): 130-135.
15. R. R. Briefel and C. L. Johnson, Secular trends in dietary intake in the United States, *Annual Review of Nutrition* 24 (2004): 401-431.
16. B. M. Popkin, Global nutrition dynamics: The world is shifting rapidly toward a diet linked with noncommunicable diseases, *American Journal of Clinical Nutrition* 84 (2006): 289-298; D. Yach and coauthors, The global burden of chronic diseases: Overcoming impediments to prevention and control, *Journal of the American Medical Association* 291 (2004): 2616-2622.
17. A. Jemal and coauthors, Trends in the leading causes of death in the United States, 1970-2002, *Journal of the American Medical Association* 294 (2005): 1255-1259.
18. A. H. Mokdad and coauthors, Actual causes of death in the United States, 2000, *Journal of the American Medical Association* 291 (2004): 1238-1245.

ANSWERS

Nutrition Calculations

1. a.
$$5 \text{ g protein} \times 4 \text{ kcal/g} = 20 \text{ kcal protein}$$
$$30 \text{ g carbohydrate} \times 4 \text{ kcal/g} = 120 \text{ kcal carbohydrate}$$
$$11 \text{ g fat} \times 9 \text{ kcal/g} = 99 \text{ kcal fat}$$
$$\text{Total} = 239 \text{ kcal}$$

b.
$$20 \text{ kcal} \div 239 \text{ kcal} \times 100 = 8.4\% \text{ kcal from protein}$$
$$120 \text{ kcal} \div 239 \text{ kcal} \times 100 = 50.2\% \text{ kcal from carbohydrate}$$
$$99 \text{ kcal} \div 239 \text{ kcal} \times 100 = 41.4\% \text{ kcal from fat}$$
$$\text{Total} = 100\%.$$

c.
$$1 \text{ g protein} = 4 \text{ kcal protein}$$
$$13 \text{ g carbohydrate} = 52 \text{ kcal carbohydrate}$$
$$146 \text{ total kcal} - 56 \text{ kcal (protein + carbohydrate)}$$
$$= 90 \text{ kcal alcohol}$$
$$90 \text{ kcal alcohol} \div 7 \text{ g/kcal} = 12.9 \text{ g alcohol}$$

2. No. 15 g protein $\times$ 4 kcal/g = 60 kcal

Study Questions (multiple choice)

1. d   2. b   3. c   4. d   5. d   6. a   7. c   8. d
9. c   10. a

Nutrition Information and Misinformation—On the Net and in the News

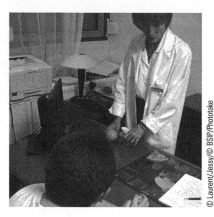

© Laurent/Jessy/© BSIP/Phototake

How can people distinguish valid nutrition information from misinformation? One excellent approach is to notice *who* is providing the information. The "who" behind the information is not always evident, though, especially in the world of electronic media. Keep in mind that *people* develop CD-ROMs and create websites on the Internet, just as people write books and report the news. In all cases, consumers need to determine whether the person is qualified to provide nutrition information.

This highlight begins by examining the unique potential as well as the problems of relying on the Internet and the media for nutrition information. It continues with a discussion of how to identify reliable nutrition information that applies to all resources, including the Internet and the news. (The glossary on p. 32 defines related terms.)

Nutrition on the Net

Got a question? The **Internet** has an answer. The Internet offers endless opportunities to obtain high-quality information, but it also delivers an abundance of incomplete, misleading, or inaccurate information.[1] Simply put: anyone can publish anything.

With hundreds of millions of **websites** on the **World Wide Web,** searching for nutrition information can be an overwhelming experience—much like walking into an enormous bookstore with millions of books, magazines, newspapers, and videos. And like a bookstore, the Internet offers no guarantees of the accuracy of the information found there—much of which is pure fiction.

When using the Internet, keep in mind that the quality of health-related information available covers a broad range.[2] You must evaluate websites for their accuracy, just like every other source. The accompanying "How to" provides tips for determining whether a website is reliable.

One of the most trustworthy sites used by scientists and others is the National Library of Medicine's PubMed, which provides free access to over 10 million abstracts (short descriptions) of research papers published in scientific journals around the world. Many abstracts provide links to websites where full articles are available. Figure H1-1 introduces this valuable resource.

Did you receive the e-mail warning about Costa Rican bananas causing the disease "necrotizing fasciitis"? If so, you've been scammed by Internet misinformation. When nutrition information arrives in unsolicited e-mails, be suspicious if:

- The person sending it to you didn't write it and you cannot determine who did or if that person is a nutrition expert
- The phrase "Forward this to everyone you know" appears
- The phrase "This is not a hoax" appears; chances are that it is
- The news is sensational and you've never heard about it from legitimate sources
- The language is emphatic and the text is sprinkled with capitalized words and exclamation marks
- No references are given or, if present, are of questionable validity when examined
- The message has been debunked on websites such as **www.quackwatch.org** or **www.urbanlegends.com**

Nutrition in the News

Consumers get much of their nutrition information from television news and magazine reports, which have heightened awareness of how diet influences the development of diseases. Consumers benefit from news coverage of nutrition when they learn to make lifestyle changes that will improve their health. Sometimes, however, when magazine articles or television programs report nutrition trends, they mislead consumers and create confusion. They often tell a lopsided story based on a few testimonials instead of presenting the results of research studies or a balance of expert opinions.

Tight deadlines and limited understanding sometimes make it difficult to provide a thorough report. Hungry for the latest news, the media often report scientific findings prematurely—without benefit of careful interpretation, replication, and peer review.[3] Usually, the reports present findings from a single, recently released study, making the news current and controversial. Consequently, the public receives diet and health news quickly, but not always in perspective. Reporters may twist inconclusive findings into "meaningful discoveries" when pressured to write catchy headlines and sensational stories.

As a result, "surprising new findings" seem to contradict one another, and consumers feel frustrated and betrayed. Occasionally, the reports are downright false, but more often the apparent contradictions are simply the normal result of science at work. A single study contributes to the big picture, but when viewed alone, it can easily distort the image. To be meaningful, the conclusions of any study must be presented cautiously within the context of other research findings.

Identifying Nutrition Experts

Regardless of whether the medium is electronic, print, or video, consumers need to ask whether the person behind the information is qualified to speak on nutrition. If the creator of an Internet website recommends eating three pineapples a day to lose weight, a trainer at the gym praises a high-protein diet, or a health-store clerk suggests an herbal supplement, should you believe these people? Can you distinguish between accurate news reports and infomercials on television? Have you noticed that many televised nutrition messages are presented by celebrities, fitness experts, psychologists, food editors, and chefs—that is, almost anyone except a **dietitian?** When you are confused or need sound dietary advice, whom should you ask?

Physicians and Other Health Care Professionals

Many people turn to physicians or other health care professionals for dietary advice, expecting them to know about all health-related matters. But are they the best sources of accurate and current information on nutrition? Only about 30 percent of all medical schools in the United States require students to take a separate nutrition course; less than half require the minimum 25 hours of nutrition instruction recommended by the National Academy of Sciences.[4] By comparison, most students reading this text are taking a nutrition class that provides an average of 45 hours of instruction.

The **American Dietetic Association (ADA)** asserts that standardized nutrition education should be included

---

HOW TO Determine Whether a Website Is Reliable

To determine whether a website offers reliable nutrition information, ask the following questions:

- **Who?** Who is responsible for the site? Is it staffed by qualified professionals? Look for the authors' names and credentials. Have experts reviewed the content for accuracy?
- **When?** When was the site last updated? Because nutrition is an ever-changing science, sites need to be dated and updated frequently.
- **Where?** Where is the information coming from? The three letters following the dot in a Web address identify the site's affiliation. Addresses ending in "gov" (government), "edu" (educational institute), and "org" (organization) generally provide reliable information; "com" (commercial) sites represent businesses and, depending on their qualifications

and integrity, may or may not offer dependable information.
- **Why?** Why is the site giving you this information? Is the site providing a public service or selling a product? Many commercial sites provide accurate information, but some do not. When money is the prime motivation, be aware that the information may be biased.

If you are satisfied with the answers to all of the questions above, then ask this final question:

- **What?** What is the message, and is it in line with other reliable sources? Information that contradicts common knowledge should be questioned. Many reliable sites provide links to other sites to facilitate your quest for knowledge, but this provision alone does not guarantee a reputable intention. Be aware that any site can link to any other site without permission.

---

in the curricula for all health care professionals: physicians, nurses, physician's assistants, dental hygienists, physical and occupational therapists, social workers, and all others who provide services directly to clients. When these professionals understand the relevance of nutrition in the treatment and prevention of disease and have command of reliable nutrition information, then all the people they serve will also be better informed.

FIGURE H1-1 PUBMED (www.pubmed.gov): Internet Resource for Scientific Nutrition References

The U.S. National Library of Medicine's PubMed website offers tutorials to help teach beginners to use the search system effectively. Often, simply visiting the site, typing a query in the "Search for" box, and clicking "Go" will yield satisfactory results.

For example, to find research concerning calcium and bone health, typing "calcium bone" nets over 30,000 results. Try setting limits on dates, types of articles, languages, and other criteria to obtain a more manageable number of abstracts to peruse.

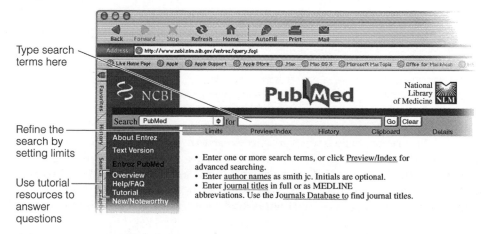

Type search terms here

Refine the search by setting limits

Use tutorial resources to answer questions

- Enter one or more search terms, or click Preview/Index for advanced searching.
- Enter author names as smith jc. Initials are optional.
- Enter journal titles in full or as MEDLINE abbreviations. Use the Journals Database to find journal titles.

GLOSSARY

accredited: approved; in the case of medical centers or universities, certified by an agency recognized by the U.S. Department of Education.

American Dietetic Association (ADA): the professional organization of dietitians in the United States. The Canadian equivalent is Dietitians of Canada, which operates similarly.

certified nutritionists or **certified nutritional consultants** or **certified nutrition therapists:** a person who has been granted a document declaring his or her authority as a nutrition professional; see also nutritionalist.

correspondence schools: schools that offer courses and degrees by mail. Some correspondence schools are accredited; others are not.

dietetic technician: a person who has completed a minimum of an associate's degree from an accredited university or college and an approved dietetic technician program that includes a supervised practice experience. See also dietetic technician, registered (DTR).

dietetic technician, registered (DTR): a dietetic technician who has passed a national examination and maintains registration through continuing professional education.

dietitian: a person trained in nutrition, food science, and diet planning. See also registered dietitian.

DTR: see dietetic technician, registered.

fraudulent: the promotion, for financial gain, of devices, treatments, services, plans, or products (including diets and supplements) that alter or claim to alter a human condition without proof of safety or effectiveness. (The word quackery comes from the term quacksalver, meaning a person who quacks loudly about a miracle product— a lotion or a salve.)

Internet (the net): a worldwide network of millions of computers linked together to share information.

license to practice: permission under state or federal law, granted on meeting specified criteria, to use a certain title (such as dietitian) and offer certain services. **Licensed dietitians** may use the initials **LD** after their names.

misinformation: false or misleading information.

nutritionist: a person who specializes in the study of nutrition. Note that this definition does not specify qualifications and may apply not only to registered dietitians but also to self-described experts whose training is questionable. Most states have licensing laws that define the scope of practice for those calling themselves nutritionists.

public health dietitians: dietitians who specialize in providing nutrition services through organized community efforts.

RD: see registered dietitian.

registered dietitian (RD): a person who has completed a minimum of a bachelor's degree from an accredited university or college, has completed approved course work and a supervised practice program, has passed a national examination, and maintains registration through continuing professional education.

registration: listing; with respect to health professionals, listing with a professional organization that requires specific course work, experience, and passing of an examination.

websites: Internet resources composed of text and graphic files, each with a unique URL (Uniform Resource Locator) that names the site (for example, www.usda.gov).

World Wide Web (the web, commonly abbreviated www): a graphical subset of the Internet.

Most health care professionals appreciate the connections between health and nutrition. Those who have specialized in clinical nutrition are especially well qualified to speak on the subject. Few, however, have the time or experience to develop diet plans and provide detailed diet instructions for clients. Often they wisely refer clients to a qualified nutrition expert—a **registered dietitian (RD).**

Registered Dietitians (RD)

A registered dietitian (RD) has the educational background necessary to deliver reliable nutrition advice and care.[5] To become an RD, a person must earn an undergraduate degree requiring about 60 semester hours in nutrition, food science, and other related subjects; complete a year's clinical internship or the equivalent; pass a national examination administered by the ADA; and maintain up-to-date knowledge and **registration** by participating in required continuing education activities such as attending seminars, taking courses, or writing professional papers.

Some states allow anyone to use the title dietitian or **nutritionist,** but others allow only an RD or people with specified qualifications to call themselves dietitians. Many states provide a further guarantee: a state registration, certification, or **license to practice.** In this way, states identify people who have met minimal standards of education and experience. Still, these state standards may fall short of those defining an RD. Similarly, some alternative educational programs qualify their graduates as **certified nutritionists, certified nutritional consultants,** or **certified nutrition therapists—** terms that sound authoritative but lack the credentials of an RD.[6]

Dietitians perform a multitude of duties in many settings in most communities. They work in the food industry, pharmaceutical companies, home health agencies, long-term care institutions, private practice, public health departments, research centers, education settings, fitness centers, and hospitals. Depending on their work settings, dietitians can assume a number of different job responsibilities and positions. In hospitals, administrative dietitians manage the foodservice system; clinical dietitians provide client care; and nutrition support team dietitians coordinate nutrition care with other health care professionals. In the food industry, dietitians conduct research, develop products, and market services.

Public health dietitians who work in government-funded agencies play a key role in delivering nutrition services to people in the community. Among their many roles, public health dietitians help plan, coordinate, and evaluate food assistance programs; act as consultants to other agencies; manage finances; and much more.

Other Dietary Employees

In some facilities, a **dietetic technician** assists registered dietitians in both administrative and clinical responsibilities. A dietetic technician has been educated and trained to work under the guidance of a registered dietitian; upon passing a national examination, the title changes to **dietetic technician, registered (DTR).**

In addition to the dietetic technician, other dietary employees may include clerks, aides, cooks, porters, and other assistants. These dietary employees do not have extensive formal training in nutrition, and their ability to provide accurate information may be limited.

Identifying Fake Credentials

In contrast to registered dietitians, thousands of people obtain fake nutrition degrees and claim to be nutrition consultants or doctors of "nutrimedicine." These and other such titles may sound meaningful, but most of these people lack the established credentials and training of an ADA-sanctioned dietitian. If you look closely, you can see signs of their fake expertise.

Consider educational background, for example. The minimum standards of education for a dietitian specify a bachelor of science (BS) degree in food science and human nutrition or related fields from an **accredited** college or university.* Such a degree generally requires four to five years of study. In contrast, a fake nutrition expert may display a degree from a six-month correspondence course. Such a degree simply falls short. In some cases, businesses posing as legitimate **correspondence schools** offer even less—they sell certificates to anyone who pays the fees. To obtain these "degrees," a candidate need not attend any classes, read any books, or pass any examinations.

To safeguard educational quality, an accrediting agency recognized by the U.S. Department of Education (DOE) certifies that certain schools meet criteria established to ensure that an institution provides complete and accurate schooling. Unfortunately, fake nutrition degrees are available from schools "accredited" by more than 30 phony accrediting agencies. Acquiring false credentials is especially easy today, with **fraudulent** businesses operating via the Internet.

Knowing the qualifications of someone who provides nutrition information can help you determine whether that person's advice might be harmful or helpful. Don't be afraid to ask for credentials. The accompanying "How to" lists credible sources of nutrition information.

Red Flags of Nutrition Quackery

Figure H1-2 (p. 34) features eight red flags consumers can use to identify nutrition **misinformation.** Sales of unproven and

Figure H1-2 (p. 34)

HOW TO Find Credible Sources of Nutrition Information

Government agencies, volunteer associations, consumer groups, and professional organizations provide consumers with reliable health and nutrition information. Credible sources of nutrition information include:

- Nutrition and food science departments at a university or community college
- Local agencies such as the health department or County Cooperative Extension Service
- Government health agencies such as:
  - Department of Agriculture (USDA)   **www.usda.gov**
  - Department of Health and Human Services (DHHS)   **www.os.dhhs.gov**
  - Food and Drug Administration (FDA)   **www.fda.gov**
  - Health Canada   **www.hc-sc.gc.ca/nutrition**
- Volunteer health agencies such as:
  - American Cancer Society   **www.cancer.org**
  - American Diabetes Association   **www.diabetes.org**
  - American Heart Association   **www.americanheart.org**
- Reputable consumer groups such as:
  - American Council on Science and Health   **www.acsh.org**
  - Federal Citizen Information Center   **www.pueblo.gsa.gov**
  - International Food Information Council   **ific.org**
- Professional health organizations such as:
  - American Dietetic Assocation   **www.eatright.org**
  - American Medical Association   **www.ama-assn.org**
  - Dietitians of Canada   **www.dietitians.ca**
- Journals such as:
  - *American Journal of Clinical Nutrition*   **www.ajcn.org**
  - *New England Journal of Medicine*   **www.nejm.org**
  - *Nutrition Reviews*   **www.ilsi.org**

dangerous products have always been a concern, but the Internet now provides merchants with an easy and inexpensive way to reach millions of customers around the world. Because of the difficulty in regulating the Internet, fraudulent and illegal sales of medical products have hit a bonanza. As is the case with the air, no one owns the Internet, and similarly, no one has control over the pollution. Countries have different laws regarding sales of drugs, dietary supplements, and other health products, but applying these laws to the Internet marketplace is almost impossible. Even if illegal activities could be defined and identified, finding the person responsible for a particular website is not always possible. Websites can open and close in a blink of a cursor. Now, more than ever, consumers must heed the caution "Buyer beware."

In summary, when you hear nutrition news, consider its source. Ask yourself these two questions: Is the person providing the information qualified to speak on nutrition? Is the information based on valid scientific research? If not, find a better source. After all, your health depends on it.

---

* To ensure the quality and continued improvement of nutrition and dietetics education programs, an ADA agency known as the Commission on Accreditation for Dietetics Education (CADE) establishes and enforces eligibility requirements and accreditation standards for programs preparing students for careers as registered dietitians or dietetic technicians. Programs meeting those standards are accredited by CADE.

FIGURE H1-2 Red Flags of Nutrition Quackery

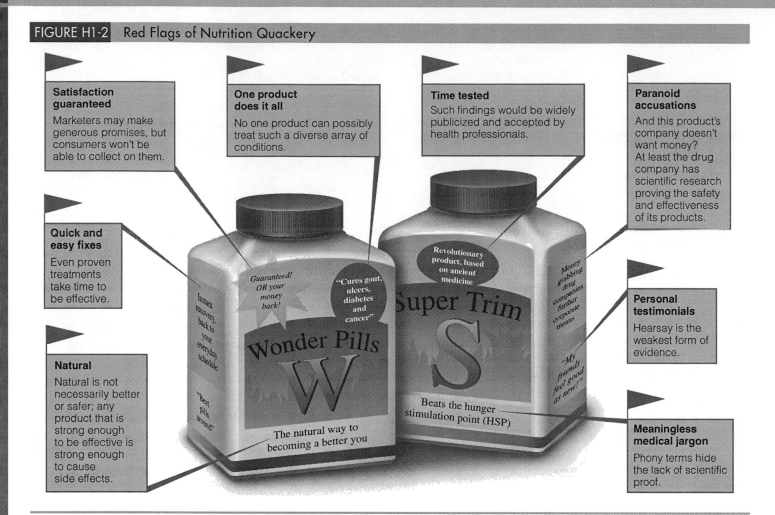

Satisfaction guaranteed
Marketers may make generous promises, but consumers won't be able to collect on them.

One product does it all
No one product can possibly treat such a diverse array of conditions.

Time tested
Such findings would be widely publicized and accepted by health professionals.

Paranoid accusations
And this product's company doesn't want money? At least the drug company has scientific research proving the safety and effectiveness of its products.

Quick and easy fixes
Even proven treatments take time to be effective.

Natural
Natural is not necessarily better or safer; any product that is strong enough to be effective is strong enough to cause side effects.

Personal testimonials
Hearsay is the weakest form of evidence.

Meaningless medical jargon
Phony terms hide the lack of scientific proof.

Guaranteed! OR your money back!

Instant recovery, back to your everyday schedule

"Best pills around"

"Cures gout, ulcers, diabetes and cancer"

Wonder Pills
W

The natural way to becoming a better you

Revolutionary product, based on ancient medicine

Super Trim
S

Money grabbing drug companies further corporate means

"My friends feel good as new!"

Beats the hunger stimulation point (HSP)

NUTRITION ON THE NET

ThomsonNOW
For furthur study of topics covered in this Highlight, log on to **www.thomsonedu.com/thomsonnow**. Go to Chapter 1, then to Highlights Nutrition on the Net.

- Visit the National Council Against Health Fraud: **www.ncahf.org**
- Find a registered dietitian in your area from the American Dietetic Association: **www.eatright.org**
- Find a nutrition professional in Canada from the Dietitians of Canada: **www.dietitians.ca**
- Find out whether a correspondence school is accredited from the Distance Education and Training Council's Accrediting Commission: **www.detc.org**
- Find useful and reliable health information from the Health on the Net Foundation: **www.hon.ch**

- Find out whether a school is properly accredited for a dietetics degree from the American Dietetic Association: **www.eatright.org/cade**
- Obtain a listing of accredited institutions, professionally accredited programs, and candidates for accreditation from the American Council on Education: **www.acenet.edu**
- Learn more about quackery from Stephen Barrett's Quackwatch: **www.quackwatch.org**
- Check out health-related hoaxes and urban legends: **www.cdc.gov/hoax_rumors.htm** and **www.urbanlegends.com/**
- Find reliable research articles: **www.pubmed.gov**

REFERENCES

1. Position of the American Dietetic Association: Food and nutrition misinformation, *Journal of the American Dietetic Association* 106 (2006): 601-607.
2. G. Eysenbach and coauthors, Empirical studies assessing the quality of health information for consumers on the World Wide Web: A systematic review, *Journal of the American Medical Association* 287 (2002): 2691-2700.
3. L. M. Schwartz, S. Woloshin, and L. Baczek, Media coverage of scientific meetings: Too much, too soon? *Journal of the American Medical Association* 287 (2002): 2859-2863.
4. K. M. Adams and coauthors, Status of nutrition education in medical schools, *American Journal of Clinical Nutrition* 83 (2006): 941S-944S.
5. Position of the American Dietetic Association: The roles of registered dieticians and dietetic technicians, registered in health promotion and disease prevention, *Journal of the American Dietetic Association* 106 (2006): 1875-1884.
6. Nutritionist imposters and how to spot them, *Nutrition and the M.D.*, September 2004, pp. 4-6.

© PhotoLink/Getty Images

Thomson Throughout this chapter, the
NOW! ThomsonNOW logo indicates
an opportunity for online
self-study, linking you to interactive tutorials and
videos based on your level of understanding.

www.thomsonedu.com/thomsonnow

How To: Practice Problems

Nutrition Portfolio Journal

Nutrition Calculations: Practice Problems

Nutrition in Your Life

You make food choices—deciding what to eat and how much to eat—
more than 1000 times every year. We eat so frequently that it's easy to
choose a meal without giving any thought to its nutrient contributions or
health consequences. Even when we want to make healthy choices, we
may not know which foods to select or how much to consume. With a
few tools and tips, you can learn to plan a healthy diet.

Planning a Healthy Diet

CHAPTER OUTLINE

Principles and Guidelines • Diet-Planning Principles • Dietary Guidelines for Americans

Diet-Planning Guides • USDA Food Guide • Exchange Lists • Putting the Plan into Action • From Guidelines to Groceries

Food Labels • The Ingredient List • Serving Sizes • Nutrition Facts • The Daily Values • Nutrient Claims • Health Claims • Structure-Function Claims • Consumer Education

HIGHLIGHT 2 Vegetarian Diets

Chapter 1 explained that the body's many activities are supported by the nutrients delivered by the foods people eat. Food choices made over years influence the body's health, and consistently poor choices increase the risks of developing chronic diseases. This chapter shows how a person can select from the tens of thousands of available foods to create a diet that supports health. Fortunately, most foods provide several nutrients, so one trick for wise diet planning is to select a combination of foods that deliver a full array of nutrients. This chapter begins by introducing the diet-planning principles and dietary guidelines that assist people in selecting foods that will deliver nutrients without excess energy (kcalories).

Principles and Guidelines

How well you nourish yourself does not depend on the selection of any one food. Instead, it depends on the selection of many different foods at numerous meals over days, months, and years. Diet-planning principles and dietary guidelines are key concepts to keep in mind whenever you are selecting foods—whether shopping at the grocery store, choosing from a restaurant menu, or preparing a home-cooked meal.

Diet-Planning Principles

Diet planners have developed several ways to select foods. Whatever plan or combination of plans they use, though, they keep in mind the six basic diet-planning principles ◆ listed in the margin.

Adequacy **Adequacy** means that the diet provides sufficient energy and enough of all the nutrients to meet the needs of healthy people. Take the essential nutrient iron, for example. Because the body loses some iron each day, people have to replace it by eating foods that contain iron. A person whose diet fails to provide enough iron-rich foods may develop the symptoms of iron-deficiency anemia: the person may feel weak, tired, and listless; have frequent headaches; and find that even the smallest amount of muscular work brings disabling fatigue. To prevent these deficiency symptoms, a person must include foods that supply adequate iron. The same is true for all the other essential nutrients introduced in Chapter 1.

◆ Diet-planning principles:
- **A**dequacy
- **B**alance
- k**C**alorie (energy) control
- Nutrient **D**ensity
- **M**oderation
- **V**ariety

adequacy (dietary): providing all the essential nutrients, fiber, and energy in amounts sufficient to maintain health.

To ensure an adequate and balanced diet, eat a variety of foods daily, choosing different foods from each group.

◆ Balance in the diet helps to ensure adequacy.

◆ Nutrient density promotes adequacy and kcalorie control.

Balance The art of balancing the diet involves consuming enough—but not too much—of each type of food. The essential minerals calcium and iron, taken together, illustrate the importance of dietary **balance**. Meats, fish, and poultry are rich in iron but poor in calcium. Conversely, milk and milk products are rich in calcium but poor in iron. Use some meat or meat alternates for iron; use some milk and milk products for calcium; and save some space for other foods, too, because a diet consisting of milk and meat alone would not be adequate. ◆ For the other nutrients, people need whole grains, vegetables, and fruits.

kCalorie (Energy) Control Designing an adequate diet without overeating requires careful planning. Once again, balance plays a key role. The amount of energy coming into the body from foods should balance with the amount of energy being used by the body to sustain its metabolic and physical activities. Upsetting this balance leads to gains or losses in body weight. The discussion of energy balance and weight control in Chapters 8 and 9 examines this issue in more detail, but the key to **kcalorie control** is to select foods of high **nutrient density**.

Nutrient Density To eat well without overeating, select foods that deliver the most nutrients for the least food energy. Consider foods containing calcium, for example. You can get about 300 milligrams of calcium from either 1½ ounces of cheddar cheese or 1 cup of fat-free milk, but the cheese delivers about twice as much food energy (kcalories) as the milk. The fat-free milk, then, is twice as calcium dense as the cheddar cheese; it offers the same amount of calcium for half the kcalories. Both foods are excellent choices for adequacy's sake alone, but to achieve adequacy while controlling kcalories, ◆ the fat-free milk is the better choice. (Alternatively, a person could select a low-fat cheddar cheese.) The many bar graphs that appear in Chapters 10 through 13 highlight the most nutrient-dense choices, and the accompanying "How to" describes how to compare foods based on nutrient density.

ThomsonNOW
To practice comparing the nutrient density of foods, log on to **www.thomsonedu.com/thomsonnow**, go to Chapter 2, then go to How To.

balance (dietary): providing foods in proportion to each other and in proportion to the body's needs.

kcalorie (energy) control: management of food energy intake.

nutrient density: a measure of the nutrients a food provides relative to the energy it provides. The more nutrients and the fewer kcalories, the higher the nutrient density.

HOW TO Compare Foods Based on Nutrient Density

One way to evaluate foods is simply to notice their nutrient contribution *per serving:* 1 cup of milk provides about 300 milligrams of calcium, and ½ cup of fresh, cooked turnip greens provides about 100 milligrams. Thus a serving of milk offers three times as much calcium as a serving of turnip greens. To get 300 milligrams of calcium, a person could choose either 1 cup of milk or 1½ cups of turnip greens.

Another valuable way to evaluate foods is to consider their nutrient density—their nutrient contribution *per kcalorie.* Fat-free milk delivers about 85 kcalories with its 300 milligrams of calcium. To calculate the nutrient density, divide milligrams by kcalories:

$$\frac{300 \text{ mg calcium}}{85 \text{ kcal}} = 3.5 \text{ mg per kcal}$$

Do the same for the fresh turnip greens, which provide 15 kcalories with the 100 milligrams of calcium:

$$\frac{100 \text{ mg calcium}}{15 \text{ kcal}} = 6.7 \text{ mg per kcal}$$

The more milligrams per kcalorie, the greater the nutrient density. Turnip greens are more calcium dense than milk. They provide more calcium *per kcalorie* than milk, but milk offers more calcium *per serving.* Both approaches offer valuable information, especially when combined with a realistic appraisal. What matters most is which are you more likely to consume—1½ cups of turnip greens or 1 cup of milk? You can get 300 milligrams of calcium from either, but the greens will save you about 40 kcalories (the savings would be even greater if you usually use whole milk).

Keep in mind, too, that calcium is only one of the many nutrients that foods provide. Similar calculations for protein, for example, would show that fat-free milk provides more protein both *per kcalorie* and *per serving* than turnip greens—that is, milk is more protein dense. Combining variety with nutrient density helps to ensure the adequacy of all nutrients.

Just like a person who has to pay for rent, food, clothes, and tuition on a limited budget, we have to obtain iron, calcium, and all the other essential nutrients on a limited energy allowance. Success depends on getting many nutrients for each kcalorie "dollar." For example, a can of cola and a handful of grapes may both provide about the same number of kcalories, but the grapes deliver many more nutrients. A person who makes nutrient-dense choices, such as fruit instead of cola, can meet daily nutrient needs on a lower energy budget. Such choices support good health.

Foods that are notably low in nutrient density—such as potato chips, candy, and colas—are sometimes called **empty-kcalorie foods**. The kcalories these foods provide are called "empty" because they deliver energy (from sugar, fat, or both) with little, or no, protein, vitamins, or minerals.

Moderation Foods rich in fat and sugar provide enjoyment and energy but relatively few nutrients. In addition, they promote weight gain when eaten in excess. A person practicing **moderation** ◆ eats such foods only on occasion and regularly selects foods low in solid fats and added sugars, a practice that automatically improves nutrient density. Returning to the example of cheddar cheese versus fat-free milk, the fat-free milk not only offers the same amount of calcium for less energy, but it also contains far less fat than the cheese.

◆ Moderation contributes to adequacy, balance, and kcalorie control.

Variety A diet may have all of the virtues just described and still lack **variety**, if a person eats the same foods day after day. People should select foods from each of the food groups daily and vary their choices within each food group from day to day for several reasons. First, different foods within the same group contain different arrays of nutrients. Among the fruits, for example, strawberries are especially rich in vitamin C while apricots are rich in vitamin A. Variety improves nutrient adequacy.[1] Second, no food is guaranteed entirely free of substances that, in excess, could be harmful. The strawberries might contain trace amounts of one contaminant, the apricots another. By alternating fruit choices, a person will ingest very little of either contaminant. (Contamination of foods is discussed in Chapter 19.) Third, as the adage goes, variety is the spice of life. A person who eats beans frequently can enjoy pinto beans in Mexican burritos today, garbanzo beans in Greek salad tomorrow, and baked beans with barbecued chicken on the weekend. Eating nutritious meals need never be boring.

Dietary Guidelines for Americans

What should a person eat to stay healthy? The answers can be found in the *Dietary Guidelines for Americans 2005*. These guidelines provide science-based advice to promote health and to reduce risk of chronic diseases through diet and physical activity.[2] Table 2-1 presents the nine *Dietary Guidelines* topics with their key recommendations. These key recommendations, along with additional recommendations for specific population groups, also appear throughout the text as their subjects are discussed. The first three topics focus on choosing nutrient-dense foods within energy needs, maintaining a healthy body weight, and engaging in regular physical activity. The fourth topic, "Food Groups to Encourage," focuses on the selection of a variety of fruits and vegetables, whole grains, and milk. The next four topics advise people to choose sensibly in their use of fats, carbohydrates, salt, and alcoholic beverages (for those who partake). Finally, consumers are reminded to keep foods safe. Together, the *Dietary Guidelines* point the way toward better health. Table 2-2 presents Canada's *Guidelines for Healthy Eating*.

Some people might wonder why *dietary* guidelines include recommendations for physical activity. The simple answer is that most people who maintain a healthy body weight do more than eat right. They also exercise—the equivalent of 60 minutes or more of moderately intense physical activity daily. As you will see repeatedly throughout this text, food and physical activity choices are integral partners in supporting good health.

empty-kcalorie foods: a popular term used to denote foods that contribute energy but lack protein, vitamins, and minerals.

moderation (dietary): providing enough but not too much of a substance.

variety (dietary): eating a wide selection of foods within and among the major food groups.

TABLE 2-1   Key Recommendations of the *Dietary Guidelines for Americans 2005*

Adequate Nutrients within Energy Needs

- Consume a variety of nutrient-dense foods and beverages within and among the basic food groups; limit intakes of saturated and *trans* fats, cholesterol, added sugars, salt, and alcohol.
- Meet recommended intakes within energy needs by adopting a balanced eating pattern, such as the USDA Food Guide (see pp. 41–47).

Weight Management

- To maintain body weight in a healthy range, balance kcalories from foods and beverages with kcalories expended (see Chapters 8 and 9).
- To prevent gradual weight gain over time, make small decreases in food and beverage kcalories and increase physical activity.

Physical Activity

- Engage in regular physical activity and reduce sedentary activities to promote health, psychological well-being, and a healthy body weight.
- Achieve physical fitness by including cardiovascular conditioning, stretching exercises for flexibility, and resistance exercises or calisthenics for muscle strength and endurance.

Food Groups to Encourage

- Consume a sufficient amount of fruits, vegetables, milk and milk products, and whole grains while staying within energy needs.
- Select a variety of fruits and vegetables each day, including selections from all five vegetable subgroups (dark green, orange, legumes, starchy vegetables, and other vegetables) several times a week. Make at least half of the grain selections whole grains. Select fat-free or low-fat milk products.

Fats

- Consume less than 10 percent of kcalories from saturated fats and less than 300 milligrams of cholesterol per day, and keep *trans* fats consumption as low as possible (see Chapter 5).
- Keep total fat intake between 20 and 35 percent of kcalories; choose from mostly polyunsaturated and monounsaturated fat sources such as fish, nuts, and vegetable oils.
- Select and prepare foods that are lean, low fat, or fat-free and low in saturated and/or *trans* fats.

Carbohydrates

- Choose fiber-rich fruits, vegetables, and whole grains often.
- Choose and prepare foods and beverages with little added sugars (see Chapter 4).
- Reduce the incidence of dental caries by practicing good oral hygiene and consuming sugar- and starch-containing foods and beverages less frequently.

Sodium and Potassium

- Choose and prepare foods with little salt (less than 2300 milligrams sodium or approximately 1 teaspoon salt daily). At the same time, consume potassium-rich foods, such as fruits and vegetables (see Chapter 12).

Alcoholic Beverages

- Those who choose to drink alcoholic beverages should do so sensibly and in moderation (up to one drink per day for women and up to two drinks per day for men).
- Some individuals should not consume alcoholic beverages (see Highlight 7).

Food Safety

- To avoid microbial foodborne illness, keep foods safe: clean hands, food contact surfaces, and fruits and vegetables; separate raw, cooked, and ready-to-eat foods; cook foods to a safe internal temperature; chill perishable food promptly; and defrost food properly.
- Avoid unpasteurized milk and products made from it; raw or undercooked eggs, meat, poultry, fish, and shellfish; unpasteurized juices; raw sprouts.

NOTE: These guidelines are intended for adults and healthy children ages 2 and older.
SOURCE: The *Dietary Guidelines for Americans 2005*, available at **www.healthierus.gov/dietaryguidelines**.

TABLE 2-2   Canada's *Guidelines for Healthy Eating*

- Enjoy a variety of foods.
- Emphasize cereals, breads, other grain products, vegetables, and fruits.
- Choose lower-fat dairy products, leaner meats, and foods prepared with little or no fat.
- Achieve and maintain a healthy body weight by enjoying regular physical activity and healthy eating.
- Limit salt, alcohol, and caffeine.

SOURCE: These guidelines derive from *Action Towards Healthy Eating—Canada's Guidelines for Healthy Eating and Recommended Strategies for Implementation*.

IN SUMMARY

A well-planned diet delivers adequate nutrients, a balanced array of nutrients, and an appropriate amount of energy. It is based on nutrient-dense foods, moderate in substances that can be detrimental to health, and varied in its selections. The 2005 *Dietary Guidelines* apply these principles, offering practical advice on how to eat for good health.

Diet-Planning Guides

To plan a diet that achieves all of the dietary ideals just outlined, a person needs tools as well as knowledge. Among the most widely used tools for diet planning are **food group plans** that build a diet from clusters of foods that are similar in nutrient content. Thus each group represents a set of nutrients that differs somewhat from the nutrients supplied by the other groups. Selecting foods from each of the groups eases the task of creating an adequate and balanced diet.

USDA Food Guide

The 2005 *Dietary Guidelines* encourage consumers to adopt a balanced eating plan, such as the USDA's Food Guide (see Figure 2-1 on pp. 42–43). The USDA Food Guide assigns foods to five major groups ◆ and recommends daily amounts of foods from each group to meet nutrient needs. In addition to presenting the food groups, the figure lists the most notable nutrients of each group, the serving equivalents, and the foods within each group sorted by nutrient density. Chapter 16 provides a food guide for young children, and Appendix I presents Canada's food group plan, the *Food Guide to Healthy Eating*.

◆ Five food groups:
  • Fruits
  • Vegetables
  • Grains
  • Meat and legumes
  • Milk

Dietary Guidelines for Americans 2005

Meet recommended intakes within energy needs by adopting a balanced eating pattern, such as the USDA Food Guide or the DASH eating plan. (The DASH eating plan is presented in Chapter 12.)

◆ Chapter 8 explains how to determine energy needs. For an approximation, turn to the DRI Estimated Energy Requirement (EER) on the inside front cover.

Recommended Amounts All food groups offer valuable nutrients, and people should make selections from each group daily. Table 2-3 specifies the amounts of foods from each group needed daily to create a healthful diet for several energy (kcalorie) levels. ◆ Estimated daily kcalorie needs for sedentary and active men and

food group plans: diet-planning tools that sort foods into groups based on nutrient content and then specify that people should eat certain amounts of foods from each group.

TABLE 2-3	Recommended Daily Amounts from Each Food Group							
	1600 kcal	**1800 kcal**	**2000 kcal**	**2200 kcal**	**2400 kcal**	**2600 kcal**	**2800 kcal**	**3000 kcal**
Fruits	1½ c	1½ c	2 c	2 c	2 c	2 c	2½ c	2½ c
Vegetables	2 c	2½ c	2½ c	3 c	3 c	3½ c	3½ c	4 c
Grains	5 oz	6 oz	6 oz	7 oz	8 oz	9 oz	10 oz	10 oz
Meat and legumes	5 oz	5 oz	5½ oz	6 oz	6½ oz	6½ oz	7 oz	7 oz
Milk	3 c	3 c	3 c	3 c	3 c	3 c	3 c	3 c
Oils	5 tsp	5 tsp	6 tsp	6 tsp	7 tsp	8 tsp	8 tsp	10 tsp
Discretionary kcalorie allowance	132 kcal	195 kcal	267 kcal	290 kcal	362 kcal	410 kcal	426 kcal	512 kcal

FIGURE 2-1 USDA Food Guide, 2005

Key:
- ● Foods generally high in nutrient density (choose most often)
- ▲ Foods lower in nutrient density (limit selections)

FRUITS

© Polara Studios, Inc.

Consume a variety of fruits and no more than one-third of the recommended intake as fruit juice.

These foods contribute folate, vitamin A, vitamin C, potassium, and fiber.

> ½ c fruit is equivalent to ½ c fresh, frozen, or canned fruit; 1 small fruit; ¼ c dried fruit; ½ c fruit juice.

● Apples, apricots, avocados, bananas, blueberries, cantaloupe, cherries, grapefruit, grapes, guava, kiwi, mango, oranges, papaya, peaches, pears, pineapples, plums, raspberries, strawberries, watermelon; dried fruit (dates, figs, raisins); unsweetened juices.

▲ Canned or frozen fruit in syrup; juices, punches, ades, and fruit drinks with added sugars; fried plantains.

VEGETABLES

© Polara Studios, Inc.

Choose a variety of vegetables from all five subgroups several times a week.

These foods contribute folate, vitamin A, vitamin C, vitamin K, vitamin E, magnesium, potassium, and fiber.

> ½ c vegetables is equivalent to ½ c cut-up raw or cooked vegetables; ½ c cooked legumes; ½ c vegetable juice; 1 c raw, leafy greens.

● Dark green vegetables: Broccoli and leafy greens such as arugula, beet greens, bok choy, collard greens, kale, mustard greens, romaine lettuce, spinach, and turnip greens.

● Orange and deep yellow vegetables: Carrots, carrot juice, pumpkin, sweet potatoes, and winter squash (acorn, butternut).

● Legumes: Black beans, black-eyed peas, garbanzo beans (chickpeas), kidney beans, lentils, navy beans, pinto beans, soybeans and soy products such as tofu, and split peas.

● Starchy vegetables: Cassava, corn, green peas, hominy, lima beans, and potatoes.

● Other vegetables: Artichokes, asparagus, bamboo shoots, bean sprouts, beets, brussels sprouts, cabbages, cactus, cauliflower, celery, cucumbers, eggplant, green beans, iceberg lettuce, mushrooms, okra, onions, peppers, seaweed, snow peas, tomatoes, vegetable juices, zucchini.

▲ Baked beans, candied sweet potatoes, coleslaw, French fries, potato salad, refried beans, scalloped potatoes, tempura vegetables.

GRAINS

© Polara Studios, Inc.

Make at least half of the grain selections whole grains.

These foods contribute folate, niacin, riboflavin, thiamin, iron, magnesium, selenium, and fiber.

> 1 oz grains is equivalent to 1 slice bread; ½ c cooked rice, pasta, or cereal; 1 oz dry pasta or rice; 1 c ready-to-eat cereal; 3 c popped popcorn.

● Whole grains (amaranth, barley, brown rice, buckwheat, bulgur, millet, oats, quinoa, rye, wheat) and whole-grain, low-fat breads, cereals, crackers, and pastas; popcorn.

● Enriched bagels, breads, cereals, pastas (couscous, macaroni, spaghetti), pretzels, rice, rolls, tortillas.

▲ Biscuits, cakes, cookies, cornbread, crackers, croissants, doughnuts, French toast, fried rice, granola, muffins, pancakes, pastries, pies, presweetened cereals, taco shells, waffles.

FIGURE 2-1 USDA Food Guide, 2005, continued

MEAT, POULTRY, FISH, LEGUMES, EGGS, AND NUTS

© Polara Studios, Inc.

Make lean or low-fat choices. Prepare them with little, or no, added fat.

Meat, poultry, fish, and eggs contribute protein, niacin, thiamin, vitamin B_6, vitamin B_{12}, iron, magnesium, potassium, and zinc; legumes and nuts are notable for their protein, folate, thiamin, vitamin E, iron, magnesium, potassium, zinc, and fiber.

> 1 oz meat is equivalent to 1 oz cooked lean meat, poultry, or fish; 1 egg; $\frac{1}{4}$ c cooked legumes or tofu; 1 tbs peanut butter; $\frac{1}{2}$ oz nuts or seeds.

● Poultry (no skin), fish, shellfish, legumes, eggs, lean meat (fat-trimmed beef, game, ham, lamb, pork); low-fat tofu, tempeh, peanut butter, nuts (almonds, filberts, peanuts, pistachios, walnuts) or seeds (flaxseeds, pumpkin seeds, sunflower seeds).

▲ Bacon; baked beans; fried meat, fish, poultry, eggs, or tofu; refried beans; ground beef; hot dogs; luncheon meats; marbled steaks; poultry with skin; sausages; spare ribs.

MILK, YOGURT, AND CHEESE

© Polara Studios, Inc.

Make fat-free or low-fat choices. Choose lactose-free products or other calcium-rich foods if you don't consume milk.

These foods contribute protein, riboflavin, vitamin B_{12}, calcium, magnesium, potassium, and, when fortified, vitamin A and vitamin D.

> 1 c milk is equivalent to 1 c fat-free milk or yogurt; $1\frac{1}{2}$ oz fat-free natural cheese; 2 oz fat-free processed cheese.

● Fat-free milk and fat-free milk products such as buttermilk, cheeses, cottage cheese, yogurt; fat-free fortified soy milk.

▲ 1% low-fat milk, 2% reduced-fat milk, and whole milk; low-fat, reduced-fat, and whole-milk products such as cheeses, cottage cheese, and yogurt; milk products with added sugars such as chocolate milk, custard, ice cream, ice milk, milk shakes, pudding, sherbet; fortified soy milk.

OILS

Matthew Farruggio

Select the recommended amounts of oils from among these sources.

These foods contribute vitamin E and essential fatty acids (see Chapter 5), along with abundant kcalories.

> 1 tsp oil is equivalent to 1 tbs low-fat mayonnaise: 2 tbs light salad dressing: 1 tsp vegetable oil; 1 tsp soft margarine.

● Liquid vegetable oils such as canola, corn, flaxseed, nut, olive, peanut, safflower, sesame, soybean, and sunflower oils; mayonnaise, oil-based salad dressing, soft *trans*-free margarine.

● Unsaturated oils that occur naturally in foods such as avocados, fatty fish, nuts, olives, seeds (flaxseeds, sesame seeds), and shellfish.

SOLID FATS AND ADDED SUGARS

Matthew Farruggio

Limit intakes of food and beverages with solid fats and added sugars.

Solid fats deliver saturated fat and *trans* fat, and intake should be kept low. Solid fats and added sugars contribute abundant kcalories but few nutrients, and intakes should not exceed the discretionary kcalorie allowance—kcalories to meet energy needs after all nutrient needs have been met with nutrient-dense foods. Alcohol also contributes abundant kcalories but few nutrients, and its kcalories are counted among discretionary kcalories. See Table 2-3 for some discretionary kcalorie allowances.

▲ Solid fats that occur in foods naturally such as milk fat and meat fat (see ▲ in previous lists).

▲ Solid fats that are often added to foods such as butter, cream cheese, hard margarine, lard, sour cream, and shortening.

▲ Added sugars such as brown sugar, candy, honey, jelly, molasses, soft drinks, sugar, and syrup.

▲ Alcoholic beverages include beer, wine, and liquor.

TABLE 2-4	Estimated Daily kCalorie Needs for Adults	
	Sedentary[a]	**Active**[b]
Women		
19–30 yr	2000	2400
31–50 yr	1800	2200
51+ yr	1600	2100
Men		
19–30 yr	2400	3000
31–50 yr	2200	2900
51+ yr	2000	2600

[a]Sedentary describes a lifestyle that includes only the activities typical of day-to-day life.
[b]Active describes a lifestyle that includes physical activity equivalent to walking more than 3 miles per day at a rate of 3 to 4 miles per hour, in addition to the activities typical of day-to-day life. kCalorie values for active people reflect the midpoint of the range appropriate for age and gender, but within each group, older adults may need fewer kcalories and younger adults may need more.
NOTE: In addition to gender, age, and activity level, energy needs vary with height and weight (see Chapter 8 and Appendix F).

◆ Reminder: *Phytochemicals* are the nonnutrient compounds found in plant-derived foods that have biological activity in the body.

◆ The USDA nutrients of concern are fiber, vitamin A, vitamin C, vitamin E, and the minerals calcium, magnesium, and potassium.

legumes (lay-GYOOMS, LEG-yooms): plants of the bean and pea family, with seeds that are rich in protein compared with other plant-derived foods.

women are shown in Table 2-4. A sedentary young women needing 2000 kcalories a day, for example, would select 2 cups of fruit; $2^1/_2$ cups of vegetables (dispersed among the vegetable subgroups); 6 ounces of grain foods (with at least half coming from whole grains); $5^1/_2$ ounces of meat, poultry, or fish, or the equivalent of **legumes**, eggs, seeds, or nuts; and 3 cups of milk or yogurt, or the equivalent amount of cheese or fortified soy products. Additionally, a small amount of unsaturated oil, such as vegetable oil, or the oils of nuts, olives, or fatty fish, is required to supply needed nutrients.

All vegetables provide an array of vitamins, fiber, and the mineral potassium, but some vegetables are especially good sources of certain nutrients and beneficial phytochemicals. ◆ For this reason, the USDA Food Guide sorts the vegetable group into five subgroups. The dark green vegetables deliver the B vitamin folate; the orange vegetables provide vitamin A; legumes supply iron and protein; the starchy vegetables contribute carbohydrate energy; and the other vegetables fill in the gaps and add more of these same nutrients.

In a 2000-kcalorie diet, then, the recommended $2^1/_2$ cups of daily vegetables should be varied among the subgroups over a week's time, as shown in Table 2-5. In other words, consuming $2^1/_2$ cups of potatoes or even nutrient-rich spinach every day for seven days does *not* meet the recommended vegetable intakes. Potatoes and spinach make excellent choices when consumed in balance with vegetables from other subgroups. Intakes of vegetables are appropriately averaged over a week's time—it is not necessary to include every subgroup every day.

Notable Nutrients As Figure 2-1 notes, each food group contributes key nutrients. This feature provides flexibility in diet planning because a person can select any food from a food group and receive similar nutrients. For example, a person can choose milk, cheese, or yogurt and receive the same key nutrients. Importantly, foods provide not only these key nutrients, but small amounts of other nutrients and phytochemicals as well.

Because legumes contribute the same key nutrients—notably, protein, iron, and zinc—as meats, poultry, and fish, they are included in the same food group. For this reason, legumes are useful as meat alternatives, and they are also excellent sources of fiber and the B vitamin folate. To encourage frequent consumption, the USDA Food Guide also includes legumes as a subgroup of the vegetable group. Thus legumes count in either the vegetable group or the meat and legume group. In general, people who regularly eat meat, poultry, and fish count legumes as a vegetable, and vegetarians and others who seldom eat meat, poultry, or fish count legumes in the meat and legumes group.

The USDA Food Guide encourages greater consumption from certain food groups to provide the nutrients most often lacking ◆ in the diets of Americans. In general, most people need to eat:

- *More* dark green vegetables, orange vegetables, legumes, fruits, whole grains, and low-fat milk and milk products

TABLE 2-5	Recommended Weekly Amounts from the Vegetable Subgroups							

Table 2-3 specifies the recommended amounts of total vegetables per *day*. This table shows those amounts dispersed among five vegetable subgroups per *week*.

Vegetable Subgroups	1600 kcal	1800 kcal	2000 kcal	2200 kcal	2400 kcal	2600 kcal	2800 kcal	3000 kcal
Dark green	2 c	3 c	3 c	3 c	3 c	3 c	3 c	3 c
Orange and deep yellow	1½ c	2 c	2 c	2 c	2 c	2½ c	2½ c	2½ c
Legumes	2½ c	3 c	3 c	3 c	3 c	3½ c	3½ c	3½ c
Starchy	2½ c	3 c	3 c	6 c	6 c	7 c	7 c	9 c
Other	5½ c	6½ c	6½ c	7 c	7 c	8½ c	8½ c	10 c

- *Less* refined grains, total fats (especially saturated fat, *trans* fat, and cholesterol), added sugars, and total kcalories

Nutrient Density The USDA Food Guide provides a foundation for a healthy diet by emphasizing nutrient-dense options within each food group. By consistently selecting nutrient-dense foods, a person can obtain all the nutrients needed and still keep kcalories under control. In contrast, eating foods that are low in nutrient density makes it difficult to get enough nutrients without exceeding energy needs and gaining weight. For this reason, consumers should select low-fat foods from each group and foods without added fats or sugars—for example, fat-free milk instead of whole milk, baked chicken without the skin instead of hot dogs, green beans instead of French fries, orange juice instead of fruit punch, and whole-wheat bread instead of biscuits. Notice that the key in Figure 2-1 indicates which foods *within each group* are high or low in nutrient density. Oil is a notable exception: even though oil is pure fat and therefore rich in kcalories, a small amount of oil from sources such as nuts, fish, or vegetable oils is necessary every day to provide nutrients lacking from other foods. Consequently these high-fat foods are listed among the nutrient-dense foods (see Highlight 5 to learn why).

Dietary Guidelines for Americans 2005

Consume a variety of nutrient-dense foods and beverages within and among the basic food groups while choosing foods that limit the intake of saturated and *trans* fats, cholesterol, added sugars, salt, and alcohol.

Discretionary kCalorie Allowance At each kcalorie level, people who consistently choose nutrient-dense foods may be able to meet their nutrient needs without consuming their full allowance of kcalories. The difference between the kcalories needed to supply nutrients and those needed for energy—known as the **discretionary kcalorie allowance**—is illustrated in Figure 2-2. Table 2-3 (p. 41) includes the discretionary kcalorie allowance for several kcalorie levels. A person with discretionary kcalories available might choose to:

- Eat additional nutrient-dense foods, such as an extra serving of skinless chicken or a second ear of corn.

- Select a few foods with fats or added sugars, such as reduced-fat milk or sweetened cereal.

- Add a little fat or sugar to foods, such as butter or jelly on toast.

- Consume some alcohol. (Highlight 7 explains why this may not be a good choice for some individuals.)

Alternatively, a person wanting to lose weight might choose to:

- *Not* use the kcalories available from the discretionary kcalorie allowance.

Added fats and sugars are always counted as discretionary kcalories. The kcalories from the fat in higher-fat milks and meats are also counted among discretionary kcalories. It helps to think of fat-free milk as "milk" and whole milk or reduced-fat milk as "milk with added fat." Similarly, "meats" should be the leanest; other cuts are "meats with added fat." Puddings and other desserts made from whole milk provide discretionary kcalories from both the sugar added to sweeten them and the naturally occurring fat in the whole milk they contain. Even fruits, vegetables, and grains can carry discretionary kcalories into the diet in the form of peaches canned in syrup, scalloped potatoes, or high-fat crackers.

Discretionary kcalories must be counted separately from the kcalories of the nutrient-dense foods of which they may be a part. A fried chicken leg, for example, provides discretionary kcalories from two sources: the naturally occurring fat of the chicken skin and the added fat absorbed during frying. The kcalories of the skinless chicken underneath are not discretionary kcalories—they are necessary to provide the nutrients of chicken.

FIGURE 2-2 Discretionary kCalorie Allowance for a 2000-kCalorie Diet Plan

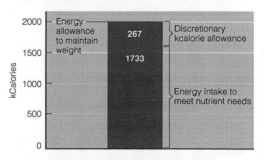

discretionary kcalorie allowance: the kcalories remaining in a person's energy allowance after consuming enough nutrient-dense foods to meet all nutrient needs for a day.

◆ For quick and easy estimates, visualize each portion as being about the size of a common object:
- 1 c fruit or vegetables = a baseball
- $1/4$ c dried fruit = a golf ball
- 3 oz meat = a deck of cards
- 2 tbs peanut butter = a marshmallow
- $1^1/_2$ oz cheese = 6 stacked dice
- $1/2$ c ice cream = a racquetball
- 4 small cookies = 4 poker chips

Serving Equivalents Recommended serving amounts for fruits, vegetables, and milk are measured in cups and those for grains and meats, in ounces. Figure 2-1 provides equivalent measures among the foods in each group specifying, for example, that 1 ounce of grains is equivalent to 1 slice of bread or $1/2$ cup of cooked rice.

A person using the USDA Food Guide can become more familiar with measured portions by determining the answers to questions such as these: ◆ What portion of a cup is a small handful of raisins? Is a "helping" of mashed potatoes more or less than a half-cup? How many ounces of cereal do you typically pour into the bowl? How many ounces is the steak at your favorite restaurant? How many cups of milk does your glass hold? Figure 2-1 (pp. 42–43) includes the serving sizes and equivalent amounts for foods within each group.

Mixtures of Foods Some foods—such as casseroles, soups, and sandwiches—fall into two or more food groups. With a little practice, users can learn to see these mixtures of foods as items from various food groups. For example, from the USDA Food Guide point of view, a taco represents four different food groups: the taco shell from the grains group; the onions, lettuce, and tomatoes from the "other vegetables" group; the ground beef from the meat group; and the cheese from the milk group.

Vegetarian Food Guide Vegetarian diets rely mainly on plant foods: grains, vegetables, legumes, fruits, seeds, and nuts. Some vegetarian diets include eggs, milk products, or both. People who do not eat meats or milk products can still use the USDA Food Guide to create an adequate diet.[3] ◆ The food groups are similar, and the amounts for each serving remain the same. Highlight 2 defines vegetarian terms and provides details on planning healthy vegetarian diets.

Ethnic Food Choices People can use the USDA Food Guide and still enjoy a diverse array of culinary styles by sorting ethnic foods into their appropriate food groups. For example, a person eating Mexican foods would find tortillas in the grains group, jicama in the vegetable group, and guava in the fruit group. Table 2-6 features ethnic food choices.

TABLE 2-6	Ethnic Food Choices				
	Grains	Vegetables	Fruits	Meats and legumes	Milk
Asian	Rice, noodles, millet	Amaranth, baby corn, bamboo shoots, chayote, bok choy, mung bean sprouts, sugar peas, straw mushrooms, water chestnuts, kelp	Carambola, guava, kumquat, lychee, persimmon, melons, mandarin orange	Soybeans and soy products such as soy milk and tofu, squid, duck eggs, pork, poultry, fish and other seafood, peanuts, cashews	Usually excluded
Mediterranean	Pita pocket bread, pastas, rice, couscous, polenta, bulgur, focaccia, Italian bread	Eggplant, tomatoes, peppers, cucumbers, grape leaves	Olives, grapes, figs	Fish and other seafood, gyros, lamb, chicken, beef, pork, sausage, lentils, fava beans	Ricotta, provolone, parmesan, feta, mozzarella, and goat cheeses; yogurt
Mexican	Tortillas (corn or flour), taco shells, rice	Chayote, corn, jicama, tomato salsa, cactus, cassava, tomatoes, yams, chilies	Guava, mango, papaya, avocado, plantain, bananas, oranges	Refried beans, fish, chicken, chorizo, beef, eggs	Cheese, custard

© Becky Luigart-Stayner/Corbis
© Photo Disc/Getty Images
© Photo Disc/Getty Images

MyPyramid—Steps to a Healthier You The USDA created an educational tool called MyPyramid to illustrate the concepts of the *Dietary Guidelines* and the USDA Food Guide. Figure 2-3 presents a graphic image of MyPyramid, which was designed to encourage consumers to make healthy food and physical activity choices every day.

The abundant materials that support MyPyramid help consumers choose the kinds and amounts of foods to eat each day (**MyPyramid.gov**). In addition to creating a personal plan, consumers can find tips to help them improve their diet and lifestyle by "taking small steps each day."

◆ **MyPyramid.gov** offers information on vegetarian diets in its Tips & Resources section.

Exchange Lists

Food group plans are particularly well suited to help a person achieve dietary adequacy, balance, and variety. **Exchange lists** provide additional help in achieving kcalorie control and moderation. Originally developed for people with diabetes, exchange systems have proved useful for general diet planning as well.

Unlike the USDA Food Guide, which sorts foods primarily by their vitamin and mineral contents, the exchange system sorts foods according to their energy-nutrient contents. Consequently, foods do not always appear on the exchange list where you might first expect to find them. For example, cheeses are grouped with meats because, like meats, cheeses contribute energy from protein and fat but provide negligible carbohydrate. (In the USDA Food Guide presented earlier, cheeses are grouped with milk because they are milk products with similar calcium contents.)

exchange lists: diet-planning tools that organize foods by their proportions of carbohydrate, fat, and protein. Foods on any single list can be used interchangeably.

FIGURE 2-3 MyPyramid: Steps to a Healthier You

The multiple colors of the pyramid illustrate variety: each color represents one of the five food groups, plus one for oils. Different widths of colors suggest the proportional contribution of each food group to a healthy diet.

The name, slogan, and website present a personalized approach.

A person climbing steps reminds consumers to be physically active each day.

The narrow slivers of color at the top imply moderation in foods rich in solid fats and added sugars.

The wide bottom represents nutrient-dense foods that should make up the bulk of the diet.

Greater intakes of grains, vegetables, fruits, and milk are encouraged by the width of orange, green, red, and blue, respectively.

MyPyramid
STEPS TO A HEALTHIER YOU
MyPyramid.gov

| GRAINS | VEGETABLES | FRUITS | OILS | MILK | MEAT & BEANS |

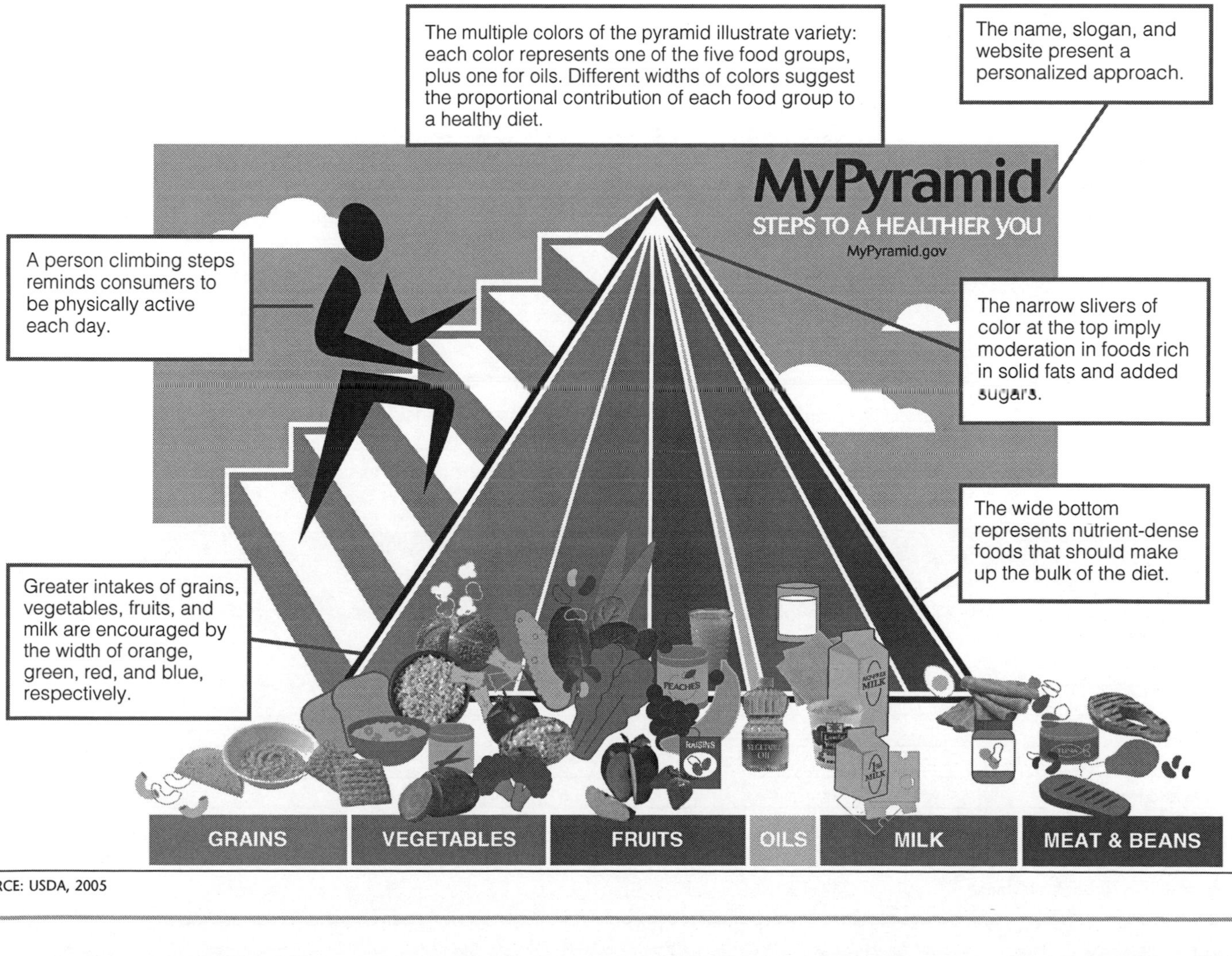

SOURCE: USDA, 2005

Most bagels today weigh in at 4 ounces or more—meaning that a person eating one of these large bagels for breakfast is actually getting four or more grain servings, not one.

For similar reasons, starchy vegetables such as corn, green peas, and potatoes are listed with grains on the starch list in the exchange system, rather than with the vegetables. Likewise, olives are not classed as a "fruit" as a botanist would claim; they are classified as a "fat" because their fat content makes them more similar to oil than to berries. Bacon and nuts are also on the fat list to remind users of their high fat content. These groupings highlight the characteristics of foods that are significant to energy intake. To learn more about this useful diet-planning tool, study Appendix G, which gives details of the exchange system used in the United States, and Appendix I, which provides details of *Beyond the Basics,* a similar diet-planning system used in Canada.

Putting the Plan into Action

Familiarizing yourself with each of the food groups is the first step in diet planning. Table 2-7 shows how to use the USDA Food Guide to plan a 2000-kcalorie diet. The amounts listed from each of the food groups (see the second column of the table) were taken from Table 2-3 (p. 41). The next step is to assign the food groups to meals (and snacks), as in the remaining columns of Table 2-7.

Now, a person can begin to fill in the plan with real foods to create a menu. For example, the breakfast calls for 1 ounce grain, ½ cup fruit, and 1 cup milk. A person might select a bowl of cereal with banana slices and milk:

1 cup cereal = 1 ounce grain

1 small banana = ½ cup fruit

1 cup fat-free milk = 1 cup milk

Or ½ bagel and a bowl of cantaloupe pieces topped with yogurt:

½ small bagel = 1 ounce grain

½ cup melon pieces = ½ cup fruit

1 cup fat-free plain yogurt = 1 cup milk

Then the person can continue to create a diet plan by creating menus for lunch, dinner, and snacks. The final plan might look like the one in Figure 2-4. With the addition of a small amount of oils, this sample diet plan provides about 1850 kcalories and adequate amounts of the essential nutrients.

As you can see, we all make countless food-related decisions daily—whether we have a plan or not. Following a plan, such as the USDA Food Guide, that incorporates health recommendations and diet-planning principles helps a person make wise decisions.

From Guidelines to Groceries

Dietary recommendations emphasize nutrient-rich foods such as whole grains, fruits, vegetables, lean meats, fish, poultry, and low-fat milk products. You can design such a diet for yourself, but how do you begin? Start with the foods you enjoy

TABLE 2-7	Diet Planning Using the USDA Food Guide					

This diet plan is one of many possibilities. It follows the amounts of foods suggested for a 2000-kcalorie diet as shown in Table 2-3 on p. 41 (with an extra ½ cup of vegetables).

Food Group	Amounts	Breakfast	Lunch	Snack	Dinner	Snack
Fruits	2 c	½ c		½ c	1 c	
Vegetables	2½ c		1 c		1½ c	
Grains	6 oz	1 oz	2 oz	½ oz	2 oz	½ oz
Meat and legumes	5½ oz		2 oz		3½ oz	
Milk	3 c	1 c		1 c		1 c
Oils	5½ tsp		1½ tsp		4 tsp	
Discretionary kcalorie allowance	267 kcal					

FIGURE 2-4 A Sample Diet Plan and Menu

This sample menu provides about 1850 kcalories and meets dietary recommendations to provide 45 to 65 percent of its kcalories from carbohydrate, 20 to 35 percent from fat, and 10 to 35 percent from protein. Some discretionary kcalories were spent on the fat in the low-fat cheese and in the sugar added to the graham crackers; about 150 discretionary kcalories remain available in this 2000-kcalorie diet plan.

Amounts	✳ SAMPLE MENU ✳	Energy (kcal)
Breakfast		
1 oz whole grains	1 c whole-grain cereal	108
1 c milk	1 c fat-free milk	83
½ c fruit	1 small banana (sliced)	105
Lunch		
2 oz whole grains, 2 oz meats	1 turkey sandwich on roll	272
1½ tsp oils	1½ tbs low-fat mayonnaise	75
1 c vegetables	1 c vegetable juice	53
Snack		
½ oz whole grains	4 whole-wheat, reduced-fat crackers	86
1 c milk	1½ oz low-fat cheddar cheese	74
½ c fruit	1 small apple	72
Dinner		
½ c vegetables	1 c salad	8
1 oz meats	¼ c garbanzo beans	71
2 tsp oils	2 tbs oil-based salad dressing and olives	81
½ c vegetables, 2½ oz meats, 2 oz enriched grains	Spaghetti with meat sauce	425
½ c vegetables	½ c green beans	22
2 tsp oils	2 tsp soft margarine	67
1 c fruit	1 c strawberries	49
Snack		
½ oz whole grains	3 graham crackers	90
1 c milk	1 c fat-free milk	83

© Polara Studios, Inc.

© Polara Studios, Inc.

© Polara Studios, Inc.

© Quest

© Quest

processed foods: foods that have been treated to change their physical, chemical, microbiological, or sensory properties.

fortified: the addition to a food of nutrients that were either not originally present or present in insignificant amounts. Fortification can be used to correct or prevent a widespread nutrient deficiency or to balance the total nutrient profile of a food.

refined: the process by which the coarse parts of a food are removed. When wheat is refined into flour, the bran, germ, and husk are removed, leaving only the endosperm.

enriched: the addition to a food of nutrients that were lost during processing so that the food will meet a specified standard.

whole grain: a grain milled in its entirety (all but the husk), not refined.

eating. Then try to make improvements, little by little. When shopping, think of the food groups, and choose nutrient-dense foods within each group.

Be aware that many of the 50,000 food options available today are **processed foods** that have lost valuable nutrients and gained sugar, fat, and salt as they were transformed from farm-fresh foods to those found in the bags, boxes, and cans that line grocery-store shelves. Their value in the diet depends on the starting food and how it was prepared or processed. Sometimes these foods have been **fortified** to improve their nutrient contents.

Grains When shopping for grain products, you will find them described as *refined, enriched,* or *whole grain.* These terms refer to the milling process and the making of grain products, and they have different nutrition implications (see Figure 2-5). **Refined** foods may have lost many nutrients during processing; **enriched** products may have had some nutrients added back; and **whole-grain** products may be rich in fiber and all the nutrients found in the original grain. As such, whole-grain products support good health and should account for at least half of the grains daily.

When it became a common practice to refine the wheat flour used for bread by milling it and throwing away the bran and the germ, consumers suffered a tragic loss of many nutrients.[4] As a consequence, in the early 1940s Congress passed legislation requiring that all grain products that cross state lines be enriched with iron,

---

FIGURE 2-5 | A Wheat Plant

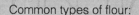

The protective coating of **bran** around the kernel of grain is rich in nutrients and fiber.

The **endosperm** contains starch and proteins.

The **germ** is the seed that grows into a wheat plant, so it is especially rich in vitamins and minerals to support new life.

The outer **husk** (or **chaff**) is the inedible part of a grain.

Whole-grain products contain much of the germ and bran, as well as the endosperm; that is why they are so nutritious.

Common types of flour:

- *Refined flour*—finely ground endosperm that is usually enriched with nutrients and bleached for whiteness; sometimes called *white flour.*
- *Wheat flour*—any flour made from the endosperm of the wheat kernel.
- *Whole-wheat flour*—any flour made from the entire wheat kernel.

The difference between *white flour* and *white wheat* is noteworthy. Typically, *white flour* refers to refined flour (as defined above). Most flour—whether refined, white, or whole wheat—is made from red wheat. Whole-grain products made from red wheat are typically brown and full flavored.

To capture the health benefits of whole grains for consumers who prefer white bread, manufacturers have been experimenting with an albino variety of wheat called *white wheat.* Whole-grain products made from white wheat provide the nutrients and fiber of a whole grain with a light color and natural sweetness. Read labels carefully—white bread is a whole-grain product only if it is made from whole white wheat.

Refined grain products contain only the endosperm. Even with nutrients added back, they are not as nutritious as whole-grain products, as the next figure shows.

© Thomas Harm/Tom Peterson/Quest Photographic Inc.

Dietary Guidelines for Americans 2005

Consume 3 or more ounce-equivalents of whole-grain products per day, with the rest of the recommended grains coming from enriched or whole-grain products. In general, at least half the grains should come from whole grains.

thiamin, riboflavin, and niacin. In 1996, this legislation was amended to include folate, a vitamin considered essential in the prevention of some birth defects. Most grain products that have been refined, such as rice, wheat pastas like macaroni and spaghetti, and cereals (both cooked and ready-to-eat types), have subsequently been enriched, ◆ and their labels say so.

Enrichment doesn't make a slice of bread rich in these added nutrients, but people who eat several slices a day obtain significantly more of these nutrients than they would from unenriched bread. Even though the enrichment of flour helps to prevent deficiencies of these nutrients, it fails to compensate for losses of many other nutrients and fiber. As Figure 2-6 shows, whole-grain items still outshine the enriched ones. Only *whole-grain* flour contains all of the nutritive portions of the grain. Whole-grain products, such as brown rice or oatmeal, provide more nutrients and fiber and contain less salt and sugar than flavored, processed rice or sweetened cereals.

Speaking of cereals, ready-to-eat breakfast cereals are the most highly fortified foods on the market. Like an enriched food, a *fortified* food has had nutrients added during processing, but in a fortified food, the added nutrients may not have been present in the original product. (The terms *fortified* and *enriched* may be used interchangeably.[5]) Some breakfast cereals made from refined flour and fortified with high doses of vitamins and minerals are actually more like supplements disguised

◆ Grain enrichment nutrients:
- Iron
- Thiamin
- Riboflavin
- Niacin
- Folate

FIGURE 2-6 Nutrients in Bread

Whole-grain bread is more nutritious than other breads, even enriched bread. For iron, thiamin, riboflavin, niacin, and folate, enriched bread provides about the same quantities as whole-grain bread and significantly more than unenriched bread. For fiber and the other nutrients (those shown here as well as those not shown), enriched bread provides less than whole-grain bread.

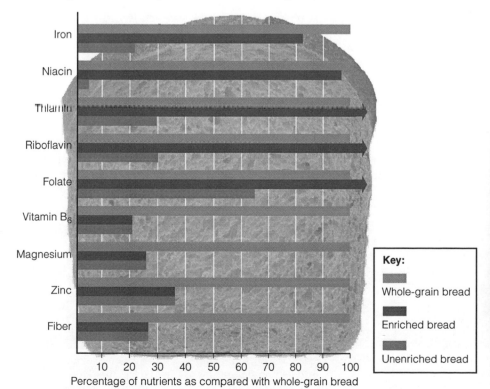

Percentage of nutrients as compared with whole-grain bread

Key:
- Whole-grain bread
- Enriched bread
- Unenriched bread

When shopping for bread, look for the descriptive words *whole grain* or *whole wheat* and check the fiber contents on the Nutrition Facts panel of the label—the more fiber, the more likely the bread is a whole-grain product.

FIGURE 2-7 Eat 5 to 9 a Day for Better Health

The "5 to 9 a Day" campaign (**www.5aday.gov**) encourages consumers to eat a variety of fruits and vegetables. Because "everyone benefits from eating more," the campaign's slogan and messages are being revised to say *Fruits and Veggies—More Matters*.

as cereals than they are like whole grains. They may be nutritious—with respect to the nutrients added—but they still may fail to convey the full spectrum of nutrients that a whole-grain food or a mixture of such foods might provide. Still, fortified foods help people meet their vitamin and mineral needs.[6]

Vegetables Posters in the produce section of grocery stores encourage consumers to "eat 5 a day." Such efforts are part of a national educational campaign to increase fruit and vegetable consumption to 5 to 9 servings every day (see Figure 2-7). To help consumers remember to eat a variety of fruits and vegetables, the campaign provides practical tips, such as selecting from each of five colors.

Choose fresh vegetables often, especially dark green leafy and yellow-orange vegetables like spinach, broccoli, and sweet potatoes. Cooked or raw, vegetables are good sources of vitamins, minerals, and fiber. Frozen and canned vegetables without added salt are acceptable alternatives to fresh. To control fat, energy, and sodium intakes, limit butter and salt on vegetables.

Choose often from the variety of legumes available. ◆ They are an economical, low-fat, nutrient- and fiber-rich food choice.

◆ Legumes include a variety of beans and peas:
- Adzuki beans
- Black beans
- Black-eyed peas
- Fava beans
- Garbanzo beans
- Great northern beans
- Kidney beans
- Lentils
- Lima beans
- Navy beans
- Peanuts
- Pinto beans
- Soybeans
- Split peas

Dietary Guidelines for Americans 2005

Choose a variety of fruits and vegetables each day. In particular, select from all five vegetable subgroups (dark green, orange, legumes, starchy vegetables, and other vegetables) several times a week.

Fruit Choose fresh fruits often, especially citrus fruits and yellow-orange fruits like cantaloupes and peaches. Frozen, dried, and canned fruits without added sugar are acceptable alternatives to fresh. Fruits supply valuable vitamins, minerals, fibers, and phytochemicals. They add flavors, colors, and textures to meals, and their natural sweetness makes them enjoyable as snacks or desserts.

Combining legumes with foods from other food groups creates delicious meals.

Add rice to red beans for a hearty meal.

Enjoy a Greek salad topped with garbanzo beans for a little ethnic diversity.

A bit of meat and lots of spices turn kidney beans into chili con carne.

Fruit juices are healthy beverages but contain little dietary fiber compared with whole fruits. Whole fruits satisfy the appetite better than juices, thereby helping people to limit food energy intakes. For people who need extra food energy, though, juices are a good choice. Be aware that sweetened fruit "drinks" or "ades" contain mostly water, sugar, and a little juice for flavor. Some may have been fortified with vitamin C or calcium but lack any other significant nutritional value.

Dietary Guidelines for Americans 2005

Consume a sufficient amount of fruits and vegetables while staying within energy needs.

Meat, Fish, and Poultry Meat, fish, and poultry provide essential minerals, such as iron and zinc, and abundant B vitamins as well as protein. To buy and prepare these foods without excess energy, fat, and sodium takes a little knowledge and planning. When shopping in the meat department, choose fish, poultry, and lean cuts of beef and pork named "round" or "loin" (as in top round or pork tenderloin). As a guide, "prime" and "choice" cuts generally have more fat than "select" cuts. Restaurants usually serve prime cuts. Ground beef, even "lean" ground beef, derives most of its food energy from fat. Have the butcher trim and grind a lean round steak instead. Alternatively, **textured vegetable protein** can be used instead of ground beef in a casserole, spaghetti sauce, or chili, saving fat kcalories.

Weigh meat after it is cooked and the bones and fat are removed. In general, 4 ounces of raw meat is equal to about 3 ounces of cooked meat. Some examples of 3-ounce portions of meat include 1 medium pork chop, $^{1}/_{2}$ chicken breast, or 1 steak or hamburger about the size of a deck of cards. To keep fat intake moderate, bake, roast, broil, grill, or braise meats (but do not fry them in fat); remove the skin from poultry after cooking; trim visible fat before cooking; and drain fat after cooking. Chapter 5 offers many additional strategies for moderating fat intake.

Milk Shoppers find a variety of fortified foods in the dairy case. Examples are milk, to which vitamins A and D have been added, and soy milk, ◆ to which calcium, vitamin D, and vitamin B_{12} have been added. In addition, shoppers may find **imitation foods** (such as cheese products), **food substitutes** (such as egg substitutes), and functional foods ◆ (such as margarine with added plant sterols). As food technology advances, many such foods offer alternatives to traditional choices that may help people who want to reduce their fat and cholesterol intakes. Chapter 5 gives other examples.

When shopping, choose fat-free ◆ or low-fat milk, yogurt, and cheeses. Such selections help consumers meet their vitamin and mineral needs within their energy and fat allowances.[7] Milk products are important sources of calcium, but can provide too much sodium and fat if not selected with care.

Dietary Guidelines for Americans 2005

Consume 3 cups per day of fat-free or low-fat milk or equivalent milk products.

IN SUMMARY

Food group plans such as the USDA Food Guide help consumers select the types and amounts of foods to provide adequacy, balance, and variety in the diet. They make it easier to plan a diet that includes a balance of grains, vegetables, fruits, meats, and milk products. In making any food choice, remember to view the food in the context of your total diet. The combination of many different foods provides the abundance of nutrients that is so essential to a healthy diet.

◆ Be aware that not all soy milks have been fortified. Read labels carefully.

◆ Reminder: *Functional foods* contain physiologically active compounds that provide health benefits beyond basic nutrition.

◆ Milk descriptions.
  - **Fat-free** milk may also be called **nonfat**, **skim**, **zero-fat**, or **no-fat**.
  - **Low-fat** milk refers to 1% milk.
  - **Reduced-fat** milk refers to 2% milk; it may also be called **less-fat**.

textured vegetable protein: processed soybean protein used in vegetarian products such as soy burgers.

imitation foods: foods that substitute for and resemble another food, but are nutritionally inferior to it with respect to vitamin, mineral, or protein content. If the substitute is not inferior to the food it resembles and if its name provides an accurate description of the product, it need not be labeled "imitation."

food substitutes: foods that are designed to replace other foods.

Food Labels

Many consumers read food labels to help them make healthy choices.[8] Food labels appear on virtually all processed foods, and posters or brochures provide similar nutrition information for fresh meats, fruits, and vegetables (see Figure 2-8). A few foods need not carry nutrition labels: those contributing few nutrients, such as plain coffee, tea, and spices; those produced by small businesses; and those prepared and sold in the same establishment. Producers of some of these items, however, voluntarily use labels. Even markets selling nonpackaged items voluntarily present nutrient information, either in brochures or on signs posted at the point of purchase. Restaurants need not supply complete nutrition information for menu items unless claims such as "low fat" or "heart healthy" have been made. When ordering such items, keep in mind that restaurants tend to serve extra-large portions—two to three times standard serving sizes. A "low-fat" ice cream, for example, may have only 3 grams of fat per ½ cup, but you may be served 2 cups for a total of 12 grams of fat and all their accompanying kcalories.

FIGURE 2-8 Example of a Food Label

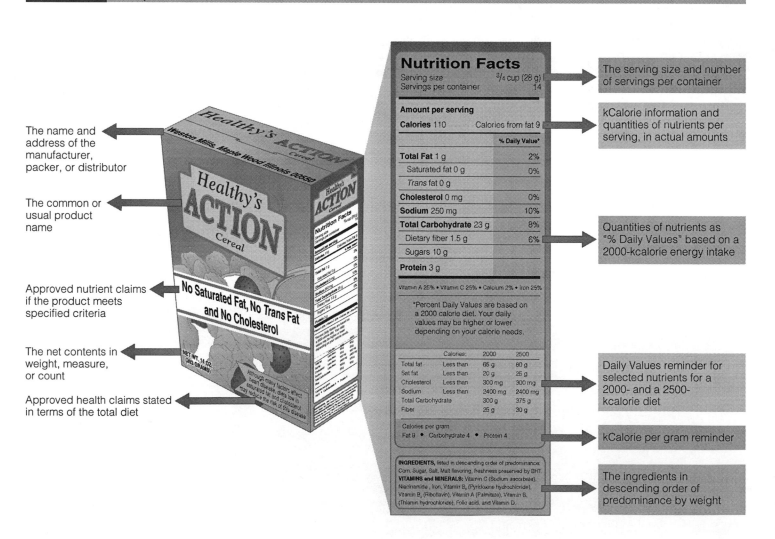

The Ingredient List

All packaged foods must list all ingredients on the label in descending order of predominance by weight. Knowing that the first ingredient predominates by weight, consumers can glean much information. Compare these products, for example:

- A beverage powder that contains "sugar, citric acid, natural flavors . . ." versus a juice that contains "water, tomato concentrate, concentrated juices of carrots, celery . . ."
- A cereal that contains "puffed milled corn, sugar, corn syrup, molasses, salt . . ." versus one that contains "100 percent rolled oats"
- A canned fruit that contains "sugar, apples, water" versus one that contains simply "apples, water"

In each of these comparisons, consumers can see that the second product is the more nutrient dense.

Serving Sizes

Because labels present nutrient information *per serving*, they must identify the size of the serving. The Food and Drug Administration (FDA) has established specific serving sizes for various foods and requires that all labels for a given product use the same serving size. For example, the serving size for all ice creams is $1/2$ cup and for all beverages, 8 fluid ounces. This facilitates comparison shopping. Consumers can see at a glance which brand has more or fewer kcalories or grams of fat, for example. Standard serving sizes are expressed in both common household measures, such as cups, and metric measures, such as milliliters, to accommodate users of both types of measures (see Table 2-8).

When examining the nutrition facts on a food label, consumers need to compare the serving size on the label with how much they actually eat and adjust their calculations accordingly. For example, if the serving size is four cookies and you only eat two, then you need to cut the nutrient and kcalorie values in half; similarly, if you eat eight cookies, then you need to double the values. Notice, too, that small bags or individually wrapped items, such as chips or candy bars, may contain more than a single serving. The number of servings per container is listed just below the serving size.

Be aware that serving sizes on food labels are not always the same as those of the USDA Food Guide.[9] For example, a serving of rice on a food label is 1 cup, whereas in the USDA Food Guide it is $1/2$ cup. Unfortunately, this discrepancy, coupled with each person's own perception (oftentimes misperception) of standard serving sizes, sometimes creates confusion for consumers trying to follow recommendations.

Nutrition Facts

In addition to the serving size and the servings per container, the FDA requires that the "Nutrition Facts" panel on food labels present nutrient information in two ways—in quantities (such as grams) and as percentages of standards called the **Daily Values.** The Nutrition Facts panel must provide the nutrient amount, percent Daily Value, or both for the following:

- Total food energy (kcalories)
- Food energy from fat (kcalories)
- Total fat (grams and percent Daily Value)
- Saturated fat (grams and percent Daily Value)
- *Trans* fat (grams)
- Cholesterol (milligrams and percent Daily Value)
- Sodium (milligrams and percent Daily Value)

TABLE 2-8	Household and Metric Measures

- 1 teaspoon (tsp) = 5 milliliters (mL)
- 1 tablespoon (tbs) = 15 mL
- 1 cup (c) = 240 mL
- 1 fluid ounce (fl oz) = 30 mL
- 1 ounce (oz) = 28 grams (g)

NOTE: The Aids to Calculation section at the back of the book provides additional weights and measures.

Daily Values (DV): reference values developed by the FDA specifically for use on food labels.

Consumers read food labels to learn about the nutrient contents of a food or to compare similar foods.

- Total carbohydrate, which includes starch, sugar, and fiber (grams and percent Daily Value)
- Dietary fiber (grams and percent Daily Value)
- Sugars, which includes both those naturally present in and those added to the food (grams)
- Protein (grams)

The labels must also present nutrient content information as a percentage of the Daily Values for the following vitamins and minerals:

- Vitamin A
- Vitamin C
- Iron
- Calcium

The Daily Values

The FDA developed the Daily Values for use on food labels because comparing nutrient amounts against a standard helps make the numbers more meaningful to consumers. Table 2-9 presents the Daily Value standards for nutrients that are required to provide this information. Food labels list the amount of a nutrient in a product as a percentage of its Daily Value. A person reading a food label might wonder, for example, whether 1 milligram of iron or calcium is a little or a lot. As Table 2-9 shows, the Daily Value for iron is 18 milligrams, so 1 milligram of iron is enough to notice—it is more than 5 percent, and that is what the food label will say. But because the Daily Value for calcium on food labels is 1000 milligrams, 1 milligram of calcium is insignificant, and the food label will read "0%."

The Daily Values reflect dietary recommendations for nutrients and dietary components that have important relationships with health. The "% Daily Value" column on a label provides a ballpark estimate of how individual foods contribute to the total diet. It compares key nutrients in a serving of food with the goals of a person consuming 2000 kcalories per day. A 2000-kcalorie diet is considered about right for sedentary younger women, active older women, and sedentary older men.

TABLE 2-9	Daily Values for Food Labels	

Food labels must present the "% Daily Value" for these nutrients.

Food Component	Daily Value	Calculation Factors
Fat	65 g	30% of kcalories
Saturated fat	20 g	10% of kcalories
Cholesterol	300 mg	—
Carbohydrate (total)	300 g	60% of kcalories
Fiber	25 g	11.5 g per 1000 kcalories
Protein	50 g	10% of kcalories
Sodium	2400 mg	—
Potassium	3500 mg	—
Vitamin C	60 mg	—
Vitamin A	1500 µg	—
Calcium	1000 mg	—
Iron	18 mg	—

NOTE: Daily Values were established for adults and children over 4 years old. The values for energy-yielding nutrients are based on 2000 kcalories a day. For fiber, the Daily Value was rounded up from 23.

Young children and sedentary older women may need fewer kcalories. Most labels list, at the bottom, Daily Values for both a 2000-kcalorie and a 2500-kcalorie diet, but the "% Daily Value" column on all labels applies only to a 2000-kcalorie diet. A 2500-kcalorie diet is considered about right for many men, teenage boys, and active younger women. People who are exceptionally active may have still higher energy needs. Labels may also provide a reminder of the kcalories in a gram of carbohydrate, fat, and protein just below the Daily Value information (review Figure 2-8).

People who consume 2000 kcalories a day can simply add up all of the "% Daily Values" for a particular nutrient to see if their diet for the day fits recommendations. People who require more or less than 2000 kcalories daily must do some calculations to see how foods compare with their personal nutrition goals. They can use the calculation column in Table 2-9 or the suggestions presented in the accompanying "How to" feature.

Daily Values help consumers see easily whether a food contributes "a little" or "a lot" of a nutrient. ◆ For example, the "% Daily Value" column on a label of macaroni and cheese may say 20 percent for fat. This tells the consumer that each serving of this food contains about 20 percent of the day's allotted 65 grams of fat. A person consuming 2000 kcalories a day could simply keep track of the percentages of Daily Values from foods eaten in a day and try not to exceed 100 percent. Be aware that for some nutrients (such as fat and sodium) you will want to select foods with a low "% Daily Value" and for others (such as calcium and fiber) you will want a high "% Daily Value." To determine whether a particular food is a wise choice, a consumer needs to consider its place in the diet among all the other foods eaten during the day.

Daily Values also make it easy to compare foods. For example, a consumer might discover that frozen macaroni and cheese has a Daily Value for fat of 20 percent, whereas macaroni and cheese prepared from a boxed mix has a Daily Value of 15 percent. By comparing labels, consumers who are concerned about their fat intakes can make informed decisions.

The Daily Values used on labels are based in part on values from the 1968 Recommended Dietary Allowances. Since 1997, Dietary Reference Intakes that reflect scientific research on diet and health have been released. Efforts to update the Daily Values based on these current recommendations and to make labels more effective and easier to understand are underway.[10]

◆ % Daily Values:
- ≥ 20% = high or excellent source
- 10-19% = good source
- ≤ 5% = low

HOW TO Calculate Personal Daily Values

The Daily Values on food labels are designed for a 2000-kcalorie intake, but you can calculate a personal set of Daily Values based on your energy allowance. Consider a 1500-kcalorie intake, for example. To calculate a daily goal for fat, multiply energy intake by 30 percent:

$$1500 \text{ kcal} \times 0.30 \text{ kcal from fat}$$
$$= 450 \text{ kcal from fat}$$

The "kcalories from fat" are listed on food labels, so you can add all the "kcalories from fat" values for a day, using 450 as an upper limit. A person who prefers to count grams of fat can divide this 450 kcalories from fat by 9 kcalories per gram to determine the goal in grams:

$$450 \text{ kcal from fat} \div 9 \text{ kcal/g}$$
$$= 50 \text{ g fat}$$

Alternatively, a person can calculate that 1500 kcalories is 75 percent of the 2000-kcalorie intake used for Daily Values:

$$1500 \text{ kcal} \div 2000 \text{ kcal} = 0.75$$
$$0.75 \times 100 = 75\%$$

Then, instead of trying to achieve 100 percent of the Daily Value, a person consuming 1500 kcalories will aim for 75 percent. Similarly, a person consuming 2800 kcalories would aim for 140 percent:

$$2800 \text{ kcal} \div 2000 \text{ kcal} = 1.40 \text{ or } 140\%$$

Table 2-9 includes a calculation column that can help you estimate your personal daily value for several nutrients.

ThomsonNOW
To calculate your personal daily values, log on to **www.thomsonedu.com/thomsonnow**, then go to Chapter 2, then go to How To.

Nutrient Claims

Have you noticed phrases such as "good source of fiber" on a box of cereal or "rich in calcium" on a package of cheese? These and other **nutrient claims** may be used on labels as long as they meet FDA definitions, which include the conditions under which each term can be used. For example, in addition to having less than 2 milligrams of cholesterol, a "cholesterol-free" product may not contain more than 2 grams of saturated fat and *trans* fat combined per serving. The accompanying glossary defines nutrient terms on food labels, including criteria for foods described as "low," "reduced," and "free."

Some descriptions *imply* that a food contains, or does not contain, a nutrient. Implied claims are prohibited unless they meet specified criteria. For example, a claim that a product "contains no oil" *implies* that the food contains no fat. If the product is truly fat-free, then it may make the no-oil claim, but if it contains another source of fat, such as butter, it may not.

nutrient claims: statements that characterize the quantity of a nutrient in a food.

GLOSSARY OF TERMS ON FOOD LABELS

GENERAL TERMS

free: "nutritionally trivial" and unlikely to have a physiological consequence; synonyms include "without," "no," and "zero." A food that does not contain a nutrient naturally may make such a claim, but only as it applies to all similar foods (for example, "applesauce, a fat-free food").

good source of: the product provides between 10 and 19% of the Daily Value for a given nutrient per serving.

healthy: a food that is low in fat, saturated fat, cholesterol, and sodium and that contains at least 10% of the Daily Values for vitamin A, vitamin C, iron, calcium, protein, or fiber.

high: 20% or more of the Daily Value for a given nutrient per serving; synonyms include "rich in" or "excellent source."

less: at least 25% less of a given nutrient or kcalories than the comparison food (see individual nutrients); synonyms include "fewer" and "reduced."

light or **lite:** one-third fewer kcalories than the comparison food; 50% or less of the fat or sodium than the comparison food; any use of the term other than as defined must specify what it is referring to (for example, "light in color" or "light in texture").

low: an amount that would allow frequent consumption of a food without exceeding the Daily Value for the nutrient. A food that is naturally low in a nutrient may make such a claim, but only as it applies to all similar foods (for example, "fresh cauliflower, a low-sodium food"); synonyms include "little," "few," and "low source of."

more: at least 10% more of the Daily Value for a given nutrient than the comparison food; synonyms include "added" and "extra."

organic: on food labels, that at least 95% of the product's ingredients have been grown and processsed according to USDA regulations defining the use of fertilizers, herbicides, insecticides, fungicides, preservatives, and other chemical ingredients (see Chapter 19).

ENERGY

kcalorie-free: fewer than 5 kcal per serving.

low kcalorie: 40 kcal or less per serving.

reduced kcalorie: at least 25% fewer kcalories per serving than the comparison food.

FAT AND CHOLESTEROL[a]

percent fat-free: may be used only if the product meets the definition of *low fat* or *fat-free* and must reflect the amount of fat in 100 g (for example, a food that contains 2.5 g of fat per 50 g can claim to be "95 percent fat free").

fat-free: less than 0.5 g of fat per serving (and no added fat or oil); synonyms include "zero-fat," "no-fat," and "nonfat."

low fat: 3 g or less fat per serving.

less fat: 25% or less fat than the comparison food.

saturated fat-free: less than 0.5 g of saturated fat and 0.5 g of *trans* fat per serving.

low saturated fat: 1 g or less saturated fat and less than 0.5 g of *trans* fat per serving.

less saturated fat: 25% or less saturated fat and *trans* fat combined than the comparison food.

trans **fat-free:** less than 0.5 g of *trans* fat and less than 0.5 g of saturated fat per serving.

cholesterol-free: less than 2 mg cholesterol per serving and 2 g or less saturated fat and *trans* fat combined per serving.

low cholesterol: 20 mg or less cholesterol per serving and 2 g or less saturated fat and *trans* fat combined per serving.

less cholesterol: 25% or less cholesterol than the comparison food (reflecting a reduction of at least 20 mg per serving), and 2 g or less saturated fat and *trans* fat combined per serving.

extra lean: less than 5 g of fat, 2 g of saturated fat and *trans* fat combined, and 95 mg of cholesterol per serving and per 100 g of meat, poultry, and seafood.

lean: less than 10 g of fat, 4.5 g of saturated fat and *trans* fat combined, and 95 mg of cholesterol per serving and per 100 g of meat, poultry, and seafood.

CARBOHYDRATES: FIBER AND SUGAR

high fiber: 5 g or more fiber per serving. A high-fiber claim made on a food that contains more than 3 g fat per serving and per 100 g of food must also declare total fat.

sugar-free: less than 0.5 g of sugar per serving.

SODIUM

sodium-free and **salt-free:** less than 5 mg of sodium per serving.

low sodium: 140 mg or less per serving.

very low sodium: 35 mg or less per serving.

[a]Foods containing more than 13 grams total fat per serving or per 50 grams of food must indicate those contents immediately after a cholesterol claim. As you can see, all cholesterol claims are prohibited when the food contains more than 2 grams saturated fat and *trans* fat combined per serving.

Health Claims

Until 2003, the FDA held manufacturers to the highest standards of scientific evidence before approving **health claims** on food labels. Consumers reading "Diets low in sodium may reduce the risk of high blood pressure," for example, knew that the FDA had examined enough scientific evidence to establish a clear link between diet and health. Such reliable health claims make up the FDA's "A" list (see Table 2-10). The FDA refers to these health claims as "unqualified"—not that they lack the necessary qualifications, but that they can stand alone without further explanation or qualification.

These reliable health claims still appear on some food labels, but finding them may be difficult now that the FDA has created three additional categories of claims based on scientific evidence that is less conclusive (see Table 2-11). These categories were added after a court ruled: "Holding only the highest scientific standard for claims interferes with commercial free speech." Food manufacturers had argued that they should be allowed to inform consumers about possible benefits based on less than clear and convincing evidence. The FDA must allow manufacturers to provide information about nutrients and foods that show preliminary promise in preventing disease. These health claims are "qualified"—not that they meet the necessary qualifications, but that they require a qualifying explanation. For example, "Very limited and preliminary research suggests that eating one-half to one cup of tomatoes and/or tomato sauce a week may reduce the risk of prostate cancer. FDA concludes that there is little scientific evidence supporting the claim." Consumer groups argue that such information is confusing. Even with required disclaimers for health claims graded "B," "C," or "D," distinguishing "A" claims from others is difficult, as the next section shows. (Health claims on supplement labels are presented in Highlight 10.)

Structure-Function Claims

Unlike health claims, which require food manufacturers to collect scientific evidence and petition the FDA, **structure-function claims** can be made without any FDA approval. Product labels can claim to "slow aging," "improve memory," and "build strong bones" without any proof. The only criterion for a structure-function claim is that it must not mention a disease or symptom. Unfortunately, structure-function claims can be deceptively similar to health claims. Consider these statements:

- "May reduce the risk of heart disease."
- "Promotes a healthy heart."

Most consumers do not distinguish between these two types of claims.[11] In the statements above, for example, the first is a health claim that requires FDA approval and the second is an unproven, but legal, structure-function claim. Table 2-12 lists examples of structure-function claims.

TABLE 2-10 Food Label Health Claims—The "A" List

- Calcium and reduced risk of osteoporosis
- Sodium and reduced risk of hypertension
- Dietary saturated fat and cholesterol and reduced risk of coronary heart disease
- Dietary fat and reduced risk of cancer
- Fiber-containing grain products, fruits, and vegetables and reduced risk of cancer
- Fruits, vegetables, and grain products that contain fiber, particularly soluble fiber, and reduced risk of coronary heart disease
- Fruits and vegetables and reduced risk of cancer
- Folate and reduced risk of neural tube defects
- Sugar alcohols and reduced risk of tooth decay
- Soluble fiber from whole oats and from psyllium seed husk and reduced risk of heart disease
- Soy protein and reduced risk of heart disease
- Whole grains and reduced risk of heart disease and certain cancers
- Plant sterol and plant stanol esters and heart disease
- Potassium and reduced risk of hypertension and stroke

health claims: statements that characterize the relationship between a nutrient or other substance in a food and a disease or health-related condition.

structure-function claims: statements that characterize the relationship between a nutrient or other substance in a food and its role in the body.

TABLE 2-11 The FDA's Health Claims Report Card

Grade	Level of Confidence in Health Claim	Required Label Disclaimers
A	High: Significant scientific agreement	These health claims do not require disclaimers; see Table 2-10 for examples.
B	Moderate: Evidence is supportive but not conclusive	"[Health claim.] Although there is scientific evidence supporting this claim, the evidence is not conclusive."
C	Low: Evidence is limited and not conclusive	"Some scientific evidence suggests [health claim]. However, FDA has determined that this evidence is limited and not conclusive."
D	Very low: Little scientific evidence supporting this claim	"Very limited and preliminary scientific research suggests [health claim]. FDA concludes that there is little scientific evidence supporting this claim."

TABLE 2-12 Examples of Structure-Function Claims

- Builds strong bones
- Promotes relaxation
- Improves memory
- Boosts the immune system
- Supports heart health
- Defends your health
- Slows aging
- Guards against colds
- Lifts your spirits

NOTE: Structure-function claims cannot make statements about diseases. See Table 2-10 on p. 59 for examples of health claims.

Consumer Education

Because labels are valuable only if people know how to use them, the FDA has designed several programs to educate consumers. Consumers who understand how to read labels are best able to apply the information to achieve and maintain healthful dietary practices.

Table 2-13 shows how the messages from the 2005 *Dietary Guidelines,* the USDA Food Guide, and food labels coordinate with each other. To promote healthy eating and physical activity, the "Healthier US Initiative" coordinates the efforts of national educational programs developed by government agencies.[12] The mission of this initiative is to deliver simple messages that will motivate consumers to make small changes in their eating and physical activity habits to yield big rewards.

TABLE 2-13 From Guidelines to Groceries

Dietary Guidelines	USDA Food Guide/MyPyramid	Food Labels
Adequate nutrients within energy needs	Select the recommended amounts from each food group at the energy level appropriate for your energy needs.	Look for foods that describe their vitamin, mineral, or fiber contents as a *good source* or *high.*
Weight management	Select nutrient-dense foods and beverages within and among the food groups. Limit high-fat foods and foods and beverages with added fats and sugars. Use appropriate portion sizes.	Look for foods that describe their kcalorie contents as *free, low, reduced, light,* or *less.*
Physical activity	Be phyisically active for at least 30 minutes most days of the week. Children and teenagers should be physically active for 60 minutes every day, or most days.	
Food groups to encourage	Select a variety of fruits each day. Include vegetables from all five subgroups (dark green, orange, legumes, starchy vegetables, and other vegetables) several times a week. Make at least half of the grain selections whole grains. Select fat-free or low-fat milk products.	Look for foods that describe their fiber contents as *good source* or *high.* Look for foods that provide at least 10% of the Daily Value for fiber, vitamin A, vitamin C, iron, and calcium from a variety of sources.
Fats	Choose foods within each group that are lean, low fat, or fat-free. Choose foods within each group that have little added fat.	Look for foods that describe their fat, saturated fat, *trans* fat, and cholesterol contents as *free, less, low, light, reduced, lean,* or *extra lean.* Look for foods that provide no more than 5% of the Daily Value for fat, saturated fat, and cholesterol.
Carbohydrates	Choose fiber-rich fruits, vegetables, and whole grains often. Choose foods and beverages within each group that have little added sugars.	Look for foods that describe their sugar contents as *free* or *reduced.* A food may be high in sugar if its ingredients list begins with or contains several of the following: *sugar, sucrose, fructose, maltose, lactose, honey, syrup, corn syrup, high-fructose corn syrup, molasses, evaporated cane juice,* or *fruit juice concentrate.*
Sodium and potassium	Choose foods within each group that are low in salt or sodium. Choose potassium-rich foods such as fruits and vegetables.	Look for foods that describe their salt and sodium contents as *free, low,* or *reduced.* Look for foods that provide no more than 5% of the Daily Value for sodium. Look for foods that provide at least 10% of the Daily Value for potassium.
Alcoholic beverages	Use sensibly and in moderation (no more than one drink a day for women and two drinks a day for men).	*Light* beverages contain fewer kcalories and less alcohol than regular versions.
Food safety		Follow the *safe handling instructions* on packages of meat and other safety instructions, such as *keep refrigerated,* on packages of perishable foods.

IN SUMMARY

Food labels provide consumers with information they need to select foods that will help them meet their nutrition and health goals. When labels contain relevant information presented in a standardized, easy-to-read format, consumers are well prepared to plan and create healthful diets.

This chapter provides the links to go from dietary guidelines to buying groceries and offers helpful tips for selecting nutritious foods. For additional information on foods, including organic foods, irradiated foods, genetically modified foods, and more, turn to Chapter 19.

 Nutrition Portfolio

ThomsonNOW™
www.thomsonedu.com/thomsonnow

The secret to making healthy food choices is learning to incorporate the 2005 *Dietary Guidelines* and the USDA Food Guide into your decision-making process.

■ Compare the foods you typically eat daily with the USDA Food Guide recommendations for your energy needs (see Table 2-3 on p. 41 and Table 2-4 on p. 44), making note of which food groups are usually over- or underrepresented.

■ Describe your choices within each food group from day to day and include realistic suggestions for enhancing the variety in your diet.

■ Write yourself a letter describing the dietary changes you can make to improve your chances of enjoying good health.

NUTRITION ON THE NET

ThomsonNOW™
For further study of topics covered in this chapter, log on to **www.thomsonedu.com/thomsonnow**. Go to Chapter 2, then to Nutrition on the Net.

• Search for "diet" and "food labels" at the U.S. Government health information site: **www.healthfinder.gov**

• Learn more about the *Dietary Guidelines for Americans.* **www.healthierus.gov/dietaryguidelines**

• Find Canadian information on nutrition guidelines and food labels at: **www.hc-sc.gc.ca**

• Learn more about the USDA Food Guide and MyPyramid: **mypyramid.gov**

• Visit the USDA Food Guide section (including its ethnic/cultural pyramids) of the U.S. Department of Agriculture: **www.nal.usda.gov/fnic**

• Visit the Traditional Diet Pyramids for various ethnic groups at Oldways Preservation and Exchange Trust: **www.oldwayspt.org**

• Search for "exchange lists" at the American Diabetes Association: **www.diabetes.org**

• Learn more about food labeling from the Food and Drug Administration: **www.cfsan.fda.gov**

• Search for "food labels" at the International Food Information Council: **www.ific.org**

• Assess your diet at the CNPP Interactive Healthy Eating Index: **www.usda.gov/cnpp**

• Get healthy eating tips from the "5 a day" programs: **www.5aday.gov** or **www.5aday.org**

NUTRITION CALCULATIONS

ThomsonNOW™ For additional practice log on to **www.thomsonedu.com/thomsonnow**. Go to Chapter 2, then to Nutrition Calculations.

These problems will give you practice in doing simple nutrition-related calculations. Although the situations are hypothetical, the numbers are real, and calculating the answers (check them on p. 63) provides a valuable nutrition lesson. Be sure to show your calculations for each problem.

1. *Read a food label.* Look at the cereal label in Figure 2-8 and answer the following questions:
   a. What is the size of a serving of cereal?
   b. How many kcalories are in a serving?
   c. How much fat is in a serving?
   d. How many kcalories does this represent?
   e. What percentage of the kcalories in this product comes from fat?
   f. What does this tell you?
   g. What is the % Daily Value for fat?
   h. What does this tell you?
   i. Does this cereal meet the criteria for a low-fat product (refer to the glossary on p. 58)?
   j. How much fiber is in a serving?
   k. Read the Daily Value chart on the lower section of the label. What is the Daily Value for fiber?
   l. What percentage of the Daily Value for fiber does a serving of the cereal contribute? Show the calculation the label-makers used to come up with the % Daily Value for fiber.
   m. What is the predominant ingredient in the cereal?
   n. Have any nutrients been added to this cereal (is it fortified)?

2. *Calculate a personal Daily Value.* The Daily Values on food labels are for people with a 2000-kcalorie intake.
   a. Suppose a person has a 1600-kcalorie energy allowance. Use the calculation factors listed in Table 2-9 to calculate a set of personal "Daily Values" based on 1600 kcalories. Show your calculations.
   b. Revise the % Daily Value chart of the cereal label in Figure 2-8 based on your "Daily Values" for a 1600-kcalorie diet.

STUDY QUESTIONS

ThomsonNOW
To assess your understanding of chapter topics, take the Student Practice Test and explore the modules recommended in your Personalized Study Plan. Log onto **www.thomsonedu.com/thomsonnow**.

These questions will help you review this chapter. You will find the answers in the discussions on the pages provided.

1. Name the diet-planning principles and briefly describe how each principle helps in diet planning. (pp. 37–39)

2. What recommendations appear in the *Dietary Guidelines for Americans*? (pp. 39–40)

3. Name the five food groups in the USDA Food Guide and identify several foods typical of each group. Explain how such plans group foods and what diet-planning principles the plans best accommodate. How are food group plans used, and what are some of their strengths and weaknesses? (pp. 41–47)

4. Review the *Dietary Guidelines*. What types of grocery selections would you make to achieve those recommendations? (pp. 40, 48–53)

5. What information can you expect to find on a food label? How can this information help you choose between two similar products? (pp. 54–57)

6. What are the Daily Values? How can they help you meet health recommendations? (pp. 55–57)

7. Describe the differences between nutrient claims, health claims, and structure-function claims. (pp. 58–59)

These multiple choice questions will help you prepare for an exam. Answers can be found on p. 63.

1. The diet-planning principle that provides all the essential nutrients in sufficient amounts to support health is:
   a. balance.
   b. variety.
   c. adequacy.
   d. moderation.

2. A person who chooses a chicken leg that provides 0.5 milligram of iron and 95 kcalories instead of two tablespoons of peanut butter that also provide 0.5 milligram of iron but 188 kcalories is using the principle of nutrient:
   a. control.
   b. density.
   c. adequacy.
   d. moderation.

3. Which of the following is consistent with the *Dietary Guidelines for Americans*?
   a. Choose a diet restricted in fat and cholesterol.
   b. Balance the food you eat with physical activity.
   c. Choose a diet with plenty of milk products and meats.
   d. Eat an abundance of foods to ensure nutrient adequacy.

4. According to the USDA Food Guide, added fats and sugars are counted as:
   a. meats and grains.
   b. nutrient-dense foods.
   c. discretionary kcalories.
   d. oils and carbohydrates.

5. Foods within a given food group of the USDA Food Guide are similar in their contents of:
   a. energy.
   b. proteins and fibers.
   c. vitamins and minerals.
   d. carbohydrates and fats.

6. In the exchange system, each portion of food on any given list provides about the same amount of:
   a. energy.
   b. satiety.
   c. vitamins.
   d. minerals.

7. Enriched grain products are fortified with:
   a. fiber, folate, iron, niacin, and zinc.
   b. thiamin, iron, calcium, zinc, and sodium.
   c. iron, thiamin, riboflavin, niacin, and folate.
   d. folate, magnesium, vitamin B_6, zinc, and fiber.

8. Food labels list ingredients in:
   a. alphabetical order.
   b. ascending order of predominance by weight.
   c. descending order of predominance by weight.
   d. manufacturer's order of preference.

9. "Milk builds strong bones" is an example of a:
   a. health claim.
   b. nutrition fact.
   c. nutrient content claim.
   d. structure-function claim.

10. Daily Values on food labels are based on a:
    a. 1500-kcalorie diet.
    b. 2000-kcalorie diet.
    c. 2500-kcalorie diet.
    d. 3000-kcalorie diet.

REFERENCES

1. S. P. Murphy and coauthors, Simple measures of dietary variety are associated with improved dietary quality, *Journal of the American Dietetic Association* 106 (2006): 425–429.
2. U.S. Department of Agriculture and U.S. Department of Health and Human Services, *Dietary Guidelines for Americans, 2005*, available at www.healthierus.gov/dietaryguidelines.
3. Position of the American Dietetic Association and Dietitians of Canada: Vegetarian diets, *Journal of the American Dietetic Association* 103 (2003): 748–765.
4. J. R. Backstrand, The history and future of food fortification in the United States: A public health perspective, *Nutrition Reviews* 60 (2002): 15–26.
5. As cited in 21 Code of Federal Regulations— Food and Drugs, Section 104.20, 45 *Federal Register* 6323, January 25, 1980, as amended in 58 *Federal Register* 2228, January 6, 1993.
6. Position of the American Dietetic Association: Food fortification and nutritional supple-

ments, *Journal of the American Dietetic Association* 105 (2005): 1300–1311.
7. R. Ranganathan and coauthors, The nutritional impact of dairy product consumption on dietary intakes of adults (1995–1996): The Bogalusa Heart Study, *Journal of the American Dietetic Association* 105 (2005): 1391–1400; L. G. Weinberg, L. A. Berner, and J. E. Groves, Nutrient contributions of dairy foods in the United States, Continuing Survey of Food Intakes by Individuals, 1994–1996, 1998, *Journal of the American Dietetic Association* 104 (2004): 895–902.
8. L. LeGault and coauthors, 2000–2001 Food Label and Package Survey: An update on prevalence of nutrition labeling and claims on processed, packaged foods, *Journal of the American Dietetic Association* 104 (2004): 952–958.
9. D. Herring and coauthors, Serving sizes in the Food Guide Pyramid and on the nutrition facts label: What's different and why? *Family*

Economics and Nutrition Review 14 (2002): 71–73.
10. Dietary Reference Intakes (DRIs) for food labeling, *American Journal of Clinical Nutrition* 83 (2006): suppl; T. Philipson, Government perspective: Food labeling, *American Journal of Clinical Nutrition* 82 (2005): 262S–264S; The National Academy of Sciences, Dietary Reference Intakes: Guiding principles for nutrition labeling and fortification (2004), http://www.nap.edu/openbook/0309091438/html/R1.html.
11. P. Williams, Consumer understanding and use of health claims for foods, *Nutrition Reviews* 63 (2005): 256–264.
12. K. A. Donato, National health education programs to promote healthy eating and physical activity, *Nutrition Reviews* 64 (2006): S65–S70.

ANSWERS

Nutrition Calculations

1. a. ¾ cup (28 g)
   b. 110 kcalories
   c. 1 g fat
   d. 9 kcalories
   e. 9 kcal ÷ 110 kcal = 0.08
      0.08 × 100 = 8%
   f. This cereal derives 8 percent of its kcalories from fat
   g. 2%
   h. A serving of this cereal provides 2 percent of the 65 grams of fat recommended for a 2000-kcalorie diet
   i. Yes
   j. 1.5 g fiber
   k. 25 g
   l. 1.5 g ÷ 25 g = 0.06
      0.06 × 100 = 6%
   m. Corn
   n. Yes

2. a. Daily Values for 1600-kcalorie diet:
      Fat: 1600 kcal × 0.30 = 480 kcal from fat
         480 kcal ÷ 9 kcal/g = 53 g fat

Saturated fat: 1600 kcal × 0.10 = 160 kcal from saturated fat
      160 kcal ÷ 9 kcal/g = 18 g saturated fat

Cholesterol: 300 mg

Carbohydrate: 1600 kcal × 0.60 = 960 kcal from carbohydrate
      960 kcal ÷ 4 kcal/g = 240 g carbohydrate

Fiber: 1600 kcal ÷ 1000 kcal = 1.6
      1.6 × 11.5 g = 18.4 g fiber

Protein: 1600 kcal × 0.10 = 160 kcal from protein
      160 kcal ÷ 4 kcal/g = 40 g protein

Sodium: 2400 mg

Potassium: 3500 mg

b.

Total fat	2%	(1 g ÷ 53 g)
Saturated fat	0%	(0 g ÷ 18 g)
Cholesterol	0%	(no calculation needed)
Sodium	10%	(no calculation needed)
Total carbohydrate	10%	(23 g ÷ 240 g)
Dietary fiber	8%	(1.5 g ÷ 18.4 g)

Study Questions (multiple choice)

1. c   2. b   3. b   4. c   5. c   6. a   7. c   8. c
9. d   10. b

Vegetarian Diets

The waiter presents this evening's specials: a fresh spinach salad topped with mandarin oranges, raisins, and sunflower seeds, served with a bowl of pasta smothered in a mushroom and tomato sauce and topped with grated parmesan cheese. Then this one: a salad made of chopped parsley, scallions, celery, and tomatoes mixed with bulgur wheat and dressed with olive oil and lemon juice, served with a spinach and feta cheese pie. Do these meals sound good to you? Or is something missing . . . a pork chop or ribeye, perhaps?

Would vegetarian fare be acceptable to you some of the time? Most of the time? Ever? Perhaps it is helpful to recognize that dietary choices fall along a continuum—from one end, where people eat no meat or foods of animal origin, to the other end, where they eat generous quantities daily. Meat's place in the diet has been the subject of much research and controversy, as this highlight will reveal. One of the missions of this highlight, in fact, is to identify the *range* of meat intakes most compatible with health. The health benefits of a primarily vegetarian diet seem to have encouraged many people to eat more vegetarian meals. The popular press refers to these "part-time vegetarians" who eat small amounts of meat from time to time as "flexitarians."

People who choose to exclude meat and other animal-derived foods from their diets today do so for many of the same reasons the Greek philosopher Pythagoras cited in the sixth century B.C.: physical health, ecological responsibility, and philosophical concerns. They might also cite world hunger issues, economic reasons, ethical concerns, or religious beliefs as motivating factors. Whatever their reasons—and even if they don't have a particular reason—people who exclude meat will be better prepared to plan well-balanced meals if they understand the nutrition and health implications of vegetarian diets.

Vegetarians generally are categorized, not by their motivations, but by the foods they choose to exclude (see the glossary below). Some people exclude red meat only; some also exclude chicken or fish; others also exclude eggs; and still others exclude milk and milk products as well. In fact, finding agreement on the definition of the term *vegetarian* is a challenge.[1]

As you will see, though, the foods a person *excludes* are not nearly as important as the foods a person *includes* in the diet. Vegetarian diets that include a variety of whole grains, vegetables, legumes, nuts, and fruits offer abundant complex carbohydrates and fibers, an assortment of vitamins and minerals, a mixture of phytochemicals, and little fat—characteristics that reflect current dietary recommendations aimed at promoting health and reducing obesity. Each of these foods—whole grains, vegetables, legumes, nuts, and fruits—independently reduces the risk for several chronic diseases.[2] This highlight examines the health benefits and potential problems of vegetarian diets and shows how to plan a well-balanced vegetarian diet.

GLOSSARY

lactovegetarians: people who include milk and milk products, but exclude meat, poultry, fish, seafood, and eggs from their diets.
 • **lacto** = milk

lacto-ovo-vegetarians: people who include milk, milk products, and eggs, but exclude meat, poultry, fish, and seafood from their diets.
 • **ovo** = egg

macrobiotic diets: extremely restrictive diets limited to a few grains and vegetables; based on metaphysical beliefs and not on nutrition. A macrobiotic diet might consist of brown rice, miso soup, and sea vegetables, for example.

meat replacements: products formulated to look and taste like meat, fish, or poultry; usually made of textured vegetable protein.

omnivores: people who have no formal restriction on the eating of any foods.
 • **omni** = all
 • **vores** = to eat

tempeh (TEM-pay): a fermented soybean food, rich in protein and fiber.

textured vegetable protein: processed soybean protein used in vegetarian products such as soy burgers; see also *meat replacements*.

tofu (TOE-foo): a curd made from soybeans, rich in protein and often fortified with calcium; used in many Asian and vegetarian dishes in place of meat.

vegans (VEE-gans): people who exclude all animal-derived foods (including meat, poultry, fish, eggs, and dairy products) from their diets; also called **pure vegetarians, strict vegetarians,** or **total vegetarians.**

vegetarians: a general term used to describe people who exclude meat, poultry, fish, or other animal-derived foods from their diets.

Health Benefits of Vegetarian Diets

Research on the health implications of vegetarian diets would be relatively easy if vegetarians differed from other people only in not eating meat. Many vegetarians, however, have also adopted lifestyles that may differ from many **omnivores**: they typically use no tobacco or illicit drugs, use little (if any) alcohol, and are physically active. Researchers must account for these lifestyle differences before they can determine which aspects of health correlate just with diet. Even then, *correlations* merely reveal what health factors *go with* the vegetarian diet, not what health effects may be *caused by* the diet. Despite these limitations, research findings suggest that well-planned vegetarian diets offer sound nutrition and health benefits to adults.[3] Dietary patterns that include very little, if any, meat may even increase life expectancy.[4]

Weight Control

In general, vegetarians maintain a lower and healthier body weight than nonvegetarians.[5] Vegetarians' lower body weights correlate with their high intakes of fiber and low intakes of fat. Because obesity impairs health in a number of ways, this gives vegetarians a health advantage.

Blood Pressure

Vegetarians tend to have lower blood pressure and lower rates of hypertension than nonvegetarians. Appropriate body weight helps to maintain a healthy blood pressure, as does a diet low in total fat and saturated fat and high in fiber, fruits, vegetables, and soy protein.[6] Lifestyle factors also influence blood pressure: smoking and alcohol intake raise blood pressure, and physical activity lowers it.

Heart Disease

The incidence of heart disease and related deaths is much lower for vegetarians than for meat eaters. The dietary factor most directly related to heart disease is saturated animal fat, and in general, vegetarian diets are lower in total fat, saturated fat, and cholesterol than typical meat-based diets.[7] The fats common in plant-based diets—the monounsaturated fats of olives, seeds, and nuts and the polyunsaturated fats of vegetable oils—are associated with a decreased risk of heart disease.[8] Furthermore, vegetarian diets are generally higher in dietary fiber, antioxidant vitamins, and phytochemicals—all factors that help control blood lipids and protect against heart disease.[9]

Many vegetarians include soy products such as **tofu** in their diets. Soy products may help to protect against heart disease because they contain polyunsaturated fats, fiber, vitamins, and minerals, and little saturated fat.[10] Even when intakes of energy, protein, carbohydrate, total fat, saturated fat, unsaturated fat, alcohol, and fiber are the same, people eating meals based on tofu have lower blood cholesterol and triglyceride levels than those

eating meat. Some research suggests that soy protein and phytochemicals may be responsible for some of these health benefits (as Highlight 13 explains in greater detail).[11]

Cancer

Vegetarians have a significantly lower rate of cancer than the general population. Their low cancer rates may be due to their high intakes of fruits and vegetables (as Highlight 11 explains). In fact, the ratio of vegetables to meat may be the most relevant dietary factor responsible for cancer prevention.[12]

Some scientific findings indicate that vegetarian diets are associated not only with lower cancer mortality in general, but also with lower incidence of cancer at specific sites as well, most notably, colon cancer.[13] People with colon cancer seem to eat more meat, more saturated fat, and fewer vegetables than do people without colon cancer. High-protein, high-fat, low-fiber diets create an environment in the colon that promotes the development of cancer in some people. A high-meat diet has been associated with stomach cancer as well.[14]

Other Diseases

In addition to obesity, hypertension, heart disease, and cancer, vegetarian diets may help prevent diabetes, osteoporosis, diverticular disease, gallstones, and rheumatoid arthritis.[15] These health benefits of a vegetarian diet depend on wise diet planning.

Vegetarian Diet Planning

The vegetarian has the same meal-planning task as any other person—using a variety of foods to deliver all the needed nutrients within an energy allowance that maintains a healthy body weight (as discussed in Chapter 2). Vegetarians who include milk products and eggs can meet recommendations for most nutrients about as easily as nonvegetarians. Such diets provide enough energy, protein, and other nutrients to support the health of adults and the growth of children and adolescents.

Vegetarians who exclude milk products and eggs can select legumes, nuts, and seeds and products made from them, such as peanut butter, **tempeh**, and tofu, from the meat group. Those who do not use milk can use soy "milk"—a product made from soybeans that provides similar nutrients if fortified with calcium, vitamin D, and vitamin B_{12}.

The MyPyramid resources include tips for planning vegetarian diets using the USDA Food Guide. In addition, several food guides have been developed specifically for vegetarian diets.[16] They all address the particular nutrition concerns of vegetarians, but differ slightly. Figure H2-1 presents one version. When selecting from the vegetable and fruit groups, vegetarians should emphasize particularly good sources of calcium and iron, respectively. Green leafy vegetables, for example, provide almost five times as much calcium per serving as other vegetables. Similarly, dried fruits deserve special notice in the fruit group because they deliver six

FIGURE H2-1   An Example of a Vegetarian Food Pyramid

Review Figure 2–1 and Table 2–3 to find recommended daily amounts from each food group, serving size equivalents, examples of common foods within each group, and the most notable nutrients for each group. Tips for planning a vegetarian diet can be found at **MyPyramid.gov.**

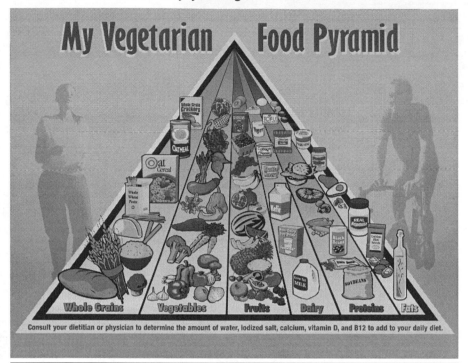

SOURCE: © GC Nutrition Council, 2006, adapted from USDA 2005 Dietary Guidelines and www.mypyramid.gov. Copies can be ordered from 301-680-6717.

times as much iron as other fruits. The milk group features fortified soy milks for those who do not use milk, cheese, or yogurt. The meat group is called "proteins" and includes legumes, soy products, nuts, and seeds. A group for oils encourages the use of vegetable oils, nuts, and seeds rich in unsaturated fats and omega-3 fatty acids. To ensure adequate intakes of vitamin B_{12}, vitamin D, and calcium, vegetarians need to select fortified foods or take supplements daily. The vegetarian food pyramid is flexible enough that a variety of people can use it: people who have adopted various vegetarian diets, those who want to make the transition to a vegetarian diet, and those who simply want to include more plant-based meals in their diet. Like MyPyramid, this vegetarian food pyramid also encourages physical activity.

Most vegetarians easily obtain large quantities of the nutrients that are abundant in plant foods: thiamin, folate, and vitamins B_6, C, A, and E. Vegetarian food guides help to ensure adequate intakes of the main nutrients vegetarian diets might otherwise lack: protein, iron, zinc, calcium, vitamin B_{12}, vitamin D, and omega-3 fatty acids.

Protein

The protein RDA for vegetarians is the same as for others, although some have suggested that it should be higher because of the lower digestibility of plant proteins.[17] **Lacto-ovo-vegetarians,** who use animal-derived foods such as milk and eggs, receive high-quality proteins and are likely to meet their protein needs. Even those

who adopt only plant-based diets are likely to meet protein needs provided that their energy intakes are adequate and the protein sources varied.[18] The proteins of whole grains, legumes, seeds, nuts, and vegetables can provide adequate amounts of all the amino acids. An advantage of many vegetarian sources of protein is that they are generally lower in saturated fat than meats and are often higher in fiber and richer in some vitamins and minerals.

Vegetarians sometimes use **meat replacements** made of **textured vegetable protein** (soy protein). These foods are formulated to look and taste like meat, fish, or poultry. Many of these products are fortified to provide the vitamins and minerals found in animal sources of protein. A wise vegetarian learns to use a variety of whole, unrefined foods often and commercially prepared foods less frequently. Vegetarians may also use soy products such as tofu to bolster protein intake.

Iron

Getting enough iron can be a problem even for meat eaters, and those who eat no meat must pay special attention to their iron intake. The iron in plant foods such as legumes, dark green leafy vegetables, iron-fortified cereals, and whole-grain breads and cereals is poorly absorbed.[19] Because iron absorption from a vegetarian diet is low, the iron RDA for vegetarians is higher than for others (see Chapter 13 for more details).

Fortunately, the body seems to adapt to a vegetarian diet by absorbing iron more efficiently. Furthermore, iron absorption is enhanced by vitamin C, and vegetarians typically eat many vitamin C–rich fruits and vegetables. Consequently, vegetarians suffer no more iron deficiency than other people do.[20]

Zinc

Zinc is similar to iron in that meat is its richest food source, and zinc from plant sources is not well absorbed.[21] In addition, soy, which is commonly used as a meat alternative in vegetarian meals, interferes with zinc absorption. Nevertheless, most vegetarian adults are not zinc deficient. Perhaps the best advice to vegetarians regarding zinc is to eat a variety of nutrient-dense foods; include whole grains, nuts, and legumes such as black-eyed peas, pinto beans, and kidney beans; and maintain an adequate energy intake. For those who include seafood in their diets, oysters, crabmeat, and shrimp are rich in zinc.

Calcium

The calcium intakes of **lactovegetarians** are similar to those of the general population, but people who use no milk products risk deficiency. Careful planners select calcium-rich foods, such as calcium-fortified juices, soy milk, and breakfast cereals, in ample quantities regularly. This advice is especially important for children and adolescents. Soy formulas for infants are fortified with calcium and can be used in cooking, even for adults. Other good calcium sources include figs, some legumes, some green vegetables such as broccoli and turnip greens, some nuts such as almonds, certain seeds such as sesame seeds, and calcium-set tofu.* The choices should be varied because calcium absorption from some plant foods may be limited (as Chapter 12 explains).

Vitamin B$_{12}$

The requirement for vitamin B$_{12}$ is small, but this vitamin is found only in animal-derived foods. Consequently, vegetarians, in general, and **vegans** who eat no foods of animal original, in particular, may not get enough vitamin B$_{12}$ in their diets.[22] Fermented soy products such as tempeh may contain some vitamin B$_{12}$ from the bacteria, but unfortunately, much of the vitamin B$_{12}$ found in these products may be an inactive form. Seaweeds such as nori and chlorella supply some vitamin B$_{12}$, but not much, and excessive intakes of these foods can lead to iodine toxicity. To defend against vitamin B$_{12}$ deficiency, vegans must rely on vitamin B$_{12}$-fortified sources (such as soy milk or breakfast cereals) or supplements. Without vitamin B$_{12}$, the nerves suffer damage, leading to such health consequences as loss of vision.

Vitamin D

People who do not use vitamin D–fortified foods and do not receive enough exposure to sunlight to synthesize adequate vitamin D may need supplements to defend against bone loss. This is particularly important for infants, children, and older adults. In northern climates during winter months, young children on vegan diets can readily develop rickets, the vitamin D–deficiency disease.

Omega-3 Fatty Acids

Both Chapter 5 and Highlight 5 describe the health benefits of unsaturated fats, most notably the omega-3 fatty acids com-

---

*Calcium salts are often added during processing to coagulate the tofu.

monly found in fatty fish. To obtain sufficient amounts of omega-3 fatty acids, vegetarians need to consume flaxseed, walnuts, soybeans, and their oils.

Healthy Food Choices

In general, adults who eat vegetarian diets have lowered their risks of mortality and several chronic diseases, including obesity, high blood pressure, heart disease, and cancer. But there is nothing mysterious or magical about the vegetarian diet; vegetarianism is not a religion like Buddhism or Hinduism, but merely an eating plan that selects plant foods to deliver needed nutrients. The quality of the diet depends not on whether it includes meat, but on whether the other food choices are nutritionally sound. A diet that includes ample fruits, vegetables, whole grains, legumes, nuts, and seeds is higher in fiber, antioxidant vitamins, and phytochemicals, and lower in saturated fats than meat-based diets. Variety is key to nutritional adequacy in a vegetarian diet. Restrictive plans, such as **macrobiotic diets,** that limit selections to a few grains and vegetables cannot possibly deliver a full array of nutrients.

If not properly balanced, any diet—vegetarian or otherwise—can lack nutrients. Poorly planned vegetarian diets typically lack iron, zinc, calcium, vitamin B$_{12}$, and vitamin D; without planning, the meat eater's diet may lack vitamin A, vitamin C, folate, and fiber, among others. Quite simply, the negative health aspects of any diet, including vegetarian diets, reflect poor diet planning. Careful attention to energy intake and specific problem nutrients can ensure adequacy.

Keep in mind, too, that diet is only one factor influencing health. Whatever a diet consists of, its context is also important: no smoking, alcohol consumption in moderation (if at all), regular physical activity, adequate rest, and medical attention when needed all contribute to a healthy life. Establishing these healthy habits early in life seems to be the most important step one can take to reduce the risks of later diseases (as Highlight 16 explains).

NUTRITION ON THE NET

ThomsonNOW™
For furthur study of topics covered in this Highlight, log on to **www.thomsonedu.com/thomsonnow**. Go to Chapter 2, then to Highlights Nutrition on the Net.

- Search for "vegetarian" at the Food and Drug Administration's site: **www.fda.gov**

- Visit the Vegetarian Resource Group: **www.vrg.org**
- Review another vegetarian diet pyramid developed by Oldways Preservation & Exchange Trust: **www.oldwayspt.org**

REFERENCES

1. S. I. Barr and G. E. Chapman, Perceptions and practices of self-defined current vegetarian, former vegetarian, and nonvegetarian women, *Journal of the American Dietetic Association* 102 (2002): 354-360.

2. J. Sabate, The contribution of vegetarian diets to human health, *Forum of Nutrition* 56 (2003): 218-220.

3. Position of the American Dietetic Association and Dietitians of Canada: Vegetarian diets, *Journal of the American Dietetic Association* 103 (2003): 748-765; J. Sabaté, The contribution of vegetarian diets to health and disease: A paradigm shift? *American Journal of Clinical Nutrition* 78 (2003): 502S-507S.

4. P. N. Singh, J. Sabaté, and G. E. Fraser, Does low meat consumption increase life expectancy in humans? *American Journal of Clinical Nutrition* 78 (2003): 526S-532S.

5. P. K. Newby, K. L. Tucker, and A. Wolk, Risk of overweight and obesity among semivegetarian, lactovegetarian, and vegan women, *American Journal of Clinical Nutrition* 81 (2005): 1267-1274; N. Brathwaite and coauthors, Obesity, diabetes, hypertension, and vegetarian status among Seventh-Day Adventists in Barbados, *Ethnicity and Disease* 13 (2003): 34-39; E. H. Haddad and J. S. Tanzman, What do vegetarians in the United States eat? *American Journal of Clinical Nutrition* 78 (2003): 626S-632S.

6. S. E. Berkow and N. D. Barnard, Blood pressure regulation and vegetarian diets, *Nutrition Reviews* 63 (2005): 1-8; L. J. Appel, The effects of protein intake on blood pressure and cardiovascular disease, *Current Opinion in Lipidology* 14 (2003): 55-59.

7. J. E. Cade and coauthors, The UK Women's Cohort Study: Comparison of vegetarians, fish-eaters, and meat-eaters, *Public Health Nutrition* 7 (2004): 871-878; E. H. Haddad and J. S. Tanzman, What do vegetarians in the United States eat? *American Journal of Clinical Nutrition* 78 (2003): 626S-632S.

8. *Third Report of the National Cholesterol Education Program (NCEP) Expert Panel on Detection, Evaluation, and Treatment of High Blood Cholesterol in Adults (Adult Treatment Panel III)*, NIH publication no. 02-5215 (Bethesda, Md.: National Heart, Lung, and Blood Institute, 2002).

9. F. B. Hu, Plant-based foods and prevention of cardiovascular disease: An overview, *American Journal of Clinical Nutrition* 78 (2003): 544S-551S.

10. F. M. Sacks and coauthors, Soy protein, isoflavones, and cardiovascular health: An American Heart Association Science Advisory for professionals from the Nutrition Committee, *Circulation* 113 (2006): 1034-1044.

11. B. L. McVeigh and coauthors, Effect of soy protein varying in isoflavone content on serum lipids in healthy young men, *American Journal of Clinical Nutrition* 83 (2006): 244-251; D. Lukaczer and coauthors, Effect of a low glycemic index diet with soy protein and phytosterols on CVD risk factors in postmenopausal women, *Nutrition* 22 (2006): 104-113; M. S. Rosell and coauthors, Soy intake and blood cholesterol concentrations: A cross-sectional study of 1033 pre- and postmenopausal women in the Oxford arm of the European Prospective Investigation into Cancer and Nutrition, *American Journal of Clinical Nutrition* 80 (2004): 1391-1396; S. Tonstad, K. Smerud, and L. Hoie, A comparison of the effects of 2 doses of soy protein or casein on serum lipids, serum lipoproteins, and plasma total homocysteine in hypercholesterolemic subjects, *American Journal of Clinical Nutrition* 76 (2002): 78-84.

12. M. Kapiszewska, A vegetable to meat consumption ratio as a relevant factor determining cancer preventive diet: The Mediterranean versus other European countries, *Forum of Nutrition* 59 (2006): 130–153.

13. M. H. Lewin and coauthors, Red meat enhances the colonic formation of the DNA adduct O6-carboxymethyl guanine: Implications for colorectal cancer risk, *Cancer Research* 66 (2006): 1859-1865.

14. H. Chen and coauthors, Dietary patterns and adenocarcinoma of the esophagus and distal stomach, *American Journal of Clinical Nutrition* 75 (2002): 137-144.

15. C. Leitzmann, Vegetarian diets: What are the advantages? *Forum of Nutrition* 57 (2005): 147-156.

16. M. Virginia, V. Melina, and A. R. Mangels, A new food guide for North American vegetarians, *Journal of the American Dietetic Association* 103 (2003): 771-775; C. A. Venti and C. S. Johnston, Modified food guide pyramid for lactovegetarians and vegans, *Journal of Nutrition* 132 (2002): 1050-1054.

17. Venti and Johnston, 2002; V. Messina and A. R. Mangels, Considerations in planning vegan diets: Children, *Journal of the American Dietetic Association* 101 (2001): 661-669.

18. Position of the American Dietetic Association and Dietitians of Canada, 2003.

19. J. R. Hunt, Moving toward a plant-based diet: Are iron and zinc at risk? *Nutrition Reviews* 60 (2002): 127-134.

20. C. L. Larsson and G. K. Johansson, Dietary intake and nutritional status of young vegans and omnivores in Sweden, *American Journal of Clinical Nutrition* 76 (2002): 100-106.

21. Hunt, 2002.

22. W. Herrmann and coauthors, Vitamin B12 status, particularly holotranscobalamin II and methylmalonic acid concentrations, and hyperhomocysteinemia in vegetarians, *American Journal of Clinical Nutrition* 78 (2003): 131-136.

chapter 1

Training and Competition Nutrition

The aim of this book is to examine sports nutrition in the context of real-life practice. In the following chapters we examine principles of sports nutrition as they apply to the training and competition performances of specific athletes and sporting teams. Before we tackle such variations and specialized applications, we need to discuss the background that underpins them. This chapter provides an overview of current nutrition guidelines for athletes and physically active people, separated into goals for the training diet and strategies for competition nutrition.

Goals of Training Nutrition

The benefits of a sound diet are most obvious in the area of competition performance, where nutrition strategies help athletes perform their best by reducing or delaying the onset of factors that would otherwise cause fatigue. However, daily eating patterns are probably even more important, because they help athletes achieve the platform from which they are ready to compete. The major role of the daily diet is to supply athletes with fuel and nutrients needed to optimize the adaptations achieved during training and to recover quickly between workouts. Athletes must also eat to stay in good health and to achieve and maintain an optimal physique. A summary of the goals of the training diet is provided in the highlight box on page 2.

Goal 1

Meet the energy and fuel requirements needed to support a training program.

The energy requirements of individual athletes are influenced by their body size, growth, pursuit of weight loss or gain, and, most important, the energy cost of their training load (frequency, duration, and intensity of training sessions). The training programs of athletes vary according

to their event, their caliber, and the time of the athletic season. An athlete's energy intake is of interest for several reasons (Burke 2001b):

- Energy intake determines the potential for achieving the athlete's requirements for energy-containing macronutrients (especially protein and carbohydrate) and the food needed to provide vitamins, minerals, and other non-energy-containing dietary compounds required for optimal function and health.

- Energy intake assists the manipulation of muscle mass and body fat levels to achieve the specific physique that is ideal for athletic performance

- Energy intake affects the function of hormonal and immune systems.

- Energy intake challenges the practical limits to food intake set by issues such as food availability and gastrointestinal comfort.

Results from dietary surveys reveal that male athletes typically report daily energy intakes varying from 12 to 20 MJ (~4,000-5,000 kcal) over prolonged periods, with endurance-training athletes reporting higher energy intakes when these values are expressed relative to body mass than those in nonendurance sports (Burke, Cox, et al. 2001). The expected (absolute) energy requirements of a female athlete should be ~20% to 30% less than her male counterpart, principally to take into account her smaller size. However, most dietary surveys report that even when energy intake is expressed per kilogram of body mass, the reported energy intakes of female athletes are still substantially lower than those reported by an equivalent male group (Burke, Cox, et al. 2001). Of course, the results of dietary surveys do not necessarily represent the actual and habitual energy intakes of athletes. Rather, these surveys provide an estimation of what athletes report eating during a particular period of time. Dietary surveys are limited by athletes' abilities to accurately report what they consumed as well as degree to which the study period provides a true representation of usual eating patterns. In general, dietary surveys

Goals of Sports Nutrition

For training, athletes should do the following:

1. Meet the energy and fuel requirements needed to support a training program
2. Achieve and maintain an ideal physique for their event; manipulate training and nutrition to achieve a level of body mass, body fat, and muscle mass that is consistent with good health and good performance
3. Enhance adaptation and recovery between training sessions by providing all the nutrients associated with these processes
4. Refuel and rehydrate well during each training session to perform optimally at each session
5. Practice any intended competition nutrition strategies so that beneficial practices can be identified and fine-tuned
6. Maintain optimal health and function, especially by meeting the increased needs for some nutrients resulting from heavy training
7. Reduce the risk of sickness and injury during heavy training periods by maintaining healthy physique and energy balance and by supplying nutrients believed to assist immune function (e.g., consume carbohydrate during prolonged exercise sessions)
8. Make well-considered decisions about the use of supplements and specialized sport foods that have been shown to enhance training performance or meet training nutrition needs
9. Eat for long-term health by following healthy eating guidelines
10. Enjoy food and the pleasure of sharing meals

For competition, athletes should do the following:

1. In weight-division sports, achieve the competition weight division with minimal harm to health or performance
2. Fuel up adequately before an event by consuming carbohydrate and tapering exercise during the days before the event according to the importance and duration of the event; use carbohydrate-loading strategies when appropriate before events of greater than 90 min duration
3. Top up carbohydrate stores with a preevent meal or snack during the 1 to 4 hr before competition
4. Keep hydration at an acceptable level during the event by drinking appropriate amounts of fluids before, during, and after the event
5. Consume carbohydrate during events of greater than 1 hr duration or where body carbohydrate stores become depleted
6. Achieve fluid and food intake before and during the event without causing gastrointestinal discomfort or upsets
7. Promote recovery after the event, particularly during multiday competitions such as tournaments and stage races
8. During a prolonged competition program, ensure that competition eating does not compromise overall energy and nutrient intake goals
9. Make well-considered decisions about the use of supplements and specialized sport foods that have been shown to enhance competition performance or meet competition needs

underestimate the true intakes of most people, because many participants undereat or underreport their usual intake while being investigated (Schoeller 1995).

Although most individuals are able to achieve remarkable energy balance over long periods, the athlete is often faced with the challenge of managing energy intakes that are either extremely high or extremely low. High energy intakes are expected where athletes have a large body mass to support, extremely high training or exercise loads, or the additional energy requirement for growth or purposeful increase in lean body mass. Such athletes are often recommended to consume extra energy, particularly in the form of carbohydrate or protein, at special times or in greater quantities than would be provided in an everyday diet or dictated by their appetite and hunger. These athletes may also need to consume energy during and after exercise when the availability of foods and fluids, or opportunities to consume them, are limited. Practical issues interfering with the achievement of energy intake goals during postexercise recovery include loss of appetite and fatigue, poor access to suitable foods, and distraction from other activities.

Conversely, other athletes need to restrict energy intake to reduce or maintain low levels of body mass and fat. This can be difficult to achieve in the face of hunger, customary eating patterns, or the eating habits of peers. These athletes may also need to address their requirements for other nutrients within a reduced energy allowance. Specialized advice from a sports dietitian often helps athletes achieve their optimal energy intake. Principles that may assist in achieving such goals include being organized to have suitable foods on hand in a busy day, choosing foods that are either compact and easy to eat or high in satiety value, and considering the micronutrient and macronutrient content of food within the framework of total energy allowances.

Dietary surveys reveal that some athletes report large energy intakes, commensurate with energy requirements of prolonged daily training or competition sessions or efforts to gain muscle size and strength. However, many endurance athletes, particularly females, appear to consume lower energy intakes than would be expected; in fact, their reported intake often appears to be insufficient to support their training loads let alone basal energy requirements (for review of studies, see Barr 1987; Manore and Thompson 2006).

Apparently low energy intakes can be explained as an artifact of dietary survey methodology or because the athlete was observed during a period of loss of body weight or fat—negative energy balance (Burke 2001b). However, an alternative and more worrying explanation is that some athletes are energy efficient—that is, they can balance their basal metabolic needs and the energy cost of eating and exercise at a substantially lower than predicted energy intake (Manore and Thompson 2006). Most sports dietitians are familiar with the frustration voiced by athletes who claim that they can't reduce their weight or body fat levels despite "hardly eating anything." The situation may be worse for female athletes, who already face strong societal pressure to be lean yet naturally carry higher levels of body fat despite undertaking substantial training loads.

There is research evidence both to support (Thompson et al. 1995) and to contradict (Edwards et al. 1993) the presence of energy efficiency in groups of athletes. Some athletes may truly have low energy requirements attributable to a reduction in resting metabolic rate accompanying energy restriction, low activity levels outside the training program, or an efficient exercise technique. In some cases, however, the energy discrepancy exists or is exacerbated by underrecording or undereating during the period of investigation (Edwards et al. 1993; Schulz et al. 1992). It is suspected that athletes who are conscious of weight and physique or dissatisfied with their body image are at highest risk of significant underestimation errors when completing dietary surveys (Edwards et al. 1993; Fogelholm

et al. 1995; Schulz et al. 1992). Reporting errors can be minimized when athletes are motivated to receive a true dietary assessment and when they have been trained to enhance record-keeping skills. Nevertheless, researchers and practitioners should be cautious in interpreting self-reported assessments of dietary intake.

Adequate energy intake is important to maintain health and achieve sound eating practices; there is evidence that restricted energy intake, or energy drain, is a direct cause of metabolic and reproductive disorders in female and possibly male athletes (Loucks 2004). Adequate energy intake is also important in providing adequate quantities of macronutrients and micronutrients needed to achieve most of the other goals of training and competition.

Goal 2

Achieve and maintain an ideal physique for their event; manipulate training and nutrition to achieve a level of body mass, body fat, and muscle mass that is consistent with good health and good performance.

Physical characteristics, including height, limb lengths, body mass, muscle mass, and body fat, can all play a role in sports performance. An athlete's physique is determined both by inherited characteristics and by the conditioning effects of his or her training program and diet. A number of techniques are available to assess body fat levels or other aspects of physique. These range from techniques that are best suited to the laboratory (e.g., hydrodensitometry and dual-energy X-ray absorptiometry scans) to protocols that can be taken into the field. Useful information about body composition can be collected from anthropometric data such as measurements of skinfold (subcutaneous) fat, body girths, and circumferences (Kerr 2006). Coaches or sports scientists who make these assessments on athletes should be trained appropriately to minimize their measurement error and to understand the limitations of their assessments.

Often, coaches or athletes set rigid criteria for an ideal physique, based on the characteristics of other successful competitors. Although such information is useful, it fails to take into account the considerable variability in the physical characteristics of athletes, even between individuals in the same sport. It also fails to acknowledge that some athletes need many years of training and maturation to achieve their ideal shape and body composition. Therefore, it is dangerous to establish rigid physique prescriptions for individuals. A preferable strategy is to determine a range of acceptable values for body fat and body mass within each sport and then monitor the health and performance of individual athletes within this range. Sequential profiling of an athlete can be used to monitor the development of physical characteristics that are associated with good performance for that individual as well as identify the changes in physique that can be expected over a season or period of specialized training.

Some athletes easily achieve the body composition that is best suited to their sport. Others may need to manipulate characteristics such as muscle mass or body fat levels through changes in diet and training. An increase in muscle mass is desired by many athletes whose performance is linked to size, strength, or power. In addition to the increase in muscle mass and strength that occurs during adolescence, particularly in males, specific muscle hypertrophy is sometimes pursued through a program of progressive muscle overload. An important nutritional requirement to support such a program is adequate energy. Energy is required for the manufacture of new muscle tissue as well as to provide fuel for the training program that supplied the stimulus for this muscle growth. Many athletes do not achieve a sufficiently positive energy balance to optimize muscle gains during a strength-training program. Specialized nutrition advice can help the athlete improve this situation by making energy-dense foods and drinks accessible and easy to consume (Burke 2001b). Despite the interest in gaining muscle size and strength, there is little rigorous scientific study of the amount of energy required, the optimal ratio of macronutrients supplying this energy, and the requirements for micronutrients to enhance this process.

Because protein forms the most significant structural component of muscle, it is tempting to hypothesize that an increase in dietary protein will stimulate muscle gain. Many strength-trained athletes consume very large amounts of protein, in excess of 2 to 3 g per kilogram of body mass per day (two to three times the recommended intakes for protein in most countries), in the belief that this will enhance the gains from resistance training programs. However, the value of very high protein intakes in optimizing muscle gains remains unsupported by the scientific literature (Lemon 1991b). Instead, there is recent evidence that timing the intake of protein after or even before a resistance training session is a useful strategy to increase net protein balance (Rasmussen et al. 2000; Tipton et al. 2001). Issues related to the protein needs of athletes are discussed separately, within goals 3 and 6.

A reduction in body mass, particularly through loss of body fat, is a common nutritional goal of athletes. There are situations when an athlete is clearly carrying excess body fat and will improve his or her health and performance by reducing these levels. Loss of body fat should be achieved through a program based on a sustained and moderate energy deficit. Counseling from a sports nutrition expert can help the athlete to decrease dietary energy intake and, perhaps, increase energy expenditure through aerobic exercise or daily physical activity. Athletes are not immune to fad diets and other quick weight loss gimmicks promoted to the general community, often preferring the scales to reflect an immediate reduction rather than undertaking the steps to achieve a slower but consistent reduction of body fat. The disadvantages of many quick weight loss strategies range from failure to achieve any loss of fat to the impairment of performance attributable to inadequate fuel intake or dehydration. Recently, attention has been drawn to the deaths of several high-profile athletes in association

Excess body fat may occur because of heredity or lifestyle factors or because the athlete has suddenly altered energy expenditure without making a compensatory change in energy intake—for example, failing to reduce energy intake while injured or taking a break from training.

with their attempts to lose weight. Although these athletes were believed to have preexisting medical conditions, other practices in common included severe restriction of fluid and food intake while in heavy training.

In some sports, a low body mass or body fat level offers distinct advantages to performance. Such benefits can be seen in terms of the energy cost of movement (e.g., distance running, cycling), the physics of movement in a tight space or against gravity (e.g., gymnastics, diving, cycling uphill), or aesthetics (e.g., gymnastics, bodybuilding). In many such weight-conscious or body fat–conscious sports, athletes strive to achieve minimum body fat levels or at least try to reduce their body fat below the level that seems natural or healthy for them. In the short term, this may improve performance. However, the long-term disadvantages include outcomes related to having very low body fat stores as well as the problems associated with unsound weight loss methods. Excessive training, chronically low intakes of energy and nutrients, and psychological distress are often involved in fat loss strategies and may cause long-term damage to health, happiness, or performance. The special issues related to making weight in weight-category sports will be discussed separately (goal 11).

Ideal weight and body fat targets for a sporting group should be set in terms of ranges, and weight control for an individual athlete should consider measures of long-term health and performance as well as the athlete's ability to eat a diet that is adequate in energy and nutrients and free of unreasonable food-related stress. Some racial groups or individuals are naturally light and have low levels of body fat or can achieve these without paying a substantial penalty. Furthermore, some athletes vary their body fat levels over a season so that very low levels are achieved only for a specific and short time. In general, however, athletes should not undertake strategies to minimize body fat levels unless they can be sure there are no side effects or disadvantages. Although it is difficult to get reliable figures on the prevalence of eating disorders or disordered eating behavior and body image among athletes, there appears to be a higher risk of problems among female athletes and among athletes in sports that require specific weight targets or low body fat levels (Beals and Manore 1994; Sundgot-Borgen 2000; Wilmore 1991). Even where clinical eating disorders do not exist, many athletes appear to be restrained eaters, reporting not only energy intakes that are considerably less than expected energy requirements but also considerable stress related to food intake (Beals and Manore 1994). The female athlete triad, the coexistence of disordered eating or energy restriction, menstrual dysfunction, and osteopenia (Loucks and Nattiv 2005), has received considerable publicity as a potential outcome of the excessive pursuit of thinness by female athletes; this is discussed in greater detail in goal 7. Expert advice from sports medicine professionals, including dietitians, psychologists, and physicians, is important in the early detection and management of problems related to body composition and nutrition.

Goal 3

Enhance adaptation and recovery between training sessions by providing all the nutrients associated with these processes.

There is some evidence, or at least sound theories, that the requirements for many nutrients are increased as a result of prolonged exercise. Acute requirements for carbohydrate and fluid in relation to exercise are relatively easy to identify and are discussed in greater detail in goals 4 and 6. However, to maintain optimal health and function, the athlete will also need to meet any increases in protein and micronutrient requirements arising from their commitment to regular prolonged exercise. In general, two dietary factors underpin the athlete's success in achieving increases in nutrient intakes: adequate intake of total energy, and focus on a wide variety of nutrient-rich foods. When these factors are in place, most athletes will be able to achieve their increased needs for protein and micronutrients.

Prolonged daily training may increase protein requirements, not only to support muscle gain and repair of damaged body tissues but also to meet the small contribution that protein oxidation makes to the fuel requirements of prolonged exercise (for reviews, see Lemon 2000; Tarnopolsky 2006). Although athletes undertaking recreational or light training activities will normally meet their protein needs within the daily recommendations prepared for the general population, sports nutrition guidelines often recommend higher protein intakes for athletes in heavy training. Table 1.1 summarizes some of the recommendations for both strength and endurance athletes in heavy training or competition, with the acknowledgement that athletes experiencing growth spurts (e.g., adolescent athletes) will also have an increased protein need. These recommendations are somewhat equivocal (Tipton and Wolfe 2004), because they have been derived from short-term studies of athletic populations, using methods with recognized

Table 1.1   Guidelines for Protein Intakes for Athletes and Physically Active People

Population	Estimates of maximum protein need for males (g·kg^{-1}·day^{-1})
Sedentary people	0.8-1.0
Recreational exercisers	0.8-1.0
Serious resistance athletes: early phase of training	1.5-1.7
Serious resistance trained athletes: established training program	1.0-1.2
Serious endurance athlete	1.2-1.6
Adolescent athletes	1.5-2.0
Female athletes	15% lower than males

Data from Lemon 2000; Tarnopolsky 2006.

shortcomings. Furthermore, they may not take into account such issues as long-term adaptation to a training stimulus or dietary intake. However, it is likely that these recommendations reflect the range of maximal protein needs for athletes who are not undertaking pharmacological stimulation of muscular development. Negative energy balance (Butterfield 1987) and inadequate carbohydrate intake during heavy training (Brouns et al. 1989) can both increase the protein intake required to maintain nitrogen balance.

Although the higher protein needs of athletes continue to be debated, current sports nutrition guidelines do not promote the need for special high-protein diets or protein supplements (Tipton and Wolfe 2004). Dietary surveys of free-living athletes find that most sports people already report protein intakes within or above the raised protein intake targets summarized in table 1.1, largely as a result of the increased energy allowances that accompany training. Athletes at risk of inadequate protein intakes are those with restricted energy intakes and unusual dietary practices (e.g., excessively high carbohydrate diets with poorly chosen vegetarian practices). Although large amounts of protein-rich foods or expensive protein supplements are considered unnecessary, sport foods such as liquid meal supplements and sport bars may allow the athlete to achieve high intake of energy or protein at strategic times. Nutritional strategies that promote the protein response to exercise are discussed under goal 6.

Vitamins and minerals play important roles as co-factors for key reactions in energy metabolism or the synthesis of new tissues. Athletes need to know whether a heavy program of exercise increases their requirement for micronutrients and whether the intake of additional amounts of vitamins and minerals will enhance performance by supercharging these key reactions. Dietary surveys of athletes show that when moderate to high energy intakes are consumed from a wide variety of nutrient-rich foods, reported intakes of vitamins and minerals are well in excess of population recommendations and are likely to meet any increases in micronutrient demand caused by training. In addition, research has failed to show clear evidence of an increase in performance following vitamin supplementation, except in the case where a preexisting deficiency was corrected (see Fogelholm 2006).

This information indicates no justification for routine vitamin and mineral supplementation by athletes. However, not all athletes achieve variety or adequate energy intake in their eating plans. Suboptimal intake of micronutrients may occur in athletes who are restrained or disordered eaters and those following fad diets. Other risk factors for a restricted food range include poor practical nutrition skills, inadequate finances, and an overcommitted lifestyle that limits access to food and causes erratic meal schedules. The best long-term management plan is to educate athletes to improve the quality and quantity of their food intake. However, a vitamin and mineral supplement, providing a broad range of micronutrients in doses similar to daily recommendations, may be useful when the athlete is unwilling or unable to make dietary changes or is traveling to places with an uncertain food supply.

An inadequate iron status is the most likely micronutrient deficiency among athletic populations, just as it is within the general community. Inadequate iron status can reduce exercise performance via suboptimal levels of hemoglobin and perhaps also via changes in the muscle including reduced myoglobin and iron-related enzymes (Hood et al. 1992). Because exercise itself alters many of the measures of iron status, because of changes in plasma volume or the acute phase response to stress, it is sometimes hard to distinguish between true iron deficiency and the normal effect of strenuous training or competition. Reduction of blood hemoglobin concentrations that results from the expansion of plasma volume in response to endurance training, often termed *sports anemia*, does not impair exercise performance (for review, see Deakin 2006). It can be useful to collect a long-term history of iron status results from the individual athlete to establish what is normal for him or her and how parameters may vary across the training season or with different interventions. Athletes often believe that more is better regarding hemoglobin levels. However, in the absence of hemoconcentration secondary to dehydration, very high hemoglobin levels are usually explained by genetic individuality or banned practices such as blood-doping or the use of the drug erythropoietin. As such they are not possible for most athletes to achieve.

Despite initial conflict in the literature, there is now evidence that iron depletion in the absence of anemia (i.e., reduced serum ferritin concentrations) may impair exercise performance (for review, see Deakin 2006). In addition, athletes with reduced iron stores complain of feeling fatigued and failing to recover between a series of competition or training sessions. Because low ferritin levels may become progressively lower and eventually lead to iron-deficiency anemia, there is merit in monitoring athletes deemed to be at high risk of iron depletion and implementing an intervention as soon as iron status appears to decline substantially or to symptomatic levels. Many experts and practitioners use the cutoff point of a ferritin concentration of less than 20 to 30 ng/ml.

The evaluation and management of iron status in athletes should be undertaken by a sports physician and considered on an individual basis. The publicity during the 1990s surrounding iron deficiency in athletes probably led to an overestimate of the true prevalence of the problem. It is tempting for the fatigued athlete and his or her coach to self-diagnose iron deficiency and to self-medicate with iron supplements that are available over the counter. However, there are dangers in self-prescription or long-term supplementation in the absence of medical follow-up. Iron supplementation is not a replacement for medical and dietary assessment and therapy, because it typically fails to correct underlying problems that have caused iron drain—iron requirements and losses exceeding iron intake. Chronic supplementation with high doses of iron carries a risk of iron overload, especially in males for whom the genetic traits for hemochromatosis are more prevalent. Iron supplements can also interfere with the absorption of other minerals such as zinc and copper.

Of course, prevention and treatment of iron deficiency may include iron supplementation. However, the manage-

Risk Factors for Iron Deficiency in Athletes

Predictors of Increased Iron Requirements

- Recent growth spurt in adolescents
- Pregnancy (current or within the past year)

Predictors of Increased Iron Losses or Iron Malabsorption

- Sudden increase in heavy training load, particularly running on hard surfaces, causing an increase in intravascular hemolysis
- Gastrointestinal bleeding (e.g., some anti-inflammatory drugs, ulcers)
- Gastrointestinal diseases involving malabsorption (e.g., Crohn's disease, ulcerative colitis, parasitic infestation, coeliac disease)
- Heavy menstrual blood losses
- Excessive blood losses such as frequent nosebleeds, recent surgery, substantial contact injuries
- Frequent blood donation

Predictors of Inadequate Intake of Bioavailable Iron

- Chronic low energy intake (<2,000 kcal or 8 MJ per day)
- Vegetarian eating—especially poorly constructed diets in which alternative food sources of iron are ignored (e.g., legumes, nuts, and seeds)
- Fad diets or erratic eating patterns
- Restricted variety of foods in diet; failure to match iron-containing foods with dietary factors that promote iron absorption
- Overconsumption of micronutrient-poor convenience foods and sport foods (e.g., high-carbohydrate powders, gels)
- Very high carbohydrate diet with high fiber content and infrequent intake of meats, fish, and chicken
- Natural food diets: failure to consume iron-fortified cereal foods such as commercial breakfast cereals and bread

ment plan should be based on long-term interventions to reverse iron drain—reducing excessive iron losses and increasing dietary iron. Risk factors for iron depletion in athletes are summarized in the highlight box on this page. Dietary interventions to improve iron status need not only to increase total iron intake but also to increase the bioavailability of dietary iron. The heme form of iron found in meat, fish, and poultry is better absorbed than organic or nonheme iron found in plant foods such as fortified and whole-grain cereal foods, legumes, and green leafy vegetables (Hallberg 1981, Monsen 1988). However, iron bioavailability can be manipulated by matching iron-rich foods with dietary elements that promote iron absorption (e.g., vitamin C and other food acids, "meat factor" found in animal flesh) and by reducing the interaction with iron inhibitory factors (e.g., phytates in fiber-rich cereals, tannins in tea) (Hallberg 1981, Monsen 1988). Changes to iron intake should be achieved with eating patterns that are compatible with the athlete's other nutrition goals (e.g., achieving fuel requirements for sport, achieving desired physique). Such education is often a specialized task, requiring the expertise of a sports dietitian.

Some athletes are at risk of problems with calcium status and bone health. Low bone density in athletes seems contradictory, because exercise is considered to be one of the best protectors of bone health. However, a serious outcome of the menstrual disturbances frequently reported by female athletes is the high risk of either direct loss of bone density or failure to optimize the gain in peak bone mass that should occur during the 10 to 15 years after the onset of puberty (for review, see Kerr et al. 2006). Because this problem is primarily related to an abnormal hormonal environment rather than inadequate calcium intake, it is discussed in more detail under goal 7.

Goals 4 and 5

Refuel and rehydrate well during each training session to perform optimally at each session. Practice any intended competition nutrition strategies so that beneficial practices can be identified and fine-tuned.

The maintenance of fuel status and fluid balance plays an important role in the performance of exercise and forms the basis of most of the special nutrition strategies undertaken for competition. Of course, many of the same physiological challenges that cause fatigue also occur during exercise sessions undertaken in the training phase. Therefore, the nutritional strategies for competition (goals 14 and 15) should also be built into the training program. This will allow the athlete to achieve optimal performance and adaptations to training. In addition, he or she can practice any intended competition strategies to identify and fine-tune a successful plan.

There is considerable variability between athletes and events, even in the same sport, in relation to nutritional challenges, opportunity for nutritional support, and response to nutritional intake. Therefore, the training situation offers each athlete a chance to find the intake of fluid and food that will be practical and valuable for future competitive events. For example, by monitoring changes in body mass over training sessions undertaken in simulation of an event, athletes can gauge their predicted competition sweat losses. They can then experiment with the types of drinks that are made available in an event under the same conditions or regulations and assess the outcomes in terms of fluid balance, gastrointestinal comfort, and performance. A number of practical issues prevent the theoretical ideal of achieving a fluid intake that matches most of the athlete's sweat losses (e.g., 80% of the body weight that is lost during the session). Sometimes, these issues can be addressed—for example, to train with a gradually increasing fluid intake or new drinking plan, so that the skills of drinking on the run are improved or gastrointestinal tolerance is increased. On other occasions, the barriers to fluid replacement are insurmountable, and the athlete must then be prepared for such consequences. Issues related to refueling during exercise can be tackled with a similar logic.

Goal 6

Maintain optimal health and function, especially by meeting the increased needs for some nutrients resulting from heavy training.

Recovery is a major challenge for the elite athlete, who undertakes two or even three workouts each day during certain phases of the training cycle, with 4 to 24 hr between each session. But it can also be a concern for recreational athletes who train once or twice a day in preparation for a special endurance event such as a marathon or triathlon. Recovery involves a complex range of processes of restoration and adaptation to physiological stress of exercise, including these:

- Restoration of muscle and liver glycogen stores
- Replacement of fluid and electrolytes lost in sweat
- Synthesis of new protein following the catabolic state and damage induced by the exercise
- Responses of the immune system

Issues of Postexercise Recovery

Recovery nutrition goals are specific to each athlete and each workout and may be determined by some of the following factors:

The physiological or homeostatic challenges caused by the workout, including
- the extent of fuel depletion (principally glycogen),
- the extent of dehydration, and
- the extent of muscle damage or protein catabolism

The goals associated with enhanced performance or adaptation to the exercise session, including
- increases in muscle size or strength,
- reductions in body fat levels,
- increases in content of functional proteins (e.g., enzymes) or manufacture of functional cells or tissues (e.g., red blood cells, capillaries), and
- the importance of fuel or hydration status in the subsequent exercise bout

The duration of the period between workouts, including
- total recovery time and
- other commitments or needs during the recovery period (e.g., sleep, drug testing, travel)

The availability of nutrients for intake during the recovery period, including
- the athlete's total energy budget,
- food availability, and
- the athlete's appetite and opportunity to consume foods and drinks during recovery period

In the training situation, with correct planning of the workload and the recovery time, such adaptation allows the body to become fitter, stronger, faster, or otherwise better suited to the chosen exercise task.

Recovery has become a buzzword used ubiquitously throughout the sporting world, and recovery eating strategies are often promoted to athletes with an almost "one size fits all" approach. In fact, recovery can encompass a variety of different priorities or goals according to the individual athlete and his or her specific training or competition session (see the highlight box on this page for a summary). Athletes and coaches should be educated to better recognize the specificity of postexercise nutrition goals and to plan a strategy for postworkout eating practices. Detailed information regarding postexercise refueling (Burke, Kiens, et al. 2004) and rehydration (Shirreffs et al. 2004) strategies is available and is summarized next, along with the accumulating information on practices that enhance net protein balance following exercise.

Despite improved fluid intake practices during exercise (see goal 14), most athletes can expect to be at least mildly dehydrated at the end of their session. Ideally, the athlete should aim to fully restore fluid losses after workouts so that the next workout can be commenced in fluid balance. This is difficult in situations where moderate to high levels of hypohydration have been incurred (e.g., a fluid deficit equivalent to 2-5% body mass or greater) and the interval between sessions is less than 6 to 8 hr. In normal circumstances, the daily replacement of fluid losses and maintenance of fluid balance are well regulated by thirst and urine losses. However, under conditions of stress such as exercise, environmental heat, and cold or altitude, thirst may not be a sufficient stimulus for maintaining euhydration (Greenleaf 1992) There may be a lag of 4 to 24 hr before body fluid levels are restored in an acute situation of hypohydration, and success of postexercise rehydration depends on how much the athlete drinks and then how much of this fluid is retained and re-equilibrated within body fluid compartments.

After exercise, many people fail to drink sufficient volumes of fluid to restore fluid balance. This is known as involuntary dehydration in recognition of the fact that the dehydrated individual has no desire to rehydrate even when fluids and opportunity are available (Nadel et al. 1990). Numerous factors have been involved in determining the voluntary fluid intake of individuals, including behavioral patterns and social customs, as well as a genetic predisposition to be a "reluctant" or "good" drinker (Greenleaf 1992). Flavoring of drinks is known to contribute to voluntary fluid intake, with studies reporting greater fluid intake during postexercise recovery with sweetened drinks than with plain water (Carter and Gisolfi 1989) (see figure 1.1). The intake of sodium in or with a fluid helps to maintain plasma osmolality while plasma volume is being restored, thus preserving thirst (Nose et al. 1988). The temperature of drinks is also important, and although very cold fluids (0°C) may be regarded as the most pleasurable, cool drinks (15°C) are more likely to be consumed quickly and in larger quantities (Hubbard et al. 1990).

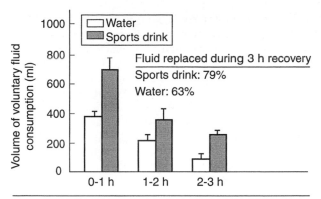

Figure 1.1 Participants who were observed over the 3 hr following dehydrating exercise consumed larger volumes of fluid when a flavored carbohydrate–electrolyte beverage (sport drink) was provided than in another trial providing only water. Regardless of drink choice, voluntary fluid intake decreased with time and failed to replace total fluid losses by the end of the 3 hr period.

* = P<0.05

Reprinted from Carter and Gisolfi 1989.

Because sweating and obligatory urine losses continue during the recovery phase, athletes must replace more than their postexercise fluid deficit to achieve fluid restoration. Typically, a volume of fluid equivalent to ~150% of the postexercise fluid deficit must be consumed to compensate for these ongoing losses and ensure that fluid balance is achieved over the first 4 to 6 hr of recovery (Shirreffs et al. 1996). Whether the pattern of fluid intake influences rehydration has been investigated, where intakes of larger amounts of fluid in the immediate postexercise period were compared with the same total volume of fluid being spread equally over 5 to 6 hr of recovery (Kovacs et al. 2002). Early replacement of large volumes of fluid was associated with better restoration of fluid balance during the first hours of recovery despite an increase in urinary output; however, differences in fluid restoration between hydration patterns disappeared by 5 to 6 hr of recovery. In another study, spacing fluid intake over several hours of recovery after exercise was more effective in restoring fluid balance because of lower urine losses than was consuming fluid as a large bolus immediately after the exercise (Archer and Shirreffs 2001). Of course, factors such as gastric comfort need to be considered in postexercise rehydration practices, especially if the athlete needs to perform another exercise session within the next hours.

Fluid replacement alone will not guarantee that rehydration goals are achieved. Unless there is simultaneous replacement of the electrolytes lost in sweat, particularly sodium, consumption of large amounts of fluid will simply result in large urine losses (Shirreffs et al. 1996). The addition of sodium to rehydration fluids has been shown to better maintain equilibrium between plasma volume and plasma osmolality, reduce urine losses, and enhance net fluid balance at the end of 6 hr of recovery (Maughan and Leiper 1995; Shirreffs et al. 1996). In contrast, with no or little sodium replacement, participants were still substantially dehydrated at the end of the 6 hr recovery period, despite drinking 150% of the volume of their postexercise fluid deficit (see figure 1.2). On a practical note, fluid replacement without sodium intake may return a false positive for good hydration status, at least in the acute phase of recovery. The production of copious amounts of clear urine, or urine with a low osmolality and specific gravity, may be useful as an overall sign of euhydration, particularly when early morning urine is used to monitor day-to-day variations in hydration (Shirreffs and Maughan 1998). However, during the hours immediately after a substantial fluid deficit is replaced without attention to sodium losses, athletes are likely to produce large amounts of urine with characteristics suggesting the return of fluid balance, when in reality they are still in substantial fluid deficit (Kovacs et al. 1999). An additional disadvantage of

failing to replace sodium losses when rehydration occurs in the late part of the day is that large urine losses may occur overnight, causing frequent trips to the restroom and interrupted sleep.

The optimal sodium level in a rehydration drink appears to be ~50 to 80 mmol/L (Maughan and Leiper 1995), as is provided in oral rehydration solutions manufactured for the treatment of diarrhea. This is considerably higher than the concentrations found in commercial carbohydrate–electrolyte drinks, or sport drinks (typically 10-25 mmol/L), and may be unpalatable to many athletes. Sport drinks may confer some rehydration advantages over plain water, in terms of palatability as well as fluid retention (Gonzalez-Alonso et al. 1992). Nevertheless, where maximum fluid retention is desired, there may be benefits in increasing the sodium levels of rehydration fluids to levels above those provided in typical sport drinks (Maughan and Leiper 1995). Alternatively, sodium may be ingested during postexercise recovery via everyday foods containing sodium or by adding salt to meals. These methods are all effective in enhancing rehydration (Maughan et al. 1996; Ray et al. 1998). In addition, food consumption may provide a social or psychological stimulus to increase voluntary fluid intake and further enhance rehydration goals (Hubbard et al. 1990).

Because caffeine and alcohol increase diuresis, consumption of alcoholic and caffeine-containing drinks during postexercise recovery may result in greater fluid losses compared with other fluids (Gonzalez-Alonso et al. 1992; Shirreffs and Maughan 1997). Athletes are often told that caffeine-containing beverages such as tea, coffee, and cola or guarana drinks are not suitable rehydration fluids and should be avoided in situations where there is a risk of developing dehydration, such as during and after exercise or during air travel. However, a recent review of caffeine and hydration status found that there is a lack of rigorously collected data to show that caffeine intake impairs fluid status (Armstrong 2002). This report concluded that the effect of caffeine on diuresis is overstated and may be minimal in people who are habitual caffeine users. In addition, increased fluid losses from caffeine-containing or low-alcohol drinks may be more than offset by the increased voluntary intake of fluids that are well liked by the athlete or part of social rituals and eating behaviors. If athletes are suddenly asked to remove such beverages from their diets, or postexercise meals, they may not compensate by drinking an equal volume of other less familiar or well-liked fluids. Of course, the intake of large amounts of alcoholic beverages after exercise will interfere with recovery, particularly by distracting the athlete from following recommended dietary practices and by promoting high-risk behavior (Burke and Maughan 2000).

The depletion of muscle glycogen provides a strong drive for its own resynthesis (Zachwieja et al. 1991). Muscle glycogen synthesis follows a biphasic response consisting of a rapid early phase for 30 to 60 min (non–insulin dependent) followed by a slow phase (insulin dependent) lasting up to several days (Ivy and Kuo 1998; Piehl 1974). The restoration of muscle glycogen takes priority over that of liver glycogen, and even in the absence of carbohydrate

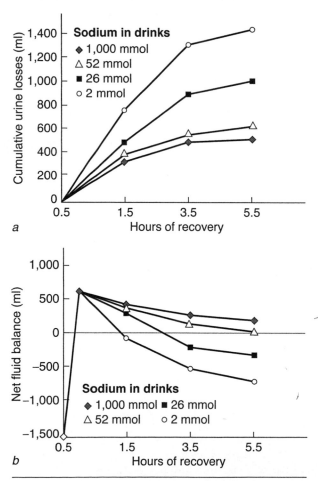

Figure 1.2 *(a)* Effect of sodium replacement on hydration. The presence of sodium in fluids consumed after exercise (replacing 150% of the fluid deficit) reduced urine losses and *(b)* enhanced net fluid balance at the end of 6 hr of recovery. The optimal level of sodium appears to be about 50 mmol/L, because a greater sodium concentration did not further enhance the effect. With little or no sodium replacement, participants were still dehydrated at the end of the 6 hr recovery period.

Reprinted from Maughan and Leiper 1995.

intake after exercise it occurs at a low rate (hourly rate of 1-2 mmol/kg wet weight [ww] muscle), with some of the substrate being provided through gluconeogenesis (Maehlum and Hermansen 1978). High-intensity exercise, resulting in high postexercise levels of lactate, is associated with rapid recovery of glycogen stores in the absence of additional carbohydrate feeding (Hermansen and Vaage 1977). After moderate-intensity exercise, however, high rates of muscle glycogen synthesis are dependent on provision of a dietary source of carbohydrate.

Maximal rates of muscle glycogen storage reported during the first 12 hr of recovery are within the range of 5 to 10 mmol/kg ww/hr (for review, see Jentjens and Jeukendrup 2003a). Given a mean storage rate of 5 to 6 mmol/kg ww/hr, 20 to 24 hr of recovery is required following exercise depletion for normalization of muscle glycogen levels (100-120 mmol/kg ww) (Coyle 1991). However, because the training and competition schedules of many athletes often provide considerably less time than this, these athletes may compromise subsequent performance by beginning with inadequate muscle fuel stores. Several factors that are within the control of the athlete can enhance or impair the rate of muscle glycogen storage (see highlight box on this page).

The major dietary factor involved in postexercise refueling is the amount of carbohydrate consumed. As long as total energy intake as adequate (Tarnopolsky et al. 2001), increased carbohydrate intake promotes increased muscle glycogen storage until the threshold for glycogen synthesis is reached (figure 1.3). Until recently, guidelines for athletes stated that optimal glycogen storage is achieved when ~1 to 1.5 g of carbohydrate is consumed every hour in the early stages of recovery, leading to a total carbohydrate of 6 to 10 g/kg of body mass (BM) over 24 hr (American College of Sports Medicine et al. 2000). However, these guidelines were developed on the basis of maximum glycogen storage during a passive recovery period and may both overestimate the carbohydrate needs of athletes who do not substantially deplete glycogen stores in their daily training and underestimate the daily refueling needs of athletes with extremely high training or competition workloads. For example, cyclists undertaking 2 hr of training each day were found to have higher muscle glycogen stores after 7 days of a daily carbohydrate intake of 12 g/kg BM compared with an intake of 10 $g \cdot kg^{-1} \cdot day^{-1}$ (Coyle et al. 2001). In addition, cyclists in the Tour de France, who compete in daily stages lasting at least 6 hr, have been reported to consume 12 to 13 g of carbohydrate per kilogram of BM each day (Saris et al. 1989). These situations have been incorporated into revised guidelines for the carbohydrate needs of athletes that recognize different carbohydrate needs based on exercise load (see table 1.2).

Factors That Influence the Rate of Muscle Glycogen Restoration

Factors that enhance the rate of restoration

- Depletion of glycogen stores—the lower the stores, the faster the rate of recovery
- Immediate intake of carbohydrate after exercise—starts effective recovery immediately
- Adequate amounts of carbohydrate and total energy intake
  - About 1 g per kilogram of the athlete's body mass within first hour of recovery
  - 7 to 12 g/kg over 24 hr
- Focus on carbohydrate-rich foods with a high glycemic index
- Perhaps, frequent intake of carbohydrate (every 15-60 min) during first hours of recovery
- In the situation where carbohydrate intake is below threshold for glycogen storage, addition of protein to carbohydrate meals and snacks

Factors that have minimal effect on rate of restoration

- Gentle exercise during recovery
- Over long-term recovery, frequency of meals and snacks (provided total amount of carbohydrate is adequate)
- When total carbohydrate intake meets threshold for glycogen storage, intake of other macronutrients (e.g., protein or fat)

Factors that reduce the rate of restoration

- Damage to the muscle (contact injury or delayed-onset muscle soreness caused by eccentric exercise)
- Delay in intake of carbohydrate after exercise (postpones the start of effective recovery)
- Inadequate intake of carbohydrate
- Inadequate total energy intake
- Reliance on carbohydrate-rich foods with a low glycemic index
- Prolonged, strenuous exercise during the recovery period

The type and timing of carbohydrate intake may affect the rate of glycogen restoration, and it is hypothesized that strategies that enhance blood glucose availability or insulin levels might enhance glycogen synthesis. For example, moderate and high glycemic index carbohydrate-rich foods and drinks appear to promote greater glycogen storage than meals based on low glycemic index carbohydrate foods (Burke et al. 1993). However, the mechanisms may include additional factors such as the malabsorption of low glycemic index carbohydrate rather than differences in the glycemic and insulinemic response to such foods alone (Burke, Collier, et al. 1996). The form of the carbohydrate—fluids or solids—does not appear to affect glycogen synthesis (Keizer et al. 1986; Reed et al. 1989) .

Early research indicated that glycogen synthesis was enhanced by the addition of protein to carbohydrate snacks consumed after exercise, an observation that was explained by the protein-stimulated enhancement of the insulin response (Zawadzki et al. 1992). However, these findings have been refuted in other studies (Jentjens et al. 2001; Van Hall, Shirreffs, et al. 2000), especially when the energy contents of protein or amino acids included in recovery feedings were matched (Burke et al. 1995; Carrithers et al. 2000; Roy and Tarnopolsky 1998; Tarnopolsky et al. 1997; Van Loon et al. 2000). The current consensus is that co-ingestion of protein or amino acids with carbohydrate does not clearly enhance glycogen synthesis. Any benefits to muscle glycogen storage are limited to the first hour of recovery (Ivy et al. 2002) or to situations where protein is added to an amount of carbohydrate or pattern of intake that is below the threshold for maximal glycogen synthesis. Of course, the intake of protein within carbohydrate-rich recovery meals may allow the athlete to meet other nutritional goals including the enhancement of net protein balance after exercise. Nevertheless, excessively large amounts of protein and fat in an athlete's diet may displace carbohydrate foods within the athlete's energy requirements and gastric comfort, thereby indirectly interfering with glycogen storage by preventing adequate carbohydrate intake.

Athletes have been advised to enhance recovery by consuming carbohydrate as soon as possible after the completion of a workout. The highest rates of muscle glycogen storage occur during the first hour after exercise (Ivy et al. 1988), attributable to activation of glycogen synthase by glycogen depletion (Wojtaszewski et al. 2001) and exercise-induced increases in muscle membrane permeability and insulin sensitivity (Richter et al. 1989). Carbohydrate feeding immediately after exercise takes advantage of these effects, with higher rates of glycogen storage during the first 2 hr of recovery, slowing thereafter to the more typical rates of storage (Ivy et al. 1988). The most important consideration, however, is that failure to consume carbohydrate in the immediate phase of postexercise recovery leads to very low rates of glycogen restoration until feeding occurs. Therefore, early intake of carbohydrate following strenuous exercise is valuable because it provides an immediate source of substrate to the muscle cell to start effective recovery, and it takes advantage of a period of moderately

enhanced glycogen synthesis. Although early feeding may be important when there is only 4 to 8 hr between exercise sessions (Ivy et al. 1988), it may have less impact over a longer recovery period. For example, there was no difference in glycogen storage after 8 and 24 hr of recovery whether carbohydrate consumption was begun immediately after exercise or delayed for 2 hr (Parkin et al. 1997) (see figure 1.4, a and b). It appears that when the interval between exercise sessions is short, athletes should begin to consume carbohydrate as soon as possible to maximize the effective recovery time. However, when longer recovery periods are available, athletes can choose their preferred meal schedule as long as total carbohydrate intake goals are achieved. It is not always practical to consume substantial meals or snacks immediately after the finish of a strenuous workout.

The frequency of food intake has also been studied. Restoration of muscle glycogen over 24 hr was the same whether a given amount of carbohydrate was fed as two or seven meals (Costill et al. 1981) or as four large meals or 16 hourly snacks (Burke, Collier, et al. 1996) despite differences in insulin and glucose responses. In contrast, very high rates of glycogen synthesis during the first 4 to 6 hr of recovery have been reported when large amounts of carbohydrate were fed at 15 to 30 min intervals (Doyle et al. 1993; Jentjens et al. 2001; Van Hall, Shirreffs, et al. 2000; Van Loon et al. 2000) and have been attributed to the higher sustained insulin and glucose profiles achieved by such a feeding protocol. The effects of enhanced insulin and glucose concentrations on glycogen storage may be important during the first hours of recovery or when total carbohydrate intake is below the threshold of maximum glycogen storage. However, during longer periods of recovery or when total carbohydrate intake is above this threshold, manipulations of plasma substrates and hormones within physiological ranges do not add further benefit. In summary, meeting total carbohydrate requirements is more important than the pattern of intake, at least for long-term recovery, and the athlete is advised to choose a food schedule that is practical and comfortable. Small frequent meals may be useful in overcoming the gastric discomfort often associated with eating large amounts of bulky, high-carbohydrate foods, but additional benefits to glycogen storage may also occur directly during the early recovery phase.

Many of the adaptations stimulated by exercise are underpinned by changes in various proteins in the muscle cell, including regulatory proteins, found in the mitochondria and sarcoplasma, and the structural or myofibrillar proteins. The body protein pool is highly dynamic, undergoing constant synthesis from, and breakdown to, free amino acids that are exchanged between intracellular and plasma pools. During exercise there is a change in the balance, with rates of breakdown exceeding those of synthesis; a goal of postexercise recovery is to reverse this situation so that over time, the magnitude of positive protein balance outweighs that of negative protein balance. This reversal can occur through an increase in protein synthesis, a decrease in protein breakdown, or a combination of both. Although the exact processes are not well explained, experience suggests that endurance exercise increases muscle oxidative capacity by preferentially stimulating the net synthesis of the mitochondrial and sarcoplasmic proteins, whereas a net increase in myofibrillar proteins explains the hypertrophy following resistance training.

The specific study of muscle protein balance is complex and relatively new (Tipton and Wolfe 2001). Our knowledge is based on studies of the acute response to exercise and dietary interventions, although fortunately, recent research shows that the first few hours following an exercise or dietary intervention provide a representative picture of 24 hr muscle protein balance (Tipton et al. 2003). The majority of studies have been undertaken using resistance training as the mode of exercise, using untrained participants. Although the postexercise period is characterized by an improvement in net protein balance, in the absence of nutritional support, net protein balance in the muscle remains negative (Phillips et al. 1997; Phillips et al. 1999). In contrast, the delivery of a source of amino acids following resistance exercise causes a net gain in muscle protein balance, principally attributable to an increase in rates of muscle protein synthesis rather than changes in muscle protein breakdown (Tipton et al. 1999). This effect can be produced by the intake of essential amino acids alone (Borsheim et al. 2002) and is further enhanced when the amino acids are provided immediately before the resistance training session, rather than after exercise (Tipton et al. 2001). The minimum amount of amino acids needed to produce an effect and the amount required for an optimal effect are currently unknown; however, there are dramatic responses to the intake of as little as 3 to 6 g of essential amino acids—10 to 20 g of high-quality protein (Borsheim et al. 2002; Tipton et al. 2001)—and there is evidence of both a dose response (Borsheim et al. 2002) and continued responses to repeated intake of recovery snacks (Miller et al. 2003).

Intake of carbohydrate after resistance exercise stimulates insulin secretion and decreases the normal stimulation of muscle protein breakdown (Biolo et al. 1999). The combination of carbohydrate and amino acids after exercise might optimize muscle protein synthesis by increasing synthesis and reducing breakdown; however, the available research suggests that the enhancement of protein synthesis is small (Miller et al. 2003). The major effect of carbohydrate intake on protein synthesis appears to be delayed for several hours (Borsheim, Cree, et al. 2004), and there may be value in delaying the intake of amino acids to coincide with the peak of the insulin action. Such protocols need to be studied. Nevertheless, the combined intake of carbohydrate and protein is a sensible strategy for recovery from resistance training because it addresses needs for refueling as well as the protein response. There is less information regarding nutritional interventions for postexercise protein balance following endurance exercise. However, there is some evidence that protein and carbohydrate intake enhances net protein balance following prolonged cycling and that early intake of recovery meals (1 hr) has greater benefits than delayed intake (3 hr) (Levenhagen et al. 2001).

More research is needed to elucidate optimal feeding practices for postexercise protein recovery. Issues that should be addressed include the amounts of amino acids needed to achieve desired outcomes, the effects of different types of whole proteins (i.e., foods), the interaction of protein and carbohydrate, the optimal timing of intake of nutrients, differential effects in well-trained athletes versus untrained subjects, and the response to different exercise stimuli. Also needed are the complex end-point studies that can prove that various interventions enhance training adaptations and competition performance. Until such research is completed, it makes sense for the athlete to address recovery goals with an integrated nutritional approach, which includes choosing foods and drinks that provide valuable sources of both protein and carbohydrate in post- and preevent meals (see table 1.3).

Table 1.3   Carbohydrate-Rich Choices Suitable for Special Issues in Sport

Carbohydrate-rich choices for preevent meals	Carbohydrate-rich foods suitable for intake during exercise (50 g of carbohydrate portions)

• Breakfast cereal + low-fat milk + fresh or canned fruit
• Muffins or crumpets + jam or honey
• Pancakes + syrup
• Toast + baked beans (this is a high-fiber choice)
• Creamed rice (made with low-fat milk)
• Rolls or sandwiches
• Fruit salad + low-fat fruit yogurt
• Spaghetti with tomato or low-fat sauce
• Baked potatoes with low-fat filling
• Fruit smoothie (low-fat milk + fruit + yogurt or ice cream)
• Liquid meal supplement
	• 600-800 ml of sport drink
	• 2 sachets of sport gel
	• 1-1.5 sport bars
	• 2 cereal bars or granola bars
	• Large bread roll filled with
	  -jam, honey, or cheese
	  -2 bananas or 3 medium pieces of other fruit
	  -60 g of jelly confectionery
	• 450 ml of cola drinks
	• 80 g chocolate bar
	• 100 g of fruit bread or cake
	• 80 dried fruit or 120 g of trail mix

Recovery snacks, to be eaten postexercise, or preexercise in the case of resistance training to promote refueling and protein responses (Each serving provides 50 g of carbohydrate and at least 10 g of protein.)	Portable carbohydrate-rich foods suitable for the traveling athlete
• 250-350 ml of liquid meal supplement, milk shake, or fruit smoothie • 500 ml of flavored low-fat milk • Sport bar + 200 ml of sport drink • 60 g (1.5-2 cups) of breakfast cereal with 1/2 cup of milk • 1 round of sandwiches with cheese, meat, or chicken filling, and 1 large piece of fruit or 300 ml of sport drink • 1 cup of fruit salad with 200 g of fruit-flavored yogurt or custard • 200 g of fruit-flavored yogurt or 300 ml of flavored milk and 30 to 35 g cereal bar • 2 crumpets or English muffins with thick spread of peanut butter • 250 g of baked beans on 2 slices of toast • 250 g (large) baked potato with cottage cheese or grated cheese filling • 150 g thick-crust pizza	• Breakfast cereal (and skim milk powder) • Cereal bars, granola bars • Dried fruit, trail mixes • Rice crackers, dry biscuits • Spreads: jam, honey • Sport bars • Liquid meal supplements: powder and ready-to-drink forms • Sport drink

Goal 7

Reduce the risk of sickness and injury during heavy training periods by maintaining healthy physique and energy balance and by supplying nutrients believed to assist immune function.

An athlete's ability to train consistently rests on remaining healthy and injury-free. Meeting known nutrient needs is important for general health and well-being. However, several issues related to sport and exercise merit special comment. The first involves the immunosuppression that is known to accompany prolonged and strenuous training, whereas the other concerns disturbances of the athlete's

hormonal system with potential implications for illness and bone integrity.

Prolonged exhaustive exercise is known to cause a transient impairment of various immune system parameters and the potential for an increased risk of illness (for review, see Pedersen et al. 1999). Various nutritional interventions such as supplementation with glutamine, echinacea, and antioxidants have failed to provide a clear and consistent improvement to the athlete's immune status or health (Gleeson and Bishop 2000). Recent studies have found that carbohydrate status may play an important role in maintaining effective immune function in athletes. Disturbed immune function may occur through two principal mechanisms related to low carbohydrate intake: direct immunosuppression attributable to the depletion of glucose, which is a key substrate for the high metabolic needs of immune cells, and indirect impairment via increased concentration of stress hormones (Gleeson et al. 2001). Studies in which carbohydrate is consumed during prolonged continuous exercise (Henson et al. 1999; Nehlsen-Cannarella et al. 1997) or in high amounts in the preexercise diet (Gleeson et al. 1998) have shown that there is less disturbance to immune system parameters during the postexercise period than when the athlete is deprived of carbohydrate. However, not all studies have found an enhancement of the distribution and function of immune parameters, especially when the exercise involves a inter-mittent high-intensity protocol (Bishop et al. 1999) or is carried out to the point of fatigue (Henson et al. 2000). The ideal study to find that long-term dietary practices correlate with reduced frequency or severity of illness in athletes is yet to be undertaken. Notwithstanding these limitations, the current literature supports the importance of adequate carbohydrate intake for the health of the athlete. Although the primary benefit is the availability of fuel supply, leading to better training or competition performance, protection of the immune system may be a secondary but substantial benefit of carbohydrate intake strategies.

Lengthy periods of restricted energy intake by female athletes are associated with menstrual dysfunction, hor-monal disturbances, and energy conservation (Loucks 2001), with the hormone leptin providing a potential link between energy availability and the hormones responsible for reproductive and metabolic function (Thong and Graham 1999). Male athletes who undertake periods of severe energy restriction are also likely to suffer some of these effects. A variety of causes of menstrual dysfunc-tion in female athletes have been suggested, and there is a large degree of individuality in response to risk factors (for review, see Manore 2002). Nevertheless, energy drain, or low energy availability—chronic periods of restricted energy intake in conjunction with high energy expendi-ture—appears to be an underlying factor in many cases of menstrual dysfunction (Loucks et al. 1998). Disordered eating and food-related stress are frequently related to menstrual dysfunction. Recent research has shown that low energy availability directly impairs bone formation and resorption (Ihle and Loucks 2004) as well as having an indirect effect on bones arising from menstrual dysfunction and altered hormonal environment. The cluster of disor-dered eating, amenorrhea, and osteopenia became known during the 1990s as the female athlete triad (Yeager et al. 1993), in recognition that female athletes are at increased risk of developing one or more of these problems and that the causes and outcomes are often closely linked. Indi-vidually, or in combination, these problems can directly impair athletic health. Significantly, they will reduce the athlete's career span by increasing her risk of illness and injury, including stress fractures. Long-term problems such as an increased risk of osteoporosis in later life and chronic suboptimal nutritional status might also be expected.

Although awareness of the female athlete triad has focused attention on menstrual dysfunction and has highlighted the seriousness of the triad, criticism of the initial "packaging" of the syndrome (Khan et al. 2002; Nattiv 2002) has helped broader definitions and recom-mendations to evolve. A diagnosis of the first definition of the female athlete triad required extreme cutoff points for the following:

- Eating disorders: described as a wide range of harm-ful eating behaviors used to achieve a reduction of weight or body fat, with the spectrum ranging from restricted food intake to frank cases of eating disorders
- Amenorrhea: described as primary or secondary amenorrhea according to standard definitions
- Osteoporosis: described as a bone mineral density more than 2.5 standard deviations below the mean value for young adults

The more recent concept of the female athlete triad (Loucks and Nattiv 2005) targets energy availability, men-strual health, and bone density. It considers that each of these issues involves a continuum between optimal health and frank disorder and that the athlete should be alert to any change in her status of any issue. In other words, ath-letes must be educated about the benefits of early diagnosis and treatment of problems and the likelihood that negative outcomes occur at a much earlier stage than previously considered. The detection, prevention, and management of the female athlete triad, or individual elements within it (Beals and Manore 2002), require expertise and, ideally, the teamwork of sports physicians, dietitians, psycholo-gists, coaches, and fitness advisors. Dietary intervention is important to correct factors that underpin menstrual dysfunction as well as those that contribute to suboptimal bone density. Dietary goals include adequate energy intake and the reversal of disordered eating or suboptimal intake. Adequate calcium intake is important for bone health, and requirements may be increased to 1,200 to 1,500 mg/day in athletes with impaired menstrual function. Where adequate calcium intake cannot be met through dietary means, usu-ally through use of low-fat dairy foods or calcium-enriched soy alternatives, a calcium supplement may be considered. There is some doubt about the degree of reversibility of bone loss and in particular the restoration of a strong bone formation, particularly in cases of long-term loss (Drinkwater et al. 1986). Prevention or early intervention is clearly the preferred option.

....

Copyright Acknowledgements *(Practical Sports Nutrition)*

Reprinted, with permission, from L. Burke, 2007, *Practical Sports Nutrition,* (Champaign, IL: Human Kinetics), 1-16.

With the exception of the following:

Figure 1.1: Reprinted by permission from Wolters Kluwer Health; **Figure 1.2:** With kind permission from Springer Science+Business Media: *European Journal of Applied Physiology*, "Sodium intake and post-exercise rehydration in man," 71(4), 1995, p. 311-319, R.J. Maughan.

Foodcollection/Getty Images

Thomson NOW! Throughout this chapter, the ThomsonNOW logo indicates an opportunity for online self-study, linking you to interactive tutorials and videos based on your level of understanding.

www.thomsonedu.com/thomsonnow

Figure 3.8: Animated! The Digestive Fate of a Sandwich

Figure 3.11: Animated! The Vascular System

Nutrition Portfolio Journal

Nutrition in Your Life

Have you ever wondered what happens to the food you eat after you swallow it? Or how your body extracts nutrients from food? Have you ever marveled at how it all just seems to happen? Follow foods as they travel through the digestive system. Learn how a healthy digestive system transforms whatever food you give it—whether sirloin steak and potatoes or tofu and brussels sprouts—into the nutrients that will nourish the cells of your body.

Digestion, Absorption, and Transport

CHAPTER OUTLINE

Digestion • Anatomy of the Digestive Tract • The Muscular Action of Digestion • The Secretions of Digestion • The Final Stage

Absorption • Anatomy of the Absorptive System • A Closer Look at the Intestinal Cells

The Circulatory Systems • The Vascular System • The Lymphatic System

The Health and Regulation of the GI Tract • Gastrointestinal Bacteria • Gastrointestinal Hormones and Nerve Pathways • The System at Its Best

HIGHLIGHT 3 Common Digestive Problems

This chapter takes you on the journey that transforms the foods you eat into the nutrients featured in the later chapters. Then it follows the nutrients as they travel through the intestinal cells and into the body to do their work. This introduction presents a general overview of the processes common to all nutrients; later chapters discuss the specifics of digesting and absorbing individual nutrients.

Digestion

Digestion is the body's ingenious way of breaking down foods into nutrients in preparation for **absorption.** In the process, it overcomes many challenges without any conscious effort on your part. Consider these challenges:

1. Human beings breathe, eat, and drink through their mouths. Air taken in through the mouth must go to the lungs; food and liquid must go to the stomach. The throat must be arranged so that swallowing and breathing don't interfere with each other.

2. Below the lungs lies the diaphragm, a dome of muscle that separates the upper half of the major body cavity from the lower half. Food must pass through this wall to reach the stomach.

3. The materials within the digestive tract should be kept moving forward, slowly but steadily, at a pace that permits all reactions to reach completion.

4. To move through the system, food must be lubricated with fluids. Too much would form a liquid that would flow too rapidly; too little would form a paste too dry and compact to move at all. The amount of fluids must be regulated to keep the intestinal contents at the right consistency to move smoothly along.

5. When the digestive enzymes break food down, they need it in a finely divided form, suspended in enough liquid so that every particle is accessible. Once digestion is complete and the needed nutrients have been absorbed out of the tract and into the body, the system must excrete the remaining residue. Excreting all the water along with the solid residue, however, would be both wasteful and messy. Some water must be withdrawn to leave a paste just solid enough to be smooth and easy to pass.

6. The enzymes of the digestive tract are designed to digest carbohydrate, fat, and protein. The walls of the tract, composed of living cells, are also made of

digestion: the process by which food is broken down into absorbable units.
 • **digestion** = take apart

absorption: the uptake of nutrients by the cells of the small intestine for transport into either the blood or the lymph.
 • **absorb** = suck in

The process of digestion transforms all kinds of *foods* into *nutrients*.

◆ The process of chewing is called **mastication** (mass-tih-KAY-shun).

---

carbohydrate, fat, and protein. These cells need protection against the action of the powerful digestive juices that they secrete.

7. Once waste matter has reached the end of the tract, it must be excreted, but it would be inconvenient and embarrassing if this function occurred continuously. Provision must be made for periodic, voluntary evacuation.

The following sections show how the body elegantly and efficiently handles these challenges.

Anatomy of the Digestive Tract

The **gastrointestinal (GI) tract** is a flexible muscular tube that extends from the mouth, through the esophagus, stomach, small intestine, large intestine, and rectum to the anus. Figure 3-1 traces the path followed by food from one end to the other. In a sense, the human body surrounds the GI tract. The inner space within the GI tract, called the **lumen,** is continuous from one end to the other. (GI anatomy terms appear in boldface type and are defined in the accompanying glossary.) Only when a nutrient or other substance finally penetrates the GI tract's wall does it enter the body proper; many materials pass through the GI tract without being digested or absorbed.

Mouth The process of digestion begins in the **mouth.** As you chew, ◆ your teeth crush large pieces of food into smaller ones, and fluids from foods, beverages, and salivary glands blend with these pieces to ease swallowing. Fluids also help dissolve the food so that you can taste it; only particles in solution can react with taste buds. When stimulated, the taste buds detect one, or a combination, of the four basic taste sensations: sweet, sour, bitter, and salty. Some scientists also include the flavor associated with monosodium glutamate, sometimes called *savory* or its Asian name, *umami* (oo-MOM-ee). In addition to these chemical triggers, aroma, texture, and temperature also affect a food's flavor. In fact, the sense of smell is thousands of times more sensitive than the sense of taste.

The tongue allows you not only to taste food, but also to move food around the mouth, facilitating chewing and swallowing. When you swallow a mouthful of

gastrointestinal (GI) tract: the digestive tract. The principal organs are the stomach and intestines.
- **gastro** = stomach
- **intestinalis** = intestine

GLOSSARY OF GI ANATOMY TERMS

These terms are listed in order from start to end of the digestive system.

lumen (LOO-men): the space within a vessel, such as the intestine.

mouth: the oral cavity containing the tongue and teeth.

pharynx (FAIR-inks): the passageway leading from the nose and mouth to the larynx and esophagus, respectively.

epiglottis (epp-ih-GLOTT-iss): cartilage in the throat that guards the entrance to the trachea and prevents fluid or food from entering it when a person swallows.
- **epi** = upon (over)
- **glottis** = back of tongue

esophagus (ee-SOFF-ah-gus): the food pipe; the conduit from the mouth to the stomach.

sphincter (SFINK-ter): a circular muscle surrounding, and able to close, a body opening. Sphincters are found at specific points along

the GI tract and regulate the flow of food particles.
- **sphincter** = band (binder)

esophageal (ee-SOF-ah-GEE-al) **sphincter:** a sphincter muscle at the upper or lower end of the esophagus. The *lower esophageal sphincter* is also called the *cardiac sphincter.*

stomach: a muscular, elastic, saclike portion of the digestive tract that grinds and churns swallowed food, mixing it with acid and enzymes to form chyme.

pyloric (pie-LORE-ic) **sphincter:** the circular muscle that separates the stomach from the small intestine and regulates the flow of partially digested food into the small intestine; also called *pylorus* or *pyloric valve.*
- **pylorus** = gatekeeper

small intestine: a 10-foot length of small-diameter intestine that is the major site of digestion of

food and absorption of nutrients. Its segments are the duodenum, jejunum, and ileum.

gallbladder: the organ that stores and concentrates bile. When it receives the signal that fat is present in the duodenum, the gallbladder contracts and squirts bile through the bile duct into the duodenum.

pancreas: a gland that secretes digestive enzymes and juices into the duodenum. (The pancreas also secretes hormones into the blood that help to maintain glucose homeostasis.)

duodenum (doo-oh-DEEN-um, doo-ODD-num): the top portion of the small intestine (about "12 fingers' breadth" long in ancient terminology).
- **duodecim** = twelve

jejunum (je-JOON-um): the first two-fifths of the small intestine beyond the duodenum.

ileum (ILL-ee-um): the last segment of the small intestine.

ileocecal (ill-ee-oh-SEEK-ul) **valve:** the sphincter separating the small and large intestines.

large intestine or **colon** (COAL-un): the lower portion of intestine that completes the digestive process. Its segments are the ascending colon, the transverse colon, the descending colon, and the sigmoid colon.
- **sigmoid** = shaped like the letter S (sigma in Greek)

appendix: a narrow blind sac extending from the beginning of the colon that stores lymph cells.

rectum: the muscular terminal part of the intestine, extending from the sigmoid colon to the anus.

anus (AY-nus): the terminal outlet of the GI tract.

digestive system: all the organs and glands associated with the ingestion and digestion of food.

FIGURE 3–1 The Gastrointestinal Tract

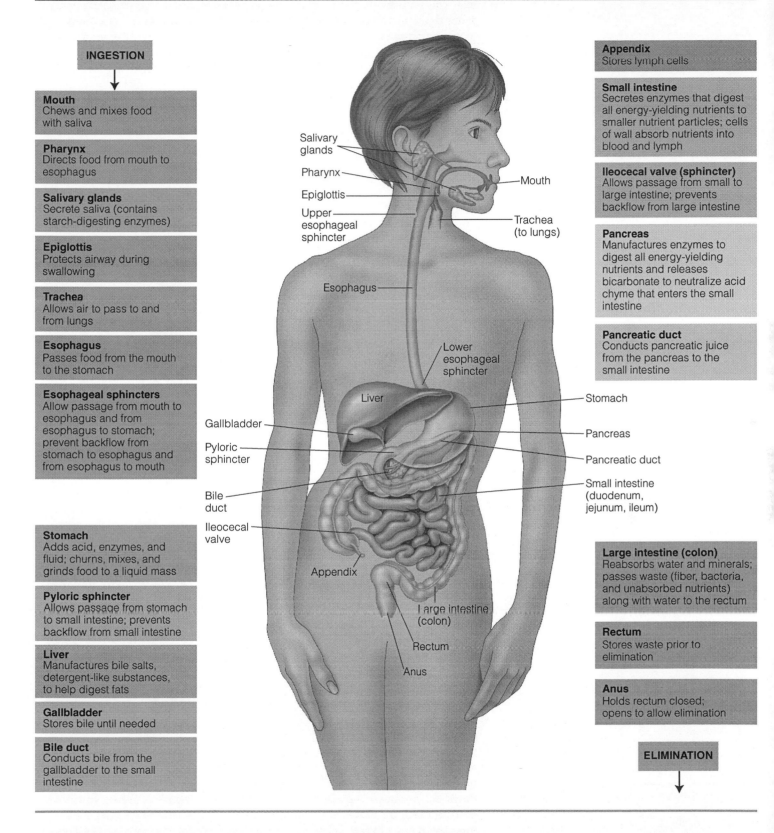

INGESTION

Mouth
Chews and mixes food with saliva

Pharynx
Directs food from mouth to esophagus

Salivary glands
Secrete saliva (contains starch-digesting enzymes)

Epiglottis
Protects airway during swallowing

Trachea
Allows air to pass to and from lungs

Esophagus
Passes food from the mouth to the stomach

Esophageal sphincters
Allow passage from mouth to esophagus and from esophagus to stomach; prevent backflow from stomach to esophagus and from esophagus to mouth

Stomach
Adds acid, enzymes, and fluid; churns, mixes, and grinds food to a liquid mass

Pyloric sphincter
Allows passage from stomach to small intestine; prevents backflow from small intestine

Liver
Manufactures bile salts, detergent-like substances, to help digest fats

Gallbladder
Stores bile until needed

Bile duct
Conducts bile from the gallbladder to the small intestine

Appendix
Stores lymph cells

Small intestine
Secretes enzymes that digest all energy-yielding nutrients to smaller nutrient particles; cells of wall absorb nutrients into blood and lymph

Ileocecal valve (sphincter)
Allows passage from small to large intestine; prevents backflow from large intestine

Pancreas
Manufactures enzymes to digest all energy-yielding nutrients and releases bicarbonate to neutralize acid chyme that enters the small intestine

Pancreatic duct
Conducts pancreatic juice from the pancreas to the small intestine

Large intestine (colon)
Reabsorbs water and minerals; passes waste (fiber, bacteria, and unabsorbed nutrients) along with water to the rectum

Rectum
Stores waste prior to elimination

Anus
Holds rectum closed; opens to allow elimination

ELIMINATION

Salivary glands
Pharynx
Epiglottis
Upper esophageal sphincter
Mouth
Trachea (to lungs)
Esophagus
Lower esophageal sphincter
Liver
Gallbladder
Pyloric sphincter
Bile duct
Ileocecal valve
Appendix
Stomach
Pancreas
Pancreatic duct
Small intestine (duodenum, jejunum, ileum)
Large intestine (colon)
Rectum
Anus

food, it passes through the **pharynx,** a short tube that is shared by both the **digestive system** and the respiratory system. To bypass the entrance to your lungs, the **epiglottis** closes off your air passages so that you don't choke when you swallow, thus resolving the first challenge. (Choking is discussed on pp. 92–93.) After a mouthful of food has been swallowed, it is called a **bolus.**

bolus (BOH-lus): a portion; with respect to food, the amount swallowed at one time.
• **bolos** = lump

Esophagus to the Stomach The **esophagus** has a **sphincter** muscle at each end. During a swallow, the upper **esophageal sphincter** opens. The bolus then slides down the esophagus, which passes through a hole in the diaphragm (challenge 2) to the **stomach.** The lower esophageal sphincter at the entrance to the stomach closes behind the bolus so that it proceeds forward and doesn't slip back into the esophagus (challenge 3). The stomach retains the bolus for a while in its upper portion. Little by little, the stomach transfers the food to its lower portion, adds juices to it, and grinds it to a semiliquid mass called **chyme.** Then, bit by bit, the stomach releases the chyme through the **pyloric sphincter,** which opens into the **small intestine** and then closes behind the chyme.

Small Intestine At the beginning of the small intestine, the chyme bypasses the opening from the common bile duct, which is dripping fluids (challenge 4) into the small intestine from two organs outside the GI tract—the **gallbladder** and the **pancreas.** The chyme travels on down the small intestine through its three segments—the **duodenum,** the **jejunum,** and the **ileum**—almost 10 feet of tubing coiled within the abdomen.*

Large Intestine (Colon) Having traveled the length of the small intestine, the remaining contents arrive at another sphincter (challenge 3 again): the **ileocecal valve,** at the beginning of the **large intestine (colon)** in the lower right side of the abdomen. Upon entering the colon, the contents pass another opening. Any intestinal contents slipping into this opening would end up in the **appendix,** a blind sac about the size of your little finger. The contents bypass this opening, however, and travel along the large intestine up the right side of the abdomen, across the front to the left side, down to the lower left side, and finally below the other folds of the intestines to the back of the body, above the **rectum.**

As the intestinal contents pass to the rectum, the colon withdraws water, leaving semisolid waste (challenge 5). The strong muscles of the rectum and anal canal hold back this waste until it is time to defecate. Then the rectal muscles relax (challenge 7), and the two sphincters of the **anus** open to allow passage of the waste.

The Muscular Action of Digestion

In the mouth, chewing, the addition of saliva, and the action of the tonguetransform food into a coarse mash that can be swallowed. After swallowing, you are generally unaware of all the activity that follows. As is the case with so much else that happens in the body, the muscles of the digestive tract meet internal needs without any conscious effort on your part. They keep things moving ◆ at just the right pace, slow enough to get the job done and fast enough to make progress.

Peristalsis The entire GI tract is ringed with circular muscles. Surrounding these rings of muscle are longitudinal muscles. When the rings tighten and the long muscles relax, the tube is constricted. When the rings relax and the long muscles tighten, the tube bulges. This action—called **peristalsis**—occurs continuously and pushes the intestinal contents along (challenge 3 again). (If you have ever watched a lump of food pass along the body of a snake, you have a good picture of how these muscles work.)

The waves of contraction ripple along the GI tract at varying rates and intensities depending on the part of the GI tract and on whether food is present. For example, waves occur three times per minute in the stomach, but they speed up to ten times per minute when chyme reaches the small intestine. When you have just eaten a meal, the waves are slow and continuous; when the GI tract is empty, the intestine is quiet except for periodic bursts of powerful rhythmic waves. Peristalsis,

◆ The ability of the GI tract muscles to move is called their **motility** (moh-TIL-ih-tee).

chyme (KIME): the semiliquid mass of partly digested food expelled by the stomach into the duodenum.
- **chymos** = juice

peristalsis (per-ih-STALL-sis): wavelike muscular contractions of the GI tract that push its contents along.
- **peri** = around
- **stellein** = wrap

* The small intestine is almost 2½ times shorter in living adults than it is at death, when muscles are relaxed and elongated.

along with sphincter muscles located at key places, keeps things moving along.

Stomach Action The stomach has the thickest walls and strongest muscles of all the GI tract organs. In addition to the circular and longitudinal muscles, it has a third layer of diagonal muscles that also alternately contract and relax (see Figure 3-2). These three sets of muscles work to force the chyme downward, but the pyloric sphincter usually remains tightly closed, preventing the chyme from passing into the duodenum of the small intestine. As a result, the chyme is churned and forced down, hits the pyloric sphincter, and remains in the stomach. Meanwhile, the stomach wall releases gastric juices. When the chyme is completely liquefied, the pyloric sphincter opens briefly, about three times a minute, to allow small portions of chyme to pass through. At this point, the chyme no longer resembles food in the least.

Segmentation The circular muscles of the intestines rhythmically contract and squeeze their contents (see Figure 3-3). These contractions,

FIGURE 3–2 Stomach Muscles

The stomach has three layers of muscles.

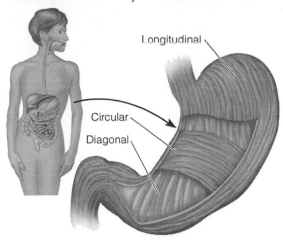

FIGURE 3–3 Peristalsis and Segmentation

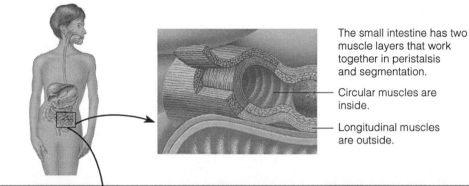

The small intestine has two muscle layers that work together in peristalsis and segmentation.

Circular muscles are inside.

Longitudinal muscles are outside.

PERISTALSIS

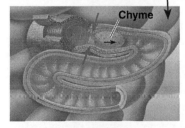

The inner circular muscles contract, tightening the tube and pushing the food forward in the intestine.

When the circular muscles relax, the outer longitudinal muscles contract, and the intestinal tube is loose.

As the circular and longitudinal muscles tighten and relax, the chyme moves ahead of the constriction.

SEGMENTATION

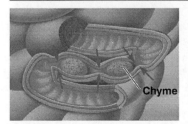

Circular muscles contract, creating segments within the intestine.

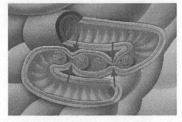

As each set of circular muscles relaxes and contracts, the chyme is broken up and mixed with digestive juices.

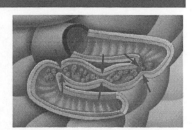

These alternating contractions, occurring 12 to 16 times per minute, continue to mix the chyme and bring the nutrients into contact with the intestinal lining for absorption.

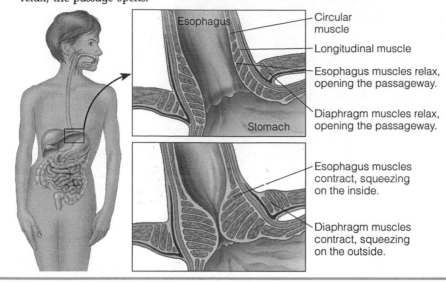

FIGURE 3–4 An Example of a Sphincter Muscle

When the circular muscles of a sphincter contract, the passage closes; when they relax, the passage opens.

- Esophagus
- Circular muscle
- Longitudinal muscle
- Esophagus muscles relax, opening the passageway.
- Diaphragm muscles relax, opening the passageway.
- Stomach
- Esophagus muscles contract, squeezing on the inside.
- Diaphragm muscles contract, squeezing on the outside.

FIGURE 3–5 The Salivary Glands

The salivary glands secrete saliva into the mouth and begin the digestive process. Given the short time food is in the mouth, salivary enzymes contribute little to digestion.

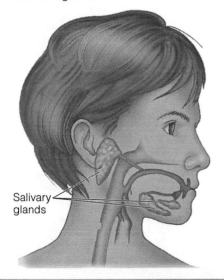

- Salivary glands

segmentation (SEG-men-TAY-shun): a periodic squeezing or partitioning of the intestine at intervals along its length by its circular muscles.

reflux: a backward flow.
- **re** = back
- **flux** = flow

catalyst (CAT-uh-list): a compound that facilitates chemical reactions without itself being changed in the process.

called **segmentation,** mix the chyme and promote close contact with the digestive juices and the absorbing cells of the intestinal walls before letting the contents move slowly along. Figure 3-3 illustrates peristalsis and segmentation.

Sphincter Contractions Sphincter muscles periodically open and close, allowing the contents of the GI tract to move along at a controlled pace (challenge 3 again). At the top of the esophagus, the upper esophageal sphincter opens in response to swallowing. At the bottom of the esophagus, the lower esophageal sphincter (sometimes called the cardiac sphincter because of its proximity to the heart) prevents **reflux** of the stomach contents. At the bottom of the stomach, the pyloric sphincter, which stays closed most of the time, holds the chyme in the stomach long enough for it to be thoroughly mixed with gastric juice and liquefied. The pyloric sphincter also prevents the intestinal contents from backing up into the stomach. At the end of the small intestine, the ileocecal valve performs a similar function, allowing the contents of the small intestine to empty into the large intestine. Finally, the tightness of the rectal muscle is a kind of safety device; together with the two sphincters of the anus, it prevents elimination until you choose to perform it voluntarily (challenge 7). Figure 3-4 illustrates how sphincter muscles contract and relax to close and open passageways.

The Secretions of Digestion

The breakdown of food into nutrients requires secretions from five different organs: the salivary glands, the stomach, the pancreas, the liver (via the gallbladder), and the small intestine. These secretions enter the GI tract at various points along the way, bringing an abundance of water (challenge 3 again) and a variety of enzymes.

Enzymes are formally introduced in Chapter 6, but for now a simple definition will suffice. An enzyme is a protein that facilitates a chemical reaction—making a molecule, breaking a molecule apart, changing the arrangement of a molecule, or exchanging parts of molecules. As a **catalyst,** the enzyme itself remains unchanged. The enzymes involved in digestion facilitate a chemical reaction known as **hydrolysis**—the addition of water *(hydro)* to break *(lysis)* a molecule into smaller pieces. The glossary (p. 77) identifies some of the common **digestive enzymes** and related terms; later chapters introduce specific enzymes. When learning about enzymes, it helps to know that the word ending *-ase* denotes an enzyme. Enzymes are often identified by the organ they come from and the compounds they work on. *Gastric lipase,* for example, is a stomach enzyme that acts on lipids, whereas *pancreatic lipase* comes from the pancreas (and also works on lipids).

Saliva The **salivary glands,** shown in Figure 3-5, squirt just enough **saliva** to moisten each mouthful of food so that it can pass easily down the esophagus (challenge 4). (Digestive **glands** and their secretions are defined in the glossary on

p. 78.) The saliva contains water, salts, mucus, and enzymes that initiate the digestion of carbohydrates. Saliva also protects the teeth and the linings of the mouth, esophagus, and stomach from attack by substances that might harm them.

Gastric Juice In the stomach, **gastric glands** secrete **gastric juice,** a mixture of water, enzymes, and **hydrochloric acid,** which acts primarily in protein digestion. The acid is so strong that it causes the sensation of heartburn if it happens to reflux into the esophagus. Highlight 3, following this chapter, discusses heartburn, ulcers, and other common digestive problems.

The strong acidity of the stomach prevents bacterial growth and kills most bacteria that enter the body with food. It would destroy the cells of the stomach as well, but for their natural defenses. To protect themselves from gastric juice, the cells of the stomach wall secrete **mucus,** a thick, slippery, white substance that coats the cells, protecting them from the acid, enzymes, and disease-causing bacteria that might otherwise harm them (challenge 6).

Figure 3-6 shows how the strength of acids is measured—in **pH** ◆ units. Note that the acidity of gastric juice registers below "2" on the pH scale—stronger than vinegar. The stomach enzymes work most efficiently in the stomach's strong acid, but the salivary enzymes, which are swallowed with food, do not work in acid this strong. Consequently, the salivary digestion of carbohydrate gradually ceases when the stomach acid penetrates each newly swallowed bolus of food. When they enter the stomach, salivary enzymes become just other proteins to be digested.

Pancreatic Juice and Intestinal Enzymes By the time food leaves the stomach, digestion of all three energy nutrients (carbohydrates, fats, and proteins) has begun, and the action gains momentum in the small intestine. There the pancreas contributes digestive juices by way of ducts leading into the duodenum. The **pancreatic juice** contains enzymes that act on all three energy nutrients, and the cells of the intestinal wall also possess digestive enzymes on their surfaces.

In addition to enzymes, the pancreatic juice contains sodium **bicarbonate,** which is basic or alkaline—the opposite of the stomach's acid (review Figure 3-6). The pancreatic juice thus neutralizes the acidic chyme arriving in the small intestine from the stomach. From this point on, the chyme remains at a neutral or slightly alkaline pH. The enzymes of both the intestine and the pancreas work best in this environment.

Bile Bile also flows into the duodenum. The **liver** continuously produces bile, which is then concentrated and stored in the gallbladder. The gallbladder squirts

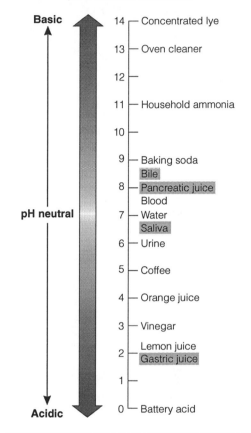

FIGURE 3–6 The pH Scale

A substance's acidity or alkalinity is measured in pH units. The pH is the negative logarithm of the hydrogen ion concentration. Each increment represents a tenfold increase in concentration of hydrogen particles. This means, for example, that a pH of 2 is 1000 times stronger than a pH of 5.

pH of common substances:

Basic

14 — Concentrated lye
13 — Oven cleaner
12
11 — Household ammonia
10
9 — Baking soda
   Bile
8 — Pancreatic juice
   Blood

pH neutral

7 — Water
   Saliva
6 — Urine
5 — Coffee
4 — Orange juice
3 — Vinegar
   Lemon juice
2 — Gastric juice
1
0 — Battery acid

Acidic

◆ The lower the pH, the higher the H⁺ ion concentration and the stronger the acid. A pH above 7 is alkaline, or base (a solution in which OH⁻ ions predominate).

GLOSSARY OF DIGESTIVE ENZYMES

digestive enzymes: proteins found in digestive juices that act on food substances, causing them to break down into simpler compounds.

-ase (ACE): a word ending denoting an enzyme. The word beginning often identifies the compounds the enzyme works on. Examples include:
- **carbohydrase** (KAR-boe-HIGH-drase), an enzyme that hydrolyzes carbohydrates.
- **lipase** (LYE-pase), an enzyme that hydrolyzes lipids (fats).

- **protease** (PRO-tee-ase), an enzyme that hydrolyzes proteins.

hydrolysis (high-DROL-ih-sis): a chemical reaction in which a major reactant is split into two products, with the addition of a hydrogen atom (H) to one and a hydroxyl group (OH) to the other (from water, H_2O). (The noun is **hydrolysis**; the verb is **hydrolyze**.)
- **hydro** = water
- **lysis** = breaking

pH: the unit of measure expressing a substance's acidity or alkalinity.

GLOSSARY OF DIGESTIVE GLANDS AND THEIR SECRETIONS

These terms are listed in order from start to end of the digestive tract.

glands: cells or groups of cells that secrete materials for special uses in the body. Glands may be **exocrine** (EKS-oh-crin) **glands,** secreting their materials "out" (into the digestive tract or onto the surface of the skin), or **endocrine** (EN-doe-crin) **glands,** secreting their materials "in" (into the blood).
• **exo** = outside
• **endo** = inside
• **krine** = to separate

salivary glands: exocrine glands that secrete saliva into the mouth.

saliva: the secretion of the salivary glands. Its principal enzyme begins carbohydrate digestion.

gastric glands: exocrine glands in the stomach wall that secrete gastric juice into the stomach.
• **gastro** = stomach

gastric juice: the digestive secretion of the gastric glands of the stomach.

hydrochloric acid: an acid composed of hydrogen and chloride atoms (HCl) that is normally produced by the gastric glands.

mucus (MYOO-kus): a slippery substance secreted by cells of the GI lining (and other body linings) that protects the cells from exposure to digestive juices (and other destructive agents). The lining of the GI tract with its coat of mucus is a **mucous membrane.** (The noun is **mucus;** the adjective is **mucous.**)

liver: the organ that manufactures bile. (The liver's many other functions are described in Chapter 7.)

bile: an emulsifier that prepares fats and oils for digestion; an exocrine secretion made by the liver, stored in the gallbladder, and released into the small intestine when needed.

emulsifier (ee-MUL-sih-fire): a substance with both water-soluble and fat-soluble portions that promotes the mixing of oils and fats in a watery solution.

pancreatic (pank-ree-AT-ic) **juice:** the exocrine secretion of the pancreas, containing enzymes for the digestion of carbohydrate, fat, and protein as well as bicarbonate, a neutralizing agent. The juice flows from the pancreas into the small intestine through the pancreatic duct. (The pancreas also has an endocrine function, the secretion of insulin and other hormones.)

bicarbonate: an alkaline compound with the formula HCO_3 that is secreted from the pancreas as part of the pancreatic juice. (Bicarbonate is also produced in all cell fluids from the dissociation of carbonic acid to help maintain the body's acid-base balance.)

---

the bile into the duodenum of the small intestine when fat arrives there. Bile is not an enzyme; it is an **emulsifier** that brings fats into suspension in water so that enzymes can break them down into their component parts. Thanks to all these secretions, the three energy-yielding nutrients are digested in the small intestine (the summary on p. 80 provides a table of digestive secretions and their actions).

stools: waste matter discharged from the colon; also called **feces** (FEE-seez).

The Final Stage

At this point, the three energy-yielding nutrients—carbohydrate, fat, and protein—have been disassembled and are ready to be absorbed. Most of the other nutrients—vitamins, minerals, and water—need no such disassembly; some vitamins and minerals are altered slightly during digestion, but most are absorbed as they are. Undigested residues, such as some fibers, are not absorbed. Instead, they continue through the digestive tract, providing a semisolid mass that helps exercise the muscles and keep them strong enough to perform peristalsis efficiently. Fiber also retains water, accounting for the pasty consistency of **stools,** and thereby carries some bile acids, some minerals, and some additives and contaminants with it out of the body.

By the time the contents of the GI tract reach the end of the small intestine, little remains but water, a few dissolved salts and body secretions, and undigested materials such as fiber. These enter the large intestine (colon).

In the colon, intestinal bacteria ferment some fibers, producing water, gas, and small fragments of fat that provide energy for the cells of the colon. The colon itself retrieves all materials that the body can recycle—water and dissolved salts (see Figure 3-7). The waste that is finally excreted has little or nothing of value left in it. The body has extracted all that it can use from the food. Figure 3-8 summarizes digestion by following a sandwich through the GI tract and into the body.

FIGURE 3–7 The Colon

The colon begins with the ascending colon rising upward toward the liver. It becomes the transverse colon as it turns and crosses the body toward the spleen. The descending colon turns downward and becomes the sigmoid colon, which extends to the rectum. Along the way, the colon mixes the intestinal contents, absorbs water and salts, and forms stools.

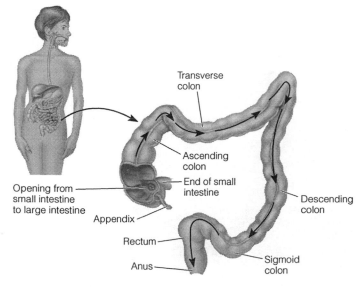

Transverse colon
Ascending colon
End of small intestine
Opening from small intestine to large intestine
Appendix
Descending colon
Rectum
Sigmoid colon
Anus

FIGURE 3–8 *Animated!* The Digestive Fate of a Sandwich

To review the digestive processes, follow a peanut butter and banana sandwich on whole-wheat, seasame seed bread through the GI tract. As the graph on the right illustrates, digestion of the energy nutrients begins in different parts of the GI tract, but all are ready for absorption by the time they reach the end of the small intestine.

ThomsonNOW"
To test your understanding of these concepts, log on to **www .thomsonedu.com/login**

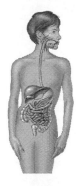

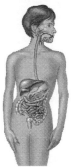

MOUTH: CHEWING AND SWALLOWING, WITH LITTLE DIGESTION

Carbohydrate digestion begins as the salivary enzyme starts to break down the starch from bread and peanut butter.
Fiber covering on the sesame seeds is crushed by the teeth, which exposes the nutrients inside the seeds to the upcoming digestive enzymes.

STOMACH: COLLECTING AND CHURNING, WITH SOME DIGESTION

Carbohydrate digestion continues until the mashed sandwich has been mixed with the gastric juices; the stomach acid of the gastric juices inactivates the salivary enzyme, and carbohydrate digestion ceases.
Proteins from the bread, seeds, and peanut butter begin to uncoil when they mix with the gastric acid, making them available to the gastric protease enzymes that begin to digest proteins.
Fat from the peanut butter forms a separate layer on top of the watery mixture.

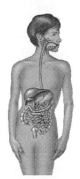

SMALL INTESTINE: DIGESTING AND ABSORBING

Sugars from the banana require so little digestion that they begin to traverse the intestinal cells immediately on contact.
Starch digestion picks up when the pancreas sends pancreatic enzymes to the small intestine via the pancreatic duct. Enzymes on the surfaces of the small intestinal cells complete the process of breaking down starch into small fragments that can be absorbed through the intestinal cell walls and into the hepatic portal vein.
Fat from the peanut butter and seeds is emulsified with the watery digestive fluids by bile. Now the pancreatic and intestinal lipases can begin to break down the fat to smaller fragments that can be absorbed through the cells of the small intestinal wall and into the lymph.
Protein digestion depends on the pancreatic and intestinal proteases. Small fragments of protein are liberated and absorbed through the cells of the small intestinal wall and into the hepatic portal vein.
Vitamins and minerals are absorbed.

Note: Sugars and starches are members of the carbohydrate family.

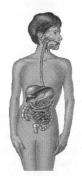

LARGE INTESTINE: REABSORBING AND ELIMINATING

Fluids and some minerals are absorbed.
Some fibers from the seeds, whole-wheat bread, peanut butter, and banana are partly digested by the bacteria living there, and some of these products are absorbed.
Most fibers pass through the large intestine and are excreted as feces; some fat, cholesterol, and minerals bind to fiber and are also excreted.

ABSORPTION

EXCRETION

IN SUMMARY

As Figure 3-1 shows, food enters the mouth and travels down the esophagus and through the upper and lower esophageal sphincters to the stomach, then through the pyloric sphincter to the small intestine, on through the ileocecal valve to the large intestine, past the appendix to the rectum, ending at the anus. The wavelike contractions of peristalsis and the periodic squeezing of segmentation keep things moving at a reasonable pace. Along the way, secretions from the salivary glands, stomach, pancreas, liver (via the gallbladder), and small intestine deliver fluids and digestive enzymes.

Summary of Digestive Secretions and Their Major Actions

Organ or Gland	Target Organ	Secretion	Action
Salivary glands	Mouth	Saliva	Fluid eases swallowing; salivary enzyme breaks down **carbohydrate.***
Gastric glands	Stomach	Gastric juice	Fluid mixes with bolus; hydrochloric acid uncoils **proteins**; enzymes break down proteins; mucus protects stomach cells.*
Pancreas	Small intestine	Pancreatic juice	Bicarbonate neutralizes acidic gastric juices; pancreatic enzymes break down **carbohydrates, fats,** and **proteins.**
Liver	Gallbladder	Bile	Bile stored until needed.
Gallbladder	Small intestine	Bile	Bile emulsifies **fat** so enzymes can attack.
Intestinal glands	Small intestine	Intestinal juice	Intestinal enzymes break down **carbohydrate, fat,** and **protein** fragments; mucus protects the intestinal wall.

* Saliva and gastric juices also contain lipases, but most fat breakdown occurs in the small intestines.

Absorption

Within three or four hours after you have eaten a dinner of beans and rice (or spinach lasagna, or steak and potatoes) with vegetable, salad, beverage, and dessert, your body must find a way to absorb the molecules derived from carbohydrate, protein, and fat digestion—and the vitamin and mineral molecules as well. Most absorption takes place in the small intestine, one of the most elegantly designed organ systems in the body. Within its 10-foot length, which provides a surface area equivalent to a tennis court, the small intestine engulfs and absorbs the nutrient molecules. To remove the molecules rapidly and provide room for more to be absorbed, a rush of circulating blood continuously washes the underside of this surface, carrying the absorbed nutrients away to the liver and other parts of the body. Figure 3-9 describes how nutrients are absorbed by simple diffusion, facilitated diffusion, or active transport. Later chapters provide details on specific nutrients. Before following nutrients through the body, we must look more closely at the anatomy of the absorptive system.

Anatomy of the Absorptive System

The inner surface of the small intestine looks smooth and slippery, but when viewed through a microscope, it turns out to be wrinkled into hundreds of folds. Each fold is contoured into thousands of fingerlike projections, as numerous as the hairs on velvet fabric. These small intestinal projections are the **villi**. A single villus, magnified still more, turns out to be composed of hundreds of cells, each covered with its own microscopic hairs, the **microvilli** (see Figure 3-10 on p. 82). In the crevices between the villi lie the **crypts**—tubular glands that secrete the intestinal juices into the small intestine. Nearby **goblet cells** secrete mucus.

Food must first be digested and absorbed before the body can use it.

Foodcollection/Getty Images

villi (VILL-ee, VILL-eye): fingerlike projections from the folds of the small intestine; singular **villus.**

microvilli (MY-cro-VILL-ee, MY-cro-VILL-eye): tiny, hairlike projections on each cell of every villus that can trap nutrient particles and transport them into the cells; singular **microvillus.**

crypts (KRIPTS): tubular glands that lie between the intestinal villi and secrete intestinal juices into the small intestine.

goblet cells: cells of the GI tract (and lungs) that secrete mucus.

FIGURE 3-9   Absorption of Nutrients

Absorption of nutrients into intestinal cells typically occurs by simple diffusion, facilitated diffusion, or active transport.

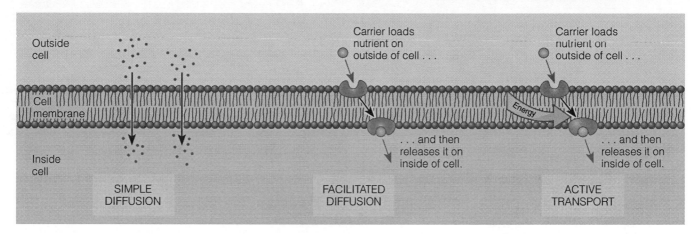

SIMPLE DIFFUSION	FACILITATED DIFFUSION	ACTIVE TRANSPORT
Some nutrients (such as water and small lipids) are absorbed by simple diffusion. They cross into intestinal cells freely.	Some nutrients (such as the water-soluble vitamins) are absorbed by facilitated diffusion. They need a specific carrier to transport them from one side of the cell membrane to the other. (Alternatively, facilitated diffusion may occur when the carrier changes the cell membrane in such a way that the nutrients can pass through.)	Some nutrients (such as glucose and amino acids) must be absorbed actively. These nutrients move against a concentration gradient, which requires energy.

The villi are in constant motion. Each villus is lined by a thin sheet of muscle, so it can wave, squirm, and wriggle like the tentacles of a sea anemone. Any nutrient molecule small enough to be absorbed is trapped among the microvilli that coat the cells and then drawn into the cells. Some partially digested nutrients are caught in the microvilli, digested further by enzymes there, and then absorbed into the cells.

A Closer Look at the Intestinal Cells

The cells of the villi are among the most amazing in the body, for they recognize and select the nutrients the body needs and regulate their absorption. ◆ As already described, each cell of a villus is coated with thousands of microvilli, which project from the cell's membrane (review Figure 3-10). In these microvilli, and in the membrane, lie hundreds of different kinds of enzymes and "pumps," which recognize and act on different nutrients. Descriptions of specific enzymes and "pumps" for each nutrient are presented in the following chapters where appropriate; the point here is that the cells are equipped to handle all kinds and combinations of foods and nutrients.

◆ The problem of food contaminants, which may be absorbed defenselessly by the body, is the subject of Chapter 19.

Specialization in the GI Tract A further refinement of the system is that the cells of successive portions of the intestinal tract are specialized to absorb different nutrients. The nutrients that are ready for absorption early are absorbed near the top of the tract; those that take longer to be digested are absorbed farther down. Registered dietitians and medical professionals who treat digestive disorders learn the specialized absorptive functions of different parts of the GI tract so that if one part becomes dysfunctional, the diet can be adjusted accordingly.

The Myth of "Food Combining" The idea that people should not eat certain food combinations (for example, fruit and meat) at the same meal, because the digestive system cannot handle more than one task at a time, is a myth. The art of "food combining" (which actually emphasizes "food separating") is based on this idea, and it represents faulty logic and a gross underestimation of the body's capabilities. In fact, the contrary is often true; foods eaten together can enhance each

FIGURE 3–10 The Small Intestinal Villi

Absorption of nutrients into intestinal cells typically occurs by simple diffusion or active transport.

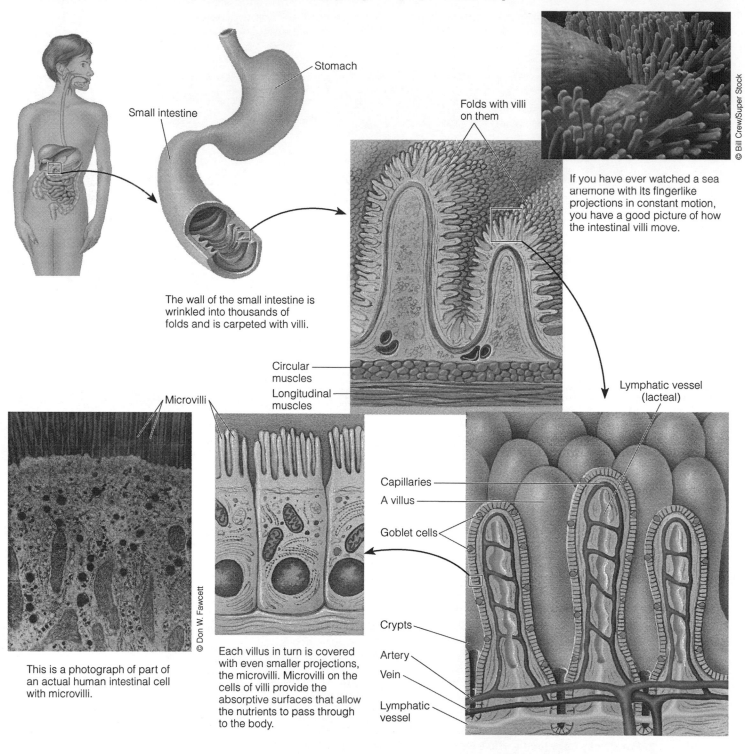

Stomach

Small intestine

Folds with villi on them

© Bill Crew/Super Stock

If you have ever watched a sea anemone with its fingerlike projections in constant motion, you have a good picture of how the intestinal villi move.

The wall of the small intestine is wrinkled into thousands of folds and is carpeted with villi.

Circular muscles

Longitudinal muscles

Lymphatic vessel (lacteal)

Microvilli

Capillaries

A villus

Goblet cells

Crypts

Artery

Vein

Lymphatic vessel

© Don W. Fawcett

This is a photograph of part of an actual human intestinal cell with microvilli.

Each villus in turn is covered with even smaller projections, the microvilli. Microvilli on the cells of villi provide the absorptive surfaces that allow the nutrients to pass through to the body.

other's use by the body. For example, vitamin C in a pineapple or other citrus fruit can enhance the absorption of iron from a meal of chicken and rice or other iron-containing foods. Many other instances of mutually beneficial interactions are presented in later chapters.

Preparing Nutrients for Transport When a nutrient molecule has crossed the cell of a villus, it enters either the bloodstream or the lymphatic system. Both transport systems supply vessels to each villus, as shown in Figure 3-10. The water-soluble nutrients and the smaller products of fat digestion are released directly into the bloodstream and guided directly to the liver where their fate and destination will be determined.

The larger fats and the fat-soluble vitamins are insoluble in water, however, and blood is mostly water. The intestinal cells assemble many of the products of fat digestion into larger molecules. These larger molecules cluster together with special proteins, forming chylomicrons. ◆ Because these chylomicrons cannot pass into the capillaries, they are released into the lymphatic system instead; the chylomicrons move through the lymph and later enter the bloodstream at a point near the heart, thus bypassing the liver at first. Details follow.

◆ Chylomicrons (kye-lo-MY-cronz) are described in Chapter 5.

IN SUMMARY

The many folds and villi of the small intestine dramatically increase its surface area, facilitating nutrient absorption. Nutrients pass through the cells of the villi and enter either the blood (if they are water soluble or small fat fragments) or the lymph (if they are fat soluble).

The Circulatory Systems

Once a nutrient has entered the bloodstream, it may be transported to any of the cells in the body, from the tips of the toes to the roots of the hair. The circulatory systems deliver nutrients wherever they are needed.

The Vascular System

The vascular, or blood circulatory, system is a closed system of vessels through which blood flows continuously, with the heart serving as the pump (see Figure 3-11, p. 84). As the blood circulates through this system, it picks up and delivers materials as needed.

All the body tissues derive oxygen and nutrients from the blood and deposit carbon dioxide and other wastes back into the blood. The lungs exchange carbon dioxide (which leaves the blood to be exhaled) and oxygen (which enters the blood to be delivered to all cells). The digestive system supplies the nutrients to be picked up. In the kidneys, wastes other than carbon dioxide are filtered out of the blood to be excreted in the urine.

Blood leaving the right side of the heart circulates through the lungs and then back to the left side of the heart. The left side of the heart then pumps the blood out of the **aorta** through **arteries** to all systems of the body. The blood circulates in the **capillaries,** where it exchanges material with the cells and then collects into **veins,** which return it again to the right side of the heart. In short, blood travels this simple route:

- Heart to arteries to capillaries to veins to heart

The routing of the blood leaving the digestive system has a special feature. The blood is carried to the digestive system (as to all organs) by way of an artery, which (as in all organs) branches into capillaries to reach every cell. Blood leaving the digestive system, however, goes by way of a vein. The **hepatic portal vein** directs blood not back to the heart, but to another organ—the liver. This vein *again* branches into *capillaries* so that every cell of the liver has access to the blood. Blood leaving the liver then *again* collects into a vein, called the **hepatic vein,** which returns blood to the heart.

The route is:

- Heart to arteries to capillaries (in intestines) to hepatic portal vein to capillaries (in liver) to hepatic vein to heart

aorta (ay-OR-tuh): the large, primary artery that conducts blood from the heart to the body's smaller arteries.

arteries: vessels that carry blood from the heart to the tissues.

capillaries (CAP-ill-aries): small vessels that branch from an artery. Capillaries connect arteries to veins. Exchange of oxygen, nutrients, and waste materials takes place across capillary walls.

veins (VANES): vessels that carry blood to the heart.

hepatic portal vein: the vein that collects blood from the GI tract and conducts it to capillaries in the liver.
- **portal** = gateway

hepatic vein: the vein that collects blood from the liver capillaries and returns it to the heart.
- **hepatic** = liver

FIGURE 3–11 *Animated!* The Vascular System

ThomsonNOW™
To test your understanding of these concepts, log on to **www .thomsonedu.com/login**

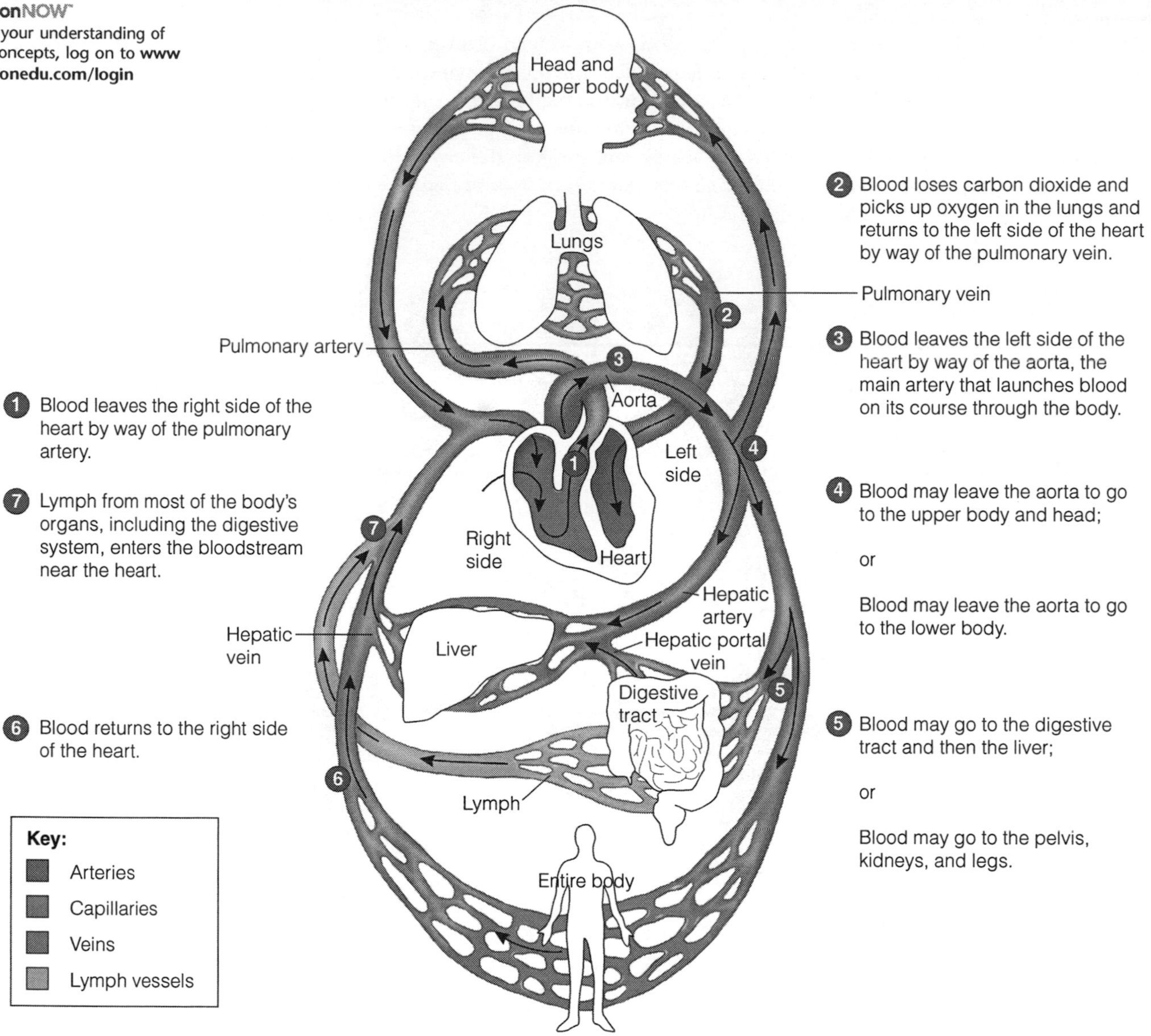

2 Blood loses carbon dioxide and picks up oxygen in the lungs and returns to the left side of the heart by way of the pulmonary vein.

Pulmonary vein

3 Blood leaves the left side of the heart by way of the aorta, the main artery that launches blood on its course through the body.

4 Blood may leave the aorta to go to the upper body and head;

or

Blood may leave the aorta to go to the lower body.

5 Blood may go to the digestive tract and then the liver;

or

Blood may go to the pelvis, kidneys, and legs.

1 Blood leaves the right side of the heart by way of the pulmonary artery.

7 Lymph from most of the body's organs, including the digestive system, enters the bloodstream near the heart.

6 Blood returns to the right side of the heart.

Key:
- ■ Arteries
- ■ Capillaries
- ■ Veins
- ■ Lymph vessels

Labels in diagram: Head and upper body, Lungs, Pulmonary artery, Aorta, Left side, Right side, Heart, Hepatic artery, Hepatic portal vein, Digestive tract, Hepatic vein, Liver, Lymph, Entire body

Figure 3-12 shows the liver's key position in nutrient transport. An anatomist studying this system knows there must be a reason for this special arrangement. The liver's placement ensures that it will be first to receive the nutrients absorbed from the GI tract. In fact, the liver has many jobs to do in preparing the absorbed nutrients for use by the body. It is the body's major metabolic organ.

You might guess that, in addition, the liver serves as a gatekeeper to defend against substances that might harm the heart or brain. This is why, when people ingest poisons that succeed in passing the first barrier (the intestinal cells), the liver quite often suffers the damage—from viruses such as hepatitis, from drugs such as barbiturates or alcohol, from toxins such as pesticide residues, and from contaminants such as mercury. Perhaps, in fact, you have been undervaluing your liver, not knowing what heroic tasks it quietly performs for you.

The Lymphatic System

The **lymphatic system** provides a one-way route for fluid from the tissue spaces to enter the blood. Unlike the vascular system, the lymphatic system has

lymphatic (lim-FAT-ic) **system:** a loosely organized system of vessels and ducts that convey fluids toward the heart. The GI part of the lymphatic system carries the products of fat digestion into the bloodstream.

FIGURE 3–12 The Liver

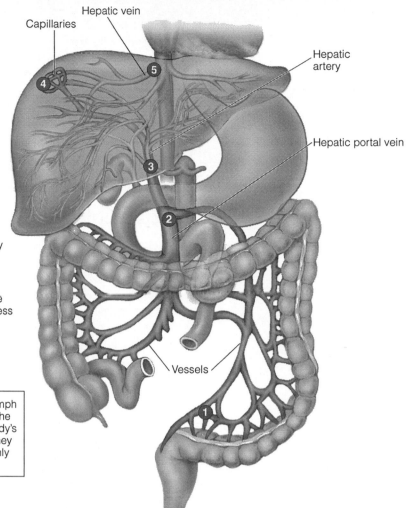

1 Vessels gather up nutrients and reabsorbed water and salts from all over the digestive tract.

Not shown here:
Parallel to these vessels (veins) are other vessels (arteries) that carry oxygen-rich blood from the heart to the intestines.

2 The vessels merge into the hepatic portal vein, which conducts all absorbed materials to the liver.

3 The hepatic artery brings a supply of freshly oxygenated blood (not loaded with nutrients) from the lungs to supply oxygen to the liver's own cells.

4 Capillaries branch all over the liver, making nutrients and oxygen available to all its cells and giving the cells access to blood from the digestive system.

5 The hepatic vein gathers up blood in the liver and returns it to the heart.

In contrast, nutrients absorbed into lymph do not go to the liver first. They go to the heart, which pumps them to all the body's cells. The cells remove the nutrients they need, and the liver then has to deal only with the remnants.

Hepatic vein

Capillaries

Hepatic artery

Hepatic portal vein

Vessels

---

no pump; instead, **lymph** circulates *between* the cells of the body and collects into tiny vessels. The fluid moves from one portion of the body to another as muscles contract and create pressure here and there. Ultimately, much of the lymph collects in the **thoracic duct** behind the heart. The thoracic duct opens into the **subclavian vein,** where the lymph enters the bloodstream. Thus nutrients from the GI tract that enter lymphatic vessels ◆ (large fats and fat-soluble vitamins) ultimately enter the bloodstream, circulating through arteries, capillaries, and veins like the other nutrients, with a notable exception—they bypass the liver at first.

Once inside the vascular system, the nutrients can travel freely to any destination and can be taken into cells and used as needed. What becomes of them is described in later chapters.

◆ The lymphatic vessels of the intestine that take up nutrients and pass them to the lymph circulation are called **lacteals** (LACK-tee-als).

lymph (LIMF): a clear yellowish fluid that is similar to blood except that it contains no red blood cells or platelets. Lymph from the GI tract transports fat and fat-soluble vitamins to the bloodstream via lymphatic vessels.

thoracic (thor-ASS-ic) **duct:** the main lymphatic vessel that collects lymph and drains into the left subclavian vein.

subclavian (sub-KLAY-vee-an) **vein:** the vein that provides passageway from the lymphatic system to the vascular system.

IN SUMMARY

Nutrients leaving the digestive system via the blood are routed directly to the liver before being transported to the body's cells. Those leaving via the lymphatic system eventually enter the vascular system but bypass the liver at first.

The Health and Regulation of the GI Tract

◆ Factors influencing GI function:
- Physical immaturity
- Aging
- Illness
- Nutrition

This section describes the bacterial conditions and hormonal regulation of a healthy GI tract, but many factors ◆ can influence normal GI function. For example, peristalsis and sphincter action are poorly coordinated in newborns, so infants tend to "spit up" during the first several months of life. Older adults often experience constipation, in part because the intestinal wall loses strength and elasticity with age, which slows GI motility. Diseases can also interfere with digestion and absorption and often lead to malnutrition. Lack of nourishment, in general, and lack of certain dietary constituents such as fiber, in particular, alter the structure and function of GI cells. Quite simply, GI tract health depends on adequate nutrition.

Gastrointestinal Bacteria

◆ Bacteria in the intestines are sometimes referred to as **flora** or **microflora.**

An estimated 10 trillion bacteria ◆ representing some 400 or more different species and subspecies live in a healthy GI tract. The prevalence of different bacteria in various parts of the GI tract depends on such factors as pH, peristalsis, diet, and other microorganisms. Relatively few microorganisms can live in the low pH of the stomach with its relatively rapid peristalsis, whereas the neutral pH and slow peristalsis of the lower small intestine and the large intestine permit the growth of a diverse and abundant bacterial population.[1]

Most of these bacteria normally do the body no harm and may actually do some good. Provided that the normal intestinal flora are thriving, infectious bacteria have a hard time establishing themselves to launch an attack on the system.

◆ Food components (such as fibers) that are not digested in the small intestine, but are used instead as food by bacteria to encourage their growth are called **prebiotics.**

Diet is one of several factors that influence the body's bacterial population and environment. Consider **yogurt,** for example.[2] Yogurt contains *Lactobacillus* and other living bacteria. These microorganisms are considered **probiotics** because they change the conditions and native bacterial colonies in the GI tract in ways that seem to benefit health.[3] The potential GI health benefits of probiotics include helping to alleviate diarrhea, constipation, inflammatory bowel disease, ulcers, allergies, and lactose intolerance; enhance immune function; and protect against colon cancer.[4] Some probiotics may have adverse effects under certain circumstances.[5] Research studies continue to explore how diet influences GI bacteria and which foods—with their probiotics—affect GI health.

◆ Vitamins produced by bacteria include:
- Biotin
- Folate
- Vitamin B_6
- Vitamin B_{12}
- Vitamin K

GI bacteria also digest fibers and complex proteins.[6] ◆ In doing so, the bacteria produce nutrients such as short fragments of fat that the cells of the colon use for energy. Bacteria in the GI tract also produce several vitamins, ◆ including a significant amount of vitamin K, although the amount is insufficient to meet the body's total need for that vitamin.

Gastrointestinal Hormones and Nerve Pathways

yogurt: milk product that results from the fermentation of lactic acid in milk by *Lactobacillus bulgaricus* and *Streptococcus thermophilus.*

probiotics: living microorganisms found in foods that, when consumed in sufficient quantities, are beneficial to health.
- **pro** = for
- **bios** = life

homeostasis (HOME-ee-oh-STAY-sis): the maintenance of constant internal conditions (such as blood chemistry, temperature, and blood pressure) by the body's control systems. A homeostatic system is constantly reacting to external forces to maintain limits set by the body's needs.
- **homeo** = the same
- **stasis** = staying

The ability of the digestive tract to handle its ever-changing contents routinely illustrates an important physiological principle that governs the way all living things function—the principle of **homeostasis.** Simply stated, survival depends on body conditions staying about the same; if they deviate too far from the norm, the body must "do something" to bring them back to normal. The body's regulation of digestion is one example of homeostatic regulation. The body also regulates its temperature, its blood pressure, and all other aspects of its blood chemistry in similar ways.

Two intricate and sensitive systems coordinate all the digestive and absorptive processes: the hormonal (or endocrine) system and the nervous system. Even before the first bite of food is taken, the mere thought, sight, or smell of food can trigger a response from these systems. Then, as food travels through the GI tract, it either stimulates or inhibits digestive secretions by way of messages that are carried from one section of the GI tract to another by both **hormones** ◆ and nerve pathways. (Appendix A presents a brief summary of the body's hormonal system and nervous system.)

Notice that the kinds of regulation described next are all examples of *feedback* mechanisms. A certain condition demands a response. The response changes that condition, and the change then cuts off the response. Thus the system is self-correcting. Examples follow:

- *The stomach normally maintains a pH between 1.5 and 1.7. How does it stay that way?* Food entering the stomach stimulates cells in the stomach wall to release the hormone **gastrin.** Gastrin, in turn, stimulates the stomach glands to secrete the components of hydrochloric acid. When pH 1.5 is reached, the acid itself turns off the gastrin-producing cells. They stop releasing gastrin, and the glands stop producing hydrochloric acid. Thus the system adjusts itself.

  Nerve receptors in the stomach wall also respond to the presence of food and stimulate the gastric glands to secrete juices and the muscles to contract. As the stomach empties, the receptors are no longer stimulated, the flow of juices slows, and the stomach quiets down.

- *The pyloric sphincter opens to let out a little chyme, then closes again. How does it know when to open and close?* When the pyloric sphincter relaxes, acidic chyme slips through. The cells of the pyloric muscle on the intestinal side sense the acid, causing the pyloric sphincter to close tightly. Only after the chyme has been neutralized by pancreatic bicarbonate and the juices surrounding the pyloric sphincter have become alkaline can the muscle relax again. This process ensures that the chyme will be released slowly enough to be neutralized as it flows through the small intestine. This is important because the small intestine has less of a mucous coating than the stomach does and so is not as well protected from acid.

- *As the chyme enters the intestine, the pancreas adds bicarbonate to it so that the intestinal contents always remain at a slightly alkaline pH. How does the pancreas know how much to add?* The presence of chyme stimulates the cells of the duodenum wall to release the hormone **secretin** into the blood. When secretin reaches the pancreas, it stimulates the pancreas to release its bicarbonate-rich juices. Thus, whenever the duodenum signals that acidic chyme is present, the pancreas responds by sending bicarbonate to neutralize it. When the need has been met, the cells of the duodenum wall are no longer stimulated to release secretin, the hormone no longer flows through the blood, the pancreas no longer receives the message, and it stops sending pancreatic juice. Nerves also regulate pancreatic secretions.

- *Pancreatic secretions contain a mixture of enzymes to digest carbohydrate, fat, and protein. How does the pancreas know how much of each type of enzyme to provide?* This is one of the most interesting questions physiologists have asked. Clearly, the pancreas does know what its owner has been eating, and it secretes enzyme mixtures tailored to handle the food mixtures that have been arriving recently (over the last several days). Enzyme activity changes proportionately in response to the amounts of carbohydrate, fat, and protein in the diet. If a person has been eating mostly carbohydrates, the pancreas makes and secretes mostly carbohydrases; if the person's diet has been high in fat, the pancreas produces more lipases; and so forth. Presumably, hormones from the GI tract, secreted in response to meals, keep the pancreas informed as to its digestive tasks. The day or two lag between the time a person's diet changes dramatically and the time digestion of the new diet becomes efficient explains why dietary changes can "upset digestion" and should be made gradually.

◆ In general, any gastrointestinal hormone may be called an **enterogastrone** (EN-ter-oh-GAS-trone), but the term refers specifically to any hormone that slows motility and inhibits gastric secretions.

hormones: chemical messengers. Hormones are secreted by a variety of glands in response to altered conditions in the body. Each hormone travels to one or more specific target tissues or organs, where it elicits a specific response to maintain homeostasis.

gastrin: a hormone secreted by cells in the stomach wall. Target organ: the glands of the stomach. Response: secretion of gastric acid.

secretin (see-CREET-in): a hormone produced by cells in the duodenum wall. Target organ: the pancreas. Response: secretion of bicarbonate-rich pancreatic juice.

◆ The inactive precursor of an enzyme is called a **proenzyme** or **zymogen** (ZYE-mo-jen).
- **pro** = before
- **zym** = concerning enzymes
- **gen** = to produce

• *Why don't the digestive enzymes damage the pancreas?* The pancreas protects itself from harm by producing an inactive form of the enzymes. ◆ It releases these proteins into the small intestine where they are activated to become enzymes. In pancreatitis, the digestive enzymes become active within the infected pancreas, causing inflammation and damaging the delicate pancreatic tissues.

• *When fat is present in the intestine, the gallbladder contracts to squirt bile into the intestine to emulsify the fat. How does the gallbladder get the message that fat is present?* Fat in the intestine stimulates cells of the intestinal wall to release the hormone **cholecystokinin (CCK).** This hormone, traveling by way of the blood to the gallbladder, stimulates it to contract, releasing bile into the small intestine. Cholescystokinin also travels to the pancreas, stimulates it to secrete its juices, releasing bicarbonate and enzymes into the small intestine. Once the fat in the intestine is emulsified and enzymes have begun to work on it, the fat no longer provokes release of the hormone, and the message to contract is canceled. (By the way, fat emulsification can continue even after a diseased gallbladder has been surgically removed because the liver can deliver bile directly to the small intestine.)

• *Fat and protein take longer to digest than carbohydrate does. When fat or protein is present, intestinal motility slows to allow time for its digestion. How does the intestine know when to slow down?* Cholecystokinin is released in response to fat or protein in the small intestine. In addition to its role in fat emulsification and digestion, cholecystokinin slows GI tract motility. Slowing the digestive process helps to maintain a pace that allows all reactions to reach completion. Hormonal and nervous mechanisms like these account for much of the body's ability to adapt to changing conditions.

Table 3-1 summarizes the actions of these GI hormones.

Once a person has started to learn the answers to questions like these, it may be hard to stop. Some people devote their whole lives to the study of physiology. For now, however, these few examples illustrate how all the processes throughout the digestive system are precisely and automatically regulated without any conscious effort.

IN SUMMARY

A diverse and abundant bacteria population support GI health. The regulation of GI processes depends on the coordinated efforts of the hormonal system and the nervous system; together, digestion and absorption transform foods into nutrients.

cholecystokinin (COAL-ee-SIS-toe-KINE-in), or **CCK:** a hormone produced by cells of the intestinal wall. Target organ: the gallbladder. Response: release of bile and slowing of GI motility.

The System at Its Best

This chapter describes the anatomy of the digestive tract on several levels: the sequence of digestive organs, the cells and structures of the villi, and the selective ma-

TABLE 3-1	The Primary Actions of GI Hormones			
Hormone:	Responds to:	Secreted from:	Stimulates:	Response:
Gastrin	Food in the stomach	Stomach wall	Stomach glands	Hydrochloric acid secreted into the stomach
Secretin	Acidic chyme in the small intestine	Duodenal wall	Pancreas	Bicarbonate-rich juices secreted into the small intestine
Cholecystokinin	Fat or protein in the small intestine	Intestinal wall	Gallbladder	Bile secreted into the duodenum
			Pancreas	Bicarbonate- and enzyme-rich juices secreted into the small intestine

chinery of the cell membranes. The intricate architecture of the digestive system makes it sensitive and responsive to conditions in its environment. Several different kinds of GI tract cells confer specific immunity against intestinal diseases such as inflammatory bowel disease. In addition, secretions from the GI tract—saliva, mucus, gastric acid, and digestive enzymes—not only help with digestion, but also defend against foreign invaders. Together the GI's team of bacteria, cells, and secretions defend the body against numerous challenges.[7] Knowing the optimal conditions will help you to make choices that promote the best functioning of the system.

One indispensable condition is good health of the digestive tract itself. This health is affected by such lifestyle factors as sleep, physical activity, and state of mind. Adequate sleep allows for repair and maintenance of tissue and removal of wastes that might impair efficient functioning. Activity promotes healthy muscle tone. Mental state influences the activity of regulatory nerves and hormones; for healthy digestion, you should be relaxed and tranquil at mealtimes.

Nourishing foods and pleasant conversations support a healthy digestive system.

Another factor in GI health is the kind of meals you eat. Among the characteristics of meals that promote optimal absorption of nutrients are those mentioned in Chapter 2: balance, moderation, variety, and adequacy. Balance and moderation require having neither too much nor too little of anything. For example, too much fat can be harmful, but some fat is beneficial in slowing down intestinal motility and providing time for absorption of some of the nutrients that are slow to be absorbed.

Variety is important for many reasons, but one is that some food constituents interfere with nutrient absorption. For example, some compounds common in high-fiber foods such as whole-grain cereals, certain leafy green vegetables, and legumes bind with minerals. To some extent, then, the minerals in those foods may become unavailable for absorption. These high-fiber foods are still valuable, but they need to be balanced with a variety of other foods that can provide the minerals.

As for adequacy—in a sense, this entire book is about dietary adequacy. But here, at the end of this chapter, is a good place to underline the interdependence of the nutrients. It could almost be said that every nutrient depends on every other. All the nutrients work together, and all are present in the cells of a healthy digestive tract. To maintain health and promote the functions of the GI tract, you should make balance, moderation, variety, and adequacy features of every day's menus.

Nutrition Portfolio

ThomsonNOW™
www.thomsonedu.com/login

A healthy digestive system can adjust to almost any diet and can handle any combination of foods with ease.

■ Describe the physical and emotional environment that typically surrounds your meals, including how it affects you and how it might be improved.

■ Detail any GI discomforts you may experience regularly and include suggestions to alleviate or prevent their occurrence (see Highlight 3).

■ List any changes you can make in your eating habits to promote overall GI health.

NUTRITION ON THE NET

ThomsonNOW™
For further study of topics covered in this chapter, log on to **www.thomsonedu** **.com/thomsonnow**. Go to Chapter 3, then to Nutrition on the Net.

- Visit the Center for Digestive Health and Nutrition: **www.gihealth.com**

- Visit the patient information section of the American College of Gastroenterology: **www.acg.gi.org**

STUDY QUESTIONS

ThomsonNOW™
To assess your understanding of chapter topics, take the Student Practice Test and explore the modules recommended in your Personalized Study Plan. Log onto **www.thomsonedu.com/thomsonnow**.

These questions will help you review this chapter. You will find the answers in the discussions on the pages provided.

1. Describe the challenges associated with digesting food and the solutions offered by the human body. (pp. 71–80)

2. Describe the path food follows as it travels through the digestive system. Summarize the muscular actions that take place along the way. (pp. 72–76)

3. Name five organs that secrete digestive juices. How do the juices and enzymes facilitate digestion? (pp. 76–78)

4. Describe the problems associated with absorbing nutrients and the solutions offered by the small intestine. (pp. 80–83)

5. How is blood routed through the digestive system? Which nutrients enter the bloodstream directly? Which are first absorbed into the lymph? (pp. 83–85)

6. Describe how the body coordinates and regulates the processes of digestion and absorption. (pp. 86–88)

7. How does the composition of the diet influence the functioning of the GI tract? (p. 89)

8. What steps can you take to help your GI tract function at its best? (p. 89)

These multiple choice questions will help you prepare for an exam. Answers can be found on p. 91.

1. The semiliquid, partially digested food that travels through the intestinal tract is called:
   a. bile.
   b. lymph.
   c. chyme.
   d. secretin.

2. The muscular contractions that move food through the GI tract are called:
   a. hydrolysis.
   b. sphincters.
   c. peristalsis.
   d. bowel movements.

3. The main function of bile is to:
   a. emulsify fats.

   b. catalyze hydrolysis.
   c. slow protein digestion.
   d. neutralize stomach acidity.

4. The pancreas neutralizes stomach acid in the small intestine by secreting:
   a. bile.
   b. mucus.
   c. enzymes.
   d. bicarbonate.

5. Which nutrient passes through the GI tract mostly undigested and unabsorbed?
   a. fat
   b. fiber
   c. protein
   d. carbohydrate

6. Absorption occurs primarily in the:
   a. mouth.
   b. stomach.
   c. small intestine.
   d. large intestine.

7. All blood leaving the GI tract travels first to the:
   a. heart.
   b. liver.
   c. kidneys.
   d. pancreas.

8. Which nutrients leave the GI tract by way of the lymphatic system?
   a. water and minerals
   b. proteins and minerals
   c. all vitamins and minerals
   d. fats and fat-soluble vitamins

9. Digestion and absorption are coordinated by the:
   a. pancreas and kidneys.
   b. liver and gallbladder.
   c. hormonal system and the nervous system.
   d. vascular system and the lymphatic system.

10. Gastrin, secretin, and cholecystokinin are examples of:
    a. crypts.
    b. enzymes.
    c. hormones.
    d. goblet cells.

REFERENCES

1. P. B. Eckburg and coauthors, Diversity of the human intestinal microbial flora, *Science* 308 (2005): 1635-1638; W. L. Hao and Y. K. Lee, Microflora of the gastrointestinal tract: A review, *Methods in Molecular Biology* 268 (2004): 491-502.

2. O. Adolfsson, S. N. Meydani, and R. M. Russell, Yogurt and gut function, *American Journal of Clinical Nutrition* 80 (2004): 245-256.

3. C. C. Chen and W. A. Walker, Probiotics and prebiotics: Role in clinical disease states, *Advances in Pediatrics* 52 (2005): 77-113; M. E. Sanders, Probiotics: Considerations for human health, *Nutrition Reviews* 61 (2003): 91-99; M. H. Floch and J. Hong-Curtiss, Probiotics and functional foods in gastrointestinal disorders, *Current Gastroenterology Reports* 3 (2001): 343-350; Probiotics and prebiotics, *American Journal of Clinical Nutrition (supp.)* 73 (2001): entire issue.

4. S. Santosa, E. Farnworth, P. J. H. Jones, Probiotics and their potential health claims, *Nutrition Reviews* 64 (2006): 265-274; S. J. Salminen, M. Gucimonde, and E. Isolauri, Probiotics that modify disease risk, *American Society for Nutritional Sciences* 135 (2005): 1294-1298; F. Guarner and coauthors, Should yoghurt cultures be considered probiotic? *British Journal of Nutrition* 93 (2005): 783-786; J. M. Saavedra and A. Tschernia, Human studies with probiotics and prebiotics: Clinical implications, *British Journal of Nutrition* 87 (2002): S241-S246; P. Marteau and M. C. Boutron-Ruault, Nutritional advantages of probiotics and prebiotics, *British Journal of Nutrition* 87 (2002): S153-S157; G. T. Macfarlane and J. H. Cummings, Probiotics, infection and immunity, *Current Opinion in Infectious Diseases* 15 (2002): 501-506; L. Kopp-Hoolihan, Prophylactic and therapeutic uses of probiotics: A review, *Journal of the American Dietetic Association* 101 (2001): 229-238; M. B. Roberfroid, Prebiotics and probiotics: Are they functional foods? *American Journal of Clinical Nutrition* 71 (2000): 1682S-1687S.

5. J. Ezendam and H. van Loveren, Probiotics: Immunomodulation and evaluation of safety and efficacy, *Nutrition Reviews* 64 (2006): 1-14.

6. J. M. Wong and coauthors, Colonic health: Fermentation and short chain fatty acids, *Journal of Clinical Gastroenterology* 40 (2006): 235-243; S. Bengmark, Colonic food: Pre- and probiotics, *American Journal of Gastroenterology* 95 (2000): S5-S7.

7. P. Bourlioux and coauthors, The intestine and its microflora are partners for the protection of the host: Report on the Danone Symposium "The Intelligent Intestine," held in Paris, June 14, 2002, *American Journal of Clinical Nutrition* 78 (2003): 675-683.

ANSWERS

Study Questions (multiple choice)

1. c   2. c   3. a   4. d   5. b   6. c   7. b   8. d
9. c   10. c

Common Digestive Problems

© Corbis

The facts of anatomy and physiology presented in Chapter 3 permit easy understanding of some common problems that occasionally arise in the digestive tract. Food may slip into the air passages instead of the esophagus, causing choking. Bowel movements may be loose and watery, as in diarrhea, or painful and hard, as in constipation. Some people complain about belching, while others are bothered by intestinal gas. Sometimes people develop medical problems such as an ulcer. This highlight describes some of the symptoms of these common digestive problems and suggests strategies for preventing them (the glossary on p. 94 defines the relevant terms).

Choking

A person chokes when a piece of food slips into the **trachea** and becomes lodged so securely that it cuts off breathing (see Figure H3-1). Without oxygen, the person may suffer brain damage or die. For this reason, it is imperative that everyone learns to recognize a person grabbing his or her own throat as the international signal for choking (shown in Figure H3-2) and act promptly.

The choking scenario might read like this. A person is dining in a restaurant with friends. A chunk of food, usually meat, becomes lodged in his trachea so firmly that he cannot make a sound. No sound can be made because the **larynx** is in the trachea and makes sounds only when air is pushed across it. Often he chooses to suffer alone rather than "make a scene in public." If he tries to communicate distress to his friends, he must depend on pantomime. The friends are bewildered by his antics and become terribly worried when he "faints" after a few minutes without air. They call for an ambulance, but by the time it arrives, he is dead from suffocation.

To help a person who is choking, first ask this critical question: "Can you make any sound at all?" If so, relax. You have time to decide what you can do to help. Whatever you do, *do not* hit him on the back—the particle may become lodged more firmly in his air passage. If the person cannot make a sound, shout for help and perform the **Heimlich maneuver** (described in Figure H3-2). You would do well to take a life-saving course and practice these techniques because you will have no time for hesitation if you are called upon to perform this death-defying act.

Almost any food can cause choking, although some are cited more often than others: chunks of meat, hot dogs, nuts, whole grapes, raw carrots, marshmallows, hard or sticky candies, gum, popcorn, and peanut butter. These foods are particularly difficult for young children to safely chew and swallow. In 2000, more than 17,500 children (under 15 years old) in the United States choked; most of them choked on food, and 160 of them choked to death.[1] Always remain alert to the dangers of choking whenever young children are eating. To prevent choking, cut food into small pieces, chew thoroughly before swallowing, don't talk or laugh with food in your mouth, and don't eat when breathing hard.

Vomiting

Another common digestive mishap is **vomiting.** Vomiting can be a symptom of many different diseases or may arise in situations that upset the body's equilibrium, such as air or sea travel. For whatever reason, the contents of the stomach are propelled up through the esophagus to the mouth and expelled.

FIGURE H3-1	Normal Swallowing and Choking

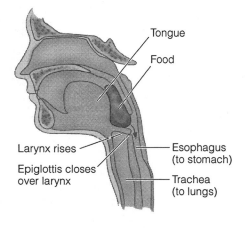

Tongue

Food

Larynx rises

Epiglottis closes over larynx

Esophagus (to stomach)

Trachea (to lungs)

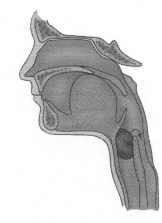

Swallowing. The epiglottis closes over the larynx, blocking entrance to the lungs via the trachea. The red arrow shows that food is heading down the esophagus normally.

Choking. A choking person cannot speak or gasp because food lodged in the trachea blocks the passage of air. The red arrow points to where the food should have gone to prevent choking.

FIGURE H3-2　First Aid for Choking

The first-aid strategy most likely to succeed is abdominal thrusts, sometimes called the Heimlich maneuver. Only if all else fails, open the person's mouth by grasping both his tongue and lower jaw and lifting. Then, and *only if* you can see the object, use your finger to sweep it out and begin rescue breathing.

The universal signal for choking is when a person grabs his throat. It alerts others to the need for assistance. If this happens, stand behind the person, and wrap your arms around him. Place the thumb side of one fist snugly against his body, slightly above the navel and below the rib cage. Grasp your fist with your other hand and give him a sudden strong hug inward and upward. Repeat thrusts as necessary.

If you are choking and need to self-administer first aid, place the thumb side of one fist slightly above your navel and below your rib cage, grasp the fist with your other hand, and then press inward and upward with a quick motion. If this is unsuccessful, quickly press your upper abdomen over any firm surface such as the back of a chair, a countertop, or a railing.

Self-induced vomiting, such as occurs in bulimia nervosa, also has serious consequences. In addition to fluid and salt imbalances, repeated vomiting can cause irritation and infection of the pharynx, esophagus, and salivary glands; erosion of the teeth and gums; and dental caries. The esophagus may rupture or tear, as may the stomach. Sometimes the eyes become red from pressure during vomiting. Bulimic behavior reflects underlying psychological problems that require intervention. (Bulimia nervosa is discussed fully in Highlight 8.)

Projectile vomiting is also serious. The contents of the stomach are expelled with such force that they leave the mouth in a wide arc like a bullet leaving a gun. This type of vomiting requires immediate medical attention.

Diarrhea

Diarrhea is characterized by frequent, loose, watery stools. Such stools indicate that the intestinal contents have moved too quickly through the intestines for fluid absorption to take place, or that water has been drawn from the cells lining the intestinal tract and added to the food residue. Like vomiting, diarrhea can lead to considerable fluid and salt losses, but the composition of the fluids is different. Stomach fluids lost in vomiting are highly acidic, whereas intestinal fluids lost in diarrhea are nearly neutral. When fluid losses require medical attention, correct replacement is crucial.

Diarrhea is a symptom of various medical conditions and treatments. It may occur abruptly in a healthy person as a result of infections (such as food poisoning) or as a side effect of medications. When used in large quantities, food ingredients such as the sugar alternative sorbitol and the fat alternative olestra may also cause diarrhea in some people. If a food is responsible, then that food must be omitted from the diet, at least temporarily. If medication is responsible, a different medicine, when possible, or a different form (injectable versus oral, for example) may alleviate the problem.

Diarrhea may also occur as a result of disorders of the GI tract, such as irritable bowel syndrome or colitis. **Irritable bowel syndrome** is one of the most common GI disorders and is characterized by a disturbance in the motility of the GI tract.[2] In most cases, GI contractions are stronger and last longer than normal, forcing intestinal contents through quickly and causing gas, bloating, and diarrhea. In some cases, however, GI contractions are weaker than normal, slowing the passage of intestinal contents and causing constipation. The exact cause of irritable bowel syndrome is not known, but researchers believe nerves and hormones are involved. The condition seems to worsen for some

If vomiting continues long enough or is severe enough, the muscular contractions will extend beyond the stomach and carry the contents of the duodenum, with its green bile, into the stomach and then up the esophagus. Although certainly unpleasant and wearying for the nauseated person, vomiting such as this is no cause for alarm. Vomiting is one of the body's adaptive mechanisms to rid itself of something irritating. The best advice is to rest and drink small amounts of liquids as tolerated until the nausea subsides.

A physician's care may be needed, however, when large quantities of fluid are lost from the GI tract, causing dehydration. With massive fluid loss from the GI tract, all of the body's other fluids redistribute themselves so that, eventually, fluid is taken from every cell of the body. Leaving the cells with the fluid are salts that are absolutely essential to the life of the cells, and they must be replaced. Replacement is difficult if the vomiting continues, and intravenous feedings of saline and glucose may be necessary while the physician diagnoses the cause of the vomiting and begins corrective therapy.

In an infant, vomiting is likely to become serious early in its course, and a physician should be contacted soon after onset. Infants have more fluid between their body cells than adults do, so more fluid can move readily into the digestive tract and be lost from the body. Consequently, the body water of infants becomes depleted and their body salt balance upset faster than in adults.

GLOSSARY

acid controllers: medications used to prevent or relieve indigestion by suppressing production of acid in the stomach; also called **H2 blockers.** Common brands include Pepcid AC, Tagamet HB, Zantac 75, and Axid AR.

antacids: medications used to relieve indigestion by neutralizing acid in the stomach. Common brands include Alka-Seltzer, Maalox, Rolaids, and Tums.

belching: the expulsion of gas from the stomach through the mouth.

colitis (ko-LYE-tis): inflammation of the colon.

colonic irrigation: the popular, but potentially harmful practice of "washing" the large intestine with a powerful enema machine.

constipation: the condition of having infrequent or difficult bowel movements.

defecate (DEF-uh-cate): to move the bowels and eliminate waste.
- **defaecare** = to remove dregs

diarrhea: the frequent passage of watery bowel movements.

diverticula (dye-ver-TIC-you-la): sacs or pouches that develop in the weakened areas of the intestinal wall (like bulges in an inner tube where the tire wall is weak).
- **divertir** = to turn aside

diverticulitis (DYE-ver-tic-you-LYE-tis): infected or inflamed diverticula.
- **itis** = infection or inflammation

diverticulosis (DYE-ver-tic-you-LOH-sis): the condition of having diverticula. About one in every six people in Western countries develops diverticulosis in middle or later life.
- **osis** = condition

enemas: solutions inserted into the rectum and colon to stimulate a bowel movement and empty the lower large intestine.

gastroesophageal reflux: the backflow of stomach acid into the esophagus, causing damage to the cells of the esophagus and the sensation of heartburn. **Gastroesophageal reflux disease (GERD)** is characterized by symptoms of reflux occurring two or more times a week.

heartburn: a burning sensation in the chest area caused by backflow of stomach acid into the esophagus.

Heimlich (HIME-lick) **maneuver (abdominal thrust maneuver):** a technique for dislodging an object from the trachea of a choking person (see Figure H3-2); named for the physician who developed it.

hemorrhoids (HEM-oh-royds): painful swelling of the veins surrounding the rectum.

hiccups (HICK-ups): repeated cough-like sounds and jerks that are produced when an involuntary spasm of the diaphragm muscle sucks air down the windpipe; also spelled *hiccoughs.*

indigestion: incomplete or uncomfortable digestion, usually accompanied by pain, nausea, vomiting, heartburn, intestinal gas, or belching.
- **in** = not

irritable bowel syndrome: an intestinal disorder of unknown cause. Symptoms include abdominal discomfort and cramping, diarrhea, constipation, or alternating diarrhea and constipation.

larynx: the upper part of the air passageway that contains the vocal cords; also called the voice box (see Figure H3-1).

laxatives: substances that loosen the bowels and thereby prevent or treat constipation.

mineral oil: a purified liquid derived from petroleum and used to treat constipation.

peptic ulcer: a lesion in the mucous membrane of either the stomach (a gastric ulcer) or the duodenum (a duodenal ulcer).
- **peptic** = concerning digestion

trachea (TRAKE-ee-uh): the air passageway from the larynx to the lungs; also called the *windpipe.*

ulcer: a lesion of the skin or mucous membranes characterized by inflammation and damaged tissues. See also *peptic ulcer.*

vomiting: expulsion of the contents of the stomach up through the esophagus to the mouth.

---

people when they eat certain foods or during stressful events. These triggers seem to aggravate symptoms but not cause them. Dietary treatment hinges on identifying and avoiding individual foods that aggravate symptoms; small meals may also be beneficial. People with **colitis,** an inflammation of the large intestine, may also suffer from severe diarrhea. They often benefit from complete bowel rest and medication. If treatment fails, surgery to remove the colon and rectum may be necessary.

Treatment for diarrhea depends on cause and severity, but it always begins with rehydration.[3] Mild diarrhea may subside with simple rest and extra liquids (such as clear juices and soups) to replace fluid losses. However, call a physician if diarrhea is bloody or if it worsens or persists—especially in an infant, young child, elderly person, or person with a compromised immune system. Severe diarrhea can be life threatening.

Constipation

Like diarrhea, **constipation** describes a symptom, not a disease. Each person's GI tract has its own cycle of waste elimination, which depends on its owner's health, the type of food eaten, when it was eaten, and when the person takes time to **defecate.** What's normal for some people may not be normal for others. Some people have bowel movements three times a day; others may have them three times a week. The symptoms of constipation include straining during bowel movements, hard stools, and infrequent bowel movements (fewer than three per week).[4] Ab-

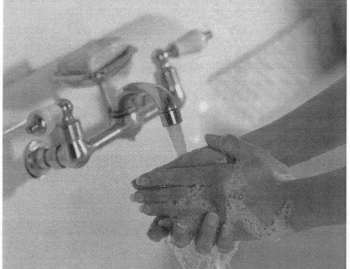

Personal hygiene (such as regular hand washing with soap and water) and safe food preparation (as described in Chapter 19) are easy and effective steps to take in preventing diarrheal diseases.

© Ariel Skelley/Corbis

dominal discomfort, headaches, backaches, and the passing of gas sometimes accompany constipation.

Often a person's lifestyle may cause constipation. Being too busy to respond to the defecation signal is a common complaint. If a person receives the signal to defecate and ignores it, the signal may not return for several hours. In the meantime, water continues to be withdrawn from the fecal matter, so when the person does defecate, the stools are dry and hard. In such a case, a person's daily regimen may need to be revised to allow time to have a bowel movement when the body sends its signal. One possibility is to go to bed earlier in order to rise earlier, allowing ample time for a leisurely breakfast and a movement.

Although constipation usually reflects lifestyle habits, in some cases it may be a side effect of medication or may reflect a medical problem such as tumors that are obstructing the passage of waste. If discomfort is associated with passing fecal matter, seek medical advice to rule out disease. Once this has been done, dietary or other measures for correction can be considered.

One dietary measure that may be appropriate is to increase dietary fiber to 20 to 25 grams per day over the course of a week or two. Fibers found in fruits, vegetables, and whole grains help to prevent constipation by increasing fecal mass. In the GI tract, fiber attracts water, creating soft, bulky stools that stimulate bowel contractions to push the contents along. These contractions strengthen the intestinal muscles. The improved muscle tone, together with the water content of the stools, eases elimination, reducing the pressure in the rectal veins and helping to prevent **hemorrhoids.** Chapter 4 provides more information on fiber's role in maintaining a healthy colon and reducing the risks of colon cancer and diverticulosis. **Diverticulosis** is a condition in which the intestinal walls develop bulges in weakened areas, most commonly in the colon (see Figure H3-3). These bulging pockets, known as **diverticula,** can worsen constipation, entrap feces, and become painfully infected and inflamed **(diverticulitis)**. Treatment may require hospitalization, antibiotics, or surgery.

Drinking plenty of water in conjunction with eating high-fiber foods also helps to prevent constipation. The increased bulk physically stimulates the upper GI tract, promoting peristalsis throughout. Similarly, physical activity improves the muscle tone and motility of the digestive tract. As little as 30 minutes of physical activity a day can help prevent or alleviate constipation.

Eating prunes—or "dried plums" as some have renamed them—can also be helpful. Prunes are high in fiber and also contain a laxative substance.* If a morning defecation is desired, a person can drink prune juice at bedtime; if the evening is preferred, the person can drink prune juice with breakfast.

These suggested changes in lifestyle or diet should correct chronic constipation without the use of **laxatives, enemas,** or **mineral oil,** although television commercials often try to persuade people otherwise. One of the fallacies often perpetrated by advertisements is that one person's successful use of a product is a good recommendation for others to use that product.

As a matter of fact, diet changes that relieve constipation for one person may increase the constipation of another. For instance, increasing fiber intake stimulates peristalsis and helps the person with a sluggish colon. Some people, though, have a spastic type of constipation, in which peristalsis promotes strong contractions that close off a segment of the colon and prevent passage; for these people, increasing fiber intake would be exactly the wrong thing to do.

A person who seems to need products such as laxatives frequently should seek a physician's advice. One potentially harmful but currently popular practice is **colonic irrigation**—the internal washing of the large intestine with a powerful enema machine. Such an extreme cleansing is not only unnecessary, but it can be hazardous, causing illness and death from equipment contamination, electrolyte depletion, and intestinal perforation. Less extreme practices can cause problems, too. Frequent use of laxatives and enemas can lead to dependency; upset the body's fluid, salt, and mineral balances; and, in the case of mineral oil, interfere with the absorption of fat-soluble vitamins. (Mineral oil dissolves the vitamins but is not itself absorbed. Instead, it leaves the body, carrying the vitamins with it.)

Belching and Gas

Many people complain of problems that they attribute to excessive gas. For some, **belching** is the complaint. Others blame intestinal gas for abdominal discomforts and embarrassment. Most people believe that the problems occur after they eat certain foods. This may be the case with intestinal gas, but belching results from swallowing air. The best advice for belching seems to be to eat slowly, chew thoroughly, and relax while eating.

Everyone swallows a little bit of air with each mouthful of food, but people who eat too fast may swallow too much air and then have to belch. Ill-fitting dentures, carbonated beverages, and chewing gum can also contribute to the swallowing of air with resultant belching. Occasionally, belching can be a sign of a more serious disorder, such as gallbladder disease or a peptic ulcer.

FIGURE H3-3 Diverticula in the Colon

Diverticula may develop anywhere along the GI tract, but they are most common in the colon.

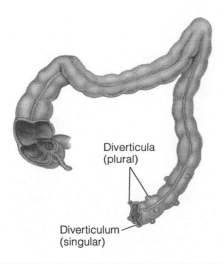

Diverticula
(plural)

Diverticulum
(singular)

---

* This substance is dihydroxyphenyl isatin.

People troubled by gas need to determine which foods bother them and then eat those foods in moderation.

People who eat or drink too fast may also trigger **hiccups,** the repeated spasms that produce a cough-like sound and jerky movement. Normally, hiccups soon subside and are of no medical significance, but they can be bothersome. The most effective cure is to hold the breath for as long as possible, which helps to relieve the spasms of the diaphragm.

Although expelling gas can be a humiliating experience, it is quite normal. (People who experience painful bloating from mal-

absorption diseases, however, require medical treatment.) Healthy people expel several hundred milliliters of gas several times a day. Almost all (99 percent) of the gases expelled—nitrogen, oxygen, hydrogen, methane, and carbon dioxide—are odorless. The remaining "volatile" gases are the infamous ones.

Foods that produce gas usually must be determined individually. The most common offenders are foods rich in the carbohydrates—sugars, starches, and fibers. When partially digested carbohydrates reach the large intestine, bacteria digest them, giving off gas as a by-product. People can test foods suspected of forming gas by omitting them individually for a trial period to see if there is any improvement.

Heartburn and "Acid Indigestion"

Almost everyone has experienced **heartburn** at one time or another, usually soon after eating a meal. Medically known as **gastroesophageal reflux,** heartburn is the painful sensation a person feels behind the breastbone when the lower esophageal sphincter allows the stomach contents to reflux into the esophagus (see Figure H3-4). This may happen if a person eats or drinks too much (or both). Tight clothing and even changes of position (lying down, bending over) can cause it, too, as can some medications and smoking. Weight gain and overweight increase the frequency, severity, and duration of heartburn symptoms.[5] A defect of the sphincter muscle itself is a possible, but less common, cause.

If the heartburn is not caused by an anatomical defect, treatment is fairly simple. To avoid such misery in the future, the person needs to learn to eat less at a sitting, chew food more thoroughly, and eat it more slowly. Additional strategies are presented in Table H3-1 at the end of this highlight.

As far as "acid indigestion" is concerned, recall from Chapter 3 that the strong acidity of the stomach is a desirable condition—television commercials for **antacids** and **acid controllers** notwithstanding. People who overeat or eat too quickly are likely to suffer from **indigestion.** The muscular reaction of the stomach to unchewed lumps or to being overfilled may be so violent that it upsets normal peristalsis. When this happens, overeaters may taste the stomach acid and feel pain. Responding to advertisements, they may reach for antacids or acid controllers. Both of these drugs were originally designed to treat GI illnesses such as ulcers. As is true of most over-the-counter medicines, antacids and acid

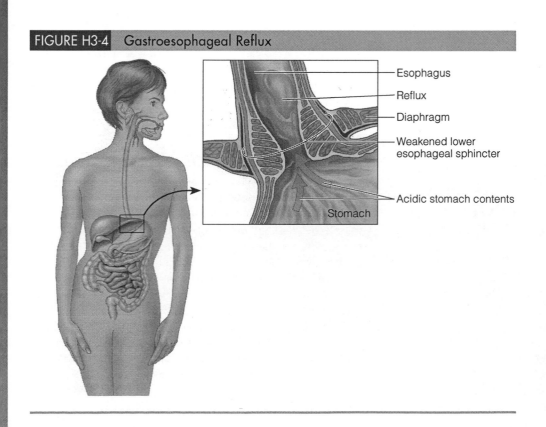

FIGURE H3-4 Gastroesophageal Reflux

- Esophagus
- Reflux
- Diaphragm
- Weakened lower esophageal sphincter
- Acidic stomach contents
- Stomach

controllers should be used only infrequently for occasional heartburn; they may mask or cause problems if used regularly. Acid-blocking drugs weaken the defensive mucous barrier of the GI tract, thereby increasing the risks of infections such as pneumonia, especially in vulnerable populations like the elderly.[6] Instead of self-medicating, people who suffer from frequent and regular bouts of heartburn and indigestion should try the strategies presented in the table below. If problems continue, they may need to see a physician, who can prescribe specific medication to control gastroesophageal reflux. Without treatment, the repeated splashes of acid can severely damage the cells of the esophagus, creating a condition known as Barrett's esophagus.[7] At that stage, the risk of cancer in the throat or esophagus increases dramatically. To repeat, if symptoms persist, see a doctor—don't self-medicate.

Ulcers

Ulcers are another common digestive problem. An **ulcer** is a lesion (a sore) and a **peptic ulcer** is a lesion in the lining of the stomach (gastric ulcers) or the duodenum of the small intestine (duodenal ulcers). The compromised lining is left unprotected and exposed to gastric juices, which can be painful. In some cases, ulcers can cause internal bleeding. If GI bleeding is excessive, iron deficiency may develop. Ulcers that perforate the GI lining can pose life-threatening complications.

Many people naively believe that an ulcer is caused by stress or spicy foods, but this is not the case. The stomach lining in a healthy person is well protected by its mucous coat. What, then, causes ulcers to form?

Three major causes of ulcers have been identified: bacterial infection with *Helicobacter pylori* (commonly abbreviated *H. pylori*);

the use of certain anti-inflammatory drugs such as aspirin, ibuprofen, and naproxen; and disorders that cause excessive gastric acid secretion. Most commonly, ulcers develop in response to *H. pylori* infection.[8] The cause of the ulcer dictates the type of medication used in treatment. For example, people with ulcers caused by infection receive antibiotics, whereas those with ulcers caused by medicines discontinue their use. In addition, all treatment plans aim to relieve pain, heal the ulcer, and prevent recurrence.

The regimen for ulcer treatment is to treat for infection, eliminate any food that routinely causes indigestion or pain, and avoid coffee and caffeine- and alcohol-containing beverages. Both regular and decaffeinated coffee stimulate acid secretion and so aggravate *existing* ulcers.

Ulcers and their treatments highlight the importance of not self-medicating when symptoms persist. People with *H. pylori* infection often take over-the-counter acid controllers to relieve the pain of their ulcers when, instead, they need physician-prescribed antibiotics. Suppressing gastric acidity not only fails to heal the ulcer, but it also actually worsens inflammation during an *H. pylori* infection. Furthermore, *H. pylori* infection has been linked with stomach cancer, making prompt diagnosis and appropriate treatment essential.[9]

Table H3-1 summarizes strategies to prevent or alleviate common GI problems. Many of these problems reflect hurried lifestyles. For this reason, many of their remedies require that people slow down and take the time to eat leisurely; chew food thoroughly to prevent choking, heartburn, and acid indigestion; rest until vomiting and diarrhea subside; and heed the urge to defecate. In addition, people must learn how to handle life's day-to-day problems and challenges without overreacting and becoming upset; learn how to relax, get enough sleep, and enjoy life. Remember, "what's eating you" may cause more GI distress than what you eat.

TABLE H3-1	Strategies to Prevent or Alleviate Common GI Problems		
GI Problem	**Strategies**	**GI Problem**	**Strategies**
Choking	• Take small bites of food. • Chew thoroughly before swallowing. • Don't talk or laugh with food in your mouth. • Don't eat when breathing hard.	Heartburn	• Eat small meals. • Drink liquids between meals. • Sit up while eating; elevate your head when lying down. • Wait 3 hours after eating before lying down. • Wait 2 hours after eating before exercising. • Refrain from wearing tight-fitting clothing. • Avoid foods, beverages, and medications that aggravate your heartburn. • Refrain from smoking cigarettes or using tobacco products. • Lose weight if overweight.
Diarrhea	• Rest. • Drink fluids to replace losses. • Call for medical help if diarrhea persists.		
Constipation	• Eat a high-fiber diet. • Drink plenty of fluids. • Exercise regularly. • Respond promptly to the urge to defecate.	Ulcer	• Take medicine as prescribed by your physician. • Avoid coffee and caffeine- and alcohol-containing beverages. • Avoid foods that aggravate your ulcer. • Minimize aspirin, ibuprofen, and naproxen use. • Refrain from smoking cigarettes.
Belching	• Eat slowly. • Chew thoroughly. • Relax while eating.		
Intestinal gas	• Eat bothersome foods in moderation.		

NUTRITION ON THE NET

ThomsonNOW™
For furthur study of topics covered in this Highlight, log on to **www .thomsonedu.com/thomsonnow**. Go to Chapter 3, then to Highlights Nutrition on the Net.

- Search for "choking," "vomiting," "diarrhea," "constipation," "heartburn," "indigestion," and "ulcers" at the U.S. Government health information site: **www.healthfinder.gov**

- Visit the Center for Digestive Health and Nutrition: **www.gihealth.com**

- Visit the Digestive Diseases section of the National Institute of Diabetes, Digestive, and Kidney Diseases: **www.niddk.nih.gov/health/health.htm**

- Visit the patient information section of the American College of Gastroenterology: **www.acg.gi.org**

- Learn more about *H. pylori* from the Helicobacter Foundation: **www.helico.com**

REFERENCES

1. K. Gotsch, J. L. Annest, and P. Holmgreen, Nonfatal choking-related episodes among children-United States, 2001, *Morbidity and Mortality Weekly Report* 51 (2002): 945-948.
2. B. J. Horwitz and R. S. Fisher, The irritable bowel syndrome, *New England Journal of Medicine* 344 (2001): 1846-1850.
3. N. M. Thielman and R. L. Guerrant, Acute infectious diarrhea, *New England Journal of Medicine* 350 (2004): 38-47.
4. A. Lembo and M. Camilleri, Chronic constipation, *New England Journal of Medicine* 349 (2003): 1360-1368.
5. B. C. Jacobson and coauthors, Body-mass index and symptoms of gastroesophageal reflux in women, *New England Journal of Medicine* 354 (2006): 2340-2348.
6. R. J. F. Laheij and coauthors, Risk of community-acquired pneumonia and use of gastric acid-suppressive drugs, *Journal of the American Medical Association* 292 (2004): 1955-1960.
7. N. Shaheen and D. F. Ransohoff, Gastroesophageal reflux, Barrett's esophagus, and esophageal cancer: Scientific review, *Journal of the American Medical Association* 287 (2002): 1972-1981.
8. S. Suerbaum and P. Michetti, Helicobacter pylori infection, *New England Journal of Medicine* 347 (2002): 1175-1186.
9. N. Uemura and coauthors, Helicobacter pylori infection and the development of gastric cancer, *New England Journal of Medicine* 345 (2001): 784-789.

© Burke/Triolo Productions/FoodPix/Jupiter Images

Thomson NOW! Throughout this chapter, the ThomsonNOW logo indicates an opportunity for online self-study, linking you to interactive tutorials and videos based on your level of understanding.

www.thomsonedu.com/login

Figure 7.5: Animated! Glycolysis: Glucose-to-Pyruvate

Figure 7.10: Animated! Fatty Acid-to-Acetyl CoA

Figure 7.18: Animated! The TCA Cycle

Figure 7.19: Animated! Electron Transport Chain and ATP Synthesis

Nutrition Portfolio Journal

Nutrition in Your Life

You eat breakfast and hustle off to class. After lunch, you study for tomorrow's exam. Dinner is followed by an evening of dancing. Do you ever think about how the food you eat powers the activities of your life? What happens when you don't eat—or when you eat too much? Learn how the cells of your body transform carbohydrates, fats, and proteins into energy—and what happens when you give your cells too much or too little of any of these nutrients. Discover the metabolic pathways that lead to body fat and those that support physical activity. It's really quite fascinating.

Metabolism: Transformations and Interactions

CHAPTER OUTLINE

Chemical Reactions in the Body

Breaking Down Nutrients for Energy • Glucose • Glycerol and Fatty Acids • Amino Acids • Breaking Down Nutrients for Energy—In Summary • The Final Steps of Catabolism

Energy Balance • Feasting—Excess Energy • The Transition from Feasting to Fasting • Fasting—Inadequate Energy

HIGHLIGHT 7 Alcohol and Nutrition

Energy makes it possible for people to breathe, ride bicycles, compose music, and do everything else they do. All the energy that sustains human life initially comes from the sun—the ultimate source of energy. As Chapter 1 explained, *energy* is the capacity to do work. Although every aspect of our lives depends on energy, the concept of energy can be difficult to grasp because it cannot be seen or touched, and it manifests in various forms, including heat, mechanical, electrical, and chemical energy. In the body, heat energy maintains a constant body temperature, and electrical energy sends nerve impulses. Energy is stored in foods and in the body as chemical energy.

During **photosynthesis**, plants make simple sugars from carbon dioxide and capture the sun's light energy in the chemical bonds of those sugars. Then human beings eat either the plants or animals that have eaten the plants. These foods provide energy, but how does the body obtain that energy from foods? This chapter answers that question by following the nutrients that provide the body with **fuel** through a series of reactions that release energy from their chemical bonds. As the bonds break, they release energy in a controlled version of the same process by which wood burns in a fire. Both wood and food have the potential to provide energy. When wood burns in the presence of oxygen, it generates heat and light (energy), steam (water), and some carbon dioxide and ash (waste). Similarly, during **metabolism,** the body releases energy, water, and carbon dioxide.

By studying metabolism, you will understand how the body uses foods to meet its needs and why some foods meet those needs better than others. Readers who are interested in weight control will discover which foods contribute most to body fat and which to select when trying to gain or lose weight safely. Physically active readers will discover which foods best support endurance activities and which to select when trying to build lean body mass.

photosynthesis: the process by which green plants use the sun's energy to make carbohydrates from carbon dioxide and water.
• **photo** = light
• **synthesis** = put together (making)

fuel: compounds that cells can use for energy. The major fuels include glucose, fatty acids, and amino acids; other fuels include ketone bodies, lactate, glycerol, and alcohol.

metabolism: the sum total of all the chemical reactions that go on in living cells. Energy metabolism includes all the reactions by which the body obtains and expends the energy from food.
• **metaballein** = change

Chemical Reactions in the Body

Earlier chapters introduced some of the body's chemical reactions: the making and breaking of the bonds in carbohydrates, lipids, and proteins. Metabolism is the sum of these and all the other chemical reactions that go on in living cells; *energy metabolism* includes all the ways the body obtains and uses energy from food.

The Site of Metabolic Reactions—Cells The human body is made up of trillions of cells, and each cell busily conducts its metabolic work all the time. (Appendix A presents a brief summary of the structure and function of the cell.) Figure 7-1 depicts a typical cell and shows where the major reactions of energy metabolism take place. The type and extent of metabolic activities vary depending on the type of cell, but of all the body's cells, the liver cells are the most versatile and metabolically active. Table 7-1 offers insights into the liver's work.

The Building Reactions—Anabolism Earlier chapters described how condensation reactions combine the basic units of energy-yielding nutrients to build body compounds. Glucose molecules may be joined together to make glycogen chains. Glycerol and fatty acids may be assembled into triglycerides. Amino acids may be linked together to make proteins. Each of these reactions starts with small, simple compounds and uses them as building blocks to form larger, more complex structures. Because such reactions involve doing work, they require energy. The building up of body compounds is known as **anabolism.** Anabolic reactions are represented in this book, wherever possible, with "up" arrows in chemical diagrams (such as those shown in Figure 7-2).

> **anabolism** (an-AB-o-lism): reactions in which small molecules are put together to build larger ones. Anabolic reactions require energy.
> • **ana** = up

FIGURE 7-1 A Typical Cell (Simplified Diagram)

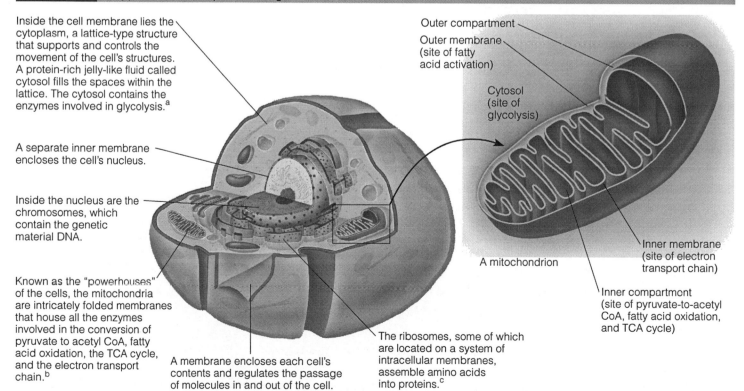

Inside the cell membrane lies the cytoplasm, a lattice-type structure that supports and controls the movement of the cell's structures. A protein-rich jelly-like fluid called cytosol fills the spaces within the lattice. The cytosol contains the enzymes involved in glycolysis.[a]

A separate inner membrane encloses the cell's nucleus.

Inside the nucleus are the chromosomes, which contain the genetic material DNA.

Known as the "powerhouses" of the cells, the mitochondria are intricately folded membranes that house all the enzymes involved in the conversion of pyruvate to acetyl CoA, fatty acid oxidation, the TCA cycle, and the electron transport chain.[b]

A membrane encloses each cell's contents and regulates the passage of molecules in and out of the cell.

The ribosomes, some of which are located on a system of intracellular membranes, assemble amino acids into proteins.[c]

Outer compartment

Outer membrane (site of fatty acid activation)

Cytosol (site of glycolysis)

A mitochondrion

Inner membrane (site of electron transport chain)

Inner compartment (site of pyruvate-to-acetyl CoA, fatty acid oxidation, and TCA cycle)

---

[a] Glycolysis is introduced on p. 219.
[b] The conversion of pyruvate to acetyl CoA, fatty acid oxidation, the TCA cycle, and the electron transport chain are described later in the chapter..
[c] Figure 6-7 on p. 188 describes protein synthesis.

TABLE 7-1 Metabolic Work of the Liver

The liver is the most active processing center in the body. When nutrients enter the body from the digestive tract, the liver receives them first; then it metabolizes, packages, stores, or ships them out for use by other organs. When alcohol, drugs, or poisons enter the body, they are also sent directly to the liver; here they are detoxified and their by-products shipped out for excretion. An enthusiastic anatomy and physiology professor once remarked that given the many vital activities of the liver, we should express our feelings for others by saying, "I love you with all my liver," instead of "with all my heart." Granted, this declaration lacks romance, but it makes a valid point. Here are just some of the many jobs performed by the liver. To renew your appreciation for this remarkable organ, review Figure 3-12 on p. 85.

Carbohydrates:

- Converts fructose and galactose to glucose
- Makes and stores glycogen
- Breaks down glycogen and releases glucose
- Breaks down glucose for energy when needed
- Makes glucose from some amino acids and glycerol when needed
- Converts excess glucose to fatty acids

Lipids:

- Builds and breaks down triglycerides, phospholipids, and cholesterol as needed
- Breaks down fatty acids for energy when needed
- Packages extra lipids in lipoproteins for transport to other body organs
- Manufactures bile to send to the gallbladder for use in fat digestion
- Makes ketone bodies when necessary

Proteins:

- Manufactures nonessential amino acids that are in short supply
- Removes from circulation amino acids that are present in excess of need and converts them to other amino acids or deaminates them and converts them to glucose or fatty acids
- Removes ammonia from the blood and converts it to urea to be sent to the kidneys for excretion
- Makes other nitrogen-containing compounds the body needs (such as bases used in DNA and RNA)
- Makes plasma proteins such as clotting factors

Other:

- Detoxifies alcohol, other drugs, and poisons; prepares waste products for excretion
- Helps dismantle old red blood cells and captures the iron for recycling
- Stores most vitamins and many minerals

FIGURE 7-2 Anabolic and Catabolic Reactions Compared

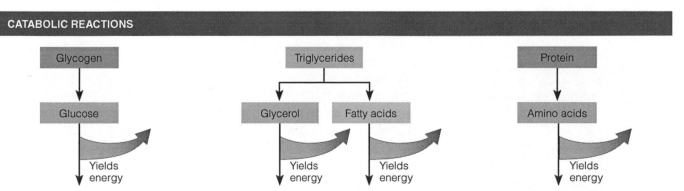

Anabolic reactions include the making of glycogen, triglycerides, and protein; these reactions require differing amounts of energy.

Catabolic reactions include the breakdown of glycogen, triglycerides, and protein; the further catabolism of glucose, glycerol, fatty acids, and amino acids releases differing amounts of energy. Much of the energy released is captured in the bonds of adenosine triphosphate (ATP).

NOTE: You need not memorize a color code to understand the figures in this chapter, but you may find it helpful to know that blue is used for carbohydrates, yellow for fats, and red for proteins.

FIGURE 7-3 ATP (Adenosine Triphosphate)

ATP is one of the body's high-energy molecules. Notice that the bonds connecting the three phosphate groups have been drawn as wavy lines, indicating a high-energy bond. When these bonds are broken, energy is released.

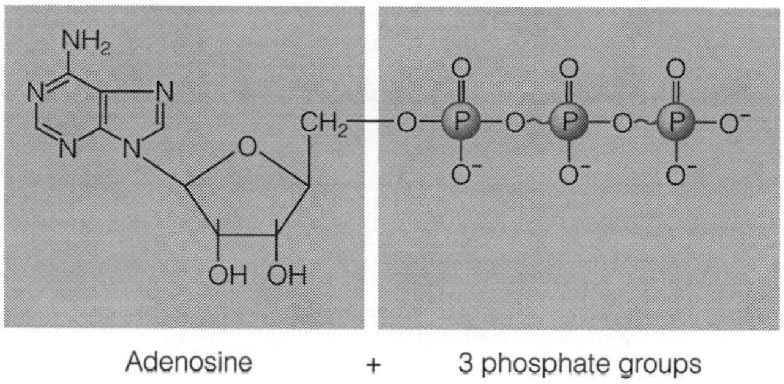

Adenosine + 3 phosphate groups

◆ ATP = A-P~P~P.
(Each ~ denotes a "high-energy" bond.)

◆ Reminder: *Enzymes* are protein catalysts—proteins that facilitate chemical reactions without being changed in the process.

◆ The general term for substances that facilitate enzyme action is **cofactors**; they include both organic coenzymes made from vitamins and inorganic substances such as minerals.

catabolism (ca-TAB-o-lism): reactions in which large molecules are broken down to smaller ones. Catabolic reactions release energy.
• **kata** = down

ATP or **adenosine** (ah-DEN-oh-seen) **triphosphate** (try-FOS-fate): a common high-energy compound composed of a purine (adenine), a sugar (ribose), and three phosphate groups.

coupled reactions: pairs of chemical reactions in which some of the energy released from the breakdown of one compound is used to create a bond in the formation of another compound.

coenzymes: complex organic molecules that work with enzymes to facilitate the enzymes' activity. Many coenzymes have B vitamins as part of their structures (Figure 10-1 on p. 327 in Chapter 10 illustrates coenzyme action).
• **co** = with

The Breakdown Reactions—Catabolism The breaking down of body compounds is known as **catabolism;** catabolic reactions release energy and are represented, wherever possible, by "down" arrows in chemical diagrams (as in Figure 7-2, p. 215). Earlier chapters described how hydrolysis reactions break down glycogen to glucose, triglycerides to fatty acids and glycerol, and proteins to amino acids. When the body needs energy, it breaks down any or all of these four basic units into even smaller units, as described later.

The Transfer of Energy in Reactions—ATP High-energy storage compounds in the body capture some of the energy released during the breakdown of glucose, glycerol, fatty acids, and amino acids from foods. One such compound is **ATP (adenosine triphosphate).** ATP, as its name indicates, contains three phosphate groups (see Figure 7-3). ◆ The bonds connecting the phosphate groups are often described as "high-energy" bonds, referring to the bonds' readiness to release their energy. The negative charges on the phosphate groups make ATP vulnerable to hydrolysis. Whenever cells do any work that requires energy, hydrolytic reactions readily break these high-energy bonds of ATP, splitting off one or two phosphate groups and releasing their energy.

Quite often, the hydrolysis of ATP occurs simultaneously with reactions that will use that energy—a metabolic duet known as **coupled reactions.** Figure 7-4 illustrates how the body captures and releases energy in the bonds of ATP. In essence, the body uses ATP to transfer the energy released during catabolic reactions to power its anabolic reactions. The body converts the chemical energy of food to the chemical energy of ATP with about 50 percent efficiency, radiating the rest as heat.[1] Energy is lost as heat again when the body uses the chemical energy of ATP to do its work—moving muscles, synthesizing compounds, or transporting nutrients, for example.

The Helpers in Metabolic Reactions—Enzymes and Coenzymes Metabolic reactions almost always require enzymes ◆ to facilitate their action. In many cases, the enzymes need assistants to help them. Enzyme helpers are called **coenzymes.** ◆

Coenzymes are complex organic molecules that associate closely with most enzymes but are not proteins themselves. The relationships between various coenzymes and their respective enzymes may differ in detail, but one thing is true of all: without its coenzyme, an enzyme cannot function. Some of the B vitamins serve as coenzymes that participate in the energy metabolism of glucose, glycerol, fatty acids, and amino acids (Chapter 10 provides more details).

FIGURE 7-4 Transfer of Energy by ATP—A Coupled Reaction

The breakdown of ATP (adenosine triphosphate) to ADP (adenosine diphosphate) releases energy that can be used to power another reaction (such as the synthesis of a needed compound). The simultaneous occurrence of one reaction releasing energy and another reaction using the energy is called a coupled reaction.

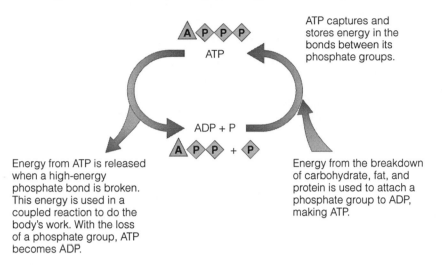

ATP captures and stores energy in the bonds between its phosphate groups.

Energy from ATP is released when a high-energy phosphate bond is broken. This energy is used in a coupled reaction to do the body's work. With the loss of a phosphate group, ATP becomes ADP.

Energy from the breakdown of carbohydrate, fat, and protein is used to attach a phosphate group to ADP, making ATP.

IN SUMMARY

During digestion the energy-yielding nutrients—carbohydrates, lipids, and proteins—are broken down to glucose (and other monosaccharides), glycerol, fatty acids, and amino acids. Aided by enzymes and coenzymes, the cells use these products of digestion to build more complex compounds (anabolism) or break them down further to release energy (catabolism). High-energy compounds such as ATP may capture the energy released during catabolism.

Breaking Down Nutrients for Energy

Chapters 4, 5, and 6 laid the groundwork for the study of metabolism; a brief review may be helpful. During digestion, the body breaks down the three energy-yielding nutrients—carbohydrates, lipids, and proteins—into four basic units that can be absorbed into the blood:

- From carbohydrates—glucose (and other monosaccharides)
- From fats (triglycerides)—glycerol and fatty acids
- From proteins—amino acids

The body uses carbohydrates and fats for most of its energy needs. Amino acids are used primarily as building blocks for proteins, but they also enter energy pathways, contributing about 10 to 15 percent of the day's energy use. Look for these four basic units—glucose, glycerol, fatty acids, and amino acids—to appear again and again in the metabolic reactions described in this chapter. Alcohol also enters many of the metabolic pathways; Highlight 7 focuses on how alcohol disrupts metabolism and how the body handles it.

Glucose, glycerol, fatty acids, and amino acids are the basic units derived from food, but a molecule of each of these compounds is made of still smaller units, the atoms—carbons, nitrogens, oxygens, and hydrogens. During catabolism, the body

All the energy used to keep the heart beating, the brain thinking, and the legs running comes from the carbohydrates, fats, and proteins in foods.

© Chris Cole/The Image Bank/Getty Images

◆ A healthy diet provides:
  • 45–65% kcalories from carbohydrate
  • 10–35% kcalories from protein
  • 20–35% kcalories from fat

pyruvate (PIE-roo-vate): a 3-carbon compound that plays a key role in energy metabolism.

$$CH_3$$
$$|$$
$$C=O$$
$$|$$
$$COOH$$

acetyl CoA (ASS-eh-teel, or ah-SEET-il, coh-AY): a 2-carbon compound (**acetate,** or **acetic acid,** shown in Figure 5-1 on p. 140) to which a molecule of CoA is attached.

CoA (coh-AY): coenzyme A; the coenzyme derived from the B vitamin pantothenic acid and central to energy metabolism.

TCA cycle or **tricarboxylic** (try-car-box-ILL-ick) **acid cycle:** a series of metabolic reactions that break down molecules of acetyl CoA to carbon dioxide and hydrogen atoms; also called the **Kreb's cycle** after the biochemist who elucidated its reactions.

electron transport chain: the final pathway in energy metabolism that transports electrons from hydrogen to oxygen and captures the energy released in the bonds of ATP.

separates these atoms from one another. To follow this action, recall how many carbons are in the "backbones" of these compounds:

  • Glucose has 6 carbons:

  • Glycerol has 3 carbons:

  • A fatty acid usually has an even number of carbons, commonly 16 or 18 carbons:*

  • An amino acid has 2, 3, or more carbons with a nitrogen attached:**

Full chemical structures and reactions appear both in the earlier chapters and in Appendix C; this chapter diagrams the reactions using just the compounds' carbon and nitrogen backbones.

As you will see, each of the compounds—glucose, glycerol, fatty acids, and amino acids—starts down a different path. Along the way, two new names appear—**pyruvate** (a 3-carbon structure) and **acetyl CoA** (a 2-carbon structure with a coenzyme, **CoA,** attached)—and the rest of the story falls into place around them.† Two major points to notice in the following discussion:

  • Pyruvate can be used to make glucose.

  • Acetyl CoA cannot be used to make glucose.

A key to understanding these metabolic pathways is learning which fuels can be converted to glucose and which cannot. The parts of protein and fat that can be converted to pyruvate *can* provide glucose for the body, whereas the parts that are converted to acetyl CoA *cannot* provide glucose but can readily provide fat. The body must have glucose to fuel the activities of the central nervous system and red blood cells. Without glucose from food, the body will devour its own lean (protein-containing) tissue to provide the amino acids to make glucose. Therefore, to keep this from happening, the body needs foods that can provide glucose—primarily carbohydrate. Giving the body only fat, which delivers mostly acetyl CoA, puts it in the position of having to break down protein tissue to make glucose. Giving the body only protein puts it in the position of having to convert protein to glucose. Clearly, the best diet ◆ provides ample carbohydrate, adequate protein, and some fat.

Eventually, all of the energy-yielding nutrients can enter the common pathways of the **TCA cycle** and the **electron transport chain.** (Similarly, people from three different cities can all enter an interstate highway and travel to the same destination.) The TCA cycle and electron transport chain have central roles in energy metabolism and receive full attention later in the chapter. First, the text describes how each of the energy-yielding nutrients is broken down to acetyl CoA and other compounds in preparation for their entrance into these final energy pathways.

---

* The figures in this chapter show 16- or 18-carbon fatty acids. Fatty acids may have 4 to 20 or more carbons, with chain lengths of 16 and 18 carbons most prevalent.
** The figures in this chapter usually show amino acids as compounds of 2, 3, or 5 carbons arranged in a straight line, but in reality amino acids may contain other numbers of carbons and assume other structural shapes (see Appendix C).
† The term *pyruvate* means a salt of *pyruvic acid.* (Throughout this book, the ending *–ate* is used interchangeably with *–ic acid;* for our purposes they mean the same thing.)

Glucose

What happens to glucose, glycerol, fatty acids, and amino acids during energy metabolism can best be understood by starting with glucose. This discussion features glucose because of its central role in carbohydrate metabolism and because liver cells can convert the other monosaccharides (fructose and galactose) to compounds that enter the same energy pathways.

Glucose-to-Pyruvate The first pathway glucose takes on its way to yield energy is called **glycolysis** (glucose splitting).* Figure 7-5 shows a simplified drawing of glycolysis. (This pathway actually involves several steps and several enzymes, which

---

* Glycolysis takes place in the cytosol of the cell (see Figure 7-1, p. 214).

> **glycolysis** (gly-COLL-ih-sis): the metabolic breakdown of glucose to pyruvate. Glycolysis does not require oxygen (anaerobic).
> • **glyco** = glucose
> • **lysis** = breakdown

FIGURE 7-5	*Animated!* Glycolysis: Glucose-to-Pyruvate

This simplified overview of glycolysis illustrates the steps in the process of converting glucose to pyruvate. Appendix C provides more details.

ThomsonNOW
To test your understanding of these concepts, log on to **www.thomsonedu.com/thomsonnow**

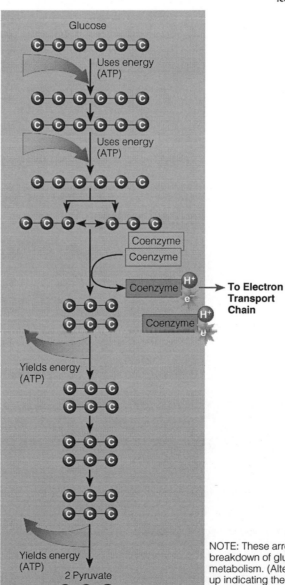

A little ATP is used to start glycolysis.

Galactose and fructose enter glycolysis at different places, but all continue on the same pathway.

In a series of reactions, the 6-carbon glucose is converted to other 6-carbon compounds, which eventually split into two interchangeable 3-carbon compounds.

A little ATP is produced, and coenzymes carry the hydrogens and their electrons to the electron transport chain.

These 3-carbon compounds are converted to pyruvate. Glycolysis of one molecule of glucose produces two molecules of pyruvate.

To Electron Transport Chain

NOTE: These arrows point down indicating the breakdown of glucose to pyruvate during energy metabolism. (Alternatively, the arrows could point up indicating the making of glucose from pyruvate, but that is not the focus of this discussion.)

are shown in Appendix C.) In a series of reactions, the 6-carbon glucose is converted to similar 6-carbon compounds before being split in half, forming two 3-carbon compounds. These 3-carbon compounds continue along the pathway until they are converted to pyruvate. Thus the net yield of one glucose molecule is two pyruvate molecules. The net yield of energy at this point is small; to start glycolysis, the cell uses a little energy and then produces only a little more than it had to invest initially.* In addition, as glucose breaks down to pyruvate, hydrogen atoms with their electrons are released and carried to the electron transport chain by coenzymes made from the B vitamin niacin. A later section of the chapter explains how oxygen accepts the electrons and combines with the hydrogens to form water and how the process captures energy in the bonds of ATP.

This discussion focuses primarily on the breakdown of glucose for energy, but if needed, cells in the liver (and to some extent, the kidneys) can make glucose again from pyruvate in a process similar to the reversal of glycolysis. Making glucose requires energy, however, and a few different enzymes. Still, glucose can be made from pyruvate, so the arrows between glucose and pyruvate could point up as well as down. ◆

Pyruvate's Options Pyruvate may enter either an **anaerobic** or an **aerobic** energy pathway. When the body needs energy quickly—as occurs when you run a quarter mile as fast as you can—pyruvate is converted to lactate in an anaerobic pathway. When energy expenditure proceeds at a slower pace—as occurs when you ride a bike for an hour—pyruvate breaks down to acetyl CoA in an aerobic pathway. The following paragraphs explain these pathways.

Pyruvate-to-Lactate As mentioned earlier, coenzymes carry the hydrogens from glucose breakdown to the electron transport chain. If the electron transport chain is unable to accept these hydrogens, as may occur when cells lack sufficient **mitochondria** (review Figure 7-1, p. 214) or in the absence of sufficient oxygen, pyruvate can accept the hydrogens. As Figure 7-6 shows, by accepting the hydrogens, pyruvate becomes

---

* The cell uses 2 ATP to begin the breakdown of glucose to pyruvate, but it then gains 4 ATP for a net gain of 2 ATP.

◆ Glucose may go "down" to make pyruvate, or pyruvate may go "up" to make glucose, depending on the cell's needs.

anaerobic (AN-air-ROE-bic): not requiring oxygen.
- **an** = not

aerobic (air-ROE-bic): requiring oxygen.

mitochondria (my-toh-KON-dree-uh): the cellular organelles responsible for producing ATP; made of membranes (lipid and protein) with enzymes mounted on them.
- **mitos** = thread (referring to their slender shape)
- **chondros** = cartilage (referring to their external appearance)

FIGURE 7-6 Pyruvate-to-Lactate

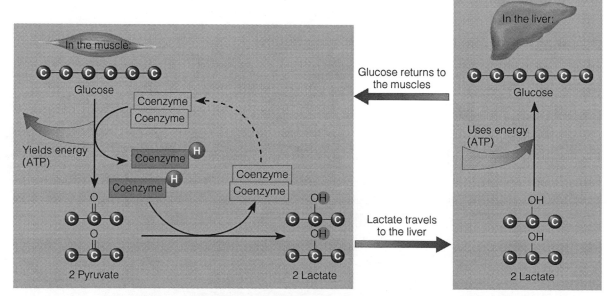

Working muscles break down most of their glucose molecules anaerobically to pyruvate. If the cells lack sufficient mitochondria or in the absence of sufficient oxygen, pyruvate can accept the hydrogens from glucose breakdown and become lactate. This conversion frees the coenzymes so that glycolysis can continue.

Liver enzymes can convert lactate to glucose, but this reaction requires energy. The process of converting lactate from the muscles to glucose in the liver that can be returned to the muscles is known as the Cori cycle.

lactate, and the coenzymes are freed to return to glycolysis to pick up more hydrogens. In this way, glucose can continue providing energy anaerobically for a while (see the left side of Figure 7-6).

The production of lactate occurs to a limited extent even at rest. During high-intensity exercise, however, the muscles rely heavily on anaerobic glycolysis to produce ATP quickly and the concentration of lactate increases dramatically. The rapid rate of glycolysis produces abundant pyruvate and releases hydrogen-carrying coenzymes more rapidly than the mitochondria can handle them. To enable exercise to continue at this intensity, pyruvate is converted to lactate and coenzymes are released, which allows glycolysis to continue (as mentioned earlier). The accumulation of lactate in the muscles coincides with—but is not the cause of—the subsequent drop in blood pH, burning pain, and fatigue that are commonly associated with intense exercise.[2] In fact, making lactate from pyruvate consumes two hydrogen ions, which actually diminishes acidity and improves the performance of tired muscles.[3] A person performing the same exercise following endurance training actually experiences less discomfort—in part because the number of mitochondria in the muscle cells have increased. This adaptation improves the mitochondria's ability to keep pace with the muscles' demand for energy.

One possible fate of lactate is to be transported from the muscles to the liver. There the liver can convert the lactate produced in muscles to glucose, which can then be returned to the muscles. This recycling process is called the **Cori cycle** (see Figure 7-6). (Muscle cells cannot recycle lactate to glucose because they lack a necessary enzyme.)

Whenever carbohydrates, fats, or proteins are broken down to provide energy, oxygen is always ultimately involved in the process. The role of oxygen in metabolism is worth noticing, for it helps our understanding of physiology and metabolic reactions. Chapter 14 describes the body's use of the energy nutrients to fuel physical activity, but the facts just presented offer a sneak preview. The breakdown of glucose-to-pyruvate-to-lactate proceeds without oxygen—it is anaerobic. This anaerobic pathway yields energy quickly, but it cannot be sustained for long—a couple of minutes at most. Conversely, the aerobic pathways produce energy more slowly, but because they can be sustained for a long time, their total energy yield is greater.

Pyruvate-to-Acetyl CoA If the cell needs energy and oxygen is available, pyruvate molecules enter the mitochondria of the cell (review Figure 7-1, p. 214). There a carbon group (COOH) from the 3-carbon pyruvate is removed to produce a 2-carbon compound that bonds with a molecule of CoA, becoming acetyl CoA. The carbon group from pyruvate becomes carbon dioxide, which is released into the blood, circulated to the lungs, and breathed out. Figure 7-7 diagrams the pyruvate-to-acetyl CoA reaction.

The step from pyruvate to acetyl CoA is metabolically irreversible: a cell cannot retrieve the shed carbons from carbon dioxide to remake pyruvate and then glucose. It is a one-way step and is therefore shown with only a "down" arrow in Figure 7-8.

The anaerobic breakdown of glucose-to-pyruvate-to-lactate is the major source of energy for short, intense exercise.

FIGURE 7-7 Pyruvate-to-Acetyl CoA

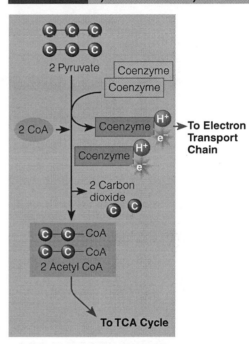

Each pyruvate loses a carbon as carbon dioxide and picks up a molecule of CoA, becoming acetyl CoA. The arrow goes only one way (down) because the step is not reversible. Result: 1 glucose yields 2 pyruvate, which yield 2 carbon dioxide and 2 acetyl CoA.

FIGURE 7-8 The Paths of Pyruvate and Acetyl CoA

Pyruvate may follow several reversible paths, but the path from pyruvate to acetyl CoA is irreversible.

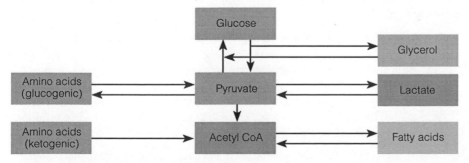

NOTE: Amino acids that can be used to make glucose are called *glucogenic*; amino acids that are converted to acetyl CoA are called *ketogenic*.

lactate: a 3-carbon compound produced from pyruvate during anaerobic metabolism.

Cori cycle: the path from muscle glycogen to glucose to pyruvate to lactate (which travels to the liver) to glucose (which can travel back to the muscle) to glycogen; named after the scientist who elucidated this pathway.

FIGURE 7-9 Glucose Enters the Energy Pathway

This figure combines Figure 7-5 and Figure 7-7 to show the breakdown of glucose-to-pyruvate-to-acetyl CoA. Details of the TCA cycle and the electron transport chain are given later and in Appendix C.

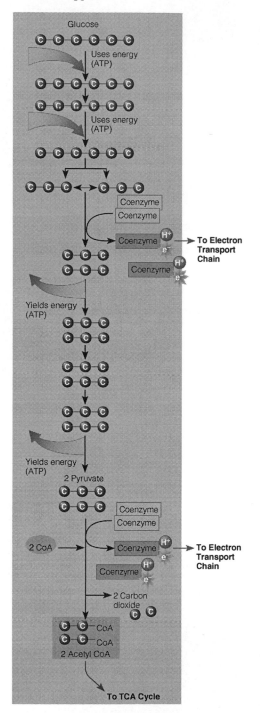

Acetyl CoA's Options Acetyl CoA has two main functions—it may be used to synthesize fats or to generate ATP. When ATP is abundant, acetyl CoA makes fat, the most efficient way to store energy for later use when energy may be needed. Thus any molecule that can make acetyl CoA—including glucose, glycerol, fatty acids, and amino acids—can make fat. In reviewing Figure 7-8, notice that acetyl CoA can be used as a building block for fatty acids, but it cannot be used to make glucose or amino acids.

When ATP is low and the cell needs energy, acetyl CoA may proceed through the TCA cycle, releasing hydrogens, with their electrons, to the electron transport chain. The story of acetyl CoA continues on p. 227 after a discussion of how fat and protein arrive at the same crossroads. For now, know that when acetyl CoA from the breakdown of glucose enters the aerobic pathways of the TCA cycle and electron transport chain, much more ATP is produced than during glycolysis. The role of glycolysis is to provide energy for short bursts of activity and to prepare glucose for later energy pathways.

IN SUMMARY

The breakdown of glucose to energy begins with glycolysis, a pathway that produces pyruvate. Keep in mind that glucose can be synthesized only from pyruvate or compounds earlier in the pathway. Pyruvate may be converted to lactate anaerobically or to acetyl CoA aerobically. Once the commitment to acetyl CoA is made, glucose is not retrievable; acetyl CoA cannot go back to glucose. Figure 7-9 summarizes the breakdown of glucose.

Glycerol and Fatty Acids

Once glucose breakdown is understood, fat and protein breakdown are easily learned, for all three eventually enter the same metabolic pathways. Recall that triglycerides can break down to glycerol and fatty acids.

Glycerol-to-Pyruvate Glycerol is a 3-carbon compound like pyruvate but with a different arrangement of H and OH on the C. As such, glycerol can easily be converted to another 3-carbon compound that can go either "up" the pathway to form glucose or "down" to form pyruvate and then acetyl CoA (review Figure 7-8, p. 221).

Fatty Acids-to-Acetyl CoA Fatty acids are taken apart 2 carbons at a time in a series of reactions known as **fatty acid oxidation.*** Figure 7-10 illustrates fatty acid oxidation and shows that in the process, each 2-carbon fragment splits off and combines with a molecule of CoA to make acetyl CoA. As each 2-carbon fragment breaks off from a fatty acid during oxidation, hydrogens and their electrons are released and carried to the electron transport chain by coenzymes made from the B vitamins riboflavin and niacin. Figure 7-11 (p. 224) summarizes the breakdown of fats.

Fatty Acids Cannot Be Used to Synthesize Glucose When carbohydrate is unavailable, the liver cells can make glucose from pyruvate and other 3-carbon compounds, such as glycerol, but they cannot make glucose from the 2-carbon fragments of fatty acids. In chemical diagrams, the arrow between pyruvate and acetyl CoA always points only one way—down—and fatty acid fragments enter the metabolic path below this arrow (review Figure 7-8, p. 221). The down arrow indicates that fatty acids cannot be used to make glucose.

---

fatty acid oxidation: the metabolic breakdown of fatty acids to acetyl CoA; also called **beta oxidation.**

---

* Oxidation of fatty acids occurs in the mitochondria of the cells (see Figure 7-1, p. 214).

FIGURE 7-10   *Animated!* Fatty Acid-to-Acetyl CoA

Fatty acids are broken apart into 2-carbon fragments that combine with CoA to make acetyl CoA.

ThomsonNOW™
To test your understanding of these concepts, log on to **www .thomsonedu.com/thomsonnow**

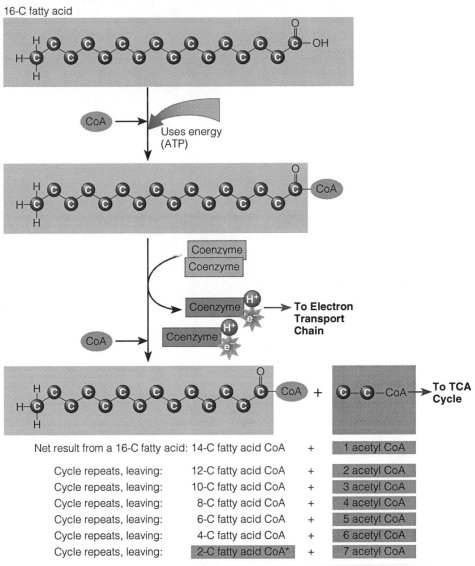

The fatty acid is first activated by coenzyme A.

Uses energy (ATP)

As each carbon-carbon bond is cleaved, hydrogens and their electrons are released, and coenzymes pick them up.

To Electron Transport Chain

Another CoA joins the chain, and the bond at the second carbon (the beta-carbon) weakens. Acetyl CoA splits off, leaving a fatty acid that is two carbons shorter.

To TCA Cycle

The shorter fatty acid enters the pathway and the cycle repeats, releasing more hydrogens with their electrons and more acetyl CoA. The molecules of acetyl CoA enter the TCA cycle, and the coenzymes carry the hydrogens and their electrons to the electron transport chain.

Net result from a 16-C fatty acid: 14-C fatty acid CoA + 1 acetyl CoA

Cycle repeats, leaving:	12-C fatty acid CoA	+	2 acetyl CoA
Cycle repeats, leaving:	10-C fatty acid CoA	+	3 acetyl CoA
Cycle repeats, leaving:	8-C fatty acid CoA	+	4 acetyl CoA
Cycle repeats, leaving:	6-C fatty acid CoA	+	5 acetyl CoA
Cycle repeats, leaving:	4-C fatty acid CoA	+	6 acetyl CoA
Cycle repeats, leaving:	2-C fatty acid CoA*	+	7 acetyl CoA

*Notice that 2-C fatty acid CoA = acetyl CoA, so that the final yield from a 16-C fatty acid is 8 acetyl CoA.

The significance of fatty acids not being able to make glucose is that red blood cells and the brain and nervous system depend primarily on glucose as fuel. Remember that almost all dietary fats are triglycerides and that triglycerides contain only one small molecule of glycerol with three fatty acids. The glycerol can yield glucose, ◆ but that represents only 3 of the 50 or so carbon atoms in a triglyceride—about 5 percent of its weight (see Figure 7-12). The other 95 percent cannot be converted to glucose.

◆ Reminder: The making of glucose from non-carbohydrate sources is called *gluconeogenesis*. The glycerol portion of a triglyceride and most amino acids can be used to make glucose (review Figure 7-8, p. 221). The liver is the major site of gluconeogenesis, but the kidneys become increasingly involved under certain circumstances, such as starvation.

IN SUMMARY

The body can convert the small glycerol portion of a triglyceride to either pyruvate (and then glucose) or acetyl CoA. The fatty acids of a triglyceride, on the other hand, cannot make glucose, but they can provide abundant acetyl CoA. Acetyl CoA may then enter the TCA cycle to release energy or combine with other molecules of acetyl CoA to make body fat.

FIGURE 7-11   *Animated!* Fats Enter the Energy Pathway

ThomsonNOW™
To test your understanding of
these concepts, log on to **www**
.thomsonedu.com/thomsonnow

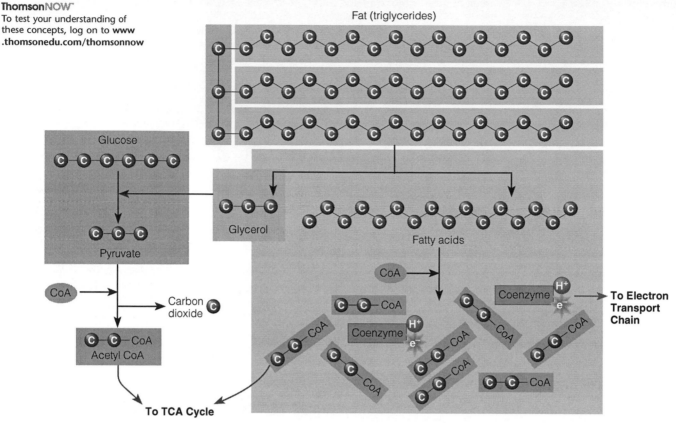

Glycerol enters the glycolysis pathway about midway between glucose and pyruvate and can be converted to either. Fatty acids are broken down into 2-carbon fragments that combine with CoA to form acetyl CoA (shown in Figure 7-10). Result: a 16-carbon fatty acid yields 8 acetyl CoA.

FIGURE 7-12   The Carbons of a Typical Triglyceride

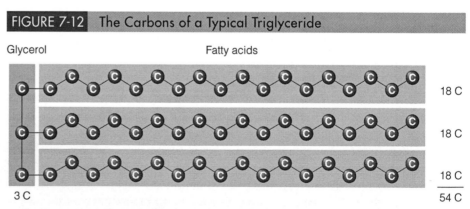

A typical triglyceride contains only one small molecule of glycerol (3 C) but has three fatty acids (each commonly 16 C or 18 C, or about 48 C to 54 C in total). Only the glycerol portion of a triglyceride can yield glucose.

Amino Acids

The preceding two sections have described how the breakdown of carbohydrate and fat produces acetyl CoA, which can enter the pathways that provide energy for the body's use. One energy-yielding nutrient remains: protein or, rather, the amino acids of protein.

FIGURE 7-13 Amino Acids Enter the Energy Pathway

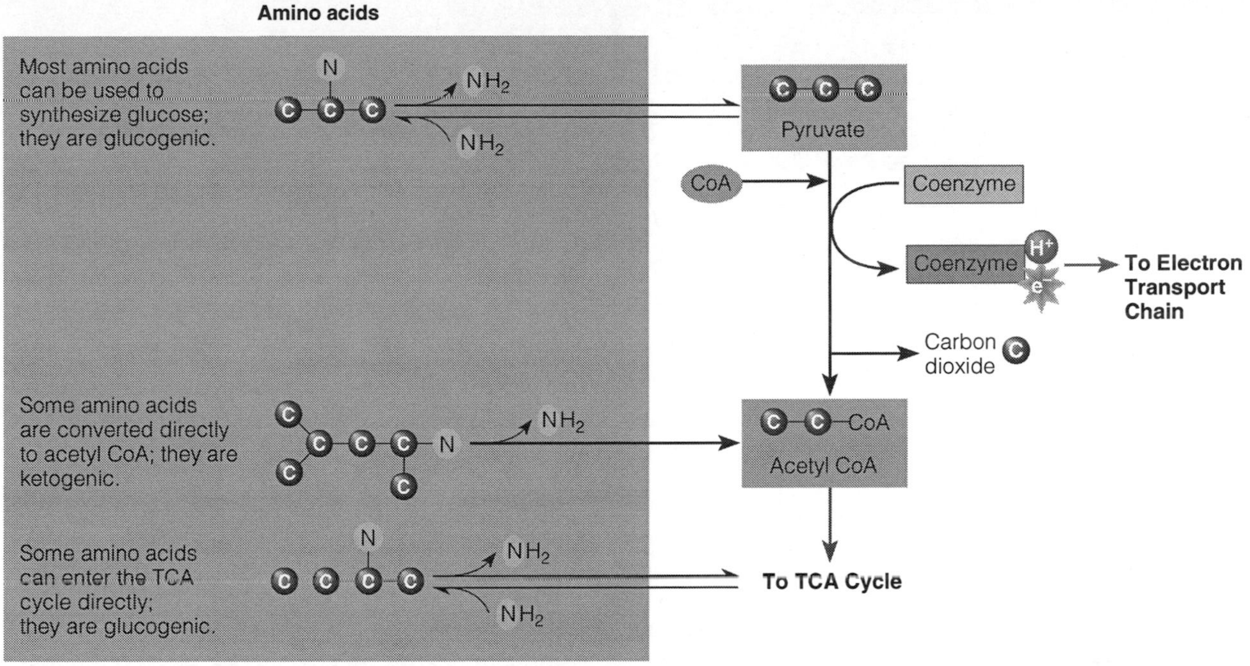

NOTE: The arrows from pyruvate and the TCA cycle to amino acids are possible only for *nonessential* amino acids; remember, the body cannot make essential amino acids.

Amino Acids-to-Acetyl CoA Before entering the metabolic pathways, amino acids are deaminated (that is, they lose their nitrogen-containing amino group) and then they are catabolized in a variety of ways. As Figure 7-13 illustrates, some amino acids can be converted to pyruvate, others are converted to acetyl CoA, and still others enter the TCA cycle directly as compounds other than acetyl CoA.

Amino Acids-to-Glucose As you might expect, amino acids that are used to make pyruvate can provide glucose, whereas those used to make acetyl CoA can provide additional energy or make body fat but cannot make glucose. ◆ Amino acids entering the TCA cycle directly can continue in the cycle and generate energy; alternatively, they can generate glucose.[4] Thus protein, unlike fat, is a fairly good source of glucose when carbohydrate is not available.

Deamination When amino acids are metabolized for energy or used to make glucose or fat, they must be deaminated first. Two products result from deamination. One is the carbon structure without its amino group—often a **keto acid** (see Figure 7-14, p. 226). The other product is **ammonia** (NH_3), a toxic compound chemically identical to the strong-smelling ammonia in bottled cleaning solutions. Ammonia is a base, and if the body produces larger quantities than it can handle, the blood's critical acid-base balance becomes upset.

Transamination As the discussion of protein in Chapter 6 pointed out, only some amino acids are essential; others can be made in the body, given a source of nitrogen. By transferring an amino group from one amino acid to its corresponding keto acid, cells can make a new amino acid and a new keto acid, as shown in Figure 7-15 (p. 226). Through many such **transamination** reactions, involving many different keto acids, the liver cells can synthesize the nonessential amino acids.

Ammonia-to-Urea in the Liver The liver continuously produces small amounts of ammonia in deamination reactions. Some of this ammonia provides the nitrogen

◆ Amino acids that can make glucose via either pyruvate or TCA cycle intermediates are *glucogenic;* amino acids that are degraded to acetyl CoA are *ketogenic.*

keto (KEY-toe) **acid:** an organic acid that contains a carbonyl group (C=O).

ammonia: a compound with the chemical formula NH_3; produced during the deamination of amino acids.

transamination (TRANS-am-ih-NAY-shun): the transfer of an amino group from one amino acid to a keto acid, producing a new nonessential amino acid and a new keto acid.

FIGURE 7-14 Deamination and Synthesis of a Nonessential Amino Acid

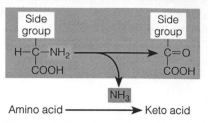

The deamination of an amino acid produces ammonia (NH_3) and a keto acid.

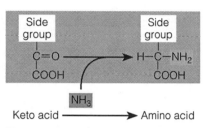

Given a source of NH_3, the body can make nonessential amino acids from keto acids.

FIGURE 7-16 Urea Synthesis

When amino acids are deaminated, ammonia is produced. The liver detoxifies ammonia before releasing it into the bloodstream by combining it with another waste product, carbon dioxide, to produce urea. See Appendix C for details.

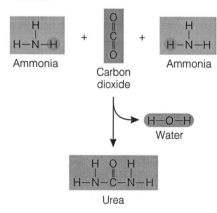

FIGURE 7-15 Transamination and Synthesis of a Nonessential Amino Acid

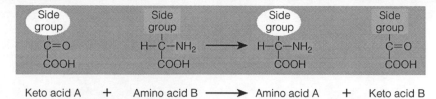

Keto acid A + Amino acid B ⟶ Amino acid A + Keto acid B

The body can transfer amino groups (NH_2) from an amino acid to a keto acid, forming a new *nonessential* amino acid and a new keto acid. Transamination reactions require the vitamin B_6 coenzyme.

needed for the synthesis of nonessential amino acids (review Figure 7-14). The liver quickly combines any remaining ammonia with carbon dioxide to make **urea**, a much less toxic compound. Figure 7-16 provides a greatly oversimplified diagram of urea synthesis; details are shown in Appendix C.

Urea Excretion via the Kidneys Liver cells release urea into the blood, where it circulates until it passes through the kidneys (see Figure 7-17). The kidneys then remove urea from the blood for excretion in the urine. Normally, the liver efficiently captures all the ammonia, makes urea from it, and releases the urea into the blood; then the kidneys clear all the urea from the blood. This division of labor allows easy diagnosis of diseases of both organs. In liver disease, blood ammonia will be high; in kidney disease, blood urea will be high.

Urea is the body's principal vehicle for excreting unused nitrogen, and the amount of urea produced increases with protein intake. To keep urea in solution, the body needs water. For this reason, a person who regularly consumes a high-protein diet (say, 100 grams a day or more) must drink plenty of water to dilute and excrete urea from the body. Without extra water, a person on a high-protein diet risks dehydration because the body uses its water to rid itself of urea. This explains some of the water loss that accompanies high-protein diets. Such losses may make high-protein diets *appear* to be effective, but water loss, of course, is of no value to the person who wants to lose body fat (as Highlight 9 explains).

IN SUMMARY

The body can use some amino acids to produce glucose, whereas others can be used either to generate energy or to make fat. Before an amino acid enters any of these metabolic pathways, its nitrogen-containing amino group must be removed through deamination. Deamination, which produces ammonia (NH_3), may be used to make nonessential amino acids and other nitrogen-containing compounds; the rest is cleared from the body via urea synthesis in the liver and excretion via the kidneys.

Breaking Down Nutrients for Energy— In Summary

To review the ways the body can use the energy-yielding nutrients, see the summary table (p. 227). To obtain energy, the body uses glucose and fatty acids as its primary fuels and amino acids to a lesser extent. To make glucose, the body can use all carbohydrates and most amino acids, but it can convert only 5 percent of fat (the glycerol portion) to glucose. To make proteins, the body needs amino acids. It can use glucose to make some nonessential amino acids when nitrogen is available; it cannot use fats to make body proteins. Finally, when energy is consumed beyond the body's needs, all three energy-yielding nutrients can contribute to body fat stores.

urea (you-REE-uh): the principal nitrogen-excretion product of protein metabolism. Two ammonia fragments are combined with carbon dioxide to form urea.

IN SUMMARY

Nutrient	Yields Energy?	Yields Glucose?	Yields Amino Acids and Body Proteins?	Yields Fat Stores?[a]
Carbohydrates (glucose)	Yes	Yes	Yes—when nitrogen is available, can yield *nonessential* amino acids	Yes
Lipids (fatty acids)	Yes	No	No	Yes
Lipids (glycerol)	Yes	Yes—when carbohydrate is unavailable	Yes—when nitrogen is available, can yield *nonessential* amino acids	Yes
Proteins (amino acids)	Yes	Yes—when carbohydrate is unavailable	Yes	Yes

[a]When energy intake exceeds needs, any of the energy-yielding nutrients can contribute to body fat stores.

The Final Steps of Catabolism

Thus far the discussion has followed each of the energy-yielding nutrients down three different pathways. All lead to the point where acetyl CoA enters the TCA cycle. The TCA cycle reactions take place in the inner compartment of the mitochondria. Examine the structure of the mitochondria shown in Figure 7-1 (p. 214). The significance of its structure will become evident as details unfold.

The TCA Cycle Acetyl CoA enters the TCA cycle, a busy metabolic traffic center. The TCA cycle is called a cycle, but that doesn't mean it regenerates acetyl CoA. Acetyl CoA goes one way only—down to two carbon dioxide molecules and a coenzyme (CoA). The TCA cycle is a circular path, though, in the sense that a 4-carbon compound known as **oxaloacetate** is needed in the first step and synthesized in the last step.

Oxaloacetate's role in replenishing the TCA cycle is critical. When oxaloacetate is insufficient, the TCA cycle slows down, and the cells face an energy crisis. Oxaloacetate is made primarily from pyruvate, although it can also be made from certain amino acids. Importantly, oxaloacetate cannot be made from fat. That oxaloacetate must be available for acetyl CoA to enter the TCA cycle underscores the importance of carbohydrates in the diet. A diet that provides ample carbohydrate ensures an adequate supply of oxaloacetate (because glucose produces pyruvate during glycolysis). (Highlight 9 presents more information on the consequences of low-carbohydrate diets.)

As Figure 7-18 shows, oxaloacetate is the first 4-carbon compound to enter the TCA cycle. Oxaloacetate picks up acetyl CoA (a 2-carbon compound), drops off one carbon (as carbon dioxide), then another carbon (as carbon dioxide), and returns to pick up another acetyl CoA. As for the acetyl CoA, its carbons go only one way—to carbon dioxide (see Appendix C for additional details).*

---

* Actually, the carbons that enter the cycle in acetyl CoA may not be the exact ones that are given off as carbon dioxide. In one of the steps of the cycle, a 6-carbon compound of the cycle becomes symmetrical, both ends being identical. Thereafter it loses carbons to carbon dioxide at one end or the other. Thus only half of the carbons from acetyl CoA are given off as carbon dioxide in any one turn of the cycle; the other half become part of the compound that returns to pick up another acetyl CoA. It is true to say, though, that for each acetyl CoA that enters the TCA cycle, 2 carbons are given off as carbon dioxide. It is also true that with each turn of the cycle, the energy equivalent of one acetyl CoA is released.

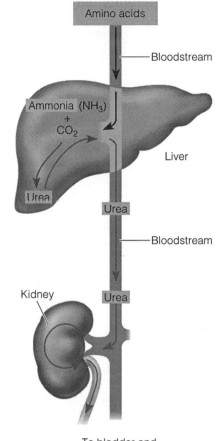

FIGURE 7-17 Urea Excretion

The liver and kidneys both play a role in disposing of excess nitrogen. Can you see why the person with liver disease has high blood ammonia, whereas the person with kidney disease has high blood urea? (Figure 12-2 provides details of how the kidneys work.)

Amino acids

Bloodstream

Ammonia (NH_3) + CO_2

Liver

Urea

Urea

Bloodstream

Kidney

Urea

To bladder and out of body

---

oxaloacetate (OKS-ah-low-AS-eh-tate): a carbohydrate intermediate of the TCA cycle.

FIGURE 7-18 *Animated!* The TCA Cycle

Oxaloacetate, a compound made primarily from pyruvate, starts the TCA cycle. The 4-carbon oxaloacetate joins with the 2-carbon acetyl CoA to make a 6-carbon compound. This compound is changed a little to make a new 6-carbon compound, which releases carbons as carbon dioxide, becoming a 5- and then a 4-carbon compound. Each reaction changes the structure slightly until finally the original 4-carbon oxaloacetate forms again and picks up another acetyl CoA—from the breakdown of glucose, glycerol, fatty acids, and amino acids—and starts the cycle over again. The breakdown of acetyl CoA releases hydrogens with their electrons, which are carried by coenzymes made from the B vitamins niacin and riboflavin to the electron transport chain. (For more details, see Appendix C.)

ThomsonNOW™
To test your understanding of these concepts, log on to www.thomsonedu.com/thomsonnow

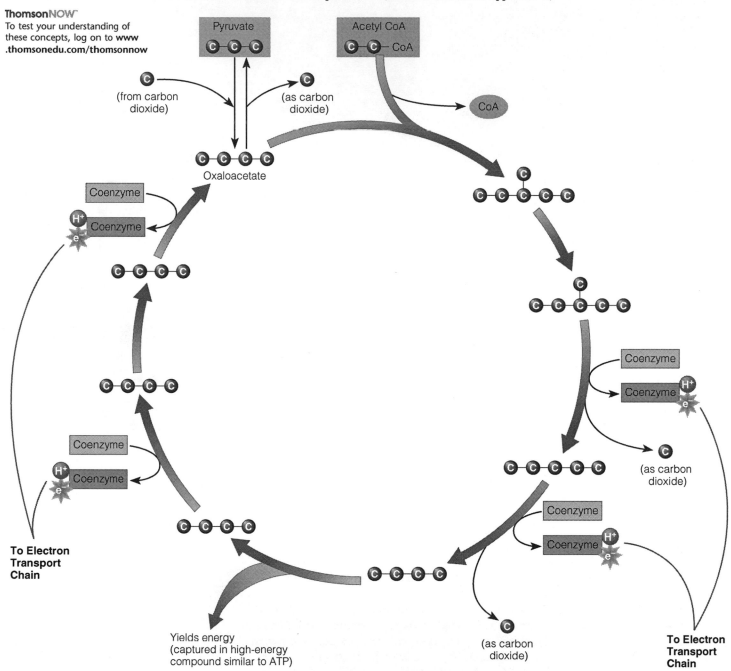

NOTE: Knowing that glucose produces pyruvate during glycolysis and that oxaloacetate must be available to start the TCA cycle, you can understand why the complete oxidation of fat requires carbohydrate.

As acetyl CoA molecules break down to carbon dioxide, hydrogen atoms with their electrons are removed from the compounds in the cycle. Each turn of the TCA cycle releases a total of eight electrons. Coenzymes made from the B vitamins niacin and riboflavin receive the hydrogens and their electrons from the TCA cycle and transfer them to the electron transport chain—much like a taxi cab that picks up passengers in one location and drops them off in another.

The Electron Transport Chain In the final pathway, the electron transport chain, energy is captured in the high-energy bonds of ATP. The electron transport chain consists of a series of proteins that serve as electron "carriers." These carriers are mounted in sequence on the inner membrane of the mitochondria (review Figure 7-1 on p. 214). As the coenzymes deliver their electrons from the TCA cycle, glycolysis, and fatty acid oxidation to the electron transport chain, each carrier receives the electrons and passes them on to the next carrier. These electron carriers continue passing the electrons down until they reach oxygen at the end of the chain. Oxygen (O) accepts the electrons and combines with hydrogen atoms (H) to form water (H_2O). ◆ That oxygen must be available for energy metabolism explains why it is essential to life.

As electrons are passed from carrier to carrier, enough energy is released to pump hydrogen ions across the membrane to the outer compartment of the mitochondria. The rush of hydrogen ions back into the inner compartment powers the synthesis of ATP. In this way, energy is captured in the bonds of ATP. The ATP leaves the mitochondria and enters the cytoplasm, where it can be used for energy. Figure 7-19 provides a simple diagram of the electron transport chain (see Appendix C for details).

The kCalories-per-Gram Secret Revealed Of the three energy-yielding nutrients, fat provides the most energy per gram. ◆ The reason may be apparent in Figure 7-20 (p. 230), which compares a fatty acid with a glucose molecule. Notice that nearly all the bonds in the fatty acid are between carbons and hydrogens. Oxygen can be added to all of them (forming carbon dioxide with the carbons and water with the hydrogens). As this happens, hydrogens are released to coenzymes heading

◆ The results of the electron transport chain:
- O_2 consumed
- H_2O and CO_2 produced
- Energy captured in ATP

◆ Fat = 9 kcal/g
Carbohydrate = 4 kcal/g
Protein = 4 kcal/g

FIGURE 7-19 *Animated!* Electron Transport Chain and ATP Synthesis

ThomsonNOW™
To test your understanding of these concepts, log on to **www**.thomsonedu.com/thomsonnow

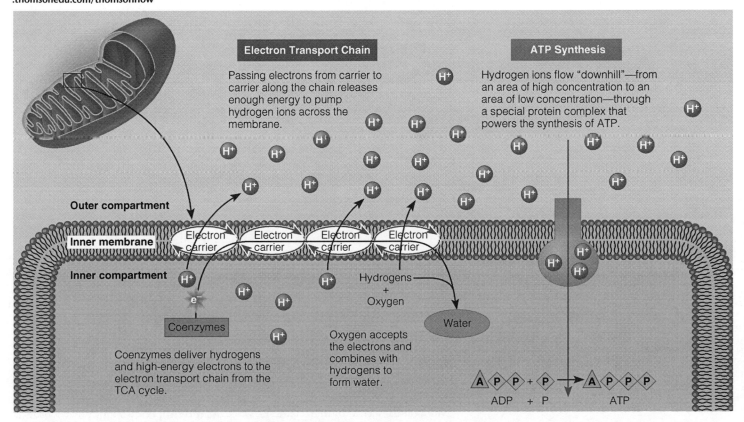

Electron Transport Chain

Passing electrons from carrier to carrier along the chain releases enough energy to pump hydrogen ions across the membrane.

ATP Synthesis

Hydrogen ions flow "downhill"—from an area of high concentration to an area of low concentration—through a special protein complex that powers the synthesis of ATP.

Outer compartment

Inner membrane — Electron carrier | Electron carrier | Electron carrier | Electron carrier

Inner compartment

Coenzymes deliver hydrogens and high-energy electrons to the electron transport chain from the TCA cycle.

Oxygen accepts the electrons and combines with hydrogens to form water.

Hydrogens + Oxygen → Water

ADP + P → ATP

FIGURE 7-20 Chemical Structures of a Fatty Acid and Glucose Compared

To ease comparison, the structure shown here for glucose is not the ring structure shown in Chapter 4, but an alternative way of drawing its chemical structure.

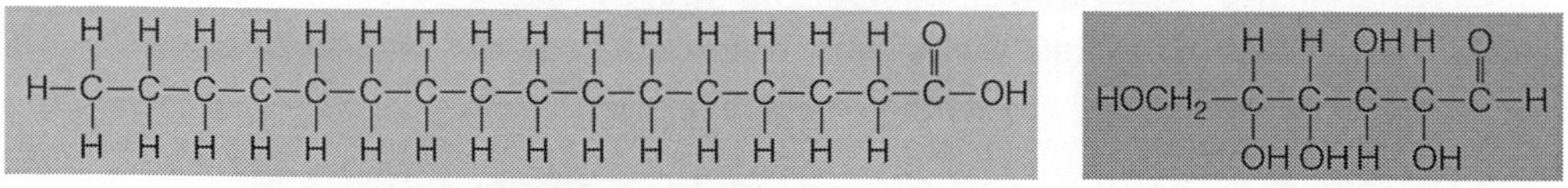

Fatty acid

Glucose

for the electron transport chain. In glucose, on the other hand, an oxygen is already bonded to each carbon. Thus there is less potential for oxidation, and fewer hydrogens are released when the remaining bonds are broken.

Because fat contains many carbon-hydrogen bonds that can be readily oxidized, it sends numerous coenzymes with their hydrogens and electrons to the electron transport chain where that energy can be captured in the bonds of ATP. This explains why fat yields more kcalories per gram than carbohydrate or protein. (Remember that each ATP holds energy and that kcalories measure energy; thus the more ATP generated, the more kcalories have been collected.) For example, one glucose molecule will yield 30 to 32 ATP when completely oxidized.[5] In comparison, one 16-carbon fatty acid molecule will yield 129 ATP when completely oxidized. Fat is a more efficient fuel source. Gram for gram, fat can provide much more energy than either of the other two energy-yielding nutrients, making it the body's preferred form of energy storage. (Similarly, you might prefer to fill your car with a fuel that provides 130 miles per gallon versus one that provides 30 miles per gallon.)

IN SUMMARY

After a balanced meal, the body handles the nutrients as follows. The digestion of carbohydrate yields glucose (and other monosaccharides); some is stored as glycogen, and some is broken down to pyruvate and acetyl CoA to provide energy. The acetyl CoA can then enter the TCA cycle and electron transport chain to provide more energy. The digestion of fat yields glycerol and fatty acids; some are reassembled and stored as fat, and others are broken down to acetyl CoA, which can enter the TCA cycle and electron transport chain to provide energy. The digestion of protein yields amino acids, most of which are used to build body protein or other nitrogen-containing compounds, but some amino acids may be broken down through the same pathways as glucose to provide energy. Other amino acids enter directly into the TCA cycle, and these, too, can be broken down to yield energy.

In summary, although carbohydrate, fat, and protein enter the TCA cycle by different routes, the final pathways are common to all energy-yielding nutrients. These pathways are all shown in Figure 7-21. Instead of dismissing this figure as "too busy," take a few moments to appreciate the busyness of it all. Consider that this figure is merely an overview of energy metabolism, and then imagine how busy a cell really is during the metabolism of hundreds of compounds, each of which may be involved in several reactions, each requiring an enzyme.

Energy Balance

Every day, a healthy diet delivers over a thousand kcalories from foods, and the active body uses most of them to do its work. As a result, body weight changes little, if at all. Maintaining body weight reflects that the body's energy budget is balanced.

FIGURE 7-21 The Central Pathways of Energy Metabolism

In reviewing these pathways, notice that:

- All of the energy-yielding nutrients—protein, carbohydrates, and fat—can be broken down to acetyl CoA, which can enter the TCA cycle.
- Many of these reactions release hydrogen atoms with their electrons, which are carried by coenzymes to the electron transport chain, where ATP is synthesized.
- In the end, oxygen is consumed, water and carbon dioxide are produced, and energy is captured in ATP.

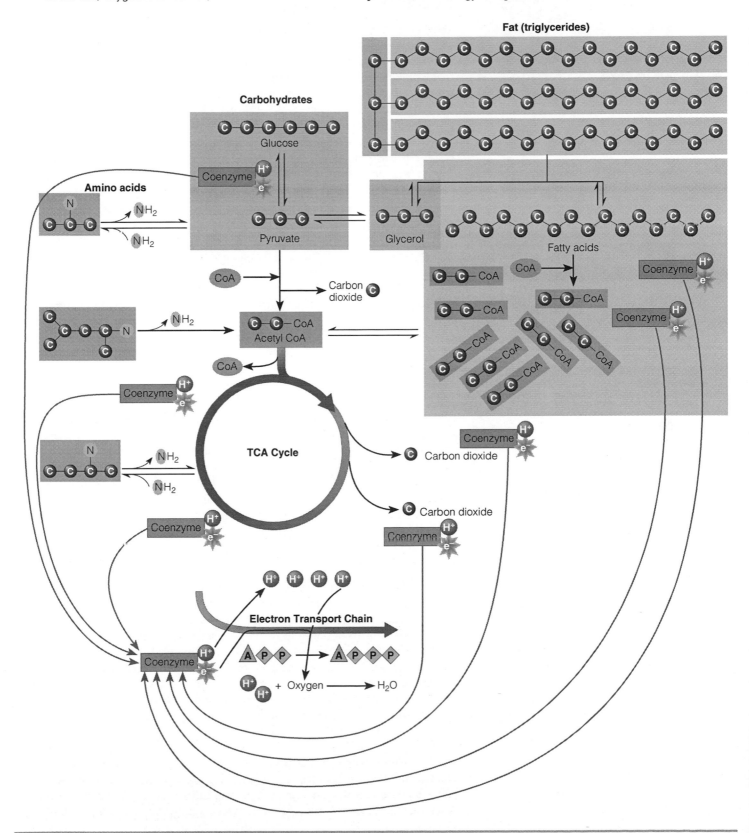

People can enjoy bountiful meals such as this without storing body fat, provided that they expend as much energy as they take in.

Some people, however, eat too much or exercise too little and get fat; others eat too little or exercise too much and get thin. The metabolic details have already been described; the next sections review them from the perspective of the body fat gained or lost. The possible reasons why people gain or lose weight are explored in Chapter 8.

Feasting—Excess Energy

When a person eats too much, metabolism favors fat formation. Fat cells enlarge regardless of whether the excess in kcalories derives from protein, carbohydrate, or fat. The pathway from dietary fat to body fat, however, is the most direct (requiring only a few metabolic steps) and the most efficient (costing only a few kcalories). To convert a dietary triglyceride to a triglyceride in adipose tissue, the body removes two of the fatty acids from the glycerol backbone, absorbs the parts, and puts them (and others) together again. By comparison, to convert a molecule of sucrose, the body has to split glucose from fructose, absorb them, dismantle them to pyruvate and acetyl CoA, assemble many acetyl CoA molecules into fatty acid chains, and finally attach fatty acids to a glycerol backbone to make a triglyceride for storage in adipose tissue. Quite simply, the body uses much less energy to convert dietary fat to body fat than it does to convert dietary carbohydrate to body fat. On average, storing excess energy from dietary fat as body fat uses only 5 percent of the ingested energy intake, but storing excess energy from dietary carbohydrate as body fat requires 25 percent of the ingested energy intake.

The pathways from excess protein and excess carbohydrate to body fat are not only indirect and inefficient, but they are also less preferred by the body (having other priorities for using these nutrients). Before entering fat storage, protein must first tend to its many roles in the body's lean tissues, and carbohydrate must fill the glycogen stores. Simply put, using these two nutrients to make fat is a low priority for the body. Still, if eaten in abundance, any of the energy-yielding nutrients can be made into fat.

This chapter has described each of the energy-yielding nutrients individually, but cells use a mixture of these fuels. How much of which nutrient is in the fuel mix depends, in part, on its availability from the diet. (The proportion of each fuel also depends on physical activity, as Chapter 14 explains.) Dietary protein and dietary carbohydrate influence the mixture of fuel used during energy metabolism. Usually, protein's contribution to the fuel mix is relatively minor and fairly constant, but protein oxidation does increase when protein is eaten in excess. Similarly, carbohydrate eaten in excess significantly enhances carbohydrate oxidation. In contrast, fat oxidation does *not* respond to dietary fat intake, especially when dietary changes occur abruptly. The more protein or carbohydrate in the fuel mix, the less fat contributes to the fuel mix. Instead of being oxidized, fat accumulates in storage. Details follow.

Excess Protein Recall from Chapter 6 that the body cannot store excess amino acids as such; it has to convert them to other compounds. Contrary to popular opinion, a person cannot grow muscle simply by overeating protein. Lean tissue such as muscle develops in response to a stimulus such as hormones or physical activity. When a person overeats protein, the body uses the surplus first by replacing normal daily losses and then by increasing protein oxidation. The body achieves protein balance this way, but any increase in protein oxidation displaces fat in the fuel mix. Any additional protein is then deaminated and the remaining carbons are used to make fatty acids, which are stored as triglycerides in adipose tissue. Thus a person can grow fat by eating too much protein.

People who eat huge portions of meat and other protein-rich foods may wonder why they have weight problems. Not only does the fat in those foods lead to fat storage, but the protein can, too, when energy intake exceeds energy needs. Many fad weight-loss diets encourage high protein intakes based on the false assumption that protein builds only muscle, not fat (see Highlight 9 for more details).

Excess Carbohydrate Compared with protein, the proportion of carbohydrate in the fuel mix changes more dramatically when a person overeats. The body handles abundant carbohydrate by first storing it as glycogen, but glycogen storage areas are limited and fill quickly. Because maintaining glucose balance is critical, the body uses glucose frugally when the diet provides only small amounts and freely when stores are abundant. In other words, glucose oxidation rapidly adjusts to the dietary intake of carbohydrate.

Excess glucose can also be converted to fat directly, but this is a minor pathway.[6] As mentioned earlier, converting glucose to fat is energetically expensive and does not occur until after glycogen stores have been filled. Even then, only a little, if any, new fat is made from carbohydrate.[7]

Nevertheless, excess dietary carbohydrate can lead to weight gain when it displaces fat in the fuel mix. When this occurs, carbohydrate spares both dietary fat and body fat from oxidation—an effect that may be more pronounced in overweight people than in lean people.[8] The net result: excess carbohydrate contributes to obesity or at least to the maintenance of an overweight body.

Excess Fat Unlike excess protein and carbohydrate, which both enhance their own oxidation, eating too much fat does not promote fat oxidation.[9] Instead, excess dietary fat moves efficiently into the body's fat stores; almost all of the excess is stored.

IN SUMMARY

If energy intake exceeds the body's energy needs, the result will be weight gain—regardless of whether the excess intake is from protein, carbohydrate, or fat. The difference is that the body is much more efficient at storing energy when the excess derives from dietary fat.

The Transition from Feasting to Fasting

Figure 7-22 (p. 234) shows the metabolic pathways operating in the body as it shifts from feasting (part A) to fasting (parts B and C). After a meal, glucose, glycerol, and fatty acids from foods are used as needed and then stored. Later, as the body shifts from a fed state to a fasting one, it begins drawing on these stores. Glycogen and fat are released from storage to provide more glucose, glycerol, and fatty acids for energy.

Energy is needed all the time. Even when a person is asleep and totally relaxed, the cells of many organs are hard at work. In fact, this work—the cells' work that maintains all life processes ◆ without any conscious effort—represents about two-thirds of the total energy a person spends in a day. The small remainder is the work that a person's muscles perform voluntarily during waking hours.

◆ The cells' work that maintains all life processes refers to the body's *basal metabolism,* which is described in Chapter 8.

The body's top priority is to meet the cells' needs for energy, and it normally does this by periodic refueling—that is, by eating several times a day. When food is not available, the body turns to its own tissues for other fuel sources. If people choose not to eat, we say they are fasting; if they have no choice, we say they are starving. The body makes no such distinction. In either case, the body is forced to draw on its reserves of carbohydrate and fat and, within a day or so, on its vital protein tissues as well.

Fasting—Inadequate Energy

During fasting, carbohydrate, fat, and protein are all eventually used for energy—fuel must be delivered to every cell. As the fast begins, glucose from the liver's stored glycogen and fatty acids from the adipose tissue's stored fat are both flowing into

FIGURE 7-22 Feasting and Fasting

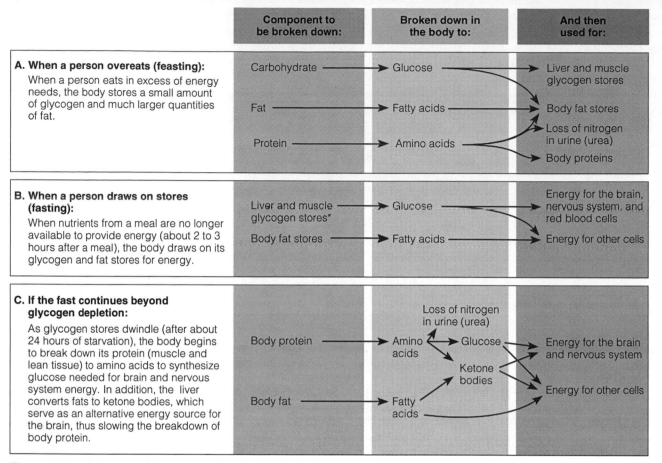

	Component to be broken down:	Broken down in the body to:	And then used for:

A. When a person overeats (feasting):
When a person eats in excess of energy needs, the body stores a small amount of glycogen and much larger quantities of fat.

Carbohydrate → Glucose → Liver and muscle glycogen stores
Fat → Fatty acids → Body fat stores
Protein → Amino acids → Loss of nitrogen in urine (urea)
Body proteins

B. When a person draws on stores (fasting):
When nutrients from a meal are no longer available to provide energy (about 2 to 3 hours after a meal), the body draws on its glycogen and fat stores for energy.

Liver and muscle glycogen stores* → Glucose → Energy for the brain, nervous system, and red blood cells
Body fat stores → Fatty acids → Energy for other cells

C. If the fast continues beyond glycogen depletion:
As glycogen stores dwindle (after about 24 hours of starvation), the body begins to break down its protein (muscle and lean tissue) to amino acids to synthesize glucose needed for brain and nervous system energy. In addition, the liver converts fats to ketone bodies, which serve as an alternative energy source for the brain, thus slowing the breakdown of body protein.

Body protein → Amino acids → Glucose → Loss of nitrogen in urine (urea)
Glucose → Energy for the brain and nervous system
Ketone bodies
Body fat → Fatty acids → Energy for other cells

*The muscles' stored glycogen provides glucose only for the muscle in which the glycogen is stored.

---

cells, then breaking down to yield acetyl CoA, and finally delivering energy to power the cells' work. Several hours later, however, most of the glucose is used up—liver glycogen is exhausted and blood glucose begins to fall. Low blood glucose serves as a signal that promotes further fat breakdown and release of amino acids from muscles.

Glucose Needed for the Brain At this point, most of the cells are depending on fatty acids to continue providing their fuel. But red blood cells and the cells of the nervous system need glucose. Glucose is their primary energy fuel, and even when other energy fuels are available, glucose must be present to permit the energy-metabolizing machinery of the nervous system to work. Normally, the brain and nerve cells—which weigh only about three pounds—consume about half of the to-tal *glucose* used each day (about 500 kcalories' worth). About one-fourth of the *energy* the adult body uses when it is at rest is spent by the brain; in children, it can be up to one-half.

Protein Meets Glucose Needs The red blood cells' and brain's special require-ments for glucose pose a problem for the fasting body. The body can use its stores of fat, which may be quite generous, to furnish most of its cells with energy, but the red blood cells are completely dependent on glucose, ◆ and the brain and nerves prefer energy in the form of glucose. Amino acids that yield pyruvate can be used to make glucose, and to obtain the amino acids, body proteins must be broken down. For this reason, body protein tissues such as muscle and liver always break down to some ex-tent during fasting. The amino acids that can't be used to make glucose are used as an energy source for other body cells.

The breakdown of body protein is an expensive way to obtain glucose. In the first few days of a fast, body protein provides about 90 percent of the needed glu-

◆ Red blood cells contain no mitochondria. Review Figure 7-1 (p. 214) to fully appreciate why red blood cells must depend on glucose for energy.

cose; glycerol, about 10 percent. If body protein losses were to continue at this rate, death would ensue within three weeks, regardless of the quantity of fat a person had stored. Fortunately, fat breakdown also increases with fasting—in fact, fat breakdown almost doubles, providing energy for other body cells and glycerol for glucose production.

The Shift to Ketosis As the fast continues, the body finds a way to use its fat to fuel the brain. It adapts by combining acetyl CoA fragments derived from fatty acids to produce an alternate energy source, ketone bodies (Figure 7-23). Normally produced and used only in small quantities, ketone bodies ◆ can provide fuel for some brain cells. Ketone body production rises until, after about ten days of fasting, it is meeting much of the nervous system's energy needs. Still, many areas of the brain rely exclusively on glucose, and to produce it, the body continues to sacrifice protein—albeit at a slower rate than in the early days of fasting.

When ketone bodies contain an acid group (COOH), they are called keto acids. Small amounts of keto acids are a normal part of the blood chemistry, but when their concentration rises, the pH of the blood drops. This is ketosis, a sign that the body's chemistry is going awry. Elevated blood ketones (ketonemia) are excreted in the urine (ketonuria). A fruity odor on the breath (known as acetone breath) develops, reflecting the presence of the ketone acetone.

Suppression of Appetite Ketosis also induces a loss of appetite. As starvation continues, this loss of appetite becomes an advantage to a person without access to food, because the search for food would be a waste of energy. When the person finds food and eats again, the body shifts out of ketosis, the hunger center gets the message that food is again available, and the appetite returns. Highlight 9 includes a discussion of the risks of ketosis-producing diets in its review of popular weight-loss diets.

Slowing of Metabolism In an effort to conserve body tissues for as long as possible, the hormones of fasting slow metabolism. As the body shifts to the use of ketone bodies, it simultaneously reduces its energy output and conserves both its fat and its lean tissue. Still the lean (protein-containing) organ tissues shrink in mass and perform less metabolic work, reducing energy expenditures. As the muscles waste, they can do less work and so demand less energy, reducing expenditures further. Although fasting may promote dramatic *weight* loss, a low-kcalorie diet better supports *fat* loss while retaining lean tissue.

◆ Reminder: *Ketone bodies* are compounds produced during the incomplete breakdown of fat when glucose is not available.

FIGURE 7-23 Ketone Body Formation

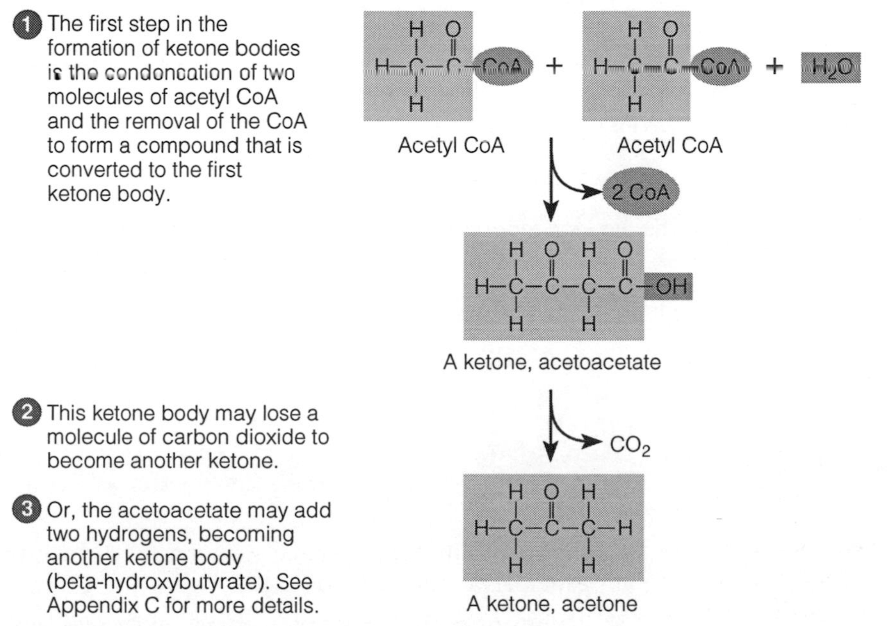

1 The first step in the formation of ketone bodies is the condensation of two molecules of acetyl CoA and the removal of the CoA to form a compound that is converted to the first ketone body.

Acetyl CoA + Acetyl CoA + H₂O → A ketone, acetoacetate (2 CoA)

2 This ketone body may lose a molecule of carbon dioxide to become another ketone.

3 Or, the acetoacetate may add two hydrogens, becoming another ketone body (beta-hydroxybutyrate). See Appendix C for more details.

A ketone, acetone

Symptoms of Starvation The adaptations just described—slowing of energy output and reduction in fat loss—occur in the starving child, the hungry homeless adult, the fasting religious person, the adolescent with anorexia nervosa, and the malnourished hospital patient. Such adaptations help to prolong their lives and explain the physical symptoms of starvation: wasting; slowed heart rate, respiration, and metabolism; lowered body temperature; impaired vision; organ failure; and reduced resistance to disease.[10] Psychological effects of food deprivation include depression, anxiety, and food-related dreams.

The body's adaptations to fasting are sufficient to maintain life for a long time—up to two months. Mental alertness need not be diminished, and even some physical energy may remain unimpaired for a surprisingly long time. These remarkable adaptations, however, should not prevent anyone from recognizing the very real hazards that fasting presents.

IN SUMMARY

When fasting, the body makes a number of adaptations: increasing the breakdown of fat to provide energy for most of the cells, using glycerol and amino acids to make glucose for the red blood cells and central nervous system, producing ketones to fuel the brain, suppressing the appetite, and slowing metabolism. All of these measures conserve energy and minimize losses.

This chapter has probed the intricate details of metabolism at the level of the cells, exploring the transformations of nutrients to energy and to storage compounds. Several chapters and highlights build on this information. The highlight that follows this chapter shows how alcohol disrupts normal metabolism. Chapter 8 describes how a person's intake and expenditure of energy are reflected in body weight and body composition. Chapter 9 examines the consequences of unbalanced energy budgets—overweight and underweight. Chapter 10 shows the vital roles the B vitamins play as coenzymes assisting all the metabolic pathways described here. And Chapter 14 revisits metabolism to show how it supports the work of physically active people and how athletes can best apply that information in their choices of foods to eat.

ThomsonNOW™
www.thomsonedu.com/thomsonnow

Nutrition Portfolio

All day, every day, your cells dismantle carbohydrates, fats, and proteins, with the help of vitamins, minerals, and water, releasing energy to meet your body's immediate needs or storing it as fat for later use.

- Describe what types of foods best support aerobic and anaerobic activities.

- Consider whether you eat more protein, carbohydrate, or fat than your body needs.

- Explain how a low-carbohydrate diet forces your body into ketosis.

STUDY QUESTIONS

ThomsonNOW™
To assess your understanding of chapter topics, take the Student Practice Test and explore the modules recommended in your Personalized Study Plan. Log onto www.thomsonedu.com/thomsonnow.

These questions will help you review the chapter. You will find the answers in the discussions on the pages provided.

1. Define metabolism, anabolism, and catabolism; give an example of each. (pp. 213–216)

2. Name one of the body's high-energy molecules, and describe how it is used. (pp. 216–217)

3. What are coenzymes, and what service do they provide in metabolism? (p. 216)

4. Name the four basic units, derived from foods, that are used by the body in metabolic transformations. How many carbons are in the "backbones" of each? (pp. 217–218)

5. Define aerobic and anaerobic metabolism. How does insufficient oxygen influence metabolism? (pp. 220–221)

6. How does the body dispose of excess nitrogen? (pp. 225–227)

7. Summarize the main steps in the metabolism of glucose, glycerol, fatty acids, and amino acids. (pp. 226–228)

8. Describe how a surplus of the three energy nutrients contributes to body fat stores. (pp. 219–226)

9. What adaptations does the body make during a fast? What are ketone bodies? Define ketosis. (pp. 233–236)

10. Distinguish between a loss of *fat* and a loss of *weight,* and describe how each might happen. (pp. 235–236)

These multiple choice questions will help you prepare for an exam. Answers can be found below.

1. Hydrolysis is an example of a(n):
   a. coupled reaction.
   b. anabolic reaction.
   c. catabolic reaction.
   d. synthesis reaction.

2. During metabolism, released energy is captured and transferred by:
   a. enzymes.
   b. pyruvate.
   c. acetyl CoA.
   d. adenosine triphosphate.

3. Glycolysis:
   a. requires oxygen.
   b. generates abundant energy.
   c. converts glucose to pyruvate.
   d. produces ammonia as a by-product.

4. The pathway from pyruvate to acetyl CoA:
   a. produces lactate.
   b. is known as gluconeogenesis.
   c. is metabolically irreversible.
   d. requires more energy than it produces.

5. For complete oxidation, acetyl CoA enters:
   a. glycolysis.
   b. the TCA cycle.
   c. the Cori cycle.
   d. the electron transport chain.

6. Deamination of an amino acid produces:
   a. vitamin B_6 and energy.
   b. pyruvate and acetyl CoA.
   c. ammonia and a keto acid.
   d. carbon dioxide and water.

7. Before entering the TCA cycle, each of the energy-yielding nutrients is broken down to:
   a. ammonia.
   b. pyruvate.
   c. electrons.
   d. acetyl CoA.

8. The body stores energy for future use in:
   a. proteins.
   b. acetyl CoA.
   c. triglycerides.
   d. ketone bodies.

9. During a fast, when glycogen stores have been depleted, the body begins to synthesize glucose from:
   a. acetyl CoA.
   b. amino acids.
   c. fatty acids.
   d. ketone bodies.

10. During a fast, the body produces ketone bodies by:
    a. hydrolyzing glycogen.
    b. condensing acetyl CoA.
    c. transaminating keto acids.
    d. converting ammonia to urea.

REFERENCES

1. R. H. Garrett and C. M. Grisham, *Biochemistry* (Belmont, Calif.: Thomson Brooks/Cole, 2005), p. 73.
2. R. A. Robergs, F. Ghiasvand, and D. Parker, Biochemistry of exercise-induced metabolic acidosis, *American Journal of Physiology-Regulatory, Integrative and Comparative Physiology* 287 (2004): R502-R516.
3. T. H. Pederson and coauthors, Intracellular acidosis enhances the excitability of working muscle, *Science* 305 (2004): 1144-1147.
4. S. S. Gropper, J. L. Smith, and J. L. Groff, *Advanced Nutrition and Human Metabolism* (Belmont, Calif.: Wadsworth/Thomson Learning, 2005), p. 198.

5. Garrett and Grisham, 2005, p. 669.
6. M. K. Hellerstein, No common energy currency: De novo lipogenesis as the road less traveled, *American Journal of Clinical Nutrition* 74 (2001): 707-708.
7. R. M. Devitt and coauthors, De novo lipogenesis during controlled overfeeding with sucrose or glucose in lean and obese women, *American Journal of Clinical Nutrition* 74 (2001): 707-708.
8. I. Marques-Lopes and coauthors, Postprandial de novo lipogenesis and metabolic changes induced by a high-carbohydrate, low-fat meal in lean and overweight men,

American Journal of Clinical Nutrition 73 (2001): 253-261.
9. E. J. Parks, Macronutrient Metabolism Group Symposium on "Dietary fat: How low should we go?" Changes in fat synthesis influenced by dietary macronutrient content, *Proceedings of the Nutrition Society* 61 (2002): 281-286.
10. C. A. Jolly, Dietary restriction and immune function, *Journal of Nutrition* 134 (2004): 1853-1856.

ANSWERS

Study Questions (multiple choice)

1. c   2. d   3. c   4. c   5. b   6. c   7. d   8. c
9. b   10. b

Alcohol and Nutrition

Richard Dunkley/Getty Images

With the understanding of metabolism gained from Chapter 7, you are in a position to understand how the body handles alcohol, how alcohol interferes with metabolism, and how alcohol impairs health and nutrition. Before examining alcohol's damaging effects, it may be appropriate to mention that drinking alcohol in *moderation* may have some health benefits, including reduced risks of heart attacks, strokes, dementia, diabetes, and osteoporosis.[1] Moderate alcohol consumption may lower mortality from all causes, but only in adults age 35 and older.[2] No health benefits are evident before middle age.[3] Importantly, any benefits of alcohol must be weighed against the many harmful effects described in this highlight, as well as the possibility of alcohol abuse.

Alcohol in Beverages

To the chemist, **alcohol** refers to a class of organic compounds containing hydroxyl (OH) groups (the accompanying glossary defines alcohol and related terms). The glycerol to which fatty acids are attached in triglycerides is an example of an alcohol to a chemist. To most people, though, *alcohol* refers to the intoxicating ingredient in **beer, wine,** and **distilled liquor (hard liquor).** The chemist's name for this particular alcohol is *ethyl alcohol,* or **ethanol.** Glycerol has 3 carbons with 3 hydroxyl groups attached; ethanol has only 2 carbons and 1 hydroxyl group (see Figure H7-1). The remainder of this highlight talks about the particular alcohol, ethanol, but refers to it simply as *alcohol.*

Alcohols affect living things profoundly, partly because they act as lipid solvents. Their ability to dissolve lipids out of cell membranes allows alcohols to penetrate rapidly into cells, destroying cell structures and thereby killing the cells. For this reason, most alcohols are toxic in relatively small amounts; by the same token, because they kill microbial cells, they are useful as disinfectants.

Ethanol is less toxic than the other alcohols. Sufficiently diluted and taken in small enough doses, its action in the brain produces an effect that people seek—not with zero risk, but with a low enough risk (if the doses are low enough) to be tolerable. Used in this way, alcohol is a **drug**—that is, a substance that modifies body functions. Like all drugs, alcohol both offers benefits and poses hazards. The 2005 *Dietary Guidelines* advise "those who choose to drink alcoholic beverages to do so sensibly and in moderation."

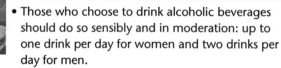

Dietary Guidelines for Americans 2005

- Those who choose to drink alcoholic beverages should do so sensibly and in moderation: up to one drink per day for women and two drinks per day for men.

- Alcoholic beverages should not be consumed by some individuals, including those who cannot restrict their alcohol intake, women of childbearing age who may become pregnant, pregnant and lactating women, children and adolescents, individuals taking medications that can interact with alcohol, and those with specific medical conditions.

- Alcoholic beverages should be avoided by individuals engaging in activities that require attention, skill, or coordination, such as driving or operating machinery.

The term **moderation** is important when describing alcohol use. How many drinks constitute moderate use, and how much is "a drink"? First, a **drink** is any alcoholic beverage that delivers $1/2$ ounce of *pure ethanol:*

- 5 ounces of wine
- 10 ounces of wine cooler
- 12 ounces of beer
- $1^1/2$ ounces of distilled liquor (80 proof whiskey, scotch, rum, or vodka)

Beer, wine, and liquor deliver different amounts of alcohol. The amount of alcohol in distilled liquor is stated as **proof:** 100 proof liquor is 50 percent alcohol, 80 proof is 40 percent alcohol, and so forth. Wine and beer have less alcohol than distilled liquor, although some fortified wines and beers have more alcohol than the regular varieties (see photo caption on p. 239).

FIGURE H7-1	Two Alcohols: Glycerol and Ethanol

Glycerol is the alcohol used to make triglycerides.

Ethanol is the alcohol in beer, wine, and distilled liquor.

GLOSSARY

acetaldehyde (ass-et-AL-duh-hide): an intermediate in alcohol metabolism.

alcohol: a class of organic compounds containing hydroxyl (OH) groups.

alcohol abuse: a pattern of drinking that includes failure to fulfill work, school, or home responsibilities; drinking in situations that are physically dangerous (as in driving while intoxicated); recurring alcohol-related legal problems (as in aggravated assault charges); or continued drinking despite ongoing social problems that are caused by or worsened by alcohol.

alcohol dehydrogenase (dee-high-DROJ-eh-nayz): an enzyme active in the stomach and the liver that converts ethanol to acetaldehyde.

alcoholism: a pattern of drinking that includes a strong craving for alcohol, a loss of control and an inability to stop drinking once begun, withdrawal symptoms (nausea, sweating, shakiness, and anxiety) after heavy drinking, and the need for increasing amounts of alcohol to feel "high."

antidiuretic hormone (ADH): a hormone produced by the pituitary gland in response to dehydration (or a high sodium concentration in the blood). It stimulates the kidneys to reabsorb more water and therefore prevents water loss in urine (also called *vasopressin*). (This ADH should not be confused with the enzyme alcohol dehydrogenase, which is also sometimes abbreviated ADH.)

beer: an alcoholic beverage brewed by fermenting malt and hops.

cirrhosis (seer-OH-sis): advanced liver disease in which liver cells turn orange, die, and harden, permanently losing their function; often associated with alcoholism.

• **cirrhos** = an orange

distilled liquor or **hard liquor:** an alcoholic beverage made by fermenting and distilling grains; sometimes called *distilled spirits*.

drink: a dose of any alcoholic beverage that delivers ½ oz of pure ethanol:
• 5 oz of wine
• 10 oz of wine cooler
• 12 oz of beer

• 1½ oz of hard liquor (80 proof whiskey, scotch, rum, or vodka)

drug: a substance that can modify one or more of the body's functions.

ethanol: a particular type of alcohol found in beer, wine, and distilled liquor; also called *ethyl alcohol* (see Figure H7-1). Ethanol is the most widely used—and abused—drug in our society. It is also the only legal, nonprescription drug that produces euphoria.

fatty liver: an early stage of liver deterioration seen in several diseases, including kwashiorkor and alcoholic liver disease. Fatty liver is characterized by an accumulation of fat in the liver cells.

fibrosis (fye-BROH-sis): an intermediate stage of liver deterioration seen in several diseases, including viral hepatitis and alcoholic liver disease. In fibrosis, the liver cells lose their function and assume the characteristics of connective tissue cells (fibers).

MEOS or **microsomal** (my-krow-SO-mal) **ethanol-oxidizing system:** a system of enzymes in the liver that oxidize not only alcohol but also several classes of drugs.

moderation: in relation to alcohol consumption, not more than two drinks a day for the average-size man and not more than one drink a day for the average-size woman.

NAD (nicotinamide adenine dinucleotide): the main coenzyme form of the vitamin niacin. Its reduced form is NADH.

narcotic (nar-KOT-ic): a drug that dulls the senses, induces sleep, and becomes addictive with prolonged use.

proof: a way of stating the percentage of alcohol in distilled liquor. Liquor that is 100 proof is 50% alcohol; 90 proof is 45%, and so forth.

Wernicke-Korsakoff (VER-nee-key KORE-sah-kof) **syndrome:** a neurological disorder typically associated with chronic alcoholism and caused by a deficiency of the B vitamin thiamin; also called *alcohol-related dementia*.

wine: an alcoholic beverage made by fermenting grape juice.

Each of these servings equals one drink.

Wines contain 7 to 24 percent alcohol by volume; those containing 14 percent or more must state their alcohol content on the label, whereas those with less than 14 percent may simply state "table wine" or "light wine." Beers typically contain less than 5 percent alcohol by volume and malt liquors, 5 to 8 percent; regulations vary, with some states requiring beer labels to show the alcohol content and others prohibiting such statements.

Second, because people have different tolerances for alcohol, it is impossible to name an exact daily amount of alcohol that is appropriate for everyone. Authorities have attempted to identify amounts that are acceptable for most healthy people. An accepted definition of moderation is up to two drinks per day for men and up to one

drink per day for women. (Pregnant women are advised to abstain from alcohol, as Highlight 15 explains.) Notice that this advice is stated as a maximum, not as an average; seven drinks one night a week would not be considered moderate, even though one a day would be. Doubtless some people could consume slightly more; others could not handle nearly so much without risk. The amount a person can drink safely is highly individual, depending on genetics, health, gender, body composition, age, and family history.

Alcohol in the Body

From the moment an alcoholic beverage enters the body, alcohol is treated as if it has special privileges. Unlike foods, which require time for digestion, alcohol needs no digestion and is quickly absorbed across the walls of an empty stomach, reaching the brain within a few minutes. Consequently, a person can immediately feel euphoric when drinking, especially on an empty stomach.

When the stomach is full of food, alcohol has less chance of touching the walls and diffusing through, so its influence on the brain is slightly delayed. This information leads to a practical tip: eat snacks when drinking alcoholic beverages. Carbohydrate snacks slow alcohol absorption and high-fat snacks slow peristalsis, keeping the alcohol in the stomach longer. Salty snacks make a person thirsty; to quench thirst, drink water instead of more alcohol.

The stomach begins to break down alcohol with its **alcohol dehydrogenase** enzyme. Women produce less of this stomach enzyme than men; consequently, more alcohol reaches the intestine for absorption into the bloodstream. As a result, women absorb more alcohol than men of the same size who drink the same amount of alcohol. Consequently, they are more likely to become more intoxicated on less alcohol than men. Such differences between men and women help explain why women have a lower alcohol tolerance and a lower recommendation for moderate intake.

In the small intestine, alcohol is rapidly absorbed. From this point on, alcohol receives priority treatment: it gets absorbed and metabolized before most nutrients. Alcohol's priority status helps to ensure a speedy disposal and reflects two facts: alcohol cannot be stored in the body, and it is potentially toxic.

Alcohol Arrives in the Liver

The capillaries of the digestive tract merge into veins that carry the alcohol-laden blood to the liver. These veins branch and rebranch into capillaries that touch every liver cell. Liver cells are the only other cells in the body that can make enough of the alcohol dehydrogenase enzyme to oxidize alcohol at an appreciable rate. The routing of blood through the liver cells gives them the chance to dispose of some alcohol before it moves on.

Alcohol affects every organ of the body, but the most dramatic evidence of its disruptive behavior appears in the liver. If liver cells could talk, they would describe alcohol as demanding, egocentric, and disruptive of the liver's efficient way of running its business. For example, liver cells normally prefer fatty acids as their fuel, and they like to package excess fatty acids into triglycerides and ship them out to other tissues. When alcohol is present, however, the liver cells are forced to metabolize alcohol and let the fatty acids accumulate, sometimes in huge stockpiles. Alcohol metabolism can also permanently change liver cell structure, impairing the liver's ability to metabolize fats. As a result, heavy drinkers develop fatty livers.

The liver is the primary site of alcohol metabolism.[4] It can process about 1/2 ounce of *ethanol* per hour (the amount in a typical drink), depending on the person's body size, previous drinking experience, food intake, and general health. This maximum rate of alcohol breakdown is set by the amount of alcohol dehydrogenase available. If more alcohol arrives at the liver than the enzymes can handle, the extra alcohol travels to all parts of the body, circulating again and again until liver enzymes are finally available to process it. Another practical tip derives from this information: drink slowly enough to allow the liver to keep up—no more than one drink per hour.

The amount of alcohol dehydrogenase enzyme present in the liver varies with individuals, depending on the genes they have inherited and on how recently they have eaten. Fasting for as little as a day forces the body to degrade its proteins, including the alcohol-processing enzymes, and this can slow the rate of alcohol metabolism by half. Drinking after not eating all day thus causes the drinker to feel the effects more promptly for two reasons: rapid absorption and slowed breakdown. By maintaining higher blood alcohol concentrations for longer times, alcohol can anesthetize the brain more completely (as described later in this highlight).

The alcohol dehydrogenase enzyme breaks down alcohol by removing hydrogens in two steps. (Figure H7-2 provides a simplified diagram of alcohol metabolism; Appendix C provides the chemical details.) In the first step, alcohol dehydrogenase oxidizes alcohol to **acetaldehyde.** High concentrations of acetaldehyde in the brain and other tissues are responsible for many of the damaging effects of **alcohol abuse.**

FIGURE H7-2 Alcohol Metabolism

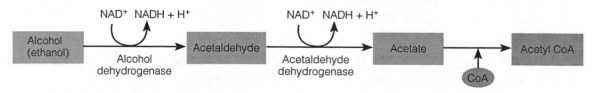

The conversion of alcohol to acetyl CoA requires the B vitamin niacin in its role as the coenzyme NAD. When the enzymes oxidize alcohol, they remove H atoms and attach them to NAD. Thus NAD is used up and NADH accumulates. (Note: More accurately, NAD+ is converted to NADH + H+.)

FIGURE H7-3 Alternate Route for Acetyl CoA: To Fat

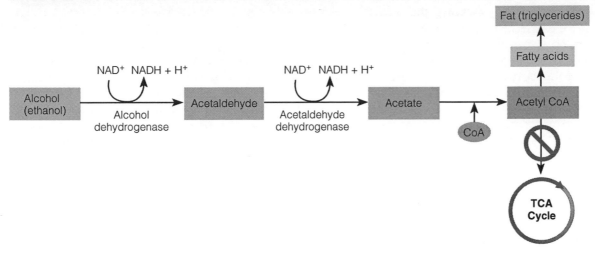

Acetyl CoA molecules are blocked from getting into the TCA cycle by the high level of NADH. Instead of being used for energy, the acetyl CoA molecules become building blocks for fatty acids.

In the second step, a related enzyme, acetaldehyde dehydrogenase, converts acetaldehyde to acetate, which is then converted to acetyl CoA—the "crossroads" compound introduced in Chapter 7 that can enter the TCA cycle to generate energy. These reactions produce hydrogen ions (H+). The B vitamin niacin, in its role as the coenzyme **NAD (nicotinamide adenine dinucleotide),** helpfully picks up these hydrogen ions (becoming NADH). Thus, whenever the body breaks down alcohol, NAD diminishes and NADH accumulates. (Chapter 10 presents information on NAD and the other coenzyme roles of the B vitamins.)

Alcohol Disrupts the Liver

During alcohol metabolism, the multitude of other metabolic processes for which NAD is required, including glycolysis, the TCA cycle, and the electron transport chain, falter. Its presence is sorely missed in these energy pathways because it is the chief carrier of the hydrogens that travel with their electrons along the electron transport chain. Without adequate NAD, these energy pathways cannot function. Traffic either backs up, or an alternate route is taken. Such changes in the normal flow of energy pathways have striking physical consequences.

For one, the accumulation of hydrogen ions during alcohol metabolism shifts the body's acid-base balance toward acid. For another, the accumulation of NADH slows the TCA cycle, so pyruvate and acetyl CoA build up. Excess acetyl CoA then takes the route to fatty acid synthesis (as Figure H7-3 illustrates), and fat clogs the liver.

As you might expect, a liver overburdened with fat cannot function properly. Liver cells become less efficient at performing a number of tasks. Much of this inefficiency impairs a person's nutritional health in ways that cannot be corrected by diet alone. For example, the liver has difficulty activating vitamin D, as well as producing and releasing bile. To overcome such problems, a person needs to stop drinking alcohol.

The synthesis of fatty acids accelerates with exposure to alcohol. Fat accumulation can be seen in the liver after a single night of heavy drinking. **Fatty liver,** the first stage of liver deterioration seen in heavy drinkers, interferes with the distribution of nutrients and oxygen to the liver cells. Fatty liver is reversible with abstinence from alcohol. If fatty liver lasts long enough, however, the liver cells will die and form fibrous scar tissue. This second stage of liver deterioration is called **fibrosis.** Some liver cells can regenerate with good nutrition and abstinence from alcohol, but in the most advanced stage, **cirrhosis,** damage is the least reversible.

The fatty liver has difficulty generating glucose from protein. Without gluconeogenesis, blood glucose can plummet, leading to irreversible damage to the central nervous system.

The lack of glucose together with the overabundance of acetyl CoA sets the stage for ketosis. The body uses the acetyl CoA to make ketone bodies; their acidity pushes the acid-base balance further toward acid and suppresses nervous system activity.

Excess NADH also promotes the making of lactate from pyruvate. The conversion of pyruvate to lactate uses the hydrogens from NADH and restores some NAD, but a lactate buildup has serious consequences of its own—it adds still further to the body's acid burden and interferes with the excretion of another acid, uric acid, causing inflammation of the joints.

Alcohol alters both amino acid and protein metabolism. Synthesis of proteins important in the immune system slows down, weakening the body's defenses against infection. Protein deficiency can develop, both from a diminished synthesis of protein and from a poor diet. Normally, the cells would at least use the amino acids from the protein foods a person eats, but the drinker's liver deaminates the amino acids and uses the carbon fragments primarily to make fat or ketones. Eating well does not protect the drinker from protein depletion; a person has to stop drinking alcohol.

The liver's priority treatment of alcohol affects its handling of drugs as well as nutrients. In addition to the dehydrogenase enzyme already described, the liver possesses an enzyme system that metabolizes *both* alcohol and several other types of drugs. Called the **MEOS (microsomal ethanol-oxidizing system)**, this system handles about one-fifth of the total alcohol a person consumes. At high blood concentrations or with repeated exposures, alcohol stimulates the synthesis of enzymes in the MEOS. The result is a more efficient metabolism of alcohol and tolerance to its effects.

As a person's blood alcohol rises, alcohol competes with—and wins out over—other drugs whose metabolism also relies on the MEOS. If a person drinks and uses another drug at the same time, the MEOS will dispose of alcohol first and metabolize the drug more slowly. While the drug waits to be handled later, the dose may build up so that its effects are greatly amplified—sometimes to the point of being fatal.

In contrast, once a heavy drinker stops drinking and alcohol is no longer competing with other drugs, the enhanced MEOS metabolizes drugs much faster than before. As a result, determining the correct dosages of medications can be challenging.

This discussion has emphasized the major way that the blood is cleared of alcohol—metabolism by the liver—but there is another way. About 10 percent of the alcohol leaves the body through the breath and in the urine. This is the basis for the breath and urine tests for drunkenness. The amounts of alcohol in the breath and in the urine are in proportion to the amount still in the bloodstream and brain. In nearly all states, legal drunkenness is set at 0.10 percent or less, reflecting the relationship between alcohol use and traffic and other accidents.

Alcohol Arrives in the Brain

Alcohol is a **narcotic.** People used it for centuries as an anesthetic because it can deaden pain. But alcohol was a poor anesthetic because one could never be sure how much a person would need and how much would be a fatal dose. Consequently, new, more predictable anesthetics have replaced alcohol. Nonetheless, alcohol continues to be used today as a kind of social anesthetic to help people relax or to relieve anxiety. People think that alcohol is a stimulant because it seems to relieve inhibitions. Actually, though, it accomplishes this by sedating *inhibitory* nerves, which are more numerous than excitatory nerves. Ultimately, alcohol acts as a depressant and affects all the nerve cells. Figure H7-4 describes alcohol's effects on the brain.

It is lucky that the brain centers respond to a rising blood alcohol concentration in the order described in Figure H7-4 because a person usually passes out before managing to drink a lethal dose. It is possible, though, to drink so fast that the effects of alcohol continue to accelerate after the person has passed out. Occasionally, a person dies from drinking enough to stop the heart before passing out. Table H7-1 shows the blood alcohol levels that correspond to progressively greater intoxication, and Table H7-2 shows the brain responses that occur at these blood levels.

Like liver cells, brain cells die with excessive exposure to alcohol. Liver cells may be replaced, but not all brain cells can regenerate. Thus some heavy drinkers suffer permanent brain damage.

FIGURE H7-4 Alcohol's Effects on the Brain

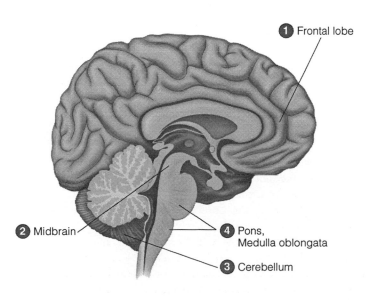

① Frontal lobe
② Midbrain
③ Cerebellum
④ Pons, Medulla oblongata

① Judgment and reasoning centers are most sensitive to alcohol. When alcohol flows to the brain, it first sedates the frontal lobe, the center of all conscious activity. As the alcohol molecules diffuse into the cells of these lobes, they interfere with reasoning and judgment.

② Speech and vision centers in the midbrain are affected next. If the drinker drinks faster than the rate at which the liver can oxidize the alcohol, blood alcohol concentrations rise: the speech and vision centers of the brain become sedated.

③ Voluntary muscular control is then affected. At still higher concentrations, the cells in the cerebellum responsible for coordination of voluntary muscles are affected, including those used in speech, eye-hand coordination, and limb movements. At this point people under the influence stagger or weave when they try to walk, or they may slur their speech.

④ Respiration and heart action are the last to be affected. Finally, the conscious brain is completely subdued, and the person passes out. Now the person can drink no more; this is fortunate because higher doses would anesthetize the deepest brain centers that control breathing and heartbeat, causing death.

TABLE H7-1	Alcohol Doses and Approximate Blood Level Percentages for Men and Women

Drinks[a] — **Body Weight in Pounds—Men**

Drinks[a]	100	120	140	160	180	200	220	240	ONLY SAFE DRIVING LIMIT
	00	00	00	00	00	00	00	00	
1	.04	.03	.03	.02	.02	.02	.02	.02	IMPAIRMENT BEGINS
2	.08	.06	.05	.05	.04	.04	.03	.03	
3	.11	.09	.08	.07	.06	.06	.05	.05	DRIVING SKILLS SIGNIFICANTLY AFFECTED
4	.15	.12	.11	.09	.08	.08	.07	.06	
5	.19	.16	.13	.12	.11	.09	.09	.08	
6	.23	.19	.16	.14	.13	.11	.10	.09	
7	.26	.22	.19	.16	.15	.13	.12	.11	LEGALLY INTOXICATED
8	.30	.25	.21	.19	.17	.15	.14	.13	
9	.34	.28	.24	.21	.19	.17	.15	.14	
10	.38	.31	.27	.23	.21	.19	.17	.16	

Drinks[a] — **Body Weight in Pounds—Women**

Drinks[a]	90	100	120	140	160	180	200	220	240	ONLY SAFE DRIVING LIMIT
	00	00	00	00	00	00	00	00	00	
1	.05	.05	.04	.03	.03	.03	.02	.02	.02	IMPAIRMENT BEGINS
2	.10	.09	.08	.07	.06	.05	.05	.04	.04	
3	.15	.14	.11	.10	.09	.08	.07	.06	.06	DRIVING SKILLS SIGNIFICANTLY AFFECTED
4	.20	.18	.15	.13	.11	.10	.09	.08	.08	
5	.25	.23	.19	.16	.14	.13	.11	.10	.09	
6	.30	.27	.23	.19	.17	.15	.14	.12	.11	
7	.35	.32	.27	.23	.20	.18	.16	.14	.13	LEGALLY INTOXICATED
8	.40	.36	.30	.26	.23	.20	.18	.17	.15	
9	.45	.41	.34	.29	.26	.23	.20	.19	.17	
10	.51	.45	.38	.32	.28	.25	.23	.21	.19	

NOTE: In some states, driving under the influence is proved when an adult's blood contains 0.08 percent alcohol, and in others, 0.10. Many states have adopted a "zero-tolerance" policy for drivers under age 21, using 0.02 percent as the limit.

[a]Taken within an hour or so; each drink equivalent to ½ ounce pure ethanol.

SOURCE: National Clearinghouse for Alcohol and Drug Information

TABLE H7-2	Alcohol Blood Levels and Brain Responses

Blood Alcohol Concentration	Effect on Brain
0.05	Impaired judgment, relaxed inhibitions, altered mood, increased heart rate
0.10	Impaired coordination, delayed reaction time, exaggerated emotions, impaired peripheral vision, impaired ability to operate a vehicle
0.15	Slurred speech, blurred vision, staggered walk, seriously impaired coordination and judgment
0.20	Double vision, inability to walk
0.30	Uninhibited behavior, stupor, confusion, inability to comprehend
0.40 to 0.60	Unconsciousness, shock, coma, death (cardiac or respiratory failure)

NOTE: Blood alcohol concentration depends on a number of factors, including alcohol in the beverage, the rate of consumption, the person's gender, and body weight. For example, a 100-pound female can become legally drunk (≥0.10 concentration) by drinking three beers in an hour, whereas a 220-pound male consuming that amount at the same rate would have a 0.05 blood alcohol concentration.

Whether alcohol impairs cognition in moderate drinkers is unclear.[5]

People who drink alcoholic beverages may notice that they urinate more, but they may be unaware of the vicious cycle that results. Alcohol depresses production of **antidiuretic hormone (ADH),** a hormone produced by the pituitary gland that retains water—consequently, with less ADH, more water is lost. Loss of body water leads to thirst, and thirst leads to more drinking. Water will relieve dehydration, but the thirsty drinker may drink alcohol instead, which only worsens the problem. Such information provides another practical tip: drink water when thirsty and before each alcoholic drink. Drink an extra glass or two before going to bed. This strategy will help lessen the effects of a hangover.

Water loss is accompanied by the loss of important minerals. As Chapters 12 and 13 explain, these minerals are vital to the body's fluid balance and to many chemical reactions in the cells, including muscle action. Detoxification treatment includes restoration of mineral balance as quickly as possible.

Alcohol and Malnutrition

For many moderate drinkers, alcohol does not suppress food intake and may actually stimulate appetite. Moderate drinkers usually consume alcohol as *added* energy—on top of their normal food intake. In addition, alcohol in moderate doses is efficiently metabolized. Consequently, alcohol can contribute to body fat and weight gain—either by inhibiting oxidation or by being converted to fat.[6] Metabolically, alcohol is almost as efficient as fat in promoting obesity; each ounce of alcohol represents about a half-ounce of fat. Alcohol's contribution to body fat is most evident in the central obesity that commonly accompanies alcohol consumption, popularly—and appropriately—known as the "beer belly."[7] Alcohol in heavy doses, though, is not efficiently metabolized, generating more heat than fat. Heavy drinkers usually consume alcohol as *substituted* energy—instead of their normal food intake. They tend to eat poorly and suffer malnutrition.

Alcohol is rich in energy (7 kcalories per gram), but as with pure sugar or fat, the kcalories are empty of nutrients. The more alcohol people drink, the less likely that they will eat enough food to obtain adequate nutrients. The more kcalories spent on alcohol, the fewer kcalories available to spend on nutritious foods. Table H7-3 (p. 244) shows the kcalorie amounts of typical alcoholic beverages.

Chronic alcohol abuse not only displaces nutrients from the diet, but it also interferes with the body's metabolism of nutrients. Most dramatic is alcohol's effect on the B vitamin folate. The liver loses its ability to retain folate, and the kidneys increase their excretion of it. Alcohol abuse creates a folate deficiency that devastates digestive

TABLE H7-3	kCalories in Alcoholic Beverages and Mixers	
Beverage	**Amount (oz)**	**Energy (kcal)**
Beer		
Regular	12	150
Light	12	78–131
Nonalcoholic	12	32–82
Distilled liquor (gin, rum, vodka, whiskey)		
80 proof	1½	100
86 proof	1½	105
90 proof	1½	110
Liqueurs		
Coffee liqueur, 53 proof	1½	175
Coffee and cream liqueur, 34 proof	1½	155
Crème de menthe, 72 proof	1½	185
Mixers		
Club soda	12	0
Cola	12	150
Cranberry juice cocktail	8	145
Diet drinks	12	2
Ginger ale or tonic	12	125
Grapefruit juice	8	95
Orange juice	8	110
Tomato or vegetable juice	8	45
Wine		
Dessert	3½	110–135
Nonalcoholic	8	14
Red or rosé	3½	75
White	3½	70
Wine cooler	12	170

system function. The intestine normally releases and retrieves folate continuously, but it becomes damaged by folate deficiency and alcohol toxicity, so it fails to retrieve its own folate and misses any that may trickle in from food as well. Alcohol also interferes with the action of folate in converting the amino acid homocysteine to methionine. The result is an excess of homocysteine, which has been linked to heart disease, and an inadequate supply of methionine, which slows the production of new cells, especially the rapidly dividing cells of the intestine and the blood. The combination of poor folate status and alcohol consumption has also been implicated in promoting colorectal cancer.

The inadequate food intake and impaired nutrient absorption that accompany chronic alcohol abuse frequently lead to a deficiency of another B vitamin—thiamin. In fact, the cluster of thiamin-deficiency symptoms commonly seen in chronic **alcoholism** has its own name—the **Wernicke-Korsakoff syndrome.** This syndrome is characterized by paralysis of the eye muscles, poor muscle coordination, impaired memory, and damaged nerves; it and other alcohol-related memory problems may respond to thiamin supplements.

Acetaldehyde, an intermediate in alcohol metabolism (review Figure H7-2, p. 240), interferes with nutrient use, too. For example, acetaldehyde dislodges vitamin B_6 from its protective binding protein so that it is destroyed, causing a vitamin B_6 deficiency and, thereby, lowered production of red blood cells.

Malnutrition occurs not only because of lack of intake and altered metabolism but because of direct toxic effects as well. Alcohol causes stomach cells to oversecrete both gastric acid and histamine, an immune system agent that produces inflammation. Beer in particular stimulates gastric acid secretion, irritating the linings of the stomach and esophagus and making them vulnerable to ulcer formation.

Overall, nutrient deficiencies are virtually inevitable in alcohol abuse, not only because alcohol displaces food but also because alcohol directly interferes with the body's use of nutrients, making them ineffective even if they are present. Intestinal cells fail to absorb B vitamins, notably, thiamin, folate, and vitamin B_{12}. Liver cells lose efficiency in activating vitamin D. Cells in the retina of the eye, which normally process the alcohol form of vitamin A (retinol) to its aldehyde form needed in vision (retinal), find themselves processing ethanol to acetaldehyde instead. Likewise, the liver cannot convert the aldehyde form of vitamin A to its acid form (retinoic acid), which is needed to support the growth of its (and all) cells.

Regardless of dietary intake, excessive drinking over a lifetime creates deficits of all the nutrients mentioned in this discussion and more. No diet can compensate for the damage caused by heavy alcohol consumption.

Alcohol's Short-Term Effects

The effects of abusing alcohol may be apparent immediately, or they may not become evident for years to come. Among the immediate consequences, all of the following involve alcohol use:[8]

- One-quarter of all emergency-room admissions
- One-third of all suicides
- One-half of all homicides
- One-half of all domestic violence incidents
- One-half of all traffic fatalities
- One-half of all fire victim fatalities

These statistics are sobering. The consequences of heavy drinking touch all races and all segments of society—men and women, young and old, rich and poor. One group particularly hard hit by heavy drinking is college students—not because they are prone to alcoholism, but because they live in an environment and are in a developmental stage of life in which heavy drinking is considered acceptable.[9]

Heavy drinking or binge drinking (defined as at least four drinks in a row for women and five drinks in a row for men) is widespread on college campuses and poses serious health and social consequences to drinkers and nondrinkers alike.* [10] In fact, binge drinking can kill: the respiratory center of the brain becomes anesthetized, and breathing stops. Acute alcohol intoxication can cause coronary artery spasms, leading to heart attacks.

Binge drinking is especially common among college students who live in a fraternity or sorority house, attend parties frequently, engage in other risky behaviors, and have a history of binge drinking in high school. Compared with nondrinkers or moderate drinkers, people who frequently binge drink (at least three times within two weeks) are more likely to engage in unpro-

---

* This definition of binge drinking, without specification of time elapsed, is consistent with standard practice in alcohol research.

tected sex, have multiple sex partners, damage property, and assault others.[11] On average, *every day* alcohol is involved in the:[12]

- Death of 5 college students
- Sexual assault of 266 college students
- Injury of 1641 college students
- Assault of 1907 college students

Binge drinkers skew the statistics on college students' alcohol use. The median number of drinks consumed by college students is 1.5 per week, but for binge drinkers, it is 14.5. Nationally, only 20 percent of all students are frequent binge drinkers; yet they account for two-thirds of all the alcohol students report consuming and most of the alcohol-related problems.

Binge drinking is not limited to college campuses, of course, but it is most common among 18 to 24 year-olds.[13] That age group and environment seem most accepting of such behavior despite its problems. Social acceptance may make it difficult for binge drinkers to recognize themselves as problem drinkers. For this reason, interventions must focus both on educating individuals and on changing the campus social environment.[14] The damage alcohol causes only becomes worse if the pattern is not broken. Alcohol abuse sets in much more quickly in young people than in adults. Those who start drinking at an early age more often suffer from alcoholism than people who start later on. Table H7-4 lists the key signs of alcoholism.

Alcohol's Long-Term Effects

The most devastating long-term effect of alcohol is the damage done to a child whose mother abused alcohol during pregnancy. The effects of alcohol on the unborn and the message that pregnant women should not drink alcohol are presented in Highlight 15.

For nonpregnant adults, a drink or two sets in motion many destructive processes in the body, but the next day's abstinence reverses them. As long as the doses are moderate, the time between them is ample, and nutrition is adequate, recovery is probably complete.

If the doses of alcohol are heavy and the time between them short, complete recovery cannot take place. Repeated onslaughts of alcohol gradually take a toll on all parts of the body (see Table H7-5, p. 246). Compared with nondrinkers and moderate drinkers, heavy drinkers have significantly greater risks of dying

from all causes.[15] Excessive alcohol consumption is the third leading preventable cause of death in the United States.[16]

Personal Strategies

One obvious option available to people attending social gatherings is to enjoy the conversation, eat the food, and drink nonalcoholic beverages. Several nonalcoholic beverages are available that mimic the look and taste of their alcoholic counterparts. For those who enjoy champagne or beer, sparkling ciders and beers without alcohol are available. Instead of drinking a cocktail, a person can sip tomato juice with a slice of lime and a stalk of celery or just a plain cola beverage. Any of these drinks can ease conversation.

The person who chooses to drink alcohol should sip each drink slowly with food. The alcohol should arrive at the liver cells slowly enough that the enzymes can handle the load. It is best to space drinks, too, allowing about an hour or so to metabolize each drink.

If you want to help sober up a friend who has had too much to drink, don't bother walking arm in arm around the block. Walking muscles have to work harder, but muscle cells can't metabolize alcohol; only liver cells can. Remember that each person has a limited amount of the alcohol dehydrogenase enzyme that clears the blood at a steady rate. Time alone will do the job.

Nor will it help to give your friend a cup of coffee. Caffeine is a stimulant, but it won't speed up alcohol metabolism. The police say ruefully, "If you give a drunk a cup of coffee, you'll just have a wide-awake drunk on your hands." Table H7-6 (p. 246) presents other alcohol myths.

People who have passed out from drinking need 24 hours to sober up completely. Let them sleep, but watch over them. Encourage them to lie on their sides, instead of their backs. That way, if they vomit, they won't choke.

Don't drive too soon after drinking. The lack of glucose for the brain's function and the length of time needed to clear the blood of alcohol make alcohol's adverse effects linger long after its blood concentration has fallen. Driving coordination is still impaired the morning *after* a night of drinking, even if the drinking was moderate. Responsible aircraft pilots know that they must allow 24 hours for their bodies to clear alcohol completely, and they refuse to fly any sooner. The Federal Aviation Administration and major airlines enforce this rule.

TABLE H7-4 Signs of Alcoholism

- Tolerance—the person needs higher and higher intakes of alcohol to achieve intoxication
- Withdrawal—the person who stops drinking experiences anxiety, agitation, increased blood pressure, or seizures, or seeks alcohol to relieve these symptoms
- Impaired control—the person intends to have 1 or 2 drinks, but has 9 or 10 instead, or the person tries to control or quit drinking, but fails
- Disinterest—the person neglects important social, family, job, or school activities because of drinking
- Time—the person spends a great deal of time obtaining and drinking alcohol or recovering from excessive drinking
- Impaired ability—the person's intoxication or withdrawal symptoms interfere with work, school, or home
- Problems—the person continues drinking despite physical hazards or medical, legal, psychological, family, employment, or school problems

The presence of three or more of these conditions is required to make a diagnosis.

SOURCE: Adapted from *Diagnostic and Statistical Manual of Mental Disorders*, 4th ed. (Washington, D.C.: American Psychiatric Association, 1994).

TABLE H7-5 Health Effects of Heavy Alcohol Consumption

Health Problem	Effects of Alcohol
Arthritis	Increases the risk of inflamed joints
Cancer	Increases the risk of cancer of the liver, pancreas, rectum, and breast; increases the risk of cancer of the lungs, mouth, pharynx, larynx, and esophagus, where alcohol interacts synergistically with tobacco
Fetal alcohol syndrome	Causes physical and behavioral abnormalities in the fetus (see Highlight 15)
Heart disease	In heavy drinkers, raises blood pressure, blood lipids, and the risk of stroke and heart disease; when compared with those who abstain, heart disease risk is generally lower in light-to-moderate drinkers (see Chapter 18)
Hyperglycemia	Raises blood glucose
Hypoglycemia	Lowers blood glucose, especially in people with diabetes
Infertility	Increases the risks of menstrual disorders and spontaneous abortions (in women); suppresses luteinizing hormone (in women) and testosterone (in men)
Kidney disease	Enlarges the kidneys, alters hormone functions, and increases the risk of kidney failure
Liver disease	Causes fatty liver, alcoholic hepatitis, and cirrhosis
Malnutrition	Increases the risk of protein-energy malnutrition; low intakes of protein, calcium, iron, vitamin A, vitamin C, thiamin, vitamin B_6, and riboflavin; and impaired absorption of calcium, phosphorus, vitamin D, and zinc
Nervous disorders	Causes neuropathy and dementia; impairs balance and memory
Obesity	Increases energy intake, but is not a primary cause of obesity
Psychological disturbances	Causes depression, anxiety, and insomnia

NOTE: This list is by no means all-inclusive. Alcohol has direct toxic effects on all body systems.

TABLE H7-6 Myths and Truths Concerning Alcohol

Myth:	Hard liquors such as rum, vodka, and tequila are more harmful than wine and beer.
Truth:	The damage caused by alcohol depends largely on the *amount* consumed. Compared with hard liquor, beer and wine have relatively low percentages of alcohol, but they are often consumed in larger quantities.
Myth:	Consuming alcohol with raw seafood diminishes the likelihood of getting hepatitis.
Truth:	People have eaten contaminated oysters while drinking alcoholic beverages and not gotten as sick as those who were not drinking. But do not be misled: hepatitis is too serious an illness for anyone to depend on alcohol for protection.
Myth:	Alcohol stimulates the appetite.
Truth:	For some people, alcohol may stimulate appetite, but it seems to have the opposite effect in heavy drinkers. Heavy drinkers tend to eat poorly and suffer malnutrition.
Myth:	Drinking alcohol is healthy.
Truth:	Moderate alcohol consumption is associated with a lower risk for heart disease (see Chapter 18 for more details). Higher intakes, however, raise the risks for high blood pressure, stroke, heart disease, some cancers, accidents, violence, suicide, birth defects, and deaths in general. Furthermore, excessive alcohol consumption damages the liver, pancreas, brain, and heart. No authority recommends that nondrinkers begin drinking alcoholic beverages to obtain health benefits.
Myth:	Wine increases the body's absorption of minerals.
Truth:	Wine may increase the body's absorption of potassium, calcium, phosphorus, magnesium, and zinc, but the alcohol in wine also promotes the body's excretion of these minerals, so no benefit is gained.
Myth:	Alcohol is legal and, therefore, not a drug.
Truth:	Alcohol is legal for adults 21 years old and older, but it is also a drug—a substance that alters one or more of the body's functions.
Myth:	A shot of alcohol warms you up.
Truth:	Alcohol diverts blood flow to the skin making you *feel* warmer, but it actually cools the body.
Myth:	Wine and beer are mild; they do not lead to alcoholism.
Truth:	Alcoholism is not related to the kind of beverage, but rather to the quantity and frequency of consumption.
Myth:	Mixing different types of drinks gives you a hangover.
Truth:	Too much alcohol in any form produces a hangover.
Myth:	Alcohol is a stimulant.
Truth:	People think alcohol is a stimulant because it seems to relieve inhibitions, but it does so by depressing the activity of the brain. Alcohol is medically defined as a depressant drug.
Myth:	Beer is a great source of carbohydrate, vitamins, minerals, and fluids.
Truth:	Beer does provide some carbohydrate, but most of its kcalories come from alcohol. The few vitamins and minerals in beer cannot compete with rich food sources. And the diuretic effect of alcohol causes the body to lose more fluid in urine than is provided by the beer.

Look again at the drawing of the brain in Figure H7-4, and note that when someone drinks, judgment fails first. Judgment might tell a person to limit alcohol consumption to two drinks at a party, but if the first drink takes judgment away, many more drinks may follow. The failure to stop drinking as planned, on repeated occasions, is a danger sign warning that the person should not drink at all. The accompanying Nutrition on the Net provides websites for organizations that offer information about alcohol and alcohol abuse.

Ethanol interferes with a multitude of chemical and hormonal reactions in the body—many more than have been enumerated here. With heavy alcohol consumption, the potential for harm is great. The best way to escape the harmful effects of alcohol is, of course, to refuse alcohol altogether. If you do drink alcoholic beverages, do so with care, and in moderation.

NUTRITION ON THE NET

ThomsonNOW™
For furthur study of topics covered in this Highlight, log on to **www.thomsonedu.com/thomsonnow**, Go to Chapter 7, then to Highlights Nutrition on the Net.

- Search for "alcohol" at the U.S. Government health site: **www.healthfinder.gov**

- Gather information on alcohol and drug abuse from the National Clearinghouse for Alcohol and Drug Information (NCADI): **ncadi.samhsa.gov**

- Learn more about alcoholism and drug dependence from the National Council on Alcoholism and Drug Dependence (NCADD): **www.ncadd.org**

- Visit the National Institute on Alcohol Abuse and Alcoholism: **www.collegedrinkingprevention.gov**

- Find help for a family alcohol problem from Alateen and Al-Anon Family support groups: **www.al-anon.alateen.org**

- Find help for an alcohol or drug problem from Alcoholics Anonymous (AA) or Narcotics Anonymous: **www.aa.org** or **www.wsoinc.com**

- Search for "party" to find tips for hosting a safe party from Mothers Against Drunk Driving (MADD): **www.madd.org**

REFERENCES

1. D. J. Meyerhoff and coauthors, Health risks of chronic moderate and heavy alcohol consumption: How much is too much? *Alcoholism, Clinical and Experimental Research* 29 (2005): 1334-1340; J. B. Standridge, R. G. Zylstra, and S. M. Adams, Alcohol consumption: An overview of benefits and risks, *Southern Medical Journal* 97 (2004): 664-672.
2. V. Arndt and coauthors, Age, alcohol consumption, and all-cause mortality, *Annals of Epidemiology* 14 (2004): 750-753.
3. I. Connor and coauthors, The burden of death, disease, and disability due to alcohol in New Zealand, *New Zealand Medical Journal* 118 (2005): U1412.
4. L. E. Nagy, Molecular aspects of alcohol metabolism: Transcription factors involved in early ethanol-induced liver injury, *Annual Review of Nutrition* 24 (2004): 55-78.
5. D. Krahn and coauthors, Alcohol use and cognition at mid-life: The importance of adjusting for baseline cognitive ability and educational attainment, *Alcoholism: Clinical and Experimental Research* 27 (2003): 1162-1166.
6. R. A. Breslow and B. A. Smothers, Drinking patterns and body mass index in never smokers: National Health Interview Survey, 1997-2001, *American Journal of Epidemiology* 161 (2005): 368-376; M. R. Yeomans, Effects of alcohol on food and energy intake in human subjects: Evidence for passive and active over-consumption of energy, *British Journal of Nutrition* 92 (2004): S31-S34; S. G.

Wannamethee and A. G. Shaper, Alcohol, body weight, and weight gain in middle-aged men, *American Journal of Clinical Nutrition* 77 (2003): 1312-1317; E. Jequier, Pathways to obesity, *International Journal of Obesity and Related Metabolic Disorders* 26 (2002): S12-S17.
7. S. G. Wannamethee, A. G. Shaper, and P. H. Whincup, Alcohol and adiposity: Effects of quantity and type of drink and time relation with meals, *International Journal of Obesity and Related Metabolic Disorders* 29 (2005): 1436-1444; J. M. Dorn and coauthors, Alcohol drinking patterns differentially affect central adiposity as measured by abdominal height in women and men, *Journal of Nutrition* 133 (2003): 2655-2662.
8. Position paper on drug policy: Physician Leadership on National Drug Policy (PLNDP), Brown University Center for Alcohol and Addiction Studies, 2000.
9. A. M. Brower, Are college students alcoholics? *Journal of American College Health* 50 (2002): 253-255.
10. R. D. Brewer and M. H. Swahn, Binge drinking and violence, *Journal of the American Medical Association* 294 (2005): 616-618; H. Wechsler and coauthors, Trends in college binge drinking during a period of increased prevention efforts—Findings from Harvard School of Public Health College Alcohol Study Surveys: 1993-2001, *Journal of American College Health* 50 (2002): 203-217.
11. Wechsler and coauthors, 2002.

12. R. W. Hingson and coauthors, Magnitude of alcohol-related mortality and morbidity among U.S. college students ages 18-24: Changes from 1998 to 2001, *Annual Review of Public Health* 26 (2005): 259-279.
13. National Center for Health Statistics, *Chartbook on Trends in the Health of Americans*, Alcohol consumption by adults 18 years of age and over, according to selected characteristics: United States, selected years 1997-2003, (2005): 264-266.
14. A. Ziemelis, R. B. Bucknam, and A. M. Elfessi, Prevention efforts underlying decreases in binge drinking at institutions of higher learning, *Journal of American College Health* 50 (2002): 238-252.
15. A. Y. Strandberg and coauthors, Alcohol consumption, 29-y total mortality, and quality of life in men in old age, *American Journal of Clinical Nutrition* 80 (2004): 1366-1371; I. R. White, D. R. Altmann, and K. Nanchahal, Alcohol consumption and mortality: Modeling risks for men and women at different ages, *British Medical Journal* 325 (2002): 191-197.
16. Centers for Disease Control, Alcohol-attributable deaths and years of potential life lost-United States, 2001, *Morbidity and Mortality Weekly Report* 53 (2004): 866-870.

Chapter 5

Carbohydrate

© PhotoDisc

Objectives

After studying this chapter, you should be able to do the following:

- Describe the main biochemical pathways involved in carbohydrate metabolism

- Describe the changes that occur in carbohydrate metabolism at different intensities of exercise

- Describe how blood glucose concentrations are maintained and regulated

- Describe the metabolic and performance effects of carbohydrate ingestion 3 hours to 4 hours before exercise

- Describe the metabolic and performance effects of carbohydrate ingestion 1 hour before exercise

- Describe the metabolic and performance effects of carbohydrate ingestion during exercise

- Describe the mechanisms involved in glycogen synthesis

- Give generally accepted guidelines for carbohydrate intake before and during exercise

- Give generally accepted guidelines for carbohydrate intake to improve recovery in the short term and long term

- Describe the dietary requirements for carbohydrate in a variety of sports

Whereas 100 years ago beef was believed to be the most important component of an athlete's diet, nowadays pasta seems to be most important. Athletes are often advised to eat a high-carbohydrate diet, consume carbohydrate before exercise, ensure adequate carbohydrate intake during exercise, and replenish carbohydrate stores as soon as possible after exercise.

Since the beginning of the 20th century, carbohydrate intake has been known to be related to exercise performance. The availability of carbohydrate as a substrate for skeletal muscle contraction and the central nervous system (i.e., the brain) is important for endurance exercise performance. However, not only the performance of prolonged exercise but also the performance in intermittent-intensity and high-intensity exercise may be influenced by carbohydrate availability. Because carbohydrate is the most important fuel for the central nervous system, various cognitive tasks and motor skills that play a crucial role in skill sports may also be affected by carbohydrate availability.

Carbohydrate is, therefore, a very important component of the athlete's diet, and various strategies have been developed over the past 30 years to optimize carbohydrate availability and, hence, performance. Generally, these goals can be achieved by (1) carbohydrate feedings before exercise to replenish muscle and liver glycogen stores and (2) carbohydrate feeding during exercise to maintain blood glucose levels and, hence, high rates of glucose oxidation derived from the plasma. In this chapter, the effects of carbohydrate on exercise metabolism and performance are explained. The results of some classic experimental studies will be discussed, along with the practical implications arising from this work. This chapter is subdivided into four distinct sections:

- Carbohydrate in the days before competition (or training);
- Carbohydrate in the hours before competition;
- Carbohydrate during competition or training; and
- Carbohydrate after training or competition.

First, however, we start with a short historical tour, beginning with the first studies that linked carbohydrate with exercise performance.

History

Krogh and Lindhardt (1920) were probably the first investigators to recognize the importance of carbohydrate as a fuel during exercise. In their study, subjects consumed a high-fat diet for three days (bacon, butter, cream, eggs, and cabbage), followed by three days on a high-carbohydrate diet (potatoes, flour, bread, cake, marmalade, and sugar). The subjects performed a 2-hour exercise test and reported various symptoms of fatigue when they consumed the high-fat diet. However, when they consumed the high-carbohydrate diet, the exercise was reported as "easy." The investigators also demonstrated that after several days of a low-carbohydrate, high-fat diet, the average respiratory exchange ratio (RER) during 2 hours of cycling was reduced to 0.80 as compared with 0.85 to 0.90 when a mixed diet was consumed. Conversely, when subjects ate a high-carbohydrate, low-fat diet, RER was increased to 0.95.

Important observations were also made by Levine, Gordon, and Derick (1924). They measured blood glucose in some of the participants of the 1923 Boston Marathon and observed that in most runners, glucose concentrations markedly declined after the race. These investigators suggested that low blood glucose levels were a cause of fatigue. To test that hypothesis, they encouraged several participants of the same marathon one year later to consume carbohydrates during the race. This practice, in combination with a high-carbohydrate diet before the race, prevented hypoglycemia (low blood glucose) and significantly improved running performance (i.e., time to complete the race).

The importance of carbohydrate for improving exercise capacity was further demonstrated by Dill, Edwards, and Talbott (1932). These investigators let their dogs, Joe and Sally, run without feeding them carbohydrates. The dogs became hypoglycemic and fatigued after 4 hours to 6 hours. When the test was repeated with the only difference that the dogs were fed carbohydrates during exercise, the dogs ran for 17 hours to 23 hours.

Christensen (1932) showed that with increasing exercise intensity, the proportion of carbohydrate utilized increased. This work was expanded in the late 1960s, with the reintroduction of the muscle biopsy technique by a group of Scandinavian scientists (Bergstrom and Hultman 1966, 1967). These studies indicated the critical role of muscle glycogen. The improved performance after a high-carbohydrate diet was linked with the higher muscle glycogen concentrations observed after such a diet. A high-carbohydrate diet (approximately 70% of dietary energy from carbohydrate) elevated muscle glycogen stores and seemed to enhance endurance capacity compared with a normal-carbohydrate (~50%) and a low-carbohydrate (~10%) diet. These observations have led to the recommendations to carbohydrate-load (i.e., eat high-carbohydrate diets) before competition (Costill and Miller 1980; Sherman and Costill 1984).

In the 1980s, the effects of carbohydrate feeding during exercise on exercise performance and metabolism were further investigated (Coyle and Coggan 1984; Coyle et al. 1983; Coyle et al. 1986). Costill et al. (1973) were the first to study the contribution of ingested carbohydrate to total energy expenditure, and in the following years, studies were conducted using isotopic tracers (i.e., ¹⁴C-glucose or ¹³C-glucose) to investigate differences in oxidation rates and metabolism of different types of carbohydrate, different amounts of carbohydrate, different feeding schedules, and various other factors that influence the efficacy of carbohydrate ingestion. Although Costill et al. (1973) concluded that ingested carbohydrates were not oxidized to any major extent, later studies have convincingly shown that ingested carbohydrates are a very important energy source during prolonged exercise.

Role of Carbohydrate

As discussed in chapter 1, carbohydrate plays many roles in the human body, but one of its main functions is to provide energy for the contracting muscle. Glycogen is the storage form of carbohydrate and is found mainly in muscle and liver.

Muscle Glycogen

Muscle glycogen is a readily available energy source for the working muscle. The glycogen content of skeletal muscle at rest is approximately 12 g/kg to 16 g/kg w.w. (65 mmol glucosyl units/kg w.w. to 90 mmol glucosyl units/kg w.w. [see the sidebar]), equating to a total of about 300 g to 400 g of carbohydrate (see chapter 2). The rate at which muscle glycogen is oxidized is highly dependent on the exercise intensity. At low to moderate exercise intensities, most of the energy can be obtained from oxidative phosphorylation of acetyl-CoA derived from both carbohydrate and fat. As the exercise intensity increases to high levels, the energy requirements cannot be met by only the oxidation of carbohydrate and fat. Muscle glycogen becomes the most important substrate, as anaerobic energy delivery (ATP resynthesis from glycolysis) is mostly derived from the breakdown of muscle glycogen. In figure 5.1, the effects of exercise intensity on muscle glycogen breakdown are shown. At very high exercise intensities, muscle glycogen is broken down very rapidly and becomes nearly depleted in a relatively short period of time when this type of exercise is performed intermittently.

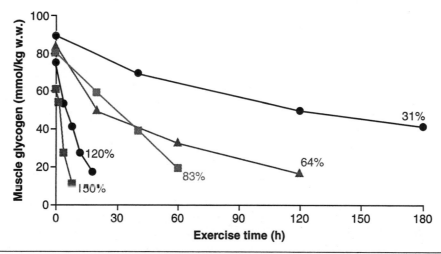

Figure 5.1 The effects of exercise intensity (shown as percentage V̇O₂max) on muscle glycogen breakdown.

Adapted, by permission, from P.D. Gollnick, K. Piehl, and B. Saltin, 1974, "Selective glycogen depletion pattern in human muscle fibers after exercise of varying intensity and at varying pedaling rates," *Journal of Physiology* 214(1): 45-57.

MUSCLE GLYCOGEN

In the literature, muscle glycogen is expressed in various ways, making possible comparison of results of different studies. The units used most frequently are mmol glycosyl (glucose) units per kilogram dry mass or per kilogram wet mass. To express the results per kg dry mass, the muscle biopsy sample must be freeze-dried. All the water is removed by placing the frozen biopsy sample in a freeze dryer. Muscle contains approximately 75% to 80% water, and to convert values from wet mass to dry mass the concentration is usually multiplied by 4.5.

Liver Glycogen

The main role of glycogen in the liver is to maintain a constant blood glucose level. Glucose is the main, and in normal circumstances the only, fuel used by the brain. The liver is often referred to as the glucoregulator or glucostat—the organ responsible for the regulation of the blood glucose concentration. An average liver weighs approximately 1.5 kg, and approximately 80 g to 110 g of glycogen is stored in the liver of an adult human in the postabsorptive state. The glycogen is broken down in the liver to glucose and then released into the circulatory system. The kidneys also store some glycogen and release glucose into the blood, but, from a quantitative point of view, the kidneys are far less important than the liver. In this book, the terms liver glucose output or **hepatic glucose output** includes the release of glucose from the liver and kidneys. This release is also often called endogenous glucose production. Glycogen that is broken down in the muscle is not released as glucose into the circulation, because muscle lacks the enzyme glucose-6-phosphatase (the enzyme that removes a phosphate group from glucose-6-phosphate). Once glucose has been phosphorylated in the muscle cell by the enzyme hexokinase (the enzyme that attaches a phosphate group to glucose), it cannot be dephosphorylated (see chapter 2).

The liver has a much higher concentration of glycogen (per kg tissue) than does muscle. Only because of the much larger mass of muscle does muscle contain more glycogen than the liver (in absolute terms, 300 g to 600 g versus 80 g to 110 g). After an overnight fast, the liver glycogen content can be reduced to very low levels (<20 g) because tissues such as the brain use glucose at a rate of about 0.1 g/min in resting conditions. During exercise, the rate of glucose utilization by tissues other than muscle does not change very much (~ 0.1 g/min).

Circulation (of blood) can be regarded as a sink (see figure 5.2) from which various tissues, and especially exercising muscle, can tap glucose. However, a very precise mechanism regulates the blood glucose concentration in this sink at 4.0 to 4.5 mmol/L. (This is equivalent to a plasma glucose concentration of 5 to 6 mmol/L because the concentration of free glucose inside the red blood cells is somewhat less than that in the plasma; see the sidebar.) When the blood glucose concentration drops, the liver releases glucose. If the demands for glucose are less, the liver produces less glucose or even takes up glucose from the bloodstream to synthesize glycogen. After a meal, for instance, when a large amount of glucose enters the liver through the hepatic portal vein, the liver uses this glucose to synthesize glycogen. Despite the changes in glucose flux, both after feeding and during exercise (or fasting), normoglycemia is usually nicely maintained.

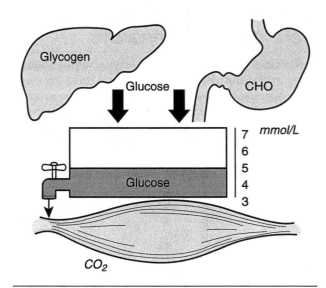

Figure 5.2 The bloodstream can be regarded as a sink in which the blood glucose concentration is accurately controlled. During exercise, muscle glucose uptake will increase dramatically, and to prevent the blood glucose concentration from dropping, the liver must produce glucose at an equally high rate.

DIFFERENCES BETWEEN WHOLE BLOOD, PLASMA, AND SERUM

Blood refers to the red liquid in our arteries and veins. It is composed of cells (red blood cells or erythrocytes, white blood cells or leukocytes, and cell fragments called platelets or thrombocytes) that are suspended in a fluid called plasma. The plasma contains proteins, lipoproteins, electrolytes, and small organic molecules such as glucose, fatty acids, glycerol, lactate, and amino acids, but by weight it is about 93% water. After taking a blood sample from a person, plasma can be separated from the cellular components by centrifugation, provided that an anticoagulant (a substance that pre-

(continued)

(continued)

vents the activation of clot formation) is added to the blood sample soon after it is collected. Typical anticoagulants that can be used include heparin, oxalate, citrate, and ethylene-diamine-tetraacetate (EDTA). If an anticoagulant is not added, the blood will clot within a matter of minutes. Centrifuging the clotted blood will separate the cellular elements and the insoluble clotting protein fibrin from the fluid; this fluid is called serum.

Hence, the difference between plasma and serum is that plasma has an anticoagulant in it and still contains soluble fibrinogen, whereas serum does not. Substances such as glucose can be measured in whole blood (after lysing all the blood cells), plasma, or serum. However, the glucose concentrations measured in each of these fluids will be a little different because the concentration of free glucose inside the red blood cells is somewhat less than that in the plasma. This means that whole blood will have a lower glucose concentration than plasma or serum. The concentration of most substances in plasma is pretty much the same as in serum, providing that the blood is not left too long to clot before centrifugation takes place. If left at room temperature, blood cell metabolism will use up glucose at a rate of about 0.5 mmol/L/h. In this situation, the serum glucose concentration will be less than that in plasma if the latter was obtained by centrifugation immediately after blood sampling.

Early studies in Scandinavia showed with liver biopsies that liver glycogen is decreased by about 50% after 1 hour of exercise at 75% $\dot{V}O_2$max. Later studies have used stable isotopes to indirectly measure the oxidation of liver glucose. These studies clearly show that liver glycogen is a significant substrate during exercise, and its importance (in absolute terms) increases when exercise intensity increases (Jeukendrup et al. 1999; Romijn 1993).

The liver can also produce glucose through gluconeogenesis. Substrates such as lactate, glycerol, pyruvate, alanine, glutamine, and some other amino acids can be used for the synthesis of glucose. These substrates are usually formed in other organs of the body and transported to the liver. For example, most of the lactate is formed in skeletal muscle, and most of the glycerol is from adipose tissue.

In resting conditions, the glucose output by the liver is approximately 150 mg/min (0.8 mmol/min). About 60% of this output (90 mg/min) is derived from the breakdown of liver glycogen, and about 40% (60 mg/min) is newly formed glucose (gluconeogenesis) (Hultman and Nilsson 1971; Nilsson and Hultman 1973). During exercise, the liver glucose output increases dramatically. During high-intensity exercise (>75% $\dot{V}O_2$max), liver glucose output increases to about 1 g/min, and the majority of this glucose is derived from the breakdown of liver glycogen (>90%). The rate of gluconeogenesis is only marginally increased during exercise compared with resting conditions. Gluconeogenesis is increased in the presence of high plasma concentrations of cortisol, epinephrine (adrenaline), and glucagon, whereas insulin has the opposite effect. The longer the exercise, the greater the relative contribution of gluconeogenesis to liver glucose production and output. During periods of starvation gluconeogenesis is increased, whereas after carbohydrate feeding gluconeogenesis is suppressed.

Regulation of Glucose Concentration

Blood glucose concentrations are normally maintained within a very narrow range (a normal resting blood glucose concentration is usually between 4.0 mmol/L and 4.5 mmol/L; plasma glucose concentrations are between 5 mmol/L and 6 mmol/L). Hormones play a key role in this regulation. In resting conditions, insulin is the most important glucoregulatory hormone. It increases the uptake of glucose into various tissues. After a meal, plasma insulin concentrations increase, and, as a result, glucose uptake by muscle, liver, and other tissues increases. Insulin promotes not only the uptake but also the storage of the glucose. Glycogen synthase activity is increased, and glycogen phosphorylase (the enzyme responsible for the breakdown of glycogen) is inhibited. Glucagon is the most important counteractive hormone. Secretion of glucagon causes the breakdown of liver glycogen and release of glucose into the circulation. Several other hormones may have a role in the regulation of blood glucose concentrations, including growth hormone, cortisol, somatostatin, and catecholamines.

During exercise, catecholamine release reduces the secretion of insulin by the pancreas, and plasma insulin concentrations can decrease to very low levels. Muscle glucose uptake is enhanced by contraction-stimulated glucose transport. As mentioned previously, however, despite dramatically increased glucose uptake by the muscle during exercise, blood glucose levels are well maintained in most conditions.

However, a situation in which a mismatch between glucose uptake and glucose production by the liver occurs is during high-intensity exercise. At an intensity of approximately 80% $\dot{V}O_2$max or more, the liver produces glucose at a higher rate than it is taken up by the muscle. This increased hepatic glucose release is most likely caused by neural feedforward mechanisms and results in slightly elevated blood glucose concentration compared with rest. Another situation in which a mismatch occurs is during the later stages of prolonged exercise. As liver glycogen becomes depleted, the rate of glucose production may become insufficient to compensate for the glucose uptake by the muscle and other tissues. As a result, hypoglycemia develops, with blood glucose levels sometimes dropping below 3 mmol/L.

Hypoglycemia

If blood glucose concentrations drop below a critical level (often 3 mmol/L), the rate of glucose uptake by the brain is insufficient to meet its metabolic requirements, and symptoms of hypoglycemia results. Hypoglycemia is characterized by a variety of symptoms, including dizziness, nausea, cold sweat, reduced mental alertness and ability to concentrate, loss of motor skill, increased heart rate, excessive hunger, and disorientation. Hypoglycemia is a common problem in exercise and sport and can be treated simply by carbohydrate consumption. Hypoglycemia has received considerable attention

because pre-exercise carbohydrate feeding seemed to induce a **rebound hypoglycemia.**

Carbohydrate Before Exercise

Carbohydrate can play an important role in the preparation for competition. Carbohydrate intake in the days before competition will mainly replenish muscle glycogen stores, whereas carbohydrate intake in the hours before competition will optimize liver glycogen stores. Because carbohydrate intake in the days before competition has distinctly different effects than carbohydrate immediately before competition, these will be discussed separately.

Carbohydrate in the Days Leading Up to Competition

Carbohydrate consumption in the days leading up to competition allows muscle glycogen stores to be fully replenished. Scandinavian researchers discovered that muscle glycogen could be supercompensated by changes in diet and exercise (Bergstrom and Hultman 1967). In a series of studies, they developed a so-called **supercompensation** protocol, which resulted in very high muscle glycogen concentrations. This diet and exercise regimen started with a glycogen depleting exercise bout (see figure 5.3a). The exercise was then followed by three days of a high-protein,

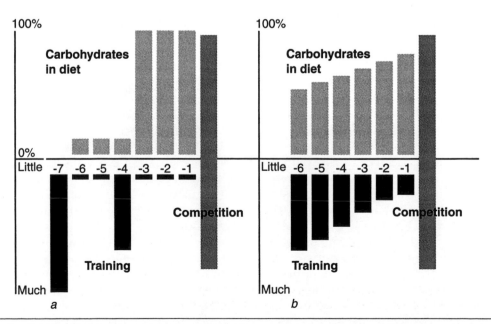

Figure 5.3 *(a)* The "classical supercompensation protocols" consisting of a glycogen-depleting exercise bout followed by 3 days of a high-protein, high-fat diet and another exhausting exercise bout on day 4, followed by a 3-day high-carbohydrate diet. *(b)* A more moderate protocol was later suggested to be almost as effective.

high-fat diet. Another exhausting exercise bout was performed on day 4, after which the subjects were placed on a high-carbohydrate diet for three days. Another group of subjects followed the same exercise protocol, but their diets were in reverse order.

Interestingly, this study revealed that the subjects who received the high-protein, high-fat, low-carbohydrate diet first followed by the high-carbohydrate diet had higher rates of muscle glycogen resynthesis. The authors, therefore, concluded that a period of carbohydrate deprivation further stimulated glycogen resynthesis when carbohydrates were given after exercise.

The regimen that was proposed is generally referred to as the "classical supercompensation protocol" (see figure 5.3a). It has been used successfully by several top athletes, including the legendary British runner Ron Hill. In fact, nowadays many marathon runners use this method to optimize their performance. Although the supercompensation protocol has been very effective in increasing muscle glycogen to very high concentrations, it also has several important (potential) disadvantages of which athletes should be aware:

- Hypoglycemia during the low-carbohydrate period
- Practical problems (difficulty in preparing such extreme diets)
- Gastrointestinal problems (especially on the low-carbohydrate diet)
- Poor recovery when no carbohydrate is ingested
- Athletes do not feel comfortable during a week without training
- Increased risk of injury
- Mood disturbances (lethargy and irritability) during low-carbohydrate period

The main problem may be the incidence of gastrointestinal problems when using this regimen. Diarrhea has often been reported on the days when the high-protein, high-fat diet is consumed. During the first three days, athletes may also experience hypoglycemia, and they may not recover very well from the exhausting exercise bout when no carbohydrate is ingested. Also, the fact that athletes cannot train in the week before an event is not ideal, because the worst punishment for most athletes seems to be asking them to avoid training. These factors may also have an impact on the mental preparation for an event.

Because of the numerous disadvantages of the classical supercompensation protocol, studies have focused on a more moderate protocol that would achieve similar results. Sherman et al. (1981) studied three types of muscle glycogen supercompensation regimens in runners. The subjects slowly reduced their training over a 6-day period from 90 minutes running at 75% $\dot{V}O_2$max to complete rest on the last day. During each taper, they ingested one of the following three diets:

- A mixed diet with 50% carbohydrate
- A low-carbohydrate diet (25% carbohydrate) for the first 3 days, followed by 3 days of a high-carbohydrate diet (70%) (classical supercompensation protocol)
- A mixed diet for the first 3 days (50% carbohydrate) followed by 3 days of a high-carbohydrate diet (70%) (moderate supercompensation protocol)

The classical protocol resulted in very high muscle glycogen stores (211 mmol/kg w.w.), thus, confirming the results of earlier studies. However, the moderate approach produced very similar muscle glycogen levels (204 mmol/kg w.w.) and therefore, a normal training taper in conjunction with a moderate-carbohydrate to high-carbohydrate diet proved just as effective as the classical supercompensation protocol. A slightly modified and commonly applied strategy of the moderate supercompensation protocol is depicted in figure 5.3b. The moderate supercompensation protocol does not have the disadvantages of the classical protocol and is the preferred regimen.

Carbohydrate loading, or increased carbohydrate stores, increases time to exhaustion (endurance capacity) on average by about 20% and reduces the time taken to complete a set task (time trial; endurance performance) by 2% to 3% (Hawley et al. 1997). However, the available studies seem to suggest that the duration of exercise has to be at least 90 minutes before performance benefits can be demonstrated. Carbohydrate loading seems to have no effect on sprint performance and high-intensity exercise up to about 30 minutes compared with normal diets (~50% carbohydrate). This finding is not unexpected, because, at these high intensities, glycogen depletion is probably not the performance-limiting factor. However, several days on a very low (<10%) carbohydrate diet after a prolonged cycle ride to exhaustion has been shown to impair endurance capacity at 100% $\dot{V}O_2$max (Maughan, Greenhaff, et al. 1997).

Carbohydrate loading has also been reported to improve performance in team sports involving high-intensity intermittent exercise and skills, such as soccer and hockey (Balsom et al. 1999), although this result has not always been confirmed. A study was performed in elite Swedish soccer players who played 2 matches separated by 3 days (Saltin 1973). One group consumed a high-carbohydrate diet, and the other group consumed a normal diet between the matches. Before the second match, muscle glycogen concentrations were 50% lower in the group that consumed the control diet. At halftime (after 45 minutes), muscle glycogen was virtually depleted in this group, whereas the high-carbohydrate group still had some glycogen left (see table 5.1). This glycogen status was related to the distance covered during the match, which was significantly lower with the control diet and low muscle glycogen concentrations. The players also spent less time sprinting and thus were believed to have impaired running performance.

Supercompensation Strategies in Sport

Although muscle glycogen is important in most endurance sports, supercompensation strategies are not always applicable. For instance in cycling, stage races consist of several days of consecutive competition. Although a supercompensation regimen can theoretically be followed before the first stage, the nature of the sport does not allow the athletes to prepare for a week. Similar problems occur in sports where consecutive competitions follow each other within 1 day to 5 days. This supercompensation protocol, however, seems very suitable for marathon running and triathlon.

Muscle glycogen supercompensation is not of great importance to individuals involved in high-intensity exercise. Muscle glycogen availability per se is not usually responsible for fatigue during high-intensity exercise, provided that the pre-exercise glycogen store is not depleted to below 25 mmol/kg w.w. (4 g/kg w.w.). Even so, athletes involved in high-intensity training do need to consume sufficient carbohydrate in their diet. It has been shown that diets very low in carbohydrate content can compromise exercise performance at intensities around 95% to 100% of the maximum oxygen uptake (Maughan, Greenhaff, et al. 1997). Glycogen availability probably does not limit performance during repeated bouts of high intensity exercise because rates of glycogenolysis and lactate production decline under these conditions.

It must also be noted that every gram of carbohydrate is stored with approximately 3 g of water, which means that storage of 500g (8,000 kJ or 2,000 kcal) of carbohydrate is accompanied by an increase in body mass of approximately 2 kg. In some sports or disciplines (especially weight-bearing activities) this increase in body mass may not be desirable.

Carbohydrate Intake 3 Hours to 5 Hours Before Exercise

Athletes should have the last fairly large meal 3 hours to 5 hours before competition. Often this meal is a breakfast, which can be very important after an overnight fast when the liver is almost depleted of glycogen. The advantages of a meal in the hours before exercise are related to the increased carbohydrate availability in muscle and liver. In the 3 hours to 5 hours before exercise, some carbohydrate is incorporated into muscle glycogen. Carbohydrate intake in the last hour before competition will not affect muscle glycogen but still has an effect on liver glycogen and increases the delivery of carbohydrate to the muscle during exercise.

Ingestion of a carbohydrate-rich meal (containing 140 to approximately 330 g carbohydrate) 3 hours to 5 hours before exercise increases muscle glycogen levels (Coyle et al. 1985) and improves exercise performance (Neufer et al. 1987). Such a meal could include carbohydrate sources such as bread and jam or honey, cereals, porridge, bananas, canned fruit,

Table 5.1 Diet and Performance in Soccer

Glycogen concentration (g/kg ww muscle)			
	Before	**Halftime**	**End**	
High-carbohydrate diet	15	4	1	
Normal diet	7	1	0	

Distance covered				
	1st half (m)	**2nd half (m)**	**Walk (%)**	**Sprint (%)**
High-carbohydrate diet	6,100	5,900	27	24
Normal diet	5,600	4,100	50	15

Reprinted, by permission, from B. Saltin, 1973, "Metabolic fundamentals in exercise," *Medicine and Science in Sports and Exercise* 5: 137-146.

and fruit juice. Following is an example of a daily diet containing 150 g of carbohydrate representing at least 80% of the energy intake:

- Meal 1: 1 large bowl of porridge with skim milk, 1 banana, 1 glass (250 ml) of sweetened orange juice
- Meal 2: 4 slices of bread with jam or honey, 1 can of a soft drink
- Meal 3: 3 cups of rice made into a light stir fry with small amounts of lean ham or chicken, peas, corn, mushrooms, and onion, and 1 glass (250 ml) of fruit juice

The enhanced performance observed in research studies is likely related to small increases in pre-exercise muscle glycogen. However, replenishing the liver glycogen levels may be even more important. Liver glycogen concentrations are substantially reduced after an overnight fast. Ingestion of carbohydrate increases these reserves and contributes, together with any ongoing absorption of the ingested carbohydrate, to the maintenance of blood glucose concentrations during the subsequent exercise bout. Plasma glucose and insulin concentrations return to basal levels within 30 minutes to 60 minutes after ingestion. However, ingestion of carbohydrate in the hours before exercise has three important effects:

- Transient fall in plasma glucose with the onset of exercise
- Increased carbohydrate oxidation and accelerated glycogen breakdown
- Blunting of FA mobilization and fat oxidation

The effects on FA mobilization can persist for a long time after carbohydrate ingestion. Montain et al. (1991) showed a blunting of FA mobilization 6 hours after ingestion of a carbohydrate meal.

These metabolic changes, however, do not appear to be detrimental to exercise performance, with an increased carbohydrate availability compensating for the greater carbohydrate utilization. No differences in exercise performance were observed after ingestion of meals that produced marked differences in plasma glucose and insulin levels (Wee et al. 1999; Jentjens and Jeukendrup 2003a; Jentjens, Cale, et al. 2003; Moseley et al. 2001). From a practical perspective, if access to carbohydrate during exercise is limited or nonexistent, ingestion of 200 g to 300 g of carbohydrate 3 hours to 4 hours before exercise may be an effective strategy for enhancing carbohydrate availability during the subsequent exercise period.

Carbohydrate Intake 30 Minutes to 60 Minutes Before Exercise

The ingestion of carbohydrate in the hour before exercise results in a large rise in plasma glucose and insulin. With the onset of exercise, however, a rapid fall in blood glucose occurs. This fall is caused by a combination of several metabolic events. First, hyperinsulinemia stimulates glucose uptake, and in addition, contractile activity further stimulates muscle glucose uptake. The exercise-induced increase in the normal liver glucose output is inhibited by carbohydrate ingestion (Marmy-Conus et al. 1996), despite ongoing absorption of the ingested carbohydrate. An enhanced uptake and oxidation of blood glucose by skeletal muscle may account for the increased carbohydrate oxidation after pre-exercise carbohydrate ingestion. In addition, in some studies, an increase in muscle glycogen degradation has been observed.

The increase in plasma FA with exercise is attenuated after pre-exercise carbohydrate ingestion as a consequence of insulin-mediated inhibition of lipolysis (Horowitz et al. 1997). Even small increases in plasma insulin (e.g., after fructose ingestion) can result in a marked reduction of lipolysis. Fat oxidation is reduced not only because of the lower plasma FA availability (Horowitz et al. 1997) but also because of inhibition of fat oxidation in skeletal muscle. Artificially increased plasma FA availability did not completely return fat oxidation to levels seen during exercise in the fasted state (Horowitz et al. 1997). Some evidence indicates that the hyperinsulinemia and hyperglycemia reduce the uptake of FA into the mitochondria (Coyle et al. 1997).

Because the metabolic effects of pre-exercise carbohydrate ingestion are a consequence of hyperglycemia and hyperinsulinemia, interest has developed in strategies that minimize the changes in plasma glucose and insulin before exercise. These strategies include the ingestion of fructose or carbohydrate types other than glucose that have a lower **glycemic index** (see the side bar for an explanation of glycemic index), varying the carbohydrate load or the ingestion schedule, the addition of fat, and the inclusion of warm-up exercise in the pre-exercise period. In general, although these various interventions do modify the metabolic response to exercise, blunting the pre-exercise glycemic and insulinemic responses appears to offer no advantage for exercise performance.

GLYCEMIC INDEX

The glycemic index (GI) refers to the increase in blood glucose and insulin in response to a standard amount of food and is determined by measuring the area under the glucose curve. The GI measurements are usually based on the ingestion of 50 g of carbohydrate and measurements of blood glucose over a 2-hour period. The greater the glucose response and the greater the area under the curve, the greater the GI of a food. A greater GI indicates a rapid absorption and delivery of the carbohydrate into the circulation. The GI is calculated using the following formula:

$$GI = \text{area under the glucose curve of test food} / \text{area under the glucose curve of reference food} \times 100$$

The reference food is usually glucose or white bread and has a glycemic index of 100. Foods are generally divided into low-GI foods, moderate-GI foods, and high-GI foods. Low-GI foods have a GI of 55 or less, moderate-GI foods have a GI between 56 and 70, and high-GI foods have a GI of 71 or higher. Apples or lentils, for example, will result in a slow and small rise of the blood glucose concentration, whereas white bread or potatoes will result in a rapid rise in the blood glucose concentration. The apples and the lentils, therefore, are classified as low-GI foods and bread and potatoes are classified as high-GI foods. A list of high-GI, moderate-GI, and low-GI foods is given in table 5.2.

Table 5.2 Glycemic Index (GI) and Glycemic Load (GL)

Food	GI	Serving size (g)	Available carbohydrate (g)	GL (per serving)
High GI (>70)				
Boiled potato	101	150	17	17
Glucose	99	10	10	10
Baked potato	85	150	30	26
Lucozade, original	95	250 (ml)	42	40
Pancakes, buckwheat	102	77	22	22
Pretzels	83	30	20	16
Scones	92	25	9	7
Gatorade	78	250 (ml)	15	12
Isostar	70	250 (ml)	18	13
Bagel	72	70	35	25
Baguette, white, plain	95	70	37	27
Cheerios cereals	74	30	20	15
Corn flakes	81	30	26	21
Shredded wheat	75	30	20	15
K-time strawberry crunch bar	77	30	25	19
Puffed rice cakes	78	25	21	17
Watermelon	72	120	6	4
Popcorn	72	20	11	8
Stir fried vegetables	73	360	75	55

(continued)

110

Food	GI	Serving size (g)	Available carbohydrate (g)	GL (per serving)
Moderate GI (56–70)				
Doughnut	67	47	23	17
Croissant	67	57	26	17
Blueberry muffin	60	57	29	17
Coca-Cola	58	250 (ml)	26	16
French baguette with butter and strawberry jam	62	70	41	26
Porridge	58	250 (ml)	22	13
Rice, white, boiled	64	150	36	23
Long-grain rice, boiled	56	150	41	23
Digestives (cookies)	59	25	16	10
Oreo cookies	64	40	32	20
Ice cream, regular	61	50	13	8
Fruit cocktail, canned	55	120	16	9
Mars bar	65	60	40	26
Snickers bar	55	60	35	19
Power bar, chocolate	56	65	42	24
Ironman PR bar	39	65	26	10
Low GI (<55)				
Honey	55	25	18	10
Potato crisps/chips	54	50	21	11
Sweet corn	54	80	17	9
Pizza Super supreme (Pizza Hut)	36	100	24	9
Wheat bread	53	30	20	11
Carrots	47	80	6	3
Orange juice	50	250 (ml)	26	13
Apple juice	40	250 (ml)	29	12
Rye bread	41	30	12	5
All Bran cereal	42	30	23	9
Baked beans	48	150	15	7
Kidney beans	28	150	25	7
Lentils	30	150	17	5
Smoothie, raspberry	33	250 (ml)	41	14
M&Ms (peanut)	33	30	17	6
Muesli	49	30	20	10
Prince Fourre chocolate cookies	52	45	30	16
Ice cream, low-fat, vanilla	50	50	6	3
Spaghetti, boiled	38	180	48	18
Chocolate milk, plain	43	50	28	12
Skim milk	32	250 (ml)	13	4
Milk, full-fat	27	250 (ml)	12	3

(continued)

(continued)

Table 5.2 *(continued)*

Food	GI	Serving size (g)	Available carbohydrate (g)	GL (per serving)
Low GI (<55)				
Yogurt	36	200	9	3
Low-fat yogurt	24	200	14	3
Apple	38	120	15	6
Banana	52	120	24	12
Orange	42	120	11	5
Grapes	46	120	18	8
Peach	42	120	11	5
Peanuts	14	50	6	1
Fructose	19	10	10	2

Reprinted, by permission, from K. Foster-Powell and J.C. Brand-Miller, "International table of glycemic index and glycemic load values: 2002," *American Journal of Clinical Nutrition.* July 76(1): 5-56.

The use of the GI as a tool is quite controversial, mainly because the GI for any given food might vary considerably between individuals. The tables usually provide an average figure that is not necessarily useful in controlling an individual's blood glucose concentration. The GI of foods is also sometimes confusing. In general, foods with large amounts of refined sugar (simple carbohydrates) have a high GI and sugars with a high fiber content and complex carbohydrates have a lower GI. However, some complex carbohydrates (starches) can have a high GI. On the other hand, adding relatively small amounts of fat to a high-GI carbohydrate can lower the GI of the food substantially. Therefore, the GI must be interpreted and used with caution. It can probably be a useful tool if its limitations and pitfalls are well understood.

The **glycemic load** (GL) is a relatively new way to assess the impact of carbohydrate consumption that takes the GI into account but gives a fuller picture than does GI alone. A GI value indicates only how rapidly a particular carbohydrate appears as glucose in the circulation but does not take into account the amount of the food that is normally consumed. For example, the carbohydrate in watermelon has a high GI, but there is not a lot of it, so watermelon's GL is relatively low. A GL of 20 or more is high, a GL of 11 to 19 is medium, and a GL of 10 or less is low. Foods that have a low GL almost always have a low GI. Foods with an intermediate or high GL range from a very low to a very high GI. The GL is calculated by multiplying the GI by the amount of carbohydrate (g) in one serving, and dividing by 100.

For example, a carrot weighing 60 g contains only 4 g of carbohydrate. To get 50 g, you would have to eat about 750 g of carrots. GL takes the GI value and multiplies it by the actual amount of carbohydrates in a serving. A GL is low if it is between 1 and 10, medium if it is between 11 and 19, and high if it is 20 or higher.

The glycemic responses during exercise after carbohydrate ingestion are determined by a number of factors related to the delivery of carbohydrate into the circulation, as well as the uptake from the circulation. Some of the factors that determine the glycemic response during exercise are

- the combined stimulatory effects of insulin and contractile activity on muscle glucose uptake;

- the balance of inhibitory and stimulatory effects of insulin and catecholamines on liver glucose output; and

- the magnitude of ongoing intestinal absorption of glucose from the ingested carbohydrate.

The metabolic alterations associated with ingestion of carbohydrate in the 30 minutes to 60 minutes before exercise have the potential to influence exercise performance. The increase in muscle glycogenolysis observed previously possibly results in an earlier onset of fatigue during exercise as suggested in a study by Foster, Costill, and Fink (1979). In contrast, the vast majority of such studies have shown either unchanged or enhanced endurance exercise performance after ingestion of carbohydrate in the hour before exercise.

Thus, the well-documented metabolic effects of pre-exercise carbohydrate ingestion and the possibility of negative consequences in susceptible individuals notwithstanding, little evidence appears to support the practice of avoiding carbohydrate ingestion in the hour before exercise, provided sufficient carbohydrate is ingested. Individual practice must be determined on the basis of individual experience with various pre-exercise carbohydrate ingestion protocols.

Finally, when carbohydrate is ingested during prolonged exercise, the potential negative effects of the pre-exercise carbohydrate feedings is reduced. When a high-GI food is ingested before exercise, it has little or no effect on metabolism and performance if carbohydrate is ingested during exercise (Burke et al. 1998).

Carbohydrate During Exercise

There is convincing evidence from numerous studies that carbohydrate feeding during exercise of about 45 minutes or longer (Jeukendrup et al. 1997; Coyle et al. 1986) can improve endurance capacity and performance. Studies have also addressed questions of which carbohydrates are most effective, what is the most effective feeding schedule, and what is the optimal amount of carbohydrate to consume. Other studies have looked at factors that could possibly influence the oxidation of ingested carbohydrate, such as muscle glycogen levels, diet, and exercise intensity. Mechanisms by which carbohydrate feeding during exercise may improve endurance performance include the following.

- Maintaining blood glucose and high levels of carbohydrate oxidation. Coyle et al. 1986 demonstrated that carbohydrate feeding during exercise at 70% $\dot{V}O_2$max prevents the drop in blood glucose that was observed when water (placebo) was ingested. In the placebo trials, the glucose concentration started to drop after 1 hour of exercise and reached extremely low concentrations (2.5 mmol/L) at exhaustion after 3 hours. With carbohydrate feeding, glucose concentrations were maintained above 3 mmol/L,

and subjects continued to exercise for 4 hours at the same intensity. Total-carbohydrate oxidation rates followed a similar pattern. A drop in carbohydrate oxidation occurred after about 1.5 hours of exercise with placebo, and high rates of carbohydrate oxidation were maintained with carbohydrate feeding. Interestingly, when subjects ingested only water and exercised to exhaustion, they were able to continue again when glucose was ingested or infused intravenously. These studies showed the importance of plasma glucose as a substrate during exercise.

- Glycogen sparing. Carbohydrate feedings during exercise "spare" liver glycogen (Bosch, Dennis, and Noakes 1994; Jeukendrup et al. 1999), and Tsintzas and Williams (1998) discussed a potential muscle glycogen sparing effect. Generally, muscle glycogen sparing is not found during cycling (Coyle et al. 1986; Jeukendrup et al. 1999), but it may be important during running (Tsintzas et al. 1995).

- Promoting glycogen synthesis during exercise. After intermittent exercise, muscle glycogen concentrations were higher when carbohydrate was ingested than when water was ingested (Yaspelkis et al. 1993). This finding could indicate a reduced muscle glycogen breakdown. However, the ingested carbohydrate was possibly used to synthesize muscle glycogen during the low-intensity exercise periods (Kuipers et al. 1986; Keizer et al. 1987).

- Affecting motor skills. Few studies have attempted to study the effect of carbohydrate drinks on motor skills. One such study investigated 13 trained tennis players and observed that when players ingested carbohydrate during a 2-hour training session (Vergauwen, Brouns, and Hespel 1998), stroke quality was improved during the final stages of prolonged play. This effect was most noticeable when the situations required fast running speed, rapid movement, and explosiveness.

- Affecting the central nervous system. Carbohydrate may also have central nervous system effects. Although direct evidence for such an effect is lacking, the brain can sense changes in the composition of the mouth and stomach contents. Evidence, for instance, suggests that taste influences mood and may also influence perception of effort. An interesting observation provides support for a central nervous system effect. When a hypoglycemic person bites a candy bar, that person's symptoms are almost immediately reduced, and the person feels better again long before the carbohydrate has reached the systemic circulation and the brain. The central nervous system effect may also explain why some studies report positive effects of carbohydrate during exercise on performance lasting approximately 1 hour (Jeukendrup et al. 1997). During exercise of such short duration, only a small amount of the carbohydrate becomes available as a substrate. Most of the ingested carbohydrate is still in the stomach or intestine. Whether the central nervous system effects of glucose feeding are mediated by sensory detection of glucose or perception of sweetness is not known, although studies with placebo solutions with identical taste to glucose solutions suggest that sweetness is not the key factor.

Feeding Strategies and Exogenous Carbohydrate Oxidation

A greater contribution of exogenous (external) fuel sources (carbohydrate) spares endogenous (internal) sources, and the notion that a greater contribution from exogenous sources increases endurance capacity is enticing. The contribution of exogenous substrates can be measured using stable (or radioactive) isotopic tracers. The principle of this technique is quite simple: The ingested substrate (e.g., glucose) is labeled and the label can be measured in expired gas after the substrate has been oxidized. The more the ingested substrate has been oxidized, the more of the label

(tracer) will be recovered in the expired gas. Knowing the amount of tracer ingested, the amount of tracer in the expired gas, and the total CO_2 production enables us to calculate exogenous substrate oxidation rates.

The typical pattern of exogenous glucose oxidation rates is shown in figure 5.4. The labeled CO_2 starts to appear 5 minutes after ingestion of the labeled carbohydrate. During the first 75 minutes to 90 minutes of exercise, **exogenous carbohydrate oxidation** continues to rise as more and more carbohydrate is emptied from the stomach and absorbed in the intestine. After 75 minutes to 90 minutes a leveling-off occurs, and the exogenous carbohydrate oxidation rate reaches its maximum value and does not increase further. Several factors have been suggested to influence exogenous carbohydrate oxidation including feeding schedule, type and amount of carbohydrate ingested, and the exercise intensity.

Feeding Schedule

The timing of carbohydrate feedings seems to have relatively little effect on exogenous carbohydrate oxidation rates. Studies in which a large bolus (100 g) of a carbohydrate in solution was given produced similar exogenous carbohydrate oxidation rates to studies in which 100 g carbohydrate was ingested at regular intervals.

Amount of Carbohydrate

From a practical point of view, the amount of carbohydrate that needs to be ingested to attain optimal

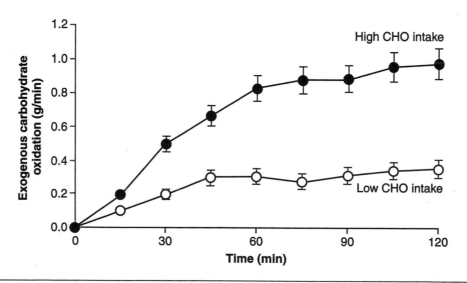

Figure 5.4 Exogenous carbohydrate oxidation during exercise. The curve shows the typical pattern of the oxidation of carbohydrate ingested at regular intervals.

Reprinted, by permission, from A.E. Jeukendrup and R. Jentjens, 2000, "Oxidation of carbohydrate feedings during prolonged exercise: Current thoughts, guidelines, and directions for future research," *Sports Medicine* 29(6): 407-424.

performance is important. The optimal amount is likely to be the amount that results in maximal exogenous oxidation rates without causing gastrointestinal problems. Rehrer, Wagenmakers, et al. (1992) studied the oxidation of different amounts of carbohydrate ingested during 80 minutes of cycling exercise at 70% $\dot{V}O_2$max. Subjects received either a 4.5% glucose solution (a total of 58 g glucose during 80 minutes of exercise) or a 17% glucose solution (220 g during 80 minutes of exercise). Total exogenous carbohydrate oxidation was measured and found to be slightly higher with the larger carbohydrate dose (42 g versus 32 g in 80 minutes). So, even though the amount of carbohydrate ingested was increased almost fourfold, the oxidation rate was barely affected. Jeukendrup et al. (1999) investigated the oxidation rates of carbohydrate intakes up to 3.00 g/min and found oxidation rates of up to 0.94 g/min at the end of 120 minutes of cycling exercise.

The results from a large number of studies were used to construct figure 5.5 (Jeukendrup and Jentjens 2000). The peak exogenous carbohydrate oxidation rates are plotted against the rate of ingestion. The maximal rate at which a single ingested carbohydrate can be oxidized is about 1.0 g/min. The horizontal line depicts the absolute maximum just below 1.1 g/min. The dotted line represents the line of identity where the rate of carbohydrate ingestion equals the rate of exogenous carbohydrate oxidation. This graph suggests that oxidation of orally ingested carbohydrate may already be optimal at ingestion rates around 1.2 g/min. Thus, athletes should ensure a carbohydrate intake of about 70 g/h for optimal

carbohydrate delivery. Adopting an ingestion rate of 70 g/h optimizes exogenous carbohydrate oxidation. Ingesting more than this amount of a single carbohydrate does not result in higher carbohydrate oxidation rates and is more likely to cause gastrointestinal discomfort. This amount of carbohydrate can be found in the following sources:

- 1 L sports drink (Gatorade, Powerade, Isostar, Lucozade Sport)
- 600 ml cola drink
- 1.5 Power bar
- 1.5 Gatorade energy bar
- Three medium bananas
- 120 g to 150 g wine gums

Type of Carbohydrate

Studies have compared the oxidation rates of various types of carbohydrate to the oxidation of ingested glucose during exercise (Jeukendrup and Jentjens 2000). Glucose is oxidized at relatively high rates (up to about 1 g/min). The other two monosaccharides, fructose and galactose, are oxidized at much lower rates because they have to be converted into glucose in the liver before they can be metabolized. They are, therefore, a relatively slow energy source.

The oxidation rates of maltose, sucrose, and glucose polymers (maltodextrins) are comparable to those of glucose. Starches with a relatively large amount of amylopectin are rapidly digested and absorbed, whereas those with a high amylose content

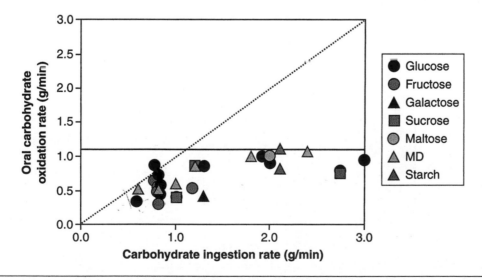

Figure 5.5 Maximal exogenous carbohydrate oxidation versus the rate of ingestion.

Reprinted, by permission, from A.E. Jeukendrup and R. Jentjens, 2000, "Oxidation of carbohydrate feedings during prolonged exercise: Current thoughts, guidelines, and directions for future research," *Sports Medicine* 29(6): 407-424.

have a relatively slow rate of hydrolysis. Ingested amylopectin is oxidized at very high rates (similar to glucose), whereas amylose is oxidized at very low rates. Carbohydrates are divided into two categories according to the rate at which they are oxidized: a higher rate group (~1 g/min) and a lower rate (~0.6 g/min). These two categories of carbohydrates are listed in figure 5.6.

Oxidized at rates of up to ~1 g/min	Oxidized at rates of up to ~0.6 g/min
Glucose	Fructose
Maltose	Galactose
Sucrose	Amylose
Maltodextrins	
Amylopectin	

Figure 5.6 Oxidation rates of ingested carbohydrate during exercise.

Reprinted, by permission, from K. Foster-Powell and J.C. Brand-Miller, "International table of glycemic index and glycemic load values: 2002," *American Journal of Clinical Nutrition* July 76(1): 5-56.

Shi et al. (1995) suggest that the inclusion of 2 or 3 different carbohydrates (glucose, fructose, and sucrose) in a drink may increase water and carbohydrate absorption despite the increased osmolality. This effect is attributed to the separate transport mechanisms across the intestinal wall for glucose, fructose, and sucrose. The monosaccharides glucose and galactose are transported across the luminal membrane by a glucose transporter called SGLT1 (see chapter 3) and fructose is transported by GLUT5. Interestingly, fructose absorption from a certain amount of the disaccharide sucrose is more rapid than the absorption of the same amount of fructose. If a combination of glucose and fructose is ingested, more carbohydrate will be absorbed and made available for oxidation. Ingestion of relatively large amounts of glucose and fructose can result in exogenous carbohydrate oxidation rates well over 1 g/min (Jentjens et al. 2004) (see figure 5.7).

Exercise Intensity

With increasing exercise intensity, the active muscle mass becomes more dependent on carbohydrate as a source of energy. Both an increased muscle glycogenolysis and an increased plasma glucose oxidation contribute to the increased energy demands (Romijn et al. 1993). Therefore exogenous carbohydrate oxidation increases with increasing exercise intensities. Indeed, Pirnay et al. (1982) reported lower exogenous carbohydrate oxidation rates at low exercise intensities compared with moderate intensities, but exogenous carbohydrate oxidation tended to level off between 51% and 64% $\dot{V}O_2$max. However, when the exercise intensity was increased from 60% to 75% $\dot{V}O_2$max, exogenous carbohydrate oxidation rates leveled off or even decreased (Pirnay et al. 1995).

Lower exogenous carbohydrate oxidation rates possibly are only observed at very low exercise intensities when the reliance on carbohydrate as an energy source is minimal. In this situation, part of the ingested carbohydrate may be directed toward nonoxidative glucose disposal (storage in the liver or muscle) rather than toward oxidation. Studies with carbohydrate ingestion during intermittent exercise have suggested that during low-intensity exercise, glycogen can be resynthesized (Kuipers et al. 1989).

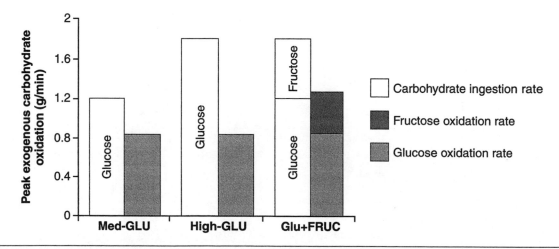

Figure 5.7 The oxidation rate of glucose plus fructose in a combined drink is higher than the oxidation rate of similar amounts of either glucose or fructose alone.

Reprinted, by permission, from A.E. Jeukendrup and R. Jentjens, 2000, "Oxidation of carbohydrate feedings during prolonged exercise: Current thoughts, guidelines, and directions for future research," *Sports Med* 29(6): 407-424.

Thus, at exercise intensities below 50% $\dot{V}O_2max$, exogenous carbohydrate oxidation increases with increasing total carbohydrate oxidation rates. Usually above approximately 60% $\dot{V}O_2max$, oxidation rates will not further increase.

Limitations to Exogenous Carbohydrate Oxidation

As discussed earlier, exogenous carbohydrate oxidation seems to be limited to rates of 1.0 g/min to 1.1 g/min (see figure 5.5). This finding is supported by most of the studies using either radioactive or stable isotopes to quantify exogenous carbohydrate oxidation during exercise. One limiting factor could be the rate of gastric emptying (see figure 5.8). However, some studies indicate that gastric emptying is unlikely to affect exogenous carbohydrate oxidation rates (Rehrer, Wagenmakers et al. 1992; Saris et al. 1993). Because in these studies only 32% to 48% of the carbohydrate delivered to the intestine was oxidized, gastric emptying was determined not to be limiting exogenous carbohydrate oxidation.

Another potential limiting factor is the rate of absorption of carbohydrate into the systemic circulation from the small intestine. Studies using a triple-lumen technique have measured glucose absorption and estimated whole-body intestinal absorption rates of a 6% glucose-electrolyte solution (Duchman et al. 1997). The estimated maximal absorption rate of the intestine ranged from 1.2 g/min to 1.7 g/min. Studies, using stable isotopes have observed a reduction in the glucose output by the liver when carbohydrate is ingested. When very large amounts of glucose are ingested, hepatic glucose output can be blocked completely (Jeukendrup et al. 1999). At low to moderate ingestion rates, no net storage of glucose occurs in the liver. Instead, all ingested glucose appears in the bloodstream. The glucose output from the liver can vary from nothing to approximately 1 g/min, when no carbohydrate is ingested, the intensity of exercise is high enough (>60% $\dot{V}O_2max$), and the duration long enough (>1 hour).

Glucose appearing in the bloodstream was taken up at rates similar to its rate of appearance (Ra), and 90% to 95% of this glucose was oxidized during exercise. When a larger dose of carbohydrate was ingested (3 g/min), the rate of appearance of glucose from the intestine was one-third of the rate of carbohydrate ingestion (0.96 g/min to 1.04 g/min). Thus, only part of the ingested carbohydrate entered the systemic circulation. However, a large proportion of the glucose appearing in the blood was taken up by tissues (presumably mainly by the muscle) and 90% to 95% was oxidized. Therefore, entrance into the systemic circulation is a limiting factor for exogenous glucose oxidation, rather than intramuscular factors. Hawley et al. (1994) bypassed both intestinal absorption and hepatic glucose uptake by infusing glucose into the circulation of subjects exercising at 70% $\dot{V}O_2max$. When large amounts of glucose were infused and subjects were hyperglycemic (10 mmol/L),

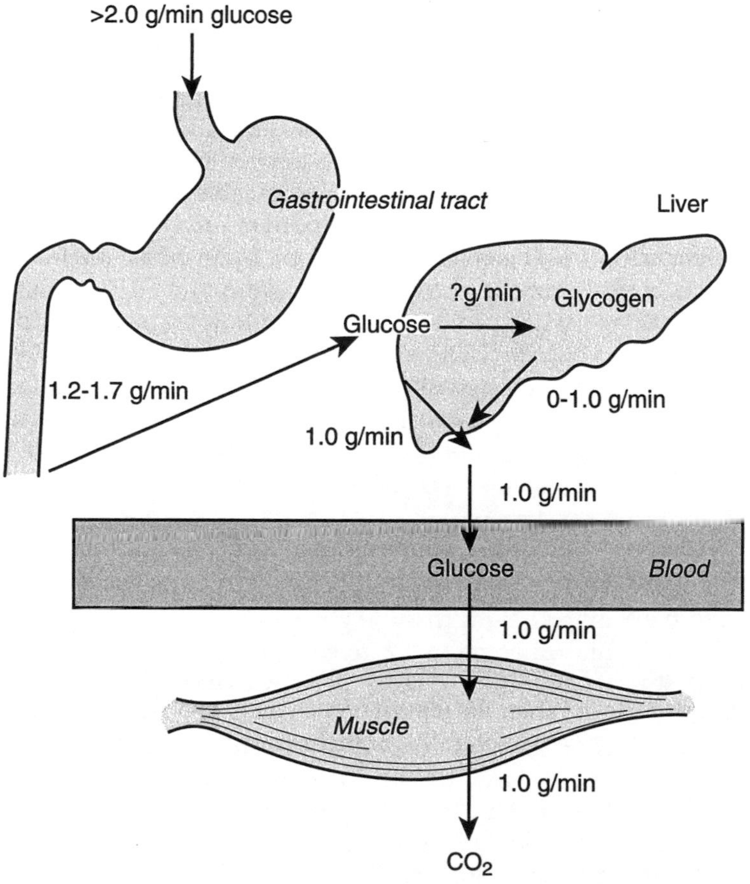

Figure 5.8 Gastric emptying of glucose, absorption, and uptake in skeletal muscle. Glucose travels from the gut after ingestion to the muscle. The suggested maximal flux at each of the stages is indicated.

Reprinted, by permission, from L.P.G. Jentjens and A.E. Jeukendrup, 2003, "Glycogen resynthesis after exercise," *Sports Medicine* 33(2): 117-144.

blood glucose oxidation rate increased substantially above 1 g/min.

Exogenous carbohydrate oxidation is limited by the rate of digestion, absorption, and subsequent transport of glucose into the systemic circulation. During high-intensity exercise (e.g., >80% $\dot{V}O_2$max), a reduced blood flow to the gut may result in a decreased absorption of glucose and water (Brouns and Beckers 1993) and hence a low rate of absorption relative to the rate of ingestion. Taken together, this information suggests that intestinal absorption is a contributing factor in limiting the oxidation of ingested carbohydrate at rates higher than 1.1 g/min, but it may not be the sole factor. The liver may also play an additional important role. Hepatic glucose output is highly regulated, and the glucose output derived from the intestine and from hepatic glycogenolysis and gluconeogenesis possibly does not exceed 1.1 g/min, even though the maximal rate of glucose absorption is slightly in excess of this rate. If supply from the intestine is too large (>1.0 g/min), glycogen synthesis may be stimulated in the liver.

Metabolic Effects of Carbohydrate Intake During Exercise

The metabolic effects of carbohydrate intake during exercise depend on various factors, including the amount ingested, the timing of the intake, and the intensity and duration of exercise. Generally, carbohydrate ingestion early in exercise has large effects on the insulin response, fat mobilization, and substrate utilization, whereas ingestion late in exercise has relatively little effect. If carbohydrate is ingested at the onset of exercise, plasma insulin concentrations rise in the first minutes of exercise and lipolysis is suppressed. FA availability is lowered and this condition may partly explain the lower fat oxidation rates observed in this situation. However, carbohydrate intake during exercise also inhibits fat oxidation by hindering the transport of FA into the mitochondria.

When carbohydrate is ingested later in exercise, the already raised catecholamine levels blunt the insulin response, and, hence, fat oxidation is less affected. Similarly, when a small amount of carbohydrate is ingested during exercise, the effect on the plasma insulin concentration is also small, whereas larger intakes result in an increased insulin response. Exercise intensity may be an important factor as well. Studies suggest that the suppressive effect of carbohydrate feeding on fat metabolism is greater at low exercise intensities than at high exercise intensities.

Carbohydrate After Exercise

The main purpose of carbohydrate intake after physical activity is to replenish depleted stores of liver and muscle glycogen. The replenishment of muscle glycogen is directly related to recovery of endurance capacity, and glycogen loading, or **carboloading,** in between training sessions has become common practice among endurance athletes.

Regulation of Glucose Uptake and Glycogen Synthesis

Glucose uptake in the muscle is through facilitated diffusion via the glucose transporter GLUT-4, which is largely responsible for transporting glucose across the sarcolemma. GLUT-4 is normally stored in intracellular vesicles but can translocate to the cell membrane, merge with the cell membrane, and allow increased transport of glucose into the cell (see figure 5.9). Both muscle contraction (through Ca^{2+} ions) and insulin secretion will stimulate the translocation of GLUT-4 and, hence, glucose transport into the cell.

After its transport across the sarcolemma, glucose is phosphorylated to glucose-6-phosphate (G6P) by the enzyme hexokinase (see figure 5.9). After phosphorylation, glucose is trapped in the muscle because the sarcolemma is impermeable to phosphorylated glucose and no transporters for G6P exists. G6P is next converted to glucose-1-phosphate (G1P) by the enzyme phosphoglucomutase, and G1P is combined with uridine triphosphate to form uridine diphosphate (UDP)–glucose and pyrophosphate (PPi) in a reaction catalyzed by 1-phosphate uridyltransferase. UDP is a carrier of glucose units and takes the glucose molecule to the terminal glucose residue of a preexisting glycogen molecule. UDP-glucose can be considered an activated glucose molecule. The UDP-glucose then forms an α-1,4 glycosidic bond, a reaction catalyzed by glycogen synthase, resulting in one long straight chain of glucose molecules. However, branch points (α-1,6 glycosidic bond) are introduced into the glycogen structure by a branching enzyme. When the length of a chain is about 12 glucose residues long, the branching enzyme detaches a chain about 7 residues long and reattaches it to a neighboring chain by an α-1,6 glycosidic bond. Branching results in the formation of a very large but compact glycogen molecule.

The rate of glycogen synthesis depends on several factors, including the activity of enzymes (especially glycogen synthase) and the transport of glucose into the cell, which, in turn, are influenced by muscle glycogen concentration and insulin. As

Carbohydrate

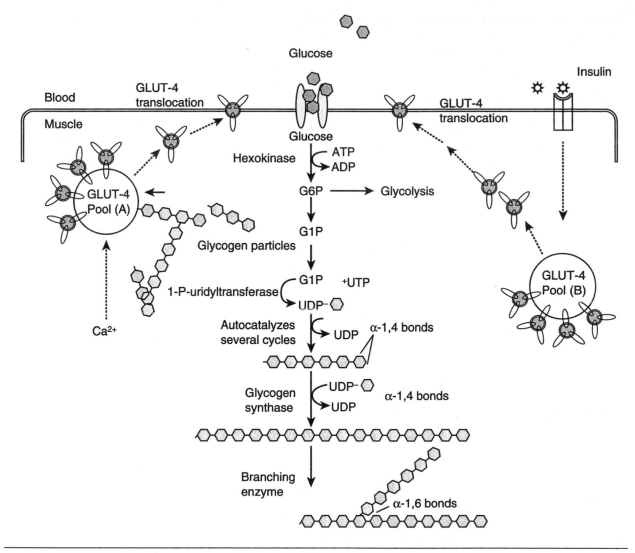

Figure 5.9 Mechanisms of glucose transport into the muscle and the synthesis of glycogen.

Reprinted, by permission, from L.P.G. Jentjens and A.E. Jeukendrup, 2003, "Glycogen resynthesis after exercise," *Sports Medicine* 33(2): 117-144.

a result of the changing activity of these enzymes and the effectiveness of these transport mechanisms, two phases can be distinguished in the process of glycogen synthesis after exercise. These phases are the initial, insulin-independent, or rapid, phase and the insulin-dependent, or slow, phase.

Rapid Phase of Glycogen Synthesis After Exercise

The rate-limiting enzyme for glycogen resynthesis after exercise, glycogen synthase, exists in an inactive D-form and an active I-form. More glycogen synthase is present in the active I-form when muscle glycogen concentrations are low (Kochan et al. 1979). As glycogen stores are replenished, more glycogen synthase

is transformed back into the D-form. Exercise activates glycogen synthase (immediately after exercise, as much as 80% of all glycogen synthase may be in the active I-form), but glycogen can only be formed if the substrate (UDP-glucose) is available. Another important factor in glycogen resynthesis, therefore, is the availability of glucose, which is mainly dependent on the glucose transport across the sarcolemma. During exercise and in the first hour after exercise, an abundance of GLUT-4 is available at the cell membrane, and glucose uptake into the muscle is facilitated. This exercise-induced effect on glucose transport, however, will last only a few hours in the absence of insulin. The increase in the permeability of the sarcolemma for glucose after exercise seems to be directly related to the amount of glycogen in the muscle. When muscle glycogen concentrations are very low, the enhanced glucose uptake may last longer. With high muscle glycogen concentrations, the effect is rapidly reversed.

Slow Phase of Glycogen Synthesis After Exercise

When the effect of the exercise-induced increase in glucose transport wears off, glycogen resynthesis occurs at a much slower rate. The rate at which glycogen synthesis occurs during the slow phase is highly dependent on the circulating insulin concentration, which will increase GLUT-4 translocation to the cell membrane and increase glucose transport into the muscle cell.

In addition, muscle contraction increases insulin sensitivity and this effect may last for several hours. This increased insulin sensitivity after exercise is thought to be an important component of the slow phase of glycogen synthesis. The glycogen synthase activity decreases during this phase as muscle glycogen is restored.

Once inside the muscle cell glucose is directed toward muscle glycogen rather than oxidation. This effect is mediated by an increased glycogen synthase activity. An increase in the amount of GLUT-4 present in the cell may also contribute to higher glycogen synthesis rates (Ren et al. 1994). After exercise, a rapid increase in GLUT-4 expression may occur, resulting in an increased synthesis of this protein, which, in turn, results in a proportional increase in insulin-stimulated glucose uptake and glycogen synthesis.

Postexercise Feeding and Rapid Recovery

A high rate of glycogen synthesis in the hours after exercise depends on the availability of substrate. In the absence of carbohydrate ingestion, glycogen resynthesis rates are very low, despite increased insulin sensitivity, increased glycogen synthase activity, and increased permeability of the sarcolemma to glucose (Ivy, Lee, et al. 1988). Often, the time to recover between successive athletic competitions or training sessions is very short. In such cases, rapid glycogen synthesis is even more important. Although muscle glycogen concentrations are unlikely to be completely restored to pre-exercise levels, all methods of carbohydrate supplementation that maximize glycogen restoration may benefit performance. Four factors have been recognized as potentially important in promoting restoration of muscle glycogen stores: (1) timing of carbohydrate intake, (2) rate of carbohydrate ingestion,

(3) the type of carbohydrate ingested, and (4) ingestion of protein and carbohydrate after exercise.

Timing of Carbohydrate Intake

The timing of carbohydrate intake can have an important effect on the rate of muscle glycogen synthesis after exercise (Ivy, Katz, et al. 1988). When carbohydrate intake is delayed until 2 hours after exercise, muscle glycogen concentration after 4 hours is 45% lower compared with ingestion of the same amount of carbohydrate immediately after exercise. Average glycogen resynthesis rates in the 2 hours after ingestion are 3 mmol/kg w.w./h to 4 mmol/kg w.w./h when carbohydrate is ingested after 2 hours and 5 mmol/kg w.w./h to 6 mmol/kg w.w./h when it is ingested immediately after exercise (see figure 5.10). When carbohydrate intake is delayed until after the rapid phase, less glucose is taken up and stored as glycogen, primarily because of decreasing insulin sensitivity after the first few hours after exercise. A substantial intake of carbohydrate immediately after exercise seems to prevent this developing insulin resistance quite effectively.

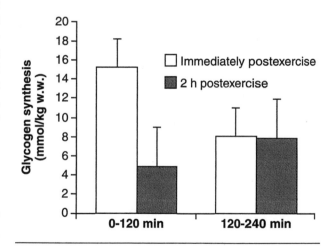

Figure 5.10 Effect of timing on muscle glycogen resynthesis.

Adapted, by permission, from J.L. Ivy, A.L. Katz, C.L. Cutler, W.M. Sherman, E.F. Cole, 1998, "Muscle glycogen synthesis after exercise: Effect of time of carbohydrate ingestion," *Journal of Applied Physiology* 64: 1480-1485.

Rate of Carbohydrate Ingestion

When no carbohydrate is ingested after exercise, the rate of muscle glycogen synthesis is extremely low (1 mmol/kg w.w./h to 2 mmol/kg w.w./h) (Ivy et al. 1988b). The ingestion of carbohydrate, especially in the first hours after exercise, results in enhanced muscle glycogen restoration, and glycogen is generally synthesized at a rate between 4.5 mmol/kg w.w./h and 11 mmol/kg w.w./h. In figure 5.11, the results of a large number of studies performed in different laboratories have been compiled. The rate of muscle glycogen synthesis plotted against the ingestion rate shows that with an increase in intake, an increase in synthesis also occurs in the first 3 hours to 5 hours after exercise. This graph shows a trend toward a higher glycogen synthesis rate when more carbohydrate is ingested, up to intakes of about 1.4 g/min, which is higher than previously suggested (Blom et al. 1987). At a given rate of carbohydrate intake, large variability exists in the rate of glycogen synthesis, probably indicating that other factors such as timing, type of carbohydrate ingested, and training are also important.

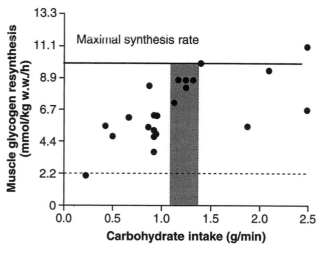

Figure 5.11 Muscle glycogen resynthesis after exercise as a function of the carbohydrate intake.

Adapted, by permission, from J.L. Ivy et al., 1988, "Muscle glycogen synthesis after exercise: Effect of time of carbohydrate ingestion," *Journal of Applied Physiology* 64: 1480-1485.

Type of Carbohydrate Ingested

Ingestion of different types of carbohydrate has different effects on glycogen synthesis. Blom et al. (1987) demonstrated that fructose ingestion resulted in slower rates of muscle glycogen synthesis after exercise compared with glucose or sucrose ingestion. Fructose must be converted to glucose in the liver before it can be used for glycogen synthesis in the muscle. Because this process takes time, glycogen synthesis occurs at a lower rate compared with a directly available carbohydrate source such as glucose. Other studies confirmed that glycogen synthesis from fructose occurs at only 50% of the rate of glycogen synthesis from glucose. In the study by Blom et al. (1987), sucrose intake resulted in similar

muscle glycogen levels 4 hours after exercise as glucose intake.

Glycogen synthesis is dependent on the GI of the meal consumed after exercise. After 6 hours of recovery, muscle glycogen is more restored with a high-GI meal compared with a low-GI meal. Thus, the absorption rate and the availability of glucose seem to be very important factors for glycogen synthesis. Low-GI foods result in lower glycogen resynthesis in the first hours after exercise.

Protein and Carbohydrate Ingestion After Exercise

Certain amino acids have a potent effect on the secretion of insulin. The effects of adding amino acids and proteins to a carbohydrate solution have been investigated to optimize glycogen synthesis. Zawadzki et al. (1992) compared glycogen resynthesis rates after ingestion of carbohydrate, protein, or carbohydrate plus protein. As expected, very little glycogen was stored when protein alone was ingested. Glycogen storage was increased when carbohydrate was ingested. However, most interestingly, glycogen storage was further increased when carbohydrate was ingested together with protein.

The increased glycogen synthesis also coincided with higher insulin levels. Van Loon et al. (2000) used a protein hydrolysate and amino acid mixture (0.8 g/kg/h carbohydrate plus 0.4 g/kg/h of protein/amino acid) that had previously been shown to result in a marked insulin response in combination with carbohydrate. When subjects ingested carbohydrate plus this protein/amino acid mixture, they observed higher glycogen resynthesis rates than when only carbohydrate was ingested. In this study, subjects also ingested an isoenergetic carbohydrate solution. Despite a larger insulin response with the added protein, glycogen resynthesis was highest with the isoenergetic amount of carbohydrate (see figure 5.12). These results suggest that insulin is an important factor, but the main limiting factor is the availability of carbohydrate. When a protein/amino acid mixture (0.4 g/kg/h) was added to a very large amount of carbohydrate (1.2 g/kg/h carbohydrate), insulin concentrations increased, but the increase did not further increase glycogen resynthesis (Jentjens et al. 2001). These studies are summarized in figure 5.12. The maximal capacity to store muscle glycogen is likely reached and, therefore, no additional effect of elevated insulin concentration is found. Thus, to achieve rapid muscle glycogen replenishment ingesting an adequate amount of carbohydrate is more important than adding protein or amino acid mixtures to a recovery meal or drink.

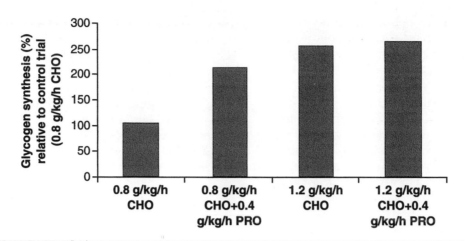

Figure 5.12 The rate of muscle glycogen synthesis after ingestion of different carbohydrate and carbohydrate-protein beverages. The synthesis rate for a drink containing 0.8 g/kg/h of carbohydrate is set at 100%, and all other synthesis rates are expressed relative to this baseline.

Solid Versus Liquid

Few studies have investigated the effect of solid versus liquid carbohydrate foods on glycogen synthesis in the early hours after exercise. Keizer et al. (1987) demonstrated that glycogen synthesis rates were similar after consumption of either a liquid or solid carbohydrate meal. However, the solid meal in this study contained slightly more carbohydrate compared with the liquid meal, and differences in fat and protein content between the two meals were substantial. Other investigators also found no difference in the rate of muscle glycogen storage between liquid and solid carbohydrate feedings. Therefore, no difference in glycogen synthesis with solid or liquid feedings is believed to exist. In the studies men-

tioned previously the investigators used a high-GI carbohydrate, probably resulting in a rapid delivery of glucose. Low-GI solid meals are likely to result in lower rates of glycogen synthesis compared with carbohydrate solutions. For further reading about glycogen synthesis after exercise, see reviews by Jentjens and Jeukendrup (2003b), Ivy (1998), and Ivy and Kuo (1998).

Muscle Glycogen, Diet, and Repeated Days of Training

Often, athletes compete or train on consecutive days, in which case, rapid replenishment of muscle glycogen appears crucial. Costill et al (1971) reported that in subjects running 16.1 km on 3 consecutive days,

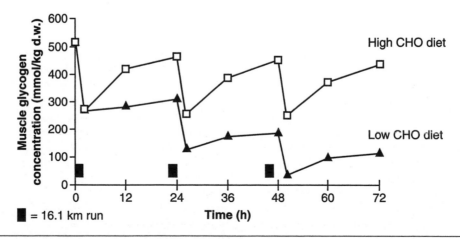

Figure 5.13 Muscle glycogen concentration after repeated bouts of running.

Reprinted, by permission, from D.L. Costill, R. Bowers, G. Branam, K. Sparks, 1971, "Muscle glycogen utilization during prolonged exercise on successive days," *Journal of Applied Physiology* 31: 834-838.

a diet containing only moderate amounts of carbohydrate (40% to 50%) may not be enough to fully restore muscle glycogen (see figure 5.13). A marked decrease in muscle glycogen occurred immediately after the run, and although some glycogen was synthesized before the run the next day, the starting muscle glycogen concentrations were lower. After 3 days of running, the muscle glycogen concentration had dropped considerably.

Sherman et al. (1993) fed subjects a diet containing either 5 g/kg b.w./day or 10 g/kg b.w./day during seven days of training. The diet containing 5 g carbohydrate/kg b.w./day resulted in a decline in muscle glycogen concentration in the first five days, which was then maintained for the remainder of the study. With the high-carbohydrate diet (10 g/kg b.w./day), muscle glycogen concentrations were maintained despite daily training.

In another study, well-trained cyclists exercised 2 hours a day at 65% $\dot{V}O_2$max (Coyle et al. 2001). They ingested a diet containing 581 g, 718 g, or 901 g of carbohydrate. These high-carbohydrate intakes made maintaining very high muscle glycogen concentrations possible (120 mmol/kg w.w., 155 mmol/kg w.w., and 185 mmol/kg w.w., respectively). The muscle glycogen concentrations were even higher than the values reported after the classical supercompensation diet. The amount of carbohydrate ingested between two exercise bouts on consecutive days is, therefore, very important in determining the total amount of muscle glycogen stored. A higher carbohydrate intake can also reduce some symptoms of overreaching (an early stage of overtraining) such as changes in mood state and feelings of fatigue, although it cannot completely prevent them. Achten, Halson, et al. (2003) observed such an effect in runners who increased their training volume and intensity and controlled their carbohydrate intake at either 5.4 g/kg b.w./day or 8.5 g/kg b.w./day.

Muscle Glycogen Restoration

Unless large amounts of carbohydrate are ingested, muscle glycogen does not normalize on a day-to-day basis (Costill et al. 1971). How much carbohydrate must we eat to replenish our glycogen stores within 24 hours? Costill et al. (1981) suggested that increasing carbohydrate intake from 150 g to 650 g results in a proportional increases in muscle glycogen. However, intakes higher than 600 g/24 h do not result in a further increase in glycogen resynthesis. More recent studies seem to suggest that with daily exercise, an almost linear increase in glycogen storage occurs in relation to carbohydrate intake (Coyle et al. 2001). These findings and others have led sports nutrition

experts to recommend increasing carbohydrate intake to 10 g/kg b.w./day to 13 g/kg b.w./day when exercising for 3 hours or more on a daily basis.

Carbohydrate Type and Long-Term Recovery

To stimulate glycogen resynthesis after exercise, the amount of carbohydrate ingested may be the most important factor, but the type of carbohydrate may also play a role. One study investigated the effects of the GI on muscle glycogen resynthesis. Subjects performed a bout of exercise that depleted their glycogen stores on two occasions and received a diet of high-GI carbohydrate on one occasion and a diet of low-GI carbohydrate on the other (Burke, Collier, and Hargreaves 1993). The total carbohydrate intake over 24 hours was 10 g/kg b.w. The increase in muscle glycogen was more than 50% greater when the high-GI carbohydrates were consumed. Therefore, high-GI foods are important for complete muscle glycogen resynthesis within 24 hours. The higher insulin responses of the high-GI meals are likely responsible for the increased glycogen synthesis.

Glycogen Loading and Long-Term Recovery

Often guidelines are expressed in percentages, which has confused the advice given to athletes. For example, a 50% carbohydrate diet may contain a very large amount of carbohydrate for a triathlete or cyclist who expends 6,000 kcal/day but contain only a small amount of carbohydrate for a distance runner who has an intake of 2,000 kcal/day. A more sensible expression of carbohydrate intake is grams/kilogram bodyweight/day.

As a general guideline, 5 g/kg b.w./day to 7 g/kg b.w./day during moderate-intensity training and 7 g/kg b.w./day to 10 g/kg b.w./day during increased training are recommended. Endurance athletes involved in extreme training programs should increase carbohydrate intake to 10 g/kg b.w./day to 13 g/kg b.w./day when exercising daily. This intake enables them to restore muscle glycogen even though they may become depleted in a training session. Recommendations for long-term recovery include

- ingesting 5-7 g/kg b.w./day during moderate intensity training;
- ingesting at least 7 g/kg b.w./day to 10 g /kg b.w./day of carbohydrate during prolonged hard training;

- ingesting 10 g/kg b.w./day to13 g /kg b.w./day of carbohydrate when performing very prolonged very hard exercise;
- choosing high-GI carbohydrates; and
- consuming sports drink to provides a convenient source of carbohydrate in the first hour after exercise when appetite is suppressed.

For optimal glycogen resynthesis, a large proportion of the carbohydrate intake should consist of high-GI foods (see table 5.2). Carbohydrate solutions have the advantage of providing fluid that will help restore fluid balance (see chapter 8).

A significant amount of ingested carbohydrate may be directed to the liver. Unfortunately, liver glycogen is very difficult to measure, and although some studies using liver biopsies were performed in the 1960s, very limited information is available about liver glycogen synthesis after exercise and its potential effect on performance. A noninvasive technique that has been used to address this problem is nuclear magnetic resonance (NMR) imaging. Using ^{13}C-NMR, Casey et al. (2000) measured liver glycogen concentrations after exercise and during 4 hours of recovery. They observed that liver glycogen resynthesis was evident after glucose and sucrose ingestion but not with water. Relatively small amounts of carbohydrate were ingested (1 g/kg b.w.), and these amounts were sufficient to initiate postexercise liver glycogen resynthesis.

What Athletes Really Do

What do athletes actually do in real life about carbohydrate intake? The many reports of dietary intake among athletes in a variety of sports are beyond the scope of this book. The interested reader is referred to an excellent publication (Burke 2001) in which this topic is discussed in great detail. The publication concluded that most male athletes achieve a dietary intake of 5 g/kg b.w./day to 7 g/kg b.w./day for regular training needs and 7 g/kg b.w./day to 10 g/kg b.w./day during periods of increased training or competition. Female athletes, in particular endurance runners, are less likely to achieve their specific carbohydrate intake targets because they sometimes try to reduce the energy intake to achieve or maintain low levels of body fat, without paying enough attention to carbohydrate intake.

Key Points

- Muscle glycogen is a readily available energy source for the working muscle. The glycogen content of skeletal muscle at rest is approximately 54 g/kg d.m.to 72 g/kg d.m. (65 mmol glucosyl units/kg w.w. to 90 mmol glucosyl units/kg w.w.), equating to a total of about 300 g to 600 g of carbohydrate.

- The main role of glycogen in the liver is to maintain a constant blood glucose level. An average liver weighs approximately 1.5 kg, and approximately 80 g to 110 g of glycogen is stored in the liver of an adult human in the postabsorptive state.

- In resting conditions, the glucose output of the liver is approximately 150 mg/min, of which 60% is derived from the breakdown of liver glycogen and about 40% is derived from gluconeogenesis. During exercise, the liver glucose output increases dramatically, up to about 1 g/min, and the majority of this glucose (>90%) is derived from the breakdown of liver glycogen.

- The classical supercompensation protocol results in very high muscle glycogen stores. However, a moderate approach results in similar muscle glycogen levels without the disadvantages of the classical protocol and is therefore the preferred regimen.

- The brain is highly dependent on glucose as a fuel. As blood glucose concentrations drop, hypoglycemia may develop, resulting in dizziness, nausea, cold sweat, reduced mental alertness and ability to concentrate, loss of motor skill, increased heart rate, excessive hunger, and disorientation.

- The primary role of carbohydrate in the days leading up to competition is to fully replenish muscle glycogen stores.

(continued)

(continued)

- Carbohydrate loading, or increased carbohydrate stores, increases time to exhaustion (endurance capacity) on average by about 20% and reduces time taken to complete a set task (time trial; endurance performance) by 2% to 3%.

- In the 3 hours to 5 hours before exercise, some carbohydrate may be incorporated into muscle glycogen, but the majority will be stored as liver glycogen.

- Carbohydrate intake in the hours before exercise results in a transient fall in plasma glucose with the onset of exercise, increases carbohydrate oxidation and accelerated glycogen breakdown, and results in a blunting of fatty acid mobilization and fat oxidation.

- Carbohydrate feeding during exercise of about 45 minutes or longer is believed to improve endurance capacity and performance. The mechanisms may be by maintaining of blood glucose levels and high carbohydrate oxidation rates, glycogen sparing, or central nervous system effects.

- Oxidation of ingested carbohydrate during exercise is dependent on the type of carbohydrate, the amount ingested, and the exercise intensity, but the maximum oxidation rate seems to be about 1 g/min.

- Ingestion of 70 g of carbohydrate per hour (1.2 g/min) is recommended during prolonged exercise.

- Multiple transportable carbohydrates (e.g. glucose and fructose) in a beverage can increase oxidation rates during exercise.

- Two phases can be distinguished in the process of glycogen synthesis after exercise, which have often been referred to as the initial, insulin-independent, or rapid phase, and the insulin-dependent, or slow, phase.

- Restoration of muscle glycogen stores after exercise may depend on the timing of carbohydrate intake, the rate of carbohydrate ingestion, the type of carbohydrate consumed, and the addition of other macronutrients (e.g., protein).

- As a general guideline, the recommended carbohydrate ingestion during periods of moderate-training intensity is 5 g/kg b.w./day to 7 g/kg b.w./day and 7 g/kg b.w./day to 10 g/kg b.w./day when training is increased. For endurance athletes who are involved in extreme training programs, increasing carbohydrate intake to 10 g/kg b.w./day to 13 g/kg b.w./day when exercising daily is generally recommended.

Key Terms

carboloading 118

exogenous carbohydrate oxidation 114

glycemic index 109

glycemic load 112

hepatic glucose output 104

rebound hypoglycemia 106

supercompensation 106

Recommended Readings

Hargreaves, M., J.A. Hawley, and A.E. Jeukendrup. 2004. Pre-exercise carbohydrate and fat ingestion: Effects on metabolism and performance. *Journal of Sports Sciences* 22: 31-38.

Hawley, J.A., E.J. Schabort, T.D. Noakes, and S.C. Dennis. 1997. Carbohydrate loading and exercise performance: An update. *Sports Medicine* 24: 73-81.

Ivy, J. 1998. Glycogen resynthesis after exercise: Effect of carbohydrate intake. *International Journal of Sports Medicine* 19: S142-S145.

Ivy, J.L., and C.-H. Kuo. 1998. Regulation of GLUT4 protein and glycogen synthase during muscle glycogen synthesis after exercise. *Acta Physiologica Scandinavica* 162: 295-304.

Jentjens, L.P.G., and A.E. Jeukendrup. 2003. Glycogen resynthesis after exercise. *Sports Medicine* 33(2): 117-144.

Jeukendrup, A.E., and R. Jentjens. 2000. Oxidation of carbohydrate feedings during prolonged exercise: Current thoughts, guidelines and directions for future research. *Sports Medicine* 29 (6): 407-424.

Maughan, R.J., and M. Gleeson. 2004. *The Biochemical Basis of Sports Performance*. Oxford University Press: Oxford.

Chapter 6

Fat

© Digital Vision Online

Objectives

After studying this chapter, you should be able to do the following:

- Describe the main biochemical pathways in fat metabolism

- Describe the changes that occur in fat metabolism at different intensities of exercise

- Discuss the factors that limit fat oxidation

- Describe the interactions between carbohydrate and fat metabolism at rest and in response to exercise

- Describe the metabolic and performance effects of fat intake 3 hours to 4 hours before exercise

- Describe the metabolic and performance effects of short-term high-fat diets

- Describe the metabolic and performance effects of long-term high-fat diets

Dietary fat is often considered the "bad guy," and excess intakes are often believed to be detrimental to performance and to cause weight gain and deterioration of health. Dietary fat, however, is also very important for athletic performance and health. Fat is an extremely important fuel for endurance exercise, along with carbohydrate, and some fat intake is required for optimal health. Dietary fat provides the essential fatty acids (EFA) that cannot be synthesized in the body.

The body's fat stores are very large in comparison with carbohydrate stores. In some forms of exercise (e.g., prolonged cycling or running), carbohydrate depletion is possibly a cause of fatigue and depletion can occur within 1 hour to 2 hours of strenuous exercise (see chapter 5). The total amount of energy stored as glycogen in the muscles and liver has been estimated to be 8,000 kJ (2,000 kcal). Fat stores can contain more than 50 times the amount of energy in carbohydrate stores. A person with a body mass of 80 kg and 15% body fat has 12 kg of fat (see table 6.1). Most of this fat is stored in subcutaneous adipose tissue, but some fat can also be found in muscle as **intramuscular triacylglycerol** (IMTG). In theory, the fat stores could provide sufficient energy for a runner to run at least 1,300 km.

Ideally, athletes would like to tap into their fat stores as much as possible and save the carbohydrate for later in a competition. Researchers, coaches, and athletes have therefore tried to devise nutritional strategies to enhance fat metabolism, spare carbohydrate stores, and, hence, improve endurance performance. Understanding the effects of various nutritional strategies requires an understanding of fat metabolism and the factors that regulate fat oxidation during exercise. This chapter, therefore, describes fat metabolism in detail and discusses different ways in which researchers and athletes have tried to enhance fat metabolism by nutritional manipulation. Finally, the effects of both low-fat and high-fat diets on metabolism, exercise performance, and health are discussed.

Fat Metabolism During Exercise

FAs that are oxidized in the mitochondria of skeletal muscle during exercise are derived from various sources. The main two sources are adipose tissue and muscle triacylglycerols. A third fuel, plasma triacylglycerol may also be utilized, but the importance of this fuel is subject to debate. Figure 6.1 gives an overview of the fat substrates and their journey to the muscle. Triacylglycerols in adipose tissue are split into FAs and glycerol. The glycerol is released into the circulation, along with some of the FAs. A small percentage of FAs is not released into the circulation but is used to form new triacylglycerols within the adipose tissue, a process called **re-esterification.** The other FAs are transported to the other tissues and taken up by skeletal muscle during exercise. Glycerol is transported to the liver, where it serves as a gluconeogenic substrate to form new glucose.

Besides the FAs in plasma, two other sources of FAs for oxidation in skeletal muscle are available. Circulating triacylglycerols (for example in **VLDL**) can temporarily bind to lipoprotein lipase (LPL), which splits off FAs that can then be taken up by the muscle. A source of fat exists inside the muscle in the form of intramuscular triacylglycerol. These triacylglycerols are split by a **hormone-sensitive lipase** (HSL), and FAs are transported into the mitochondria for oxidation in the same way FAs from plasma and plasma triacylglycerol are utilized.

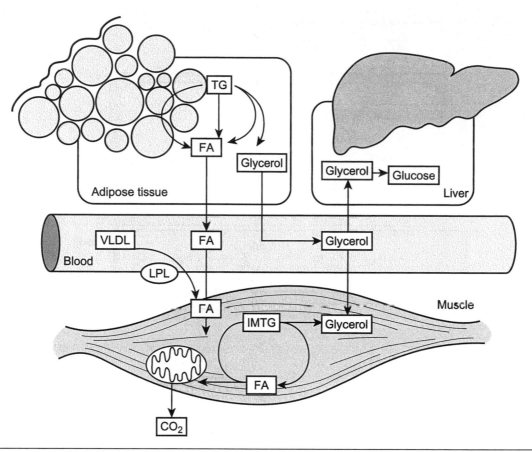

Figure 6.1 Overview of fat metabolism and the main organs involved. TG = triacylglycerol; FA = fatty acid; IMTG = intramuscular triacylglycerol; LPL = lipoprotein lipase; VLDL = very-low-density lipoprotein.

What Limits Fat Oxidation

Despite the fact that humans have large fat stores, in many situations utilizing these large amounts of fat as a fuel seems impossible. Why can fat not be oxidized at higher rates in some conditions? Because the FAs cannot be mobilized, or do other factors play a role? To find the factor that causes this limitation, we examine all the steps that are important in the process of fat oxidation: from the mobilization of FAs to the transport and the oxidation of FAs in the mitochondria itself. The steps that could potentially limit fat oxidation are

- **lipolysis,** the breakdown of triacylglycerols to FAs and glycerol;
- removal of FAs from the fat cell;
- transport of fat by the bloodstream;
- transport of FAs into the muscle cell;
- transport of FAs into the mitochondria; and
- oxidation of FAs in the β-oxidation pathway and TCA cycle.

Lipolysis in Adipocytes

Most FAs are stored in the form of triacylglycerols in subcutaneous adipose tissue. Before these FAs are oxidized, they must be mobilized and transported to the site of oxidation. The adipocyte contains hormone sensitive lipase (HSL), which splits triacylglycerols into FAs and glycerol and, as its name implies, is regulated by hormones (see figure 6.2). Conversion of the inactive form of HSL into the active form mainly depends on the sympathetic nervous system and circulating epinephrine. Insulin is probably the most important counterregulatory hormone. The glycerol released by this reaction diffuses freely into the blood. The adipocyte cannot reuse it, because the enzyme glycerokinase, which is required to phosphorylate the glycerol before re-esterification with FAs, is only present in very low concentrations. Therefore, almost all the glycerol produced by lipolysis is released into the plasma, and the measurement of glycerol in the blood is often used as a measure of lipolysis. FAs released by lipolysis are either re-esterified within the adipocyte or transported into the bloodstream for use in other tissues (see figure 6.3).

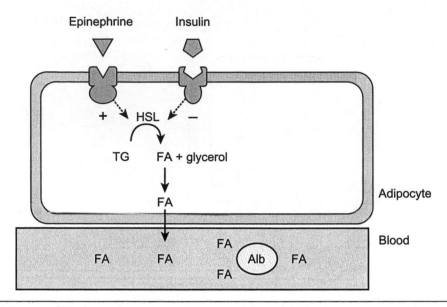

Figure 6.2 Mobilization of FAs from adipose tissue. TG = triacylglycerol; HSL = hormone-sensitive lipase; Alb = albumin.

At rest, approximately 70% of all FAs released during lipolysis are re-esterified (Wolfe et al. 1990). During exercise, re-esterification is suppressed, which results in an increased availability of FAs in the adipocyte. The availability of FAs is even more increased because lipolysis is stimulated via β-adrenoreceptors during exercise. Catecholamines released from the adrenal gland stimulate lipolysis during exercise. Lipolysis is usually in excess of the demand for FAs both at rest and during exercise. Re-esterification is, therefore, believed to play a very important role in regulating the FA mobilization. Re-esterification is dependent on the rate at which FAs are removed from the adipocyte by the blood and the rate of glycerol-3-phosphate production. Because glycerol cannot be recycled to any major extent in human adipocytes (or myocytes), the backbone for a triacylglycerol molecule is derived from glycerol-3-phosphate, an intermediate of the glycolytic pathway.

FAs are not soluble in the aqueous environment of the adipocyte cytoplasm. They are, therefore, bound to so-called FA-binding proteins (FABP) that transport the FAs to the cell membrane. At least during low-intensity to moderate-intensity exercise, the increase in lipolysis and the reduction in esterification of FAs result in a substantially increased level of FAs in the blood (Romijn et al. 1993; Wolfe et al. 1990).

Removal of FAs and Transport in the Blood

The removal of FAs from the adipocyte into the bloodstream depends on several factors, the most important being blood flow to the adipose tissue, the albumin concentration in the blood, and the number of free binding sites for FAs on the albumin molecule. Albumin is a plasma carrier protein that transports FAs. When it arrives at the target tissue (for example muscle) it binds to specific albumin-binding proteins (ABP). Binding to this protein then aids the release of FAs from albumin and their uptake.

A typical plasma albumin concentration is around 0.7 mmol/L (45 g/L) and albumin has at least three high-affinity binding sites for FAs, which provide a large capacity to bind FAs. Therefore, most FAs in the blood are bound to albumin (>99.9%) and only a small fraction (<0.1%), dissolved in the plasma water, circulate freely. Under most conditions, only a fraction of the total number of binding sites of albumin are occupied. However, during very prolonged exercise, the FA concentration in the blood can rise up to about 2 mmol/L. At this concentration the maximum capacity of albumin to bind FAs may be reached. When the FA concentration further rises, the percentage of unbound FAs increases, which is believed to be toxic for cells because of detergent-like properties of unbound FAs. These very high FA levels, however, are unusual, and the body seems to have protective mechanisms to prevent rises above 2 mmol/L. One of these mechanisms could be increased incorporation of FAs into plasma triacylglycerol. During every pass through the liver, a fraction of the FAs is extracted from the circulation and incorporated into VLDL particles.

Plasma Lipoproteins

Triacylglycerols bound to lipoproteins (VLDLs and chylomicrons) are another potential source of FAs (Havel et al. 1967). The enzyme lipoprotein lipase (LPL) in the vascular wall hydrolyzes some of the triacylglycerols in circulating lipoproteins passing through the capillary bed. As a result, FAs are released that the muscle can take up and use for oxidation. However, the FA uptake from plasma lipoprotein triacylglycerols occurs slowly and accounts for fewer than 3% of the energy expenditure during prolonged exercise (Havel et al. 1967; Issekutz et al. 1964). Therefore, it is generally believed that plasma triacylglycerols contribute only minimally to energy production during exercise. Some interesting observations need further investigation. For instance, LPL activity is significantly increased after training and after a high-fat diet; in both situations, fat oxidation is markedly increased. In addition, acute exercise also stimulates LPL activity.

Transport of FAs into the Muscle Cell

For a long time, the transport of FAs into the muscle cell was believed to be a passive process. This belief was based on early observations that FA uptake increased linearly with FA concentration. However, recently, specific carrier proteins have been identified (see figure 6.4). In the sarcolemma, at least two proteins are involved in the transport of FAs across the membrane, a specific plasma membrane FA-binding protein (FABPpm) and an FA transporter (FAT/CD36) protein. These proteins are likely to be responsible for the transport of most FAs across the sarcolemma. Animal studies indicate that the transporters become saturated at plasma FA concentrations around 1.5 mmol/L. FAT/CD36 can translocate from intracellular vesicles to the cell membrane in a similar manner as the GLUT-4 protein, indicating that FA transport can also be regulated acutely (Bonen et al. 2000). Muscle contraction increases plasma membrane FAT/CD36 and decreases the concentration of FAT/CD36 in the sarcoplasma. Along with a higher density of FAT/CD36 at the cell membrane, an increased FA transport into the cell was observed. What triggers the translocation of the FAT/CD36 to the cell membrane is currently not known. However, similar factors that result in GLUT-4 translocation might also be responsible for the translocation of FAT/CD36.

In the sarcoplasm (cytoplasm of muscle cells), the FAs are bound to another specific cytoplasmic FA-binding protein (FABPc). FABPc is thought to be responsible for the transport of FAs from the sarcolemma to the mitochondria. At present, little is known about the roles of these FA-binding proteins and transporters, and whether they are a limiting factor for fat oxidation is unknown.

Intramuscular Triacylglycerols

Another source of FAs are the IMTG stores in the muscle itself. Type I muscle fibers have higher contents of IMTG than type II muscle fibers. IMTG stores, usually located adjacent to the mitochondria as lipid

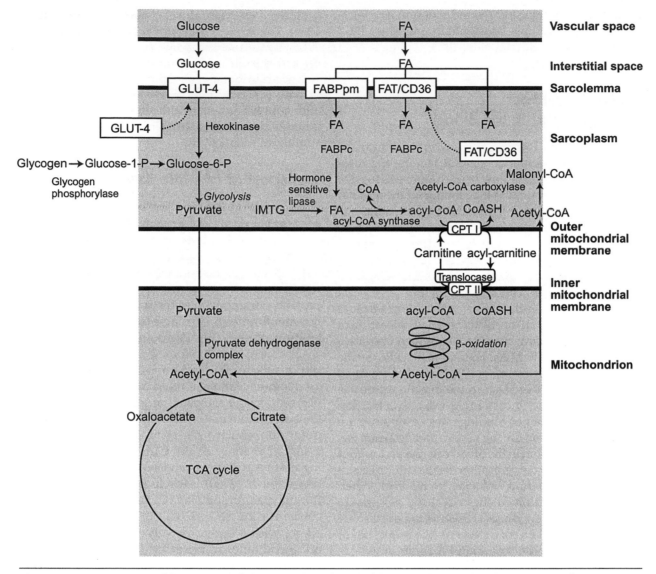

Figure 6.4 Presentation of the transport of glucose and FAs from the blood into the mitochondria. CoASH = free coenzyme A; CPT I = carnitine palmitoyl transferase I; CPT II = carnitine palmitoyl transferase II; FABP = fatty acid binding protein; IMTG = intramuscular triacylglycerol.

Reprinted, by permission, from A.E. Jeukendrup, 2002, "Regulation of skeletal muscle fat metabolism," *New York Academy of Sciences* 967: 1-19.

droplets (see figure 6.5), have been recognized as an important energy source during exercise. Studies in which muscle samples were investigated under a microscope revealed that the size of these lipid droplets decreases during exercise. Also, indirect measures of IMTG breakdown provide evidence for its use during exercise (Martin et al. 1993). The location of the droplets seems to be important as well. In trained muscle, the lipid droplets are believed to be located next to the mitochondria, whereas in untrained muscle, the lipid droplets do not seem to be linked with mitochondria at all.

Like adipose tissue, muscle contains a HSL that is activated by β-adrenergic stimulation and inhib-

ited by insulin. FAs liberated from IMTGs may be released into the blood, re-esterified, or oxidized within the muscle. Because, at least in trained muscle, the lipid droplets are located close to the mitochondria, most of the FAs released after lipolysis are assumed to be oxidized. The FAs released are bound to FABPc until they are transported into the mitochondria.

Transport of FAs into the Mitochondria

FAs in the cytoplasm may be activated by the enzyme acyl-CoA synthethase or thiokinase to form an acyl-CoA complex (often referred to as an activated FA)

The bonding between carnitine and the activated FA is the first step in the transport of the FA into the mitochondria. As carnitine binds to the FA, free CoA is released. The fatty acyl-carnitine complex is transported with a translocase and reconverted into fatty acyl-CoA at the matrix side of the inner mitochondrial membrane by the enzyme carnitine palmitoyl transferase II (CPT II). The carnitine that is released diffuses back across the mitochondrial membrane into the cytoplasm and thus becomes available again for the transport of other FAs. Fatty acyl-carnitine crosses the inner membrane in a 1:1 exchange with a molecule of free carnitine. Although short-chain FAs (SCFAs) and **medium-chain FAs** (MCFAs) are believed to freely diffuse into the mitochondrial matrix, carrier proteins with a specific maximum affinity for short-chain or medium-chain acyl-CoA transport at least some of these FAs.

β-Oxidation

Once in the mitochondrial matrix, the fatty acyl-CoA is subjected to β-oxidation, a series of reactions that splits a 2-carbon acetyl-CoA molecule of the multiple carbon FA chain (see figure 6.7). The β-oxidation pathway uses oxygen and generates some ATP through substrate-level phosphorylation. The acetyl-CoA is then oxidized in the tricarboxylic acid (TCA) cycle. The complete oxidation of FAs in the mitochondria depends on several factors, including the activity of enzymes of the β-oxidation pathway, the concentration of TCA-cycle intermediates and activity of enzymes in the TCA cycle (these factors determine the total TCA-cycle activity), and the presence of oxygen.

(see figure 6.6). This acyl-CoA complex is used for the synthesis of IMTGs, or it is bound to carnitine under the influence of the enzyme **carnitine palmitoyl transferase** I (CPT I; which is also known as carnitine acyl transferase I or CAT I), which is located at the outside of the outer mitochondrial membrane.

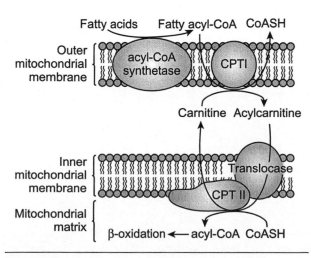

Figure 6.6 Transport of FAs into the mitochondria.

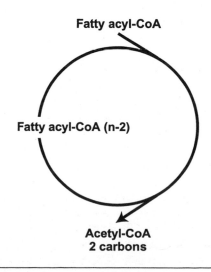

Figure 6.7 The β-oxidation process.

Fat As a Fuel During Exercise

Carbohydrate and fat are always oxidized as a mixture, and whether carbohydrate or fat is the predominant fuel depends on a variety of factors, including the intensity and duration of exercise, the level of aerobic fitness, diet, and carbohydrate intake before or during exercise. The changes in fat metabolism that occur in the transition from rest to exercise as well as the various factors that influence fat mobilization and oxidation will be discussed in the following sections.

Fat Utilization at Rest and During Exercise

After an overnight fast, most of the energy requirement is covered by the oxidation of FAs derived from adipose tissue. The rate of lipolysis in adipose tissue mostly depends on the circulating concentrations of hormones (epinephrine stimulates lipolysis and insulin inhibits lipolysis). It seems that most of the FAs liberated after lipolysis are re-esterified within the adipocyte. Some FAs enter the bloodstream, but only about half of them are oxidized. Resting plasma FA concentrations are typically between 0.2 mmol/L and 0.4 mmol/L.

When exercise is initiated, the rate of lipolysis and the rate of FA release from adipose tissue are increased. During moderate-intensity exercise, lipolysis increases approximately threefold, mainly because of an increased β-adrenergic stimulation (by catecholamines). In addition, during moderate-intensity exercise, the blood flow to adipose tissue is doubled and the rate of re-esterification is halved. Blood flow in skeletal muscle is increased dramatically, and, therefore, the delivery of FAs to the muscle is increased.

During the first 15 minutes of exercise, plasma FA concentrations usually decrease because the rate of FA uptake by the muscle exceeds the rate of FA appearance from lipolysis. Thereafter, the rate of appearance is in excess of the utilization by muscle, and plasma FA concentrations increase. The rise in FA depends on the exercise intensity. During moderate-intensity exercise, FA concentrations may reach 1 mmol/L within 60 minutes of exercise, but at higher exercise intensities, the rise in plasma FAs is very small or may even be absent.

Fat Oxidation and Exercise Duration

Fat oxidation increases as the exercise duration increases. Edwards et al. (1934) reported fat oxidation rates of over 1.0 g/min after 6 hours of running. Christensen and Hansen (1939) observed that the contribution of fat could even increase to levels as high as 90% of energy expenditure when a fatty meal was consumed, leading to fat oxidation rates of 1.5 g/min. The mechanism of this increased fat oxidation as exercise duration increases is not entirely clear but seems to be linked to the decrease in muscle glycogen stores.

Fat Oxidation and Exercise Intensity

Fat oxidation is usually the predominant fuel at low exercise intensities, whereas during high exercise intensities, carbohydrates are the major fuel. In absolute terms, fat oxidation increases as the exercise intensity increases from low to moderate intensities, even though the percentage contribution of fat may actually decrease (see figure 6.8). For the transition from light-intensity to moderate-intensity exercise, the increased fat oxidation is a direct result of the increased energy expenditure. At higher intensities of exercise (>75% $\dot{V}O_2$max) fat oxidation is inhibited and both the relative and absolute rates of fat oxidation decrease to negligible values. Achten et al. (2002, 2003) studied this relationship over a wide range of exercise intensities in a group of trained subjects and found that, on average, the maximal rates of fat oxidation were observed at 62-63% $\dot{V}O_2$max.

During exercise at 25% $\dot{V}O_2$max, most of the fat oxidized is derived from plasma FAs, and only small amounts comes from IMTGs. (Romijn et al. 1993) (see figure 6.9). However, during moderate exercise intensity (65% $\dot{V}O_2$max), the contribution of plasma FAs declines, whereas the contribution of IMTGs increases and provides about half of the FAs used for total fat oxidation (Romijn et al. 1993). Training also decreases the contribution of plasma FAs, despite a dramatic increase in total fat oxidation. This decrease in plasma FA oxidation is accounted for by a marked increase in the contribution of muscle triacylglycerols to energy expenditure.

When the exercise intensity is further increased, fat oxidation decreases, even though the rate of lipolysis is still high. The blood flow to the adipose tissue may be decreased (because of sympathetic vasoconstriction), which may result in a decreased removal of FAs from adipose tissue. During high-intensity exercise, lactate accumulation may also increase the rate of re-esterification of FAs. As a result, plasma FA concentrations are usually low during intense exercise. However, this decreased availability of FAs can only partially explain the reduced fat oxidation observed in these conditions. When Romijn et al. (1995) restored FA concentrations to levels observed at moderate exercise intensities by infusing triacylglycerols (Intralipid) and heparin, fat oxidation was only slightly increased but still lower than at moderate intensities (see the sidebar and figure 6.10). Therefore, an additional mechanism in the muscle must be responsible for the decreased fat oxidation observed during high-intensity exercise.

Sidossis et al. (1997) and Coyle et al. (1997) suggested that the decreased fat oxidation is related to the transport of FAs into the mitochondria. They observed that during high-intensity exercise, the oxidation of **long-chain FAs** is impaired, whereas the oxidation of medium chain FAs is unaffected. Because the medium-chain FAs are less dependent on

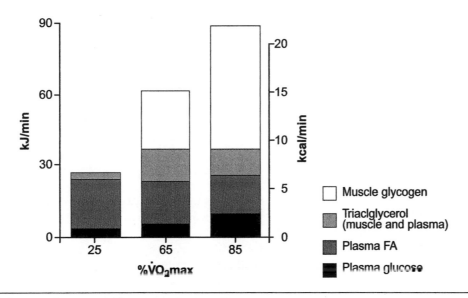

Figure 6.9 Substrate utilization at different exercise intensities.

Reprinted, by permission, from J.A. Romijn et al., 1993, "Regulation of endogenous fat and carbohydrate metabolism in relation to exercise intensity and duration," *Journal of Applied Physiology* 265: E380-E391.

TRIACYLGLYCEROL AND HEPARIN INFUSION

In order to increase plasma FA concentrations for experimental purposes, researchers have used the infusion of triacylglycerol and heparin. Because FAs are not soluble in water (plasma), they cannot be infused directly. Therefore a lipid emulsion is used (often Intralipid) in combination with a heparin injection. Heparin releases lipoprotein lipase (LPL) from the capillaries. Once LPL becomes freely available in the circulation, it starts to break down the plasma triacylglycerol, and FA concentrations rise rapidly.

(continued)

(continued)

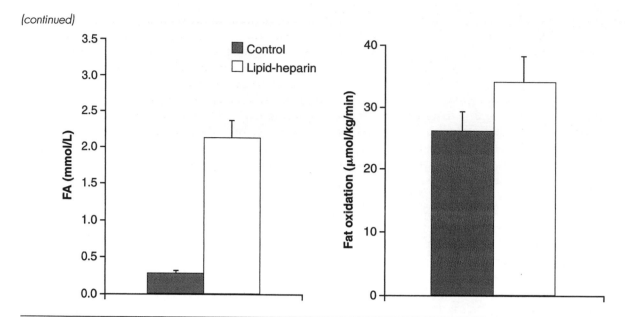

Figure 6.10 FA concentrations are usually low at high exercise intensities (>85% $\dot{V}O_2$max), which could explain the relatively low oxidation rates of fat compared with moderate exercise intensities (gray bars). When lipid and heparin are infused, high plasma FA concentrations are achieved but do not restore fat oxidation to the levels observed at moderate exercise intensities (65% $\dot{V}O_2$max).

Reprinted, by permission, from J.A. Romijn et al., 1995, "Relationship between fatty acid delivery and fatty acid oxidation during strenuous exercise," *Journal of Applied Physiology* 79(6): 1939-1945.

transport mechanisms into the mitochondria, these data provide evidence that carnitine-dependent FA transport is a limiting factor.

Fat Oxidation and Aerobic Capacity

Endurance training affects both substrate utilization and exercise capacity. Studies involving both animals and humans have established a marked adaptive increase in oxidative potential in response to increased regular physical activity (Holloszy and Booth 1976; Holloszy and Coyle 1984). A consequence and probably contributing factor to the enhanced exercise capacity after endurance training is the metabolic shift to a greater use of fat and a concomitant sparing of glycogen. The contribution of fat to total energy expenditure increases after training at both the relative and the absolute exercise intensities. The adaptations that contribute to a stimulation of fat oxidation in trained subjects include:

- increased mitochondrial density and an increase in the number of oxidative enzymes in trained muscle, which increases the capacity to oxidize fat;
- increased capillary density, which enhances FA delivery to the muscle;

- increased FABP concentrations, which may facilitate uptake of FAs across the sarcolemma; and
- increased CPT concentration, which facilitates the transport of FAs into the mitochondria.

One factor that does not seem to be influenced by training is lipolysis in adipose tissue (Klein et al. 1994) (see figure 6.11). After training, the rate of lipolysis at the same absolute exercise intensity does not seem to be affected. At the same relative exercise intensity, the rate of lipolysis is increased after training (Klein et al. 1996). An increased lipolysis of IMTG likely contributes to this increased whole-body lipolysis.

Fat Oxidation and Diet

Diet also has marked effects on fat oxidation. Generally a high-carbohydrate, low-fat diet reduces fat oxidation, whereas a high-fat, low-carbohydrate diet increases fat oxidation. Some scientists have argued that the results seen in most of these studies are the effects of the last meal, which is known to influence substrate utilization. However, Burke et al. (1999) showed that a high-fat, low-carbohydrate diet had a similar effect on substrate utilization, even after a day on a high-carbohydrate diet. The results indicate that some chronic effects of diet cannot be directly

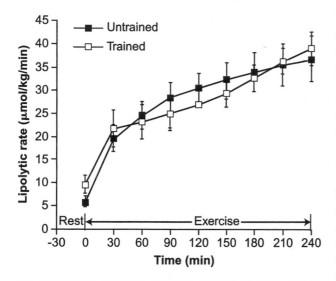

Figure 6.11 Whole-body lipolysis in trained and untrained subjects.

Reprinted, by permission, from S. Klein, E.F. Coyle, and R.R. Wolfe, 1994, "Fat metabolism during low-intensity exercise in endurance trained and untrained men," *Journal of Applied Physiology* 267: E934-E940.

explained by substrate availability. In the study by Burke et al. (1999), for example, subjects consumed a high-fat diet or a high-carbohydrate diet for 5 days followed by 1 day on a high-carbohydrate diet. The one-day high-carbohydrate intake replenished glycogen stores in both conditions, and muscle glycogen concentrations were identical. Yet large differences existed in substrate utilization between the two diets. The respiratory exchange ratio (RER) changed from 0.90 to 0.82 after 5 days on a high-fat diet. After consuming a high-carbohydrate diet for one day, RER was still lower compared with baseline values (0.87). Because these changes were not caused by alterations in substrate availability, they are likely to be related to metabolic adaptations in the muscle.

Chronic diets can have marked effects on metabolism. These effects seem only partly related to the effects of diets on substrate availability. Adaptations at the muscular level, which result in changes in substrate utilization in response to a diet, may occur already after five days.

Response to Carbohydrate Feeding

The fastest way to alter fat metabolism during exercise is probably by carbohydrate feeding. Carbohydrate increases the plasma insulin concentration, which reduces lipolysis and causes a marked reduction in FA availability. In a study by Horowitz et al. (1997), carbohydrate was ingested 1 hour before exercise. Both lipolysis and fat oxidation were reduced. Plasma

FA concentrations decreased to very low levels during exercise. However, when Intralipid was infused and heparin was injected to increase the plasma FA concentrations, fat oxidation was only partially restored. These findings indicate that a reduced availability of FAs is indeed a factor that limits fat oxidation. However, because increasing the plasma FA concentrations does not completely restore fat oxidation, other factors must play a role as well. These factors must be located inside the muscle itself.

When a large amount of glucose is ingested 1 hour before exercise, plasma insulin levels are very high at the start of exercise, whereas plasma FA and glycerol concentrations are very low (Coyle et al. 1997). This results in a 30% reduction in fat oxidation compared with no carbohydrate intake. In a study by Coyle et al. (1997), trace amounts of labeled medium-chain or long-chain FAs were infused, and the oxidation rates of these FAs were determined. The oxidation of long-chain FAs appeared to be reduced, whereas the oxidation of medium-chain FAs appeared to be unaffected (see figure 6.12). Because medium-chain FAs are not as dependent on transport mechanisms into the mitochondria, but the long-chain FAs are highly dependent on this mechanism, these results provide evidence that this transport is an important regulatory step. Although the exact mechanisms are still unclear, carbohydrate feeding before exercise reduces fat oxidation by reducing lipolysis and plasma FA availability and exerts an inhibitory effect on carnitine-dependent FA transport into the mitochondria.

Regulation of Carbohydrate and Fat Metabolism

In all situations, carbohydrate and fat together constitute most, if not all, of the energy provision. The percentage contribution of these two fuels, however, varies depending on the factors discussed previously. The rate of carbohydrate utilization during prolonged strenuous exercise is closely related to the energy needs of the working muscle. In contrast, fat utilization during exercise is not tightly regulated. No mechanisms closely match the metabolism of FAs to energy expenditure. Fat oxidation is therefore mainly influenced by fat availability and the rate of carbohydrate utilization.

Some evidence suggests that increases in plasma FA concentration can cause a decrease in the rate of muscle glycogen breakdown. This action could theoretically be beneficial, because muscle glycogen depletion is one of the prime causes of fatigue. Researchers have artificially elevated plasma FA concentrations by raising plasma triacylglycerol

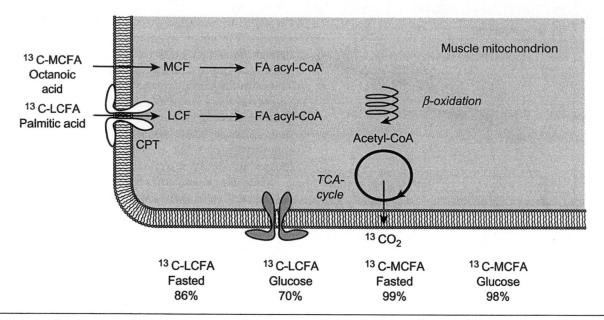

| ^{13} C-LCFA Fasted 86% | ^{13} C-LCFA Glucose 70% | ^{13} C-MCFA Fasted 99% | ^{13} C-MCFA Glucose 98% |

Figure 6.12 Oxidation of medium-chain FAs (MCFAs) and long-chain FAs (LCFAs) in the mitochondria during fasted and fed conditions (glucose). Glucose intake reduced the oxidation of LCFAs but not MCFAs. Because LCFAs use a transport protein to enter the mitochondria, and MCFAs are less dependent on this protein, glucose availability possibly regulates the entry of FA into the mitochondria.

Reprinted, by permission, from E.F. Coyle et al., 1997, "Fatty acid oxidation is directly regulated by carbohydrate metabolism during exercise," *American Journal of Physiology* 273: E268-E275.

concentrations by means of a fat meal or intravenous infusion of triacylglycerol (Intralipid), followed by a heparin injection. Using this method, it has been repeatedly shown that an increase in FA concentration can reduce carbohydrate dependence.

In a study by Costill et al. (1977), Intralipid was infused and heparin was injected during exercise at 70% $\dot{V}O_2$max. After 60 minutes, a muscle biopsy was taken and muscle glycogen was measured before and after the exercise bout. Muscle glycogen breakdown was reduced with the elevated plasma FA concentrations (see figure 6.13). Similar results were obtained when a fat feeding was given in combination with heparin infusion (Vukovich et al. 1993). Although elevating FA levels seems to reduce muscle glycogen breakdown during exercise, the mechanisms are still incompletely understood.

The classical glucose-FA cycle was originally thought to explain this interaction between carbohydrate and fat metabolism (see figure 6.14). This theory states that with an increase in plasma FA concentration, uptake of FAs increases and these FAs undergo β-oxidation in the mitochondria, in which they are broken down to acetyl-CoA. An increasing concentration of acetyl-CoA (or increased acetyl-CoA/CoA ratio) inhibits the pyruvate dehydrogenase complex that breaks down pyruvate to acetyl-CoA. Also, increased formation of acetyl-CoA from FA oxidation

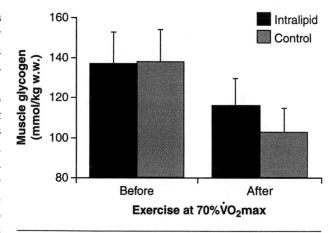

Figure 6.13 Glycogen "sparing" with increased FA availability. This increased availability of FAs was achieved by infusing a triacylglycerol emulsion with heparin.

Data from D.L. Costill et al., 1977.

in the mitochondria increases muscle citrate levels, and after diffusing into the sarcoplasm, citrate could inhibit phosphofructokinase, the rate-limiting enzyme in glycolysis. The effect of increased acetyl-CoA and citrate levels is therefore a reduction in the rate of glycolysis. This reduced glycolysis, in turn, may cause accumulation of glucose-6-phosphate (G6P) in the muscle sarcoplasm, which inhibits hexokinase activity and thus reduces muscle glucose uptake.

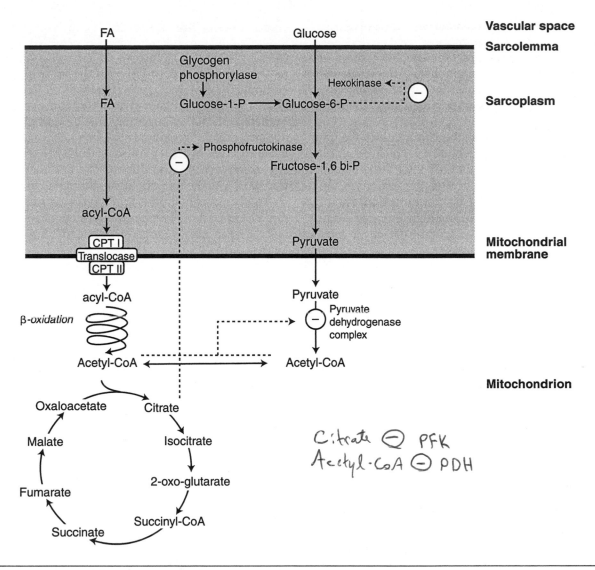

Figure 6.14 Glucose-FA cycle, or Randle cycle.

Reprinted, by permission, from A.E. Jeukendrup, 2002, "Regulation of fat metabolism in skeletal muscle," New York Academy of Sciences 967: 217-235.

With increased fat availability the disturbance in the cellular homeostasis is less. Increasing FA availability decreases intramuscular inorganic phosphate (Pi) and adenosine monophosphate (AMP) accumulation during exercise, possibly because of a greater accumulation of mitochondrial reduced nicotinamide adenine dinucleotide (NADH) (Dyck et al. 1996; Dyck et al. 1993). Pi and AMP are energy sensing signals; high concentrations indicate low energy status, whereas low concentrations reflect ample energy availability. Because Pi and AMP are known to stimulate the enzyme glycogen phosphorylase, the reduction in Pi and AMP levels may be at least partially responsible for the reduced muscle glycogen breakdown.

An alternative explanation for reduced muscle glycogen breakdown after elevation of plasma FA concentrations is given in some studies. When studied in more detail, the plasma FA concentrations appear significantly elevated (by infusion of TG and injection of heparin) compared with the control condition. The FA concentrations in the control condition, however, were below 0.2 mmol/L. Conceivably, these FA levels are too low to provide the muscle with sufficient fat substrate. As a result, muscle glycogen breakdown may have been increased in the control condition. Therefore, the observed "sparing" of glycogen with the high FA concentrations could have been caused by an increased breakdown of glycogen in the control condition. Blocking lipolysis and reducing FA availability by giving nicotinic acid or a derivative increases muscle glycogen breakdown during exercise.

A more recent theory about the regulation of carbohydrate and fat metabolism proposes that fat does not regulate carbohydrate metabolism, but rather carbohydrate regulates fat metabolism. An increase in the rate of glycolysis decreases fat oxidation. Figure 6.15 shows some of the factors that regulate carbohydrate and fat metabolism.

Regulation of fat metabolism involves the transport of FAs into the mitochondria, which is controlled mainly by the activity of CPT I. CPT I is regulated by several factors, including the malonyl-CoA (a precursor of FA synthesis) concentration. The high rate of glycogenolysis during high-intensity exercise increases the amount of acetyl-CoA in the muscle

cell, and some of this acetyl-CoA is converted to malonyl-CoA by the enzyme acetyl CoA carboxylase (ACC). Malonyl-CoA inhibits CPT I and could thus reduce the transport of FAs into the mitochondria. Although evidence suggests that malonyl-CoA may be an important regulator at rest, studies in exercising humans indicate no important role of malonyl-CoA (Odland et al. 1998; Odland et al. 1996). Reductions in intramuscular pH that may occur during high-intensity exercise may also inhibit CPT I and, hence, FA transport into the mitochondria (Starritt et al. 2000).

Another explanation is that a reduced free carnitine concentration plays a role. When glycogenolysis is accelerated, acetyl-CoA accumulates during intense

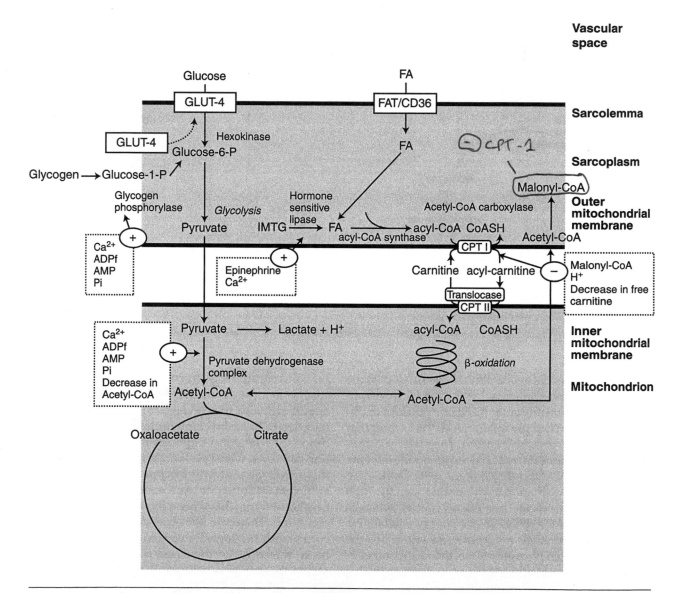

Figure 6.15 Glucose FA cycle reversed. An increase in glycolysis can reduce the FA transport into the mitochondria. CPT I = carnitine palmitoyl transferase I; CPT II = carnitine palmitoyl transferase II; ADPf = free ADP.

Reprinted, by permission, from A.E. Jeukendrup, 2002, "Regulation of metabolism in skeletal muscle," New York Academy of Sciences 967: 217-235.

exercise and some of this acetyl-CoA is bound to carnitine. As a result, the free carnitine concentration drops, and less carnitine is available to transport FAs into the mitochondria (Greenhaff and Timmons 1998). Finally, it has been proposed that pyruvate-derived acetyl-CoA competes with the FA-derived acetyl-CoA for entrance into the TCA cycle.

The rate of carbohydrate utilization during prolonged strenuous exercise is closely related to the energy needs of the working muscle. In contrast, fat utilization during exercise is not tightly regulated. No mechanisms closely match the metabolism of FAs to energy expenditure. Fat oxidation is, therefore, mainly influenced by fat availability and the rate of carbohydrate utilization. The importance of each of these factors may depend on the situation. For example, carbohydrate utilization may be a more important factor during exercise, whereas the availability of FAs may be more important at rest.

Fat Supplementation and Exercise

The effects of eating fat before or during exercise have been studied as a method to increase FA availability and increase fat oxidation in order to reduce muscle glycogen breakdown. Initial studies looked at fatty meals consisting mainly of long-chain triacylglyerols (LCTs); later studies have also looked at alternative lipid fuels such as medium-chain triacylglycerols (MCTs).

Ingestion of Long-Chain Triacylglycerols

Nutritional fats include triacylglycerols (containing mostly C16 and C18 FAs), phospholipids, and cholesterol, of which only triacylglycerols can contribute to any extent to energy provision during exercise. In contrast to carbohydrates, nutritional fats only reach the circulation slowly because they are potent inhibitors of gastric emptying. Furthermore, the digestion in the gut and absorption of fat are also rather slow processes compared with the digestion and absorption of carbohydrates.

Bile salts, produced by the liver, and lipase, secreted by the pancreas, are needed for lipolysis of the long-chain triacylglycerols (LCTs) into glycerol and 3 LCFAs or monoacylglycerol and 2 FAs. The FAs diffuse into the intestinal mucosa cells and are re-esterified in the cytoplasm to form LCTs. These LCTs are encapsulated by a coat of proteins—forming chylomicrons—to make them water soluble. These chylomicrons are then released in the lymphatic system, which ultimately drains in the systemic circulation. Exogenous LCTs enter the systemic circulation much more slowly than carbohydrates, which are absorbed as glucose (or to minor extents, as fructose or galactose) and directly enter the main circulation through the portal vein. Long-chain dietary FAs typically enter the blood 3 to 4 hours after ingestion.

The fact that these LCFAs enter the circulation in chylomicrons is also important, and the rate of breakdown of chylomicron-bound triacylglycerols by muscle is generally believed to be relatively low. The primary role of these triacylglycerols in chylomicrons may be the replenishment of IMTG stores after exercise (Oscai et al. 1990). The intake of fat during exercise should, therefore, be avoided. Many so-called "sports bars" or "energy bars," however, contain relatively large amounts of fat. Food labels of these products should be checked when choosing an energy bar.

Ingestion of Medium-Chain Triacylglycerols

Medium-chain triacylglycerols (MCTs) contain FAs with a chain length of C8 or C10. MCTs are normally present in our diet in very small quantities and they have few natural sources. Intake via these sources is small and, therefore, MCTs are often consumed as a supplement. MCTs are sold as a supplement to replace normal fat because MCTs are not stored in the body and, therefore, could help athletes lose body fat. MCT supplements are fairly popular among body builders and have been used as an alternative fuel source during exercise. (See chapter 10.)

Ingestion of Fish Oil

Fish oil is a natural source of long-chain omega-3 FAs. It contains both docosahexaenoic (DHA) and eicosapentaenoic acid (EPA). Fish oil is said to improve membrane characteristics and improve membrane function when more of these omega-3 FAs are incorporated into the lipid bilayer of the membrane. (See chapter 10.)

Effect of Diet on Fat Metabolism and Performance

Another strategy that has been used to increase fat oxidation and reduce reliance on carbohydrate stores has involved longer-term manipulations of the diet lasting days or weeks. These methods included fasting and high-fat, low-carbohydrate diets.

Fasting

Fasting has been proposed as a way to increase fat utilization, spare muscle glycogen, and improve exercise performance. In rats, short-term fasting increases plasma epinephrine and norepinephrine concentrations, stimulates lipolysis, and increases the concentration of circulating plasma FAs. These effects, in turn, increase fat oxidation and "spare" muscle glycogen, leading to a similar (Koubi et al. 1991), or even increased, running time to exhaustion in rats (Dohm et al. 1983). In humans, fasting also results in an increased concentration of circulating catecholamines, increased lipolysis, increased concentration of plasma FAs (Dohm et al. 1986), and a decreased glucose turnover (Knapik et al. 1988). Muscle glycogen concentrations, however, are unaffected by fasting for 24 hours when no strenuous exercise is performed (Knapik et al. 1988; Loy et al. 1986). Although fasting has been reported to have no effect on endurance capacity at low exercise intensities (45% $\dot{V}O_2$max), decreases in performance have been observed for exercise intensities between 50% and 100% $\dot{V}O_2$max. The observed decreased performance was not reversible by carbohydrate ingestion during exercise (Riley et al. 1988).

Some investigators argued that the effects observed in most of these studies were seen because, in the control situation, the last meal was provided 3 hours before the exercise to exhaustion. The effects, therefore, are of the feeding before exercise improving endurance capacity rather than of decreased performance after fasting. However, the studies that compared a prolonged fast (>24 hours) to a 12-hour fast also reported decreased performance (Knapik et al. 1988; Maughan and Gleeson 1988; Zinker et al. 1990) and, thus, the conclusion that fasting decreases endurance capacity seems justified. The mechanism remains unclear, although certainly liver glycogen stores are substantially depleted after a 24-hour fast. Thus, euglycemia may not be as well maintained during exercise. Some degree of metabolic acidosis may also be observed after prolonged fasting. When hepatic glycogen stores are exhausted (e.g., after 12 hours to 24 hours of total fasting), the liver produces ketone bodies (acetoacetate, β-hydroxybutyrate, and acetone) to provide an energy substrate for peripheral tissues. These keto-acids lower blood pH, although the acidosis is usually only mild.

Effects of a Short-Term High-Fat Diet

Christensen and Hansen (1939) showed that short-term exposure to a high-fat diet resulted in impaired fatigue resistance. After muscle biopsy techniques were redeveloped, a high-fat, low-carbohydrate diet was shown to result in decreased muscle glycogen levels, and this was the main factor causing lack of fatigue resistance during prolonged exercise (Bergstrom and Hultman 1967; Hultman 1967). Plasma FA concentrations are increased at rest and increase more rapidly when a low-carbohydrate diet is consumed (Conlee et al. 1990; Martin et al. 1978; Maughan et al. 1978). These changes in plasma FA concentrations are attributed to changes in the rate of lipolysis. Not only plasma FAs but also plasma glycerol concentrations are increased after a low-carbohydrate diet.

Jansson and Kaijser (1982) reported that the uptake of FAs by the muscle during 25 minutes of cycling at 65% $\dot{V}O_2$max was 82% higher in subjects receiving a low-carbohydrate diet (5%) for 5 days, compared with subjects receiving a high-carbohydrate diet (75%) for 5 days. Plasma FAs contributed 24% and 14%, respectively, to energy expenditure. Increased FA concentrations in the blood after a period of carbohydrate restriction leads to an increased ketogenesis with elevated plasma levels of β-hydroxybutyrate and acetoacetate. After a few days of high-fat feeding, the ketone body production increases 5-fold (Fery and Balasse 1983) and the arterial concentration of ketone bodies may increase 10-fold to 20-fold (Fery and Balasse 1983). During the first phase of light to moderate exercise, ketone body concentrations usually decline, and after 30 minutes to 90 minutes, they increase again (Fery and Balasse 1983; Knapik et al. 1988; Zinker et al. 1990). However, the observed plasma concentrations under those conditions are still higher after a high-fat diet compared with those associated with low-fat diets. Carbohydrate-restricted diets may also lead to an increased breakdown of muscle triacylglycerols.

Effects of a Long-Term High-Fat Diet

A 3-day to 4-day alteration in the dietary composition has been suggested to be an insufficient time to induce an adaptive response to the changed diet. A high-fat diet over a prolonged period, however, may result in a decreased utilization of carbohydrates and an increased contribution of fat to energy metabolism. In rats, adaptation to a high-fat diet leads to considerable improvements in endurance capacity (Miller et al. 1984; Simi et al. 1991) (see figure 6.16). These adaptations can be attributed to the increased number of oxidative enzymes and a decreased degradation of liver glycogen during exercise (Simi et al. 1991). The results suggest that after adaptation to a high-fat diet, the capacity to oxidize FAs instead of carbohydrates is increased because of an adaptation of the oxidative enzymes in the muscle cell. These

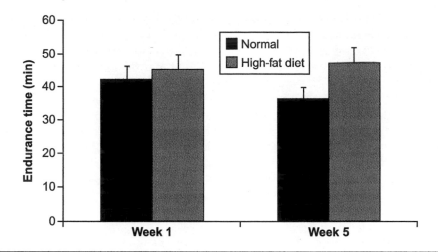

Figure 6.16 Running performance with high-fat diets in rats.

Reprinted, by permission, from W.C. Miller, R. Bryce, and R.K. Conlee, 1984, "Adaptation to a high-fat diet that increase exercise endurance in male rats" *Journal of Applied Physiology* 56(1): 78-83.

adaptations are much like the adaptations seen after endurance training.

One of the first studies that investigated the effects of prolonged high-fat diets on humans was conducted by Phinney et al. (1980). They investigated exercise performance in obese subjects who followed a high-fat diet (90% of energy intake from fat) for 6 weeks. Before and after the diet, subjects exercised at 75% $\dot{V}O_2$max until exhaustion. Subjects were able to exercise as long on the high-fat diet as they did on their normal diet, but after the high-fat diet, fat became the main substrate. Results of this study, however, may have been influenced by the fact that these subjects were not in energy balance and lost 11 kg of body weight. So, although no differences were seen in the absolute $\dot{V}O_2$max before and after the dietary period, considerable differences were apparent in the relative exercise intensity.

The observed improvement in performance may have been an artifact rather than a positive effect of the adaptation period. Therefore, Phinney and colleagues (Phinney, Bistrian, Evans, et al. 1983; Phinney, Bistrian, Wolfe, and Blackburn 1983) conducted a follow-up study in which trained subjects were studied before and after a four-week high-fat diet (<20 g/day of carbohydrates). The diet reduced the pre-exercise muscle glycogen concentration by 50%, but no difference in the average time to exhaustion at 62% to 64% $\dot{V}O_2$max before and after the diet was found. However, the results are difficult to interpret because of the large variability of the subjects' performance times (times to exhaustion). One subject exercised 57% longer, whereas other subjects showed no improvement or even had decreased times to exhaustion. Also, the exercise intensity was rela-

tively low and subjects' reliance on carbohydrates during exercise at 62% to 64% $\dot{V}O_2$max was low. In such a situation, reduced carbohydrate stores may not be limiting. Possibly at higher exercise intensities, performance would have been impaired. Nevertheless, the fact that performance was not reduced in all subjects, even though muscle glycogen levels measured before exercise were decreased by almost 50% and fat oxidation during exercise was markedly increased, is remarkable. These observations have been attributed to enzymatic adaptations (including a 44% increase in carnitine palmitoyl transferase activity and a 46% decrease in hexokinase activity) (Phinney, Bistrian, Evans, et al. 1983). In subsequent studies, a maintained or improved performance was seen at relatively low exercise intensities (60% to 65% $\dot{V}O_2$max), which are far below the intensities observed during competition. How these results translate into practical applications in training and competition for most athletes is unclear.

Eating large amounts of fat has been associated with the development of obesity and cardiovascular disease. Whether this association is also true for athletes is not known. Few studies have described the effects of high-fat diets on cardiovascular risk factors in athletes who train regularly. Pendergast et al. (1996) reported no changes in plasma LDL, HDL, or total cholesterol levels in male and female runners with diets in the range of 17% to 40% fat. Although the risk of obesity and cardiovascular disease increases with the consumption of high-fat diets in sedentary people, regular exercise or endurance training seems to attenuate these risks (Sarna and Kaprio 1994). Exposure to high-fat diets has also been associated with insulin resistance, which has recently linked to an effect of the IMTG pools on glucose ...ake (Pan et al. 1997). However, this observation ... as made in obese subjects, and whether these results can be extrapolated to athletes is not clear, especially because athletes seem to have larger IMTG stores and increased insulin sensitivity. Because little information is available about the negative effects of high-fat diets on athletes, and since the effects of these diets on performance are unclear, we suggest caution when recommending high-fat diets to athletes.

Although chronic high-fat diets induce persistent enzymatic adaptations in skeletal muscle that favor fat oxidation, the effects on performance may not be visible because muscle glycogen levels are suboptimal. A period of adaptation to a high-fat diet, followed by acute carbohydrate feeding, might theoretically induce the enzymatic adaptations in the muscle while also allowing optimizing of pre-exercise glycogen stores. If the high glycogen levels are accompanied by a slightly lower rate of glycogenolysis, an improvement in exercise capacity is expected. Indeed, in rats after 3 weeks to 8 weeks of adaptation to a high-fat diet (0% to 25% carbohydrate) followed by 3 days of carbohydrate feeding (70% carbohydrate), muscle and liver glycogen were restored to very high levels.

In humans, Helge et al. (1998) studied trained subjects who, after 7 weeks of adaptation to a high-fat diet (62% fat, 21% carbohydrate), changed to a high-carbohydrate diet (65% carbohydrate, 20% fat) for 1 week (see figure 6.17). A control group followed a high-carbohydrate diet for 8 weeks. Although exercise time to exhaustion increased from week 7 to week 8 in the group that received a high-fat diet followed by the high-carbohydrate diet, performance was less compared with the group that received the high-

carbohydrate diet for 8 weeks. Because switching to a high-carbohydrate diet after 7 weeks of a high-fat diet did not reverse the negative effects, these authors concluded that the negative effects of 7 weeks of a high-fat diet on performance are not simply caused by a lack of carbohydrate as a fuel, but rather by suboptimal adaptations to the training (i.e., improvements in endurance capacity were smaller compared with the high-carbohydrate diet).

In another study by Burke et al. (1999), trained cyclists received a high-fat diet for a relatively short period (5 days), followed by a day of carbohydrate loading on day 6. On day 7, substrate oxidation during exercise was measured, followed by a performance ride. No significant performance improvement was observed. The potential benefits of an adaptation period to a high-fat diet followed by a period of carbohydrate loading are not clear. A fat-adaptation period beyond four weeks may decrease exercise performance, which cannot be reversed by a week on a high-carbohydrate diet.

Although the hypothesis that chronic high-fat diets may increase the capacity to oxidize fat and improve exercise performance during competition is attractive, little evidence indicates that it is true. The available studies that indicate a positive effect on performance were conducted at exercise intensities lower than the normal intensities during competition. Therefore, more well-controlled studies are needed to clarify the importance of the effect of dietary carbohydrate and fat content on athletic performance and, at this time, because little information is available about the negative effects of high-fat diets for athletes, caution should be exercised when recommending a high-fat diet to athletes.

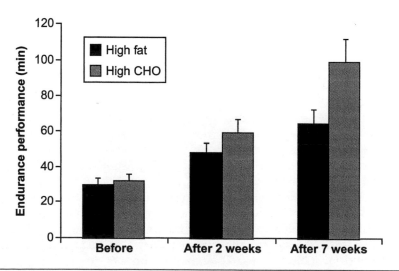

Figure 6.17 High-fat diets and performance improvements during training in humans.
Data from J.W. Helge et al., 1998 and J.W. Helge et al., 1996.

Supplements That Increase Fat Oxidation

Several nutritional supplements on the market are claimed to increase fat oxidation, increase fat loss and lean body mass, and help weight loss. Supplements that have been associated with fat oxidation are caffeine, carnitine, pyruvate, and dihydroxyacetone (see figure 6.18).

Caffeine is thought to stimulate lipolysis and the mobilization of FAs. Carnitine is believed to help transport FAs into the mitochondria. Pyruvate and dihydroxyacetone are often sold as supplements to

Caffeine	Pyruvate
Carnitine	Vanadium (vanadyl-sulphate)
Chromium	Yohimbine
Dihydroxyacetone	

Figure 6.18 Supplements that are claimed to increase fat oxidation.

increase fat oxidation. Similarly, the trace elements chromium and vanadium are claimed to promote fat oxidation and help weight loss. (See chapter 10 for further details.)

Key Points

- In contrast to carbohydrate stores, fat stores are large in humans and are regarded as practically unlimited. The stores of fat are mainly located in adipose tissue but significant amounts also exist as IMTGs.

- The steps that could potentially limit fat oxidation are lipolysis, removal of FAs from the fat cell, transport of fat by the bloodstream, transport of FAs into the muscle cell, transport of FAs into the mitochondria, or oxidation of FAs in the β-oxidation pathway and TCA cycle.

- The majority of FAs are stored in the form of triacylglycerols in subcutaneous adipose tissue, and FAs are released along with glycerol after the breakdown of triacylglycerols (lipolysis) by the enzyme hormone-sensitive lipase.

- Most FAs in the blood are bound to albumin (>99.9%).

- Transporter proteins (FAT/CD36) have been identified that are likely to be responsible for most of the transport of FAs across the sarcolemma. Once in the muscle cell, FAs are bound to FA-binding proteins.

- In the muscle, FAs are stored as IMTG, which can provide an important fuel during exercise.

- The enzyme CPT I plays a crucial role in the transport of FAs into the mitochondria.

- Carbohydrate and fat are always oxidized as a mixture, and the relative contribution of these two substrates depends on the exercise intensity and duration, the level of aerobic fitness, diet, and the carbohydrate intake before and during exercise.

- In absolute terms, fat oxidation increases as the exercise intensity increases from low to moderate intensities, even though the percentage contribution of fat may actually decrease. At higher intensities of exercise (>75% $\dot{V}O_2max$) fat oxidation is inhibited and both the relative and absolute rates of fat oxidation decrease to negligible values. In trained individuals, the maximal rates of fat oxidation were observed at 63% $\dot{V}O_2max$.

- Diet also has marked effects on fat oxidation. Generally a high-carbohydrate, low-fat diet reduces fat oxidation, whereas a high-fat, low-carbohydrate diet increases fat oxidation.

- Carbohydrate feeding before exercise reduces fat oxidation by reducing lipolysis and plasma FA availability and by an inhibition of the carnitine-dependent FA transport into the mitochondria.

(continued)

(continued)

■ The rate of carbohydrate utilization during prolonged strenuous exercise is closely related to the energy needs of the working muscle. In contrast, fat utilization during exercise is not tightly regulated. No mechanisms exist that closely match the metabolism of FAs to energy expenditure. Fat oxidation is, therefore, mainly influences by fat availability and the rate of carbohydrate utilization.

■ Long-chain triacylglycerol ingestion during exercise is not desirable, because they slow gastric emptying, they only slowly appear in the systemic circulation, and they enter the systemic circulation in chylomicrons, which are believed to be an insignificant fuel source during exercise.

■ Medium-chain triacylglycerols (MCTs) are rapidly emptied from the stomach, absorbed, and oxidized, but the ingestion of larger amounts of MCTs resulted in gastrointestinal distress. When ingested in smaller amounts MCTs do not appear to have the positive effects on performance that are often claimed.

■ Fasting increases the availability of lipid substrates, resulting in increased oxidation of FAs at rest and during exercise. However, because the liver glycogen stores are not maintained, fatigue resistance and exercise performance are impaired.

■ High-fat diets for 3 days to 5 days increase the availability of lipid substrates, but reduce the storage of glycogen. As a result, fat oxidation increases during exercise, but fatigue resistance and exercise performance are compromised.

■ Although the hypothesis that chronic high-fat diets may increase the capacity to oxidize fat and improve exercise performance during competition is attractive, little evidence indicates that the hypothesis is true.

Key Terms

carnitine palmitoyl transferase (CPT) 133

hormone-sensitive lipase 128

intramuscular triacylglycerol (IMTG) 128

lipolysis 129

long-chain FA (LCFA) 135

medium-chain FA (MCFA) 133

re-esterification 128

very low-density lipoprotein 128

Recommended Readings

Hawley, J.A., F. Brouns, and A. Jeukendrup. 1998. Strategies to enhance fat utilization during exercise. *Sports Medicine* 26:241-257.

Jeukendrup, A.E. 1999. Dietary fat and physical performance. *Current Opinion in Clinical Nutrition Metabolic Care* 2:521-526.

Jeukendrup, A.E. 2002. Regulation of skeletal muscle fat metabolism. *Annals of the New York Academy of Science* 967:217-35.

Jeukendrup, A.E. 2003. Modulation of carbohydrate and fat utilization by diet, exercise and environment. *Biochemical Society Transactions* 31: 270-1273.

Jeukendrup, A.E., W.H.M. Saris, and A.J.M. Wagenmakers. 1998. Fat metabolism during exercise: A review. Part I: Fatty acid mobilization and muscle metabolism. *International Journal of Sports Medicine* 19:231-244.

Jeukendrup, A.E., W.H.M. Saris, and A.J.M. Wagenmakers. 1998. Fat metabolism during exercise: A review. Part II: Regulation of metabolism and the effects of training. *International Journal of Sports Medicine* 19:293-302.

Jeukendrup, A.E., W.H.M. Saris, and A.J.M. Wagenmakers. 1998. Fat metabolism during exercise: A review. Part III: Effects of nutritional interventions. *International Journal of Sports Medicine* 19:371-379.

Van der Vusse, G.J., and R.S. Reneman. 1996. Lipid metabolism in muscle. In *Handbook of Physiology*, Section 12. ed. L.B. Rowell and J.T. Shephard. Oxford University Press: New York.

Chapter 7

Protein and Amino Acids

© Rob Tringali/SportsChrome USA

Objectives

After studying this chapter, you should be able to do the following:

■ Give a general description of amino acids and protein metabolism and describe the potential fate of amino acids

■ Understand the functions of protein and identify the most abundant amino acids

■ Describe the effects of training on body proteins

■ List techniques available to study protein metabolism and to discuss the advantages and disadvantages of these techniques

■ Discuss the contribution of protein to energy expenditure at rest and during exercise

■ Discuss the effect of feeding on protein synthesis and breakdown

■ Describe the recommendations generally given for strength and endurance athletes

■ Discuss the need for protein supplementation in athletes

■ Describe the potential health hazards of excess intake of protein

■ Discuss the effects of ingesting single amino acids

Debate has always raged over how much dietary protein is required for optimal athletic performance, partly because muscle contains a large proportion of the protein in a human body (about 40%). Muscle also accounts for 25% to 35% of all protein turnover in the body. Both the structural proteins that make up the myofibrils and the proteins that act as enzymes within a muscle cell change as an adaptation to exercise training. Indeed, muscle mass, muscle protein content, and muscle protein composition change in response to training.

Interest in protein consumption is very high among amateur and professional athletes. Therefore, the fact that meat, which contains high-quality protein, is a very popular protein source for athletes (especially strength athletes) is not surprising. This preference for meat probably dates back to ancient Greece where athletes in preparation for Olympic games consumed large quantities of meat.

A strong belief, especially among strength athletes, is that a large protein intake or certain protein or amino acid supplements increases muscle mass and strength. Despite the long history of protein use in sport, debate continues even over questions such as whether protein requirements are increased in athletes. Protein and amino acid metabolism is very complex, and many organs and tissues are involved. Thus, no uniform opinion exists as to what should be measured as an endpoint. For example, the effectiveness of protein intake or supplements could be assessed by measuring performance, muscle mass, or strength, or it could be measured by **nitrogen balance** over several days or by short-term methods involving the incorporation of labeled amino acids into muscle proteins.

The use of different techniques to estimate protein turnover may give different results. Therefore, the principles of the techniques and their limitations must be understood. This chapter discusses the various techniques available to investigate protein metabolism. Then, a brief overview of protein and amino acid metabolism is given. Subsequently, protein metabolism during exercise and dietary protein needs for endurance and strength-training athletes are examined. Finally, the effects of individually supplementing the diet with various amino acids is discussed.

Amino Acids

The most abundant proteins in muscle are the contractile proteins actin and myosin. Together they account for approximately 80% to 90% of all muscle protein. Muscle contains all the naturally occurring amino acids, and, thus, meat is a very valuable food.

The most abundant amino acids are the **branched-chain amino acids** (BCAAs) leucine, valine, and isoleucine, which together account for 20% of the total amino acids found in muscle protein.

Amino Acid Transport

The concentrations of amino acids in muscle and in the blood differ, suggesting that to maintain these concentration gradients, an active transport mechanism is required. Because different amino acids have different concentration gradients, different transporters move individual or groups of amino acids. Amino acid transporters are membrane-bound proteins that recognize specific amino acid shapes and chemical properties (e.g., neutral, basic, or anionic). The transporters are divided into sodium-dependent and sodium-independent carriers. Generally the sodium-dependent transporters maintain a larger gradient than the sodium-independent transporters. To date, some transporter proteins have been identified, but many more are yet to be discovered.

Amino Acid Metabolism

The metabolism of most amino acids is linked to the metabolism of other amino acids, and some amino acids can be synthesized from other amino acids. This feature is especially important in conditions of limited dietary protein intake or when metabolic requirements are increased. Some amino acids are essential and are not synthesized in the body, whereas others can be synthesized in the body (nonessential amino acids). (See chapter 1, figure 1.7.)

Amino acids are involved in a wide variety of biochemical and physiological processes, some of which are common to all and some of which are highly specific to certain amino acids. Amino acids are constantly incorporated into proteins (**protein synthesis**), and proteins are constantly broken down (protein breakdown or degradation). These processes are summarized in figure 7.1. The vast majority of the amino acids in the body are incorporated into tissue proteins, but a small pool of free amino acids also exists (about 120 g of free amino acids is present in the skeletal muscle of an adult). Amino acids are constantly extracted from the free amino acid pool for synthesis of various proteins, and breakdown of protein (**protein degradation**) makes amino acids available for the free amino acid pool.

Protein Breakdown

The breakdown of protein serves two main purposes: (1) It provides energy when some of its individual

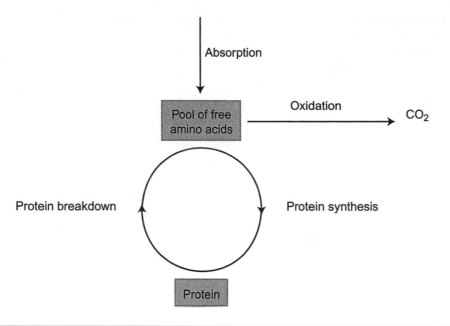

Figure 7.1 Protein metabolism. Amino acids enter the free amino acid pool from the diet (absorption) or from breakdown of protein. Amino acids leave the free amino acid pool for protein synthesis or oxidation to CO_2.

amino acids are converted into acetyl-CoA or TCA-cycle intermediates and are oxidized in the mitochondria. (2) Individual amino acids can be used for the synthesis of other compounds, including neurotransmitters (e.g., **serotonin**), hormones (e.g., epinephrine), and other peptides and proteins. This breakdown of protein and incorporation of the amino acids into a new protein links protein degradation with protein synthesis. Amino acids can also be incorporated into compounds that are not proteins. In this case, the body loses protein. For example, some amino acids are converted into glucose (gluconeogenesis) or fat (lipogenesis) and subsequently stored in adipose tissue.

Before amino acids can be oxidized, the amino group must be removed. Removal of the amino group can be achieved for some amino acids by transferring it to another molecule called a keto-acid, which results in the formation of a different amino acid. This process is called **transamination** and is catalyzed by enzymes called aminotransferases. A good example is the transfer of the amino group from the amino acid leucine to the keto-acid α-ketoglutarate forming α-ketoisocaproate (which can be further metabolized to form acetyl-CoA) and **glutamate,** respectively. Alternatively, the amino group can be removed from the amino acid to form free **ammonia** (NH_3), in a process called oxidative **deamination.** One example is the breakdown of asparagine to form aspartate and NH_3. Because free ammonia is a toxic substance, it is either used to form **glutamine** from glutamate within the muscle or is transported to the liver, where it is converted to urea

and is eventually excreted by the kidneys. Both ammonia and urea can be excreted in urine and sweat.

After the removal of the amino group from an amino acid, the remaining carbon skeleton (the keto-acid) is eventually oxidized to CO_2 in the TCA cycle. The carbon skeleton of amino acids can enter the TCA cycle in several ways. Some can be converted to acetyl-CoA and enter the TCA cycle just like acetyl-CoA from carbohydrate or fat. They can also enter the TCA cycle as α-ketoglutarate or oxaloacetate as metabolites of glutamate and aspartate, respectively (see figure 7.2).

The amino acids that can be converted into α-ketoglutarate, oxaloacetate, or pyruvate can also be used for the synthesis of glucose in the liver (gluconeogenesis). Amino acids or keto-acids that are eventually broken down to acetyl-CoA can also be used in the synthesis of FAs. Acetyl-CoA units can be used in an elongation process to form "longer" FAs by adding on to the hydrocarbon chain of the 16-carbon FA, palmitate. The following are examples of some common aminotransferase reactions:

$$\text{L-glutamate} + \text{oxaloacetate} \rightarrow$$
$$\text{α-ketoglutarate} + \text{L-aspartate}$$

$$\text{L-alanine} + \text{α-ketoglutarate} \rightarrow \text{pyruvate} + \text{L-glutamate}$$

Several amino acids undergo reversible transamination. These amino acids include alanine, aspartate, glutamate, and the BCAAs: leucine, isoleucine, and valine. The BCAAs are the only **essential amino acids** that can undergo transamination. Transamination is

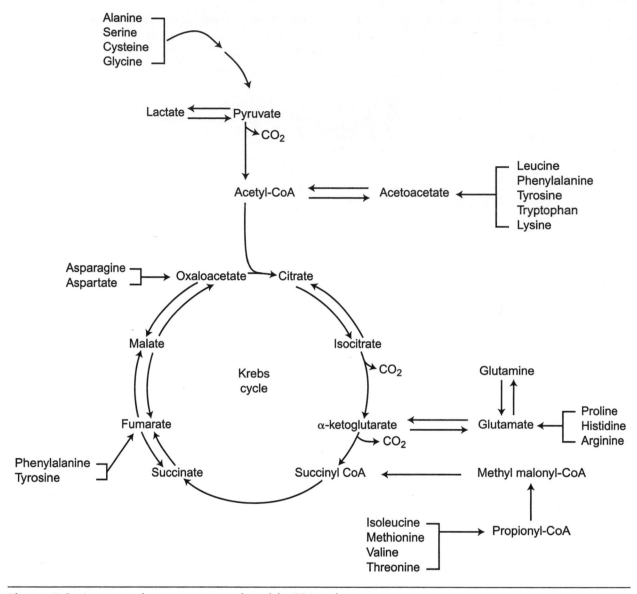

Figure 7.2 Interactions between amino acids and the TCA cycle.

usually rapid, and the main limiting factor is the fact that these processes sometimes take place in different tissues. Amino acids, thus, have to be transported via the circulation. Glutamate serves a central role in these transamination reactions because several amino acids can undergo transamination with glutamate.

Leucine
Valine
Isoleucine
Alanine } Glutamate
Aspartate
Glutamine
NH₃ + α-ketoglutarate

Most of the nitrogen from amino acid degradation is transferred to α-ketoglutarate to form glutamate and subsequently glutamine; these two amino acids are the most abundant free amino acids in muscle. Only 6 of the available 20 amino acids in protein are oxidized in significant amounts by muscle: asparagine, aspartate, glutamate, isoleucine, leucine, and valine. An outline of the pathways involved in degradation of the various amino acids is provided in table 7.1.

Amino Acid Synthesis

The discussion of synthesis of amino acids is by definition limited to the nonessential amino acids because the essential amino acids cannot be synthesized in

Table 7.1   Pathways of Amino Acid Degradation

Metabolic pathway	Important enzymes	Nitrogen end product	Carbon end product
Amino acids converted to other amino acids			
Asparagine	Asparaginase	Aspartate+NH_3	
Glutamine	Glutaminase	Glutamate+NH_3	
Arginine	Arginase	Ornithine+Urea	
Phenylalanine	Phenylalanine hydroxylase	Tyrosine	
Proline		Glutamate	
Cysteine		Taurine	
Transamination to form glutamate			
Alanine		Glutamate	Pyruvate
Aspartate		Glutamate	Oxaloacetate
Leucine		Glutamate	Ketones
Isoleucine		Glutamate	Succinate
Valine		Glutamate	Succinate
Ornithine		2 Glutamates	α-ketoglutarate
Tyrosine		Glutamate	Ketone + fumarate
Cysteine		Glutamate	Ketone + SO_4^-
Other pathways			
Serine	Serine dehydratase	NH_3	Pyruvate
Threonine	Theorine dehydratase	NH_3	Ketobutyrate
Histidine	Histidase	NH_3	Urocanate
Tryptophan		NH_3	Kynurenine
Glycine		NH_3	CO_2
Methionine		NH_3	Ketobutyrate
Lysine		2 Glutamates	Acetate

Adapted from D.E. Matthews, 1999.

the body. In figure 7.3, a summary of the synthetic pathways of nonessential amino acids is given. Again, glutamate plays a central role. Glutamate serves as the donor of nitrogen in the synthesis of many amino acids, which occurs by transferring NH_3 to a carbon skeleton precursor (keto-acid) from the TCA cycle, from another nonessential amino acid, or from an essential amino acid.

Synthesis of amino acids by the transfer of NH_3 to a carbon skeleton precursor from the TCA cycle is rarely limited because of the ample availability of the substrates (carbon skeleton precursors and NH_3). On the other hand, synthesis of amino acids from other amino acids can sometimes be limited because of limited dietary supply. Cysteine and tyrosine are special cases because they are synthesized from essential amino acids and are therefore indirectly dependent on amino acid intake.

Incorporation of Amino Acids Into Protein

Different proteins are synthesized and degraded at different rates. Generally, the proteins that have a regulatory function (such as enzymes) or that act as signals (hormones) have a relatively rapid turnover

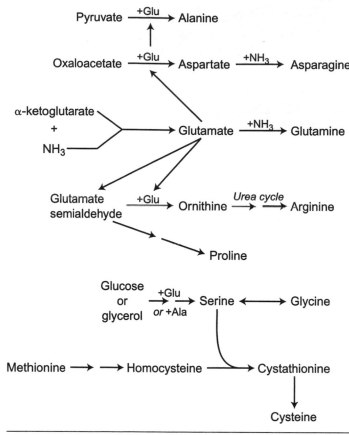

Figure 7.3 Synthetic pathways of the nonessential amino acids.
Adapted from D.E. Matthews, 1998.

(hours or days). The structural proteins, such as collagen and contractile proteins (actin and myosin), have a relatively slow turnover (days, weeks, or months). In humans who are weight stable, the overall synthesis and degradation must be in balance, which means that the nitrogen consumed equals the nitrogen excreted in urine, feces, and other routes.

Protein turnover is several times greater than the protein intake, as is illustrated in figure 7.4 for a healthy 70-kg (154-lb) person. A normal daily protein intake is approximately 90 g. In this example, the intake of protein, therefore, provides only about 25% of the amino acids that enter the free amino acid pool each day (340 g). Most of the amino acids that appear in and disappear from the free amino acid pool are derived from proteins in the gut, kidneys, and liver. Even though this protein is a relatively small portion of the total mass of protein, it represents about two-thirds of the total protein turnover because of the very rapid turnover in these tissues. Muscle has a relatively slow protein turnover and provides most of the remainder. Various techniques are used to study protein metabolism and nitrogen balance. These techniques are reviewed later in this chapter.

Incorporation of Amino Acids Into Other Compounds

Amino acids are used for the synthesis of amino acid–like compounds. A list of the most important products is provided in table 7.2. Amino acids glutamate, tyrosine, and tryptophan, for example, are precursors of neurotransmitters. Glutamate is a special amino acid in this respect because it is not only a precursor of neurotransmitters but is also a neurotransmitter itself. Tyrosine is the precursor of catecholamines (dopamine, ephinephrine, and norepinephrine) and tryptophan is the precursor of serotonin (5-hydroxytryptamine). The roles of amino acids as precursors of creatine and carnitine synthesis are discussed in more detail in chapter 10.

Techniques to Study Protein and Amino Acid Metabolism

The following is a list of currently available techniques to study protein metabolism. These techniques range from very simple techniques, such as the measurement of urea in urine, to very complex techniques involving expensive and very sophisticated equipment in combination with more invasive techniques.

- Urea concentration in urine and sweat
- 3-methylhistidine in urine (indication of myofibrillar protein breakdown)
- Nitrogen balance (nitrogen intake minus nitrogen excretion in sweat and urine)
- Arteriovenous measurements of amino acids across a tissue bed
- Radiolabeled isotopes
- Stable isotopes
- Tracer incorporation into a specific protein (protein synthesis)
- Tracer release from a specific protein (protein breakdown)
- Fractional synthetic rate (FSR)
- Fractional breakdown rates (FBR)

An overview of these techniques, including their strengths and weaknesses, is given in table 7.3.

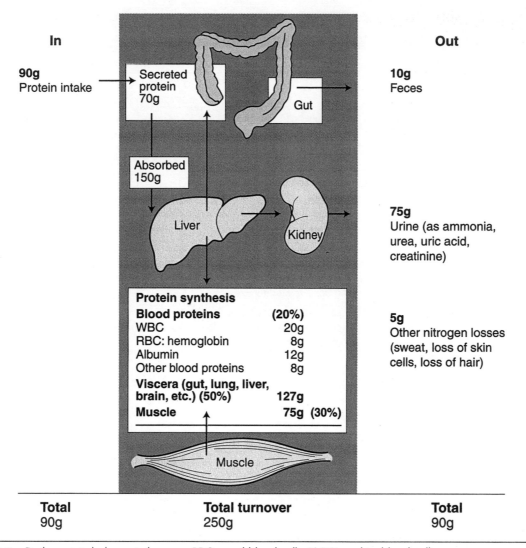

Figure 7.4 Daily protein balance in humans. RBC = red blood cells, WBC = white blood cells.

Adapted from D.E. Matthews, 1998, Proteins and amino acids. In *Modern Nutrition in Health and Disease*, edited by N.E. Shils, J.A. Olson, M. Shike, and A.C. Ross (Philadelphia: Lippincott Williams and Wilkins).

Table 7.2   Products Synthesized from Amino Acids

Product	Synthesized from	Product	Synthesized from
Creatine	Arginine Glycine Methionine	Pyrimidines	Aspartate Glutamine
Glutathione	Cysteine Taurine Glutamine	Histamine	Histidine
		Carnitine	Lysine
Neurotransmitters	Glutamate Tyrosine Tryptophan	Choline Serine	Methionine
Purines	Aspartate Glutamine Glycine	T3, T4 Epinephrine	Tyrosine

Table 7.3 Methods for Estimating Protein Metabolism

Method	Advantages	Disadvantages/Limitations
Urea concentration in urine and sweat	Easy; relatively cheap	Only rough estimate; heavily affected by diet (protein intake)
3-methylhistidine in urine	Simple measure of myofibrillar protein breakdown	Only rough estimate of myofibrillar protein breakdown; requires strict control of meat intake; does not provide information about actual changes in muscle mass
Nitrogen balance (nitrogen intake – nitrogen excretion in sweat and urine)	Accurate method when used over relatively long periods of time	Difficult and time consuming; tends to overestimate nitrogen retention; usually ignores nitrogen loss in sweat; highly dependent on subject compliance; gives no insight into metabolic pathways
Arteriovenous measurements of amino acids across a tissue bed	Gives information about net exchange of amino acids across a tissue; net uptake of essential amino acids related to rate of protein synthesis	Invasive; can have high variability, depending on blood flow measurement
Radiolabeled isotopes	Relatively cheap; relatively easy to measure; small amounts of tracer needed	Potential health risk
Stable isotopes	No health risk	Relatively expensive; sophisticated equipment needed for analyses
Tracer incorporation into a specific protein (protein synthesis)	Gives direct information about protein synthesis in a tissue	Invasive (tissue biopsies needed); relatively expensive; sophisticated equipment needed for analyses
Fractional synthetic rate (FSR) and fractional breakdown rate (FBR)	Uses stable isotopes so no health risk	Short-term measurement; does not provide information about actual changes in muscle mass; relatively expensive; sophisticated equipment needed for analyses

Urea Concentration in Urine

The amount of urea excreted in urine is an indication of whole-body protein breakdown but does not provide detailed information and only gives a very rough indication of protein breakdown. The urinary urea concentration depends on many disturbing factors, such as the level of hydration and the diet (protein intake). When urine is collected over 24 hours, the results become slightly more meaningful because total daily urea excretion can be determined, but the results are still highly dependent on protein intake.

Nitrogen Balance

Most experts in various countries have used nitrogen balance studies to determine the recommended dietary intakes for protein. Subjects are fed a diet with a certain level of protein intake, and for a time (3 days to 14 days), urine and feces are collected over 24-hour periods. The nitrogen intake (protein intake) and nitrogen excretion are measured as accurately as possible. A week or more may be required before collection reflects the adaptations to a particular diet.

Nitrogen excretion can be measured from urine, feces, and sweat. Nitrogen is detectable in feces because not all protein is completely absorbed, and some of the nitrogen secreted into the gastrointestinal tract is not reabsorbed. When nitrogen balance is measured in exercising subjects, nitrogen excretion in sweat is substantial and must be included in the measurements. Nitrogen is excreted mainly in the form of urea (about 90%) but also in creatinine, ammonia, uric acid, and other nitrogen-containing compounds. Often urinary nitrogen is the only measure taken, but nitrogen excretion is underestimated when using this measure alone.

When nitrogen intake exceeds excretion, a person is in positive nitrogen balance. When nitrogen excretion exceeds nitrogen intake, a person is in negative nitrogen balance. The latter situation cannot continue for a long time. The body uses protein, and because it does not contain large stores of protein, the breakdown and atrophy of tissues and organs will occur.

Only when nitrogen intake matches nitrogen excretion is a person in nitrogen balance.

Although the estimation of nitrogen balance is a technique that is often used, it is not easy to apply and it has been criticized for numerous reasons: It is very time consuming and involves several 24-hour periods of urine collection. It is labor intensive for the investigators. Its success is highly dependent on subject compliance. This technique also tends to underestimate nitrogen excretion and thus overestimate nitrogen retention, and it only gives a measure of the net nitrogen balance. Because of its "black box" nature, this technique does not provide any insight into the metabolic pathways involved in changes in protein metabolism.

3-Methylhistidine Excretion

Another method of estimating protein metabolism is the measurement 3-methylhistidine or N-methylhistidine excretion in the urine. When proteins are degraded, 3-methylhistidine cannot be recycled within the muscle and is excreted in the urine. The amount of 3-methylhistidine in urine is, therefore, a measure of contractile protein breakdown. The results of this relatively simple technique can be confounded by the diet. Meat and fish contain a relatively large amount of 3-methylhistidine and could cause erroneous results. The measurement of 3-methylhistidine is, therefore, only meaningful when the diet is strictly controlled. The urinary 3-methylhistidine is also highly dependent on the renal clearance rate. Thus, 3-methylhistidine excretion is often expressed relative to creatinine excretion to allow corrections for renal clearance and individual differences in muscle mass. The technique has several limitations but is regarded as a relatively easy and noninvasive way to get a rough idea of muscle protein breakdown.

Arteriovenous Differences

Nitrogen balance can also be determined across a specific organ. When arterial and venous blood across a certain tissue is sampled, the differences in the amino acid concentration gives information about the net exchange of specific amino acids. The arterial blood delivers amino acids to a tissue, and some of these amino acids are taken up and used for protein synthesis. The venous blood contains amino acids from protein breakdown. Depending on the tissue of interest, measuring arteriovenous differences (AV-differences) can be more or less invasive. For example, AV-differences from tissues like the gut, liver, and brain are very difficult to obtain. On the other hand, AV-differences across an arm or leg muscle are relatively easy to obtain. Recently, techniques have been developed to sample across adipose tissue. Independent of the tissue sampled, measurements of AV-differences always require a medically qualified person with good skills.

The AV-difference provides a measure of net uptake and release of amino acids by a tissue. The most valuable information is obtained from amino acids that are not metabolized. For example, the AV-difference of tyrosine and lysine (which are not metabolized in the muscle) reflect the difference between net amino acid uptake from protein synthesis and the release of amino acids from muscle protein breakdown. This method does not provide an insight into the various metabolic pathways in that tissue. Also, all metabolites of amino acids must be measured to get a true balance. Adding a tracer improves the value of the measurement and allows for more firm conclusions about metabolic pathways that play a role in the tissue. AV-differences of 3-methylhistidine across a muscle may be used as a specific marker of contractile protein breakdown.

Tracer Methods

Labeled tracers are used to follow amino acids in the body. These tracers have identical properties as the amino acid or metabolite they are meant to trace. They are, however, distinguishable because they either emit radiation (radioactive isotopes) or are slightly heavier (stable isotopes). Radioactive labeled tracers such as ^3H (hydrogen) and ^{14}C (carbon) have been used most often, but many laboratories now use stable isotopic tracers because, unlike radioisotopes, they do not pose a health risk. Stable isotopes have a different number of neutrons and, therefore, a different molecular mass. The difference in mass can be detected with mass spectrometry.

Stable isotopes occur naturally, and most elements have one abundant mass and up to three less abundant masses. For example, the abundant mass for hydrogen is ^1H and the less abundant mass is ^2H. For carbon the abundant and less abundant isotopes are ^{12}C and ^{13}C, respectively. Figure 7.5 lists some common stable isotopes and their abundance.

Common stable	Rare stable	Radioactive
^1H	^2H (0.02%)	^3H
^{12}C	^{13}C (1.1%)	^{14}C
^{14}N	^{15}N (0.37%)	$^{13}N*$
^{16}O	^{18}O (0.04%)	$^{17}O*$

Figure 7.5 Common stable, rare stable, and radioactive isotopes. The asterisk (*) indicates no long-lived radioisotopes for these elements.

Most tracer techniques are based on the principle of dilution. A tracer is infused, and the dilution of the tracer gives information about endogenous production of the amino acid of interest. This principle can be illustrated by a simple analogy. If you want to know the amount of water in a bucket, you can add a known amount of dye. After mixing the dye with the water, a sample of the mixture can be taken and the concentration of the dye can be determined. From the dilution of the dye, the amount of water in the bucket can be calculated. This calculation is, of course, only accurate if the exact amount of dye is known, mixing with the water is complete, and the concentration of the dye can be determined after mixing. Similar measurements can be made in a dynamic system if the dye is infused at a known constant rate. For example, a dye could be used to calculate the flow of water through a stream. The same principle can be applied by infusing a tracer into the human circulation. Several variations to this technique exist, to study whole-body protein metabolism or the metabolism of specific amino acids. Here we only discuss the principles. The interested reader should refer to other literature to learn more about stable and radioactive tracers (Wolfe 1992; Matthews 1999).

Methods have been developed to calculate the fractional synthetic rate (FSR) and fractional breakdown rate (FBR). These techniques, which use isotopic tracers, calculate the relative rate of protein breakdown and synthesis. Most of the information on protein metabolism currently available is from animal studies. Although the techniques to study protein metabolism in humans are constantly being improved, all methods have their limitations and no agreement has been reached on what method is best to use. Nevertheless, the available information allows us to draw some conclusions about exercise and protein requirements.

Protein Requirements for Exercise

Acute endurance exercise results in increased leucine oxidation. Because leucine is an essential amino acid and cannot be synthesized within the body, the implication is that dietary protein requirements are increased. Studies using a nitrogen balance technique confirm that the dietary protein requirements for athletes involved in prolonged endurance training are higher than those for sedentary individuals. However, these results have been questioned by scientists who have not found differences or even improved nitrogen and leucine balance in more active individuals.

During exercise, the uptake of glutamate and BCAA from the blood is increased. At the same time, the production and the release of alanine and glutamine by the muscle increases almost linearly with increasing exercise intensity. At exercise intensities below 70% $\dot{V}O_2$max, little or no change occurs in the concentration of amino acids in the muscle. At intensities above 70% $\dot{V}O_2$max, a sharp decrease in the intramuscular glutamate and glutamine concentrations is observed. The release of glutamine and alanine by the muscle is thought to remove ammonia from the muscle and transport it to the liver, where these amino acids can be deaminated and the ammonia is converted to urea and subsequently excreted.

In prolonged exercise or very-high-intensity exercise, the net negative protein balance that is normally observed in the hours after eating is increased. Accumulation of amino acids that are not metabolized in the muscle (for example lysine and threonine) increases. Whether this is the result of increased protein breakdown, decreased protein synthesis, or both is still unclear.

After resistance exercise, muscle protein turnover is increased because of an acceleration of both protein synthesis and degradation. Muscle protein breakdown is increased after resistance training but to a smaller degree than muscle protein synthesis (Biolo et al. 1995, 1999; Phillips et al. 1997, 1999). The elevations in protein degradation and synthesis are transient but are still present at 3 hours and 24 hours after exercise, although protein turnover returns to baseline levels after 48 hours. These results seem to apply to resistance exercise or dynamic exercise at a relatively high intensity. Low-intensity to moderate-intensity dynamic endurance exercise does not seem to have the same effects on muscle protein turnover, although studies have shown that endurance exercise may result in increased protein oxidation, especially during the later stages of very prolonged exercise and in conditions of glycogen depletion.

Protein is estimated to contribute about 5% to 15% to energy expenditure in resting conditions. During exercise, this relative contribution is likely to decrease because of an increasing importance of carbohydrate and fat as fuels. During very prolonged exercise, when carbohydrate availability becomes limited, the contribution of protein to energy expenditure may increase up to about 10% of total energy expenditure. Thus, although total protein oxidation is increased during endurance exercise, the relative contribution of protein to energy expenditure remains small. Furthermore, the oxidized amino acids do not appear to be derived from degradation of myofibrillar proteins (Kasperek and Snider 1989). In fact, only 6 of the 20 available amino acids are oxidized by muscle.

Protein Requirements for Endurance Athletes

Even though most researchers agree that exercise increases protein oxidation to some extent and this oxidation increase is accompanied by increased nitrogen losses, controversy persists over whether athletes have to eat more protein than less active individuals. Several research groups claim that evidence supports the contention that athletes should eat more protein, whereas others believes that the evidence is insufficient to make such a statement. One interesting observation is that training seems to have a protein-sparing effect. The better trained a person is, the lower the protein breakdown and oxidation during exercise. The research groups that advocate an increased protein intake for endurance athletes usually recommend an intake of 1.2 g/kg b.w. to 1.8 g/kg b.w. of protein (as opposed to the recommended intake of 0.8 g/kg b.w. of protein for the average population).

Even if protein requirements are increased, in practice athletes have no problem meeting these needs. As an extreme example, we can look at the Tour de France. Cyclists in this event compete for 3 hours to 7 hours a day, and maintaining energy balance is often problematic (Saris et al. 1989; Jeukendrup, Craig, and Hawley 2000). Nevertheless, in this situation, they seem to have no problems in maintaining nitrogen balance (Brouns et al. 1989a). With increasing food intake, the intake of protein automatically increases because many food products contain at least some protein. A study by van

Erp-Baart et al. (1989a) showed a linear relationship between energy intake and protein intake. Tour de France cyclists consumed 12% of their daily energy intake (26 MJ, or 6,500 kcal) in the form of protein, and they easily met the suggested increased requirements (~2.5 g/kg b.w./day). These results suggest that provided the energy intake matches energy expenditure on a daily basis, endurance athletes do not need to supplement their diets with protein.

Protein Requirements for Strength Athletes

Unlike endurance exercise, resistance exercise does not increase the rate of leucine oxidation to any major degree. The suggested increased dietary protein requirements are related to increased muscle bulk (hypertrophy).

The question of whether strength athletes have increased protein requirements is controversial, and the nitrogen balance studies that have been done have been criticized because they generally have been of short duration and a steady-state situation may not be established (Rennie and Tipton 2000). Gontzea, Sutzeescu, and Dumitrache (1975) showed that the negative nitrogen balance used by many to indicate increased protein needs, disappears after approximately 12 days of training (see figure 7.6). The protein requirements may, therefore, only be temporarily elevated. However, with a further increase in training load, the protein requirement is likely

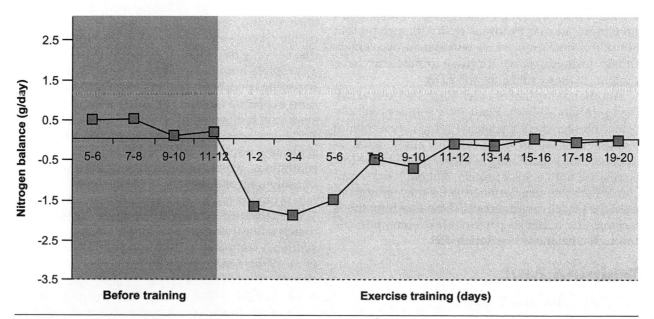

Figure 7.6 Nitrogen balance in response to exercise training.

Adapted from I. Gontzea, R. Sutzeescu, and S. Dumitrache, 1975, "The influence of adaptation to physical effort on nitrogen balance in man," *Nutrition Report International* 11(3): 231-236.

to increase again. The recommendation for protein intake for strength athletes is often 1.6 g/kg b.w./day to 1.7 g/kg b.w./day. Again, this requirement seems to be met easily with a normal diet, and no extra protein intake is needed. Protein supplements are often used but are not necessary to meet the recommended protein intake.

Protein Intake by Athletes and Athletes at Risk

The literature contains several reports of protein intake by athletes in a variety of sports. These intakes are usually self-reported but generally give a good indication of nutritional habits and can reveal whether the athlete is achieving the recommended protein intake. In the van Erp-Baart et al. study (1989a), protein intake in a variety of elite athletes was investigated. The lowest recorded intake was in a group of field hockey players, but their intake was still over 1.0 g/kg b.w./day. The highest intakes were recorded for endurance cyclists who consumed almost 3 g/kg b.w./day and bodybuilders who consumed 2.5 g/kg b.w./day. The majority of athletes therefore consume far more than the RDA for protein (0.8 g/kg b.w./day).

However, some individuals may suffer from protein deficiency, which can result in a compromise of function and ultimately to loss of body protein (atrophy). Four groups of athletes are recognized as being at risk from protein and energy deficiency: amenorrheic female runners, male wrestlers, male and female gymnasts, and female dancers. Energy intake can be very low for these groups and as a result protein intake may be low as well. Although protein intake for these groups may be adequate on average, certain individuals within these groups may have protein intakes well below the RDA.

Another group that has been suggested to be at risk is vegetarian athletes. Plant food sources typically contain lower-quality proteins, which often contain low levels of one or more essential amino acids. In addition, the digestibility of plant protein can be low compared with animal protein. Although some concern exists that vegetarian athletes may struggle to meet the protein requirements, the evidence for this is lacking, and adequate protein intake seems possible through a balanced vegetarian diet.

Training and Protein Metabolism

Training can have profound effects on muscle morphology and function. Different types of training seem to have very distinct effects. For example, strength training results in muscle hypertrophy and increased muscle mass (Jones and Rutherford 1987). Endurance training has no effect on muscle mass, but the mitochondrial density inside the muscle fibers increases dramatically (Holloszy and Coyle 1984). However, dynamic exercise training possibly results in increased muscle strength, but this increase depends on the relative intensity and the strength required to complete the training sessions.

Hypertrophy from strength training must be caused by increased protein synthesis. This protein synthesis must occur in the recovery phase between training sessions. Studies have shown that the body adapts to training by becoming more efficient with protein. Protein turnover decreases after training, and less net protein degradation occurs. In other words, after training, athletes become more efficient and "waste" less protein (Butterfield and Calloway 1984). BCAA oxidation at the same relative workload is the same in untrained and trained individuals (Lamont, McCullough, and Kalhan 1999). So although initially the protein requirement may increase, after adaptation to the training this increase seems to disappear.

Effect of Protein Intake on Protein Synthesis

Nutrition always plays a very important role in the establishment of training adaptations. In the hours after exercise, protein synthesis may exceed protein degradation but only after feeding. If feeding is delayed by 24 hours to 48 hours, net protein balance remains negative and no muscle hypertrophy occurs (Rennie and Tipton 2000). Feeding a mixed diet not only provides substrates but also results in a favorable hormonal milieu for protein synthesis. In resting conditions, higher amino acid concentrations in plasma have a stimulatory effect on protein synthesis (Bennet et al. 1990; Bennet and Rennie 1991). Increased availability of glucose and amino acids also results in increased plasma insulin concentrations, which, in turn, may cause a reduction of protein breakdown and a small increase in protein synthesis (Biolo et al. 1995; Bennet and Rennie 1991). Increased availability of amino acids immediately after exercise has a larger effect on protein synthesis compared with resting conditions (Biolo et al. 1995). Amino acids and exercise, thus, seem to have an additive effect on net protein synthesis. However, in these studies, amino acids were infused, and plasma amino acid concentrations were elevated to very high levels.

Intravenous infusion is not a practical method for athletes, and infused amino acids bypass the liver.

The liver normally extracts 20% to 90% of all amino acids after absorption in the gut (first-pass splanchnic extraction). Therefore, whether similar effects are to be expected after oral ingestion of amino acids is not clear. A follow-up study investigated this question (Tipton et al. 1999). In this study, a relatively large amount of amino acids was ingested after resistance exercise. Postexercise muscle protein balance was negative after placebo ingestion, but when amino acids were ingested, the net balance was positive mainly because of an increased muscle protein synthesis. From this study and a limited number of other studies, one can conclude that ingestion of amino acids after exercise enhances net protein synthesis.

Carbohydrate ingestion per se may not have an effect on protein synthesis. However, carbohydrate ingestion elevates plasma insulin concentrations and thereby may reduce the breakdown of protein. The combined ingestion of protein and carbohydrate seems to be preferred after exercise. The protein delivers the substrate (amino acids), and carbohydrate further increases the anabolic hormonal milieu required for net protein synthesis.

Some evidence in support of this hypothesis was recently provided by a study by Rasmussen et al. (2000). After a strenuous bout of resistance exercise, subjects were fed 6 g of essential amino acids plus 35 g of sucrose. Plasma amino acid levels increased threefold, and insulin concentrations increased 10-fold. Muscle protein synthesis increased 3.5-fold, but no increase occurred in protein breakdown (see figure 7.7). In the control condition, a net protein breakdown was observed. These results suggest that the ingestion of a relatively small amount of amino acids with a larger amount of carbohydrate can increase net muscle protein synthesis.

In the past, the amino acid needs of the body were primarily met by ingestion of whole proteins in the diet. However, over the past few years, the supplementation of individual amino acids has become

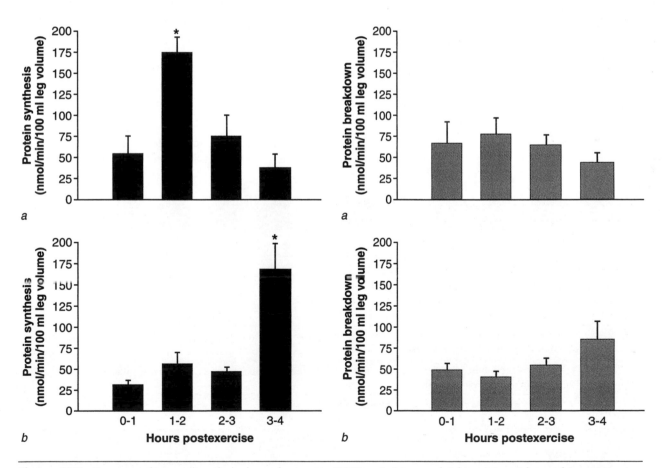

Figure 7.7 Protein synthesis with carbohydrate plus protein (CHO + Pro) ingested 1 hour (a) or 3 hours (b) post-exercise. Protein synthesis (in dark blue) was increased 1 hour to 2 hours after exercise when CHO + Pro was ingested 1 hour after exercise. When CHO + Pro ingestion was delayed, the increase in protein synthesis occurred much later. No major changes occurred in protein breakdown.

Adapted, by permission, from B.B. Rasmussen et al., 2000, "An oral essential amino acid-carbohydrate supplement enhances muscle protein anabolism after resistance exercise," *Journal of Applied Physiology* 88(2): 386-392.

increasingly popular. Technological advances have made it possible to manufacture food-grade ultrapure amino acids. The individual amino acids, called free-form amino acids, are mostly produced by bacterial fermentation.

Scientific studies are focusing on the pharmacologic and metabolic interactions of free-form amino acids. Considerable progress has been made in the area of clinical nutrition, where individual amino acids are used to reduce nitrogen losses and improve organ functions in traumatized and critically ill patients. Individual amino acids also are marketed as supplements for athletes and healthy individuals. Intake of separate amino acids are often claimed to improve exercise performance, stimulate hormone release, and improve immune function among a variety of other positive effects. The following section reviews the facts and fallacies of these claims.

Amino Acids As Ergogenic Aids

Amino acid supplements have become increasingly available and popular in certain athletic circles. Among others, weightlifters and bodybuilders consume various amino acids in attempts to stimulate the release of growth hormone from the pituitary gland, hoping that the growth hormone will, in turn, stimulate muscle development. Amino acids are also used to stimulate the release of insulin from the pancreas. Insulin is

considered an anabolic hormone because it facilitates the uptake of amino acids as well as glucose by muscle cells and increases protein and glycogen synthesis. In addition to these effects on protein synthesis, certain amino acids are claimed to provide extra fuel to the muscle and prevent fatigue by changing the concentrations of brain neurotransmitters. Other amino acids have been used in attempts to reduce immunosuppression during strenuous training, to increase ATP and PCr levels in the muscle, and to help athletes lose body weight. An overview of common claims is provided in table 7.4. Such claims are often not based on scientific evidence, and sometimes they are not even based on a sound scientific rationale.

Ingestion of amino acids can have profound physiological effects. However, amino acid metabolism is very complex. One amino acid can be converted into another, and amino acids may influence nerve impulse transmission as well as hormone secretion. Consumption of specific amino acids or even high-protein diets may lead to nutritional imbalances because overload of one amino acid may reduce the absorption of others. The following section discusses the latest scientific findings with regard to the intake of individual amino acids or combinations of amino acids.

Arginine

Infusion of some amino acids into the blood can stimulate the release of growth hormone from the pitu-

Table 7.4 Manufacturers' Claims for Amino Acids

Amino acid	Claim
Arginine	Improves immune function, increases tissue creatine levels, increases release of insulin and growth hormone, leads to fewer gastrointestinal problems, improves performance
Aspartate	Improves energy metabolism in muscle, reduces amount of fatigue causing metabolites, improves endurance performance
Glutamine	Improves immune function (fewer colds), hastens recovery after exercise, improves performance, leads to fewer gastrointestinal problems
Ornithine	Increases growth hormone and insulin release, stimulates protein synthesis and reduces protein breakdown, improves performance
BCAA	Provides fuel for working muscle, reduces fatigue, improves endurance, reduces muscle protein breakdown
Tyrosine	Increases blood concentration of catecholamines, improves fuel mobilization and metabolism during exercise
Tryptophan	Increases the release of growth hormone, improves sleep, decreases sensations of pain, improves performance
Taurine	Delays fatigue, improves performance, facilitates faster recovery, leads to less muscle damage and pain, leads to fewer gastrointestinal problems, scavenges free radicals
Glycine	Increases phosphocreatine synthesis, increases sprint performance, improves strength

itary gland. Arginine is not the only amino acid that can have such an effect. Other amino acids that may stimulate the release of hormones from endocrine glands include lysine and ornithine. The intravenous administration of arginine to adults in a dose of 30 g in 30 minutes caused a marked increase in the secretion of human pituitary growth hormone (Knopf et al. 1966; Merimee, Lillicrap, and Rabinowitz 1965). Intravenous and oral arginine administration also resulted in a marked insulin release from the α-cells of the pancreas (Dupre et al. 1968; Floyd et al. 1966). The finding that arginine increases the secretion of anabolic hormones such as human growth hormone and insulin has made arginine a very popular supplement among bodybuilders and strength athletes. However, the amounts of arginine present in sport nutritional supplements are often rather small (between 1 g/day and 2 g/day) in comparison with the intravenous doses that have been shown to have potent secretagogue actions (30 g/30 min). Well-controlled studies (double-blind, crossover) (Fogelholm et al. 1993; Lambert et al. 1993) failed to show an effect of oral L-arginine supplementation taken in low quantities on the plasma concentrations of growth hormone and insulin (measured over a 24-hour period) in male competitive weight lifters and bodybuilders. It also should be noted that the growth hormone responses that can be obtained by ingesting relatively large amounts of arginine are still smaller than those that can be obtained by 60 min of moderate intensity exercise. Furthermore, the oral ingestion of larger doses of arginine can cause severe gastrointestinal discomfort (Wagenmakers 1999a).

Although arginine infused in large quantities can have anabolic properties, oral ingestion of tolerable doses (i.e., amounts that do not cause gastrointestinal problems) do not result in increased secretion of human growth hormone and insulin. Large increases in insulin secretion can be obtained by ingestion of carbohydrate, and much larger increases in plasma growth hormone are observed during exercise than with even large doses of arginine and other individual amino acids.

Aspartate

Aspartate is often claimed to improve aerobic exercise performance. Aspartate is a precursor of the TCA-cycle intermediates and reduces plasma ammonia accumulation during exercise. Because ammonia formation is associated with fatigue, aspartate supplementation could theoretically be ergogenic.

In a study by Maughan and Sadler (1983), eight subjects cycled to exhaustion at 75% to 80% $\dot{V}O_2$max after ingestion of 6 g of aspartate (as magnesium and potassium salts) or placebo over 24 hours. No effect of aspartate supplementation was observed on plasma ammonia concentration or exercise time to exhaustion.

Branched-Chain Amino Acids

The three BCAAs, leucine, isoleucine, and valine, are not synthesized in the body. Yet they are oxidized during exercise, and they must, therefore, be replenished by the diet. In the late 1970s, BCAAs were suggested to be the third fuel for skeletal muscle after carbohydrate and fat (Goldberg and Chang 1978). BCAAs are sometimes supplied to athletes in energy drinks to provide extra fuel. Claims have also been made that BCAA supplementation can reduce net protein breakdown in muscle during exercise and reduce fatigue and enhance performance via effects on the brain.

BCAA As Fuel

As mentioned earlier, a study by Goldberg and Chang (1978) suggested that BCAAs can act as a fuel during exercise in addition to carbohydrate and fat. More recently, however, the activities of the enzymes involved in the oxidation of BCAAs were shown to be too low to allow a major contribution of BCAAs to energy expenditure (Wagenmakers et al. 1989, 1991). Detailed studies with a ^{13}C-labeled BCAA (^{13}C-leucine) showed that the oxidation of BCAAs only increases 2-fold to 3-fold during exercise, whereas the oxidation of carbohydrate and fat increases 10-fold to 20-fold (Wolfe et al. 1982; Knapik et al. 1991). Also, carbohydrate ingestion during exercise can prevent the increase in BCAA oxidation. BCAAs, therefore, do not seem to play an important role as a fuel during exercise, and from this point of view, the supplementation of BCAAs during exercise is unnecessary (Wagenmakers 1999a).

BCAA and Protein Breakdown

The claims that BCAAs reduce protein breakdown are mainly based on early in vitro studies, which showed that adding BCAAs to an incubation or perfusion medium stimulated tissue protein synthesis and inhibited protein degradation. Several in vivo studies in healthy individuals (Nair et al. 1992; Frexes-Steed et al. 1992; Louard, Barrett, and Gelfand 1990) failed to confirm the positive effect on protein balance that had been observed in vitro. No BCAA supplementation studies to date have demonstrated an improved nitrogen balance during or after exercise. Therefore, no valid scientific evidence supports the commercial claims that orally ingested BCAAs have an anticatabolic effect during and after exercise or that BCAA supplements may accelerate the repair of muscle damage after exercise (Wagenmakers 1999b).

Central Fatigue Hypothesis

The central fatigue hypothesis, which is illustrated in figure 7.8, was proposed in 1987 as an important mechanism contributing to the development of fatigue during prolonged exercise (Newsholme, Acworth, and Blomstrand 1987). This hypothesis predicts that during exercise, FAs are mobilized from adipose tissue and are transported via the blood to the muscles to serve as fuel. Because the rate of mobilization is greater than the rate of uptake by the muscle, the blood FA concentration increases. Both FAs and the amino acid tryptophan bind to albumin and compete for the same binding sites. Tryptophan is prevented from binding to albumin by the increasing FA concentration, and, therefore, the free tryptophan (fTRP) concentration and the fTRP:BCAA ratio in the blood rises. Experimental studies in humans have confirmed that these events occur. The central fatigue hypothesis predicts that the increase in the fTRP:BCAA ratio results in an increased fTRP transport across the blood-brain barrier, because BCAA and fTRP compete for carrier-mediated entry into the central nervous system by the large neutral amino acid (LNAA) transporter (Chaouloff et al. 1986; Hargreaves and Pardridge 1988). Once taken up, the conversion of tryptophan to serotonin occurs and leads to a local increase of this neurotransmitter (Hargreaves and Pardridge 1988).

Serotonin plays a role in the onset of sleep and is a determinant of mood and aggression. Therefore, the increase in serotoninergic activity might subsequently lead to central fatigue, forcing athletes to stop exercise or reduce the exercise intensity. Of course, the assumption that increased fTRP uptake leads to increased serotonin synthesis and activity of serotoninergic pathways (i.e., increased synaptic serotonin release) is a rather large leap of faith.

The central fatigue hypothesis also predicts that ingestion of BCAA will raise the plasma BCAA concentration and, hence, reduce transport of fTRP into the brain. Subsequent reduced formation of serotonin may alleviate sensations of fatigue and, in turn, improve endurance exercise performance. If the central fatigue hypothesis is correct and the ingestion of BCAAs reduces the exercise-induced increase of brain fTRP uptake and thereby delays fatigue, the opposite must also be true; that is, inges-

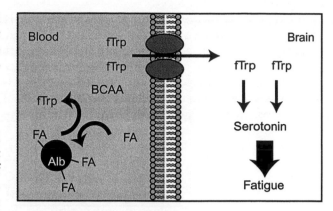

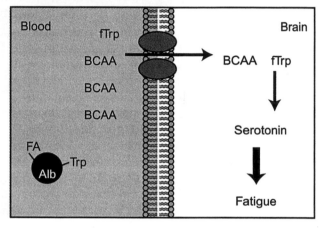

Figure 7.8 Central fatigue hypothesis.

tion of tryptophan before exercise should reduce the time to exhaustion. A few studies have included supplemental tryptophan in human subjects before or during exercise, and from these studies the conclusion must be drawn that tryptophan has no effects on exercise performance.

The effect of BCAA ingestion on physical performance was investigated for the first time in a field test by Blomstrand et al. (1991). One hundred and ninety-three male subjects were studied during a marathon in Stockholm. The subjects were randomly divided into an experimental group receiving BCAA in plain water and a placebo group receiving flavored water. The subjects also had free access to carbohydrate-containing drinks. No difference was observed in the marathon time of the 2 groups. However, when the original subject group was divided into fast and slower runners, a small significant reduction in marathon time was observed in subjects given BCAAs in the slower runners only. This study has since been criticized for its design and statistical analysis. Later studies, with various exercise and treatment designs and several forms of administration of BCAA (infusion, oral, and with and without carbohydrates), failed to find a performance effect (Varnier et al. 1994; Blomstrand et al. 1995,1997; Van Hall et al. 1995; Madsen et al. 1996). Van Hall et al. (1995) studied time-trial performance in trained cyclists consuming carbohydrate during exercise with and without BCAAs. A high and a low dose of BCAA was given, but no differences were seen in time-trial performance (see figure 7.9).

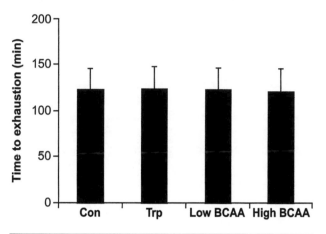

Figure 7.9 Time to exhaustion during cycling at 75% to 80% $\dot{V}O_2$max. No effect is seen with tryptophan, a small dose of branched-chain amino acids (BCAAs), or a large dose of BCAAs.

Reprinted, by permission, from G. Van Hall et al., 1995, "Ingestion of branched-chain amino acids and tryptophan during sustained exercise in man: Failure to affect performance," *Journal of Physiology* 486: 789-794.

Despite the lack of strong evidence for the efficacy of BCAA supplements, athletes continue to use them. However, normal food alternatives are available and are almost certainly cheaper. For example, a typical BCAA supplement sold in tablet form contains 100 mg valine, 50 mg of isoleucine, and 100 mg of leucine. A chicken breast (100 g) contains approximately 470 mg valine, 375 mg of isoleucine, and 656 mg leucine, the equivalent of about 7 BCAA tablets. One-fourth cup of peanuts (60 g) contains even more BCAA and is equivalent to 11 tablets.

Glutamine

Glutamine is a naturally occurring nonessential amino acid; that is, it can be synthesized in the body. It is important as a constituent of proteins and as a means of nitrogen transport between tissues. It is also important in acid-base regulation and as a precursor of the antioxidant glutathione. Glutamine is the most abundant free amino acid in human muscle and plasma. Its alleged effects can be classified as anabolic and immunostimulatory. Based somewhat

on an uncritical evaluation of the scientific literature, glutamine supplements are claimed by various manufacturers and suppliers to have the following beneficial effects:

- More rapid water absorption from the gut
- Improved intracellular fluid retention (i.e., a "volumizing" effect)
- Improved gut barrier function and reduced risk of endotoxemia
- Nutritional support for immune system and prevention of infection
- Stimulation of muscle protein synthesis and muscle tissue growth
- Stimulation of muscle glycogen resynthesis
- Reduction in muscle soreness and improved muscle tissue repair
- Enhanced buffering capacity and improved high-intensity exercise performance

The normal daily intake of glutamine from dietary protein is about 3 g/day to 6 g/day (assuming a daily protein intake of 0.8 g/kg b.m. to 1.6 g/kg b.m. of protein for a 70-kg individual). Researchers examining the effects of glutamine on the postexercise decline in plasma glutamine concentration report that a dose of about 0.1 g/kg b.w. of glutamine has to be given every 30 minutes over a 2-hour to 3-hour period to prevent the fall in the plasma glutamine concentration (Nieman and Pedersen 2000).

Glutamine is utilized at high rates by white blood cells (particularly lymphocytes) to provide energy and optimal conditions for nucleotide biosynthesis and, hence, cell proliferation (Ardawi and Newsholme 1994). Indeed, glutamine is considered important, if not essential, to lymphocytes and other rapidly dividing cell, including the gut mucosa and bone marrow stem cells. Prolonged exercise is associated with a fall in the intramuscular and plasma concentration of glutamine, and this decrease in glutamine availability has been hypothesized to impair immune function (Parry-Billings et al. 1992). Periods of very heavy training are associated with a chronic reduction in plasma glutamine levels, and this reduction may be partly responsible for the immunosuppression apparent in many endurance athletes (Parry-Billings et al. 1992). The intramuscular concentration of glutamine is related to the rate of net protein synthesis (Rennie et al. 1989), and some evidence also indicates a role for glutamine in promoting glycogen synthesis (Bowtell et al. 1999). However, the mechanisms underlying these alleged anabolic effects of glutamine remain to be elucidated.

Glutamine and Fluid Absorption

Water transport from the gut into the circulation is promoted by the presence of glucose and sodium in drinks. Water movement is determined by osmotic gradients, and the cotransport of sodium and glucose into the gut epithelial cells is accompanied by the osmotic movement of water molecules in the same direction. Glutamine is transported into gut epithelial cells by both sodium-dependent and sodium-independent mechanisms, and the addition of glutamine to oral rehydration solutions increases the rate of fluid absorption above that of ingested water alone (Silva et al. 1998). However, the potential benefits of adding glutamine to commercially available sports drinks have not be adequately tested, and any additional benefit in terms of increased rate of fluid absorption and retention is likely to be very small. Placebo-controlled studies that have investigated the effects of glutamine supplementation on extracellular buffering capacity and high-intensity exercise performance have not found any beneficial effect. Glutamine is not included in commercial sports drinks, mainly because of its relative instability in solution.

Glutamine and Muscle Protein Breakdown

Muscle protein breakdown occurs in the fasted state. Research indicates that resistance exercise reduces the extent of this protein catabolism, but an anabolic (muscle growth) response requires an intake of essential amino acids (dietary protein) in the recovery period after exercise (Rasmussen, Tipton, et al. 2000). This intake of essential amino acids promotes amino acid uptake into muscle and increases the tissue protein synthesis rate without affecting the rate of protein breakdown. Provided that ingested protein contains the eight essential amino acids, taking supplements of individual nonessential amino acids at this time is unlikely to provide any additional benefit. Protein synthesis in the tissues of the body requires the simultaneous presence of all 20 amino acids. Some evidence exists for an effect of glutamine supplements in promoting glycogen synthesis in the first few hours of recovery after exercise (Bowtell et al. 1999), but further work using optimal amounts of carbohydrate feeding after exercise needs to be done to substantiate this finding and give it practical relevance. Thus, a postexercise meal consisting of predominantly carbohydrate with some protein would seem to be the best strategy to promote both glycogen and protein synthesis in muscle after exercise (see the discussion on glycogen resynthesis in chapter 5).

Glutamine and the Immune System

Several scientists have suggested that exogenous provision of glutamine supplements may prevent muscle damage and muscle soreness and the impairment of immune function after endurance exercise. However, eccentric exercise-induced muscle damage does not affect the plasma glutamine concentration (Walsh et al. 1998), and no scientific evidence supports a beneficial effect of oral glutamine supplementation on muscle repair after exercise-induced damage, and no evidence supports reduced muscle soreness when glutamine is consumed compared with placebo. Prolonged exercise at 50% to 70% $\dot{V}O_2$max causes a 10% to 30% fall in plasma glutamine concentration that may last for several hours during recovery (Parry-Billings et al. 1992; Walsh et al. 1998; Castell and Newsholme 1997). This fall in plasma glutamine coincides with the window of opportunity for infection after prolonged exercise when an athlete is more susceptible to infections (Walsh et al. 1998).

One study showed that an oral glutamine supplement (5 g in 330 ml water) consumed immediately after and 2 hours after a marathon reduced the incidence of upper respiratory tract infection in the 7 days after the race (Castell, Poortmans, and Newsholme 1996). However, the dose given in that study was unlikely sufficient to prevent the postexercise fall in the plasma glutamine concentration. Furthermore, several recent studies (reviewed in Nieman and Pedersen [2000] and Gleeson and Bishop [2000a]) that investigated the effect of glutamine supplementation during exercise on various indices of immune function failed to find any beneficial effect.

A larger dose of glutamine (0.1 g/kg b.w.) than that given by Castell et al. (1996) ingested at 0 minutes, 30 minutes, 60 minutes, and 90 minutes after a marathon race prevented the fall in the plasma glutamine concentration but did not prevent the fall in mitogen-induced lymphocyte proliferation and lymphocyte-activated killer cell activity (Nieman and Pedersen 2000; Gleeson and Bishop 2000a). Similarly, maintaining the plasma glutamine concentration by consuming glutamine in drinks taken both during and after a prolonged bout of cycling did not affect leukocyte subset trafficking or prevent the exercise-induced fall in neutrophil function, lymphocyte proliferative response, natural killer cell activity, or salivary IgA secretion rate (Nieman and Pedersen 2000; Gleeson and Bishop 2000a). Unlike the feeding of carbohydrate during exercise, glutamine supplements seem not to affect the immune function perturbations that have been examined to date (see chapter 13 for further details).

Glutamine is thought to be relatively safe and well tolerated by most people, although administration to people with kidney disorders is not recommended. No adverse reactions to short-term glutamine supplementation have been reported, and no information is available on long-term use exceeding 1 g/day. Excessive doses may cause gastrointestinal problems.

Glycine

Glycine is a nonessential amino acid that is involved in the synthesis of phosphocreatine. Therefore, it has been theorized to have ergogenic properties. Early studies indicated improvements in strength after glycine (or gelatin that contains about 25% glycine) supplementation. However, these studies were poorly designed. Thus, the effects of glycine remain unresolved.

Ornithine

Ornithine has been suggested to stimulate growth hormone release from the pituitary gland (Evain-Brion et al. 1982) and insulin release from the pancreas. Growth hormone release after infusion of ornithine was even higher than that observed after arginine infusion. However, most ornithine supplements contain 1 g to 2 g of ornithine and this dosage does not affect the 24-hour hormone profile (Fogelholm et al. 1993). Therefore, ornithine does not seem to increase growth hormone release or increase muscle mass or strength. Although ornithine is often claimed to increase the secretion of insulin from the pancreas, a study in bodybuilders in which the effects of ornithine supplementation on insulin release was investigated failed to show any effect (Bucci et al. 1992).

Taurine

Taurine is a nonprotein amino acid and a derivative of cysteine. Taurine has recently become a popular ingredient of many sports drinks. The concentrations of taurine in the brain, heart, and muscle are high, but its role is poorly understood. It has been suggested to act as a membrane stabilizer, an antioxidant, and a neuromodulator. Taurine plays an undefined role in calcium currents in cells, influences ionic conductance in excitable membranes, and plays a role in the regulation of cell volume. Its value as a nutrition supplement is unclear.

Tyrosine

Oral doses of tyrosine (5 g to 10 g) result in increases in circulating concentrations of epinephrine, norepinephrine, and dopamine, hormones that are heavily involved in the regulation of body function during physical stress and exercise. Tyrosine supplements are used especially by strength athletes because of their supposed effect of activating metabolic pathways. However, no controlled studies show an effect of tyrosine supplementation on exercise performance. Most tyrosine supplements use a very low dosage (mg), whereas probably large doses are required to alter hormone levels. Regular supplementation of large amounts (5 g to 10 g) may have adverse health effects in the long term because it affects sympathetic nervous system activity.

Tryptophan

Tryptophan was suggested to stimulate the release of growth hormone. The most common proposed ergogenic effect, however, is based on another function. Tryptophan is the precursor of serotonin, a neurotransmitter in the brain that may induce sleepiness, decrease aggression, and elicit a mellow mood. Serotonin has also been suggested to decrease the perception of pain. Segura and Ventura (1988) hypothesized that tryptophan supplementation increases serotonin levels and the tolerance of pain and thereby improves exercise performance. They studied 12 subjects during running to exhaustion at 80% $\dot{V}O_2$max, with ingestion of tryptophan or placebo. Tryptophan was supplemented in four doses of 300 mg in the 24 hours before the endurance test, with the last doses ingested 1 hour before the test (total tryptophan ingestion, 1,200 mg). The investigators observed a 49% improvement in endurance capacity and decreased ratings of perceived exertion after tryptophan ingestion. Because a 49% performance improvement seemed somewhat unrealistic, several other investigators have challenged the results of this study (Stensrud et al. 1992; Van Hall et al. 1995).

In a study by Stensrud et al. (1992), 49 well-trained male runners were exercised to exhaustion at 100% $\dot{V}O_2$max, and no significant effect of tryptophan supplementation on endurance time was found. A very-well-controlled study by Van Hall et al. (1995) included eight cyclists given tryptophan supplements and found no effect on time to exhaustion at 70% $\dot{V}O_2$max (see figure 7.9).

Both tryptophan and BCAAs have been suggested as supplements to reduce central fatigue. Yet, the BCAAs and tryptophan have opposite effects. Whereas some claim that tryptophan reduces central fatigue (Segura and Ventura 1988), others have associated it with the development of central fatigue

(Newsholme, Blomstrand, and Ekblom 1992). Tryptophan could also exert some negative effects, including a blocking of gluconeogenesis and decreased mental alertness. Based on these studies, tryptophan does not seem to be ergogenic and may even be ergolytic in prolonged exercise.

Protein Intake and Health Risks

Excessive protein intake (more than 3 g/kg b.w./day) may have various negative effects, including kidney damage, increased blood lipoprotein levels (which has been associated with arteriosclerosis), and dehydration. The latter may occur as a result of increased nitrogen excretion in urine, which results in increased urinary volume and dehydration. Athletes consuming a high-protein diet must, therefore, increase their fluid intake to prevent dehydration. The recommended protein intakes for athletes (1.2 g/kg b.w./day to 1.8 g/kg b.w./day) and up to approximately 2 g/kg b.w./day do not seem to be harmful.

Intake of individual amino acids has no added nutritional value compared with the intake of proteins containing these amino acids. A possible advantage of the intake of individual amino acids is that larger amounts can be ingested. Purified amino acids were developed for clinical use in intravenous infusion of patients for adequate protein nutrition (particularly when oral consumption is compromised). Individual amino acids are also used as food additives to enhance the protein balance in case the diet is deficient in certain amino acids. Because individual amino acids are often ingested in pharmacological doses and the effects of such large doses are largely unknown, amino acids supplements should be treated as drugs.

In 1989, an epidemic in the United States of the eosinophilia-myalgia syndrome (EMS), a neuromuscular disorder characterized by weakness, fever, edema, rashes, bone pain, and various other symptoms was attributed to the excessive intake of L-tryptophan. L-tryptophan has been classified as neurotoxic and was banned for a while in the United States.

Key Points

- Amino acids are constantly incorporated into proteins (protein synthesis), and proteins are constantly broken down (protein breakdown or degradation) to amino acids. Some amino acids are essential and are not synthesized in the body, whereas others can be synthesized in the body (nonessential amino acids).

- Muscle contains 40% of the total protein in a human body and accounts for 25% to 35% of all protein turnover in the body. The contractile proteins actin and myosin are the most abundant proteins in muscle, together accounting for 80% to 90% of all muscle protein.

- Training has marked effects on body proteins. Both the structural proteins that make up the myofibrillar proteins and the proteins that act as enzymes within a muscle cell change as an adaptation to exercise training. Muscle mass, muscle protein composition, and muscle protein content all change in response to training.

- Methods of studying protein metabolism include nitrogen excretion, nitrogen balance, arteriovenous balance studies, and tracer methods. All methods available to measure protein turnover in humans have their limitations, and no method has been identified as the best one to use.

- Amino acids can be used to synthesize other amino acids, can be incorporated into proteins or other compounds (i.e., FAs and glucose), or can be oxidized in the TCA cycle.

- The BCAAs are the most abundant amino acids in skeletal muscle, together accounting for 20% of all amino acids in muscle. Glutamine is the most abundant free amino acid in muscle and plasma.

- Protein has been estimated to contribute up to about 15% to energy expenditure in resting conditions. During exercise, this relative contribution likely decreases because

(continued)

(continued)

of an increasing importance of carbohydrate and fat as fuels. During very prolonged exercise, when carbohydrate availability becomes limited, the contribution of protein to energy expenditure may increase up to about 10% of total energy expenditure.

■ In the hours after exercise, protein synthesis may exceed protein degradation but only after feeding. If feeding is delayed by 24 hours to 48 hours, net protein balance remains negative and no muscle hypertrophy occurs.

■ The recommended protein intake for strength athletes is generally 1.6 g/kg b.w./day to 1.7 g/kg b.w./day, about twice the value for the general population. The recommended protein intake for endurance athletes is usually 1.2 g/kg b.w./day to 1.8 g/kg b.w. of protein, although in extreme situations, the amount may rise to as much as 2.5 g/kg b.w./day.

■ With increasing food intake, the intake of protein automatically increases because many food products contain at least some protein. The relationship between energy intake and protein intake is linear.

■ Excessive protein intake (more than 3 g/kg b.w./day) may have various negative effects, including kidney damage, increased blood lipoprotein levels (which has been associated with arteriosclerosis), and dehydration.

■ Arginine infused in large quantities can have anabolic properties in patients, but oral ingestion of tolerable amounts do not result in increased secretion of human growth hormone and insulin.

■ BCAAs are among the most popular nutrition supplements. However, the evidence for claims of reduced net protein breakdown and reduced fatigue and enhanced performance via central nervous system mechanisms are not convincing.

Key Terms

ammonia (NH_3) 149

branched-chain amino acid (BCAA) 148

deamination 149

essential amino acids 149

glutamate 149

glutamine 149

nitrogen balance 148

protein degradation 148

protein synthesis 148

serotonin 149

transamination 149

Recommended Readings

McNurlan, M.A., and P.J. Garlick. 2000. Protein synthesis and degradation. In *Biochemical and Physiological Aspects of Human Nutrition*, ed. M.H. Stipanuk. Saunders: Philadelphia.

Rennie, M.J. 1996. Influence of exercise on protein and amino acid metabolism. In *Handbook of Physiology*, Section 12: Exercise: Regulation and Integration of Multiple Systems, ed. J.B. Rowell and J.T. Shepherd. Oxford University Press: New York.

Rennie, M.J., and K.D. Tipton. 2000. Protein and amino acid metabolism during and after exercise and the effects of nutrition. *Annual Review of Nutrition* 20:457-483.

Tarnopolsky, M.A. 1999. Protein and physical performance. *Current Opinion in Clinical Nutrition Metabolic Care* 2:533-537.

Wagenmakers, A.J. 1998. Protein and amino acid metabolism in human muscle. *Advances in Experimental Medicine and Biology* 441:307-319.

Wagenmakers, A.J. 1999. Amino acid supplements to improve athletic performance. *Current Opinion in Clinical Nutrition Metabolic Care* 2(6):539-544.

Chapter 8

Water Requirements and Fluid Balance

Objectives

After studying this chapter, you should be able to do the following:

- Describe how body temperature is regulated at rest and during exercise

- Describe the effect of dehydration on exercise performance

- Describe the effects of fluid intake before and during exercise on exercise performance

- Describe fluid intake strategies that help to ensure that the fluid requirements of athletes are met

- Describe the composition of drinks that are suitable for consumption by athletes during exercise and after exercise

Most athletes and coaches are aware that a reduction in the body's water content (dehydration) impairs exercise performance. However, appropriate strategies to prevent or limit dehydration during training and competition are not always followed. The hydration status of the body is determined by the balance between water intake and water loss. As with all the other nutrients, a regular and sufficient water intake is required to maintain health and physical performance. A lack of water intake causes deficiency symptoms, and failure to drink water for more than a few days can result in death. Symptoms associated with overconsumption of water can also be observed.

In most people, water accounts for 50% to 60% of the body mass. Lean body tissues (e.g., muscle, heart, and liver) contain about 75% water by mass, whereas adipose tissue contains only about 5% water by mass, as the bulk of the adipocytes are filled with triacylglycerol fat. The fat content of the body, therefore, largely determines the normal body-water content. For a healthy, lean young male weighing 70 kg (154 lb), the body water amounts to about 42 L (i.e., 60% of body weight). A healthy, lean young female weighing 70 kg has a total body-water volume of about 35 L, equivalent to 50% of her body weight (see table 8.1). The water content of the female body is less than that of the male because (1) the female body is lighter than that of the male and (2) the female body contains a higher proportion of fat (see table 8.1). Thus, for a typical female weighing 60 kg (132 lb), the body-water content is about 30 kg. The total body water is distributed among different body fluid compartments, as illustrated in table 8.2.

An important route of water (and electrolyte) loss from the body is through sweating, which is the

Table 8.1 Fat Content and Volumes of Body Fluid Compartments in Adults and Infants

Body fluid	Infants*	Adult men*	Adult women*
Plasma	4	5	4
Interstitial fluid	26	15	11
Intracellular fluid	45	40	35
Total	75	60	50
Fat	5	18	25

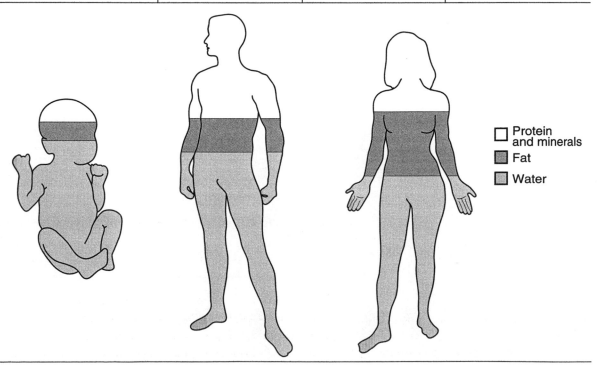

□ Protein and minerals
■ Fat
■ Water

*Values are expressed as a percentage of body mass.

Table 8.2 Distribution of Body Water[a] in a Young 70-kg (154-lb) Man

	Volume (L)	Body mass (%)	Total-body water (%)
Intracellular fluid	28	40	62.5
Extracellular fluid	14	20	37.5
Interstitial fluid	10.5	15	30
Blood plasma	3.5	5	7.5

[a]Total-body water volume = 42 L or 60% of body mass.

body's principal means of preventing excessive rises in body temperature **(hyperthermia)** during exercise in the heat. Some understanding of the regulation of body temperature is, therefore, fundamental to the discussion of fluid balance in the body and the formulation of drinks intended for consumption both during and after exercise. Hence, this chapter begins with a brief overview of heat production and **thermoregulation** during exercise, followed by a consideration of the effects of dehydration on exercise performance, before discussing the need for water and electrolyte consumption by athletes.

Thermoregulation and Exercise in the Heat

Increased muscular activity during exercise causes an increase in heat production in the body because of the inefficiency of the metabolic reactions that provide energy for muscle force development. Thermoregulation concerns the mechanisms that prevent excessive rises in body temperature.

Heat Production During Exercise

For every liter of oxygen consumed during exercise such as cycling or running, approximately 16 kJ (4 kcal) of heat is produced and only about 4 kJ (1 kcal) is actually used to perform mechanical work (to be precise, 1.0 kcal = 4.186 kJ; see chapter 3 where this work efficiency is explained in more detail). Thus, for an athlete consuming oxygen at a rate of 4 L/min during exercise, the rate of heat production in the body is about $16,000 \times 4/60 = 800$ J/s, or watts (W), or $16 \times 4 \times 60/1,000 = 3.84$ MJ/h (917 kcal/h). Only a small proportion of the heat produced in active skeletal muscle is lost from the overlying skin. Rather, most of the heat is passed to the body core via the convective flow of venous blood returning to the heart. The rate of temperature increase in the belly of the quadriceps muscle group is close to 1°

C/min (1.8° F/min) during the initial moments of high-intensity cycling (Saltin et al. 1968). This rate of heat storage cannot persist, because the muscle contractile proteins and enzymes would be inactivated by heat-induced denaturation within 10 minutes. Thus, most of the heat generated in the muscle is transferred to the body core and increases in body core temperature are sensed by thermoreceptors located in the hypothalamus. This area of the brain also receives sensory input from skin thermoreceptors and integrates this information to produce appropriate reflex effector responses—increasing blood flow to the skin and initiating sweating—to increase heat loss and limit further rises in body temperature.

Heat Storage During Exercise

During exercise at a constant work rate, heat production increases in a square-wave fashion. The set point of the hypothalamic thermostat does not change during exercise, but some heat storage does occur. When heat loss from the body equals heat production, the rise in body temperature plateaus. However, during high-intensity exercise, particularly in an environment with a high ambient temperature and high humidity, core temperature continues to rise.

During exercise at an intensity equivalent to about 80% to 90% $\dot{V}O_2$max, heat production in a fit individual may exceed 1,000 W (resting heat production is about 70 W), which could potentially increase body temperature by 1° C (1.8° F) every 4 minutes to 5 minutes if no changes occur in the body's heat-dissipating mechanisms. This estimate is based on the specific heat capacity of human tissues, which is 3.47 kJ/kg/°C (0.46 kcal/kg/°F) for lean tissue and 1.73 kJ/kg/°C (0.23 kcal/kg/°F) for fat. For a man weighing 70 kg (154 lb) with 15% body fat, the specific heat capacity of the body is $(3.47 \times 0.85) + (1.73 \times 0.15) = 3.21$ kJ/kg/°C (0.43 kcal/kg/°F). Using this value, you can calculate that at a rate of body heat production of 1,000 W, in 1 minute 1,000 J/s × 60 s = 60,000 J or 60 kJ (14.3 kcal) of heat energy is produced, which raises the body temperature of this 70 kg man by 60 kJ ÷ (70 kg × 3.21 kJ/kg/°C) = 0.27° C (0.49° F). Thus, within 12 to15 minutes, core body temperature could approach dangerous levels or exercise is terminated because of the symptoms of fatigue that occur from this degree of hyperthermia.

Problems of hyperthermia and heat injury are not restricted to prolonged exercise in a hot environment. Heat production is directly proportional to exercise intensity, so very strenuous exercise, even in a cool environment, can cause a substantial rise in body temperature.

The absolute body temperature at the end of exercise depends on the starting body temperature. A vigorous warm up causes a rise in body temperature and results in a higher final body temperature. When body temperature rises to about 39.5° C (103° F), central fatigue (i.e., in the brain rather than in the working muscles) ensues, and so a high starting temperature is undesirable for athletes exercising in a hot environment. Such large increases in body temperature during exercise tend not to occur in unfit individuals (e.g., the types who jog through a marathon in 4 hours to 6 hours) but are common in highly motivated athletes.

A body temperature of 36° to 38°C (96.8° to 100.4° F) is the normal range at rest and may rise to 38° to 40° C (100.4° to 104° F) during exercise. Further increases are commonly associated with heat exhaustion and occasionally with heatstroke, a life-threatening disorder characterized by a lack of consciousness after exertion and by clinical symptoms of damage to the brain, liver, and kidneys (Gleeson 1998; Sutton and Bar-Or 1980). The elevated core temperature associated with exercise is not regulated at its elevated level (i.e., it is not caused by a resetting of the hypothalamic thermostat). Rather, the elevated temperature is caused by the temporary imbalance between the rates of heat production and dissipation during the early stages of exercise and the rapidity with which the heat-dissipating mechanisms respond to an increase in core temperature.

Environmental Heat Stress and Heat Loss by Evaporation of Sweat

Environmental heat stress is determined by the ambient temperature, relative humidity, wind velocity, and solar **radiation** (both directly from the sun and reflected from the ground) (see figure 8.1). During exercise, the working muscles produce heat at a high rate and the body temperature rises. If the skin is hotter than the

surroundings, heat is lost from the skin by physical transfer (evaporation of sweat, **convection,** and **conduction**) to the environment. If the environment is hotter than the skin, heat is gained by convection and conduction. If the environment is saturated with water vapor (i.e., relative humidity = 100%), **evaporation** of sweat does not occur and heat is not lost from the body. The relative humidity is very important because a high humidity severely compromises the evaporative loss of sweat, and sweat must evaporate from the body surface to exert a cooling effect.

Evaporation of 1 L of water from the skin will remove 2.4 MJ (573 kcal) of heat from the body. The sweat rate during exercise has to be at least 1.6 L/hour if all the heat produced is to be dissipated by evaporative loss alone. In fact, the sweat rate probably has to be nearer 2 L/hour, because at such high sweat rates, some of the sweat rolls off the skin, which has virtually no cooling effect. A reduction in skin blood flow and sweat rate as the body becomes progressively dehydrated or a high humidity limiting evaporative loss of sweat leads to further rises in core temperature, resulting in fatigue and possible heat injury to body tissues. The latter is potentially fatal.

A useful index of environmental heat stress is the wet bulb globe temperature (WBGT), which is calculated as follows:

$$WBGT = 0.7\,T_{wb} + 0.2\,T_{bg} + 0.1\,T_{db}$$

where T_{wb} is the temperature (in °C) of a wet-bulb thermometer, T_{db} is the temperature of a dry-bulb thermometer, and T_{bg} is the temperature of a black-globe thermometer. Note the 70% bias toward the T_{wb}, which recognizes the greater relative importance of the environmental humidity. Some typical environmental scenarios and physiological responses to exercise in different environmental conditions are illustrated in table 8.3.

Heat loss via the evaporation of sweat is largely determined by the water vapor pressure (humidity) of the air close to the body surface. The local humidity may be high if inappropriate, poorly ventilated clothing is worn, reducing the convective flow of air over the skin surface. Sweat drips off the skin, rather than evaporates, and heat loss via this route is severely restricted. If exercise continues at the same intensity, body core temperature rises further, a higher sweat rate is induced, and the athlete dehydrates more rapidly. This dehydration poses further problems for the athlete because progressive dehydration impairs the ability to sweat and, consequently, to thermoregulate. At any given exercise intensity, body temperature rises faster in the dehydrated state, and this condition is commonly accompanied by a higher heart rate

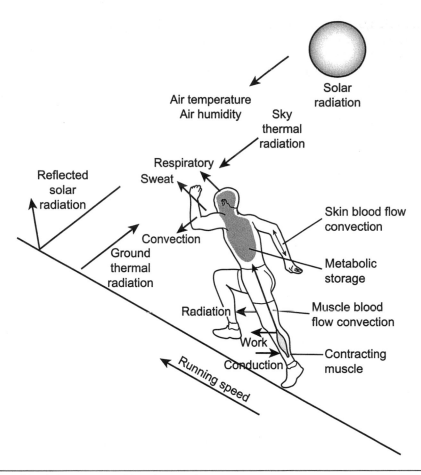

Figure 8.1 Sources of body heat-gain and heat-loss mechanisms.

Table 8.3 Sweat Loss and Heart Rates After 60 Minutes of Exercise

Ambient temperature (°C/°F)	Humidity (%)	Sweat loss (L)	Core temperature (°C/°F)	Heart rate (beats/min)
13 (55)	7	0.8	38.0 (100.4)	140
18 (64)	50	1.2	38.3 (100.9)	143
25 (77)	50	1.4	38.7 (101.6)	145
30 (86)	30	2.1	39.3 (102.7)	148
30 (86)	90	2.8	39.5 (103.1)	150
35 (95)	30	3.0	39.9 (103.8)	153

Exercise performed at about 60% to 70% $\dot{V}O_2$max under different environmental conditions.

during exercise, as shown in figure 8.2. Dehydration equivalent to the loss of only 2% body mass (i.e., the loss of about 1.5 L of water for a typical 70 kg [154 lb] male athlete) is sufficient to significantly impair exercise performance (Armstrong et al. 1985; Craig and Cummings 1966; Maughan 1991; Sawka and Pandolf 1990).

Heat Loss by Radiation and Convection

The other crucial effector mechanism in thermoregulation during exercise in the heat is the increased blood flow through the skin capillaries. This mechanism allows increased heat loss from the body core to the

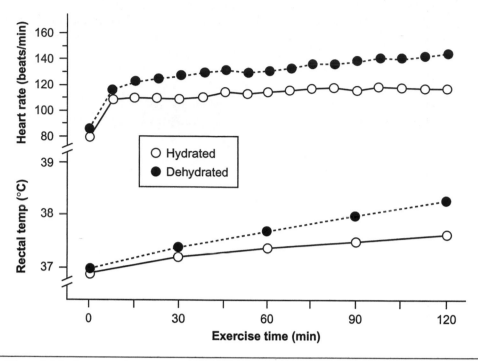

Figure 8.2 Effect of dehydration on heart rate and rectal temperature during 2 hours of cycling.

environment by radiation and convection. Radiation is the transfer of energy waves by emission from one object and absorption by another. Convection is the exchange of heat between a solid medium (e.g., the human body) and one that moves (e.g., air or water). The rate of heat transfer away from the body core is the product of the skin blood flow and the temperature difference between the core and the skin.

A high skin blood flow alone may not be sufficient to remove heat from the body core during exercise in hot, humid conditions when the skin temperature rises because of the inability to evaporate sweat. The effectiveness of this route of heat loss also largely dependent on the amount of body surface available for heat exchange and the temperature gradient between the body surface and the surrounding atmosphere. When ambient temperature is close to body temperature, heat loss via the skin blood flow is minimal. The body is then almost entirely dependent on evaporative cooling. Inappropriate clothing impairs convection and radiation of heat from the body surface, so total heat dissipation will be reduced to a critically low level.

Regulation of Body Temperature

Sensory information about body temperature is input to the central controller via nerves emanating from both deep-body and peripheral thermoreceptors. The latter, located in the skin, provide advance warning of environmental heat input. Central thermoreceptors, located in the hypothalamus, are sensitive to changes in internal core temperature and effectively monitor the temperature of blood flowing to the brain. Input from these receptors is more important than input from the peripheral receptors in eliciting appropriate effector responses designed to limit increases in body temperature. The central thermal controller, or "thermostat," located in the preoptic anterior hypothalamus also receives nonthermal sensory inputs that are capable of modulating the homeostatic regulation of body temperature.

These other inputs include nervous signals from osmoreceptors and pressure receptors, so changes in plasma osmolarity and blood volume are capable of affecting sweating and cutaneous vasodilation responses to rises in core temperature. These effects are summarized in figure 8.3. Some hormones (e.g., estrogen) and cytokines (e.g., interleukin-1 and interleukin-6) are also capable of influencing thermoregulatory responses. Interleukin-6, also known as endogenous pyrogen, is secreted from macrophages and is responsible for raising the set-point temperature of the hypothalamic "thermostat," causing the rise in core temperature during fever. The influence of other sensory inputs also appears to take place at the level of the hypothalamic neurons and is mediated by neurotransmitters, including dopamine, 5-hydroxytryptamine (5-HT or serotonin), norepinephrine (noradrenaline), and acetylcholine.

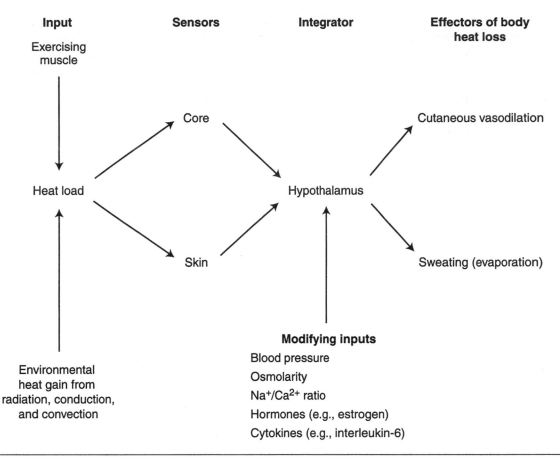

Input	Sensors	Integrator	Effectors of body heat loss

Figure 8.3 Summary of thermoregulation during exercise in the heat.

Exercise Training, Acclimitization, and Temperature Regulation

Exercise training improves temperature regulation during exercise at the same absolute work rate. To obtain thermoregulatory benefits from training, individuals must adequately stimulate thermoregulatory effector responses (viz. sweating and increased skin blood flow). In other words, they must exercise at a sufficiently high intensity. Improvements in thermoregulatory responses to exercise have consistently been seen in studies in which subjects exercised at 70% to 100% $\dot{V}O_2$max and increased their body temperature above 39° C (102.2° F). Studies in which subjects exercised at lower intensities (typically 35% to 60% $\dot{V}O_2$max) have commonly shown little or no thermoregulatory benefit in response to training.

Most serious athletes regularly exercise at intensities above 70% $\dot{V}O_2$max; such training allows individuals to achieve thermal equilibrium during exercise at 25% to 35% $\dot{V}O_2$max in desert heat conditions, but of course this exercise intensity is not race pace. However, appropriate training increases tolerance of exercise in hot conditions, and acclimation

to warm environments (achieved by exercising in a hot environment, not just resting exposure to that environment) confers further benefits in terms of the ability to regulate body temperature during exercise in the heat at higher exercise intensities (Greenleaf 1979).

Marathon runners exhibit a lower resting body temperature and have a lower sweating (and shivering) threshold. Thus, set-point temperature seems to decrease as a result of training in endurance athletes. These individuals have also been reported to have a lower resting metabolic rate in thermoneutral conditions and a lower skin temperature. This effect appears to mimic the "insulative hypothermia" reported in Australian aborigines who sleep in the cold desert night: both skin and core temperature drop, reducing the temperature gradient between the body surface and the environment, which reduces heat loss and conserves energy. Heat and cold **acclimatization** are not mutually exclusive and can occur simultaneously in the same individual.

Exercise training improves thermoregulation in the heat by an earlier onset of sweat secretion and by increasing the total amount of sweat that can be produced. Thus, training increases the sensitivity of the sweat rate/core temperature relationship, as well as decreases the internal temperature threshold for sweating. Sweat rates can vary markedly between individuals (up to a maximum of about 3 L/h), even at the same relative exercise intensity, (Maughan 1991), but evidence suggests that individuals characterized as heavy sweaters have larger sweat glands than light sweaters. Training appears to induce a hypertrophy (enlarging) of existing sweat glands, without increasing the total number.

Other adaptations to training include an increase in total blood volume and maximal cardiac output. As a result, blood flow in muscle and skin, with its heat flux, is better preserved during strenuous exercise in the heat. The body does not adapt to dehydration, so exercising in the heat without fluid intake does not confer an additional adaptation in thermoregulation. In fact, progressive dehydration during exercise in the heat reduces the sensitivity of the sweat rate/ core temperature relationship as shown in figure 8.4 and, thus, results in a relative hyperthermia and an earlier onset of fatigue (Nadel et al. 1980; Sawka, Young, Francescone, et al. 1985). In practical terms, the athlete is less able to maintain training loads, so the physiological adaptation to training is not as great. Exercising for prolonged periods in the heat without fluid intake also increases the risk of cramps and heat illness.

Effects of Dehydration on Exercise Performance

Fatigue toward the end of a prolonged sporting event may result as much from dehydration as from fuel substrate depletion. Exercise performance is impaired when an individual is dehydrated by as little as 2% of body weight. Losses in excess of 5% of body weight can decrease the capacity for work by about 30% (see figure 8.5) (Armstrong et al. 1985; Craig and Cummings 1966; Maughan 1991; Sawka and Pandolf 1990).

Sprint athletes are generally less concerned about the effects of dehydration than are endurance athletes. However, the capacity to perform high-intensity exercise, which results in exhaustion within a few minutes, is reduced by as much as 45% by prior dehydration corresponding to a loss of only 2.5% of body weight (Sawka, Young, Cadarette, et al. 1985). Although sprint events offer little opportunity for sweat loss, athletes who travel to compete in hot climates are likely to experience acute dehydration, which persists for several days and may be serious enough to have a detrimental effect on performance in competition.

Even in cool laboratory conditions, maximal aerobic power ($\dot{V}O_2$max) decreases by about 5% when persons experience fluid losses equivalent to 3% of body mass or more, as is shown in figure 8.6 (Pinchan et al. 1988). In hot conditions, similar water deficits can cause a larger decrease in $\dot{V}O_2$max. The endurance capacity during incremental exercise is decreased by marginal dehydration (fluid loss of 1% to 2% of body weight), even if water deficits do not actually result in a decrease in $\dot{V}O_2$max. Endurance capacity is impaired much more in hot environments than in cool conditions, which implies that impaired thermoregulation is an important causal factor in the reduced exercise performance associated with a body-water deficit. Dehydration also impairs endur-

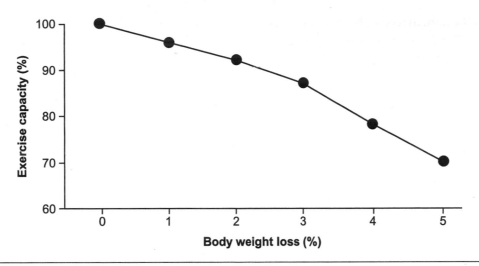

Figure 8.5 Reduction of work capacity with increasing degree of dehydration (body weight loss).

ance exercise performance. Fluid loss equivalent to 2% of body mass induced by a diuretic drug (furosemide) caused running performance at 1,500, 5,000, and 10,000 m distances to be impaired (Armstrong et al. 1985). Running performance was impaired more at the longer distances (by approximately 5% at 5,000 and 10,000 m) compared with the shortest distance (approximately 3% at 1,500 m).

A study investigated the capacity of eight subjects to perform treadmill walking (at 25% $\dot{V}O_2$max with a target time of 140 minutes) in very hot, dry conditions (49° C [120° F], 20% relative humidity) when they were euhydrated and when they were dehydrated by a 3%, 5%, or 7% loss of body mass (Sawka, Young, Francescone, et al. 1985). All eight subjects were able to

complete 140 minutes walking when euhydrated and 3% dehydrated. Seven subjects completed the walk when 5% dehydrated, but when dehydrated by 7%, six subjects stopped walking after an average of only 64 minutes. Thus, even for relatively low-intensity exercise, dehydration clearly increases the incidence of exhaustion from heat strain. Sawka et al. (1992) had subjects walk to exhaustion at 47% $\dot{V}O_2$max in the same environmental conditions as their previous study. Subjects were euhydrated and dehydrated to a loss of 8% of each individual's total-body water. Dehydration reduced exercise endurance time from 121 minutes to 55 minutes. Dehydration also appeared to reduce the core temperature a person could tolerate, as core temperature at exhaustion was about 0.4° C

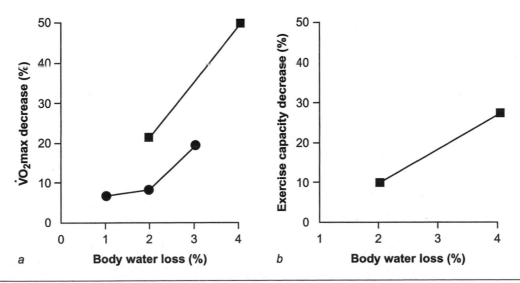

Figure 8.6 Effect of degree of dehydration (% loss of body water) on (a) decrement in maximal oxygen uptake ($\dot{V}O_2$max) and (b) reduction in physical work capacity during heat exposure.

Data from E.N. Craig and E.G. Cummings, 1966 and G. Pinchan et al., 1988.

(0.7° F) lower in the dehydrated state. The main reasons dehydration has an adverse effect on exercise performance can be summarized as follows:

- Reduction in blood volume
- Decreased skin blood flow
- Decreased sweat rate
- Decreased heat dissipation
- Increased core temperature
- Increased rate of muscle glycogen use

A reduced maximal cardiac output (i.e., the highest pumping capacity of the heart that can be achieved during exercise) is the most likely physiologic mechanism whereby dehydration decreases a person's $\dot{V}O_2$max and impairs work capacity in fatiguing exercise of an incremental nature. Dehydration causes a fall in plasma volume both at rest and during exercise, and a decreased blood volume increases blood thickness (viscosity), lowers central venous pressure, and reduces venous return of blood to the heart. During maximal exercise, these changes can decrease the filling of the heart during diastole (the phase of the cardiac cycle when the heart is relaxed and is filling with blood before the next contraction), hence, reducing stroke volume and cardiac output. Also, during exercise in the heat, the opening up of the skin blood vessels reduces the proportion of the cardiac output available to the working muscles.

Even for normally hydrated (**euhydrated**) individuals, climatic heat stress alone decreases $\dot{V}O_2$max by about 7%. Thus, both environmental heat stress and dehydration can act independently to limit cardiac output and blood delivery to the active muscles during high-intensity exercise. Dehydration also impairs the body's ability to lose heat. Both sweat rate and skin blood flow are lower at the same core temperature for the dehydrated compared with the euhydrated state (see figure 8.4) (Nadel et al. 1979 1980; Sawka and Wenger 1988). Body temperature rises faster during exercise when the body is dehydrated. The reduced sweating response in the dehydrated state is probably mediated through the effects of both a fall in blood volume (**hypovolemia**) and elevated plasma osmolarity (i.e., dissolved salt concentration) (see figure 8.7) on hypothalamic neurons. As explained previously, as core temperature rises towards about 39.5° C (103° F), sensations of fatigue ensue. This critical temperature is reached more quickly in the dehydrated state.

Dehydration not only elevates core temperature responses but also negates the thermoregulatory advantages conferred by high aerobic fitness and heat acclimatization. The effects of dehydration (5% loss of body weight) on core temperature responses in the same persons when unacclimated and when acclimated to heat are shown in figure 8.8. Heat acclimation lowered core temperature responses when subjects were euhydrated. However, when they were dehydrated, similar core temperature responses were observed for both unacclimated and acclimated states (Pinchan et al. 1988).

A person's ability to tolerate heat strain appears to be impaired when dehydrated, so the critical temperature for experiencing central fatigue is likely to be nearer 39.0° C (102.2° F) when dehydrated by more than about 5% of body mass (Sawka et al. 1992). The larger rise in core temperature during exercise in the dehydrated state is associated with a bigger catecholamine response, and these effects may lead to increased rates of glycogen breakdown in the exercising muscle, which, in turn, may contribute to earlier onset of fatigue in prolonged exercise.

Dehydration is associated with a reduced gastric emptying rate of ingested fluids during exercise in the heat. For example, one study reported a 20% to 25% reduction in gastric emptying when subjects were dehydrated by 5% of body mass (Neufer et al. 1989).

Fluid consumption should begin during the early stages of exercise in the heat, not only to minimize the degree of dehydration but also to maximize the bioavailability of ingested fluids. Dehydration poses a serious health risk in that it increases the risk of cramps, heat exhaustion, and life-threatening heat stroke (Sutton and Bar-Or 1980).

Mechanisms of Heat Illness

Heat injury is most common during exhaustive exercise in a hot, humid environment, particularly if the athlete is dehydrated. These problems affect not only highly trained athletes but also less well-trained sport participants. In fact, less well-trained individuals have less-effective thermoregulation during exercise, work less economically, use more carbohydrate for muscular work, and take longer to recover from exhausting exercise than do highly trained individuals.

During the initial stages of exercise in a hot environment, sweating begins and the skin blood vessels dilate, effecting increased heat loss from the body. However, as central blood volume and pressure fall, sympathetic nervous activity increases and the skin blood vessels constrict. A more powerful constriction of the blood vessels supplying the abdominal organs leads to cellular hypoxia in the region of the gastrointestinal tract, liver, and kidneys. Cellular hypoxia leads to the production of reactive oxygen species (ROS), including superoxide anion, hydrogen peroxide, hydroxyl radical, peroxynitrite, and nitric oxide (NO). The latter is a potent blood vessel dila-

tor, and although its production can be viewed as protective (i.e., helping to conserve some blood flow through the capillary beds of the abdominal organs), ultimately the ROS may cause damage through their actions on membranes. The ROS cause peroxidation of lipids in cellular membranes, making them leaky. In the gastrointestinal tract, this action allows the passage of bacterial toxins (endotoxins) from the gut into the systemic circulation, leading to endotoxemia (blood poisoning) and a drastic fall in blood pressure (hypotension). Increased levels of NO probably contribute to the development of hypotension. The consequences for the athlete can be heat syncope (fainting) and organ injury (see figure 8.9).

Animal studies have shown a disappearance of manganese-superoxide dismutase (Mn-SOD), an important antioxidant enzyme that deactivates ROS, after 2 hours of heat exposure and a later induction of Mn-SOD in the liver cells of animals exposed to elevated core temperatures (41° C [106° F]) over a 24-hour period. Increased levels of hemoglobin-NO, semiquinone radical (a marker of mitochondrial oxidative stress), and ceruloplasmin (a copper-binding protein with antioxidant properties) have also been found in the hepatic portal vein after exposure to heat stress.

A doubling of hepatic portal blood endotoxin levels has also been reported within 24 hours of the onset of heat exposure. Thus, ROS generation appears to increase within abdominal tissues during heat exposure. Antioxidant status is compromised within the first few hours but gradually recovers and is enhanced after 24 hours of heat exposure.

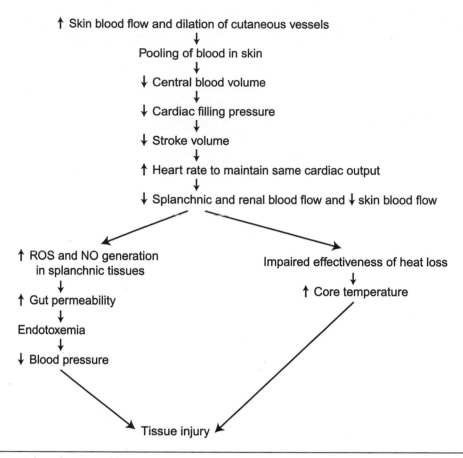

↑ Skin blood flow and dilation of cutaneous vessels
↓
Pooling of blood in skin
↓
↓ Central blood volume
↓
↓ Cardiac filling pressure
↓
↓ Stroke volume
↓
↑ Heart rate to maintain same cardiac output
↓
↓ Splanchnic and renal blood flow and ↓ skin blood flow

↑ ROS and NO generation in splanchnic tissues
↓
↑ Gut permeability
↓
Endotoxemia
↓
↓ Blood pressure

Impaired effectiveness of heat loss
↓
↑ Core temperature

Tissue injury

Figure 8.9 Potential mechanisms of heat-stress injury.

ROS generation probably increases most in areas of high metabolic activity and greatest potential for a reduction in blood flow.

This ischemia/reperfusion mechanism involving the gastrointestinal tract may play a role in the vascular dysfunction and tissue injury associated with heat stress. Further studies are warranted on the possible benefits of antioxidant supplementation in people who regularly experience very high body temperatures such as athletes who train and compete in hot, humid climates.

Effects of Fluid Intake on Exercise Performance

Oral fluid ingestion during exercise helps restore plasma volume to near pre-exercise levels and prevents the adverse effects of dehydration on muscle strength, endurance, and coordination. Elevating blood volume just before exercise by various **hyperhydration** strategies has been suggested to be effective in enhancing exercise performance, but only a few studies have directly investigated this possibility.

Pre-Exercise Hyperhydration

Because even mild dehydration has debilitating effects on exercise performance, hyperhydration (greater than normal body water content) has been hypothesized to improve thermoregulation by expanding blood volume and reducing plasma osmolarity, thereby improving heat dissipation and exercise performance. Although some studies report higher sweating rates, lower core temperatures, and lower heart rates during exercise after hyperhydration, several of these studies used control conditions that represented dehydration rather than euhydration, making results questionable. However, the findings generally support the notion that hyperhydration reduces the thermal and cardiovascular strain of exercise. Relatively few studies have directly investigated the effects of hyperhydration on exercise performance, but one well-controlled study reported that expansion of blood volume by 450 to 500 ml improved cycling time trial performance by 10% (81 minutes compared with 90 minutes).

Temporary hyperhydration is induced in test subjects by having them drink large volumes of water or water-electrolyte solutions for 1 hour to 3 hours before exercise. However, much of the fluid overload is rapidly excreted, and so expansion of the body water and blood volume is only transient. Studies in which the blood volume was directly expanded by infusion reported decreased cardiovascular strain during exercise but yielded conflicting results on sweat loss, heat dissipation, and exercise performance. Some studies that limited the rise in plasma osmolarity during exercise reported improved heat dissipation but did not address the question of whether it actually affects exercise performance.

Greater fluid retention is achieved if glycerol is added to fluids consumed before exercise. One study has reported a higher sweating rate and lower core temperature when subjects exercised in the heat after hyperhydrating with glycerol (1 g/kg b.w.) and water (21.4 ml/kg b.w.) compared with an equal volume of water alone (Lyons et al 1990). However, other studies report no thermoregulatory advantage during exercise after glycerol solution–induced hyperhydration (Inder et al. 1998; Latzka et al. 1997, 1998). In these studies, the volume of water consumed (500 ml) may have been too small. In a study by Murray et al. (1991), no indications of hyperhydration were found. Generally, however, the ingestion of 1 g/kg b.w. of glycerol with 1 to 2 liters of water seems to protect against heat stress and thus may have some health benefits when exercising in hot conditions. A recent study examined the effect of ingestion of a large bolus of water (20 ml/kg b.w.) with or without added glycerol (1 g/kg b.w.) 2 hours before 90 minutes of submaximal cycling (98% of lactate threshold) in dry, hot conditions (35° C [95° F], relative humidity = 30%) followed by a 15-minute time trial (Anderson et al. 2001). Although pre-exercise glycerol ingestion did not affect skin temperature, muscle temperature, circulating catecholamine, or muscle metabolic responses to the steady state exercise, heart and core temperature were lower than with the ingestion of water alone. Furthermore, time-trial performance (total work performed) was improved significantly by 5%. In subsequent studies, this finding could not be confirmed, even though those studies reported indications of improved thermoregulation. Thus, whether glycerol improves endurance performance in the heat remains unclear. (For more information on glycerol, see chapter 10.)

Fluid Intake During Exercise

During exercise, especially in a hot environment, dehydration can only be avoided by matching fluid consumption with sweat loss. However, this effort is difficult for a number of reasons:

- Sweat rates during strenuous exercise in the heat can be around 2 to 3 L/h. A volume of ingested fluid in the stomach of more than about 1 L feels uncomfortable for most people when exercising, so achieving fluid intakes that match sweat losses during exercise is often not practical.

- Sweat rates vary widely among different individuals under the same ambient conditions. (Figure 8.10 shows the sweat rates of individuals competing in marathon race in Scotland [Maughan 1985].) Hence, to accurately prescribe the amounts that should be drunk is difficult without knowing the athlete's sweat rate under the prevailing climatic conditions.

- Thirst is not a good indicator of body-water requirements or the degree of dehydration. In general, the sensation of thirst is not perceived until a person has lost at least 2% of body weight through sweating. As already mentioned, even this mild degree of dehydration is sufficient to impair exercise performance. Numerous studies show that ad libitum intake of water during exercise in the heat results in incomplete replacement of body-water losses (observed values of fluid intakes and losses are shown in table 8.4).

- The rules or practicalities of specific sports may limit the opportunities for drinking during competition.

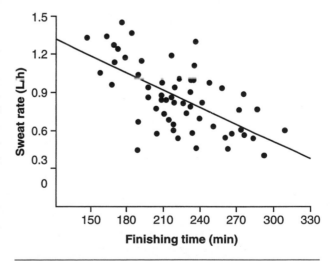

Figure 8.10 Sweat rates for subjects who competed in a marathon race held in cool (about 12° C [54° F]) conditions. The sweat rate was related to the running speed, but a large variation existed between individuals, even those running at the same speed.

Data from R.J. Maughan, 1985.

Table 8.4 Fluid Losses and Intakes of Athletes

Sport	Ambient temperature (°C/°F)	Sweat loss (mL/h)	Fluid intake (mL/h)
Marathon running	15–20 (59–68)	800–1,200	500
Soccer	10 (50)	1,000	350
	25 (77)	1,200	500
Basketball	20–25 (68–77)	1,600	1,080
Rowing	10 (50)	1,165	580
	30 (86)	1,980	960
Cycling	30 (86)	2,000	800

Because endurance exercise capacity is impaired even by mild dehydration and small decreases in plasma volume, athletes should try to minimize the extent of dehydration by ingesting fluids during exercise. Regular water intake during prolonged exercise is effective in improving both exercise capacity (time to exhaustion [see figures 8.11 and 8.12]) and exercise performance (time to complete a given amount of work [see figure 8.13]) (Fallowfield et al. 1996; Maughan et al. 1987).

Fluid intake during prolonged exercise offers the opportunity to ingest some fuel as well. The addition of carbohydrate to some drinks consumed during exercise has an additional independent effect in improving exercise performance (see figures 8.12 and 8.13) (Below et al. 1995). Further details can found in chapter 5. Too much added carbohydrate in a sports drink, although providing more fuel for the working muscles, however, decreases the amount of water that can be absorbed. In this situation, water is actually drawn out of the interstitial fluid and plasma into the lumen of the small intestine by **osmosis.** This effect is demonstrated in figure 8.14, which shows that the ingestion of a concentrated glucose solution, **hypertonic** with respect to plasma, delays the restoration of plasma volume during exercise compared with the ingestion of a **hypotonic** glucose-electrolyte drink (Maughan et al. 1987).

As long as the fluid remains hypotonic with respect to plasma, the uptake of water from the small intestine is not adversely affected. In fact, the presence of small amounts of glucose and sodium tend to slightly increase the rate of water absorption compared with pure water (Maughan and Murray 2000). Rather than to replace electrolytes lost through sweating, sodium and other electrolytes are added to sports drinks to

- increase palatability,
- maintain thirst (and therefore promote drinking),
- prevent hyponatremia (low serum sodium concentration, which can occur when individuals ingest far more water than their requirements),

- increase the rate of water uptake, and
- increase the retention of fluid.

Replacement of the electrolytes lost in sweat can normally wait until the postexercise recovery period. Fluid intake during strenuous exercise of less than 30 minutes duration offers no advantage. Gastric emptying is inhibited at high work rates, and insignificant amounts of fluid are absorbed during exercise of such short duration. For exercise lasting more than 1 hour or exercise in hot or humid conditions, consumption of carbohydrate-electrolyte sports drink is warranted. These drinks supply fluid together with carbohydrate that helps maintain blood glucose and high levels of carbohydrate oxidation. The electrolyte (sodium) content partly offsets salt losses in sweat but, perhaps more importantly, maintains the desire to drink.

Sweat-loss rates during exercise depend on exercise intensity, duration, and environmental conditions but also vary considerably among different individuals. Some people may lose up to 3 L/h of sweat during strenuous activity in a warm environment (see figure 8.15) (Sawka and Pandolf 1990), and even at low ambient temperatures of about 12° C (54° F), sweat loss can exceed 1 L/h (see figure 8.10) (Maughan 1985). Because the electrolyte composition of sweat is hypotonic to plasma (in other words, the total concentration of dissolved anions and cations is considerably lower in sweat than in plasma; see table

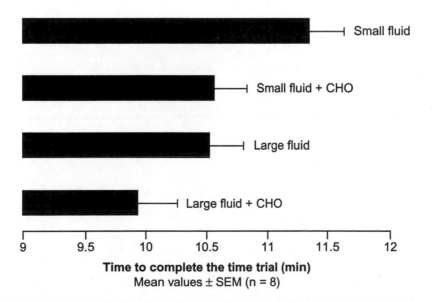

Figure 8.13 Effect of carbohydrate and fluid ingestion on a cycling time trial performed at the end of a prolonged exercise test at 31° C (88° F) in which either a small (200 ml) or large (1,330 ml) fluid volume with either zero carbohydrate or a large amount (79 g) of carbohydrate was given. Ingestion of water and carbohydrate has independent and additive effects in improving exercise performance.

Data from P. Below et al., 1995.

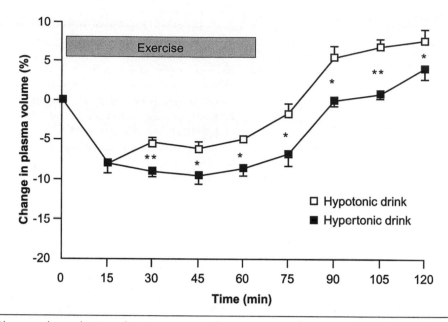

Figure 8.14 Plasma volume changes during exercise with consumption of a hypertonic or hypotonic glucose–containing beverage. Because of the faster gastric emptying and faster intestinal absorption of water, ingestion of dilute carbohydrate-electrolyte solutions (open squares) is more effective in restoring plasma volume during exercise compared with the ingestion of an equal volume of a concentrated glucose solution (closed squares).

European Journal of Applied Physiology, Metabolic and circulatory responses to the ingestion of glucose polymer and gluclose/electrolyte solutions during exercise in man, R.J. Maughan et al., 45: 356-362, 1987, © Springer-Verlag.

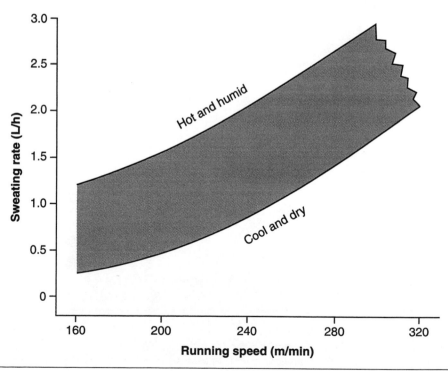

Figure 8.15 Approximate hourly sweating rates as a function of environmental conditions and running speed.

Adapted from M.N. Sawka and S.J. Mountain, 2000.

8.5), the replacement of water rather than electrolytes is the priority during exercise. Plasma volume falls by up to 20% during exercise, the magnitude of the fall being related to the relative exercise intensity. Typically, at work rates equivalent to 60% to 80% of the maximal oxygen uptake, plasma volume falls acutely by about 10% to 15% because of the increased capillary hydrostatic pressure and osmotic uptake of water into active skeletal muscle tissue. Without fluid intake, particularly in a warm, humid environment, further falls in plasma volume and increases in plasma osmolarity occur because of the loss of hypotonic sweat, as exercise proceeds.

As mentioned previously, the decrease in plasma volume that accompanies dehydration may be of particular importance in influencing work capacity. Blood flow to the muscles must be maintained at a high level to supply oxygen and fuel substrates (glucose and fatty acids), but a high blood flow to the skin is also necessary to convect heat to the body surface, where it can be dissipated. When the ambient temperature is high and plasma volume is decreased by sweat loss during prolonged exercise (as shown in figure 8.16), skin blood flow is likely to be compromised (Costill and Fink 1974), allowing central venous pressure and blood flow to the working muscle to be maintained but reducing heat loss and causing body temperature to rise to dangerous levels. To prevent dehydration, water must be replaced at a faster rate. Metabolic water production increases during exercise but not enough to compensate for water loss through sweating. Oral fluid ingestion during exercise helps restore plasma volume to near pre-exercise levels (see figure 8.16) and prevents the adverse effects of dehydration

on thermal and cardiovascular strain, muscle strength, endurance, and coordination.

A study compared time to exhaustion during cycling at 60% $\dot{V}O_2$max in warm ambient conditions (30° C [86° F]) when six subjects were given either (a) no drink, (b) 500 ml of a 15% carbohydrate-electrolyte drink immediately before exercise and 125 ml of the same drink every 10 minutes throughout exercise, or (c) 500 ml of a 2% carbohydrate-electrolyte drink immediately before exercise and 250 ml of the same drink every 10 minutes throughout exercise (Galloway and Maughan 2000). As shown in figure 8.17, with no drink, subjects fatigued after 71 minutes (median range 39 minutes to 97 minutes). With the 15% carbohydrate-electrolyte drink, they could continue for longer times (median 84 minutes, range 63 minutes to 145 minutes). However, the best performance was achieved with the 2% carbohydrate-electrolyte drink (median 118 minutes, range 83 minutes to 168 minutes). Interestingly, the median core temperature at exhaustion was the same in all 3 trials (39.5° C [103° F]). A significant fall in plasma volume occurred within the first 15 minutes of exercise on all trials. Subsequently, plasma volume remained below resting values on the no-drink and the 15% carbohydrate-electrolyte trials, but on the 2% carbohydrate-electrolyte trial, plasma volume was gradually restored during exercise.

Gonzalez-Alonso et al. (1998) showed that exercising-limb perfusion may be reduced during prolonged exercise combined with heat stress and dehydration. The maintenance of plasma volume on the 2% carbohydrate-electrolyte trial may have resulted in better perfusion of active muscles during exercise and

Table 8.5 Concentrations of Electrolytes in Sweat, Plasma, and Intracellular Water

Electrolyte	Sweat (mmol/L)	Plasma (mmol/L)	Intracellular water (mmol/L)
Cations			
Sodium	20–80	130–155	10
Potassium	4–8	3.2–5.5	150
Calcium	0.1–1.0	2.1–2.9	0.01
Magnesium	0.1–0.2	0.7–1.5	15
Anions			
Chloride	20–60	96–110	8
Bicarbonate	1–35	23–28	10
Phosphate	0.1–0.2	0.7–1.6	65
Sulphate	0.1–2.0	0.3–0.9	10

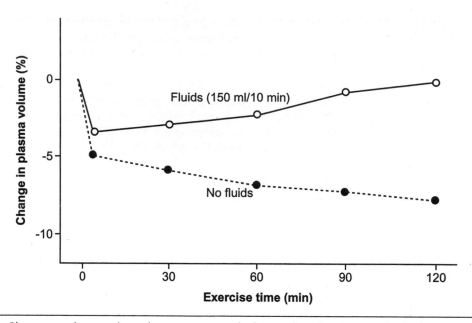

Figure 8.16 Changes in plasma volume during exercise in the heat with and without regular fluid ingestion.

Reprinted, by permission, from D.L. Costill, and W.J. Fink, 1974, "Plasma volume changes following exercise and thermal dehydration," *Journal of Applied Physiology* 37: 521-525.

may have resulted in better maintenance of cellular hydration.

Ingestion of relatively cool fluid may have an additional small benefit during exercise in the heat because the additional volume of fluid in the body after drinking adds to the body's heat-storage capacity. The improvement in heat-storage capacity can be calculated based on the specific heat capacity of water, which is 4.184 kJ/kg/°C (0.555 kcal/kg/°F). For example, the ingestion of 2 L of fluid at 10° C

(50° F) increases heat-storage capacity by $4.184 \times 2 \times (37 - 10)$ kJ = 225 kJ (54 kcal).

In the study by Galloway and Maughan (2000), subjects ingested fluids cooled to 14° C (57° F), and these investigators calculated that the extra fluid consumed on the 2% carbohydrate-electrolyte treatment (2.3 L) could have produced an 8-minute improvement in performance because of its effect in increasing body heat-storage capacity compared with the no-drink treatment.

Daily Water Balance

The typical daily water balance for a sedentary individual living in a cool or temperate climate (ambient temperature 10° to 20° C [50° to 68° F]) is shown in figure 8.18. Variable amounts of water are lost from the body through sweating in response to the requirement for thermoregulation, but for a sedentary individual in cool conditions, evaporative loss of water through the skin only amounts to about 600 ml/day. Additional water is lost in the feces (about 100 ml/day) and urine. Normally, about 800 ml to 1,600 ml of urine is produced each day. The kidneys are able to regulate the amount of water lost in urine, although even in severe dehydration, some urine is still produced to maintain fluid flow through the kidney tubules (nephrons) and excrete toxic nitrogenous wastes such as ammonia and urea. Urinary water loss is not usually less than 800 ml/day.

Environmental conditions affect a person's water requirements by altering the losses that occur by the various routes. Water losses may be 2 to 3 times greater for a sedentary individual living in a hot climate compared with a sedentary individual living in a temperate climate. These higher rates of water loss are not exclusively caused by increased sweating, but may also be incurred by a marked increase in transcutaneous and respiratory water losses. These routes of water loss are heavily influenced by the humidity of the ambient air, which may be a more important factor than the ambient temperature. Respiratory water losses are greater when the relative humidity (RH) of the ambient air is low because air breathed out of the body is fully saturated with water vapor (RH = 100%). Although these losses are quite small for a sedentary individual in a moist, warm environment (about 200 ml/day), they may be increased approximately twofold in low-humidity conditions (RH = 0% to 20%) and may rise up to 1,500 ml/day during periods of hard training in cold, dry air at altitude.

Water intake comes from drinks and food; some foods (especially plant material) have a high water content. Water in food, in fact, makes a major contribution to total water intake. Water is also produced internally (metabolic water) from the catabolism of carbohydrates, fat, and protein. For example, in the complete oxidation of 1 molecule of glucose, 6 molecules of carbon dioxide, and 6 molecules of water are produced. In a sedentary individual, metabolic water production will amount to about 300 ml/day, although most of this water is lost in expired gas, as oxidizing fuel in the body generates carbon dioxide, which stimulates breathing and, hence, increases respiratory water loss. Although an athlete increases his or her metabolic water production because of the increased rate of fuel catabolism

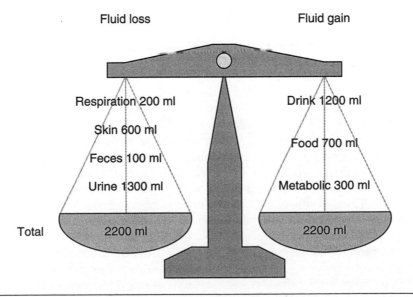

Figure 8.18 Daily water balance for a sedentary adult individual.

during exercise, this increase, again, is offset by the obligatory increase in lung ventilation and respiratory evaporative water loss.

The body's water balance is under tight regulation involving nervous and hormonal factors that respond to a number of different inputs. The osmolarity of the blood plasma is maintained within tight limits around 290 mOsmol/L. A rise or fall in the plasma osmolarity is sufficient to alter kidney function from maximum water conservation to maximum water excretion. Because sodium is the major electrolyte in the extracellular fluids (it accounts for 50% of plasma osmolarity), the maintenance of osmotic balance is closely coupled to the intake and excretion of sodium and water. Even small reductions in the plasma osmolarity invoke a marked increase in urine output (diuresis), and this increase is normally sufficient to prevent fluid overload when large volumes of water or low-electrolyte drinks such as beer are consumed. However, some cases of **hyponatremia** (low plasma sodium concentration) have been reported, usually in individuals who have ingested excessively large volumes of plain water or low-electrolyte drinks in a relatively short time.

The subjective sensation of thirst initiates the desire to drink and is therefore a key factor in the regulation of fluid intake. Although the kidneys can quite effectively conserve water or electrolytes by reducing the rate of loss, they cannot restore a fluid deficit. Only consumption of fluid can correct this imbalance. The sensation of thirst is mainly evoked by the detection of elevated plasma osmolarity (and to a lesser extent, by reductions in blood volume and pressure) by osmoreceptors located in the hypothalamus of the brain. The thirst sensation results in a profound desire to drink and an increase in the secretion of antidiuretic hormone (ADH) from the posterior pituitary gland, which acts on the kidneys to reduce urine excretion. Other factors that promote thirst are learned responses such as dryness of the mouth or throat, salty tastes, and feeling hot. Thirst is quickly alleviated by drinking fluid, and alleviation can occur before a significant amount of the fluid is absorbed in the gut. This effect suggests a role for sensory receptors in the mouth and stomach. Distension of the stomach wall appears to reduce the perception of thirst and may result in fluid ingestion being stopped prematurely. Thus, the absence of the sensation of thirst cannot be used as an indicator that fluid balance (euhydration) is established; often the perception of thirst is not present until a significant degree of dehydration has occurred.

An electrolyte imbalance commonly called "water intoxication," which results from hyponatremia (low plasma sodium) caused by excessive water consumption, is occasionally reported in endurance athletes. This condition appears to be most common among slow runners in marathon and ultramarathon races and probably arises because of the loss of sodium in sweat coupled with very high intakes (8 L to 10 L) of water (Noakes et al. 1985). The symptoms of hyponatremia are similar to those of dehydration and include mental confusion, weakness, and fainting. Therefore, this condition can be misdiagnosed when it occurs in individuals participating in endurance races. The usual treatment for dehydration is administration of fluid intravenously and orally. If this treatment is given to a hyponatremic individual, the consequences can be fatal.

Fluid Requirements for Athletes

Athletes must be fully hydrated before they train or compete because the body cannot adapt to dehydration. Training quality will suffer if an athlete becomes dehydrated during training, as will performance quality if an athlete becomes dehydrated during competition.

Ensuring Adequate Hydration Before Exercise

An adequately hydrated state can be assured by a high fluid intake in the last few days before competition. A useful check is to observe the color of the urine. It should be pale in color, although this simple test cannot be reliably used if the athlete is taking vitamin supplements, as some of the excreted water-soluble B vitamins add a yellowish hue to the urine. A clearer indication of hydration status is obtained by measuring urine osmolality. (Note that the units of osmolality are Osmol/kg, whereas osmolarity is expressed as Osmol/L.) This measurement can be done quickly and simply using a portable osmometer. A urine osmolality of over 900 mOsmol/kg definitely indicates that the athlete is relatively dehydrated; values of 100 mOsmol/kg to 300 mOsmol/kg indicate that the athlete is well hydrated. Measuring the athlete's body weight after rising and voiding each morning may also prove useful. A sudden drop in body mass on any given day is likely to indicate dehydration. Approximate fluid intake requirements in liters per day in hot, dry conditions are shown in figure 8.19. The fluid intake requirement (to maintain water balance, or euhydration) increases as ambient temperature increases and as daily energy expenditure increases.

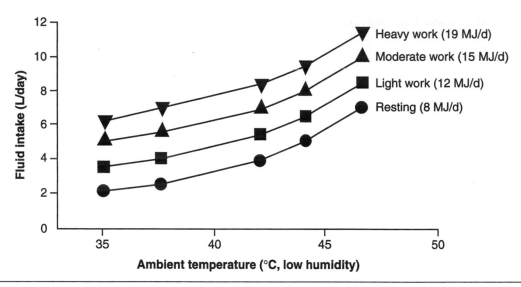

Figure 8.19 Approximate daily fluid intake requirements for individuals at rest or performing different amounts of physical work while living at different ambient temperatures.

Adapted from M.N. Sawka and S.J. Montain, 2000.

Ensuring Hydration During Exercise

Relying on feeling thirsty as the signal to drink is unreliable because a considerable degree of dehydration (certainly sufficient to impair athletic performance) can occur before the desire for fluid intake is evident. Ideally, athletes should consume enough fluids during activity to make body weight remain fairly constant before and after exercise. Guidelines for the amounts of fluid to be consumed before, during, and after exercise can only be very general because of the large interindividual sweating responses. However, the American and Canadian Dietetic Associations recommend that approximately 500 ml of fluid be consumed 2 hours before exertion, followed by another 500 ml about 15 minutes before prolonged exercise. In hot and humid environments, frequent consumption (every 15 to 20 minutes) of small volumes (120 to 180 ml) of fluid are recommended throughout exertion. Athletes should become accustomed to consuming fluid at regular intervals (with or without thirst) during training sessions so they do not experience discomfort during competition. For most persons exercising for 30 minutes to 60 minutes in moderate temperature conditions, an appropriate beverage is cool water.

Composition of Sport Drinks During Exercise

Fluid ingestion during exercise also supplies exogenous fuel substrate (usually carbohydrate) as well as helps maintain plasma volume and prevents dehydration. However, the availability of ingested fluids may be limited by the rate of gastric emptying or intestinal absorption. Gastric emptying of fluids is slowed by the addition of carbohydrate or other macronutrients that increase the osmolarity of the solution ingested. Hence, with increasing glucose concentration in the fluid ingested, the rate of fluid volume delivery to the small intestine is decreased, although the rate of glucose delivery is increased.

Water absorption in the small intestine is by osmosis and is promoted by the coupled transport of glucose and sodium. Hence, the composition of fluids to be used during exercise depends on the relative needs to replace water and provide fuel substrate. Where rehydration is the main priority (e.g., for prolonged exercise in the heat), the solution should contain some carbohydrate as glucose or glucose polymers (20 g/L to 60 g/L) and sodium (20 mmol/L to 60 mmol/L) and should not exceed isotonicity (290 mOsmol/L). Most commercially available sports drinks contain 60 g/L to 80 g/L of carbohydrate (predominantly as glucose, glucose polymers, or both, although some drinks may also contain fructose or sucrose) and 20 mmol/L to 25 mmol/L of sodium. Table 8.6 compares the compositions of several commercially available drinks that are commonly consumed by athletes during training or competition. In cool environments, where substrate provision to maintain endurance performance is more important, a more concentrated solution incorporating large amounts of glucose polymers in concentrations of 550 mmol/L to 800 mmol/L glucosyl units (100 g/L to 150 g/L) is recommended. To minimize the limitation imposed by the rate of gastric emptying, the osmolarity of the beverage should be minimized

189

Table 8.6 Compositions of Commonly Consumed Sport Drinks

Drink	Carbohydrate (g/L)	Sodium (mmol/L)	Potassium (mmol/L)	Osmolality (mOsmol/kg)
Coca-Cola	105	3	0	650
Allsport	80	10	6	516
Gatorade	60	18	3	349
Isostar	65	24	4	296
Lucozade Sport	64	23	4	280
Lucozade	180	0	0	658
Powerade (U.K.)	60	24	4	285
Powerade (U.S.)	80	5	4	381

by providing the glucose in the form of glucose polymers, and the volume of fluid in the stomach should be kept as high as is comfortable by frequent ingestion of small amounts of fluid.

The importance of practicing drinking during training is often neglected. This practice will accustom athletes to the feeling of exercising with fluid in the stomach. It also provides the opportunity to experiment with different volumes and flavorings to determine how much fluid intake athletes can tolerate and which formulations suit them best. Measuring fluid consumption and body mass changes before and after training gives an idea of the athlete's sweat rate under different environmental conditions. This information will help determine an individual athlete's requirements for fluid intake during competition.

The ideal drink for fluid replacement during exercise is one that tastes good to the athlete, does not cause gastrointestinal discomfort when consumed in large volumes (this rules out all fizzy carbonated drinks), promotes rapid gastric emptying and fluid absorption to help maintain extracellular fluid volume, and provides some energy in the form of carbohydrate for the working muscles. Cool, pleasantly flavored, sweetened beverages are preferred by exercising subjects, and the presence of sodium in the drinks seems to promote their consumption, probably by maintaining thirst.

Rehydration After Exercise

Replacement of water and electrolytes in the postexercise recovery period may be of crucial importance where repeated bouts of exercise must be performed and rehydration must be maximized in the time available. As previously mentioned, dehydration is associated with impaired thermoregulation and increased cardiovascular strain and with the loss of the thermoregulatory advantages conferred by heat acclimation and high aerobic fitness. With progressive dehydration, losses of intracellular as well as extracellular fluid volume occurs. Loss of intracellular volume may have important implications for recovery from exercise given the emerging evidence of a role for cell volume in the regulation of cell metabolism. A reduced intracellular volume reduces rates of glycogen and protein synthesis, whereas a high cell volume stimulates these processes.

The main factors influencing the effectiveness of postexercise rehydration are the volume and composition of the fluid consumed. Plain water is not the ideal rehydration beverage when rapid and complete restoration of body fluid balance is necessary and when all intake is in liquid form. Ingestion of water alone causes a rapid fall in the plasma sodium concentration and in the plasma osmolarity. These changes reduce the stimulation to drink (thirst) and increase the urine output, both of which delay the rehydration process. Plasma volume is more rapidly and completely restored if some sodium chloride (77 mmol/L, or 0.45 g/L) is added to the water consumed (Nose et al. 1988). This sodium concentration is similar to the upper limit of the sodium concentration found in sweat but is considerably higher than the sodium concentration of many commercially available sports drinks, which usually contain 10 mmol/L to 25 mmol/L (see table 8.6). Optimal rehydration after exercise can only be achieved if the sodium lost in sweat is replaced along with the water.

Shirreffs et al. (1996) showed that, provided that an adequate volume of fluid is consumed, euhydration is achieved when sodium intake is greater than sodium loss (see figure 8.20). Ingesting a beverage containing sodium not only promotes rapid fluid absorption in

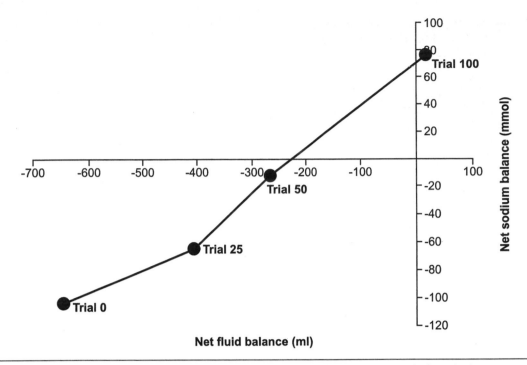

Figure 8.20 Net sodium balance plotted against net fluid balance, 6 hours after the end of a rehydration period, during which subjects ingested different drinks in a volume equivalent to 150% of sweat loss. The drinks containing sodium at a concentration of 0 mmol/L, 25 mmol/L, 50 mmol/L, or 100 mmol/L (trials 0, 25, 50, and 100, respectively) were ingested after exercise. At the end of the 6-hour rehydration period, water balance was only achieved when the sodium intake was greater than the sweat sodium loss.

Reprinted, by permission, from S.M. Shirreffs and R.J. Maughan, 2000, "Rehydration and recovery of fluid balance after exercise," *Exercise and Sport Sciences Reviews* 28(1): 27-32.

the small intestine but also allows the plasma sodium concentration to remain elevated during the rehydration period and helps maintain thirst while delaying stimulation of urine production. Sodium is the major cation in the extracellular fluid. The inclusion of potassium in the beverage consumed after exercise would be expected to enhance the replacement of intracellular water and thus promote rehydration, but currently little experimental evidence supports this expectation. The rehydration drink should also contain carbohydrate (glucose or glucose polymers) because the presence of some glucose also stimulates fluid absorption in the gut and improves beverage taste. After exercise, the uptake of glucose into the muscle for glycogen resynthesis should also promote intracellular rehydration.

Fluid Consumption After Exercise

Until recently, athletes were generally encouraged to consume a volume of fluid equivalent to their sweat loss incurred during exercise to adequately rehydrate in the postexercise recovery period. In other words, they were to consume about 1 L of fluid for every kg lost during an exercise session. This amount is insufficient because it does not take into account the obligatory urine losses that are incurred after beverage consumption over a period of hours. Existing data indicate that ingestion of 150% or more of weight loss (i.e., 1.5 L of fluid consumed during recovery for every kg of weight lost during exercise) may be required to achieve normal hydration within 6 hours after exercise (Shirreffs et al. 1996; Shirreffs and Maughan 1998, 2000 [see figure 8.21]). Current (1996) American College of Sports Medicine (ACSM) guidelines on fluid ingestion before, during, and after exercise are shown in figure 8.22.

Intake of caffeine and alcohol in the postexercise recovery period is generally discouraged because of their diuretic actions. However, the diuretic effect of alcohol appears to be blunted when consumed by persons who are moderately dehydrated after exercise in a warm environment (Shirreffs and Maughan 1997). If shandy (a mixture of beer and lemonade) is consumed in the postexercise period, then (as expected) the urinary output increases with increasing alcohol intake. However, this increase only approaches statistical significance (compared with lemonade alone) when alcohol content is around 4% w/v. This concentration of alcohol in the rehydration

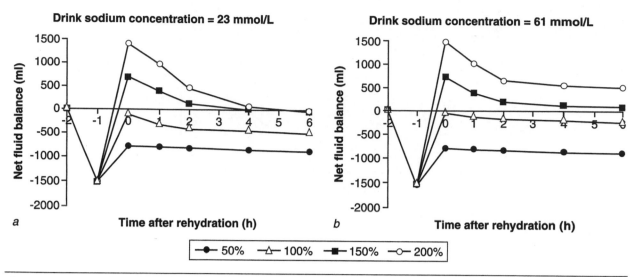

Figure 8.21 Net fluid balance plotted against time after dehydration (loss of 1,500 ml body water) induced by mild exercise in a hot environment. Zero net fluid balance represents euhydration. Drink volume ingested was half of (50%), equal to (100%), one-and-a-half times (150%), and twice (200%) the sweat loss. The drink sodium concentration was either (a) 23 mmol/L or (b) 61 mmol/L. Mild dehydration was present 6 hours after rehydration when a large volume of the low-sodium drink (23 mmol/L) was consumed, but with the same volume, hyperhydration was achieved with the high-sodium drink (61 mmol/L).

Reprinted, by permission, from S.M. Shirreffs et al., 1996, "Post-exercise rehydration in man: Effects of volume consumed and drink sodium content," Medicine and Science in Sport Exercise 28: 1260-1271..

Adequate fluid replacement helps maintain hydration and therefore promotes the health, safety, and optimal physical performance of individuals participating in regular physical activity. The following are general recommendations on the amount and composition of fluids that should be ingested in preparation for, during, and after exercise or athletic competition.

1. Individuals should consume a nutritionally balanced diet and drink adequate fluids during the 24-hour period before an event, especially during the period that includes the meal before exercise, to promote proper hydration before exercise or competition.

2. Individuals should drink about 500 ml (about 17 fl oz) of fluid about 2 hours before exercise to promote adequate hydration and allow time for excretion of excess ingested water.

3. During exercise, athletes should start drinking early and at regular intervals in an attempt to consume fluids at a rate sufficient to replace all the water lost through sweating (i.e., body weight loss), or they should consume the maximal amount that can be tolerated.

4. Ingested fluids should be cooler than ambient temperature (between 15° and 22° C [59° and 72° F]) and flavored to enhance palatability and promote fluid replacement. Fluid should be readily available and served in containers that allow adequate volumes to be ingested with ease and with minimal interruption of exercise.

5. Addition of proper amounts of carbohydrates or electrolytes to a fluid replacement solution is recommended for exercise events of duration greater than 1 hour because such additives do not significantly impair water delivery to the body and may enhance performance. For exercise of less than 1 hour, little evidence exists of physiological or physical performance differences as a result of consuming a carbohydrate-electrolyte drink and plain water.

6. During intense exercise lasting longer than 1 hour, carbohydrates should be ingested at a rate of 30 g/h to 60 g/h to maintain oxidation of carbohydrate and delay fatigue. This rate of carbohydrate delivery can be achieved without compromising fluid delivery by drinking 600 ml/h to 1,200 ml/h of solutions containing 4% to 8% carbohydrates (g/100 ml). The carbohydrates can be sugars (glucose or sucrose) or starch (e.g., maltodextrins).

7. Inclusion of sodium (0.5 g/L to 0.7 g/L of water) in the rehydration solution ingested during exercise lasting longer than 1 hour is recommended because it may enhance palatability, promote fluid retention, and possibly prevent hyponatremia in certain individuals who drink excessive quantities of fluid. Little physiological evidence suggests the need for sodium in an oral rehydration solution for enhancing intestinal water absorption as long as sodium is sufficiently available from the previous meal.

Figure 8.22 American College of Sports Medicine Guidelines on fluid intake for exercise.

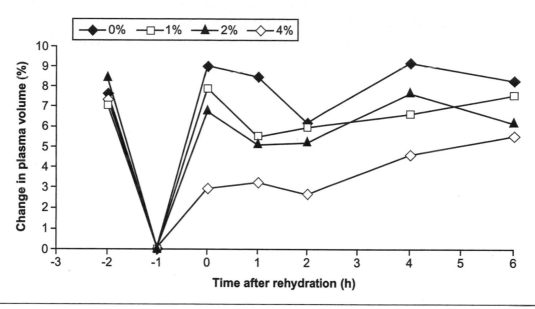

Figure 8.23 Percentage change in plasma volume with dehydration equivalent to 2% of body weight, followed by rehydration with drinks containing 0%, 1%, 2%, and 4% (w/v) alcohol in a volume equivalent to one-and-a-half times the sweat loss. Note that plasma volume restoration was delayed with the 4% alcohol drink.

Reprinted, by permission, from S.M. Shirreffs and R.J. Maughan, 1997, "Restoration of fluid balance after exercise-induced dehydration: Effect of alcohol consumption," *Journal of Applied Physiology* 83: 1152-1157.

drink is also associated with a slower rate of recovery of plasma volume, as shown in figure 8.23, whereas drinks containing 1% and 2% alcohol seem just as effective as lemonade alone.

In most circumstances, athletes should consume solid food as well as drink between exercise bouts, unless food intake is likely to result in gastrointestinal disturbances. In one study, the same fluid volume consumed as a meal-plus-water combination compared with a sports drink alone resulted in a smaller volume of urine produced and hence greater fluid retention (Maughan, Leiper, and Shirreffs 1996). The greater efficacy of the meal-plus-water treatment in restoring whole-body fluid balance was probably a consequence of its greater total sodium and potassium content. In exercise situations where sweat losses are large, the total sodium and chloride losses are high. For example, the loss of 10 L of sweat, with a sodium concentration of 50 mmol/L, amounts to a loss of about 29 g of sodium chloride.

Obviously, food intake can be important in restoring these salt losses because most commercial sports drinks do not contain more than about 25 mmol/L sodium. Rehydration after exercise can only be achieved if sweat electrolyte losses as well as water are replaced. One problem is that drinks with high-sodium content (i.e., 40 to 80 mmol/L) are unpalatable to some people, which results in reduced consumption. On the other hand, drinks with low-sodium content (e.g., most soft drinks) are much less effective for rehydration, and they also reduce the stimulus to drink.

Key Points

■ High rates of sweat secretion are necessary during hard exercise to limit the rise in body temperature that would otherwise occur. If the exercise is prolonged, body-temperature increase leads to progressive dehydration and loss of electrolytes.

■ Body temperatures of 36° to 38° C (96.8° to 100.4° F) are considered as the normal range at rest and may increase to 38° to 40° C (100.4° to 104° F) during exercise. When body temperature rises toward 39.5° C (103° F), central fatigue ensues. Further increases are commonly associated with heat exhaustion and occasionally with life-threatening heat

(continued)

(continued)

stroke, characterized by a lack of consciousness after exertion and by clinical symptoms of organ damage.

■ Some people may lose up to 2 to 3 L/h of sweat during strenuous activity in a hot environment. Even at low ambient temperatures of about 10° C (50° F), sweat loss can exceed 1 L/h.

■ Because the electrolyte composition of sweat is hypotonic to plasma, the replacement of water rather than electrolytes is the priority during exercise.

■ Fatigue towards the end of a prolonged event may result as much from the effects of dehydration as from substrate depletion. Exercise performance is impaired when an individual is dehydrated by as little as 2% of body weight, and losses in excess of 5% of body weight can decrease the capacity for work by about 30%.

■ Oral fluid ingestion during exercise helps restore plasma volume to near pre-exercise levels and prevents the adverse effects of dehydration on muscle strength, endurance, and coordination. Dehydration also poses a serious health risk in that it increases the risk of cramps, heat exhaustion, and life-threatening heat stroke.

■ Relying on feeling thirsty as the signal to drink is unreliable because a considerable degree of dehydration (certainly sufficient to impair athletic performance) can occur before the desire for fluid intake is evident. Ideally, athletes should consume adequate fluids during activity so that body weight remains fairly constant before and after exercise.

■ The composition of drinks to be taken during exercise should suit individual circumstances. Where rehydration is the main priority (e.g., for prolonged exercise in the heat), the solution should contain some carbohydrate as glucose or glucose polymers (20 to 60 g/L) and sodium (20 to 60 mmol/L) and should not exceed isotonicity (290 mOsmol/L).

■ Optimal rehydration after exercise can only be achieved if the sodium lost in sweat is replaced along with the water. Plasma volume is more rapidly and completely restored in the postexercise period if some sodium chloride is added to the water consumed. A volume equivalent to at least one-and-a-half times the sweat loss must be consumed to ensure that complete rehydration is achieved at the end of a 6-hour recovery period after exercise.

Key Terms

acclimatization 175	euhydration 178	hypertonic 182	osmosis 182
conduction 172	evaporation 172	hyponatremia 188	radiation 172
convection 172	hyperhydration 180	hypotonic 182	thermoregulation 171
dehydration 170	hyperthermia 171	hypovolemia 178	

Recommended Readings

Armstrong, L.E. 2000. *Performing in Extreme Environments.* Human Kinetics: Champaign, IL.

Maughan, R.J. 2000. Water and electrolyte loss and replacement in exercise. In *Nutrition in Sport,* ed. R.J. Maughan, 226-240. Blackwell Science: Oxford.

Maughan, R.J., and L.M. Burke. 2002. Sport nutrition. *Handbook of Sports Medicine and Sciences.* Blackwell Science: Oxford.

Maughan, R.J., and R. Murray. (eds). 2000. *Sports Drinks: Basic Science and Practical Aspects.* CRC Press: Boca Raton, FL.

Maughan, R.J., and E.R. Nadel. 2000. Temperature regulation and fluid and electrolyte balance. In *Nutrition in Sport*, ed. R. J. Maughan, 203-215. Blackwell Science: Oxford.

Sawka, M.N., W.A. Latzka, and S.J. Montain. 2000. Effects of dehydration and rehydration on performance. In *Nutrition in Sport*, ed. R.J. Maughan, 216-225. Blackwell Science: Oxford.

Shirreffs, S.M. 2000. Rehydration and recovery after exercise. In *Nutrition in Sport*, ed. R.J. Maughan, 256-265. Blackwell Science: Oxford.

Shirreffs, S.M., and R.J. Maughan. 2000. Rehydration and recovery of fluid balance after exercise. *Exercise and Sport Sciences Reviews* 28:27-32.

Chapter 11

Weight Management

© Empics

Objectives

After studying this chapter, you should be able to do the following:

- Describe the principles of methods available to measure body composition

- Compare different techniques of measuring body composition and discuss their advantages and limitations

- Categorize sports and the importance of body weight or composition

- Describe ways of losing body weight by dieting

- Describe the role of exercise in losing body weight

- Describe the benefits and risks of making weight and discuss the possibilities to minimize the risks

Body weight, or body composition, is an important determinant of performance in many sports. Some athletes try to achieve weight loss, and others try to achieve weight gain. In some sports, reducing body fat is important, whereas in other sports, increasing lean-body mass is important. In most weight-bearing activities, such as running and jumping, extra weight may be a disadvantage, though in some contact sports, such as American football and rugby, extra weight may be an advantage. Every sport has an "optimal physique," and in some sports, a specific discipline or position requires a different body type. For dancing and gymnastics, leanness is important mainly for aesthetic reasons.

The desire to lose or gain weight is not limited to competitive athletes but is also common among recreational athletes and sedentary individuals who wish to change their physical appearance. While obesity is a growing problem, images in the media create continuous pressure to be lean and well proportioned. The stereotypical athlete is particularly lean and toned. Many athletes try to lose weight through either diet or exercise or both. This chapter discusses the relationship between body composition and performance, followed by a discussion of how body composition can be assessed and, finally, the problems associated with weight loss and weight gain and the applications in various categories of sport.

Ideal Body Weight and Composition

Body size, structure, and composition are separate, yet interrelated, aspects of the body that make up the physique. Body size refers to the volume, mass, length, and surface area of the body; body structure refers to the distribution or arrangement of body parts such as the skeleton, muscle, and fat; and body composition refers to the amounts of constituents in the body. Size, structure, and composition all contribute to optimal sports performance. Evidence from sports participants in various age groups demonstrates an inverse relationship between fat mass and performance of physical activities requiring translocation of the body weight either vertically, such as in jumping, or horizontally, as in running. Excess fat is detrimental to performance in these types of activities because it adds mass to the body without additional capacity to produce force. Also, acceleration is directly proportional to force but inversely proportional to mass, so excess fat, at a given level of force application, results in slower changes in velocity and direction. Excess fat also increases the metabolic cost of physical activities that require movement of the total-body mass. Thus, in most performances involving movement of the body mass, a relatively low percentage body fat is advantageous both mechanically and metabolically.

By studying the anthropometry of high-level athletes, we can get an idea about optimum body size, structure, and composition for various sports. In some sports, a low percentage body fat is a requirement. For example, Olympic marathon runners have 3% to 4% body fat. Tour de France cyclists have between 4% and 6% body fat. Linebackers in American football have between 12% and 15% body fat, whereas defensive linemen have 16% body fat or more.

Body mass may also be dramatically different in different sports. Female distance runners may weigh 50 kg to 55 kg (110 lb to 120 lb), whereas female shot putters may weigh 75 kg to 85 kg (165 lb to 185 lb). Ballet dancers may weigh no more than 45 kg (100 lb). These body composition assessments reveal that athletes generally have physique characteristics unique to their specific sport and discipline.

Body Composition

By measuring body composition one can quantify the most important structural components of the body: muscle, bone, and fat. A variety of techniques have been developed to measure body composition (see table 11.1). Such measurements are more meaningful than the traditional weight and height relationship. Height-weight tables, such as the one shown in figure 11.1 provide a normal range of body weights for any given height. Such figures and tables have limitations, especially when applied to an athletic population. For instance, a bodybuilder (180 cm, 100 kg [6 ft, 220 lb]) may have very low body fat but could be classified as overweight. Clearly the "extra" weight is muscle and not body fat, which would lead to erroneous classification and possibly mistaken advice.

Body Mass Index

A rough but better measure than the height-weight tables is the **body mass index (BMI),** also known as Quetelet index. Also derived from body mass and height, BMI is calculated thus:

$$BMI = body\ mass\ in\ kilograms/(height\ in\ meters)^2$$

An individual who is 1.76 m (5 ft, 9 in) and weighs 72 kg (158 lb) has a BMI of $72/(1.76)^2 = 23.2$. The normal range is between 18.5 kg/m² and 25.0 kg/m². Individuals with a BMI higher than 25 kg/m² are classified as "overweight," and individuals with a BMI higher than 30 kg/m² are classified as obese.

Table 11.1 Various Techniques to Measure Body Composition

Method	Description
Anthropometry	Measurements of body segment girths to predict body fat
Skinfold thickness	Measurement of subcutaneous fat with a calliper that gives an estimation of lean-body mass and fat mass
Hydrostatic weighing (underwater weighing or hydrodensitometry)	Underwater weighing based on Archimedes' principle to estimate lean-body mass and fat mass
Air displacement plethysmography (BOD POD)	Measurement of air displacement to estimate lean-body mass and fat mass
Bioelectrical impedance analysis (BIA)	Measurement of resistance to an electrical current to estimate total-body water, lean-body mass, and fat mass
Computed tomography (CT)	Computer-assisted X-ray scan to image body tissues and measure bone mass
Duel energy x-ray absorptiometry (DEXA or DXA)	X-ray scan at two intensities to measure total-body water, lean-body mass, fat mass, and bone-mineral density

Even with this formula, the bodybuilder would be classified as overweight or even obese as the equation does not take into account body composition (BMI = $100/(1.80)^2$ = 30.9). Two individuals might have the same BMI but completely different body composition. One could achieve his body weight with mainly muscle mass as a result of hard training, whereas the other could achieve his body weight by fat deposition as a result of a sedentary lifestyle. Without information about body composition, they both might be classified as obese. In children and the elderly, the BMI is very difficult to interpret because the muscle and bone weights are changing in relationship to height.

The BMI, however, does provide useful information about risks for various diseases and is used in many epidemiological and clinical studies. For example, BMI correlates with the incidence of cardiovascular complications (hypertension and stroke), certain cancers, type II diabetes, gall stones, osteoarthritis, and renal disease (Calleet al. 1999).

Densitometry

Several techniques of **densitometry** have been developed to measure body composition and to distinguish between the most important components: carbohydrate (typically <1% of body mass), minerals (~4%), fat (~15%), protein (~20%), and water (~60%). Each of these components has a different density. Density is mass divided by volume and is usually expressed in grams per cubic centimeter (g/cm^3). The density of bone for instance is 1.3 g/cm^3 to 1.4 g/cm^3, the density of fat is 0.9 g/cm^3 and the density for fat-free (lean) tissue is 1.1 g/cm^3. A lower total-body density value represents a higher fat mass.

The Greek inventor Archimedes (287 b.c.–212 b.c) discovered a fundamental principle to assess human body composition. King Heron II of Syracuse had commissioned a goldsmith to make a crown of pure gold. When the goldsmith delivered the crown, the King noticed that the color of the gold was slightly lighter. Suspecting that some of the gold had been replaced with silver, the King asked Archimedes to invent a way to measure the gold content of the crown without melting it down. Archimedes thought very hard about this problem for several weeks. Then, stepping into a bath filled to the top with water and watching the overflow, he realized he had found a way to measure the density of an object. Archimedes jumped from the bath and ran naked through the streets, shouting his famous words "Eureka, Eureka!" Archimedes had found a way to solve the mystery of the King's crown. He reasoned that a substance must have a volume proportional to its mass, and measuring the volume of an irregularly shaped object would require submersion in water and collecting the overflow. He found that pure gold with the same mass as the crown displaced less water than the crown and that silver displaced more water (see figure 11.2). He concluded that the crown was made of a mixture of gold and silver and confirmed the king's suspicions.

Assume a 1,000-g crown that is an alloy of 70% gold and 30% silver. Because its volume is 64.6 cm³, it displaces 64.6 g of water (water has a density of 1.00 g/cm³). The crown's apparent mass in water is, thus, 1,000 g minus 64.6 g, or 935.4 g. The 1,000 g of pure gold has a volume of 51.8 cm³, and so its apparent mass in water is 1,000 minus 51.8 g, or 948.2 g. Thus, when both ends of the scale are immersed in water, there is an apparent mass of 935.4 g at one end and an apparent mass of 948.2 g at the other end, an imbal-

ance of 12.8 g. Scales from Archimedes' time could easily detect such an imbalance in mass.

The same principle can be used to distinguish between fat mass and fat-free mass in the human body (see figure 11.3). With this technique, called underwater weighing or hydrostatic weighing, a person is submerged in water and the body weight is accurately measured before and after submersion. Assume a 75-kg (165-lb) person is submerged in water and weighs 3 kg (6.6 lb) in water. According to the Archimedes' principle the loss of weight in water of 72 kg (158.4 lb) equals the weight of the displaced

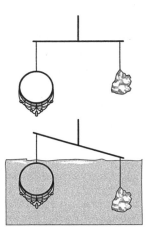

Figure 11.2 Archimedes' principle of determining the volume of an irregularly shaped object by submerging it in water and collecting the overflow. From this measurement and the weight of the object in air, the density (weight/volume) can be calculated.

water. The volume of the water displaced must be corrected for the temperature of the water at the time of weighing because the water density changes with temperature. The density is 1.00 g/cm³ at 4° C (39.2° F), but measurements are usually performed in warmer water temperatures. Without correction, the body density in our example would be 75,000/72,000 = 1.0417 g/cm³.

Siri (1956) developed a method to estimate the percentage of body fat from these measurements. The method assumes a density of 0.90 g/cm³ for the density of fat and 1.10 g/cm³ for the density of fat-free tissues. The equation for calculating the percentage body fat, often referred to as the Siri equation, is

$$\% \text{ body fat} = (495/\text{body density}) - 450$$

Using the same example of a 75-kg (165-lb) person, the percentage body fat is (495/1.0417)–450 = 25.2%. Fat mass (FM) can then be calculated as 25.2% × 75 kg = 18.9 kg and fat-free mass (FFM) is 75 kg – 18.9 kg = 56.1 kg.

Although, in general, this technique works very well and is often used as the gold standard, it has several limitations. The calculations are based on a two-compartment model (fat mass and fat-free mass). The composition of the fat-free mass can change considerably after weight training. In very muscular persons, the Siri equations will overestimate body fat and underestimate fat-free mass (Modlesky et al. 1996). A slightly modified equation may give more accurate results in this population:

$$\% \text{ body fat} = (521/\text{body density}) - 478$$

Measurements are usually made after the person has made a maximal exhalation and breath is held under water for 5 seconds to 10 seconds. This maximal exha-

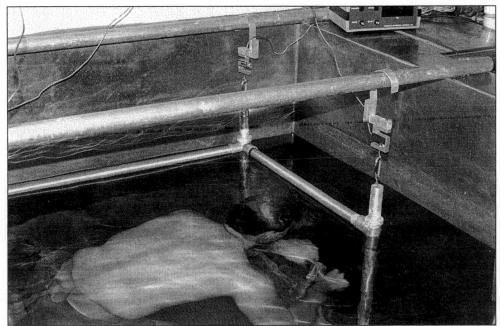

© Laura Gilkey

Figure 11.3 With the underwater, or hydrostatic, weighing technique, a person's body density is determined using Archimedes' principle.

lation is performed to reduce the air remaining in the lungs, which would otherwise exert a buoyant effect. However, even with a maximal exhalation, a residual volume remains in the lungs and, therefore, residual lung volume must be measured and corrected for. Failure to correct for residual lung volume underestimates whole-body density and, thus, overestimates fat mass. Food intake and, especially, the intake of carbonated beverages, can also affect the measurement and should be avoided in the hours before a measurement.

Skinfolds

The most frequently used technique to estimate body fat is measuring the thickness of skinfolds. These measurements are based on the interrelationships between the fat located underneath the skin (subcutaneous fat), internal fat, and whole-body density. Skinfolds can be measured using a calliper, which will usually indicate the thickness in millimeters (see figure 11.4). The skinfold should be taken and the measurement read within 2 seconds to avoid skinfold compression. Considerable experience is necessary to produce accurate skinfold measurements. When comparing skinfold thicknesses, measurements should always be taken by the same person to guarantee consistency.

Several anatomical sites can be used for skinfold measurements. The four most common sites are the biceps, triceps, subscapular, and abdominal. These sites are shown in figure 11.5. Sometimes other sites on the upper thigh and chest are used. Often the sum of 4 skinfolds is chosen, but other methods have taken the sum of 7 or even 10 skinfolds.

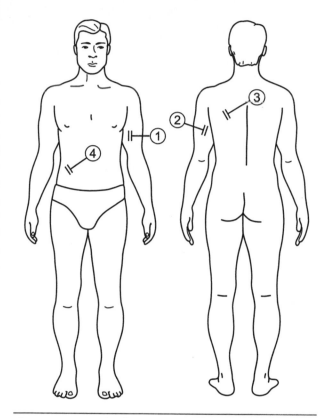

Figure 11.5 The four sites used for measuring skinfold thickness.

Adapted, by permission, from A.S. Jackson, and M.L. Pollock, 1978, "Generalized equations for predicting body density of men," *British Journal of Nutrition* 40(3): 497-504.

The sum of skinfolds can then be used to predict body density and, thence, body-fat percentage. This prediction is usually based on previous research in which the skinfold measurements were compared with the results of underwater weighing. Various experimenters have put forward equations that are used either with skinfold thickness alone or in conjunction with other measurements such as body circumference or limb lengths. Two of the most common sets of equations used are attributable to Durnin and Womersley (1974) (skinfolds alone) and to Jackson and Pollock (1978) (skinfolds and body measurements).

Once skinfold thickness has been measured using the sum of four skinfold measurements, body density can be calculated based on the equation and values

Table 11.2 Linear Regression Equations for the Calculation of Body Density

	17–19 y	20–29 y	30–39 y	40–49 y	50 y+
C	1.1620 (male)	1.1631 (male)	1.1422 (male)	1.1620 (male)	1.1715 (male)
	1.1549 (female)	1.1599 (female)	1.1423 (female)	1.1333 (female)	1.1339 (female)
M	0.0630 (male)	0.0632 (male)	0.0544 (male)	0.0700 (male)	0.0779 (male)
	0.0678 (female)	0.0717 (female)	0.0632 (female)	0.0612 (female)	0.0645 (female)

Body density = $C - [M(\log_{10}$ sum of all four skinfolds)]
From Durnin & Wormersley 1974.

shown in table 11.2 (Durnin and Womersley 1974). Read the appropriate values of C and M from the table, and solve the equation to determine body density (g/cm³) according to gender, age, and sum of the four skinfolds (in millimeters).

Percentage body fat is calculated using the Siri equation. For ease of reference, tables have also been generated for percentage body fat values for both males (see table 11.3) and females (see table 11.4)

across the whole age range based on the sum of 4 skinfold measurements, with the results shown for each 2-mm increment of skinfold thickness.

Measurements at three skinfold sites in the body (different ones for males and females as illustrated in figures 11.6 and 11.7, respectively) can also be used to estimate percentage body fat. When using three skinfold measurements, the body density equations of Jackson and Pollock are used:

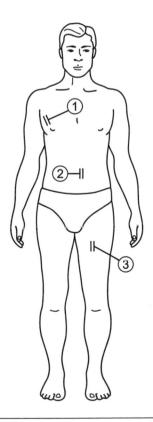

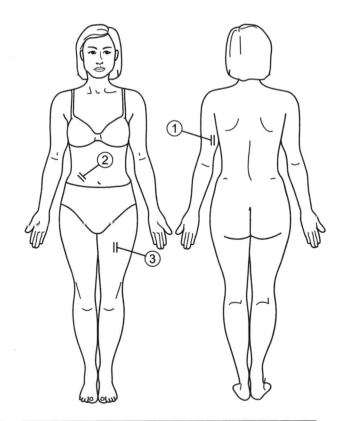

Figure 11.6 The three-site skinfold measuring system for male subjects.

Adapted, by permission, from A.S. Jackson, and M.L. Pollock, 1978, "Generalized equations for predicting body density of men," *British Journal of Nutrition* 40(3): 497-504.

Figure 11.7 The three-site skinfold measuring system for female subjects.

Adapted, by permission, from A.S. Jackson, and M.L. Pollock, 1978, "Generalized equations for predicting body density of men," *British Journal of Nutrition* 40(3): 497-504.

Table 11.3 Percentage Body Fat for Male Subjects According to Age and Skinfold Thickness

Skinfold thickness*	Age (years)				
	17–19	20–29	30–39	40–49	50+
10 mm	0.41	0.40	5.05	3.30	2.63
12 mm	2.46	2.1	6.86	5.61	5.20
14 mm	4.21	3.85	8.40	7.58	7.39
16 mm	5.74	5.38	9.74	9.31	9.31
18 mm	7.10	6.74	10.93	10.84	11.02
20 mm	8.32	7.96	12.00	12.22	12.55
22 mm	9.43	9.07	12.98	13.47	13.95
24 mm	10.45	10.09	13.87	14.62	15.23
26 mm	11.39	11.03	14.69	15.68	16.42
28 mm	12.26	11.91	15.46	16.67	17.53
30 mm	13.07	12.73	16.17	17.60	18.56
32 mm	13.84	13.49	16.84	18.47	19.53
34 mm	14.56	14.22	17.47	19.28	20.44
36 mm	15.25	14.90	18.07	20.06	21.31
38 mm	15.89	15.55	18.63	20.79	22.13
40 mm	16.51	16.17	19.17	21.49	22.92
42 mm	17.10	16.76	19.69	22.16	23.66
44 mm	17.66	17.32	20.18	22.80	24.38
46 mm	18.20	17.86	20.65	23.41	25.06
48 mm	18.71	18.37	21.10	24.00	25.72
50 mm	19.21	18.87	21.53	24.56	26.35
52 mm	19.69	19.35	21.95	25.10	26.96
54 mm	20.15	19.81	22.35	25.63	27.55
56 mm	20.59	20.26	20.73	26.13	28.11
58 mm	21.02	20.69	23.11	26.62	28.66
60 mm	21.44	21.11	23.47	27.09	29.20
62 mm	21.84	21.51	23.82	27.55	29.71
64 mm	22.23	21.90	24.16	28.00	30.21
66 mm	22.61	22.28	24.49	28.43	30.70
68 mm	22.98	22.65	24.81	28.85	31.17
70 mm	23.34	23.01	25.13	29.26	31.63
72 mm	23.69	23.36	25.43	29.66	32.07
74 mm	24.03	23.70	25.73	30.04	32.51
76 mm	24.36	24.03	26.01	30.42	32.93
78 mm	24.68	24.36	26.30	30.79	33.35
80 mm	25.00	24.67	26.57	31.15	33.75

*Sum of all four skinfolds.

Table 11.4 Percentage Body Fat for Female Subjects According to Age and Skinfold Thickness

Skinfold thickness*	Age (years)				
	17–19	20–29	30–39	40–49	50+
10 mm	5.34	4.88	8.72	11.71	12.88
12 mm	7.60	7.27	10.85	13.81	15.10
14 mm	9.53	9.30	12.68	15.59	16.99
16 mm	11.21	11.08	14.27	17.15	18.65
18 mm	12.71	12.66	15.68	18.54	20.11
20 mm	14.05	14.08	16.95	19.78	21.44
22 mm	15.28	15.38	18.10	20.92	22.64
24 mm	16.40	16.57	19.16	21.95	23.74
26 mm	17.44	17.67	20.14	22.91	24.76
28 mm	18.40	18.69	21.05	23.80	25.71
30 mm	19.30	19.64	21.90	24.64	26.59
32 mm	20.15	20.54	22.70	25.42	27.42
34 mm	20.95	21.39	23.45	26.16	28.21
36 mm	21.71	22.19	24.16	26.85	28.95
38 mm	22.42	22.95	24.84	27.51	29.65
40 mm	23.10	23.67	25.48	28.14	30.32
42 mm	23.76	24.36	26.09	28.74	30.96
44 mm	24.38	25.02	26.68	29.32	31.57
46 mm	24.97	25.65	27.24	29.87	32.15
48 mm	25.54	26.26	27.78	30.39	32.71
50 mm	26.09	26.84	28.30	30.90	33.25
52 mm	26.62	27.40	28.79	31.39	33.77
54 mm	27.13	27.94	29.27	31.86	34.27
56 mm	27.63	28.47	29.74	32.31	34.75
58 mm	28.10	28.97	30.19	32.75	35.22
60 mm	28.57	29.46	30.62	33.17	35.67
62 mm	29.01	29.94	31.04	33.58	36.11
64 mm	29.45	30.40	31.45	33.98	36.53
66 mm	29.87	30.84	31.84	34.37	36.95
68 mm	30.28	31.28	32.23	34.75	37.35
70 mm	30.67	31.70	32.60	35.11	37.74
72 mm	31.06	32.11	32.97	35.47	38.12
74 mm	31.44	32.51	33.32	35.82	38.49
76 mm	31.81	32.91	33.67	36.15	38.85
78 mm	32.17	33.29	34.00	36.48	39.20
80 mm	32.52	33.66	34.33	36.81	39.54

*Sum of all four skinfolds.

male body density = 1.0990750 − 0.0008209 (X2) + 0.0000026 (X2)² − 0.0002017 (X3) − 0.005675 (X4) + 0.018586 (X5)

where X2 = sum of the chest, abdomen, and thigh skinfolds in mm; X3 = age in years; X4 = waist circumference in cm; and X5 = forearm circumference in cm.

female body density = 1.1 470292 − 0.0009376 (X3) + 0.0000030 (X3)² − 0.0001156 (X4) − 0.0005839 (X5)

where X3 = sum of triceps, thigh, and suprailiac skinfolds, in mm; X4 = age in years; and X5 = gluteal circumference in cm.

Again, percentage body fat is then calculated using the Siri equation.

The correct tables must be used because the relationship between skinfold thickness and body fat may vary depending on gender, age, and ethnicity of the individual. Populations other than the population the equations were based on may result in large errors. Skinfold measurements, when properly taken, correlate very highly (r = 0.83 to 0.89) with hydrostatic weighing, with a standard error of only about 3% or 4%. This error should always be kept in mind when using tables or equations to convert skinfold thickness to a percentage body fat. Often sport scientists stay with the skinfold thickness measurement rather than convert it to a percentage body fat. This method is especially useful when repeated and regular measurements are made of the same athlete.

Bioelectrical Impedance Analysis

Bioelectrical impedance analysis (BIA) is based on the principle that different tissues and substances have a different impedance (resistance) to an electrical current. For example, impedance or conductivity is very different for fat tissue and water (see figure 11.8).

Electrodes are placed on different parts of the body, often the hand and foot, and if a current is applied to one of those electrodes, it can be measured at the other electrode. The less the measured resistance, the higher the body water content. Adipose tissue has a very high resistance, or impedance, whereas muscle—of which 75% is water—has a very low resistance. Based on these differential effects of applied electrical cur-

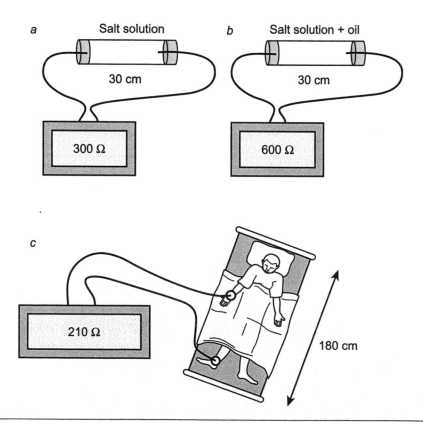

Figure 11.8 Bioelectrical impedance analysis (BIA). *(a)* If the resistance is measured to a known current in a tube with a salt solution and a known length (30 cm), the volume can be calculated. *(b)* If the same tube contains oil in addition to the salt solution, the resistance changes and a new calculation of volume is obtained. *(c)* The same principle can be applied to the human body, which can be viewed as 5 tubes (2 arms, 2 legs, and 1 trunk).

rent, BIA can be used to estimate percentage body fat, percentage lean-body mass, and percentage body water. Often BIA is used to measure body composition, but it can also be used to estimate fluid levels in different body segments.

A simple example of a device for measuring impedance is a tube containing a highly conductive salt solution and electrodes inserted at each end (see figure 11.8a). An electrical current is sent through one of the electrodes, and a resistance (Z) is measured between the two electrodes. If the length of the tube (L) and the specific resistivity (ρ) of the salt solution are known, the volume (V) can be calculated using the formula

$$V = \rho \times L^2/Z$$

If some of the salt solution is replaced with oil, the measured resistance increases and the new volume of the salt solution is calculated. By deduction the percentage of oil in the solution can be determined (see figure 11.8b). The principle is exactly the same when measuring body impedance and calculating body composition. For this purpose the measured body impedance and the subject's height are used.

Most BIA devices are tetrapolar, meaning they have 4 electrodes: 2 that apply the current and 2 that receive a signal. The device applies a current of 500 μA to 800 μA at a single frequency of 50 kHz or more, too weak to be felt by the subject.

The subject lies down on a nonconducting surface with arms not touching the trunk and legs at least 20 cm apart. Shoes and socks are removed, as well as metal objects (jewelry). The contact surfaces on the hand and ankle should be cleaned with alcohol. The resistance measured can then be used in various formulas in a similar manner to the tube examples. The body can be viewed as 5 tubes: 2 arms, 2 legs, and 1 trunk (see figure 11.8c).

The example of the tubes is an oversimplification. In reality, several factors can affect impedance and invalidate the assumptions. A larger tube increases the conductivity. Warming the tube also increases conductivity. Changes in the skin temperature, in particular, alter whole-body conductivity and have a profound effect on the measurement. A higher skin temperature results in an underestimate of the body fat content (Baumgartner et al. 1990). Often, when the measurements are performed, the subject may sweat more; a wet surface reduces impedance and underestimates body-fat content.

In humans, factors such as hydration status and distribution of water can also affect impedance. Even small changes in the hydration level can have a marked effect on the accuracy of the measurement and can influence the calculated body-fat content (Koulmann et

al. 2000; Saunders et al. 1998). If a person is dehydrated, the impedance decreases, whereas if someone drank a lot of fluid before the measurement, impedance could increase. Thus, losing body water through prior exercise or voluntary fluid restriction will overestimate body-fat content. Hyperhydration has the opposite effect and will underestimate body-fat content.

Body position is important, and the fluid shifts that occur can also affect impedance. The orientation of tissues can affect impedance. For example, a current is more easily transported along muscle fibers than against muscle fibers. The testing conditions under which BIA is run should be extremely well controlled. Usually subjects are advised as follows:

- Abstain from alcohol for 8 hours to 12 hours before the measurement.
- Avoid vigorous exercise for 8 hours to 12 hours before the measurement.
- Measurements are performed at least 2 hours after the last meal (or drink),
- Measurements are performed within 5 minutes of lying down.

BIA seems a convenient technique that needs considerable experience, expertise, and especially, control of the testing conditions. When BIA is performed in the best possible way, the results are very reliable but may not be as accurate as skinfold measurements (Broeder et al. 1997; Stolarczyk et al. 1997).

Dual Energy X-Ray Absorptiometry

Dual energy X-ray absorptiometry (DEXA or DXA) has become the clinical standard for measuring bone density. The principle is based on absorption of low-energy X-rays. The short duration of exposure gives only a minimal radiation dose.

During the measurement, the subject lies supine on a table and a source and detector probe pass across the body at relatively low speed (about 60 cm/min; a whole-body scan may take 15 minutes). The subject is exposed to these low-energy X-rays, and the loss of signal in various parts of the tissue are recorded. The measurement is performed at two different intensities, so that the instrument's software can distinguish not only between soft tissues and bone mineral content but also between lean-body mass and fat mass.

DEXA seems to be a fairly accurate technique that shows excellent agreement with other independent techniques to measure bone mineral content (Going et al. 1993: Heymsfield et al. 1990). Also, small changes in body composition can be detected with this method (Going et al. 1993).

However, DEXA may underestimate body-fat content somewhat compared with underwater weighing. In addition, with DEXA test conditions must be standardized (Kohrt 1995) because factors such as hydration status can influence the results (Elowsson et al. 1998). The software and hardware of the various commercially available DEXA scanners is different, which is also a source of error (Van Loan et al. 1995). Although DEXA has limitations, it appears to be one of the better ways to measure body composition, and it has the advantages over other methods in that it not only can distinguishes between lean-body mass and fat mass it also can assess bone density.

Computed Tomography

Computed tomography (CT) uses ionizing radiation via an X-ray beam to create images of body segments. The CT scan produces qualitative and quantitative information about the total area of the tissue investigated and the thickness and volume of tissues within an organ. With this method, fat surrounding a tissue as well as fat within a tissue can be measured.

Magnetic Resonance Imaging

With **magnetic resonance imaging** (MRI), pictures can be obtained from body tissues and compartments. The results are somewhat similar to those obtained by CT scan, but with MRI, electromagnetic radiation is used rather than ionizing radiation. Generally, MRI shows good agreement with other methods. A study found excellent agreement between MRI and underwater weighing estimates in both overweight and nonoverweight women, suggesting that MRI may be a satisfactory substitute for the more established methods of body-fat estimation in adult women. In fact, MRI showed the smallest day-to-day variation in the measurement within an individual (see figure 11.9). However, calculations of body fat from MRI scans are highly dependent on software, and this dependency can introduce an error.

Air Displacement Plethysmography

A relatively new and promising method to estimate whole-body volume is a small chamber in which air displacement is measured. The technique is called air displacement plethysmography and is marketed commercially as BOD POD (see figure 11.10). The advantage of this technique is that it is convenient for the subject because it takes place while the subject is sitting in a small chamber, measurements take only 3 minutes to 5 minutes, and the reproducibility is good.

The subject is first weighed accurately outside the BOD POD. He or she then sits in the 750 L volume

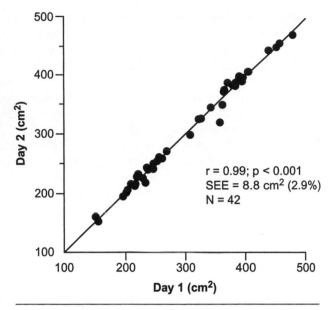

Figure 11.9 Comparison of typical in vivo magnetic resonance images obtained on 2 separate days from the same subject at the level of the midthigh. Regression between cross-sectional adipose tissue–free skeletal muscle (ATFSM) areas from 42 pairs of magnetic resonance images (6 subjects × 7 images each). SEE = SE of estimate; N = number of images. Solid line is regression line.

BOD POD, which consists of a dual chamber made out of fiberglass (see figure 11.10). The person's volume is the original volume in the chamber minus the air that has been displaced with the subject inside. The subject breathes into an air circuit to assess pulmonary gas volume, which, when subtracted from measured body volume, yields true body volume. Body density can then be calculated from body mass and body volume. Although this technique has good reproducibility, it generally gives lower percentages of body fat compared with hydrostatic weighing and DEXA (Collins et al. 1999; Wagner et al. 2000; Weyers et al. 2002).

Multicomponent Models

Multicomponent models use a combination of methods such as hydrostatic weighing, BIA, and DEXA to reduce the errors associated with using a single method (Wagner et al. 2000). While the traditional 2-component model is based on separating fat mass and FFM to determine body composition, these models assume that the density of fat-free mass is 1.1 g/cm^3 and the components that constitute the FFM (water, protein, and minerals) are constant for all individuals. These assumptions may not always hold true, and accuracy can, therefore, be improved by measuring these different components. These multicomponent models can combine measures of whole-body density with measures of body water and bone-mineral density. This approach is generally believed to give the most accurate results.

Normal Ranges of Body Weight and Body Fat

Body fat consists of essential body fat and storage fat. Essential body fat is present in the nerve tissues, bone marrow, and organs (all membranes), and we cannot lose this fat without compromising physiological function. Storage fat, on the other hand, represents an energy reserve that accumulates when excess energy is ingested and decreases when more energy is expended than consumed. Essential body fat is approximately 3% of body mass for men and 12% of body mass for women. Women are believed to have more essential body fat than men because of childbearing and hormonal functions. In general, the total body fat percentage (essential plus storage fat) is between 12% and 15% for young men and between 25% and 28% for young women (Lohman and Going 1993).

Different sports have different requirements in terms of body composition. In some contact sports such as American football or rugby, a higher body weight is generally seen as an advantage. In sports such as gymnastics, marathon running, and other weight-bearing activities, a lower body weight and high power-to-weight ratio are extremely important. Therefore, in these sports both low body fat and low body weight are necessary. In sports such as bodybuilding, increasing lean-body mass and increasing body weight without increasing body fat are desirable.

No accepted percentage body fat standards exist for athletes. The ideal body composition is highly dependent on the particular sport or discipline and should be discussed on an individual basis with the coach, physiologist, and nutritionist or dietician. Body weight and body composition should be discussed in relation to functional capacity and exercise performance.

Genetics

A significant portion of the variation in body-fat levels of individuals is genetically determined. Perhaps 25% to 40% of adiposity is the result of our genes (Bouchard 1994). Evidence from both genetic epidemiology and molecular epidemiology studies suggests that genetic factors determine the susceptibility to gaining or losing body fat in response to dietary energy intake (Perusse and Bouchard 2000). To study the influence of genetics on the effects of overfeeding, identical twins were investigated. In one study, monozygotic twins were submitted to an energy surplus of 4.2 kJ/day (1,000 kcal/day) 6 days a week for 100 days (Bouchard et al. 1990). The excess energy intake over the entire period was 353 MJ (84,000 kcal). The average gain in body mass was 8.1 kg, but considerable interindividual variation occurred. Interestingly, the variation between pairs was more than 3 times greater than the variation within pairs, suggesting an important genetic component. The variation between pairs was even greater for changes in abdominal visceral fat, indicating that the site of storage is also genetically determined.

Similarly, when identical twins completed a negative energy balance protocol by exercising over a period of 93 days without increasing energy intake, more variation occurred between pairs than within pairs. The energy deficit was estimated to be 244 MJ (58,000 kcal), and the mean body-weight loss was 5 kg. The range of weight loss, however, was 1.0 kg to 8.0 kg (see figure 11.11).

These classical early studies demonstrate a genetic factor in the development of obesity. This link has been confirmed by molecular epidemiology studies, and now more than 250 genes are believed to have the potential to influence body fatness (Rankinen et al. 2002).

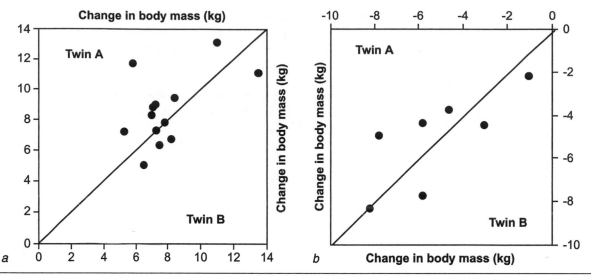

Figure 11.11 Changes in body mass in identical twins (a) after overfeeding and (b) after being subjected to a negative energy balance by exercise. Considerably more variation occurred between pairs than within pairs, strongly suggesting a genetic component in the regulation of body mass.

Adapted, by permission, from C. Bouchard et al., 1990, "The response to long-term over-feeding in identical twins," *New England Journal of Medicine* 322: 1477-1482.

Weight Loss

Many athletes, although not overweight, seek to lose body weight, particularly body fat. For some this weight loss is an advantage because it increases the power-to-weight ratio (jumping events). For others, weight loss means they can reduce the energy expenditure when competing (such as when running). Weight reduction is also common in weight-category sports in which athletes often compete well below their normal weight. Another reason why athletes want to get rid of some body fat is simply for physical appearance and to live up to the stereotype of the lean, toned, and strong athlete.

Weight loss is not always a good idea and can even be detrimental to performance. A reduction in body mass is usually accompanied by a reduction in muscle mass, and it may also reduce muscle glycogen stores. Excessive weight loss has also been associated with chronic fatigue and increased risk of injuries. Too much emphasis on losing weight can lead to the development of eating disorders, which are discussed in chapter 12. Many mistakes can be made in the weight management of the athlete, and the purpose of this chapter is to make the reader aware of some of these mistakes and to provide some guidelines on how to lose the weight in a responsible way.

Defining Goals

In conjunction with the coach and a nutritionist weight-loss goals should be established. These goals should be carefully thought out and well defined. Whether it is a good idea or not depends primarily on the current body-fat percentage. Although individual differences exist, a body-fat percentage less than 5% for men and 12% for women is not recommended. As discussed earlier, some fat is essential, and we can only lose some of the storage fat without affecting physiological function.

Goals also have to be defined with a time schedule in mind. How much weight must be lost and how soon? A realistic weight loss is about a 1 kg (2 lb) every 2 weeks, so to lose 3 kg at least 6 weeks are needed. This means reducing the energy intake by about 2,000 kJ (500 kcal) a day. A more rapid weight loss will make training difficult or impossible.

Energy and Substrate Balances

A negative energy balance is necessary to lose weight and it can be induced by reducing energy intake, by increasing energy expenditure, or by a combination of these two. However, these alterations in energy balance are just part of the picture. The macronutrient (carbohydrate, fat, and protein) intake and the expenditure of these substrates must also be considered. Excess intakes of carbohydrate and protein can be converted to fat, although this process requires energy and does not easily occur. The body increases the oxidation rate of carbohydrate and protein immediately when excess amounts are ingested. Fat, however, is different. Generally, fat is not converted into protein or carbohydrate.

Also, when excess amounts are ingested, the oxidation rates are not increased immediately, making fat more likely to be stored in adipose tissue (Abbott et al. 1988; Westerterp 1993).

The macronutrient composition of the diet, therefore, plays a very important role in the daily energy intake and expenditure (Westerterp et al. 1995), and to maintain body weight and body composition, individuals must not only be in energy balance but also be in carbohydrate, fat, and protein (and alcohol) balance. These substrate balances are influenced by a variety of genetic, environmental, cultural, and socioeconomic factors (Flatt 1995). For example, dietary intake is different in different socioeconomic classes, with the lower socioeconomic classes typically having a higher fat intake and lower carbohydrate intake than the higher socioeconomic classes. Also, clear cultural differences exist in diets as well as on acceptability of exercise. Some African countries, for example, have a very high carbohydrate intake (>70%), whereas the carbohydrate intake in the Western world is typically around 40% to 50%.

A simple example illustrates the importance of substrate balances. Someone who eats 50 g of sugar (e.g., by drinking half a liter of a soft drink) daily in addition to the normal diet is in positive energy balance by approximately 800 kJ/day (200 kcal/day). This level of intake means 292,000 kJ (73,000 kcal) a year, which over the course of 30 years amounts to 8,760 MJ (2,190,000 kcal). Assuming an energy density of adipose tissue of 19.0 kJ/g (7.7 kcal/g) this person should experience a weight gain of 284 kg (625 lb) in those 30 years. Clearly, this amount of weight gain is not reality, and this person would probably only gain a few kilograms.

The increased body weight results in an increased metabolic rate and an increased oxidation of energy substrates. Also, some of the energy ingested as carbohydrate is lost in the conversion to fat. Reducing dietary fat intake can be very effective for several reasons:

- Fat is very energy dense. It has more than twice the amount of energy as the same weight of carbohydrate or protein.
- High-fat foods generally taste good, which leads to a tendency to eat more. Studies show that increasing the fat content of the diet increases the spontaneous intake of food.
- Fat is efficiently stored and requires very little energy for digestion.
- Fat intake does not immediately increase fat oxidation.

Common Mistakes

When trying to lose weight, athletes make the following common mistakes:

- Trying to lose weight too rapidly. Like most people, athletes are impatient about weight loss. They want to see results within a couple of weeks, but unfortunately this expectation is not realistic. Although rapid weight loss is possible, this reduction is mostly dehydration, which reduces performance and the ability to train. Weight loss without performance loss has to occur slowly.
- Trying to lose weight during the on-season. Athletes often try to lose weight during the competitive season, and this effort may result in underperformance. Because hard training is difficult when the energy intake is reduced, weight loss best accomplished during the off-season.
- Not eating breakfast or lunch. Another weight-loss approach athletes have tried is skipping breakfast and sometimes also skipping lunch. Although this approach may work for some, it increases hunger feelings later in the day, and one very large evening meal, can easily compensate for the daytime reduction in food intake. Also, exercise capacity and, thus, the ability to train may be reduced without a breakfast, when liver glycogen stores may be low (see chapter 5).
- Too little carbohydrate intake. When losing body weight (being in negative energy balance), athletes risk also losing some muscle mass. However, this risk can partly be reduced by consuming relatively large amounts of carbohydrate. Carbohydrate has a protein-sparing effect.

Decreased Resting Energy Expenditure

Losing body weight becomes increasingly difficult because the body responds to the weight loss by becoming more efficient. Resting energy expenditure, or resting metabolic rate (RMR), decreases in response to weight loss (Dulloo and Jacquet 1998). This decrease in resting metabolism cannot simply be attributed to the decrease in body mass or fat-free mass. Rather, it is an autoregulatory feedback mechanism by which the body tries to preserve energy. This "food efficiency" may occur independently of a person's body mass or dieting history. It usually causes a plateau in weight loss and is a common source of frustration for dieters.

In an elegant study by Leibel et al. (1995), maintenance of a 10% reduced body weight was associated with a reduction in total energy expenditure of 25 kJ/kg FFM/day (6 kcal/kg FFM/day) in nonobese subjects (see figure 11.12). Resting energy expenditure and nonresting energy expenditure each decreased 13 kJ/kg FFM/day to 17 kJ/kg FFM/ day (3 kcal/kg FFM/day to 4 kcal/kg FFM/day). Maintenance of a 10% higher body weight was associated with an increase in total energy expenditure of 38 kJ/kg FFM/day (9 kcal/kg FFM/day). Maintenance of a reduced or elevated body weight is associated with compensatory changes in energy expenditure, which oppose the maintenance of a body weight that is different from the usual weight. This study shows that the body has compensatory mechanisms that try to maintain the normal body weight.

Female athletes, especially runners, sometimes have very low energy intakes. Despite their training load (30 km to 90 km of running a week), they may have energy intakes similar to their sedentary counterparts (Drinkwater et al. 1984; Myerson et al. 1991). Amenorrheic runners (those whose menstrual cycles are currently absent) had a significantly lower RMR than their eumenorrheic runners (those with normal monthly menstrual cycles), and their energy intake was similar, despite higher activity levels (Lebenstedt et al. 1999; Myerson et al. 1991). These findings suggest that energy efficiency or food efficiency exists. However, other reasons may account for the negative energy balance or low energy intake and expenditure in these female athletes. Not all studies of these athletes have found a reduced RMR (Beidleman et al.

1995; Wilmore et al. 1992). Alternative explanations could include inaccuracies and underreporting of food intake by these athletes or reduced physical activity in the hours they are not training.

The concept of food efficiency fits in with the theory that the body has a weight "set point." Although the interindividual differences in body weight of humans are very large, the body weight of an individual is usually fairly constant and typically varies only 0.5% over periods of 6 weeks to 10 weeks (350 g for an individual with a body mass of 70 kg). If rats are given an energy-restricted diet for several weeks, they lose body mass rapidly. However, upon being permitted to eat freely again, they restore this body mass within weeks and their weight becomes identical to their counterparts who had free access to food for the entire period. A similar change happens when rats are overfed. Evidence also exists for such a "set point" for body weight in humans (Keesey and Hirvonen 1997).

Weight Cycling: The Yo-Yo Effect

Often, weight loss is achieved with considerable effort but maintaining the new lower body weight is even more difficult. After the weight is lost, it is regained in a relatively short period of time. This effect is usually referred to as the yo-yo effect. Studies in animals have documented this pattern of **weight cycling.** After a period of food restriction and weight reduction, animals tend to regain the

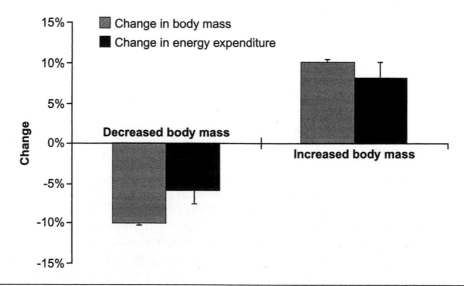

Figure 11.12 Changes in daily energy expenditure in response to weight loss or weight gain. A 10% reduction in body weight resulted in a 6% decrease in energy expenditure, and a 10% gain in body weight resulted in a 8% increase in energy expenditure. This shows that the body has compensatory mechanisms that try to maintain a normal body weight.

Adapted, by permission, from R.L. Leibel, M. Rosenbaum, and J. Hirsch, "Changes in energy expenditure resulting from altered body weight," *New England Journal of Medicine* 332(10): 621-628. Copyright © 1995 Massachusetts Medical Society. All rights reserved. Adapted with permission.

weight very quickly if they are allowed free access to food.

Several prospective studies have shown weight fluctuation (gain-loss or loss-gain) or weight variability to be associated with increased mortality, independent of the direction of weight change. However, when taking limited account of preexisting disease, studies show little evidence of negative side effects of weight cycling (Field et al. 1999; Wannamethee et al. 2002). From a public health perspective, the risks from overweight and obesity far exceed the potential risks of weight cycling.

Gender Differences in Weight Loss

Meta-analyses of studies on weight loss after aerobic-type exercise training showed that weight loss, although modest, was greater for males (Ballor and Keesey 1991). These findings confirm earlier research in males concerning exercise-training effects on body mass and body composition and extend them both to females and to a broader range of exercise types. These gender differences have been related to the differences in body-fat distribution. Women store more fat in the gluteal-femoral region, whereas men store more fat in the visceral (abdominal) depot. Fat located in the upper body and abdominal regions (central fat) is more metabolically active and, therefore, has higher rates of lipolysis in response to adrenergic stimulation. During exercise, FAs are preferentially mobilized from these regions (Wahrenberg et al. 1991). Also, postprandial fat storage may be higher in subcutaneous adipose tissue in women than in men. All of these differences may play a role in the variation in net regional fat storage between men and women (Blaak 2001) and women's greater resistance to weight loss.

Weight-Loss Methods

The various ways to lose body weight include pharmacological and surgical procedures (see figure 11.13), but here we focus on the weight-loss strategies that involve diet, exercise, or a combination of the two. Several different diets exist, some of which have been commercialized. Some diets have proved to be effective, whereas others are a list of erroneous assumptions and claims. For the athlete, distinguishing between the facts and the fallacies is often difficult. This section reviews some of the most common dietary regimens and weight-loss methods.

Energy Restriction and Reduced Fat Intake

Debate continues over whether weight loss can be achieved by reducing energy intake or by reducing fat intake only. Epidemiological evidence suggests that reducing the percentage of fat in the diet is more effective in reducing body weight than is reducing the absolute amount of fat (Sheppard et al. 1991). The most important factor, however, is the reduction in energy intake. Although both energy restriction and low-fat eating results in weight loss, energy restriction usually results in a larger reduction in energy intake than does ad libitum low-fat eating. Therefore, energy restriction may initially result in a larger weight loss, although studies show that both diets are effective over the long term (Jeffery et al. 1995; Schlundt et al. 1993).

The advantage of reduced fat intake is that relatively high carbohydrate content can be maintained, resulting in reasonable glycogen stores and better recovery. Many athletes adopt a diet that is low in fat with small reductions in the energy intake, so they can still replenish the carbohydrate stores. This type

Dietary methods

Fasting

Energy restriction

Low-fat diet

High-protein diet

High-carbohydrate diet

Low-carbohydrate ketogenic diet (Atkins diet, Sugarbusters)

Zone diet

Food-combining diet

Exercise

Regular exercise

Endurance exercise

Surgical procedures

Stomach stapling

Removal of a section of the small intestine

Liposuction

Pharmacological methods

Stimulants

Appetite suppressants

Drugs that reduce fat absorption

Figure 11.13 Methods to achieve weight loss.

of diet seems to be a sensible way of reducing weight, although suboptimal carbohydrate intake can still interfere with normal training. Thus, weight reduction should occur slowly and in the off-season.

Very-Low-Energy Diets

Very-low-energy diets (VLEDs) or very-low-calorie diets (VLCDs) diets are used as a therapy to achieve rapid weight loss in the obese. They are usually in the form of liquid meals that contain the recommended daily intakes of micronutrients but with only 1,600 kJ/day to 3,200 kJ/day (400 kcal/day to 800 kcal/day). These liquid meals contain a relatively large amount of protein to reduce muscle wasting and a relatively small amount of carbohydrate (less than 100 g/day). Such diets are very effective in reducing body weight rapidly. In the first week, the weight loss is predominantly glycogen and water. Fat and protein are lost as well during the initial phase, but these losses are a relatively small proportion of the total weight loss. After the initial rapid weight loss, the weight reduction is mainly from adipose tissue, with some losses of body protein. The increased fat oxidation results in ketosis (formation of ketone bodies, acetoacetate, and β-hydroxybutyrate). Ketone bodies have a very specific odor and can easily be detected on the breath (bad breath). Once ketosis is initiated, hunger feelings may be reduced somewhat.

Because carbohydrate intake is low, the blood glucose concentration is maintained by gluconeogenesis from various precursors (glycerol and alanine). Although increased physical activity is also encouraged when very-low-energy diets are prescribed to the obese, the diets are effective without the exercise component. Because of the associated chronic glycogen depletion, exercise capacity is severely impaired. For this reason, such diets are not advised for athletes, who would unlikely be able to complete their normal training sessions. Even in the off-season such diets are not advised, because the loss of body protein can be significant. Side effects of such diets include nausea, halitosis (bad breath), hunger (which may decrease after the initiation of ketosis), lightheadedness, and hypotension. Dehydration is also common with such diets, and electrolyte imbalances may occur.

Food-Combination Diets

Food-combination diets are based on a philosophy that certain foods should *not* be combined. Although a wide variety exists, most of these diets warn against the combination of protein and carbohydrate foods. Such combinations cause a "buildup of toxins" with "negative side effects such as weight gain." These diets are often very tempting because they promise an easy way to rapid weight loss, and these diets have worked for many individuals. When these diets are strictly followed, energy and fat intake are very likely to be reduced compared with the normal diet. The reduction in energy and fat is the reason for the success of the diet rather than the fact that certain foods were not combined. Because energy and carbohydrate intake are lower, glycogen stores are reduced, and performance as well as recovery may be impaired.

High-Protein Diets

Recommendations for increased protein consumption are among the most common approaches of popular or fad diets. Some have argued that high-protein diets suppress the appetite, which might be a mechanism for facilitated weight loss. Protein also has a larger thermic effect and a relatively low coefficient of digestibility compared with a mixed, equicaloric (isoenergetic) meal. In short-term studies, dietary protein modulates energy intake via the sensation of satiety and increases total-energy expenditure by increasing the thermic effect of feeding. Whereas these effects did not contribute to weight and fat loss in the studies in which energy intake was fixed, one ad libitum study suggests that a high-protein diet results in a greater decrease in energy intake and, therefore, greater weight and fat loss.

In terms of safety, little long-term information is available on the health effects of high-protein diets. The available data, however, indicates that consumption of protein greater than 2 times to 3 times the recommended intake contributes to urinary calcium loss and may, in the long term, predispose to bone mineral loss. Caution with these diets is recommended for individuals who may be predisposed to kidney disease and, particularly, individuals with diabetes mellitus.

The Zone Diet

The Zone diet was proposed by Barry Sears in his book, *The Zone: A Dietary Road Map* (Sears 1995). The diet opposes the traditional recommendations of a high-carbohydrate, low-fat diet for athletes. By reducing the carbohydrate intake, insulin responses are reduced and a favorable insulin to glucagon ratio is established. The benefits are increased lipolysis and improved regulation of eicosanoids, hormone-like derivatives of FAs in the body that act as cell-cell signaling molecules. The diet increases the "good" eicosanoids and decreases the "bad" eicosanoids. The "good" eicosanoids improve blood flow to the working muscle and enhance the delivery of oxygen and nutrients, eventually resulting in improved performance. To "enter the zone" the diet should consist of 40% carbohydrate, 30% fat, and 30% protein divided into a regimen of 3 meals and 2 snacks a day. The diet is also referred to as the 40:30:30 diet.

Although some arguments by Sears are scientifically sound, the book has problems, pitfalls, and errors in assumptions, and it also contains some contradictory information. Many of the promised benefits of the Zone diet are based on selective information about hormonal influences on eicosanoid metabolism. Opposing evidence is conveniently left out.

Eicosanoid metabolism is extremely complex and highly unpredictable, and previous diet manipulation studies have been unsuccessful in stimulating the synthesis of good eicosanoids relative to bad eicosanoids. Very small changes in insulin concentration are sufficient to reduce lipolysis significantly. Such effects persist for up to 6 hours after a meal. To avoid reductions in lipolysis after a meal, the carbohydrate intake must be extremely small, even less than proposed by the Zone diet. Meals with the 40:30:30 combination are very difficult to compose, unless you buy the 40:30:30 energy bars marketed by Sears.

Nevertheless, the Zone diet seems to work for some people, and anecdotal evidence indicates weight loss with the diet. The successes are expected because the Zone diet is essentially low in energy (4,000 kJ/day to 8,000 kJ/day [1,000 kcal/day to 2,000 kcal/day]). Even for athletes who train hard, the energy intake does not increase much and they are in a relatively large energy deficit.

The principle of vasodilating muscle arterioles by altering eicosanoid production is correct in theory. However, the little evidence available from human studies does not support any significant contribution of eicosanoids to active muscle vasodilation. In fact, the key eicosanoid reportedly produced in the Zone and responsible for improved muscle oxygenation is not found in skeletal muscle. Based on the best available scientific evidence, the Zone diet is more ergolytic than ergogenic to performance.

Low-Carbohydrate Diets

Some of the best-known low-carbohydrate ketogenic diets are the Atkins diet (Atkins 1992) and Sugarbusters (Andrews et al. 1998). These diets are based on the premise that reducing the carbohydrate intake results in increased fat oxidation. Ketone body production will increase, which may suppress appetite.

Ketones may also be present in urine, which could result in loss of "calories" via urine. Although all of the above may be true, the losses achieved in this diet are extremely small. The excretion of ketone bodies in urine is small and is at most 400 kJ/day to 600 kJ/day (100 kcal/day and 150 kcal/day). Such diets can be effective but not more effective than a well-balanced, energy-restricted diet. These low-carbohydrate diets are not recommended because of the relatively high fat content, which may raise blood lipids. For athletes, this diet is detrimental because of reduced glycogen stores and exercise capacity.

Exercise to Lose Weight

Exercise is another way to create a negative energy balance. In obese individuals, the effectiveness of exercise programs to achieve weight loss has been questioned because of problems with motivation, compliance with the program, and the fact that the ability to exercise is often impaired. In athletes, these factors are unlikely to be a problem. Most athletes can include exercise sessions with the specific aim of increasing energy expenditure, and they can exercise at a high enough intensity to significantly increase energy expenditure. However, athletes may have different problems. For example, coaches of athletes who compete in explosive events (e.g., sprints and jumps) are often reluctant to include aerobic exercise in their training programs. Athletes may have difficulty finding more time to exercise in addition to their normal training without compromising recovery.

Generally, however, adding exercise to a weight-loss program results in weight loss that is fat loss (Ballor and Keesey 1991; Kraemer et al. 1995; McMurray et al. 1985). The combination of exercise and diet is the most effective way to maintain a lower body weight after weight reduction. Some argue that the optimal exercise intensity is related to fat oxidation and should be the intensity with the highest fat-oxidation rates. As discussed in chapter 6, fat oxidation increases as exercise increases from low to moderate intensities, even though the percentage contribution of fat may actually decrease (see figure 6.8). The increased fat oxidation is a direct result of the increased energy expenditure when going from light-intensity to moderate-intensity exercise. At high exercise intensities (>75% $\dot{V}O_2max$), fat oxidation is inhibited, and both the relative rate and the absolute rate of fat oxidation decreases to negligible values (Achten et al. 2002). Maximal rates of fat oxidation are generally observed between 55% and 65% $\dot{V}O_2max$.

The type of exercise also affects maximal rates of fat oxidation and is significantly higher during uphill walking and running compared with cycling (Achten, Venables, Jeukendrup, et al. 2003; Arkinstall et al. 2001; Houmard et al. 1991; Nieman et al. 1998a, Nieman et al. 1998b; Snyder et al. 1993). No long-term studies have been conducted to compare different types of exercise and their effectiveness in achieving or maintaining weight loss. Also, whether exercises that optimize fat oxidation are indeed an effective way to reduce body fat remains to be determined.

Comparisons of resistance training with endurance training have demonstrated favorable effects on body composition (Broeder et al. 1997; Van Etten et al. 1994) or similar effects of resistance training compared with aerobic exercise in facilitating body-fat loss (Ballor and Keesey 1991). Resistance training seems more effective in preserving or increasing fat-free mass. In turn, the amount of metabolically active tissue also increases, and the increase is suggested to be one of the mechanisms by which exercise helps to maintain a lower body weight after weight loss through energy restriction. The exercise preserves (or even increases) muscle mass, resulting in a smaller reduction of the RMR.

Very few studies have compared the effectiveness of various types of exercise. From the current evidence, however, resistance training is at least as effective in reducing body fat as aerobic exercise. Most of the existing evidence is from studies in sedentary and obese individuals with almost no information about active individuals and trained athletes. One important factor is, of course, the duration of exercise, which largely determines the energy expended during exercise. Athletes who can spend more time exercising at relatively high exercise intensities likely have a greater opportunity to achieve a negative energy balance and, thus, lose body weight. Following are guidelines to help athletes achieve weight loss.

- Determine a realistic body-weight goal. The help of a sports dietician is likely to be needed to identify a realistic target weight.

- Do not try to lose more than about 0.5 kg/week (about 1 lb/week), and do not restrict energy intake by more than 500 kcal/day to 750 kcal/day.

- Eat more fruit and vegetables.

- Choose low-fat snacks.

- Study food labels and try to find substitutes for high-fat foods. Look not only at fat content but also at the energy content per serving.

- Limit fat add-ons such as sauces, sour cream, and high-fat salad dressings, or choose the low-fat versions of these products.

- Try to structure your eating into 5 or 6 smaller meals.

- Avoid eating very large meals.

- Make sure carbohydrate intake is high and consume carbohydrates immediately after training.

- A multivitamin and mineral supplement may be useful during periods of energy restriction. You should seek the advice of a nutritionist or dietician.

- Measure body weight daily and get measurements of body fat regularly (every 2 months). Keep a record of the changes

Making Weight and Rapid Weight-Loss Strategies

Sports in which making weight is important are those with weight categories, including judo, wrestling, rowing, and boxing. In horse racing, jockeys are weighed before and after competition to ensure that each horse will carry the precise assigned weight. In these sports, weight classes are clearly defined, and to compete in a particular weight class, body weight must be within the limits for that category at the weigh-in. Rowing, for instance, has a lightweight and a heavyweight division. In the lightweight division, male athletes are not permitted to exceed 72.5 kg (160 lb), with a crew average of 70 kg (155 lb). For females, the maximum individual weight is 59 kg (130 lb) with a crew average of 57 kg (125 lb). Weigh-ins can happen from 30 minutes to about 20 hours before competition, although sometimes the weigh-in is performed the day before the competition. Athletes commonly compete at a weight that is 2 kg to 6 kg (4 lb to 13 lb) below their normal weight, which implies that they must lose weight rapidly in the days or weeks before competition.

Most rapid weight loss is by dehydration, and athletes use various techniques to achieve it. The most common methods are energy or fluid restriction; dehydration by exercise, sauna, hotrooms, or steam rooms; diuretics, stimulants, and laxatives. Exercise is often performed in a hotroom, wearing plastic or rubber garments. This rapid weight loss mainly affects body water, glycogen content, and lean-body mass, with very little or no loss of body fat (Kelly et al. 1978; Oppliger et al. 1991). Wrestlers experience these weight-loss/weight-gain cycles about 7 to 15 times each year and approximately 100 times during a wrestling career (Tipton and Oppliger 1993).

The rapid weight loss may result in reductions in plasma volume, central blood volume, and blood flow to active tissues and increased core temperature and heart rate. The cardiovascular changes can be observed with a weight loss of approximately 2% of body weight (see chapter 8). These rapid weight-loss strategies have also been reported to alter hormone status, impede normal growth and development, affect psychological state, impair academic performance, and affect immune function. Severe dehydration can result in heat illness and even death.

In 1997, three previously healthy collegiate wrestlers in the United States died while each was engaged in a rapid weight-loss program to qualify for competition (Anonymous 1998). In the hours preceding the official weigh-in, all three wrestlers engaged in a similar rapid weight-loss regimen that promoted dehydration through perspiration and resulted in hyperthermia. The wrestlers restricted food and fluid intake and attempted to maximize sweat losses by wearing vapor-impermeable suits under cotton warm-up suits and exercising vigorously in hot environments. In response to these deaths, the National Collegiate Athletic Association (NCAA) rules were changed, and a wresting weight certification program was made mandatory to create a safer competitive environment (Davis et al. 2002). Other changes included establishing a weight class

system that better reflected the wrestling population, weigh-ins close to competition (1 hour before), weigh-ins for each day of a multiple-day tournament, and eliminating tools that are used for rapid dehydration (Davis et al. 2002). The current NCAA rules are now in line with the recommendations by the American College of Sports Medicine (ACSM) (Oppliger et al. 1996).

Weight gain is a concern for athletes in sports where a higher body weight and increased muscle mass are advantages, such as hammer throwing, discuss throwing, shotput, weightlifting, American football, and rugby. The key to gaining weight is to have a higher energy intake than energy expenditure. To increase lean-body mass rather than just fat mass, one must increase carbohydrate intake and not fat intake. Whereas the body counteracts a decrease in body weight that occurs with energy restriction by decreasing resting energy expenditure (see previous section), the body increases resting energy expenditure when the energy intake is increased in excess of the expenditure. Just as expecting large weight losses in a short period of time is unrealistic, so is expecting large weight gains within days. Realistic weight gains are between 0.2 kg/week and 1.0 kg/week (0.4 lb/week to 2 lb/week), depending on the increase in energy intake. Protein synthesis is a slow process, and even with intake of excess amounts of protein, synthesis of muscle protein takes a long time and only takes place if combined with an adequate training program. For more information on protein synthesis and gaining muscle mass, see chapter 7.

Key Points

■ Standard height-weight tables do not provide information about body composition and can be misleading when applied to individual athletes.

■ Body mass index (BMI) is often used as a rough measure of body composition. However, although BMI can be useful in epidemiological and clinical studies, it does not distinguish between muscle mass and fat mass.

■ The technique of densitometry is based on the "Archimedes principle" that the loss of weight in water is equal to the volume of the displaced water. Because body fat is less dense than water, it lets one float, whereas the fat-free mass, which is denser than water, makes one sink. After correcting for residual volume, percent fat can be calculated based on the underwater weight.

■ The sum of skinfolds can be used to estimate body fat percentage. For accuracy, values from tables that have been established for specific populations (e.g., same gender, same age range, or same ethnicity) must be used.

(continued)

(continued)

- Bioelectrical impedance analysis (BIA) is a convenient technique that needs considerable experience, expertise, and, especially, control of the environmental conditions to get reliable results. When BIA is performed in the best possible circumstances, the results may be reliable, but they may still be less accurate than skinfold measurements.

- Dual energy X-ray absorptiometry (DEXA or DXA) is based on the principle that compartments with different densities will absorb different amounts of low-energy X-rays. The advantage of DEXA is that it can distinguish not only fat mass and fat-free mass but also bone density. DEXA has become the clinical standard to measure bone density.

- Imaging technologies, such as computed tomography (CT) and magnetic resonance imaging (MRI) can visualize body fat of different parts of the body.

- An average body-fat percentage for young adults is between 12% and 15% for males and between 25% and 28% for females. Approximately 3% of body mass of males and 12% of body mass of females is essential body fat.

- A negative energy balance is required to lose weight. In addition, a negative fat balance will promote fat loss. However, the resting metabolic rate (RMR) decreases in response to weight loss. This effect is referred to as "food efficiency" and makes losing weight more difficult. A common problem is the so-called yo-yo effect, or weight cycling. After weight loss is achieved, the weight is often regained in a relatively short period of time.

- Common diet strategies to lose weight include a very-low-energy diet (VLED), low carbohydrate diets, food-combination diets, and high-protein diets. For athletes seeking to lose weight, energy restriction and reduced fat intake are recommended. This strategy allows a reasonable carbohydrate intake, enabling the athletes to perform high-intensity training without major reductions in lean-body mass (LBM).

- Exercise can help to create a negative energy balance, can help to maintain muscle mass, and may compensate for the reductions in RMR seen after weight loss.

- In weight-category sports such as judo, wrestling, rowing, and boxing, the need to "make weight" encourages athletes to try to lose weight in a relatively short period of time. Athletes should be aware of the risks of rapid weight loss. Rapid weight loss (mainly dehydration) can affect both health and performance.

- The recommended method to gain weight is maintaining a positive energy balance without increasing fat intake. Most of the excess energy intake should come from carbohydrate.

Key Terms

bioelectrical impedance analysis (BIA) 276

body mass index (BMI) 268

computed tomography 278

densitometry 269

dual energy X-ray absorptiometry 277

magnetic resonance imaging (MRI) 278

very-low-energy diets (VLED) 284

weight cycling 282

Recommended Readings

Bouchard, C. 1994. Genetics of obesity: Overview and research directions. In *The Genetics of Obesity*, ed. C. Bouchard, 223-233. CRC Press: Boca Raton, FL.

Bouchard, C., A. Tremblay, J.P. Despres, A. Nadeau, P.J. Lupien, G. Theriault, J. Dussault, S. Moorjani, S. Pinault, and G. Fournier. 1990. The response to long-term over-feeding in identical twins. *New England Journal of Medicine* 322:1477-1482.

Flatt, J.-P. 1995. Use and storage of carbohydrate and fat. *American Journal of Clinical Nutrition* 61:952S-959S.

Roche, A.F., S.B. Heymsfield, and T.G. Lohman. 1996. *Human Body Composition*. Human Kinetics: Champaign, IL.

....

Copyright Acknowledgements *(Sport Nutrition)*

Reprinted, with permission, from A. Jeukendrup and M. Gleeson, 2004, *Sport Nutrition: An Introduction to Energy Production and Performance,* (Champaign, IL: Human Kinetics), 101-196, 267-289.

With the exception of the following:

Figure 5.1: Reproduced with permission by Blackwell Publishing Ltd.; **Table 5.1:** Reprinted by permission from Wolters Kluwer Health; **Figure 5.4:** Reprinted by permission from Wolters Kluwer Health; **Figure 5.5:** Reprinted by permission from Wolters Kluwer Health; **Figure 5.7:** Reprinted by permission from Wolters Kluwer Health; **Figure 5.8:** Reprinted by permission from Wolters Kluwer Health; **Figure 5.9:** Reprinted by permission from Wolters Kluwer Health; **Figure 6.4:** Reproduced with permission by Blackwell Publishing Ltd.; **Figure 6.14:** Reproduced with permission by Blackwell Publishing Ltd.; **Figure 6.15:** Reproduced with permission by Blackwell Publishing Ltd.; **Table 7.1:** Adapted from D.E. Mathews, 1999. Proteins and amino acids. In *Modern Nutrition in Health and Disease*, ed. M.E. Shils, J.A. Olson, M.Shike, and A.C. Ross, 11-48. (Philadelphia: Lippincott Williams & Wilkins); **Figure 7.3:** Adapted from D.E. Mathews, 1998. Proteins and amino acids. In *Modern Nutrition in Health and Disease*, ed. M.E. Shils, J.A. Olson, M.Shike, and A.C. Ross, 11-48. (Philadelphia: Lippincott Williams & Wilkins); **Figure 7.4:** Adapted from D.E. Matthews, 1998. Proteins and amino acids. In *Modern Nutrition in Health and Disease*, edited by N.E. Shils, J.A. Olson, M. Shike, and A.C. Ross (Philadelphia: Lippincott Williams and Wilkins); **Figure 7.6:** Copyright Elsevier, 1975; **Figure 7.9:** Reproduced with permission by Blackwell Publishing Ltd.; **Figure 8.14:** With kind permission from Springer Science+Business Media: *European Journal of Applied Physiology*, "Metabolic and circulatory responses to the ingestion of glucose polymer and glucose/electrolyte solutions during exercise in man," 56(3), 1987, p. 356-362, R.J. Maughan. **Figure 8.20:** Reprinted by permission from Wolters Kluwer Health; **Figure 8.21:** Reprinted by permission from Wolters Kluwer Health; **Table 11.2:** Reprinted with the permission of Cambridge University Press; **Figure 11.5:** Reprinted with the permission of Cambridge University Press; **Figure 11.6:** Reprinted with the permission of Cambridge University Press; **Figure 11.7:** Reprinted with the permission of Cambridge University Press.

Dietary Reference Intakes (DRI)

The Dietary Reference Intakes (DRI) include two sets of values that serve as goals for nutrient intake—Recommended Dietary Allowances (RDA) and Adequate Intakes (AI). The RDA reflect the average daily amount of a nutrient considered adequate to meet the needs of most healthy people. If there is insufficient evidence to determine an RDA, an AI is set. AI are more tentative than RDA, but both may be used as goals for nutrient intakes. (Chapter 1 provides more details.)

In addition to the values that serve as goals for nutrient intakes (presented in the tables on these two pages), the DRI include a set of values called Tolerable Upper Intake Levels (UL). The UL represent the maximum amount of a nutrient that appears safe for most healthy people to consume on a regular basis. Turn the page for a listing of the UL for selected vitamins and minerals.

Estimated Energy Requirements (EER), Recommended Dietary Allowances (RDA), and Adequate Intakes (AI) for Water, Energy, and the Energy Nutrients

Age(yr)	Reference BMI (kg/m²)	Reference height, cm (in)	Reference weight, kg (lb)	Water[a] AI (L/day)	Energy EER[b] (kcal/day)	Carbohydrate RDA (g/day)	Total fiber AI (g/day)	Total fat AI (g/day)	Linoleic acid AI (g/day)	Linolenic acid[c] AI (g/day)	Protein RDA (g/day)[d]	Protein RDA (g/kg/day)
Males												
0–0.5	—	62 (24)	6 (13)	0.7[e]	570	60	—	31	4.4	0.5	9.1	1.52
0.5–1	—	71 (28)	9 (20)	0.8[f]	743	95	—	30	4.6	0.5	11	1.2
1–3[g]	—	86 (34)	12 (27)	1.3	1046	130	19	—	7	0.7	13	1.05
4–8[g]	15.3	115 (45)	20 (44)	1.7	1742	130	25	—	10	0.9	19	0.95
9–13	17.2	144 (57)	36 (79)	2.4	2279	130	31	—	12	1.2	34	0.95
14–18	20.5	174 (68)	61 (134)	3.3	3152[h]	130	38	—	16	1.6	52	0.85
19–30	22.5	177 (70)	70 (154)	3.7	3067[h]	130	38	—	17	1.6	56	0.8
31–50				3.7	3067[h]	130	38	—	17	1.6	56	0.8
>50				3.7	3067[h]	130	30	—	14	1.6	56	0.8
Females												
0–0.5	—	62 (24)	6 (13)	0.7[e]	520	60	—	31	4.4	0.5	9.1	1.52
0.5–1	—	71 (28)	9 (20)	0.8[f]	676	95	—	30	4.6	0.5	11	1.2
1–3[g]	—	86 (34)	12 (27)	1.3	992	130	19	—	7	0.7	13	1.05
4–8[g]	15.3	115 (45)	20 (44)	1.7	1642	130	25	—	10	0.9	19	0.95
9–13	17.4	144 (57)	37 (81)	2.1	2071	130	26	—	10	1.0	34	0.95
14–18	20.4	163 (64)	54 (119)	2.3	2368	130	26	—	11	1.1	46	0.85
19–30	21.5	163 (64)	57 (126)	2.7	2403[i]	130	25	—	12	1.1	46	0.8
31–50				2.7	2403[i]	130	25	—	12	1.1	46	0.8
>50				2.7	2403[i]	130	21	—	11	1.1	46	0.8
Pregnancy												
1st trimester				3.0	+0	175	28	—	13	1.4	+25	1.1
2nd trimester				3.0	+340	175	28	—	13	1.4	+25	1.1
3rd trimester				3.0	+452	175	28	—	13	1.4	+25	1.1
Lactation												
1st 6 months				3.8	+330	210	29	—	13	1.3	+25	1.3
2nd 6 months				3.8	+400	210	29	—	13	1.3	+25	1.3

NOTE: For all nutrients, values for infants are AI. Dashes indicate that values have not been determined.

[a] The water AI includes drinking water, water in beverages, and water in foods; in general, drinking water and other beverages contribute about 70 to 80 percent, and foods, the remainder. Conversion factors: 1 L = 33.8 fluid oz; 1 L = 1.06 qt; 1 cup = 8 fluid oz.

[b] The Estimated Energy Requirement (EER) represents the average dietary energy intake that will maintain energy balance in a healthy person of a given gender, age, weight, height, and physical activity level. The values listed are based on an "active" person at the reference height and weight and at the midpoint ages for each group until age 19. Chapter 8 and Appendix F provide equations and tables to determine estimated energy requirements.

[c] The linolenic acid referred to in this table and text is the omega-3 fatty acid known as alpha-linolenic acid.

[d] The values listed are based on reference body weights.

[e] Assumed to be from human milk.

[f] Assumed to be from human milk and complementary foods and beverages. This includes approximately 0.6 L (~3 cups) as total fluid including formula, juices, and drinking water.

[g] For energy, the age groups for young children are 1–2 years and 3–8 years.

[h] For males, subtract 10 kcalories per day for each year of age above 19.

[i] For females, subtract 7 kcalories per day for each year of age above 19.

SOURCE: Adapted from the *Dietary Reference Intakes* series, National Academies Press. Copyright 1997, 1998, 2000, 2001, 2002, 2004, 2005 by the National Academies of Sciences.

Recommended Dietary Allowances (RDA) and Adequate Intakes (AI) for Vitamins

Age (yr)	Thiamin RDA (mg/day)	Riboflavin RDA (mg/day)	Niacin RDA (mg/day)[a]	Biotin AI (µg/day)	Pantothenic acid AI (mg/day)	Vitamin B6 RDA (mg/day)	Folate RDA (µg/day)[b]	Vitamin B12 RDA (µg/day)	Choline AI (mg/day)	Vitamin C RDA (mg/day)	Vitamin A RDA (µg/day)[c]	Vitamin D AI (µg/day)[d]	Vitamin E RDA (mg/day)[e]	Vitamin K AI (µg/day)
Infants														
0–0.5	0.2	0.3	2	5	1.7	0.1	65	0.4	125	40	400	5	4	2.0
0.5–1	0.3	0.4	4	6	1.8	0.3	80	0.5	150	50	500	5	5	2.5
Children														
1–3	0.5	0.5	6	8	2	0.5	150	0.9	200	15	300	5	6	30
4–8	0.6	0.6	8	12	3	0.6	200	1.2	250	25	400	5	7	55
Males														
9–13	0.9	0.9	12	20	4	1.0	300	1.8	375	45	600	5	11	60
14–18	1.2	1.3	16	25	5	1.3	400	2.4	550	75	900	5	15	75
19–30	1.2	1.3	16	30	5	1.3	400	2.4	550	90	900	5	15	120
31–50	1.2	1.3	16	30	5	1.3	400	2.4	550	90	900	5	15	120
51–70	1.2	1.3	16	30	5	1.7	400	2.4	550	90	900	10	15	120
>70	1.2	1.3	16	30	5	1.7	400	2.4	550	90	900	15	15	120
Females														
9–13	0.9	0.9	12	20	4	1.0	300	1.8	375	45	600	5	11	60
14–18	1.0	1.0	14	25	5	1.2	400	2.4	400	65	700	5	15	75
19–30	1.1	1.1	14	30	5	1.3	400	2.4	425	75	700	5	15	90
31–50	1.1	1.1	14	30	5	1.3	400	2.4	425	75	700	5	15	90
51–70	1.1	1.1	14	30	5	1.5	400	2.4	425	75	700	10	15	90
>70	1.1	1.1	14	30	5	1.5	400	2.4	425	75	700	15	15	90
Pregnancy														
≤18	1.4	1.4	18	30	6	1.9	600	2.6	450	80	750	5	15	75
19–30	1.4	1.4	18	30	6	1.9	600	2.6	450	85	770	5	15	90
31–50	1.4	1.4	18	30	6	1.9	600	2.6	450	85	770	5	15	90
Lactation														
≤18	1.4	1.6	17	35	7	2.0	500	2.8	550	115	1200	5	19	75
19–30	1.4	1.6	17	35	7	2.0	500	2.8	550	120	1300	5	19	90
31–50	1.4	1.6	17	35	7	2.0	500	2.8	550	120	1300	5	19	90

NOTE: For all nutrients, values for infants are AI. The glossary on the inside back cover defines units of nutrient measure.

[a] Niacin recommendations are expressed as niacin equivalents (NE), except for recommendations for infants younger than 6 months, which are expressed as preformed niacin.
[b] Folate recommendations are expressed as dietary folate equivalents (DFE).
[c] Vitamin A recommendations are expressed as retinol activity equivalents (RAE).
[d] Vitamin D recommendations are expressed as cholecalciferol and assume an absence of adequate exposure to sunlight.
[e] Vitamin E recommendations are expressed as α-tocopherol.

Recommended Dietary Allowances (RDA) and Adequate Intakes (AI) for Minerals

Age (yr)	Sodium AI (mg/day)	Chloride AI (mg/day)	Potassium AI (mg/day)	Calcium AI (mg/day)	Phosphorus RDA (mg/day)	Magnesium RDA (mg/day)	Iron RDA (mg/day)	Zinc RDA (mg/day)	Iodine RDA (µg/day)	Selenium RDA (µg/day)	Copper RDA (µg/day)	Manganese AI (mg/day)	Fluoride AI (mg/day)	Chromium AI (µg/day)	Molybdenum RDA (µg/day)
Infants															
0–0.5	120	180	400	210	100	30	0.27	2	110	15	200	0.003	0.01	0.2	2
0.5–1	370	570	700	270	275	75	11	3	130	20	220	0.6	0.5	5.5	3
Children															
1–3	1000	1500	3000	500	460	80	7	3	90	20	340	1.2	0.7	11	17
4–8	1200	1900	3800	800	500	130	10	5	90	30	440	1.5	1.0	15	22
Males															
9–13	1500	2300	4500	1300	1250	240	8	8	120	40	700	1.9	2	25	34
14–18	1500	2300	4700	1300	1250	410	11	11	150	55	890	2.2	3	35	43
19–30	1500	2300	4700	1000	700	400	8	11	150	55	900	2.3	4	35	45
31–50	1500	2300	4700	1000	700	420	8	11	150	55	900	2.3	4	35	45
51–70	1300	2000	4700	1200	700	420	8	11	150	55	900	2.3	4	30	45
>70	1200	1800	4700	1200	700	420	8	11	150	55	900	2.3	4	30	45
Females															
9–13	1500	2300	4500	1300	1250	240	8	8	120	40	700	1.6	2	21	34
14–18	1500	2300	4700	1300	1250	360	15	9	150	55	890	1.6	3	24	43
19–30	1500	2300	4700	1000	700	310	18	8	150	55	900	1.8	3	25	45
31–50	1500	2300	4700	1000	700	320	18	8	150	55	900	1.8	3	25	45
51–70	1300	2000	4700	1200	700	320	8	8	150	55	900	1.8	3	20	45
>70	1200	1800	4700	1200	700	320	8	8	150	55	900	1.8	3	20	45
Pregnancy															
≤18	1500	2300	4700	1300	1250	400	27	12	220	60	1000	2.0	3	29	50
19–30	1500	2300	4700	1000	700	350	27	11	220	60	1000	2.0	3	30	50
31–50	1500	2300	4700	1000	700	360	27	11	220	60	1000	2.0	3	30	50
Lactation															
≤18	1500	2300	5100	1300	1250	360	10	13	290	70	1300	2.6	3	44	50
19–30	1500	2300	5100	1000	700	310	9	12	290	70	1300	2.6	3	45	50
31–50	1500	2300	5100	1000	700	320	9	12	290	70	1300	2.6	3	45	50

B

Tolerable Upper Intake Levels (UL) for Vitamins

Age (yr)	Niacin (mg/day)[a]	Vitamin B6 (mg/day)	Folate (µg/day)[a]	Choline (mg/day)	Vitamin C (mg/day)	Vitamin A (µg/day)[b]	Vitamin D (µg/day)	Vitamin E (mg/day)[c]
Infants								
0–0.5	—	—	—	—	—	600	25	—
0.5–1	—	—	—	—	—	600	25	—
Children								
1–3	10	30	300	1000	400	600	50	200
4–8	15	40	400	1000	650	900	50	300
9–13	20	60	600	2000	1200	1700	50	600
Adolescents								
14–18	30	80	800	3000	1800	2800	50	800
Adults								
19–70	35	100	1000	3500	2000	3000	50	1000
>70	35	100	1000	3500	2000	3000	50	1000
Pregnancy								
≤18	30	80	800	3000	1800	2800	50	800
19–50	35	100	1000	3500	2000	3000	50	1000
Lactation								
≤18	30	80	800	3000	1800	2800	50	800
19–50	35	100	1000	3500	2000	3000	50	1000

[a]The UL for niacin and folate apply to synthetic forms obtained from supplements, fortified foods, or a combination of the two.

[b]The UL for vitamin A applies to the preformed vitamin only.
[c]The UL for vitamin E applies to any form of supplemental α-tocopherol, fortified foods, or a combination of the two.

Tolerable Upper Intake Levels (UL) for Minerals

Age (yr)	Sodium (mg/day)	Chloride (mg/day)	Calcium (mg/day)	Phosphorus (mg/day)	Magnesium (mg/day)[d]	Iron (mg/day)	Zinc (mg/day)	Iodine (µg/day)	Selenium (µg/day)	Copper (µg/day)	Manganese (mg/day)	Fluoride (mg/day)	Molybdenum (µg/day)	Boron (mg/day)	Nickel (mg/day)	Vanadium (mg/day)
Infants																
0–0.5	—[e]	—[e]	—	—	—	40	4	—	45	—	—	0.7	—	—	—	—
0.5–1	—[e]	—[e]	—	—	—	40	5	—	60	—	—	0.9	—	—	—	—
Children																
1–3	1500	2300	2500	3000	65	40	7	200	90	1000	2	1.3	300	3	0.2	—
4–8	1900	2900	2500	3000	110	40	12	300	150	3000	3	2.2	600	6	0.3	—
9–13	2200	3400	2500	4000	350	40	23	600	280	5000	6	10	1100	11	0.6	—
Adolescents																
14–18	2300	3600	2500	4000	350	45	34	900	400	8000	9	10	1700	17	1.0	—
Adults																
19–70	2300	3600	2500	4000	350	45	40	1100	400	10,000	11	10	2000	20	1.0	1.8
>70	2300	3600	2500	3000	350	45	40	1100	400	10,000	11	10	2000	20	1.0	1.8
Pregnancy																
≤18	2300	3600	2500	3500	350	45	34	900	400	8000	9	10	1700	17	1.0	—
19–50	2300	3600	2500	3500	350	45	40	1100	400	10,000	11	10	2000	20	1.0	—
Lactation																
≤18	2300	3600	2500	4000	350	45	34	900	400	8000	9	10	1700	17	1.0	—
19–50	2300	3600	2500	4000	350	45	40	1100	400	10,000	11	10	2000	20	1.0	—

[d]The UL for magnesium applies to synthetic forms obtained from supplements or drugs only.
[e]Source of intake should be from human milk (or formula) and food only.

NOTE: An Upper Limit was not established for vitamins and minerals not listed and for those age groups listed with a dash (—) because of a lack of data, not because these nutrients are safe to consume at any level of intake. All nutrients can have adverse effects when intakes are excessive.

SOURCE: Adapted with permission from the *Dietary Reference Intakes* series, National Academy Press. Copyright 1997, 1998, 2000, 2001, 2002, 2005 by the National Academy of Sciences. Courtesy of the National Academy Press, Washington, D.C.

Appendixes

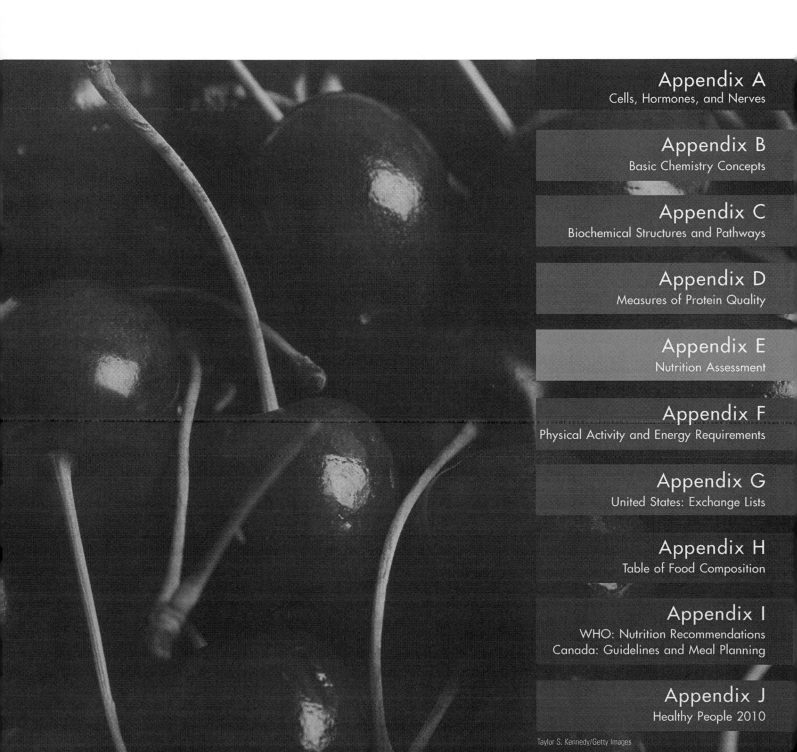

Appendix A
Cells, Hormones, and Nerves

Appendix B
Basic Chemistry Concepts

Appendix C
Biochemical Structures and Pathways

Appendix D
Measures of Protein Quality

Appendix E
Nutrition Assessment

Appendix F
Physical Activity and Energy Requirements

Appendix G
United States: Exchange Lists

Appendix H
Table of Food Composition

Appendix I
WHO: Nutrition Recommendations
Canada: Guidelines and Meal Planning

Appendix J
Healthy People 2010

Taylor S. Kennedy/Getty Images

CONTENTS

The Cell

The Hormones

The Nervous System

Putting It Together

A

GLOSSARY OF CELL STRUCTURES

cell: the basic structural unit of all living things.

cell membrane: the thin layer of tissue that surrounds the cell and encloses its contents; made primarily of lipid and protein.

chromosomes: a set of structures within the nucleus of every cell that contains the cell's genetic material, DNA, associated with other materials (primarily proteins).

cytoplasm (SIGH-toh-plazm): the cell contents, except for the nucleus.
- **cyto** = cell
- **plasm** = a form

cytosol: the fluid of cytoplasm; contains water, ions, nutrients, and enzymes.

endoplasmic reticulum (en-doh-PLAZ-mic reh-TIC-you-lum): a complex network of intracellular membranes. The **rough endoplasmic reticulum** is dotted with ribosomes, where protein synthesis takes place. The **smooth endoplasmic reticulum** bears no ribosomes.
- **endo** = inside
- **plasm** = the cytoplasm

Golgi (GOAL-gee) **apparatus:** a set of membranes within the cell where secretory materials are packaged for export.

lysosomes (LYE-so-zomes): cellular organelles; membrane-enclosed sacs of degradative enzymes.
- **lysis** = dissolution

mitochondria (my-toh-KON-dree-uh); singular **mitochondrion:** the cellular organelles responsible for producing ATP aerobically; made of membranes (lipid and protein) with enzymes mounted on them.
- **mitos** = thread (referring to their slender shape)
- **chondros** = cartilage (referring to their external appearance)

nucleus: a major membrane-enclosed body within every cell, which contains the cell's genetic material, DNA, embedded in chromosomes.
- **nucleus** = a kernel

organelles: subcellular structures such as ribosomes, mitochondria, and lysosomes.
- **organelle** = little organ

Cells, Hormones, and Nerves

This appendix is offered as an optional chapter for readers who want to enhance their understanding of how the body coordinates its activities. It presents a brief summary of the structure and function of the body's basic working unit (the cell) and of the body's two major regulatory systems (the hormonal system and the nervous system).

The Cell

The body's organs are made up of millions of cells and of materials produced by them. Each **cell** is specialized to perform its organ's functions, but all cells have common structures (see the accompanying glossary and Figure A-1). Every cell is contained within a **cell membrane.** The cell membrane assists in moving materials into and out of the cell, and some of its special proteins act as "pumps" (described in Chapter 6). Some features of cell membranes, such as microvilli (Chapter 3), permit cells to interact with other cells and with their environments in highly specific ways.

Inside the membrane lies the **cytoplasm,** which is filled with **cytosol,** or cell "fluid." The cytoplasm contains much more than just fluid, though. It is a highly organized system of fibers, tubes, membranes, particles, and subcellular **organelles** as complex as a city. These parts intercommunicate, manufacture and exchange materials, package and prepare materials for export, and maintain and repair themselves.

Within each cell is another membrane-enclosed body, the **nucleus.** Inside the nucleus are the **chromosomes,** which contain the genetic material, DNA. The DNA encodes all the instructions for carrying out the cell's activities. The role of DNA in coding for cell proteins is summarized in Figure 6-7 on p. 188. Chapter 6 also describes the variety of proteins produced by cells and the ways they perform the body's work.

Among the organelles within a cell are ribosomes, mitochondria, and lysosomes. Figure 6-7 briefly refers to the **ribosomes;** they assemble amino acids into proteins, following directions conveyed to them by RNA.

The **mitochondria** are made of intricately folded membranes that bear thousands of highly organized sets of enzymes on their inner and outer surfaces. Mitochondria are crucial to energy metabolism (described in Chapter 7) and muscles conditioned to work aerobically are packed with them. Their presence is implied whenever the TCA cycle and electron transport chain are mentioned because the mitochondria house the needed enzymes.*

The **lysosomes** are membranes that enclose degradative enzymes. When a cell needs to self-destruct or to digest materials in its surroundings, its lysosomes free their enzymes. Lysosomes are active when tissue repair or remodeling is taking place—for example, in cleaning up infections, healing wounds, shaping embryonic organs, and remodeling bones.

Besides these and other cellular organelles, the cell's cytoplasm contains a highly organized system of membranes, the **endoplasmic reticulum.** The ribosomes may either float free in the cytoplasm or be mounted on these membranes. A membranous surface dotted with ribosomes looks speckled under the microscope and is called "rough" endoplasmic reticulum; such a surface without ribosomes is called "smooth." Some intracellular membranes are organized into tubules that collect cellular materials, merge with the cell membrane, and discharge their contents to the outside of

---

*For the reactions of glycolysis, the TCA cycle, and the electron transport chain, see Chapter 7 and Appendix C. The reactions of glycolysis take place in the cytoplasm; the conversion of pyruvate to acetyl CoA takes place in the mitochondria, as do the TCA cycle and electron transport chain reactions. The mitochondria then release carbon dioxide, water, and ATP as their end products.

FIGURE A-1 The Structure of a Typical Cell

The cell shown might be one in a gland (such as the pancreas) that produces secretory products (enzymes) for export (to the intestine). The rough endoplasmic reticulum with its ribosomes produces the enzymes; the smooth reticulum conducts them to the Golgi region; the Golgi membranes merge with the cell membrane, where the enzymes can be released into the extracellular fluid.

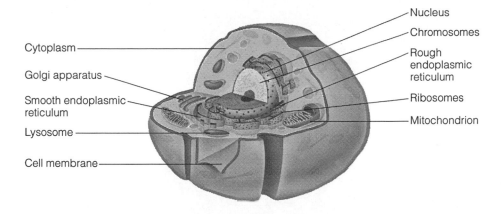

- Cytoplasm
- Golgi apparatus
- Smooth endoplasmic reticulum
- Lysosome
- Cell membrane
- Nucleus
- Chromosomes
- Rough endoplasmic reticulum
- Ribosomes
- Mitochondrion

◆ The study of hormones and their effects is **endocrinology.**

◆ The **pituitary gland** in the brain has two parts—the **anterior** (front) and the **posterior** (hind).

ribosomes (RYE-boh-zomes): protein-making organelles in cells; composed of RNA and protein.
- **ribo** = containing the sugar ribose (in RNA)
- **some** = body

the cell; these membrane systems are named the **Golgi apparatus,** after the scientist who first described them. The rough and smooth endoplasmic reticula and the Golgi apparatus are continuous with one another, so secretions produced deep in the interior of the cell can be efficiently transported to the outside and released. These and other cell structures enable cells to perform the multitudes of functions for which they are specialized.

The actions of cells are coordinated by both hormones and nerves, as the next sections show. Among the types of cellular organelles are receptors for the hormones delivering instructions that originate elsewhere in the body. Some hormones penetrate the cell and its nucleus and attach to receptors on chromosomes, where they activate certain genes to initiate, stop, speed up, or slow down synthesis of certain proteins as needed. Other hormones attach to receptors on the cell surface and transmit their messages from there. The hormones ◆ are described in the next section; the nerves, in the one following.

The Hormones

A chemical compound—a **hormone**—originates in a gland and travels in the bloodstream. The hormone flows everywhere in the body, but only its target organs respond to it, because only they possess the receptors to receive it.

The hormones, the glands they originate in, and their target organs and effects are described in this section. Many of the hormones you might be interested in are included, but only a few are discussed in detail. Figure A-2 (p. A-4) identifies the glands that produce the hormones, and the accompanying glossary defines the hormones discussed in this section.

Hormones of the Pituitary Gland and Hypothalamus

The anterior pituitary gland ◆ produces the following hormones, each of which acts on one or more target organs and elicits a characteristic response:

- **Adrenocorticotropin (ACTH)** acts on the adrenal cortex, promoting the production and release of its hormones.
- **Thyroid-stimulating hormone (TSH)** acts on the thyroid gland, promoting the production and release of thyroid hormones.
- **Growth hormone (GH)** or **somatotropin** acts on all tissues, promoting growth, fat breakdown, and the formation of antibodies.

GLOSSARY OF HORMONES

adrenocorticotropin (ad-REE-noh-KORE-tee-koh-TROP-in) or **ACTH**: a hormone, so named because it stimulates (trope) the adrenal cortex. The adrenal gland, like the pituitary, has two parts, in this case an outer portion (cortex) and an inner core (medulla). The release of ACTH is mediated by **corticotropin-releasing hormone (CRH).**

aldosterone: a hormone from the adrenal gland involved in blood pressure regulation.
- **aldo** = aldehyde

angiotensin: a hormone involved in blood pressure regulation that is activated by **renin** (REN-in), an enzyme from the kidneys.
- **angio** = blood vessels
- **tensin** = pressure
- **ren** = kidneys

antidiuretic hormone (ADH): the hormone that prevents water loss in urine (also called vasopressin).
- **anti** = against
- **di** = through
- **ure** = urine
- **vaso** = blood vessels
- **pressin** = pressure

calcitonin (KAL-see-TOH-nin): a hormone secreted by the thyroid gland that regulates (tones) calcium metabolism.

erythropoietin (eh-RITH-ro-POY-eh-tin): a hormone that stimulates red blood cell production.
- **erythro** = red (blood cell)
- **poiesis** = creating (like poetry)

estrogens: hormones responsible for the menstrual cycle and other female characteristics.
- **oestrus** = the egg-making cycle
- **gen** = gives rise to

◆ Hormones that are turned off by their own effects are said to be regulated by **negative feedback.**

---

follicle-stimulating hormone (FSH): a hormone that stimulates maturation of the ovarian follicles in females and the production of sperm in males. (The ovarian follicles are part of the female reproductive system where the eggs are produced.) The release of FSH is mediated by **follicle-stimulating hormone releasing hormone (FSH–RH).**

glucocorticoids: hormones from the adrenal cortex that affect the body's management of glucose.
• **gluco** = glucose
• **corticoid** = from the cortex

growth hormone (GH): a hormone secreted by the pituitary that regulates the cell division and protein synthesis needed for normal growth (also called **somatotropin**). The release of GH is mediated by **GH-releasing hormone (GHRH)** and **GH-inhibiting hormone (GHIH).**

hormone: a chemical messenger. Hormones are secreted by a variety of endocrine glands in response to altered conditions in the body. Each hormone travels to one or more specific target tissues or organs, where it elicits a specific response to maintain homeostasis.

luteinizing (LOO-tee-in-EYE-zing) hormone (LH): a hormone that stimulates ovulation and the development of the corpus luteum (the small tissue that develops from a ruptured ovarian follicle and secretes hormones); so called because the follicle turns yellow as it matures. In men, LH stimulates testosterone secretion. The release of LH is mediated by **luteinizing hormone–releasing hormone (LH–RH).**
• **lutein** = a yellow pigment

FIGURE A-2 The Endocrine System

These organs and glands release hormones that regulate body processes. An *endocrine gland* secretes its product directly into *(endo)* the blood; for example, the pancreas cells that produce insulin. An *exocrine gland* secretes its product(s) out *(exo)* to an epithelial surface either directly or through a duct; the sweat glands of the skin and the enzyme-producing glands of the pancreas are both examples. The pancreas is therefore both an endocrine and an exocrine gland.

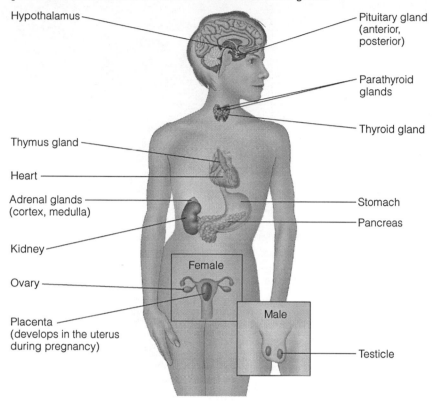

- **Follicle-stimulating hormone (FSH)** acts on the ovaries in the female, promoting their maturation, and on the testicles in the male, promoting sperm formation.

- **Luteinizing hormone (LH)** also acts on the ovaries, stimulating their maturation, the production and release of progesterone and estrogens, and ovulation; and on the testicles, promoting the production and release of testosterone.

- **Prolactin,** secreted in the female during pregnancy and lactation, acts on the mammary glands to stimulate their growth and the production of milk.

Each of these hormones has one or more signals that turn it on and another (or others) that turns it off. ◆ Among the controlling signals are several hormones from the hypothalamus:

- **Corticotropin-releasing hormone (CRH),** which promotes release of ACTH, is turned on by stress and turned off by ACTH when enough has been released.

- **TSH-releasing hormone (TRH),** which promotes release of TSH, is turned on by large meals or low body temperature.

- **GH-releasing hormone (GHRH),** which stimulates the release of growth hormone, is turned on by insulin.

- **GH-inhibiting hormone (GHIH** or **somatostatin),** which inhibits the release of GH and interferes with the release of TSH, is turned on by hypoglycemia and/or physical activity and is rapidly destroyed by body tissues so that it does not accumulate.

- **FSH/LH–releasing hormone (FSH/LH–RH)** is turned on in the female by nerve messages or low estrogen and in the male by low testosterone.
- **Prolactin-inhibiting hormone (PIH)** is turned on by high prolactin levels and off by estrogen, testosterone, and suckling (by way of nerve messages).

Let's examine some of these controls. PIH, for example, responds to high prolactin levels (remember, prolactin promotes milk production). High prolactin levels ensure that milk is made and—by calling forth PIH—ensure that prolactin levels don't get too high. But when the infant is suckling—and creating a demand for milk—PIH is not allowed to work (suckling turns off PIH). The consequence: prolactin remains high, and milk production continues. Demand from the infant thus directly adjusts the supply of milk. The need is met through the interaction of the nerves and hormones.

As another example, consider CRH. Stress, perceived in the brain and relayed to the hypothalamus, switches on CRH. On arriving at the pituitary, CRH switches on ACTH. Then ACTH acts on its target organ, the adrenal cortex, which responds by producing and releasing stress hormones. The stress hormones trigger a cascade of events involving every body cell and many other hormones.

The numerous steps required to set the stress response in motion make it possible for the body to fine-tune the response; control can be exerted at each step. These two examples illustrate what the body can do in response to two different stimuli—producing milk in response to an infant's need and gearing up for action in an emergency.

The posterior pituitary gland produces two hormones, each of which acts on one or more target cells and elicits a characteristic response:

- **Antidiuretic hormone (ADH),** or **vasopressin,** acts on the arteries, promoting their contraction, and on the kidneys, preventing water excretion. ADH is turned on whenever the blood volume is low, the blood pressure is low, or the salt concentration of the blood is high (see Chapter 12). It is turned off by the return of these conditions to normal.
- **Oxytocin** acts during late pregnancy on the uterus, inducing contractions, and during lactation on the mammary glands, causing milk ejection. Oxytocin is produced in response to reduced progesterone levels, suckling, or the stretching of the cervix.

Hormones That Regulate Energy Metabolism

Hormones produced by a number of different glands have effects on energy metabolism:

- Insulin from the pancreas beta cells is turned on by many stimuli, including raised blood glucose. It acts on cells to increase glucose and amino acid uptake into them and to promote the secretion of GHRH.
- Glucagon from the pancreas alpha cells responds to low blood glucose and acts on the liver to promote the breakdown of glycogen to glucose, the conversion of amino acids to glucose, and the release of glucose into the blood.
- Thyroxine from the thyroid gland responds to TSH and acts on many cells to increase their metabolic rate, growth, and heat production.
- Norepinephrine and epinephrine ◆ from the adrenal medulla respond to stimulation by sympathetic nerves and produce reactions in many cells that facilitate the body's readiness for fight or flight: increased heart activity, blood vessel constriction, breakdown of glycogen and glucose, raised blood glucose levels, and fat breakdown. Norepinephrine and epinephrine also influence the secretion of the many hormones from the hypothalamus that exert control on the body's other systems.
- Growth hormone (GH) from the anterior pituitary (already mentioned).
- **Glucocorticoids** from the adrenal cortex become active during times of stress and carbohydrate metabolism.

◆ Norepinephrine and epinephrine were formerly called **noradrenalin** and **adrenalin**, respectively.

oxytocin (OCK-see-TOH-sin): a hormone that stimulates the mammary glands to eject milk during lactation and the uterus to contract during childbirth.
- **oxy** = quick
- **tocin** = childbirth

progesterone: the hormone of gestation (pregnancy).
- **pro** = promoting
- **gest** = gestation (pregnancy)
- **sterone** = a steroid hormone

prolactin (proh-LAK-tin): a hormone so named because it promotes (pro) the production of milk (lacto). The release of prolactin is mediated by **prolactin-inhibiting hormone (PIH).**

relaxin: the hormone of late pregnancy.

somatostatin (GHIH): a hormone that inhibits the release of growth hormone; the opposite of **somatotropin (GH).**
- **somato** = body
- **stat** = keep the same
- **tropin** = make more

testosterone: a steroid hormone from the testicles, or testes. The steroids, as explained in Chapter 5, are chemically related to, and some are derived from, the lipid cholesterol.
- **sterone** = a steroid hormone

thyroid-stimulating hormone (TSH): a hormone secreted by the pituitary that stimulates the thyroid gland to secrete its hormones—thyroxine and triiodothyronine. The release of TSH is mediated by **TSH-releasing hormone (TRH).**

Every body part is affected by these hormones. Each different hormone has unique effects; and hormones that oppose each other are produced in carefully regulated amounts, so each can respond to the exact degree that is appropriate to the condition.

Hormones That Adjust Other Body Balances

Hormones are involved in moving calcium into and out of the body's storage deposits in the bones:

- **Calcitonin** from the thyroid gland acts on the bones, which respond by storing calcium from the bloodstream whenever blood calcium rises above the normal range. It also acts on the kidneys to increase excretion of both calcium and phosphorus in the urine. Calcitonin plays a major role in infants and young children, but is less active in adults.

- Parathyroid hormone (parathormone or PTH) from the parathyroid gland responds to the opposite condition—lowered blood calcium—and acts on three targets: the bones, which release stored calcium into the blood; the kidneys, which slow the excretion of calcium; and the intestine, which increases calcium absorption.

- Vitamin D from the skin and activated in the kidneys acts with parathyroid hormone and is essential for the absorption of calcium in the intestine.

Figure 12-12 on p. 417 diagrams the ways vitamin D and the hormones calcitonin and parathyroid hormone regulate calcium homeostasis.

Another hormone has effects on blood-making activity:

- **Erythropoietin** from the kidneys is responsive to oxygen depletion of the blood and to anemia. It acts on the bone marrow to stimulate the making of red blood cells.

Another hormone is special for pregnancy:

- **Relaxin** from the ovaries is secreted in response to the raised progesterone and estrogen levels of late pregnancy. This hormone acts on the cervix and pelvic ligaments to allow them to stretch so that they can accommodate the birth process without strain.

Other agents help regulate blood pressure:

- **Renin** (an enzyme), from the kidneys, in cooperation with **angiotensin** in the blood responds to a reduced blood supply experienced by the kidneys and acts in several ways to increase blood pressure. Renin and angiotensin also stimulate the adrenal cortex to secrete the hormone aldosterone.

- **Aldosterone,** a hormone from the adrenal cortex, targets the kidneys, which respond by reabsorbing sodium. The effect is to retain more water in the bloodstream—thus, again, raising the blood pressure. Figure 12-3 (on p. 403) in Chapter 12 provides more details.

The Gastrointestinal Hormones

Several hormones are produced in the stomach and intestines in response to the presence of food or the components of food:

- Gastrin from the stomach and duodenum stimulates the production and release of gastric acid and other digestive juices and the movement of the GI contents through the system.

- Cholecystokinin from the duodenum signals the gallbladder and pancreas to release their contents into the intestine to aid in digestion.

- Secretin from the duodenum calls forth acid-neutralizing bicarbonate from the pancreas into the intestine and slows the action of the stomach and its secretion of acid and digestive juices.

- Gastric-inhibitory peptide from the duodenum and jejunum inhibits the secretion of gastric acid and slows the process of digestion.

These hormones are defined and presented in more detail in Chapter 3.

The Sex Hormones

There are three major sex hormones:

- **Testosterone** from the testicles is released in response to LH (described earlier) and acts on all the tissues that are involved in male sexuality, promoting their development and maintenance.
- **Estrogens** from the ovaries are released in response to both FSH and LH and act similarly in females.
- **Progesterone** from the ovaries' corpus luteum and from the placenta acts on the uterus and mammary glands, preparing them for pregnancy and lactation.

This brief description of the hormones and their functions should suffice to provide an awareness of the enormous impact these compounds have on body processes. The other overall regulating agency is the nervous system.

The Nervous System

The nervous system has a central control system that can evaluate information about conditions within and outside the body, and a vast system of wiring that receives information and sends instructions. The control unit is the brain and spinal cord, called the **central nervous system;** and the vast complex of wiring between the center and the parts is the **peripheral nervous system.** The smooth functioning that results from the system's adjustments to changing conditions is homeostasis.

The nervous system has two general functions: it controls voluntary muscles in response to sensory stimuli from them, and it controls involuntary, internal muscles and glands in response to nerve-borne and chemical signals about their status. In fact, the nervous system is best understood as two systems that use the same or similar pathways to receive and transmit their messages. The **somatic nervous system** controls the voluntary muscles; the **autonomic nervous system** controls the internal organs.

When scientists were first studying the autonomic nervous system, they noticed that when something hurt one organ of the body, some of the other organs reacted as if in sympathy for the afflicted one. They therefore named the nerve network they were studying the sympathetic nervous system. The term is still used today to refer to that branch of the autonomic nervous system that responds to pain and stress. The other branch is called the parasympathetic nervous system. (Think of the sympathetic branch as the responder when homeostasis needs restoring and the parasympathetic branch as the commander of function during normal times.) Both systems transmit their messages through the brain and spinal cord. Nerves of the two branches travel side by side along the same pathways to transmit their messages, but they oppose each other's actions (see Figure A-3 on p. A-8).

An example will show how the sympathetic and parasympathetic nervous systems work to maintain homeostasis. When you go outside in cold weather, your skin's temperature receptors send "cold" messages to the spinal cord and brain. Your conscious mind may intervene at this point to tell you to zip your jacket, but let's say you have no jacket. Your sympathetic nervous system reacts to the external stressor, the cold. It signals your skin-surface capillaries to shut down so that your blood will circulate deeper in your tissues, where it will conserve heat. Your sympathetic nervous system also signals involuntary contractions of the small muscles just under the skin surface. The product of these muscle contractions is heat, and the visible result is goose bumps. If these measures do not raise your body temperature enough, then the sympathetic nerves signal your large muscle groups

GLOSSARY OF NERVOUS SYSTEM

autonomic nervous system: the division of the nervous system that controls the body's automatic responses. Its two branches are the **sympathetic** branch, which helps the body respond to stressors from the outside environment, and the **parasympathetic** branch, which regulates normal body activities between stressful times.
- **autonomos** = self-governing

central nervous system: the central part of the nervous system; the brain and spinal cord.

peripheral (puh-RIFF-er-ul) **nervous system:** the peripheral (outermost) part of the nervous system; the vast complex of wiring that extends from the central nervous system to the body's outermost areas. It contains both somatic and autonomic components.

somatic (so-MAT-ick) **nervous system:** the division of the nervous system that controls the voluntary muscles, as distinguished from the autonomic nervous system, which controls involuntary functions.
- **soma** = body

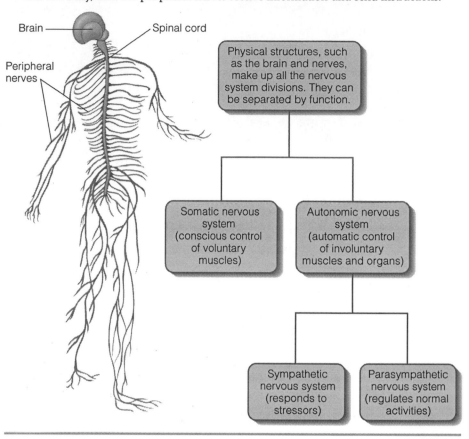

FIGURE A-3 The Organization of the Nervous System

The brain and spinal cord evaluate information about conditions within and outside the body, and the peripheral nerves receive information and send instructions.

Brain

Spinal cord

Peripheral nerves

Physical structures, such as the brain and nerves, make up all the nervous system divisions. They can be separated by function.

Somatic nervous system (conscious control of voluntary muscles)

Autonomic nervous system (automatic control of involuntary muscles and organs)

Sympathetic nervous system (responds to stressors)

Parasympathetic nervous system (regulates normal activities)

to shiver; the contractions of these large muscles produce still more heat. All of this activity helps to maintain your homeostasis (with respect to temperature) under conditions of external extremes (cold) that would throw it off balance. The cold was a stressor; the body's response was resistance.

Now let's say you come in and sit by a fire and drink hot cocoa. You are warm and no longer need all that sympathetic activity. At this point, your parasympathetic nerves take over; they signal your skin-surface capillaries to dilate again, your goose bumps to subside, and your muscles to relax. Your body is back to normal. This is recovery.

Putting It Together

The hormonal and nervous systems coordinate body functions by transmitting and receiving messages. The point-to-point messages of the nervous system travel through a central switchboard (the spinal cord and brain), whereas the messages of the hormonal system are broadcast over the airways (the bloodstream), and any organ with the appropriate receptors can pick them up. Nerve impulses travel faster than hormonal messages do—although both are remarkably swift. Whereas your brain's command to wiggle your toes reaches the toes within a fraction of a second and stops as quickly, a gland's message to alter a body condition may take several seconds or minutes to get started and may fade away equally slowly.

Together, the two systems possess every characteristic a superb communication network needs: varied speeds of transmission, along with private communication lines or public broadcasting systems, depending on the needs of the moment. The hormonal system, together with the nervous system, integrates the whole body's functioning so that all parts act smoothly together.

Biochemical Structures and Pathways

CONTENTS

Carbohydrates
Lipids
Protein: Amino Acids
Vitamins and Coenzymes
Glycolysis
Fatty Acid Oxidation
Amino Acid Degradation
The TCA Cycle
The Electron Transport Chain
Alcohol's Interference with Energy Metabolism
The Urea Cycle
Formation of Ketone Bodies

The diagrams of nutrients presented here are meant to enhance your understanding of the most important organic molecules in the human diet. Following the diagrams of nutrients are sections on the major metabolic pathways mentioned in Chapter 7—glycolysis, fatty acid oxidation, amino acid degradation, the TCA cycle, and the electron transport chain—and a description of how alcohol interferes with these pathways. Discussions of the urea cycle and the formation of ketone bodies complete the appendix.

Carbohydrates
Monosaccharides

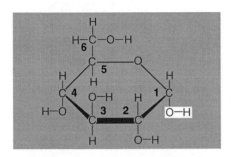

Glucose (alpha form). The ring would be at right angles to the plane of the paper. The bonds directed upward are above the plane; those directed downward are below the plane. This molecule is considered an alpha form because the OH on carbon 1 points downward.

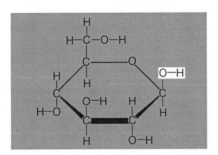

Glucose (beta form). The OH on carbon 1 points upward.
Fructose, galactose: see Chapter 4.

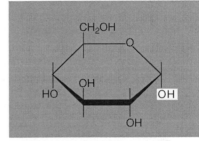

Glucose (alpha form) shorthand notation. This notation, in which the carbons in the ring and single hydrogens have been eliminated, will be used throughout this appendix.

Disaccharides

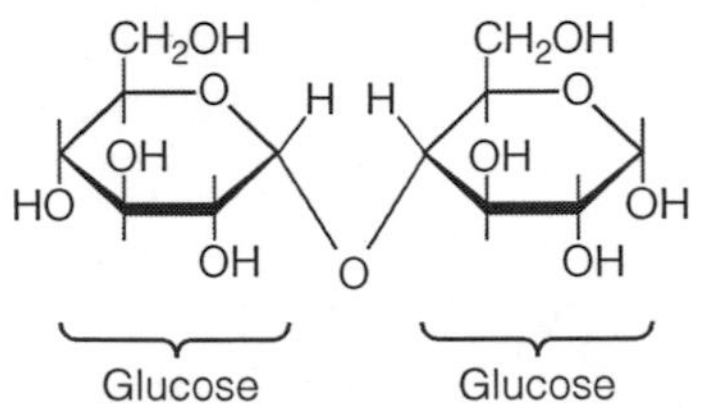

CH₂OH   CH₂OH
OH   OH
HO   OH
OH   OH
Glucose   Glucose

Maltose.

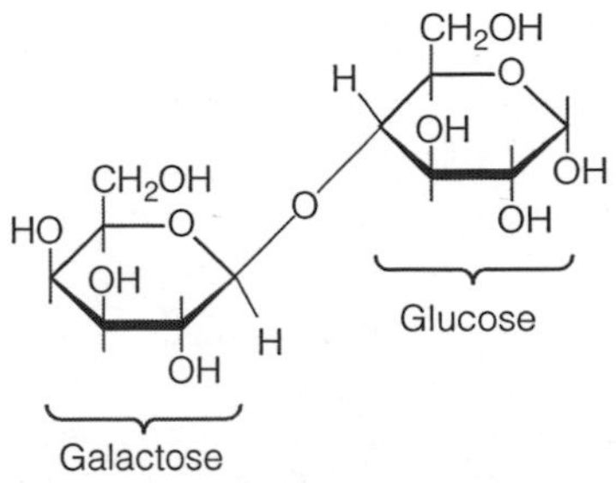

CH₂OH
OH
HO
CH₂OH
OH
Galactose
Glucose

Lactose (alpha form).

CH₂OH   CH₂OH
OH   HO
HO   CH₂OH
OH   OH
Glucose   Fructose

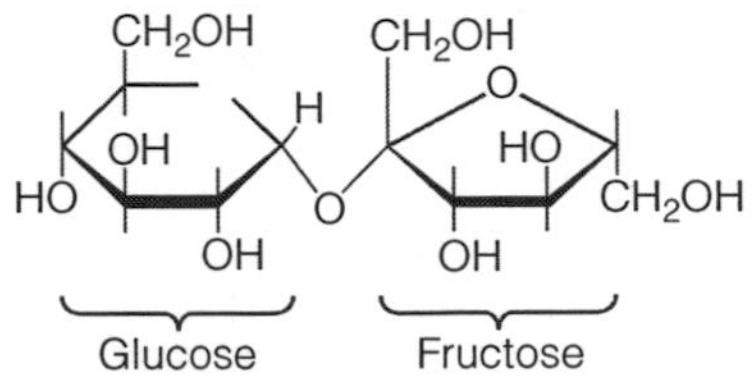

Sucrose.

Polysaccharides

As described in Chapter 4, starch, glycogen, and cellulose are all long chains of glucose molecules covalently linked together.

Amylose (unbranched starch)

Amylopectin (branched starch)

Starch. Two kinds of covalent linkages occur between glucose molecules in starch, giving rise to two kinds of chains. Amylose is composed of straight chains, with carbon 1 of one glucose linked to carbon 4 of the next (α-1,4 linkage). Amylopectin is made up of straight chains like amylose but has occasional branches arising where the carbon 6 of a glucose is also linked to the carbon 1 of another glucose (α-1,6 linkage).

Glycogen. The structure of glycogen is like amylopectin but with many more branches.

Cellulose. Like starch and glycogen, cellulose is also made of chains of glucose units, but there is an important difference: in cellulose, the OH on carbon 1 is in the beta position (see p. C-1). When carbon 1 of one glucose is linked to carbon 4 of the next, it forms a β-1,4 linkage, which cannot be broken by digestive enzymes in the human GI tract.

Fibers, such as hemicelluloses, consist of long chains of various monosaccharides.

Monosaccharides common in the backbone chain of hemicelluloses:

Xylose

Mannose

Galactose

*These structures are shown in the alpha form with the H on the carbon pointing upward and the OH pointing downward, but they may also appear in the beta form with the H pointing downward and the OH upward.

Monosaccharides common in the side chains of hemicelluloses:

Arabinose   Glucuronic acid   Galactose

Hemicelluloses. The most common hemicelluloses are composed of a backbone chain of xylose, mannose, and galactose, with branching side chains of arabinose, glucuronic acid, and galactose.

Lipids

TABLE C-1   Saturated Fatty Acids Found in Natural Fats

Saturated Fatty Acids	Chemical Formulas	Number of Carbons	Major Food Sources
Butyric	C_3H_7COOH	4	Butterfat
Caproic	$C_5H_{11}COOH$	6	Butterfat
Caprylic	$C_7H_{15}COOH$	8	Coconut oil
Capric	$C_9H_{19}COOH$	10	Palm oil
Lauric	$C_{11}H_{23}COOH$	12	Coconut oil, palm oil
Myristic[a]	$C_{13}H_{27}COOH$	14	Coconut oil, palm oil
Palmitic[a]	$C_{15}H_{31}COOH$	16	Palm oil
Stearic[a]	$C_{17}H_{35}COOH$	18	Most animal fats
Arachidic	$C_{19}H_{39}COOH$	20	Peanut oil
Behenic	$C_{21}H_{43}COOH$	22	Seeds
Lignoceric	$C_{23}H_{47}COOH$	24	Peanut oil

[a]Most common saturated fatty acids.

TABLE C-2   Unsaturated Fatty Acids Found in Natural Fats

Unsaturated Fatty Acids	Chemical Formulas	Number of Carbons	Number of Double Bonds	Standard Notation[a]	Omega Notation[b]	Major Food Sources
Palmitoleic	$C_{15}H_{29}COOH$	16	1	16:1;9	16:1ω7	Seafood, beef
Oleic	$C_{17}H_{33}COOH$	18	1	18:1;9	18:1ω9	Olive oil, canola oil
Linoleic	$C_{17}H_{31}COOH$	18	2	18:2;9,12	18:2ω6	Sunflower oil, safflower oil
Linolenic	$C_{17}H_{29}COOH$	18	3	18:3;9,12,15	18:3ω3	Soybean oil, canola oil
Arachidonic	$C_{19}H_{31}COOH$	20	4	20:4;5,8,11,14	20:4ω6	Eggs, most animal fats
Eicosapentaenoic	$C_{19}H_{29}COOH$	20	5	20:5;5,8,11,14,17	20:5ω3	Seafood
Docosahexaenoic	$C_{21}H_{31}COOH$	22	6	22:6;4,7,10,13,16,19	22:6ω3	Seafood

NOTE: A fatty acid has two ends; designated the methyl (CH_3) end and the carboxyl, or acid (COOH), end.
[a]Standard chemistry notation begins counting carbons at the acid end. The number of carbons the fatty acid contains comes first, followed by a colon and another number that indicates the number of double bonds; next comes a semicolon followed by a number or numbers indicating the positions of the double bonds. Thus the notation for linoleic acid, an 18-carbon fatty acid with two double bonds between carbons 9 and 10 and between carbons 12 and 13, is 18:2;9,12.
[b]Because fatty acid chains are lengthened by adding carbons at the acid end of the chain, chemists use the omega system of notation to ease the task of identifying them. The omega system begins counting carbons at the methyl end. The number of carbons the fatty acid contains comes first, followed by a colon and the number of double bonds; next come the omega symbol (ω) and a number indicating the position of the double bond nearest the methyl end. Thus linoleic acid with its first double bond at the sixth carbon from the methyl end would be noted 18:2ω6 in the omega system.

Protein: Amino Acids

The common amino acids may be classified into the seven groups listed on the next page. Amino acids marked with an asterisk (*) are essential.

Appendix C

1. Amino acids with aliphatic side chains, which consist of hydrogen and carbon atoms (hydrocarbons):

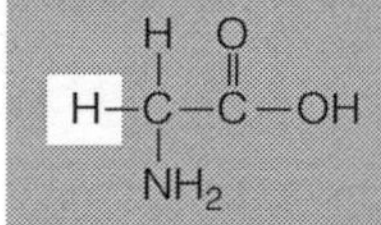

Glycine (Gly)

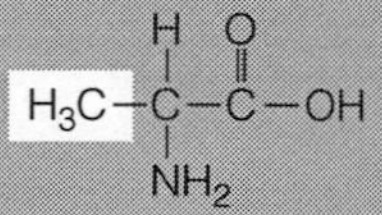

Alanine (Ala)

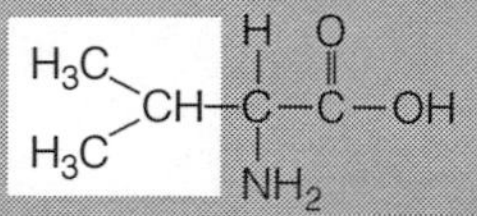

Valine* (Val)

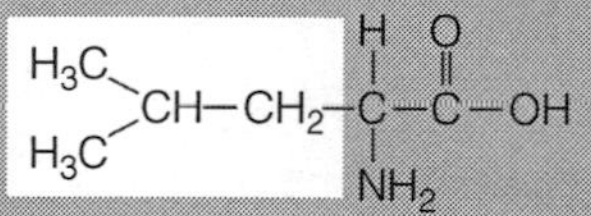

Leucine* (Leu)

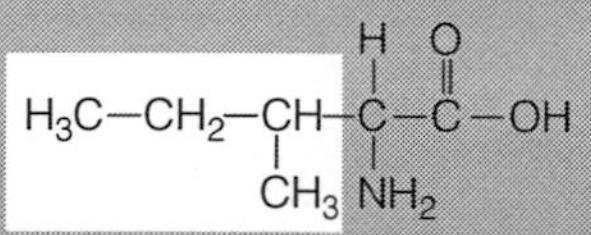

Isoleucine* (Ile)

2. Amino acids with hydroxyl (OH) side chains:

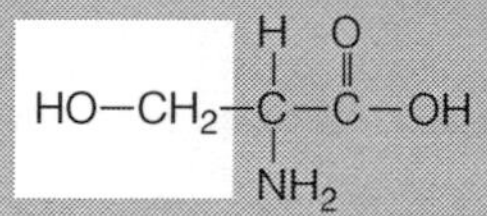

Serine (Ser)

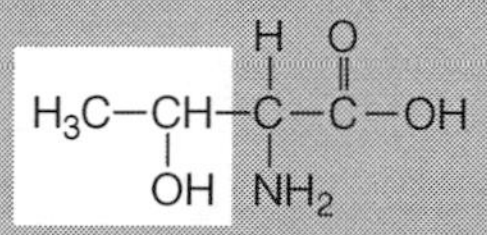

Threonine* (Thr)

3. Amino acids with side chains containing acidic groups or their amides, which contain the group NH_2:

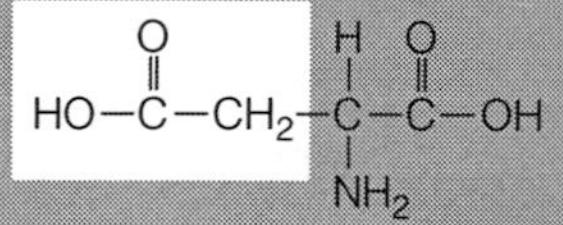

Aspartic acid (Asp)

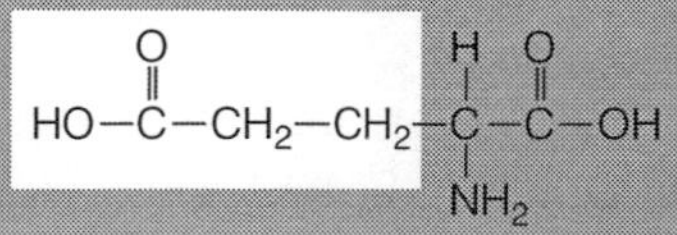

Glutamic acid (Glu)

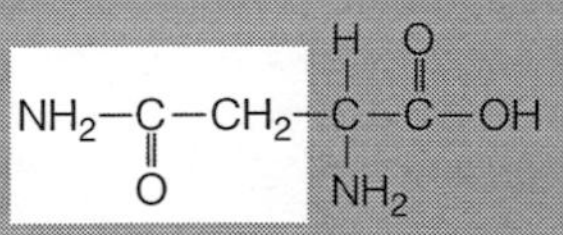

Asparagine (Asn)

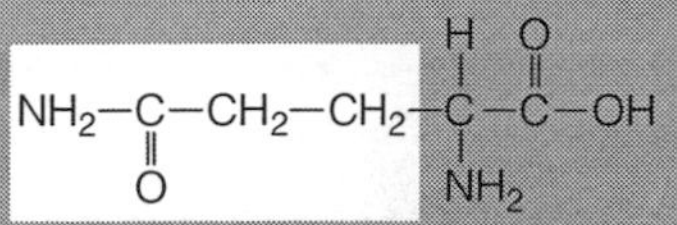

Glutamine (Gln)

4. Amino acids with basic side chains:

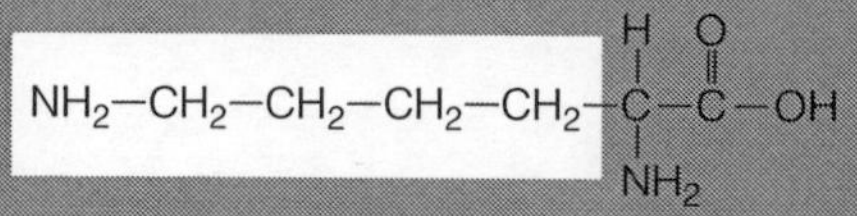

Lysine* (Lys)

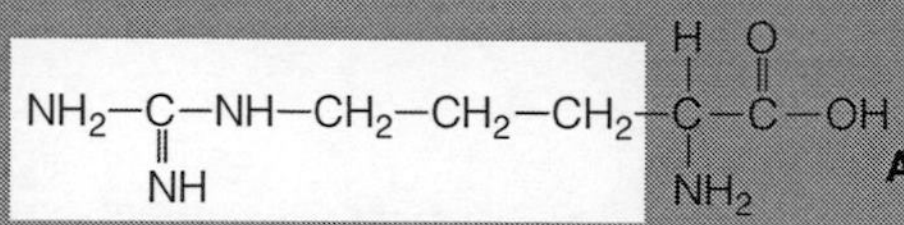

Arginine (Arg)

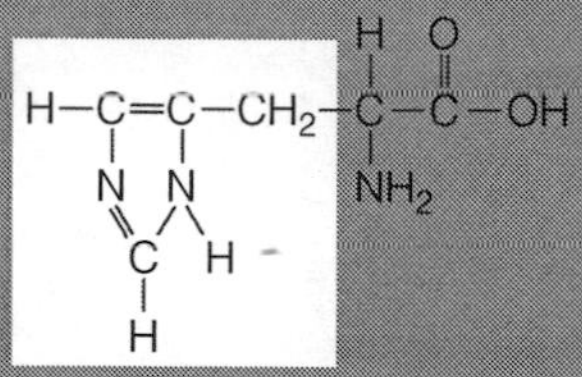

Histidine* (His)

5. Amino acids with aromatic side chains, which are characterized by the presence of at least one ring structure:

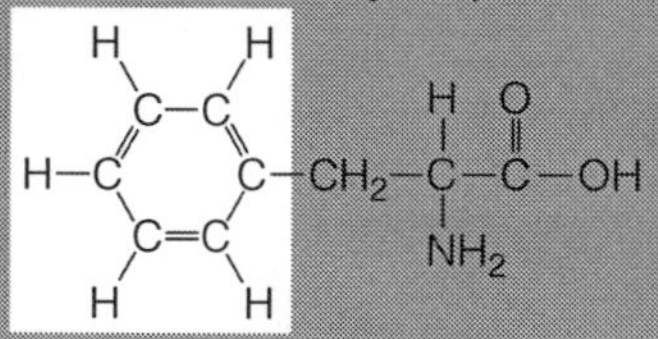

Phenylalanine* (Phe)

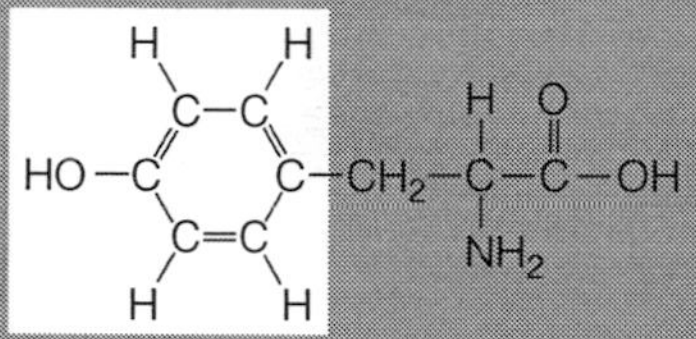

Tyrosine (Tyr)

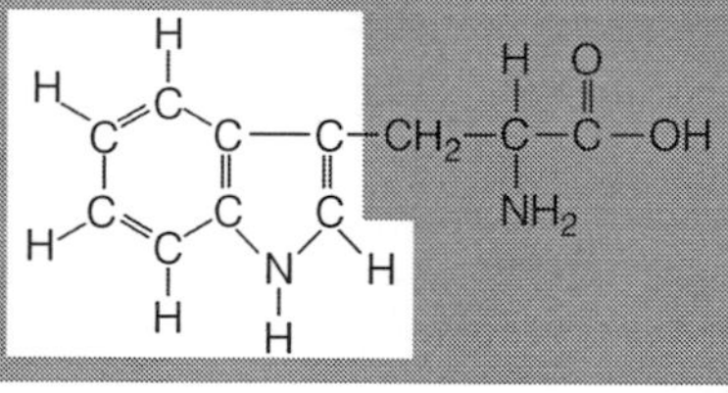

Tryptophan* (Trp)

6. Amino acids with side chains containing sulfur atoms:

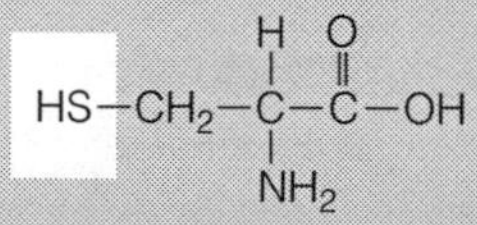

Cysteine (Cys)

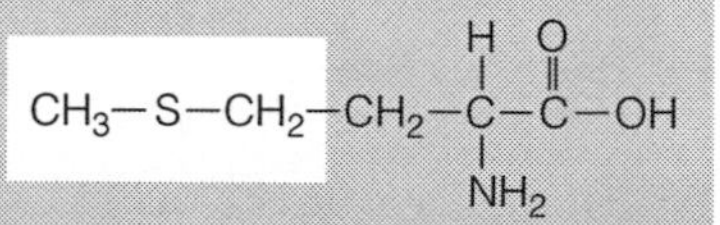

Methionine* (Met)

7. Imino acid:

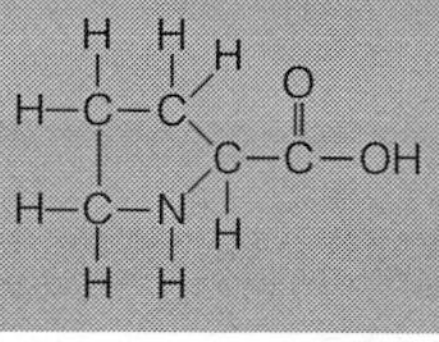

Proline (Pro)

Proline has the same chemical structure as the other amino acids, but its amino group has given up a hydrogen to form a ring.

Vitamins and Coenzymes

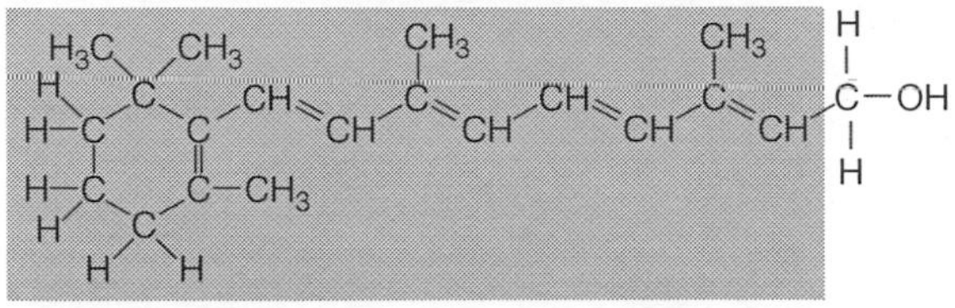

Vitamin A: retinol. This molecule is the alcohol form of vitamin A.

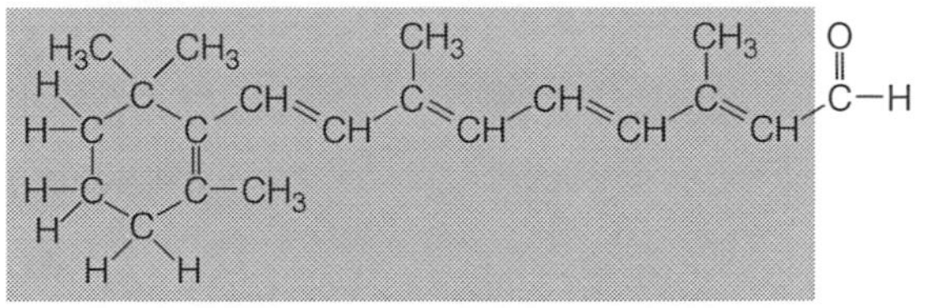

Vitamin A: retinal. This molecule is the aldehyde form of vitamin A.

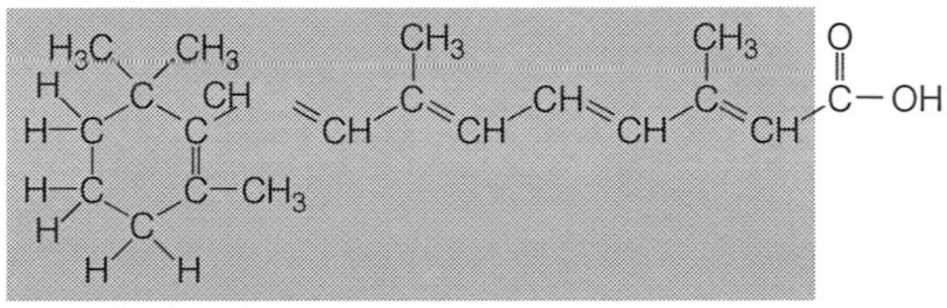

Vitamin A: retinoic acid. This molecule is the acid form of vitamin A.

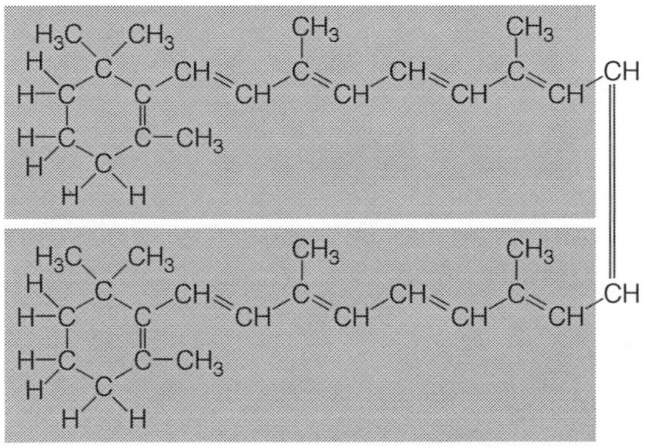

Vitamin A precursor: beta-carotene. This molecule is the carotenoid with the most vitamin A activity.

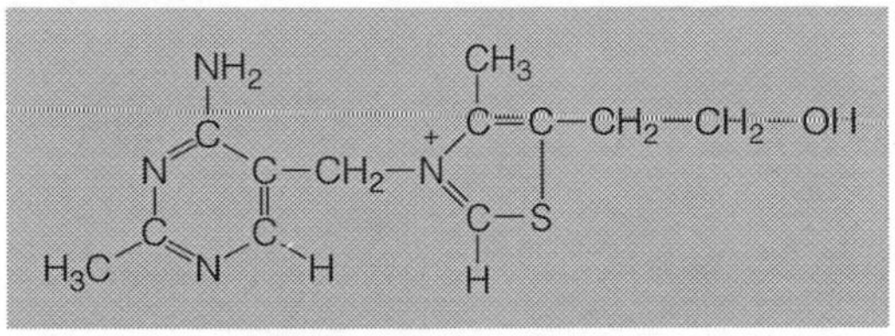

Thiamin. This molecule is part of the coenzyme thiamin pyrophosphate (TPP).

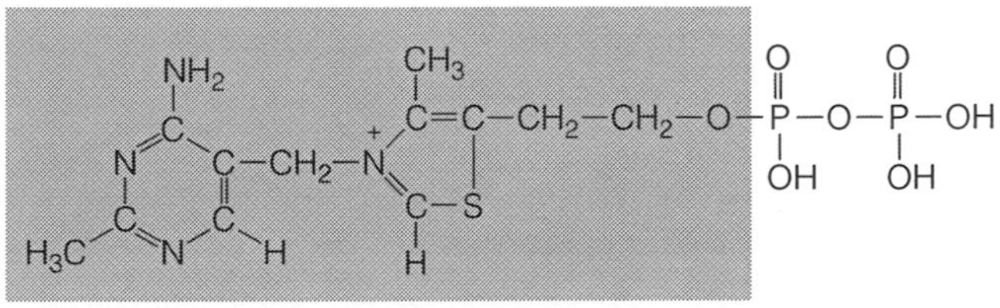

Thiamin pyrophosphate (TPP). TPP is a coenzyme that includes the thiamin molecule as part of its structure.

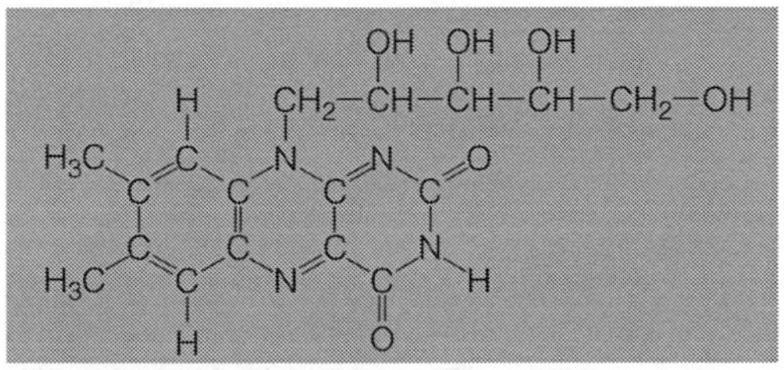

Riboflavin. This molecule is a part of two coenzymes—flavin mononucleotide (FMN) and flavin adenine dinucleotide (FAD).

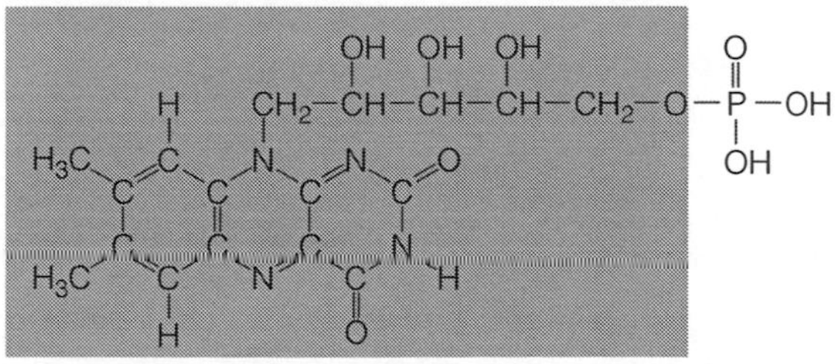

Flavin mononucleotide (FMN). FMN is a coenzyme that includes the riboflavin molecule as part of its structure.

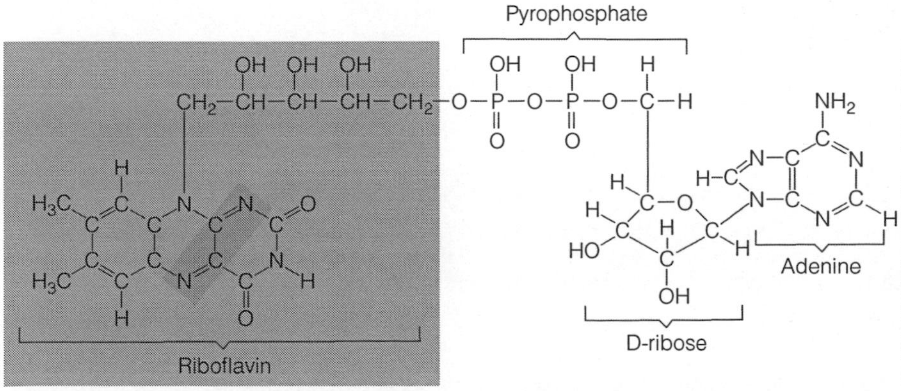

Pyrophosphate

Adenine

D-ribose

Riboflavin

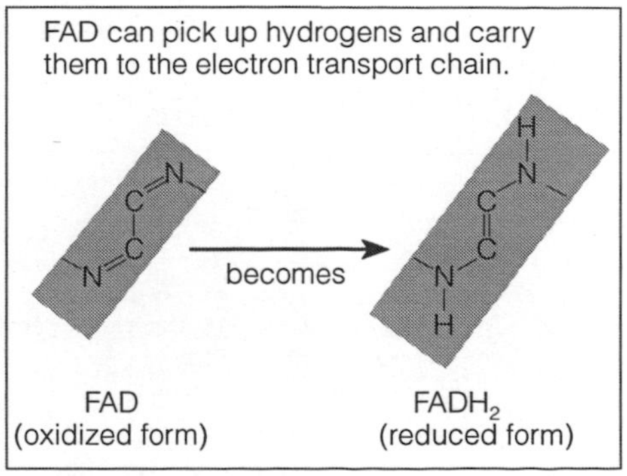

FAD can pick up hydrogens and carry them to the electron transport chain.

becomes

FAD
(oxidized form)

FADH$_2$
(reduced form)

Flavin adenine dinucleotide (FAD). FAD is a coenzyme that includes the riboflavin molecule as part of its structure.

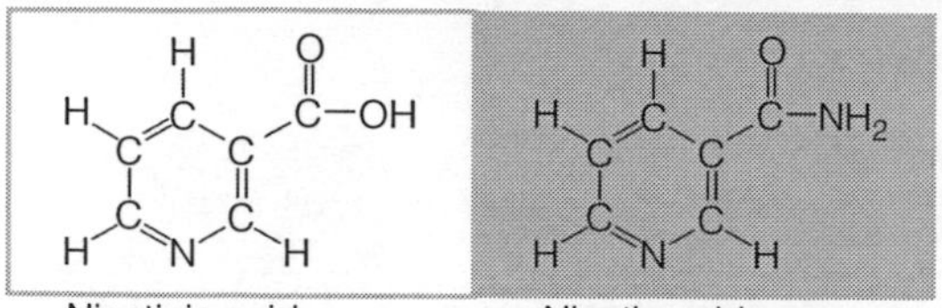

Appendix C

Nicotinic acid   Nicotinamide

Niacin (nicotinic acid and nicotinamide). These molecules are a part of two coenzymes—nicotinamide adenine dinucleotide (NAD$^+$) and nicotinamide adenine dinucleotide phosphate (NADP$^+$).

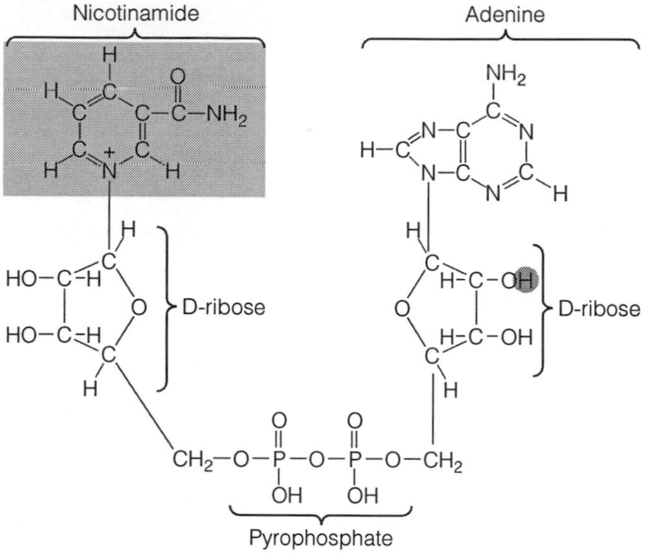

Nicotinamide   Adenine

D-ribose

D-ribose

Pyrophosphate

Nicotinamide adenine dinucleotide (NAD$^+$) and nicotinamide adenine dinucleotide phosphate (NADP$^+$). NADP has the same structure as NAD but with a phosphate group attached to the O instead of the Ⓗ.

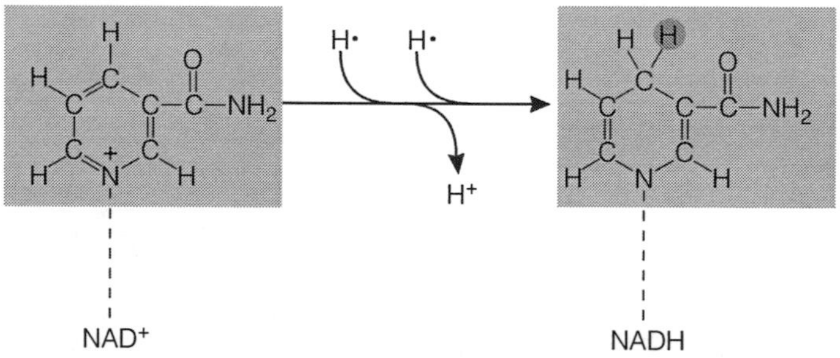

NAD$^+$ NADH

Reduced NAD$^+$ (NADH). When NAD$^+$ is reduced by the addition of H$^+$ and two electrons, it becomes the coenzyme NADH. (The dots on the H entering this reaction represent electrons—see Appendix B.)

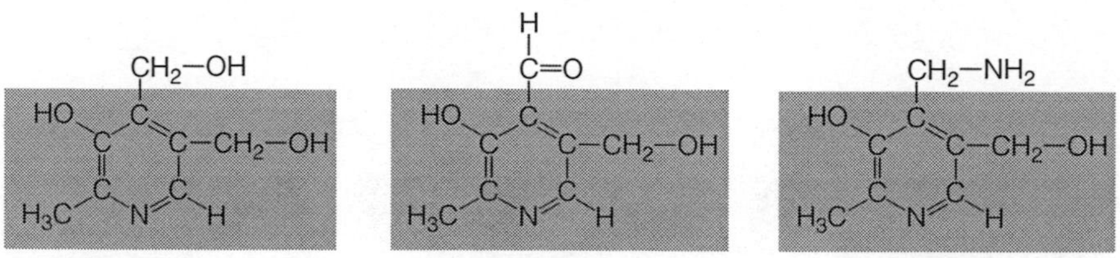

Pyridoxine   Pyridoxal   Pyridoxamine

Vitamin B$_6$ (a general name for three compounds—pyridoxine, pyridoxal, and pyridoxamine). These molecules are a part of two coenzymes—pyridoxal phosphate and pyridoxamine phosphate.

Pyridoxal phosphate (PLP) and pyridoxamine phosphate. These coenzymes include vitamin B_6 as part of their structures.

Folate (folacin or folic acid). This molecule consists of a double ring combined with a single ring and at least one glutamate (a nonessential amino acid marked in the box). Folate's biologically active form is tetrahydrofolate.

Vitamin B_{12} (cyanocobalamin). The arrows in this diagram indicate that the spare electron pairs on the nitrogens attract them to the cobalt.

Tetrahydrofolate. This active coenzyme form of folate has four added hydrogens. An intermediate form, dihydrofolate, has two added hydrogens.

Pantothenic acid. This molecule is part of coenzyme A (CoA).

Coenzyme A (CoA). Coenzyme A is a coenzyme that includes pantothenic acid as part of its structure.

Biotin.

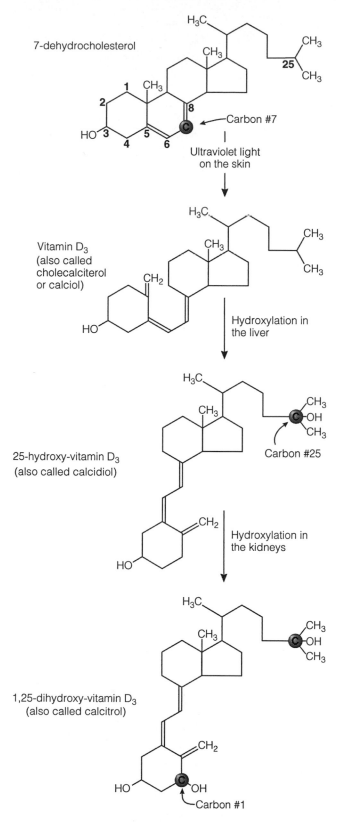

Ascorbic acid
(reduced form)

Dehydroascorbic acid
(oxidized form)

Vitamin C. Two hydrogen atoms with their electrons are lost when ascorbic acid is oxidized and gained when it is reduced again.

7-dehydrocholesterol

Carbon #7

Ultraviolet light on the skin

Vitamin D₃
(also called cholecalciterol or calciol)

Hydroxylation in the liver

25-hydroxy-vitamin D₃
(also called calcidiol)

Carbon #25

Hydroxylation in the kidneys

1,25-dihydroxy-vitamin D₃
(also called calcitrol)

Carbon #1

Vitamin D. The synthesis of active vitamin D begins with 7-dehydrocholesterol. (The carbon atoms at which changes occur are numbered.)

Vitamin E (alpha-tocopherol). The number and position of the methyl groups (CH_3) bonded to the ring structure differentiate among the tocopherols.

Tocotrienols contain double bonds here.

Vitamin K. Naturally occurring compounds with vitamin K activity include phylloquinones (from plants) and menaquinones (from bacteria).

Menadione. This synthetic compound has the same activity as natural vitamin K.

Adenosine triphosphate (ATP), the energy carrier. The cleavage point marks the bond that is broken when ATP splits to become ADP + P.

Adenosine diphosphate (ADP).

Glycolysis

Figure C-1 depicts the events of glycolysis. The following text describes key steps as numbered on the figure.

FIGURE C-1 Glycolysis

Notice that galactose and fructose enter at different places but continue on the same pathway.

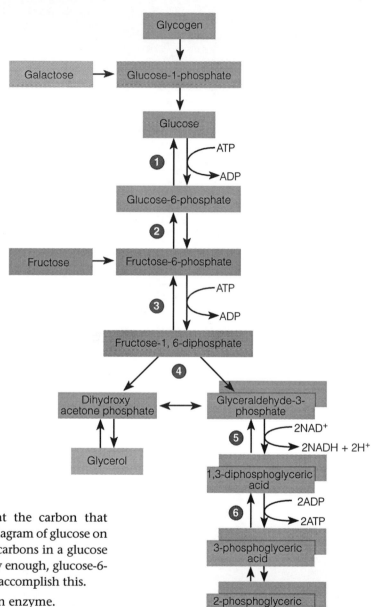

1. A phosphate is attached to glucose at the carbon that chemists call number 6 (review the first diagram of glucose on p. C-1 to see how chemists number the carbons in a glucose molecule). The product is called, logically enough, glucose-6-phosphate. One ATP molecule is used to accomplish this.

2. Glucose-6-phosphate is rearranged by an enzyme.

3. A phosphate is added in another reaction that uses another molecule of ATP. The product this time is fructose-1,6-diphosphate. At this point the six-carbon sugar has a phosphate group on its first and sixth carbons and is ready to break apart.

4. When fructose-1,6-diphosphate breaks in half, the two three-carbon compounds are not identical. Each has a phosphate group attached, but only glyceraldehyde-3-phosphate converts directly to pyruvate. The other compound, however, converts easily to glyceraldehyde-3-phosphate.

5. In the next step, enough energy is released to convert NAD^+ to $NADH + H^+$.

6. In two of the following steps ATP is regenerated.

Remember that in effect two molecules of glyceraldehyde-3-phosphate are produced from glucose; therefore, four ATP molecules are generated from each glucose molecule. Two ATP were needed to get the sequence started, so the net gain at this point is two ATP and two molecules of $NADH + H^+$. As you will see later, each $NADH + H^+$ moves to the electron transport chain to unload its hydrogens onto oxygen, producing more ATP.

Fatty Acid Oxidation

Figure C-2 presents fatty acid oxidation. The sequence is as follows.

1. The fatty acid is activated by combining with coenzyme A (CoA). In this reaction, ATP loses two phosphorus atoms (PP, or pyrophosphate) and becomes AMP (adenosine monophosphate)—the equivalent of a loss of two ATP.

2. In the next reaction, two H with their electrons are removed and transferred to FAD, forming $FADH_2$.

3. In a later reaction, two H are removed and go to NAD^+ (forming $NADH + H^+$).

4. The fatty acid is cleaved at the "beta" carbon, the second carbon from the carboxyl (COOH) end. This break results in a fatty acid that is two carbons shorter than the previous one and a two-carbon molecule of acetyl CoA. At the same time, another CoA is attached to the fatty acid, thus activating it for its turn through the series of reactions.

5. The sequence is repeated with each cycle producing an acetyl CoA and a shorter fatty acid until only a 2-carbon fatty acid remains—acetyl CoA.

In the example shown in Figure C-2, palmitic acid (a 16-carbon fatty acid) will go through this series of reactions seven times, using the equivalent of two ATP for the initial activation and generating seven $FADH_2$, seven $NADH + H^+$, and eight acetyl CoA. As you will see later, each of the seven $FADH_2$ will enter the electron transport chain to unload its hydrogens onto oxygen, yielding two ATP (for a total of 14). Similarly, each $NADH + H^+$ will enter the electron transport chain to unload its hydrogens onto oxygen, yielding three ATP (for a total of 21). Thus the oxidation of a 16-carbon fatty acid uses 2 ATP and generates 35 ATP. When the eight acetyl CoA enter the TCA cycle, even more ATP will be generated, as a later section describes.

Amino Acid Degradation

The first step in amino acid degradation is the removal of the nitrogen-containing amino group through either deamination (Figure 7-14 on p. 226) or transamination (Figure 7-15 on p. 226) reactions. Then the remaining carbon skeletons may enter the metabolic pathways at different places, as shown in Figure C-3.

The TCA Cycle

The tricarboxylic acid, or TCA, cycle is the set of reactions that break down acetyl CoA to carbon dioxide and hydrogens. To link glycolysis to the TCA cycle, pyruvate enters the mitochondrion, loses a carbon group, and bonds with a molecule of CoA to become acetyl CoA. The TCA cycle uses any substance that can be converted to acetyl CoA directly or indirectly through pyruvate.

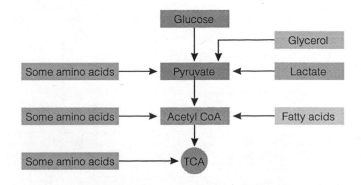

The step from pyruvate to acetyl CoA is complex. We have included only those substances that will help you understand

FIGURE C-2 Fatty Acid Oxidation

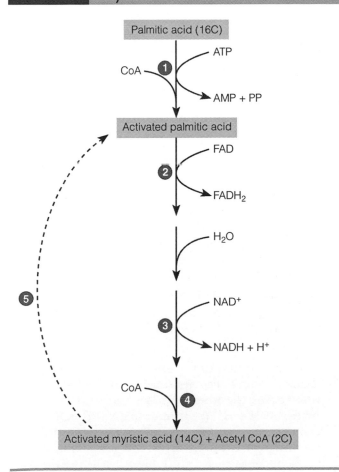

FIGURE C-3 Amino Acid Degradation

After losing their amino groups, carbon skeletons can be converted to one of seven molecules that can enter the TCA cycle (presented in Figure C-4).

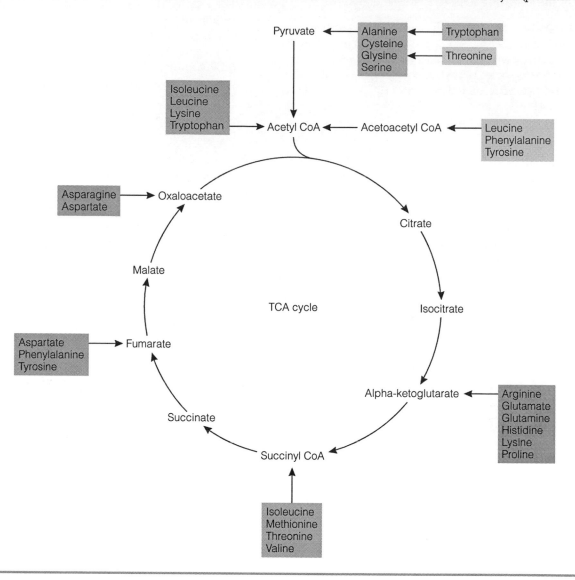

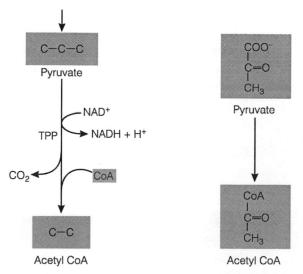

The step from pyruvate to acetyl CoA. (TPP and NAD are coenzymes containing the B vitamins thiamin and niacin, respectively.)

the transfer of energy from the nutrients. Pyruvate loses a carbon to carbon dioxide and is attached to a molecule of CoA. In the process, NAD$^+$ picks up two hydrogens with their associated electrons, becoming NADH + H$^+$.

Let's follow the steps of the TCA cycle (see the corresponding numbers in Figure C-4).

1. The two-carbon acetyl CoA combines with a four-carbon compound, oxaloacetate. The CoA comes off, and the product is a six-carbon compound, citrate.

2. The atoms of citrate are rearranged to form isocitrate.

3. Now two H (with their two electrons) are removed from the isocitrate. One H becomes attached to the NAD$^+$ with the two electrons; the other H is released as H$^+$. Thus NAD$^+$ becomes NADH + H$^+$. (Remember this NADH + H$^+$, but let's follow the carbons first.) A carbon is combined with two oxygens, forming carbon dioxide (which diffuses away into the blood and is exhaled). What is left is the five-carbon compound alpha-ketoglutarate.

FIGURE C-4 The TCA Cycle

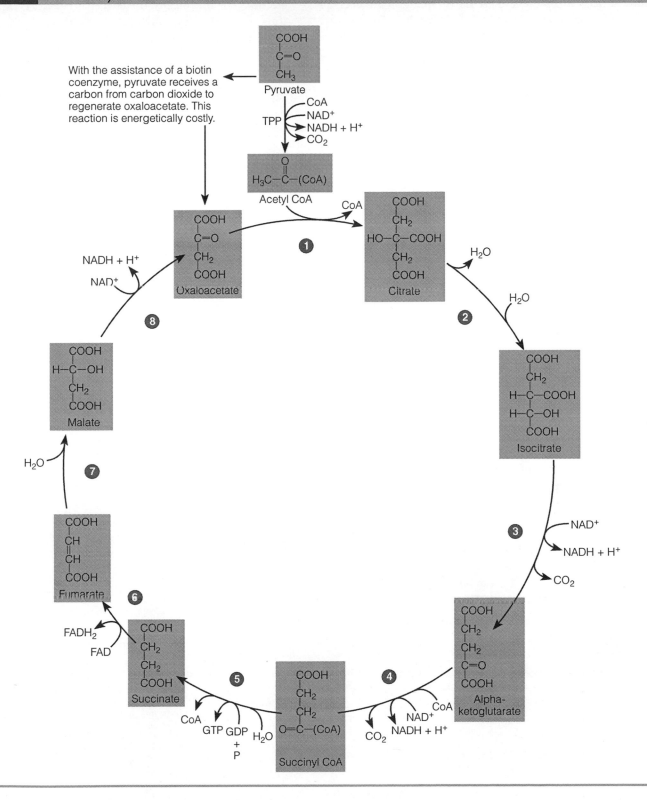

4. Now two compounds interact with alpha-ketoglutarate —a molecule of CoA and a molecule of NAD⁺. In this complex reaction, a carbon and two oxygens are removed (forming carbon dioxide); two hydrogens are removed and go to NAD^+ (forming $NADH + H^+$); and the remaining four-carbon compound is attached to the CoA, forming succinyl

CoA. (Remember this $NADH + H^+$ also. You will see later what happens to it.)

5. Now two molecules react with succinyl CoA—a molecule called GDP and one of phosphate (P). The CoA comes off, the GDP and P combine to form the high-energy compound GTP (similar to ATP), and succinate remains. (Remember this GTP.)

6. In the next reaction, two H with their electrons are removed from succinate and are transferred to a molecule of FAD (a coenzyme like NAD^+) to form $FADH_2$. The product that remains is fumarate. (Remember this $FADH_2$.)

7. Next a molecule of water is added to fumarate, forming malate.

8. A molecule of NAD^+ reacts with the malate; two H with their associated electrons are removed from the malate and form $NADH + H^+$. The product that remains is the four-carbon compound oxaloacetate. (Remember this $NADH + H^+$.)

We are back where we started. The oxaloacetate formed in this process can combine with another molecule of acetyl CoA (step 1), and the cycle can begin again, as shown in Figure C-4.

So far, we have seen two carbons brought in with acetyl CoA and two carbons ending up in carbon dioxide. But where are the energy and the ATP we promised?

A review of the eight steps of the TCA cycle shows that the compounds $NADH + H^+$ (three molecules), $FADH_2$, and GTP capture energy originally found in acetyl CoA. To see how this energy ends up in ATP, we must follow the electrons further—into the electron transport chain.

The Electron Transport Chain

The six reactions described here are those of the electron transport chain, which is shown in Figure C-5. Since oxygen is required for these reactions, and ADP and P are combined to form ATP in several of them (ADP is phosphorylated), these reactions are also called oxidative phosphorylation.

An important concept to remember at this point is that an electron is not a fixed amount of energy. The electrons that bond the H to NAD^+ in NADH have a relatively large amount of energy. In the series of reactions that follow, they release this energy in small amounts, until at the end they are attached (with H) to oxygen (O) to make water (H_2O). In some of the steps, the energy they release is captured into ATP in coupled reactions.

1. In the first step of the electron transport chain, NADH reacts with a molecule called a flavoprotein, losing its electrons (and their H). The products are NAD^+ and reduced flavoprotein. A little energy is released as heat in this reaction.

2. The flavoprotein passes on the electrons to a molecule called coenzyme Q. Again they release some energy as heat, but ADP and P bond together and form ATP, storing much of the energy. This is a coupled reaction: $ADP + P \rightarrow ATP$.

3. Coenzyme Q passes the electrons to cytochrome b. Again the electrons release energy.

4. Cytochrome b passes the electrons to cytochrome c in a coupled reaction in which ATP is formed: $ADP + P \rightarrow ATP$.

5. Cytochrome c passes the electrons to cytochrome a.

6. Cytochrome a passes them (with their H) to an atom of oxygen (O), forming water (H_2O). This is a coupled reaction in which ATP is formed: $ADP + P \rightarrow ATP$.

As Figure C-5 shows, each time NADH is oxidized (loses its electrons) by this means, the energy it releases is captured into three ATP molecules. When the electrons are passed on to water at the end, they are much lower in energy than they were originally. This completes the story of the electrons from NADH.

As for $FADH_2$, its electrons enter the electron transport chain at coenzyme Q. From coenzyme Q to water, ATP is generated in only two steps. Therefore, $FADH_2$ coming out of the TCA cycle yields just two ATP molecules.

One energy-receiving compound of the TCA cycle (GTP) does not enter the electron transport chain but gives its energy directly to ADP in a simple phosphorylation reaction. This reaction yields one ATP.

It is now possible to draw up a balance sheet of glucose metabolism (see Table C-3). Glycolysis has yielded $4 NADH + H^+$ and 4 ATP molecules and has spent 2 ATP. The 2 acetyl CoA

FIGURE C-5 The Electron Transport Chain

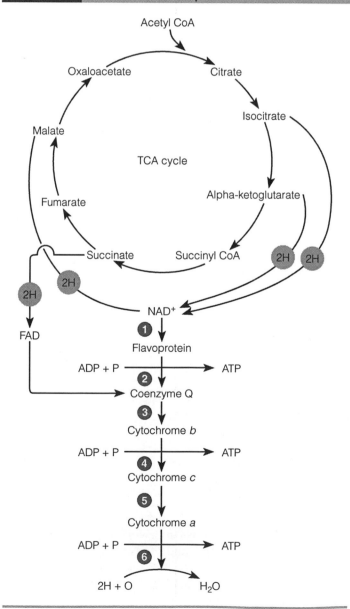

going through the TCA cycle have yielded 6 NADH + H$^+$, 2 FADH$_2$, and 2 GTP molecules. After the NADH + H$^+$ and FADH$_2$ have gone through the electron transport chain, there are 28 ATP. Added to these are the 4 ATP from glycolysis and the 2 ATP from GTP, making the total 34 ATP generated from one molecule of glucose. After the expense of 2 ATP is subtracted, there is a net gain of 32 ATP.*

A similar balance sheet from the complete breakdown of one 16-carbon fatty acid would show a net gain of 129 ATP. As mentioned earlier, 35 ATP were generated from the seven FADH$_2$ and seven NADH + H$^+$ produced during fatty acid oxidation. The eight acetyl CoA produced will each generate 12 ATP as they go through the TCA cycle and the electron transport chain, for a total of 96 more ATP. After subtracting the 2 ATP needed to activate the fatty acid initially, the net yield from one 16-carbon fatty acid: 35 + 96 − 2 = 129 ATP.

These calculations help explain why fat yields more energy (measured as kcalories) per gram than carbohydrate or protein. The more hydrogen atoms a fuel contains, the more ATP will be generated during oxidation. The 16-carbon fatty acid molecule, with its 32 hydrogen atoms, generates 129 ATP, whereas glucose, with its 12 hydrogen atoms, yields only 32 ATP.

The TCA cycle and the electron transport chain are the body's major means of capturing the energy from nutrients in ATP molecules. Other means, such as anaerobic glycolysis, contribute energy quickly, but the aerobic processes are the most efficient. Biologists and chemists understand much more about these processes than has been presented here.

Alcohol's Interference with Energy Metabolism

Highlight 7 provides an overview of how alcohol interferes with energy metabolism. With an understanding of the TCA cycle, a few more details may be appreciated. During alcohol metabolism, the enzyme alcohol dehydrogenase oxidizes alcohol to acetaldehyde while it simultaneously reduces a molecule of NAD$^+$ to NADH + H$^+$. The related enzyme acetaldehyde dehydrogenase reduces another NAD$^+$ to NADH + H$^+$ while it oxidizes acetaldehyde to acetyl CoA, the compound that enters the TCA cycle to generate energy. Thus, whenever alcohol is being metabolized in the body, NAD$^+$ diminishes, and NADH + H$^+$ accumulates. Chemists say that the body's "redox state" is altered, because NAD$^+$ can oxidize, and NADH + H$^+$ can reduce, many other body compounds. During alcohol metabolism, NAD$^+$ becomes unavailable for the multitude of reactions for which it is required.

TABLE C-3 Balance Sheet for Glucose Metabolism

		ATP
Glycolysis:	4 ATP − 2 ATP	2
1 glucose to 2 pyruvate	2 NADH + H$^+$	3-5[a]
2 pyruvate to 2 acetyl CoA	2 NADH + H$^+$	5
TCA cycle and electron transport chain:		
2 isocitrate	2 NADH + H$^+$	5
2 alpha-ketoglutarate	2 NADH + H$^+$	5
2 succinyl CoA	2 GTP	2
2 succinate	2 FADH$_2$	3
2 malate	2 NADH + H$^+$	5
Total ATP collected from one molecule glucose:		30–32

[a]Each NADH + H$^+$ from glycolysis can yield 1.5 or 2.5 ATP. See the accompanying text.

As the previous sections just explained, for glucose to be completely metabolized, the TCA cycle must be operating, and NAD$^+$ must be present. If these conditions are not met (and when alcohol is present, they may not be), the pathway will be blocked, and traffic will back up—or an alternate route will be taken. Think about this as you follow the pathway shown in Figure C-6.

In each step of alcohol metabolism in which NAD$^+$ is converted to NADH + H$^+$, hydrogen ions accumulate, resulting in a dangerous shift of the acid-base balance toward acid (Chapter 12 explains acid-base balance). The accumulation of NADH + H$^+$ slows TCA cycle activity, so pyruvate and acetyl CoA build up. This condition favors the conversion of pyruvate to lactate, which serves as a temporary storage place for hydrogens from NADH + H$^+$. The conversion of pyruvate to lactate restores some NAD$^+$, but a lactate buildup has serious consequences of its own. It adds to the body's acid burden and interferes with the excretion of uric acid, causing goutlike symptoms. Molecules of acetyl CoA become building blocks for fatty acids or ketone bodies. The making of ketone bodies consumes acetyl CoA and generates NAD$^+$; but some ketone bodies are acids, so they push the acid-base balance further toward acid.

Thus alcohol cascades through the metabolic pathways, wreaking havoc along the way. These consequences have physical effects, which Highlight 7 describes.

The Urea Cycle

Chapter 7 sums up the process by which waste nitrogen is eliminated from the body by stating that ammonia molecules combine with carbon dioxide to produce urea. This is true, but it is not the whole story. Urea is produced in a multistep process within the cells of the liver.

---

*The total may sometimes be 30 ATP. The NADH + H$^+$ generated in the cytoplasm during glycolysis pass their electrons on to shuttle molecules, which move them into the mitochondria. One shuttle, malate, contributes its electrons to the electron transport chain before the first site of ATP synthesis, yielding 5 ATP. Another, glycerol phosphate, adds its electrons into the chain beyond that first site, yielding 3 ATP. Thus sometimes 5, and sometimes 3, ATP result from the NADH + H$^+$ that arise from glycolysis. The amount depends on the cell.

FIGURE C-6 Ethanol Enters the Metabolic Path

This is a simplified version of the glucose-to-energy pathway showing the entry of ethanol. The coenzyme NAD (which is the active form of the B vitamin niacin) is the only one shown here; however, many others are involved.

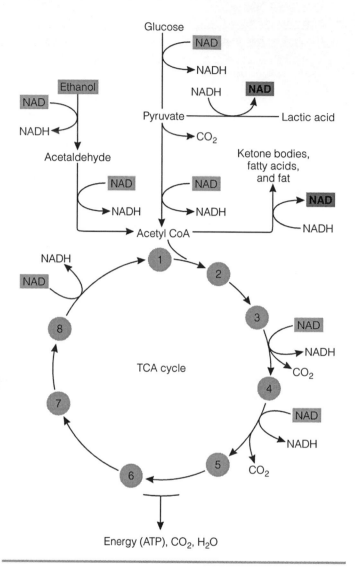

FIGURE C-7 The Urea Cycle

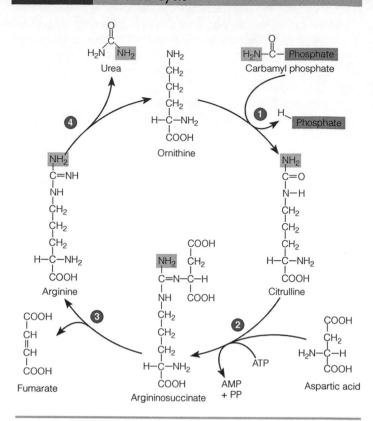

Figure C-7 shows the cycle of four reactions that follow.

1. Carbamyl phosphate combines with the amino acid ornithine, losing its phosphate group. The compound formed is citrulline.

2. Citrulline combines with the amino acid aspartic acid, to form argininosuccinate. The reaction requires energy from ATP. (ATP was shown earlier losing one phosphorus atom in a phosphate group, P, to become ADP. In this reaction, it loses two phosphorus atoms joined together, PP, and becomes adenosine monophosphate, AMP.)

3. Argininosuccinate is split, forming another acid, fumarate, and the amino acid arginine.

4. Arginine loses its terminal carbon with two attached amino groups and picks up an oxygen from water. The end product is urea, which the kidneys excrete in the urine. The compound that remains is ornithine, identical to the ornithine with which this series of reactions began, and ready to react with another molecule of carbamyl phosphate and turn the cycle again.

Ammonia, freed from an amino acid or other compound during metabolism anywhere in the body, arrives at the liver by way of the bloodstream and is taken into a liver cell. There, it is first combined with carbon dioxide and a phosphate group from ATP to form carbamyl phosphate:

$$CO_2 + NH_3 \xrightarrow[\text{2 ATP}]{\text{2 ADP + P}} H_2N-C-O-P-O^-$$

Carbon   Ammonia   Carbamyl phosphate
dioxide

Formation of Ketone Bodies

Normally, fatty acid oxidation proceeds all the way to carbon dioxide and water. However, in ketosis (discussed in Chapter 7), an intermediate is formed from the condensation of two molecules of acetyl CoA: acetoacetyl CoA. Figure C-8 shows the formation of ketone bodies from that intermediate.

FIGURE C-8   The Formation of Ketone Bodies

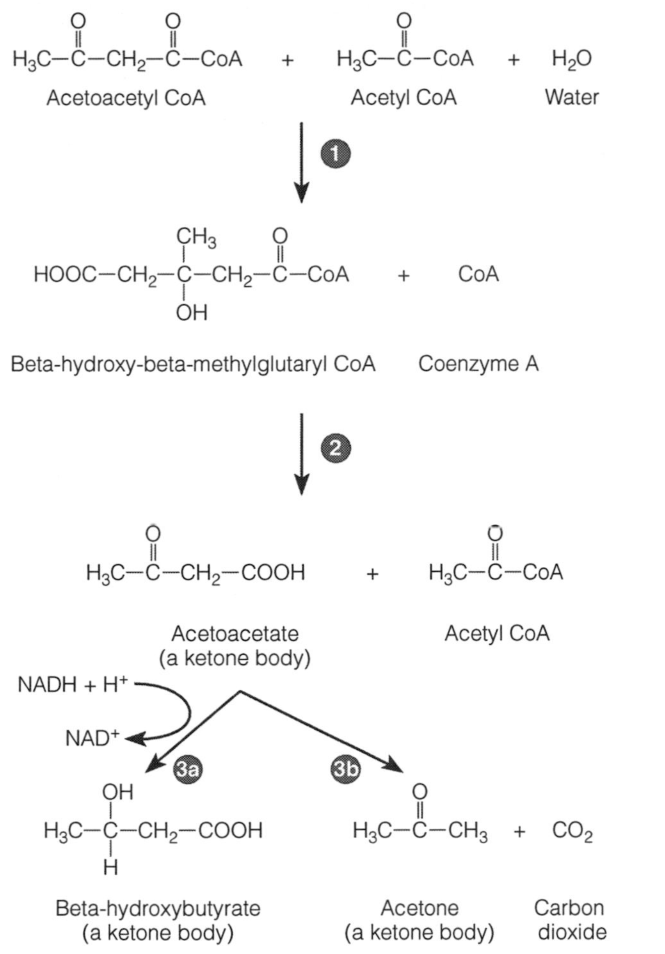

$H_3C-\overset{O}{\overset{\|}{C}}-CH_2-\overset{O}{\overset{\|}{C}}-CoA$ + $H_3C-\overset{O}{\overset{\|}{C}}-CoA$ + H_2O

Acetoacetyl CoA   Acetyl CoA   Water

1

$HOOC-CH_2-\overset{CH_3}{\underset{OH}{\overset{|}{\underset{|}{C}}}}-CH_2-\overset{O}{\overset{\|}{C}}-CoA$ + CoA

Beta-hydroxy-beta-methylglutaryl CoA   Coenzyme A

2

$H_3C-\overset{O}{\overset{\|}{C}}-CH_2-COOH$ + $H_3C-\overset{O}{\overset{\|}{C}}-CoA$

Acetoacetate   Acetyl CoA
(a ketone body)

NADH + H$^+$

NAD$^+$

3a   **3b**

$H_3C-\overset{OH}{\underset{H}{\overset{|}{\underset{|}{C}}}}-CH_2-COOH$ $H_3C-\overset{O}{\overset{\|}{C}}-CH_3$ + CO_2

Beta-hydroxybutyrate   Acetone   Carbon
(a ketone body)   (a ketone body)   dioxide

1. Acetoacetyl CoA condenses with acetyl CoA to form a six-carbon intermediate, beta-hydroxy-betamethylglutaryl CoA.

2. This intermediate is cleaved to acetyl CoA and acetoacetate.

3. Acetoactate can be metabolized either to beta-hydroxybutyrate acid (step 3a) or to acetone (3b).

Acetoacetate, beta-hydroxybutyrate, and acetone are the ketone bodies of ketosis. Two are real ketones (they have a C=O group between two carbons); the other is an alcohol that has been produced during ketone formation—hence the term *ketone bodies*, rather than ketones, to describe the three of them. There are many other ketones in nature; these three are characteristic of ketosis in the body.

CONTENTS

Amino Acid Scoring

PDCAAS

Biological Value

Net Protein Utilizatin

Protein Efficiency Ratio

GLOSSARY

amino acid scoring: a measure of protein quality assessed by comparing a protein's amino acid pattern with that of a reference protein; sometimes called **chemical scoring.**

biological value (BV): a measure of protein quality assessed by measuring the amount of protein nitrogen that is retained from a given amount of protein nitrogen absorbed.

net protein utilization (NPU): a measure of protein quality assessed by measuring the amount of protein nitrogen that is retained from a given amount of protein nitrogen eaten.

PDCAAS (protein digestibility–corrected amino acid score): a measure of protein quality assessed by comparing the amino acid score of a food protein with the amino acid requirements of preschool-age children and then correcting for the true digestibility of the protein; recommended by the FAO/WHO and used to establish protein quality of foods for Daily Value percentages on food labels.

protein efficiency ratio (PER): a measure of protein quality assessed by determining how well a given protein supports weight gain in growing rats; used to establish the protein quality for infant formulas and baby foods.

Measures of Protein Quality

In a world where food is scarce and many people's diets contain marginal or inadequate amounts of protein, it is important to know which foods contain the highest-quality protein. Chapter 6 describes protein quality, and this appendix presents different measures researchers use to assess the quality of a food protein. The accompanying glossary defines related terms.

Amino Acid Scoring

Amino acid scoring evaluates a protein's quality by determining its amino acid composition and comparing it with that of a reference protein. The advantages of amino acid scoring are that it is simple and inexpensive, it easily identifies the limiting amino acid, and it can be used to score mixtures of different proportions of two or more proteins mathematically without having to make up a mixture and test it. Its chief weaknesses are that it fails to estimate the digestibility of a protein, which may strongly affect the protein's quality; it relies on a chemical procedure in which certain amino acids may be destroyed, making the pattern that is analyzed inaccurate; and it is blind to other features of the protein (such as the presence of substances that may inhibit the digestion or utilization of the protein) that would only be revealed by a test in living animals.

Table D-1 (p. D-1) shows the reference pattern for the nine essential amino acids. To interpret the table, read, "For every 3210 units of essential amino acids, 145 must be histidine, 340 must be isoleucine, 540 must be leucine," and so on. To compare a test protein with the reference protein, the experimenter first obtains a chemical analysis of the test protein's amino acids. Then, taking 3210 units of the amino acids, the experimenter compares the amount of each amino acid to the amount found in 3210 units of essential amino acids in egg protein. For example, suppose the test protein contained (per 3210 units) 360 units of isoleucine; 500 units of leucine; 350 of lysine; and for each of the other amino acids, more units than egg protein contains. The two amino acids that are low are leucine (500 as compared with 540 in egg) and lysine (350 versus 440 in egg). The ratio, amino acid in the test protein divided by amino acid in egg, is 500/540 (or about 0.93) for leucine and 350/440 (or about 0.80) for lysine. Lysine is the limiting amino acid (the one that falls shortest compared with egg). If the protein's limiting amino acid is 80 percent of the amount found in the reference protein, it receives a score of 80.

PDCAAS

The **protein digestibility–corrected amino acid score,** or **PDCASS,** compares the amino acid composition of a protein with human amino acid requirements and corrects for digestibility. First the protein's amino acid composition is determined, and then it is compared against the amino acid requirements of preschool-age children. This comparison reveals the most limiting amino acid—the one that falls shortest compared with the reference. If a food protein's limiting amino acid is 70 percent of the amount found in the reference protein, it receives a score of 70. The amino acid score is multiplied by the food's protein digestibility percentage to determine the PDCAAS. The box on p. D-2 provides an example of how to calculate the PDCAAS, and Table D-2 (p. D-1) lists the PDCAAS values of selected foods.

Biological Value

The **biological value (BV)** of a protein measures its efficiency in supporting the body's needs. In a test of biological value, two nitrogen balance studies are done. In the first, no protein is fed, and nitrogen (N) excretions in the urine and feces are measured. It is assumed that under these conditions, N lost in the urine is the amount the body always necessarily loses by filtration into the urine each day, regardless of what protein is fed (endogenous N). The N lost in the feces (called metabolic N) is the amount the body invariably loses into the intestine each day, whether or not food protein is fed. (To help you remember the terms: endogenous N is "urinary N on a zero-protein diet"; metabolic N is "fecal N on a zero-protein diet.")

In the second study, an amount of protein slightly below the requirement is fed. Intake and losses are measured; then the BV is derived using this formula:

$$BV = \frac{N \text{ retained}}{N \text{ absorbed}} \times 100$$

The denominator of this equation expresses the amount of nitrogen *absorbed*: food N minus fecal N (excluding the metabolic N the body would lose in the feces anyway, even without food). The numerator expresses the amount of N *retained* from the N absorbed: absorbed N (as in the denominator) minus the N excreted in the urine (excluding the endogenous N the body would lose in the urine anyway, even without food). The more nitrogen retained, the higher the protein quality. (Recall that when an essential amino acid is missing, protein synthesis stops, and the remaining amino acids are deaminated and the nitrogen excreted.)

Egg protein has a BV of 100, indicating that 100 percent of the nitrogen absorbed is retained. Supplied in adequate quantity, a protein with a BV of 70 or greater can support human growth as long as energy intake is adequate. Table D-3 presents the BV for selected foods.

This method has the advantages of being based on experiments with human beings (it can be done with animals, too, of course) and of measuring actual nitrogen retention. But it is also cumbersome, expensive, and often impractical, and it is based on several assumptions that may not be valid. For example, the physiology, normal environment, or typical food intake of the subjects used for testing may not be similar to those for whom the test protein may ultimately be used. For another example, the retention of protein in the body does not necessarily mean that it is being well utilized. Considerable exchange of protein among tissues (protein turnover) occurs, but is hidden from view when only N intake and output are measured. The test of biological value wouldn't detect if one tissue were shorted.

Net Protein Utilization

Like BV, **net protein utilization (NPU)** measures how efficiently a protein is used by the body and involves two balance studies. The difference is that NPU measures retention of food nitrogen rather than food nitrogen absorbed (as in BV). The formula for NPU is:

$$NPU = \frac{N \text{ retained}}{N \text{ intake}} \times 100$$

The numerator is the same as for BV, but the denominator represents food N intake only—not N absorbed.

This method offers advantages similar to those of BV determinations and is used more frequently, with animals as the test subjects. A drawback is that if a low NPU is obtained, the test results offer no help in distinguishing between two possible causes: a poor amino acid composition of the test protein or poor digestibility. There is also a limit to the extent to which animal test results can be assumed to be applicable to human beings.

TABLE D-1	A Reference Pattern for Amino Acid Scoring of Proteins
Essential Amino Acids	**Reference Protein—Whole Egg (mg amino acid/g nitrogen)**
Histidine	145
Isoleucine	340
Leucine	540
Lysine	440
Methionine + cystine[a]	355
Phenylalanine + tyrosine[b]	580
Threonine	294
Tryptophan	106
Valine	410
Total	3210

[a]Methionine is essential and is also used to make cystine. Thus the methionine requirement is lower if cystine is supplied.
[b]Phenylalanine is essential and is also used to make tyrosine if not enough of the latter is available. Thus the phenylalanine requirement is lower if tyrosine is also supplied.

TABLE D-2	PDCAAS Values of Selected Foods
Casein (milk protein)	1.00
Egg white	1.00
Soybean (isolate)	.99
Beef	.92
Pea flour	.69
Kidney beans (canned)	.68
Chickpeas (canned)	.66
Pinto beans (canned)	.66
Rolled oats	.57
Lentils (canned)	.52
Peanut meal	.52
Whole wheat	.40

NOTE: 1.0 is the maximum PDCAAS a food protein can receive.

TABLE D-3	Biological Values (BV) of Selected Foods
Egg	100
Milk	93
Beef	75
Fish	75
Corn	72

NOTE: 100 is the maximum BV a food protein can receive.

HOW TO Measure Protein Quality Using PDCAAS

To calculate the PDCAAS (protein digestibility–corrected amino acid score), researchers first determine the amino acid profile of the test protein (in this example, pinto beans). The second column of the table below presents the essential amino acid profile for pinto beans. The third column presents the amino acid reference pattern.

To determine how well the food protein meets human needs, researchers calculate the ratio by dividing the second column by the third column (for example, 30 ÷ 18 = 1.67). The amino acid with the lowest ratio is the most limiting amino acid—in this case, methionine. Its ratio is the amino acid score for the protein—in this case, 0.84.

The amino acid score alone, however, does not account for digestibility. Protein digestibility, as determined by rat studies, yields a value of 79 percent for pinto beans. Together, the amino acid score and the digestibility value determine the PDCAAS:

$$PDCAAS =$$
protein digestibility × amino acid score
PDCAAS for pinto beans =
$$0.79 × 0.84 = 0.66$$

Thus the PDCAAS for pinto beans is 0.66. Table D-2 lists the PDCAAS values of selected foods.

The PDCAAS is used to determine the % Daily Value on food labels. To calculate the % Daily Value for protein for canned pinto beans, multiply the number of grams of protein in a standard serving (in the case of pinto beans, 7 grams per ½ cup) by the PDCAAS:

$$7 g × 0.66 = 4.62$$

This value is then divided by the recommended standard for protein (for children over age four and adults, 50 grams):

$$4.62 ÷ 50 = 0.09 \text{ (or 9%)}$$

The food label for this can of pinto beans would declare that one serving provides 7 grams protein, and if the label included a % Daily Value for protein (which is optional), the value would be 9 percent.

Essential Amino Acids	Amino Acid Profile of Pinto Beans (mg/g protein)	Amino Acid Reference Pattern (mg/g protein)	Amino Acid Score
Histidine	30.0	18	1.67
Isoleucine	42.5	25	1.70
Leucine	80.4	55	1.46
Lysine	69.0	51	1.35
Methionine (+ cystine)	21.1	25	0.84
Phenylalanine (+ tyrosine)	90.5	47	1.93
Threonine	43.7	27	1.62
Tryptophan	8.8	7	1.26
Valine	50.1	32	1.57

TABLE D-4 Protein Efficiency Ratio (PER) Values of Selected Proteins	
Casein (milk)	2.8
Soy	2.4
Glutein (wheat)	0.4

Protein Efficiency Ratio

The **protein efficiency ratio (PER)** measures the weight gain of a growing animal and compares it to the animal's protein intake. Until recently, the PER was generally accepted in the United States and Canada as the official method for assessing protein quality, and it is still used to evaluate proteins for infants.

Young rats are fed a measured amount of protein and weighed periodically as they grow. The PER is expressed as:

$$PER = \frac{\text{weight gain (g)}}{\text{protein intake (g)}}$$

This method has the virtues of economy and simplicity, but it also has many drawbacks. The experiments are time-consuming; the amino acid needs of rats are not the same as those of human beings; and the amino acid needs for growth are not the same as for the maintenance of adult animals (growing animals need more lysine, for example). Table D-4 presents PER values for selected foods.

Physical Activity and Energy Requirements

CONTENTS

Calculating Physical Activity Level
Estimating Physical Activity Level
Using a Shortcut to Estimate Total Energy Expenditure

Chapter 8 described how to calculate estimated energy requirements (EER) for adults by using an equation that accounts for gender, age, weight, height, and physical activity level. Table F-1 presents additional equations to determine the EER for infants, children, adolescents, and pregnant and lactating women.

This appendix helps you determine the correct physical activity (PA) factor to use in the equations, either by calculating the physical activity level or by estimating it. For those who prefer to bypass these steps, the appendix presents tables that provide a shortcut to estimating total energy expenditure.*

Calculating Physical Activity Level

To calculate your physical activity level, record all of your activities for a typical 24-hour day, noting the type of activity, the level of intensity, and the duration. Then, using a copy of Table F-2, find your activity in the first column (or an activity that is reasonably similar) and multiply the number of minutes spent on that activity by the factor in the third column. Put your answer in the last column and total the accumulated values for the day. Now add the subtotal of the last column to 1.1 (to account for basal energy and the thermic effect of food) as shown. This score indicates your physical activity level. Using Table F-3, find the PA factor for your age and gender that correlates with your physical activity level and use it in the energy equations presented in Table F-1.

Estimating Physical Activity Level

As an alternative to recording your activities for a day, you can use the third column of Table F-3 to decide if your daily activity is sedentary, low active, active, or very active. Find the PA factor for your age and gender that correlates with your typical physical activity level and use it in the energy equations presented in Table F-1.

Using a Shortcut to Estimate Total Energy Expenditure

The DRI Committee has developed estimates of total energy expenditure based on the equations for adults presented in Table F-1. These estimates are presented in Table F-4 for women and Table F-5 for men. You can use these tables to estimate your energy requirement—that is, the number of kcalories needed to maintain your current body weight. On the table appropriate for your gender, find your height in meters (or inches) in the left-hand column. Then follow the row across to find your weight in kilograms (or pounds). (If you can't find your exact height and weight, choose a value between the two closest ones.) Look down the column to find the number of kcalories that corresponds to your activity level.

Importantly, the values given in the tables are for 30-year-old people. Women 19 to 29 should add 7 kcalories per day for each year below age 30; older women should subtract 7 kcalories per day for each year above age 30. Similarly, men 19 to 29 should add 10 kcalories per day for each year below age 30; older men should subtract 10 kcalories per day for each year above age 30.

---

*This appendix, including the tables, is adapted from Committee on Dietary Reference Intakes, *Dietary Reference Intakes for Energy, Carbohydrate, Fiber, Fat, Fatty Acids, Cholesterol, Protein, and Amino Acids* (Washington, D.C.: National Academies Press, 2002/2005).

TABLE F-1　Equations to Determine Estimated Energy Requirement (EER)

Infants

0–3 months	EER = (89 × weight − 100) + 175
4–6 months	EER = (89 × weight − 100) + 56
7–12 months	EER = (89 × weight − 100) + 22
13–15 months	EER = (89 × weight − 100) + 20

Children and Adolescents

Boys

3–8 years	EER = 88.5 − (61.9 × age + PA × [(26.7 × weight) + (903 × height)] + 20
9–18 years	EER = 88.5 − (61.9 × age + PA × [(26.7 × weight) + (903 × height)] + 25

Girls

3–8 years	EER = 135.3 − (30.8 × age + PA × [(10.0 × weight) + (934 × height)] + 20
9–18 years	EER = 135.3 − (30.8 × age + PA × [(10.0 × weight) + (934 × height)] + 25

Adults

Men	EER = 662 − (9.53 × age + PA × [(15.91 × weight) + (539.6 × height)]
Women	EER = 354 − (6.91 × age + PA × [(9.36 × weight) + (726 × height)]

Pregnancy

1st trimester	EER = nonpregnant EER + 0
2nd trimester	EER = nonpregnant EER + 340
3rd trimester	EER = nonpregnant EER + 452

Lactation

0–6 months postpartum	EER = nonpregnant EER + 500 − 170
7–12 months postpartum	EER = nonpregnant EER + 400 − 0

NOTE: Select the appropriate equation for gender and age and insert weight in kilograms, height in meters, and age in years. See the text and Table F-3 to determine PA.

TABLE F-2　Physical Activities and Their Scores

If your activity was equivalent to this ...	Then list the number of minutes here and ...	Multiply by this factor ...	Add this column to get your physical activity level score:
Activities of Daily Living			
Gardening (no lifting)		0.0032	
Household tasks (moderate effort)		0.0024	
Lifting items continuously		0.0029	
Loading/unloading car		0.0019	
Lying quietly		0.0000	
Mopping		0.0024	
Mowing lawn (power mower)		0.0033	
Raking lawn		0.0029	
Riding in a vehicle		0.0000	
Sitting (idle)		0.0000	
Sitting (doing light activity)		0.0005	
Taking out trash		0.0019	
Vacuuming		0.0024	
Walking the dog		0.0019	
Walking from house to car or bus		0.0014	
Watering plants		0.0014	
Additional Activities			
Billiards		0.0013	
Calisthenics (no weight)		0.0029	
Canoeing (leisurely)		0.0014	
Chopping wood		0.0037	

continued

TABLE F-2 Physical Activities and Their Scores—continued

If your activity was equivalent to this ...	Then list the number of minutes here and ...	Multiply by this factor ...	Add this column to get your physical activity level score:
Additional Activities continued			
Climbing hills (carrying 11 lb load)		0.0061	
Climbing hills (no load)		0.0056	
Cycling (leisurely)		0.0024	
Cycling (moderately)		0.0045	
Dancing (aerobic or ballet)		0.0048	
Dancing (ballroom, leisurely)		0.0018	
Dancing (fast ballroom or square)		0.0043	
Golf (with cart)		0.0014	
Golf (without cart)		0.0032	
Horseback riding (walking)		0.0012	
Horseback riding (trotting)		0.0053	
Jogging (6 mph)		0.0088	
Music (playing accordion)		0.0008	
Music (playing cello)		0.0012	
Music (playing flute)		0.0010	
Music (playing piano)		0.0012	
Music (playing violin)		0.0014	
Rope skipping		0.0105	
Skating (ice)		0.0043	
Skating (roller)		0.0052	
Skiing (water or downhill)		0.0055	
Squash		0.0106	
Surfing		0.0048	
Swimming (slow)		0.0033	
Swimming (fast)		0.0057	
Tennis (doubles)		0.0038	
Tennis (singles)		0.0057	
Volleyball (noncompetitive)		0.0018	
Walking (2 mph)		0.0014	
Walking (3 mph)		0.0022	
Walking (4 mph)		0.0033	
Walking (5 mph)		0.0067	
Subtotal			
Factor for basal energy and the thermic effect of food			1.1
Your physical activity level score			

TABLE F-3 Physical Activity Equivalents and Their PA Factors

Physical Activity Level	Description	Physical Activity Equivalents	Men, 19+ yr PA Factor	Women, 19+ yr PA FActor	Boys, 3–18 yr PA Factor	Girls, 3–18 yr PA Factor
1.0 to 1.39	Sedentary	Only those physical activities required for typical daily living	1.0	1.0	1.0	1.0
1.4 to 1.59	Low active	Daily living + 30–60 min moderate activity[a]	1.11	1.12	1.13	1.16
1.6 to 1.89	Active	Daily living + ≥ 60 min moderate activity	1.25	1.27	1.26	1.31
1.9 and above	Very active	Daily living + ≥ 60 min moderate activity *and* ≥ 60 min vigorous activity *or* ≥ 120 min moderate activity	1.48	1.45	1.42	1.56

[a]Moderate activity is equivalent to walking at a pace of 3 to $4^1/2$ mph.

TABLE F-4 Total Energy Expenditure (TEE in kCalories per Day) for Women 30 Years of Age[a] at Various Levels of Activity and Various Heights and Weights

Heights m (in)	Physical Activity Level	Weight[b] kg (lb)					
1.45 (57)		38.9 (86)	45.2 (100)	52.6 (116)	63.1 (139)	73.6 (162)	84.1 (185)
		kCalories					
	Sedentary	1564	1623	1698	1813	1927	2042
	Low active	1734	1800	1912	2043	2174	2304
	Active	1946	2021	2112	2257	2403	2548
	Very active	2201	2287	2387	2553	2719	2886
1.50 (59)		41.6 (92)	48.4 (107)	56.3 (124)	67.5 (149)	78.8 (174)	90.0 (198)
		kCalories					
	Sedentary	1625	1689	1771	1894	2017	2139
	Low active	1803	1874	1996	2136	2276	2415
	Active	2025	2105	2205	2360	2516	2672
	Very active	2291	2382	2493	2671	2849	3027
1.55 (61)		44.4 (98)	51.7 (114)	60.1 (132)	72.1 (159)	84.1 (185)	96.1 (212)
		kCalories					
	Sedentary	1688	1756	1846	1977	2108	2239
	Low active	1873	1949	2081	2230	2380	2529
	Active	2104	2190	2299	2466	2632	2798
	Very active	2382	2480	2601	2791	2981	3171
1.60 (63)		47.4 (104)	55.0 (121)	64.0 (141)	76.8 (169)	89.6 (197)	102.4 (226)
		kCalories					
	Sedentary	1752	1824	1922	2061	2201	2340
	Low active	1944	2025	2168	2327	2486	2645
	Active	2185	2276	2396	2573	2750	2927
	Very active	2474	2578	2712	2914	3116	3318
1.65 (65)		50.4 (111)	58.5 (129)	68.1 (150)	81.7 (180)	95.3 (210)	108.9 (240)
		kCalories					
	Sedentary	1816	1893	1999	2148	2296	2444
	Low active	2016	2102	2556	2425	2594	2763
	Active	2267	2364	2494	2682	2871	3059
	Very active	2567	2678	2824	3039	3254	3469
1.70 (67)		53.5 (118)	62.1 (137)	72.3 (159)	86.7 (191)	101.2 (223)	115.6 (255)
		kCalories					
	Sedentary	1881	1963	2078	2235	2393	2550
	Low active	2090	2180	2345	2525	2705	2884
	Active	2350	2453	2594	2794	2994	3194
	Very active	2662	2780	2938	3166	3395	3623
1.75 (69)		56.7 (125)	65.8 (145)	76.6 (169)	91.9 (202)	107.2 (236)	122.5 (270)
		kCalories					
	Sedentary	1948	2034	2158	2325	2492	2659
	Low active	2164	2260	2437	2627	2817	3007
	Active	2434	2543	2695	2907	3119	3331
	Very active	2758	2883	3054	3296	3538	3780
1.80 (71)		59.9 (132)	69.7 (154)	81.0 (178)	97.2 (214)	113.4 (250)	129.6 (285)
		kCalories					
	Sedentary	2015	2106	2239	2416	2593	2769
	Low active	2239	2341	2529	2731	2932	3133
	Active	2519	2634	2799	3023	3247	3472
	Very active	2855	2987	3172	3428	3684	3940

continued

[a]For each year below 30, add 7 kcalories/day to TEE. For each year above 30, subtract 7 kcalories/day from TEE.
[b]These columns represent a BMI of 18.5, 22.5, 25, 30, 35, and 40, respectively.

| TABLE F-4 | Total Energy Expenditure (TEE in kCalories per Day) for Women 30 Years of Age[a] at Various Levels of Activity and Various Heights and Weights—continued |

Heights m (in)	Physical Activity Level	Weight[b] kg (lb)					
1.85 (73)		63.3 (139)	73.6 (162)	85.6 (189)	102.7 (226)	119.8 (264)	136.9 (302)
				kCalories			
	Sedentary	2083	2179	2322	2509	2695	2882
	Low active	2315	2422	2624	2836	3049	3262
	Active	2605	2727	2904	3141	3378	3615
	Very active	2954	3093	3292	3562	3833	4103
1.90 (75)		66.8 (147)	77.6 (171)	90.3 (199)	108.3 (239)	126.4 (278)	144.4 (318)
				kCalories			
	Sedentary	2151	2253	2406	2603	2800	2996
	Low active	2392	2505	2720	2944	3168	3393
	Active	2693	2821	3011	3261	3511	3760
	Very active	3053	3200	3414	3699	3984	4270
1.95 (77)		70.3 (155)	81.8 (180)	95.1 (209)	114.1 (251)	133.1 (293)	152.1 (335)
				kCalories			
	Sedentary	2221	2328	2492	2699	2906	3113
	Low active	2470	2589	2817	3053	3290	3526
	Active	2781	2917	3119	3383	3646	3909
	Very active	3154	3309	3538	3838	4139	4439

[a]For each year below 30, add 7 kcalories/day to TEE. For each year above 30, subtract 7 kcalories/day from TEE.
[b]These columns represent a BMI of 18.5, 22.5, 25, 30, 35, and 40, respectively.

| TABLE F-5 | Total Energy Expenditure (TEE in kCalories per Day) for Men 30 Years of Age[a] at Various Levels of Activity and Various Heights and Weights |

Heights m (in)	Physical Activity Level	Weight[b] kg (lb)					
1.45 (57)		38.9 (86)	47.3 (100)	52.6 (116)	63.1 (139)	73.6 (163)	84.1 (185)
				kCalories			
	Sedentary	1777	1911	2048	2198	2347	2496
	Low active	1931	2080	2225	2393	2560	2727
	Active	2127	2295	2447	2636	2826	3015
	Very active	2450	2648	2845	3075	3305	3535
1.50 (59)		41.6 (92)	50.6 (107)	56.3 (124)	67.5 (149)	78.8 (174)	90.0 (198)
				kCalories			
	Sedentary	1848	1991	2126	2286	2445	2605
	Low active	2009	2168	2312	2491	2670	2849
	Active	2215	2394	2545	2748	2951	3154
	Very active	2554	2766	2965	3211	3457	3703
1.55 (61)		44.4 (98)	54.1 (114)	60.1 (132)	72.1 (159)	84.1 (185)	96.1 (212)
				kCalories			
	Sedentary	1919	2072	2205	2376	2546	2717
	Low active	2089	2259	2401	2592	2783	2974
	Active	2305	2496	2646	2862	3079	3296
	Very active	2660	2887	3087	3349	3612	3875

continued

[a]For each year below 30, add 10 kcalories/day to TEE. For each year above 30, subtract 10 kcalories/day from TEE.
[b]These columns represent a BMI of 18.5, 22.5, 25, 30, 35, and 40, respectively.

TABLE F-5 Total Energy Expenditure (TEE in kCalories per Day) for Men 30 Years of Age[a] at Various Levels of Activity and Various Heights and Weights—continued

Heights m (in)	Physical Activity Level	Weight[b] kg (lb)					
1.60 (63)		47.4 (104)	57.6 (121)	64.0 (141)	76.8 (169)	89.6 (197)	102.4 (226)
				kCalories			
	Sedentary	1993	2156	2286	2468	2650	2831
	Low active	2171	2351	2492	2695	2899	3102
	Active	2397	2601	2749	2980	3210	3441
	Very active	2769	3010	3211	3491	3771	4051
1.65 (65)		50.4 (111)	61.3 (129)	68.1 (150)	81.7 (180)	95.3 (210)	108.9 (240)
				kCalories			
	Sedentary	2068	2241	2369	2562	2756	2949
	Low active	2254	2446	2585	2801	3017	3234
	Active	2490	2707	2854	3099	3345	3590
	Very active	2880	3136	3339	3637	3934	4232
1.70 (67)		53.5 (118)	65.0 (137)	72.3 (159)	86.7 (191)	101.2 (223)	115.6 (255)
				kCalories			
	Sedentary	2144	2328	2454	2659	2864	3069
	Low active	2338	2542	2679	2909	3139	3369
	Active	2586	2816	2961	3222	3483	3743
	Very active	2992	3265	3469	3785	4101	4417
1.75 (69)		56.7 (125)	68.9 (145)	76.6 (169)	91.9 (202)	107.2 (236)	122.5 (270)
				kCalories			
	Sedentary	2222	2416	2540	2757	2975	3192
	Low active	2425	2641	2776	3020	3263	3507
	Active	2683	2927	3071	3347	3623	3900
	Very active	3108	3396	3602	3937	4272	4607
1.80 (71)		59.9 (132)	72.9 (154)	81.0 (178)	97.2 (214)	113.4 (250)	129.6 (285)
				kCalories			
	Sedentary	2301	2507	2628	2858	3088	3318
	Low active	2513	2741	2875	3132	3390	3648
	Active	2782	3040	3183	3475	3767	4060
	Very active	3225	3530	3738	4092	4447	4801
1.85 (73)		63.3 (139)	77.0 (162)	85.6 (189)	102.7 (226)	119.8 (264)	136.9 (302)
				kCalories			
	Sedentary	2382	2599	2718	2961	3204	3447
	Low active	2602	2844	2976	3248	3520	3792
	Active	2883	3155	3297	3606	3915	4223
	Very active	3344	3667	3877	4251	4625	4999
1.90 (75)		66.8 (147)	81.2 (171)	90.3 (199)	108.3 (239)	126.4 (278)	144.4 (318)
				kCalories			
	Sedentary	2464	2693	2810	3066	3322	3579
	Low active	2693	2948	3078	3365	3652	3939
	Active	2986	3273	3414	3739	4065	4390
	Very active	3466	3806	4018	4413	4807	5202
1.95 (77)		70.3 (155)	85.6 (180)	95.1 (209)	114.1 (251)	133.1 (293)	152.1 (335)
				kCalories			
	Sedentary	2547	2789	2903	3173	3443	3713
	Low active	2786	3055	3183	3485	3788	4090
	Active	3090	3393	3533	3875	4218	4561
	Very active	3590	3948	4162	4578	4993	5409

[a]For each year below 30, add 10 kcalories/day to TEE. For each year above 30, subtract 10 kcalories/day from TEE.
[b]These columns represent a BMI of 18.5, 22.5, 25, 30, 35, and 40, respectively.

FIGURE I-1 *Eating Well with Canada's Food Guide*

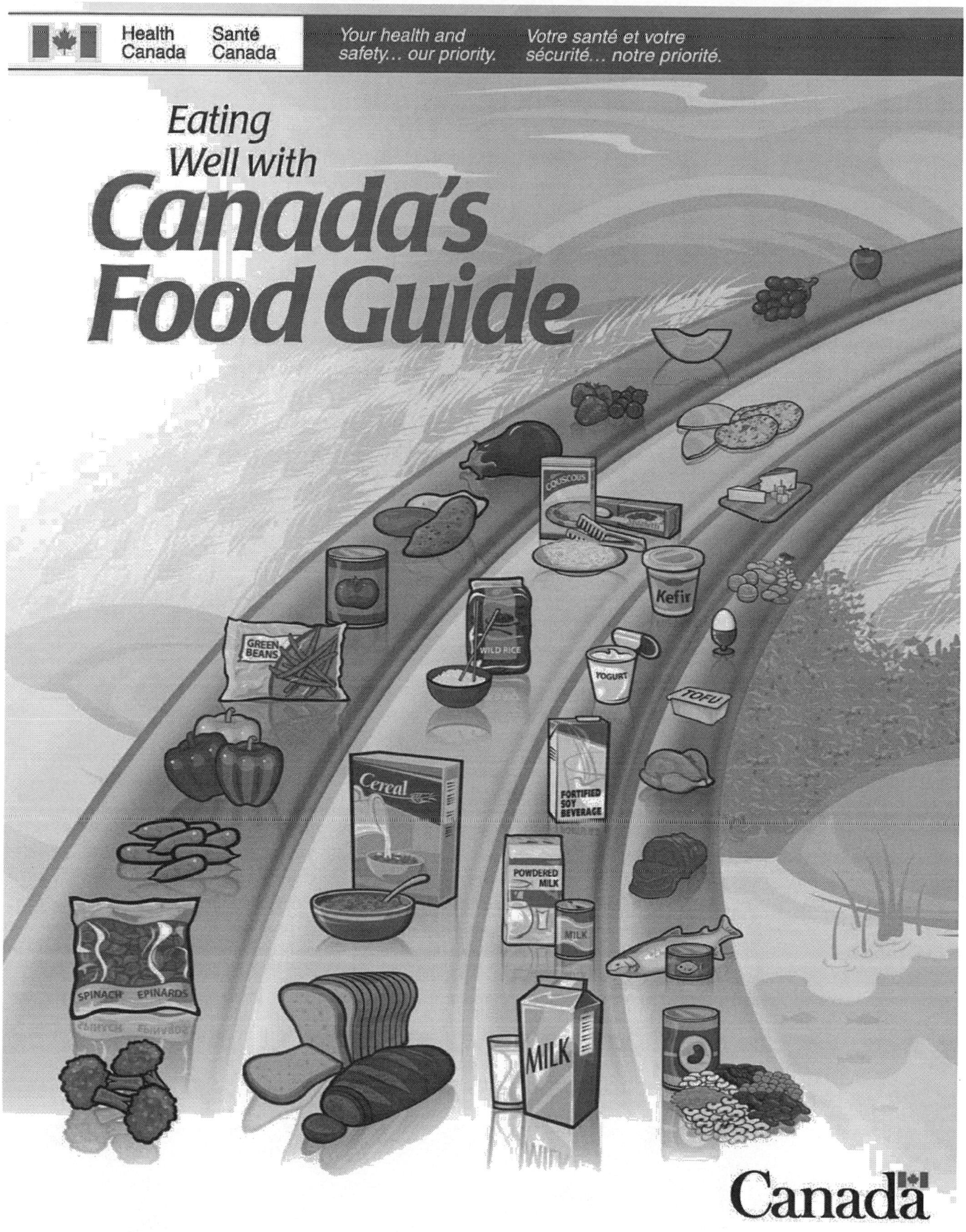

WHO: Nutrition Recommendations
Canada: Guidelines and Meal Planning

CONTENTS

Nutrition Recommendations from WHO
Eating Well with Canada's Food Guide
Canada's Meal Planning for Healthy Eating

This appendix presents nutrition recommendations from the World Health Organization (WHO) and details for Canadians on the *Eating Well with Canada's Food Guide* and the *Beyond the Basics* meal planning system.

Nutrition Recommendations from WHO

The World Health Organization (WHO) has assessed the relationships between diet and the development of chronic diseases. Its recommendations include:

- Energy: sufficient to support growth, physical activity, and a healthy body weight (BMI between 18.5 and 24.9) and to avoid weight gain greater than 11 pounds (5 kilograms) during adult life
- Total fat: 15 to 30 percent of total energy
- Saturated fatty acids: <10 percent of total energy
- Polyunsaturated fatty acids: 6 to 10 percent of total energy
- Omega-6 polyunsaturated fatty acids: 5 to 8 percent of total energy
- Omega-3 polyunsaturated fatty acids: 1 to 2 percent of total energy
- *Trans* fatty acids: <1 percent of total energy
- Total carbohydrate: 55 to 75 percent of total energy
- Sugars: <10 percent of total energy
- Protein: 10 to 15 percent of total energy
- Cholesterol: <300 mg per day
- Salt (sodium): <5 g salt per day (<2 g sodium per day), appropriately iodized
- Fruits and vegetables: ≥400 g per day (about 1 pound)
- Total dietary fiber: >25 g per day from foods
- Physical activity: one hour of moderate-intensity activity, such as walking, on most days of the week

Eating Well with Canada's Food Guide

Figure I-1 presents the 2007 *Eating Well with Canada's Food Guide,* which interprets Canada's *Guidelines for Healthy Eating* (see Table 2-2 on p. 40) for consumers and recommends a range of servings to consume daily from each of the four food groups. Additional publications, which are available from Health Canada ♦ through its website, provide many more details.

♦ Search for "Canada's food guide" at Health Canada: **www.hc-sc.gc.ca**

FIGURE I-1   *Eating Well with Canada's Food Guide*—continued

Recommended Number of Food Guide Servings per Day

	Children			Teens		Adults			
Age in Years	2-3	4-8	9-13	14-18		19-50		51+	
Sex	Girls and Boys			Females	Males	Females	Males	Females	Males
Vegetables and Fruit	4	5	6	7	8	7-8	8-10	7	7
Grain Products	3	4	6	6	7	6-7	8	6	7
Milk and Alternatives	2	2	3-4	3-4	3-4	2	2	3	3
Meat and Alternatives	1	1	1-2	2	3	2	3	2	3

The chart above shows how many Food Guide Servings you need from each of the four food groups every day.

Having the amount and type of food recommended and following the tips in *Canada's Food Guide* will help:

- Meet your needs for vitamins, minerals and other nutrients.
- Reduce your risk of obesity, type 2 diabetes, heart disease, certain types of cancer and osteoporosis.
- Contribute to your overall health and vitality.

FIGURE I-1 *Eating Well with Canada's Food Guide—continued*

What is One Food Guide Serving?
Look at the examples below.

Fresh, frozen or canned vegetables
125 mL (½ cup)

Leafy vegetables
Cooked: 125 mL (½ cup)
Raw: 250 mL (1 cup)

Fresh, frozen or canned fruits
1 fruit or 125 mL (½ cup)

100% Juice
125 mL (½ cup)

Bread
1 slice (35 g)

Bagel
½ bagel (45 g)

Flat breads
½ pita or ½ tortilla (35 g)

Cooked rice, bulgur or quinoa
125 mL (½ cup)

Cereal
Cold: 30 g
Hot: 175 mL (¾ cup)

Cooked pasta or couscous
125 mL (½ cup)

Milk or powdered milk (reconstituted)
250 mL (1 cup)

Canned milk (evaporated)
125 mL (½ cup)

Fortified soy beverage
250 mL (1 cup)

Yogurt
175 g
(¾ cup)

Kefir
175 g
(¾ cup)

Cheese
50 g (1 ½ oz.)

Cooked fish, shellfish, poultry, lean meat
75 g (2 ½ oz.)/125 mL (½ cup)

Cooked legumes
175 mL (¾ cup)

Tofu
150 g or
175 mL (¾ cup)

Eggs
2 eggs

Peanut or nut butters
30 mL (2 Tbsp)

Shelled nuts and seeds
60 mL (¼ cup)

Oils and Fats
- Include a small amount – 30 to 45 mL (2 to 3 Tbsp) – of unsaturated fat each day. This includes oil used for cooking, salad dressings, margarine and mayonnaise.
- Use vegetable oils such as canola, olive and soybean.
- Choose soft margarines that are low in saturated and trans fats.
- Limit butter, hard margarine, lard and shortening.

FIGURE I-1 *Eating Well with Canada's Food Guide—continued*

Make each Food Guide Serving count...
wherever you are – at home, at school, at work or when eating out!

▸ **Eat at least one dark green and one orange vegetable each day.**
- Go for dark green vegetables such as broccoli, romaine lettuce and spinach.
- Go for orange vegetables such as carrots, sweet potatoes and winter squash.

▸ **Choose vegetables and fruit prepared with little or no added fat, sugar or salt.**
- Enjoy vegetables steamed, baked or stir-fried instead of deep-fried.

▸ **Have vegetables and fruit more often than juice.**

▸ **Make at least half of your grain products whole grain each day.**
- Eat a variety of whole grains such as barley, brown rice, oats, quinoa and wild rice.
- Enjoy whole grain breads, oatmeal or whole wheat pasta.

▸ **Choose grain products that are lower in fat, sugar or salt.**
- Compare the Nutrition Facts table on labels to make wise choices.
- Enjoy the true taste of grain products. When adding sauces or spreads, use small amounts.

▸ **Drink skim, 1%, or 2% milk each day.**
- Have 500 mL (2 cups) of milk every day for adequate vitamin D.
- Drink fortified soy beverages if you do not drink milk.

▸ **Select lower fat milk alternatives.**
- Compare the Nutrition Facts table on yogurts or cheeses to make wise choices.

▸ **Have meat alternatives such as beans, lentils and tofu often.**

▸ **Eat at least two Food Guide Servings of fish each week.***
- Choose fish such as char, herring, mackerel, salmon, sardines and trout.

▸ **Select lean meat and alternatives prepared with little or no added fat or salt.**
- Trim the visible fat from meats. Remove the skin on poultry.
- Use cooking methods such as roasting, baking or poaching that require little or no added fat.
- If you eat luncheon meats, sausages or prepackaged meats, choose those lower in salt (sodium) and fat.

Enjoy a variety of foods from the four food groups.

Satisfy your thirst with water!

Drink water regularly. It's a calorie-free way to quench your thirst. Drink more water in hot weather or when you are very active.

* Health Canada provides advice for limiting exposure to mercury from certain types of fish. Refer to www.healthcanada.gc.ca for the latest information.

FIGURE I-1   *Eating Well with Canada's Food Guide—continued*

Advice for different ages and stages...

Children

Following *Canada's Food Guide* helps children grow and thrive.

Young children have small appetites and need calories for growth and development.

- Serve small nutritious meals and snacks each day.

- Do not restrict nutritious foods because of their fat content. Offer a variety of foods from the four food groups.

- Most of all... be a good role model.

Women of childbearing age

All women who could become pregnant and those who are pregnant or breastfeeding need a multivitamin containing **folic acid** every day. Pregnant women need to ensure that their multivitamin also contains **iron**. A health care professional can help you find the multivitamin that's right for you.

Pregnant and breastfeeding women need more calories. Include an extra 2 to 3 Food Guide Servings each day.

Here are two examples:
- Have fruit and yogurt for a snack, or

- Have an extra slice of toast at breakfast and an extra glass of milk at supper.

Men and women over 50

The need for **vitamin D** increases after the age of 50.

In addition to following *Canada's Food Guide*, everyone over the age of 50 should take a daily vitamin D supplement of 10 µg (400 IU).

How do I count Food Guide Servings in a meal?

Here is an example:

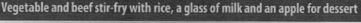

Vegetable and beef stir-fry with rice, a glass of milk and an apple for dessert		
250 mL (1 cup) mixed broccoli, carrot and sweet red pepper	=	2 **Vegetables and Fruit** Food Guide Servings
75 g (2 ½ oz.) lean beef	=	1 **Meat and Alternatives** Food Guide Serving
250 mL (1 cup) brown rice	=	2 **Grain Products** Food Guide Servings
5 mL (1 tsp) canola oil	=	part of your **Oils and Fats** intake for the day
250 mL (1 cup) 1% milk	=	1 **Milk and Alternatives** Food Guide Serving
1 apple	=	1 **Vegetables and Fruit** Food Guide Serving

FIGURE I-1 *Eating Well with Canada's Food Guide—continued*

Eat well and be active today and every day!

The benefits of eating well and being active include:

- Better overall health.
- Lower risk of disease.
- A healthy body weight.
- Feeling and looking better.
- More energy.
- Stronger muscles and bones.

Be active

To be active every day is a step towards better health and a healthy body weight.

Canada's Physical Activity Guide recommends building 30 to 60 minutes of moderate physical activity into daily life for adults and at least 90 minutes a day for children and youth. You don't have to do it all at once. Add it up in periods of at least 10 minutes at a time for adults and five minutes at a time for children and youth.

Start slowly and build up.

Eat well

Another important step towards better health and a healthy body weight is to follow *Canada's Food Guide* by:

- Eating the recommended amount and type of food each day.

- Limiting foods and beverages high in calories, fat, sugar or salt (sodium) such as cakes and pastries, chocolate and candies, cookies and granola bars, doughnuts and muffins, ice cream and frozen desserts, french fries, potato chips, nachos and other salty snacks, alcohol, fruit flavoured drinks, soft drinks, sports and energy drinks, and sweetened hot or cold drinks.

Read the label

- Compare the Nutrition Facts table on food labels to choose products that contain less fat, saturated fat, trans fat, sugar and sodium.

- Keep in mind that the calories and nutrients listed are for the amount of food found at the top of the Nutrition Facts table.

Nutrition Facts		
Per 0 mL (0 g)		
Amount		**% Daily Value**
Calories 0		
Fat 0 g		0 %
Saturates 0 g		0 %
+ Trans 0 g		
Cholesterol 0 mg		
Sodium 0 mg		0 %
Carbohydrate 0 g		0 %
Fibre 0 g		0 %
Sugars 0 g		
Protein 0 g		
Vitamin A 0 %	Vitamin C	0 %
Calcium 0 %	Iron	0 %

Limit trans fat

When a Nutrition Facts table is not available, ask for nutrition information to choose foods lower in trans and saturated fats.

Take a step today...

✓ Have breakfast every day. It may help control your hunger later in the day.

✓ Walk wherever you can – get off the bus early, use the stairs.

✓ Benefit from eating vegetables and fruit at all meals and as snacks.

✓ Spend less time being inactive such as watching TV or playing computer games.

✓ Request nutrition information about menu items when eating out to help you make healthier choices.

✓ Enjoy eating with family and friends!

✓ Take time to eat and savour every bite!

For more information, interactive tools, or additional copies visit Canada's Food Guide on-line at: www.healthcanada.gc.ca/foodguide

or contact:
Publications
Health Canada
Ottawa, Ontario K1A 0K9
E-Mail: publications@hc-sc.gc.ca
Tel.: 1-866-225-0709
Fax: (613) 941-5366
TTY: 1-800-267-1245

Également disponible en français sous le titre :
Bien manger avec le Guide alimentaire canadien

This publication can be made available on request on diskette, large print, audio-cassette and braille.

© Her Majesty the Queen in Right of Canada, represented by the Minister of Health Canada, 2007. This publication may be reproduced without permission. No changes permitted. HC Pub.: 4651 Cat.: H164-38/1-2007E ISBN: 0-662-44467-1

Canada's *Meal Planning for Healthy Eating*

Beyond the Basics: Meal Planning for Healthy Eating, Diabetes Prevention and Management is Canada's system of meal planning.[1] Similar to the U.S. exchange system, *Beyond the Basics* sorts foods into groups and defines portion sizes to help people manage their blood glucose and maintain a healthy weight. Because foods that contain carbohydrate raise blood glucose, the food groups are organized into two sections—those that contain carbohydrate (presented in Table I-1) and those that contain little or no carbohydrate (shown in Table I-2). One portion from any of the food groups listed in Table I-1 provides about 15 grams of available carbohydrate (total carbohydrate minus fiber) and counts as one carbohydrate choice. Within each group, foods are identified as those to "choose more often" (generally higher in vitamins, minerals, and fiber) and those to "choose less often" (generally higher in sugar, saturated fat, or *trans* fat).

[1] The tables for the Canadian meal planning system are adapted from *Beyond the Basics: Meal Planning for Healthy Eating, Diabetes Prevention and Management,* copyright 2005, with permission of the Canadian Diabetes Association. Additional information is available from **www.diabetes.ca**.

Key:
● Choose more often
▲ Choose less often

TABLE I-1 Food Groups that Contain Carbohydrate

1 serving = 15 g carbohydrate or 1 carbohydrate choice

Food	Measure
Grains and starches: 15 g carbohydrate, 2 g protein, 0 g fat, 286 kJ (68 kcal)	
▲ Bagel, large	¼
▲ Bagel, small	½
▲ Bannock, fried	1.5″ × 2.5″
● Bannock, whole grain baked	1.5″ × 2.5″
● Barley, cooked	125 mL (½ c)
▲ Bread, white	30 g (1 oz)
● Bread, whole grain	30 g (1 oz)
● Bulgur, cooked	125 mL (½ c)
▲ Bun, hamburger or hotdog	½
▲ Cereal, flaked unsweetened	125 mL (½ c)
● Cereal, hot	¾ c
● Chapati, whole wheat (6″)	1
● Corn	125 mL (½ c)
● Couscous, cooked	125 mL (½ c)
▲ Crackers, soda type	7
▲ Croutons	⅔ c
● English muffin, whole grain	½
▲ French fries	10
● Millet, cooked	⅓ c
▲ Naan bread (6″)	¼
▲ Pancake (4″)	1
● Pasta, cooked	125 mL (½ c)
▲ Pita bread, white (6″)	1
● Pita bread, whole wheat (6″)	1
▲ Pizza crust (12″)	1/12
● Plantain, mashed	⅓ c
● Potatoes, boiled or baked	½ medium

(continued on the next page)

TABLE I-1   Food Groups that Contain Carbohydrate—continued

1 serving = 15 g carbohydrate or 1 carbohydrate choice

Food	Measure
Grains and starches: 15 g carbohydrate, 2 g protein, 0 g fat, 286 kJ (68 kcal)	
● Rice, cooked	⅓ c
● Roti, whole wheat (6")	1
● Soup, thick type	250 mL (1 c)
● Sweet potato, mashed	⅓ c
▲ Taco shells (5")	2
● Tortilla, whole wheat (6")	1
▲ Waffle (4")	1
Fruits:15 g carbohydrate, 1 g protein, 0 g fat, 269 kJ (64 kcal)	
● Apple	1 medium
● Apple sauce, unsweetened	125 mL (½ c)
● Banana	1 small
● Blackberries	500 mL (2 c)
● Cherries	15
● Fruit, canned in juice	125 mL (½ c)
▲ Fruit, dried	50 mL (¼ c)
● Grapefruit	1 small
● Grapes	15
● Kiwi	2 medium
▲ Juice	125 mL (½ c)
● Mango	½ medium
● Melon	250 mL (1 c)
● Orange	1 medium
● Other berries	250 mL (1 c)
● Pear	1 medium
● Pineapple	¾ c
● Plum	2 medium
● Raspberries	500 mL (2 c)
● Strawberries	500 mL (2 c)
Milk and alternatives: 15 g carbohydrate, 8 g protein, variable fat, 386–651 kJ (92–155 kcal)	
● Chocolate milk, 1%	125 mL (½ c)
● Evaporated milk, canned	125 mL (½ c)
● Milk, fluid	250 mL (1 c)
● Milk powder, skim	30 mL (2 tbs)
● Soy beverage, flavored	125 mL (½ c)
● Soy beverage, plain	250 mL (1 c)
● Soy yogurt, flavored	⅓ c
● Yogurt, nonfat, plain	¾ c
● Yogurt, skim, artificially sweetened	250 mL (1 c)
Other choices (sweet foods and snacks): 15 g carbohydrate, variable protein and fat	
▲ Brownies, unfrosted	2" × 2"
▲ Cake, unfrosted	2" × 2"
▲ Cookies, arrowroot or gingersnap	3–4
▲ Jam, jelly, marmalade	15 mL (1 tbs)
● Milk pudding, skim, no sugar added	125 mL (½ c)
▲ Muffin	1 small (2")
▲ Oatmeal granola bar	1 (28 g)
● Popcorn, low fat	750 mL (3 c)
▲ Pretzels, low fat, large	7
▲ Pretzels, low fat, sticks	30
▲ Sugar, white	15 mL (3 tsp or packets)

TABLE I-2 Food Groups that Contain Little or No Carbohydrate

Food	Measure
Vegetables: To encourage consumption, most vegetables are considered "free"	
● Asparagus	
● Beans, yellow or green	
● Bean sprouts	
● Beets	
● Broccoli	
● Cabbage	
● Carrots	
● Cauliflower	
● Celery	
● Cucumber	
● Eggplant	
● Greens	
● Leeks	
● Mushrooms	
● Okra	
▲ Parsnips[a]	
▲ Peas[a]	
● Peppers	
▲ Rutabagas (turnips)[a]	
● Salad vegetables	
● Snow peas	
▲ Squash, winter[a]	
● Tomatoes	
Meat and alternatives: 0 g carbohydrate, 7 g protein, 3–5 g fat, 307 kJ (73 kcal)	
● Cheese, skim (<7% milk fat)	30 g (1 oz)
● Cheese, light (<17% milk fat)	30 g (1 oz)
▲ Cheese, regular (17–33% milk fat)	30 g (1 oz)
● Cottage cheese (1–2% milk fat)	50 mL (¼ c)
● Egg	1 large
▲ Fish, canned in oil	50 mL (¼ c)
● Fish, canned in water	50 mL (¼ c)
● Fish, fresh, cooked	30 g (1 oz)
● Hummus[b]	⅓ c
● Legumes, cooked[b]	125 mL (½ c)
● Meat, game, cooked	30 g (1 oz)

[a]These vegetables provide significant carbohydrate when more than 125 mL (½ c) is eaten.
[b]Legumes contain 15 g carbohydrate in a 125 mL (½ c) serving.

(continued on the next page)

TABLE I-2	Food Groups that Contain Little or No Carbohydrate—continued

Food	Measure
Meat and alternatives: 0 g carbohydrate, 7 g protein, 3–5 g fat, 307 kJ (73 kcal)	
● Meat, ground, lean, cooked	30 g (1 oz)
▲ Meat, ground, medium-regular, cooked	30 g (1 oz)
● Meat, lean, cooked	30 g (1 oz)
● Meat, organ or tripe, cooked	30 g (1 oz)
● Meat, prepared, low fat	30 g (1 oz)
▲ Meat, prepared, regular fat	30 g (1 oz)
▲ Meat, regular, cooked	30 g (1 oz)
● Peameal/back bacon, cooked	30 g (1 oz)
● Poultry, ground, lean, cooked	30 g (1 oz)
● Poultry, skinless, cooked	30 g (1 oz)
▲ Poultry/wings, skin on, cooked	30 g (1 oz)
● Shellfish, cooked	30 g (1 oz)
● Tofu (soybean)	½ block (100 g)
● Vegetarian meat alternatives	30 g (1 oz)
Fats: 0 g carbohydrate, 0 g protein, 5 g fat, 189 kJ (45 kcal)	
● Avocado	⅛
▲ Bacon	30 g (1 oz)
● Butter	5 mL (1 tsp)
▲ Cheese, spreadable	15 mL (1 tbs)
● Margarine, non-hydrogenated	5 mL (1 tsp)
▲ Mayonnaise, light	30 mL (2 tbs)
● Nuts	15 mL (1 tbs)
● Oil, canola or olive	5 mL (1 tsp)
● Salad dressing, regular	15 mL (1 tbs)
● Seeds	15 mL (1 tbs)
● Tahini	7.5 mL (½ tbs)
Extras: <5 g carbohydrate, 84 kJ (20 kcal)	
Broth	
Coffee	
Herbs and spices	
Ketchup	
Mustard	
Sugar-free soft drinks	
Sugar-free gelatin	
Tea	